MY BaD

Also by Jerry Scott and Jim Borgman

Zits: Sketchbook 1
Growth Spurt: Zits Sketchbook 2
Don't Roll Your Eyes at Me, Young Man!: Zits Sketchbook 3
Are We an "Us"?: Zits Sketchbook 4
Zits Unzipped: Zits Sketchbook 5
Busted!: Zits Sketchbook 6
Road Trip: Zits Sketchbook 7
Teenage Tales: Zits Sketchbook No. 8
Thrashed: Zits Sketchbook No. 9
Pimp My Lunch: Zits Sketchbook No. 10
Are We Out of the Driveway Yet?: Zits Sketchbook No. 11
Rude, Crude, and Tattooed: Zits Sketchbook No. 12
Jeremy and Mom
Pierced

Treasuries
Humongous Zits
Big Honkin' Zits
Zits: Supersized
Random Zits
Crack of Noon
Alternative Zits

MY BaD

A ZITS® Treasury by Jerry Scott and Jim Borgman

**Andrews McMeel
Publishing, LLC**

Kansas City

Zits® is syndicated internationally by King Features Syndicate, Inc. For information, write King Features Syndicate, Inc., 300 West Fifty-Seventh Street, New York, New York 10019.

 For information, write Andrews McMeel Publishing, LLC, an Andrews McMeel Universal company, 1130 Walnut Street, Kansas City, Missouri 64106.

09 10 11 12 13 BAM 10 9 8 7 6 5 4 3 2 1

ISBN-13: 978-0-7407-8090-5
ISBN-10: 0-7407-8090-5

Library of Congress Control Number: 2008940074

Zits® may be viewed online at
www.kingfeatures.com.

www.andrewsmcmeel.com

Our special thanks to Molly Choma for her help on the book design and
for her amazing patience with the !@*%# copy machine.

To Thomas Patrick Rowan,
the 1945 Château Mouton Rothschild of the legal profession.

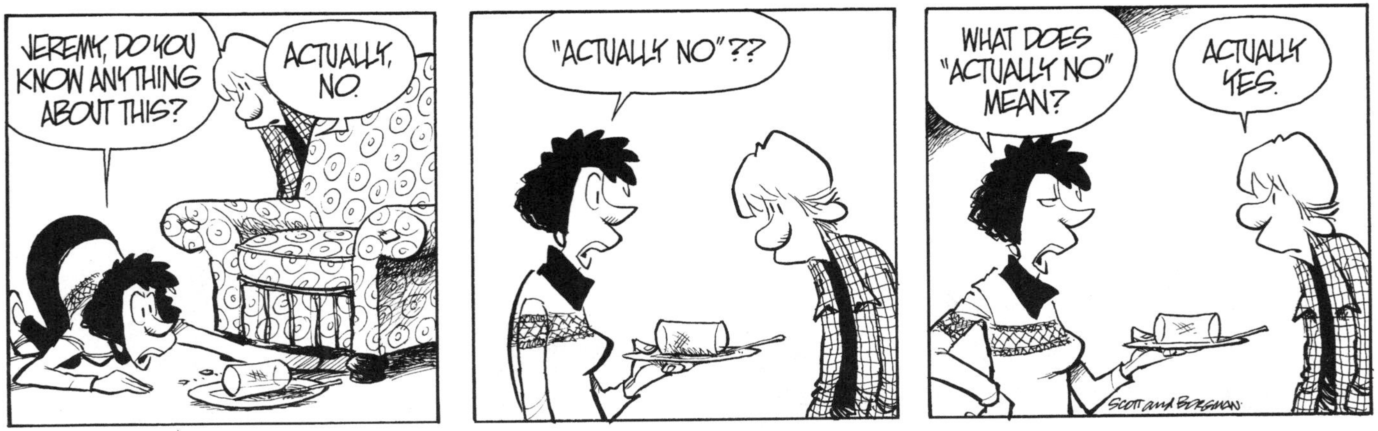
JEREMY, DO YOU KNOW ANYTHING ABOUT THIS?
ACTUALLY, NO.
"ACTUALLY NO"??
WHAT DOES "ACTUALLY NO" MEAN?
ACTUALLY YES.
SCOTT and BORGMAN

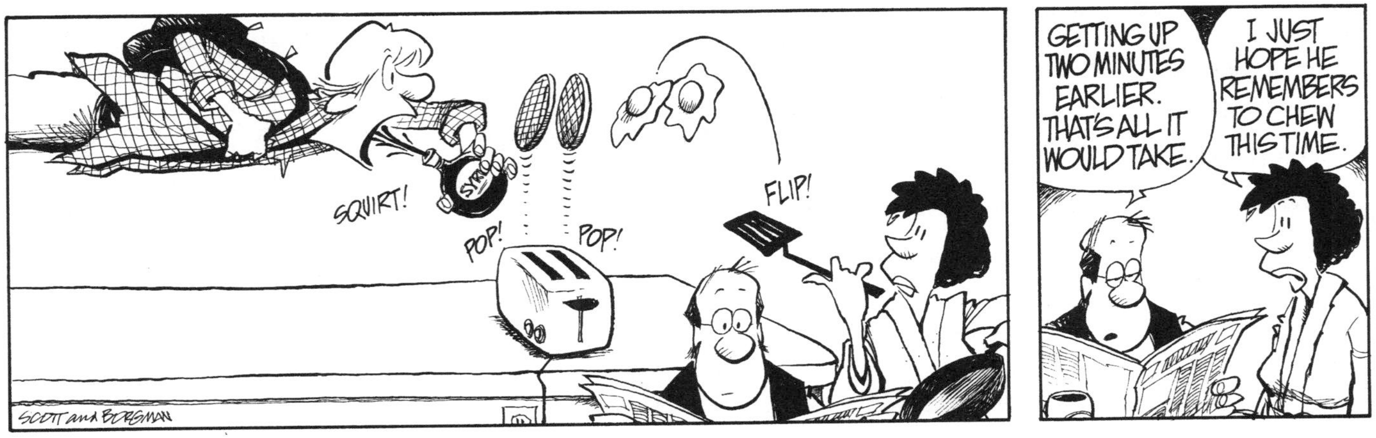
SQUIRT!
SYRUP
POP!
POP!
FLIP!
SCOTT and BORGMAN
GETTING UP TWO MINUTES EARLIER. THAT'S ALL IT WOULD TAKE.
I JUST HOPE HE REMEMBERS TO CHEW THIS TIME.

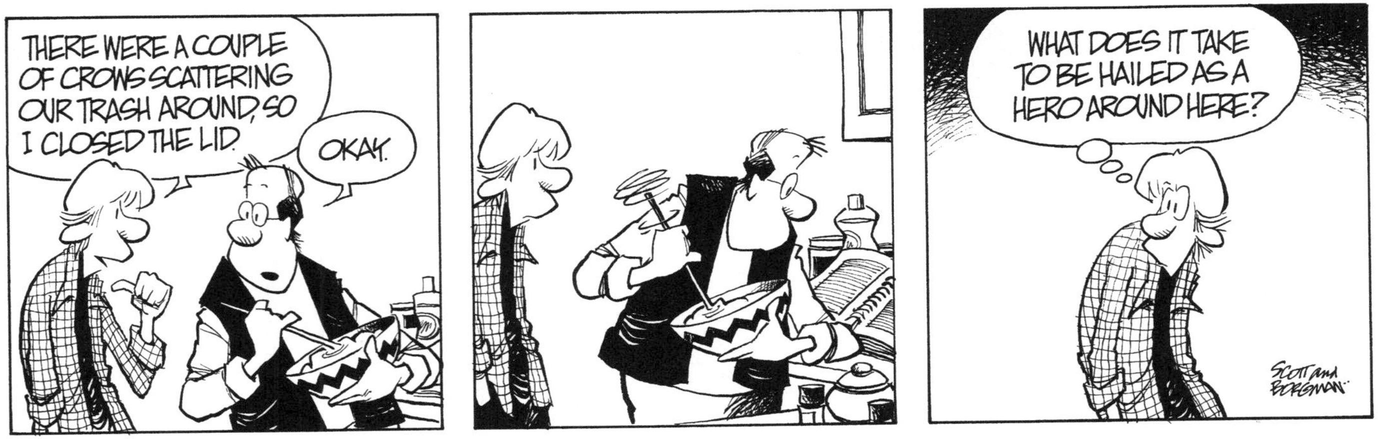
THERE WERE A COUPLE OF CROWS SCATTERING OUR TRASH AROUND, SO I CLOSED THE LID.
OKAY.
WHAT DOES IT TAKE TO BE HAILED AS A HERO AROUND HERE?
SCOTT and BORGMAN

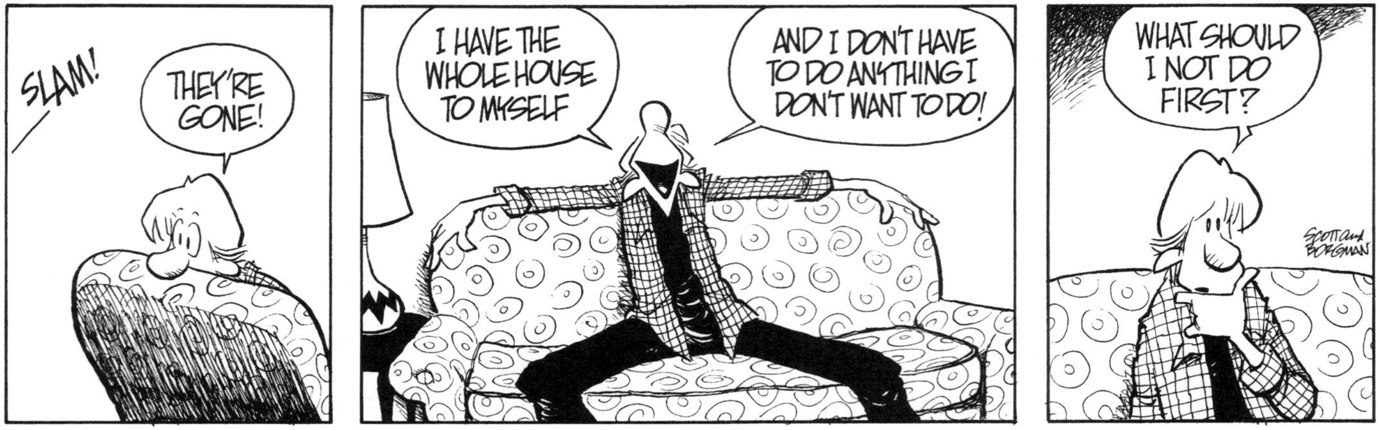
SLAM!
THEY'RE GONE!
I HAVE THE WHOLE HOUSE TO MYSELF
AND I DON'T HAVE TO DO ANYTHING I DON'T WANT TO DO!
WHAT SHOULD I NOT DO FIRST?

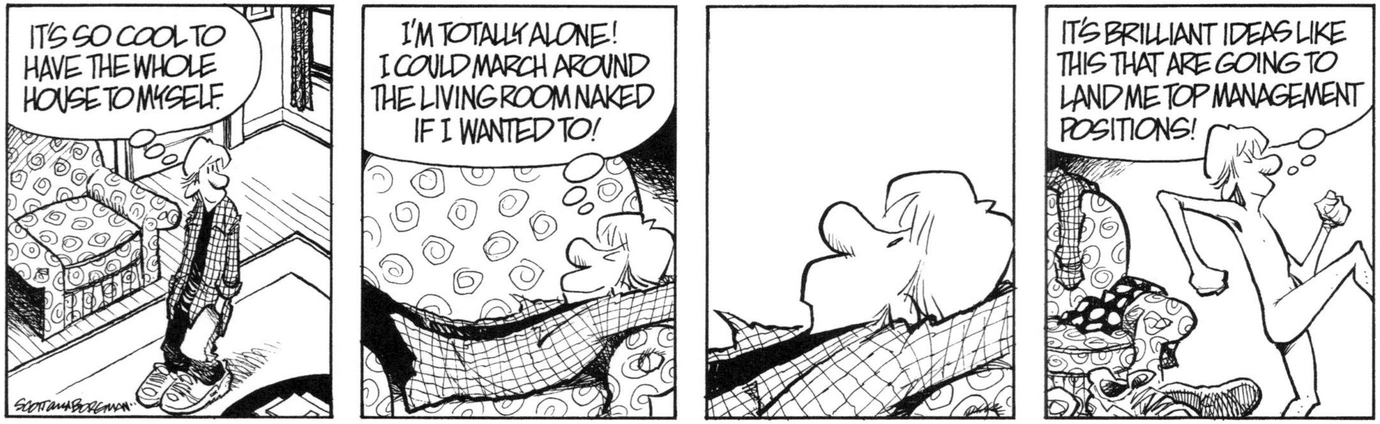
IT'S SO COOL TO HAVE THE WHOLE HOUSE TO MYSELF.
I'M TOTALLY ALONE! I COULD MARCH AROUND THE LIVING ROOM NAKED IF I WANTED TO!
IT'S BRILLIANT IDEAS LIKE THIS THAT ARE GOING TO LAND ME TOP MANAGEMENT POSITIONS!

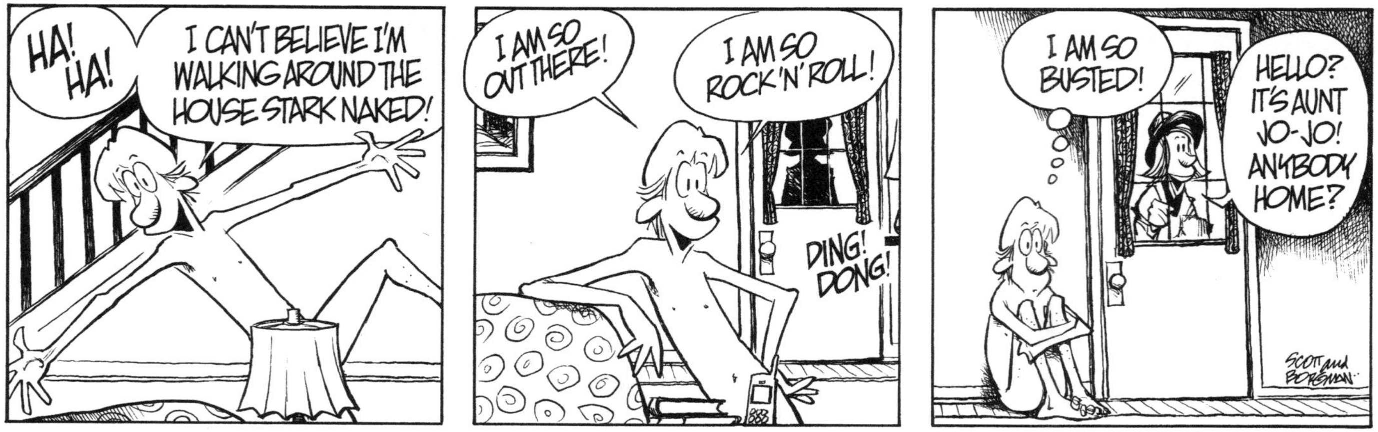
HA! HA!
I CAN'T BELIEVE I'M WALKING AROUND THE HOUSE STARK NAKED!
I AM SO OUT THERE!
I AM SO ROCK 'N' ROLL!
DING! DONG!
I AM SO BUSTED!
HELLO? IT'S AUNT JO-JO! ANYBODY HOME?

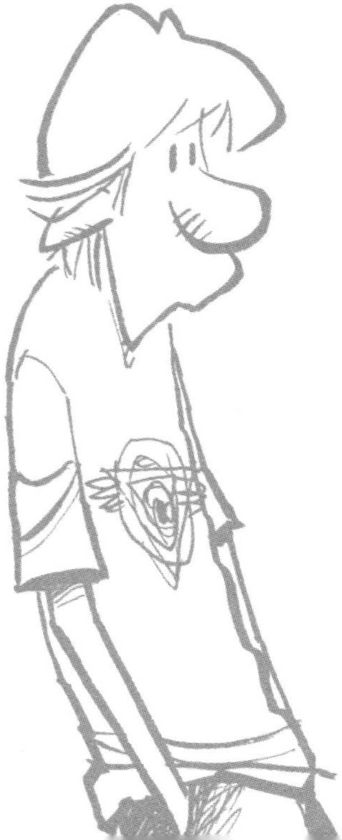

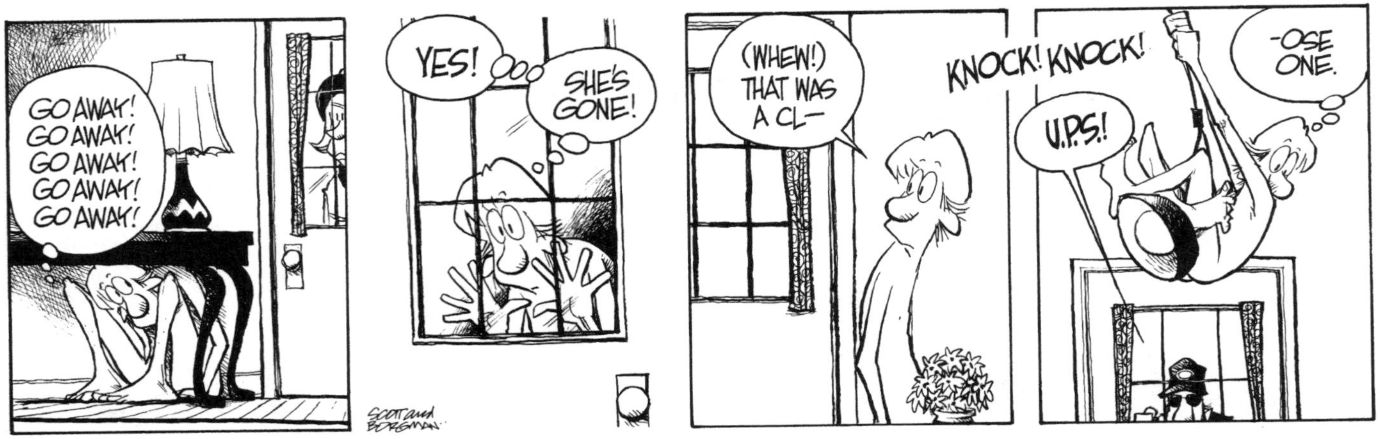
GO AWAY! GO AWAY! GO AWAY! GO AWAY! GO AWAY!
YES!
SHE'S GONE!
(WHEW!) THAT WAS A CL—
KNOCK! KNOCK!
U.P.S.!
-OSE ONE.
SCOTT and BORGMAN

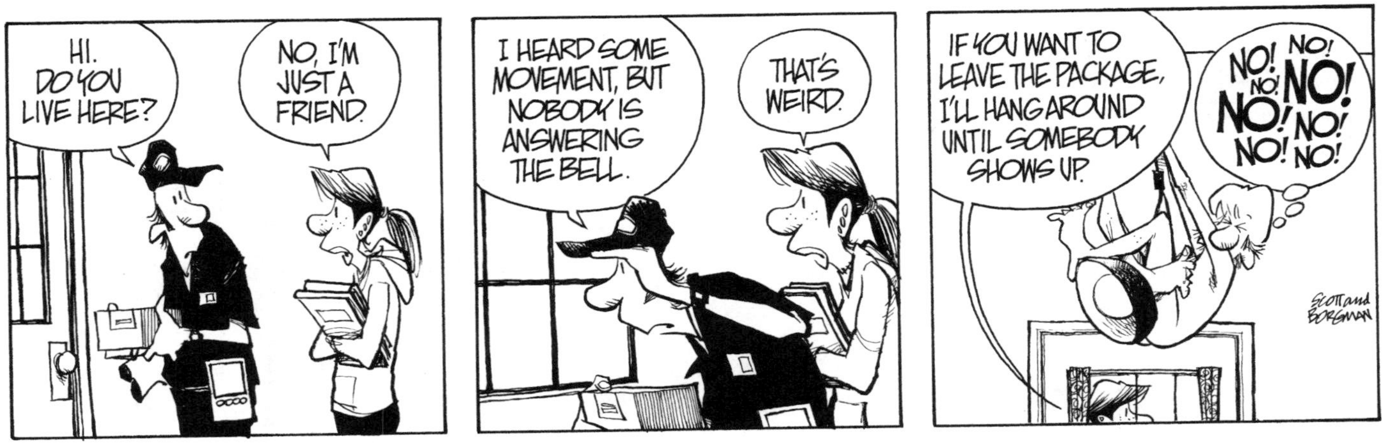
HI. DO YOU LIVE HERE?
NO, I'M JUST A FRIEND.
I HEARD SOME MOVEMENT, BUT NOBODY IS ANSWERING THE BELL.
THAT'S WEIRD.
IF YOU WANT TO LEAVE THE PACKAGE, I'LL HANG AROUND UNTIL SOMEBODY SHOWS UP.
NO! NO! NO! NO! NO! NO! NO! NO! NO!
SCOTT and BORGMAN

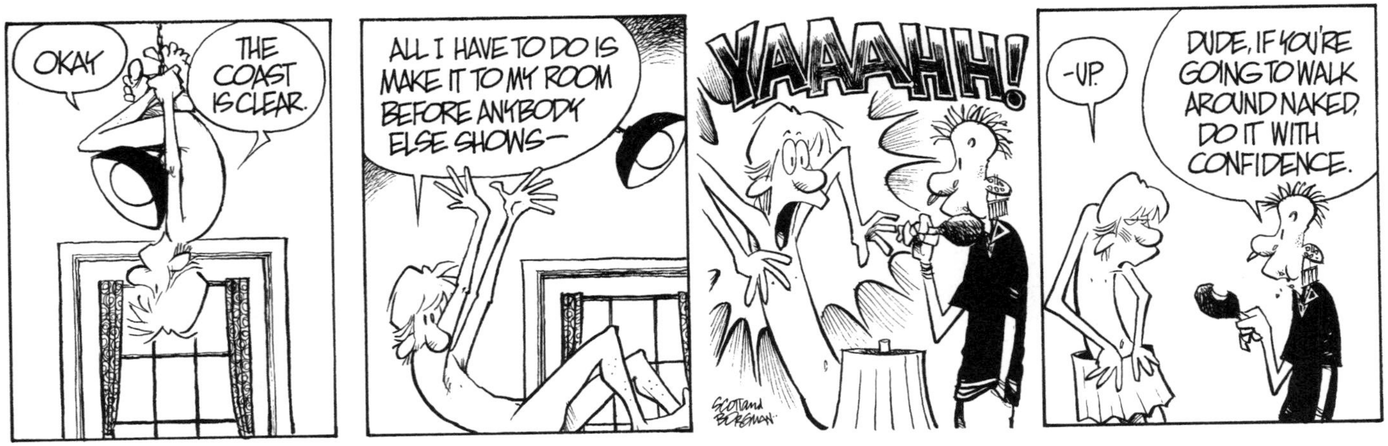
OKAY
THE COAST IS CLEAR.
ALL I HAVE TO DO IS MAKE IT TO MY ROOM BEFORE ANYBODY ELSE SHOWS—
YAAAHH!
SCOTT and BORGMAN
-UP.
DUDE, IF YOU'RE GOING TO WALK AROUND NAKED, DO IT WITH CONFIDENCE.

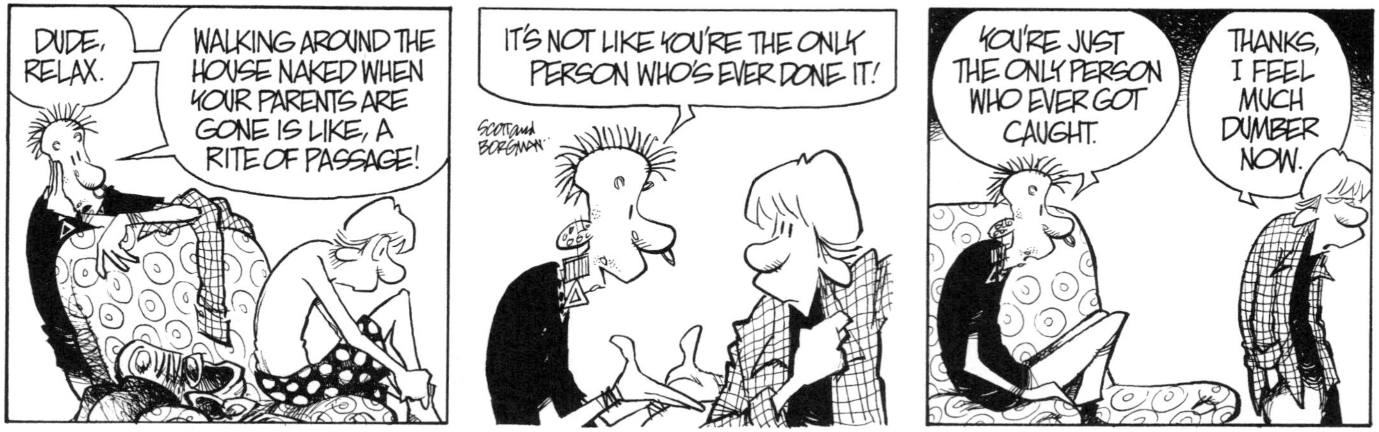
DUDE, RELAX.
WALKING AROUND THE HOUSE NAKED WHEN YOUR PARENTS ARE GONE IS LIKE, A RITE OF PASSAGE!
IT'S NOT LIKE YOU'RE THE ONLY PERSON WHO'S EVER DONE IT!
YOU'RE JUST THE ONLY PERSON WHO EVER GOT CAUGHT.
THANKS, I FEEL MUCH DUMBER NOW.

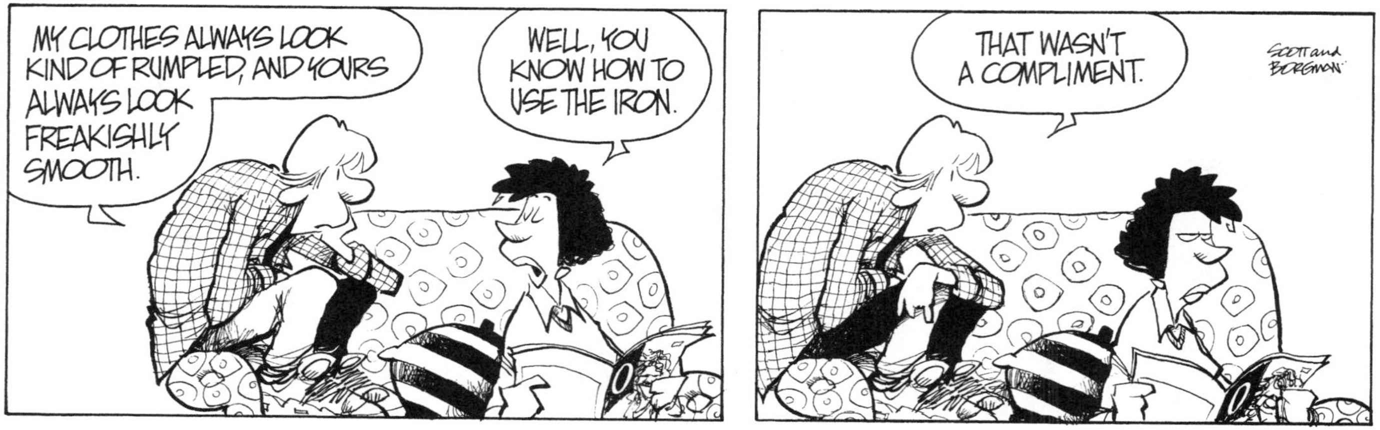
MY CLOTHES ALWAYS LOOK KIND OF RUMPLED, AND YOURS ALWAYS LOOK FREAKISHLY SMOOTH.
WELL, YOU KNOW HOW TO USE THE IRON.
THAT WASN'T A COMPLIMENT.

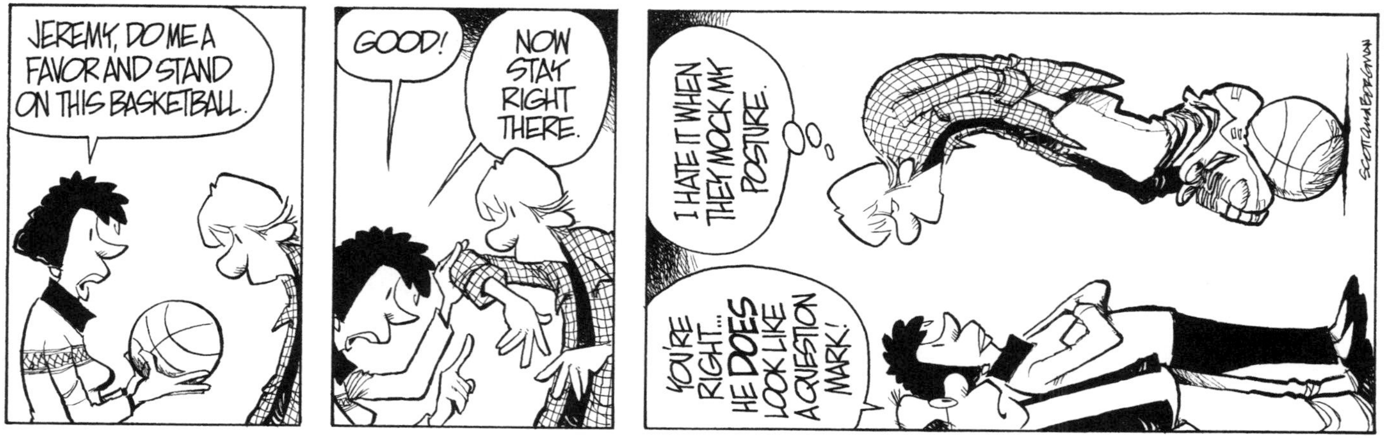
JEREMY, DO ME A FAVOR AND STAND ON THIS BASKETBALL.
GOOD!
NOW STAY RIGHT THERE.
I HATE IT WHEN THEY MOCK MY POSTURE.
YOU'RE RIGHT... HE DOES LOOK LIKE A QUESTION MARK!

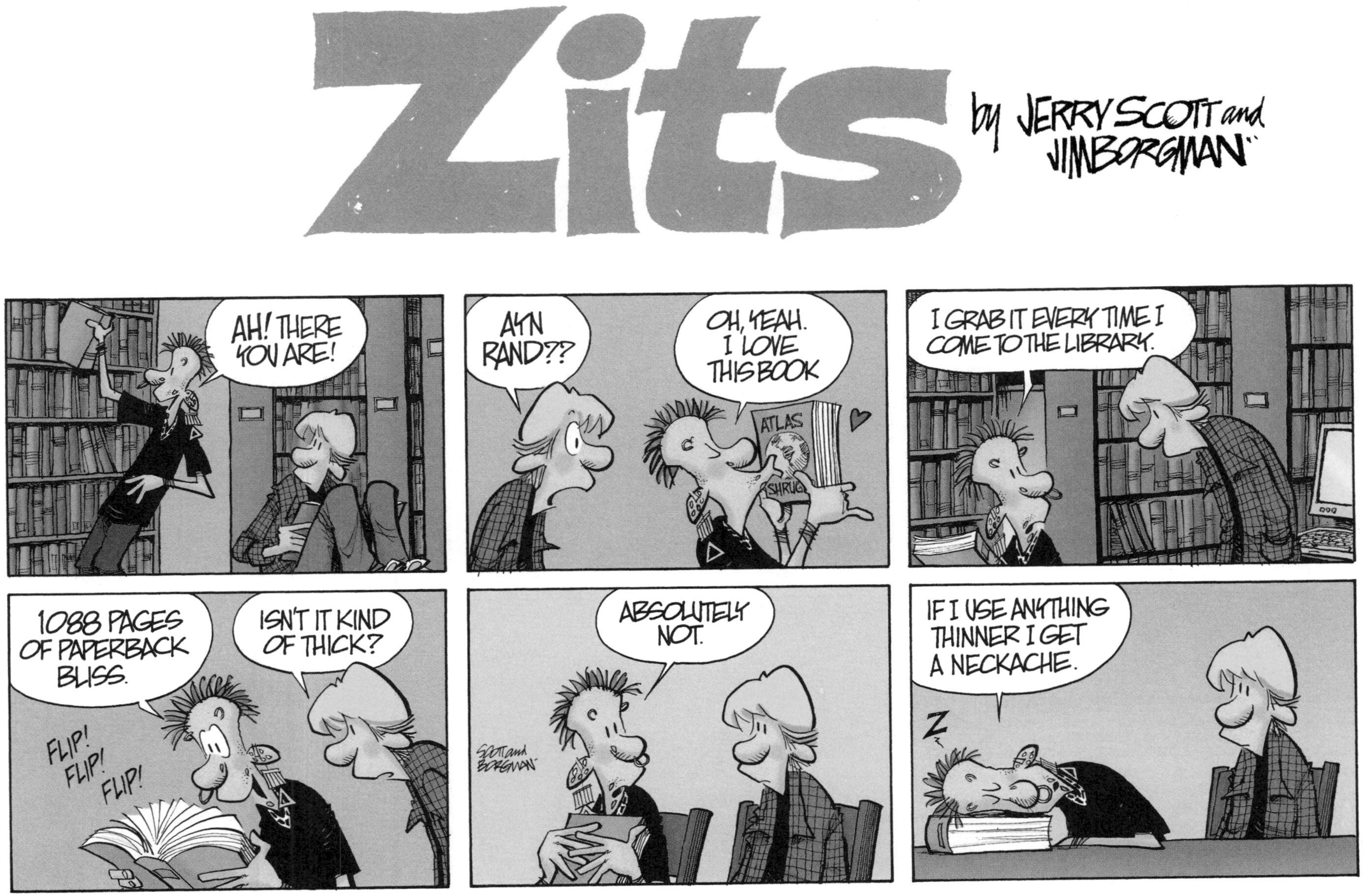
Zits
by JERRY SCOTT and JIM BORGMAN
AH! THERE YOU ARE!
AYN RAND??
OH, YEAH. I LOVE THIS BOOK
ATLAS SHRUG
I GRAB IT EVERY TIME I COME TO THE LIBRARY.
1088 PAGES OF PAPERBACK BLISS.
ISN'T IT KIND OF THICK?
FLIP! FLIP! FLIP!
ABSOLUTELY NOT.
SCOTT and BORGMAN
IF I USE ANYTHING THINNER I GET A NECKACHE.
Z

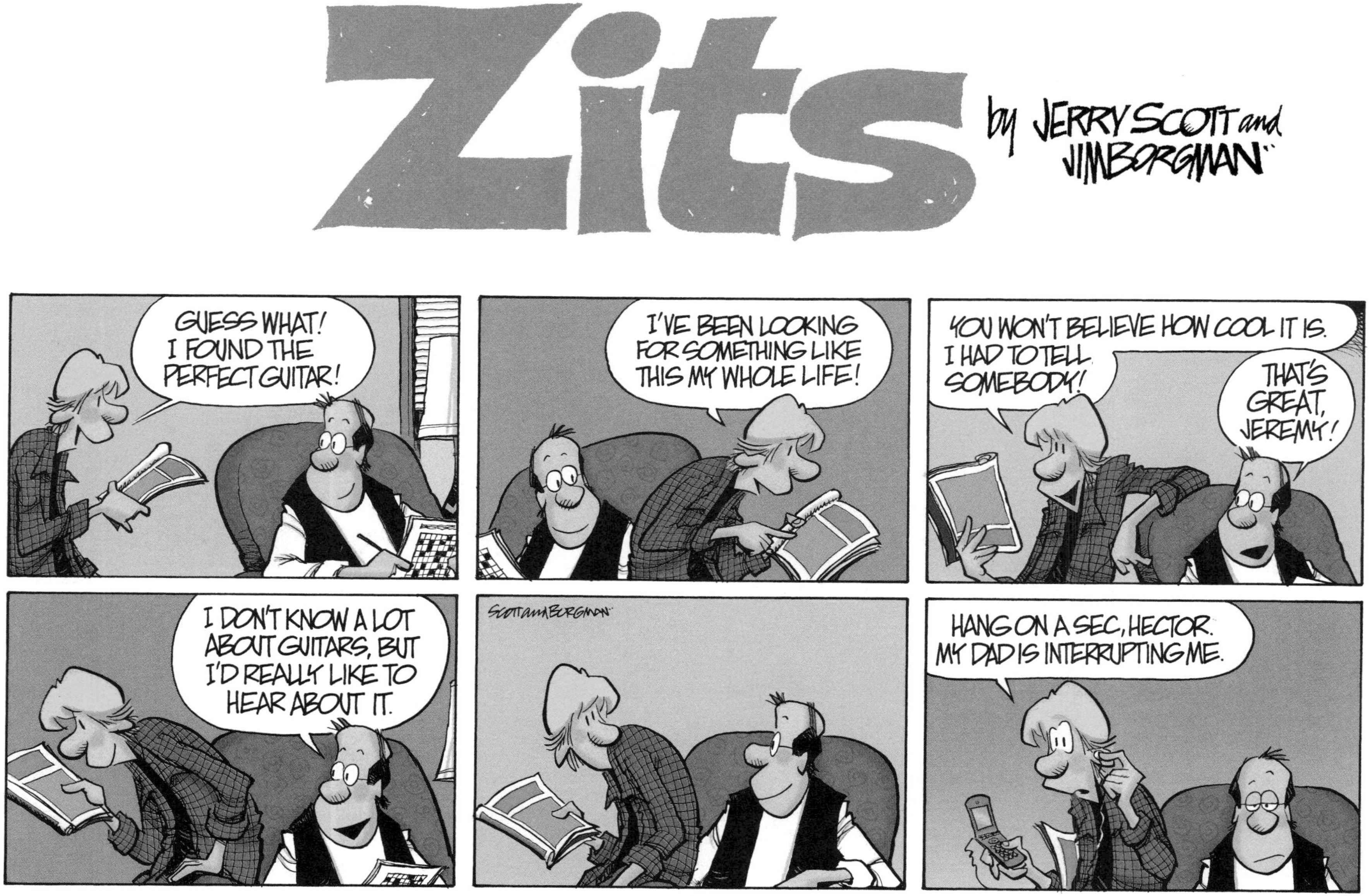
Zits
by JERRY SCOTT and JIM BORGMAN
GUESS WHAT! I FOUND THE PERFECT GUITAR!
I'VE BEEN LOOKING FOR SOMETHING LIKE THIS MY WHOLE LIFE!
YOU WON'T BELIEVE HOW COOL IT IS. I HAD TO TELL SOMEBODY!
THAT'S GREAT, JEREMY!
I DON'T KNOW A LOT ABOUT GUITARS, BUT I'D REALLY LIKE TO HEAR ABOUT IT.
SCOTT and BORGMAN
HANG ON A SEC, HECTOR. MY DAD IS INTERRUPTING ME.

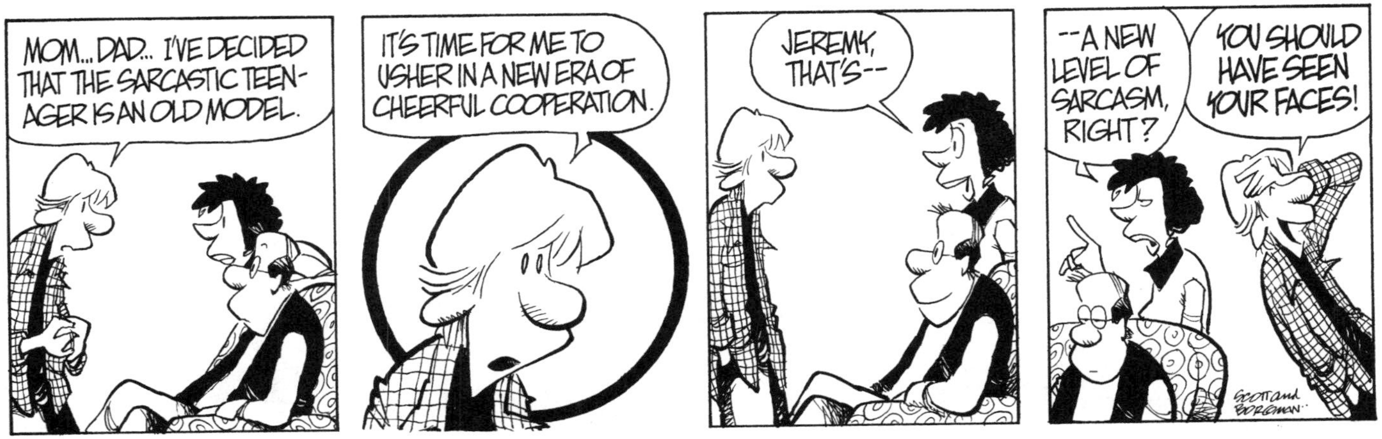
MOM... DAD... I'VE DECIDED THAT THE SARCASTIC TEEN-AGER IS AN OLD MODEL.
IT'S TIME FOR ME TO USHER IN A NEW ERA OF CHEERFUL COOPERATION.
JEREMY, THAT'S--
--A NEW LEVEL OF SARCASM, RIGHT?
YOU SHOULD HAVE SEEN YOUR FACES!
SCOTT and BORGMAN

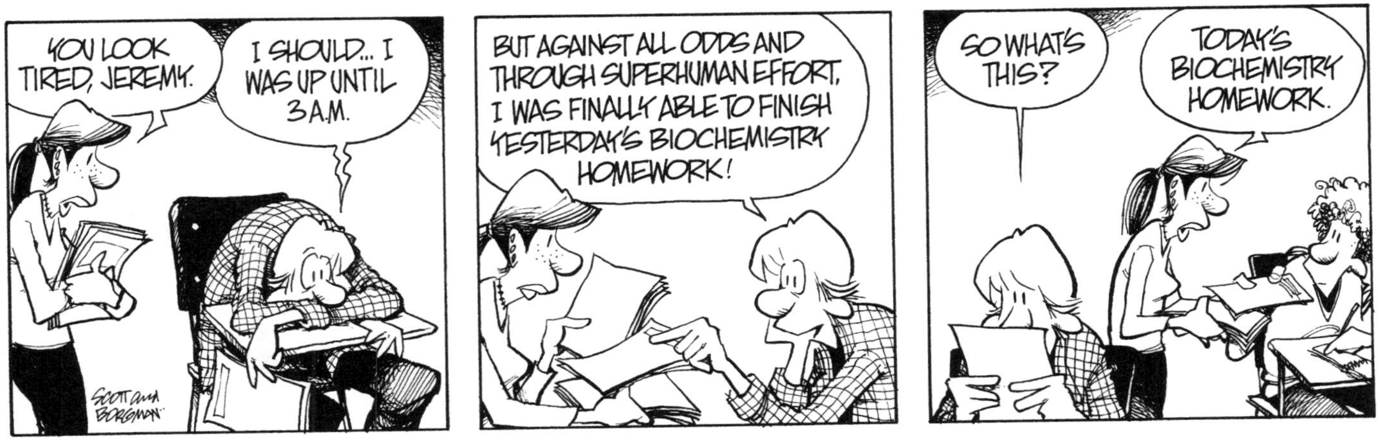
YOU LOOK TIRED, JEREMY.
I SHOULD... I WAS UP UNTIL 3 A.M.
SCOTT and BORGMAN
BUT AGAINST ALL ODDS AND THROUGH SUPERHUMAN EFFORT, I WAS FINALLY ABLE TO FINISH YESTERDAY'S BIOCHEMISTRY HOMEWORK!
SO WHAT'S THIS?
TODAY'S BIOCHEMISTRY HOMEWORK.

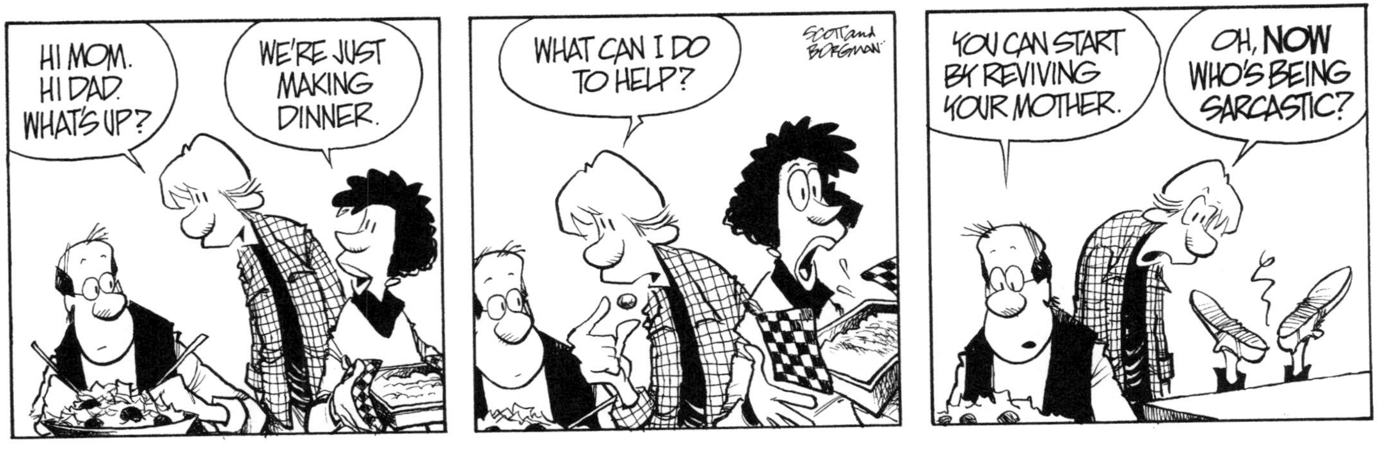
HI MOM. HI DAD. WHAT'S UP?
WE'RE JUST MAKING DINNER.
WHAT CAN I DO TO HELP?
SCOTT and BORGMAN
YOU CAN START BY REVIVING YOUR MOTHER.
OH, **NOW** WHO'S BEING SARCASTIC?

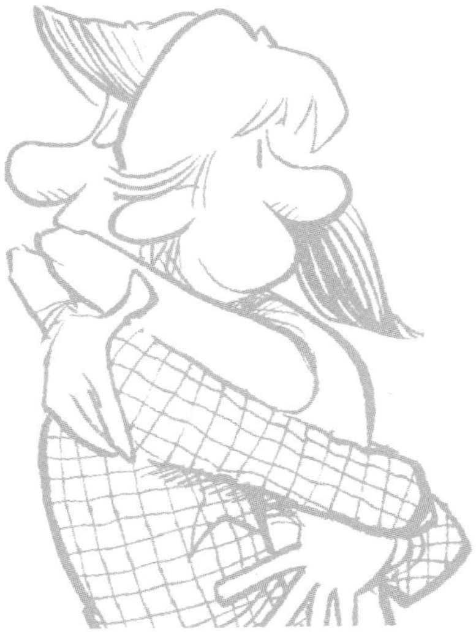

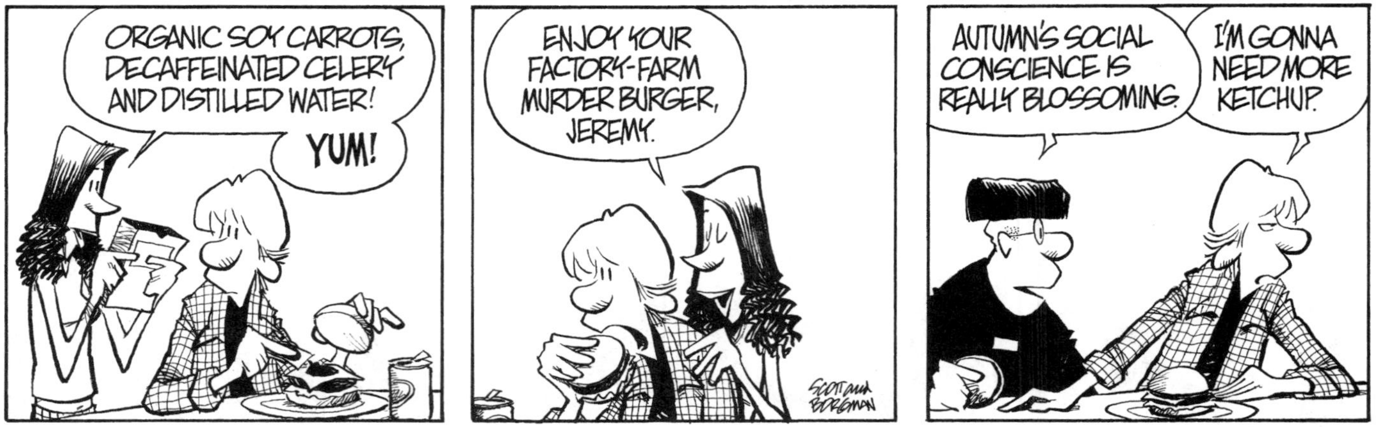
ORGANIC SOY CARROTS, DECAFFEINATED CELERY AND DISTILLED WATER!
YUM!
ENJOY YOUR FACTORY-FARM MURDER BURGER, JEREMY.
AUTUMN'S SOCIAL CONSCIENCE IS REALLY BLOSSOMING.
I'M GONNA NEED MORE KETCHUP.

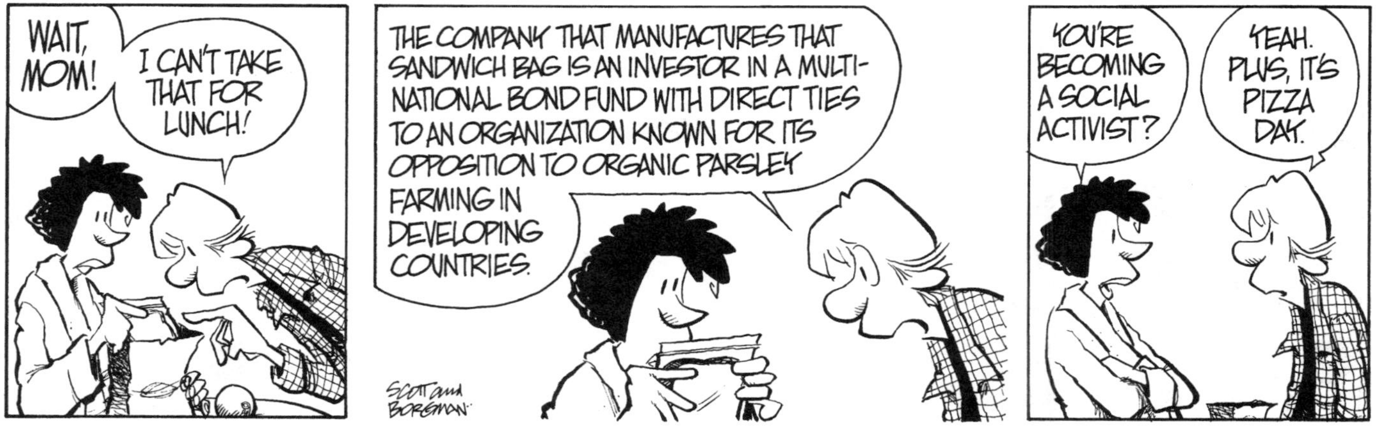
WAIT, MOM!
I CAN'T TAKE THAT FOR LUNCH!
THE COMPANY THAT MANUFACTURES THAT SANDWICH BAG IS AN INVESTOR IN A MULTI-NATIONAL BOND FUND WITH DIRECT TIES TO AN ORGANIZATION KNOWN FOR ITS OPPOSITION TO ORGANIC PARSLEY FARMING IN DEVELOPING COUNTRIES.
YOU'RE BECOMING A SOCIAL ACTIVIST?
YEAH. PLUS, IT'S PIZZA DAY.

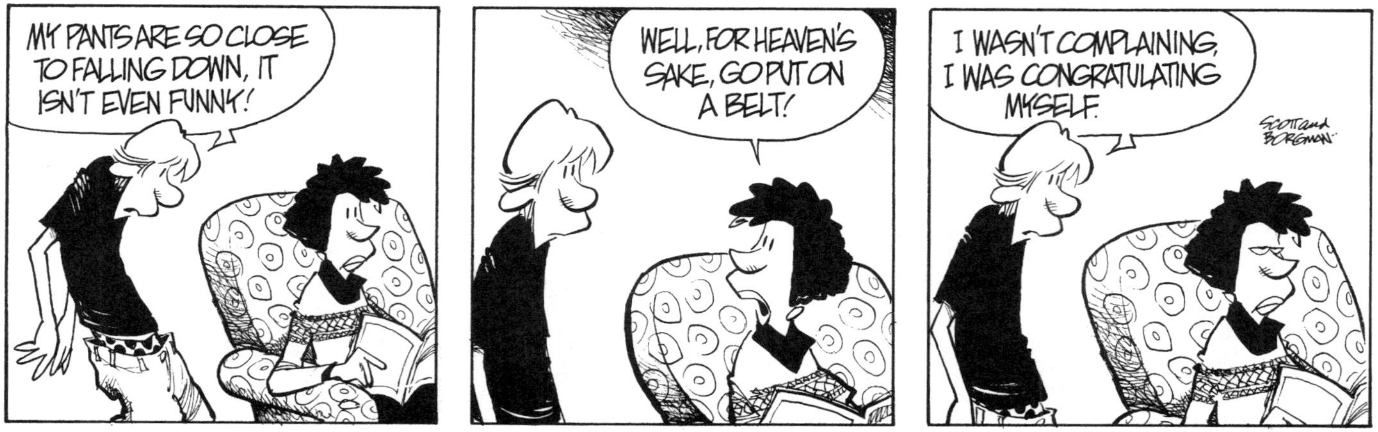
MY PANTS ARE SO CLOSE TO FALLING DOWN, IT ISN'T EVEN FUNNY!
WELL, FOR HEAVEN'S SAKE, GO PUT ON A BELT!
I WASN'T COMPLAINING, I WAS CONGRATULATING MYSELF.

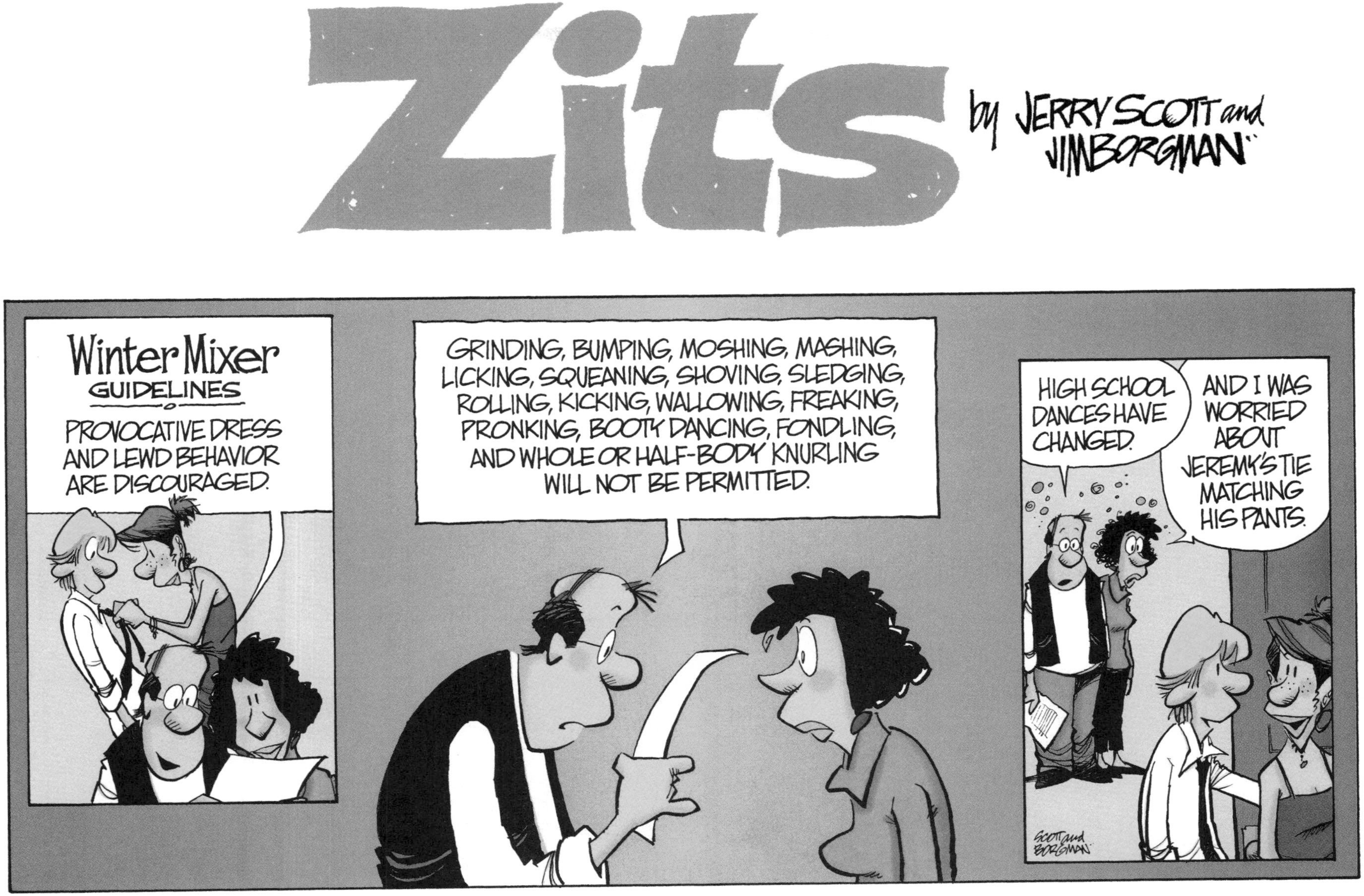
Zits
by JERRY SCOTT and JIM BORGMAN
Winter Mixer GUIDELINES
PROVOCATIVE DRESS AND LEWD BEHAVIOR ARE DISCOURAGED.
GRINDING, BUMPING, MOSHING, MASHING, LICKING, SQUEANING, SHOVING, SLEDGING, ROLLING, KICKING, WALLOWING, FREAKING, PRONKING, BOOTY DANCING, FONDLING, AND WHOLE OR HALF-BODY KNURLING WILL NOT BE PERMITTED.
HIGH SCHOOL DANCES HAVE CHANGED.
AND I WAS WORRIED ABOUT JEREMY'S TIE MATCHING HIS PANTS.
SCOTT and BORGMAN

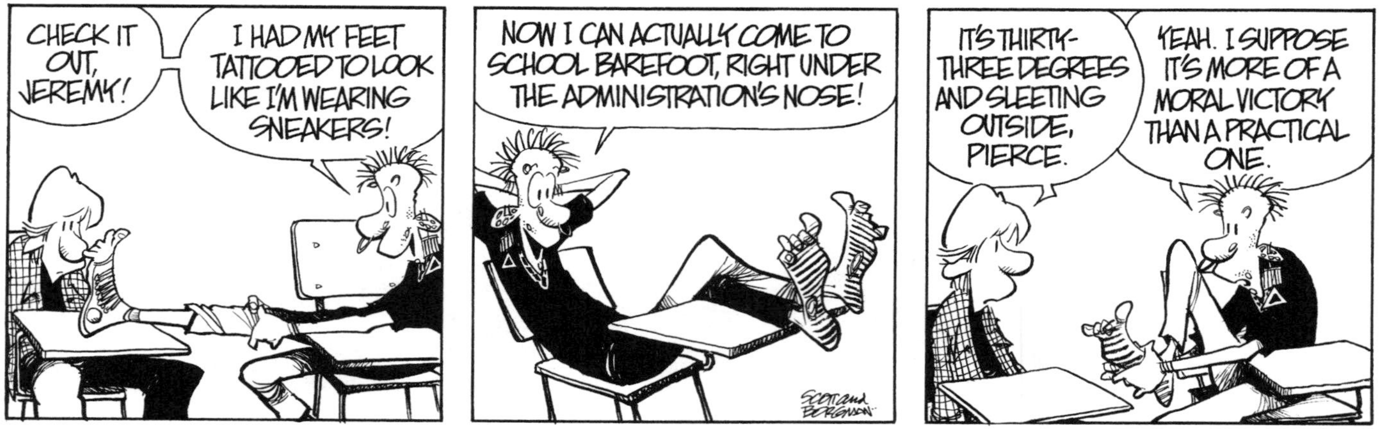
CHECK IT OUT, JEREMY!
I HAD MY FEET TATTOOED TO LOOK LIKE I'M WEARING SNEAKERS!
NOW I CAN ACTUALLY COME TO SCHOOL BAREFOOT, RIGHT UNDER THE ADMINISTRATION'S NOSE!
IT'S THIRTY-THREE DEGREES AND SLEETING OUTSIDE, PIERCE.
YEAH. I SUPPOSE IT'S MORE OF A MORAL VICTORY THAN A PRACTICAL ONE.

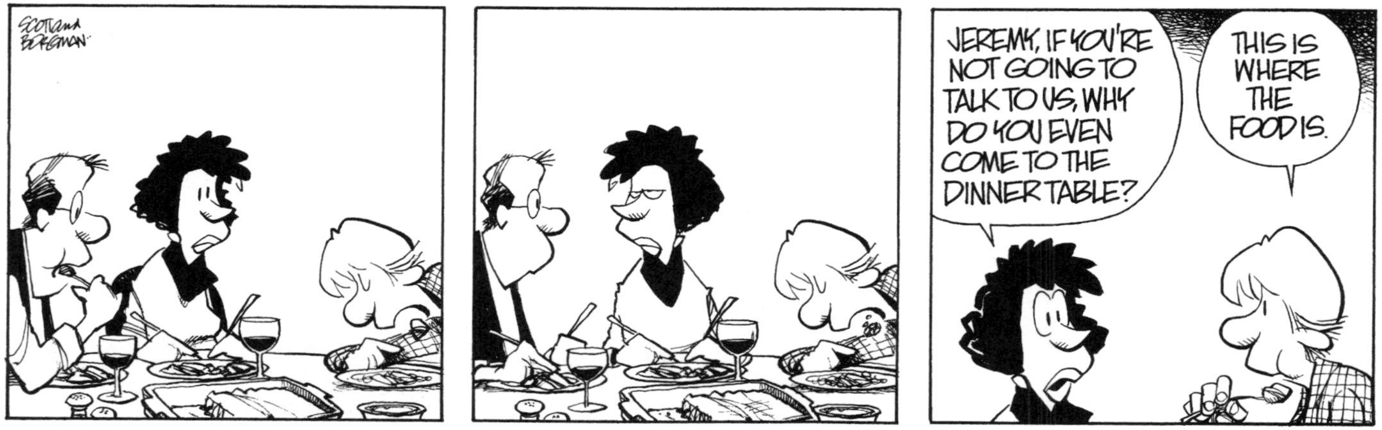
JEREMY, IF YOU'RE NOT GOING TO TALK TO US, WHY DO YOU EVEN COME TO THE DINNER TABLE?
THIS IS WHERE THE FOOD IS.

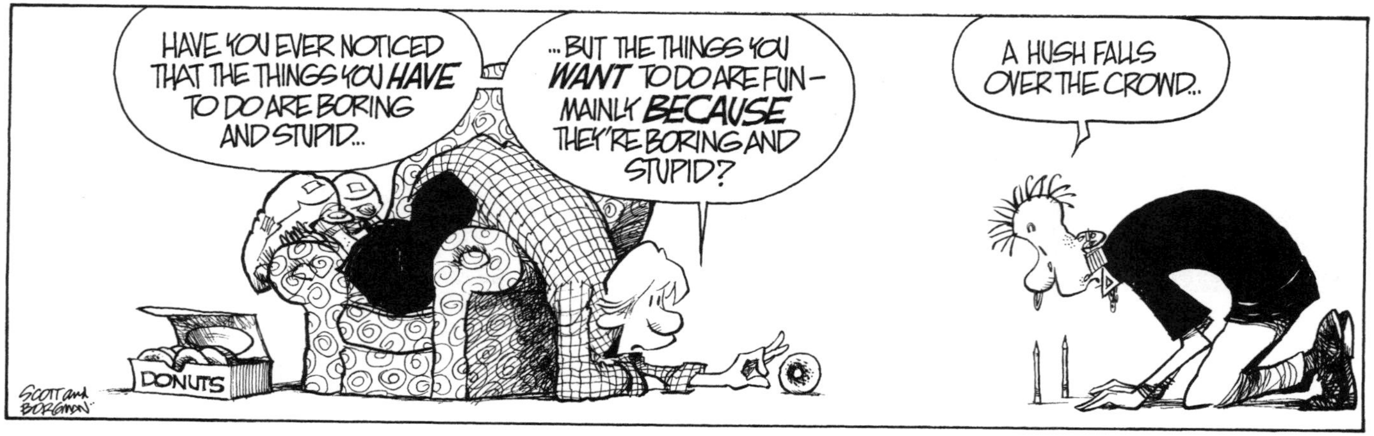
HAVE YOU EVER NOTICED THAT THE THINGS YOU HAVE TO DO ARE BORING AND STUPID...
...BUT THE THINGS YOU WANT TO DO ARE FUN-MAINLY BECAUSE THEY'RE BORING AND STUPID?
A HUSH FALLS OVER THE CROWD...
DONUTS

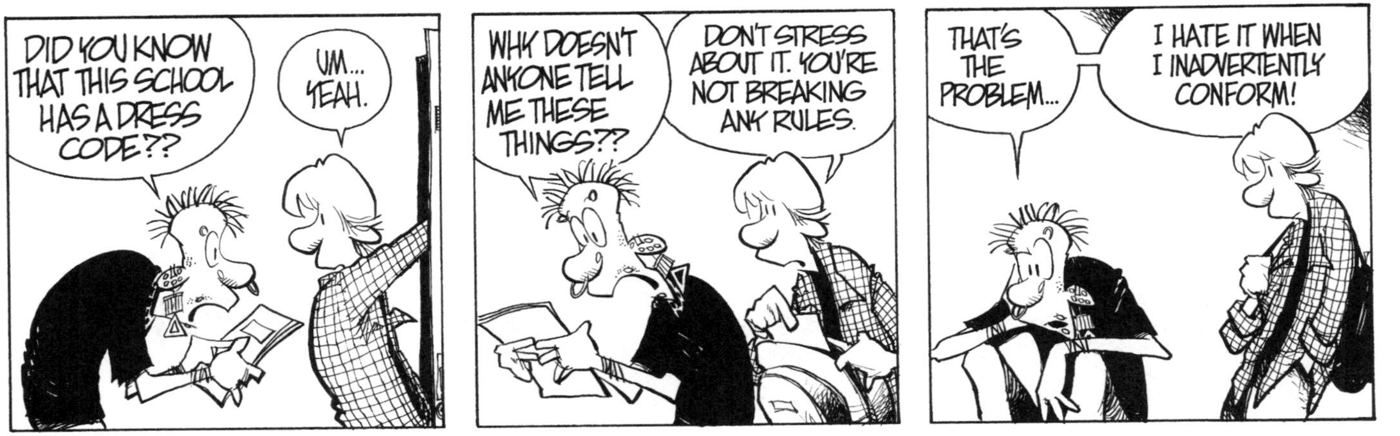
DID YOU KNOW THAT THIS SCHOOL HAS A DRESS CODE??
UM... YEAH.
WHY DOESN'T ANYONE TELL ME THESE THINGS??
DON'T STRESS ABOUT IT. YOU'RE NOT BREAKING ANY RULES.
THAT'S THE PROBLEM...
I HATE IT WHEN I INADVERTENTLY CONFORM!

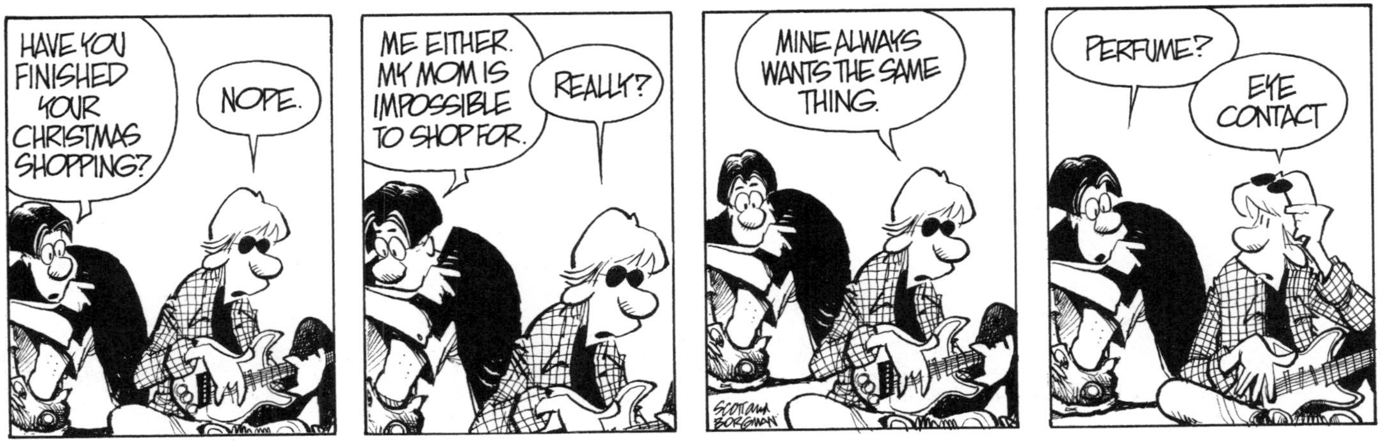
HAVE YOU FINISHED YOUR CHRISTMAS SHOPPING?
NOPE.
ME EITHER. MY MOM IS IMPOSSIBLE TO SHOP FOR.
REALLY?
MINE ALWAYS WANTS THE SAME THING.
SCOTT and BORGMAN
PERFUME?
EYE CONTACT

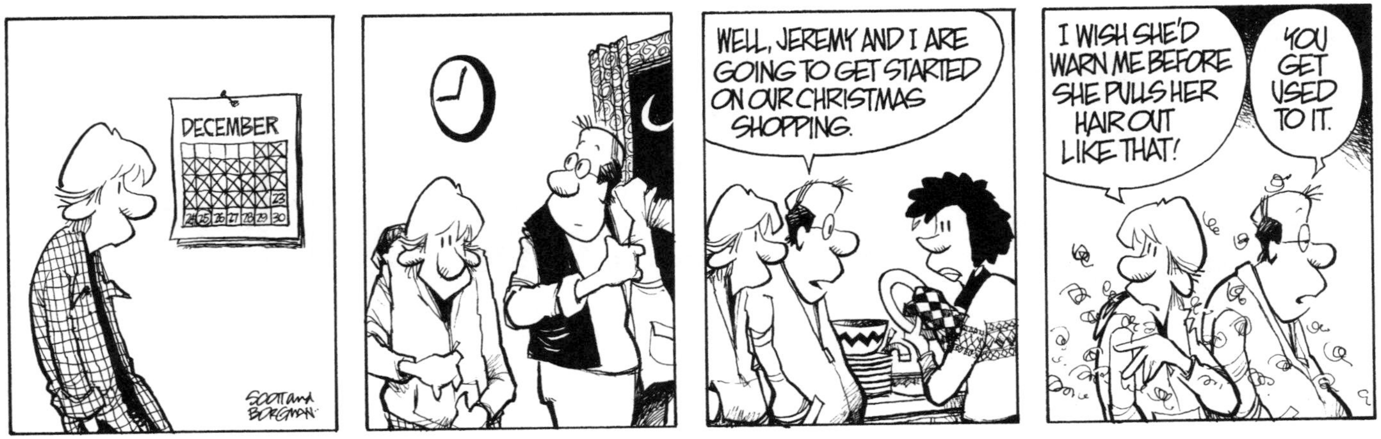
DECEMBER
SCOTT and BORGMAN
WELL, JEREMY AND I ARE GOING TO GET STARTED ON OUR CHRISTMAS SHOPPING.
I WISH SHE'D WARN ME BEFORE SHE PULLS HER HAIR OUT LIKE THAT!
YOU GET USED TO IT.

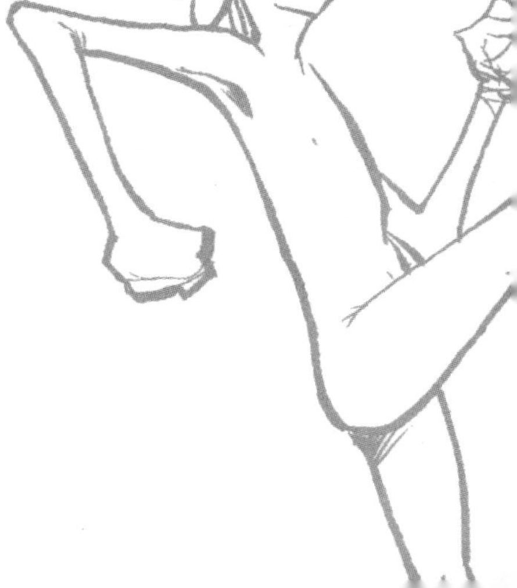

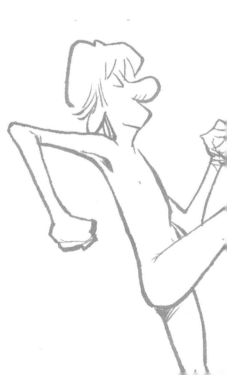

Zits

by JERRY SCOTT and JIM BORGMAN

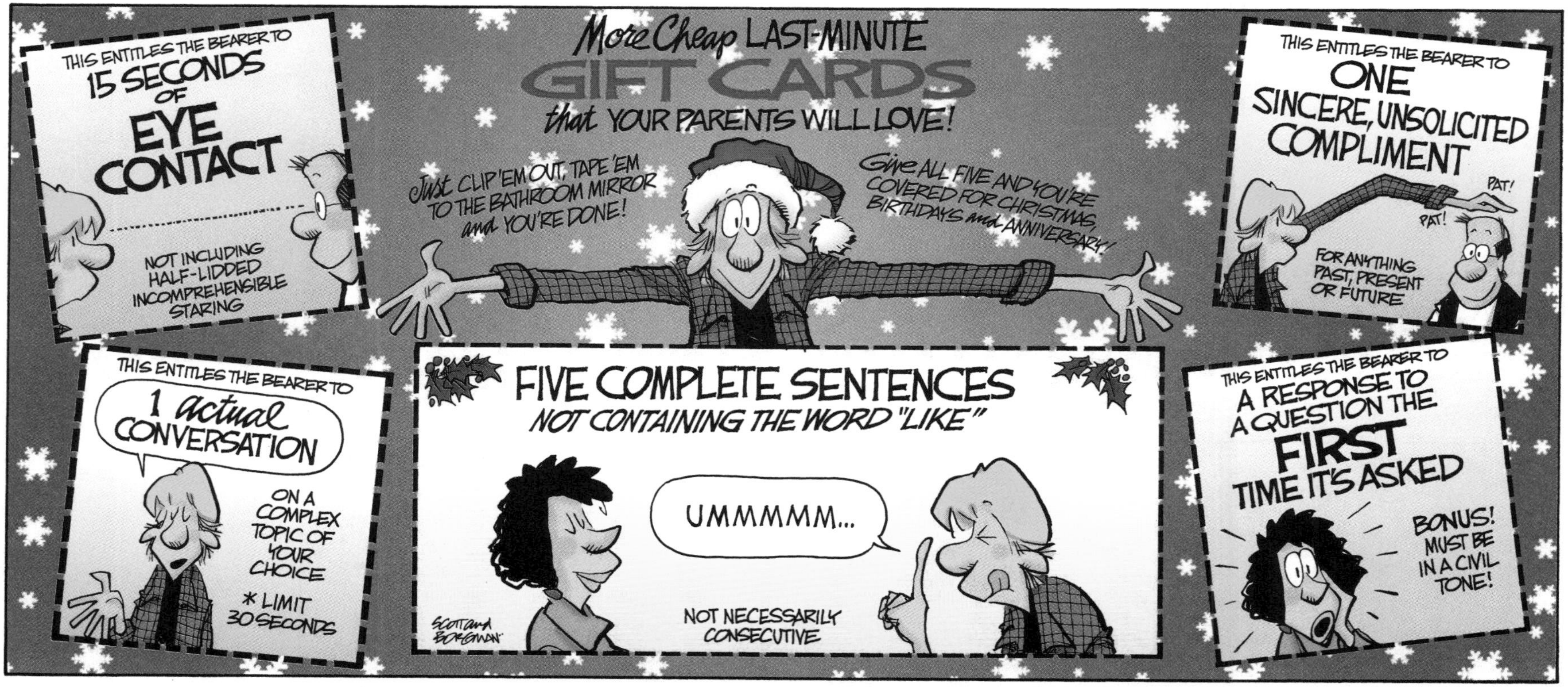
More Cheap LAST-MINUTE
GIFT CARDS
that YOUR PARENTS WILL LOVE!
Just CLIP 'EM OUT, TAPE 'EM TO THE BATHROOM MIRROR and YOU'RE DONE!
Give ALL FIVE AND YOU'RE COVERED FOR CHRISTMAS, BIRTHDAYS and ANNIVERSARY!
THIS ENTITLES THE BEARER TO
15 SECONDS OF EYE CONTACT
NOT INCLUDING HALF-LIDDED INCOMPREHENSIBLE STARING
THIS ENTITLES THE BEARER TO
ONE SINCERE, UNSOLICITED COMPLIMENT
PAT!
PAT!
FOR ANYTHING PAST, PRESENT OR FUTURE
THIS ENTITLES THE BEARER TO
1 actual CONVERSATION
ON A COMPLEX TOPIC OF YOUR CHOICE
* LIMIT 30 SECONDS
FIVE COMPLETE SENTENCES
NOT CONTAINING THE WORD "LIKE"
UMMMMM...
NOT NECESSARILY CONSECUTIVE
SCOTT and BORGMAN
THIS ENTITLES THE BEARER TO
A RESPONSE TO A QUESTION THE FIRST TIME IT'S ASKED
BONUS! MUST BE IN A CIVIL TONE!

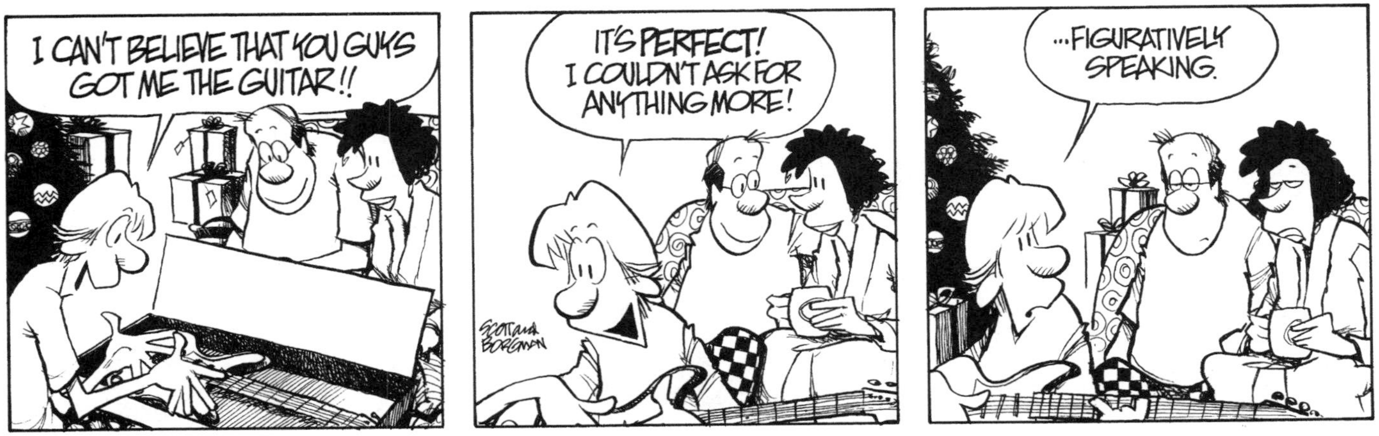
I CAN'T BELIEVE THAT YOU GUYS GOT ME THE GUITAR!!
IT'S PERFECT! I COULDN'T ASK FOR ANYTHING MORE!
SCOTT and BORGMAN
...FIGURATIVELY SPEAKING.

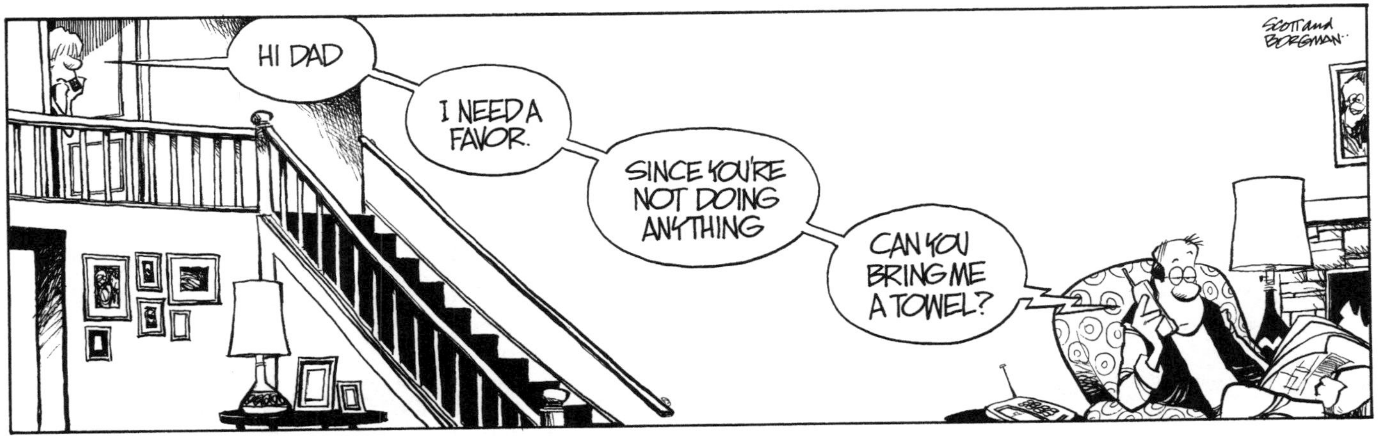
SCOTT and BORGMAN
HI DAD
I NEED A FAVOR.
SINCE YOU'RE NOT DOING ANYTHING
CAN YOU BRING ME A TOWEL?

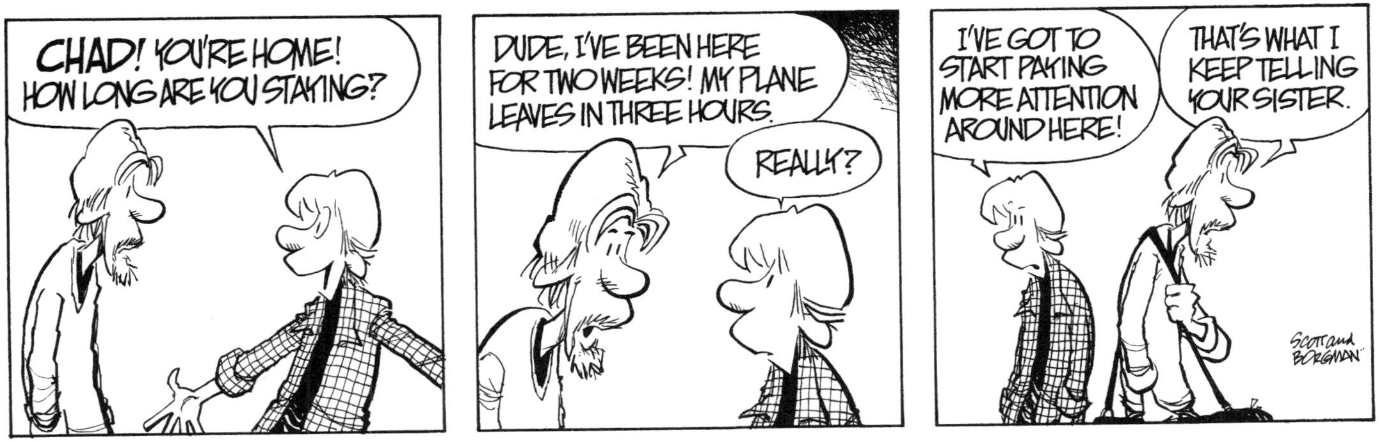
CHAD! YOU'RE HOME! HOW LONG ARE YOU STAYING?
DUDE, I'VE BEEN HERE FOR TWO WEEKS! MY PLANE LEAVES IN THREE HOURS.
REALLY?
I'VE GOT TO START PAYING MORE ATTENTION AROUND HERE!
THAT'S WHAT I KEEP TELLING YOUR SISTER.
SCOTT and BORGMAN

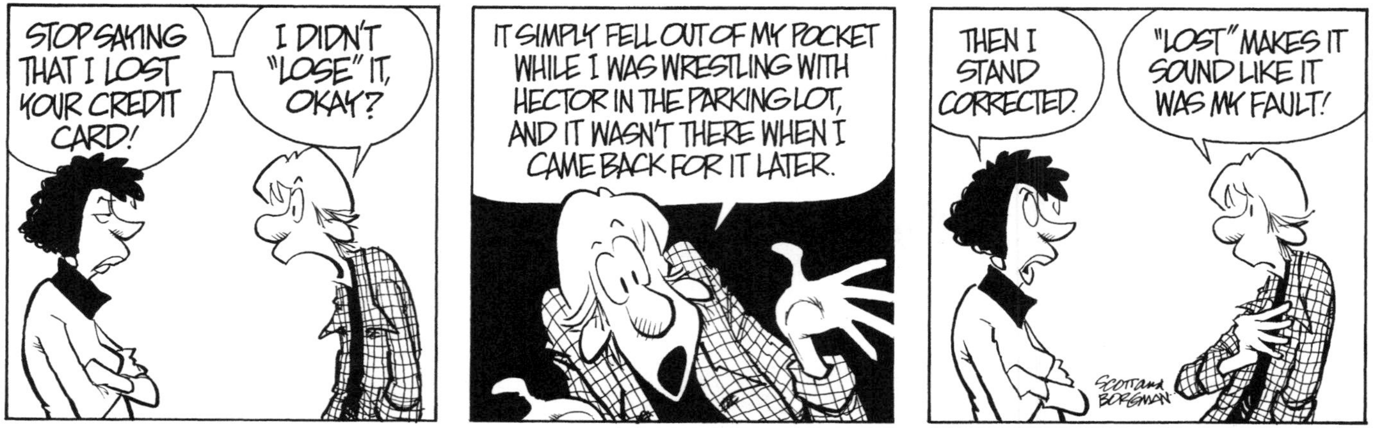
STOP SAYING THAT I LOST YOUR CREDIT CARD!
I DIDN'T "LOSE" IT, OKAY?
IT SIMPLY FELL OUT OF MY POCKET WHILE I WAS WRESTLING WITH HECTOR IN THE PARKING LOT, AND IT WASN'T THERE WHEN I CAME BACK FOR IT LATER.
THEN I STAND CORRECTED.
"LOST" MAKES IT SOUND LIKE IT WAS MY FAULT!
SCOTT and BORGMAN

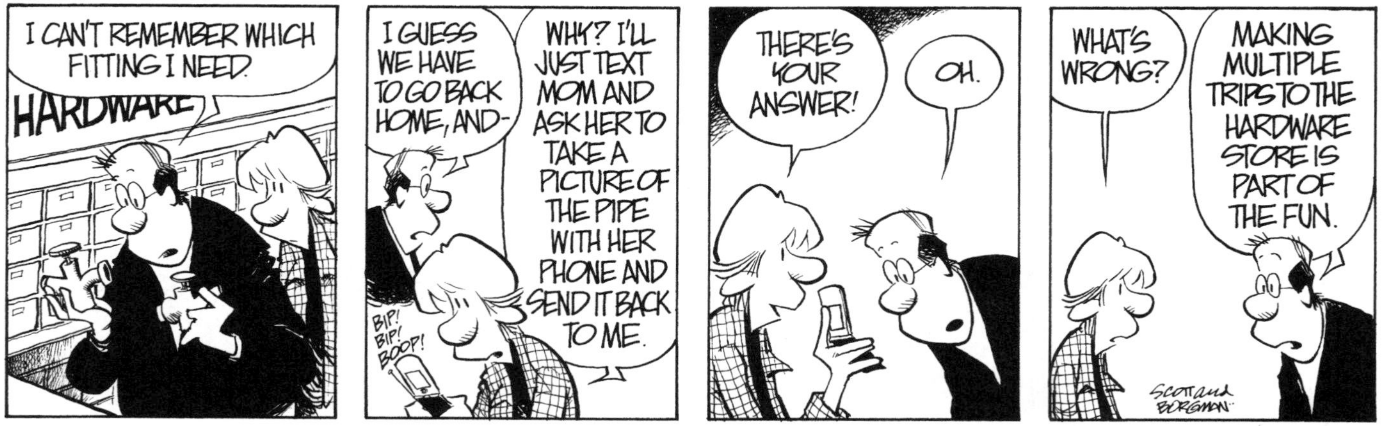
I CAN'T REMEMBER WHICH FITTING I NEED.
HARDWARE
I GUESS WE HAVE TO GO BACK HOME, AND-
WHY? I'LL JUST TEXT MOM AND ASK HER TO TAKE A PICTURE OF THE PIPE WITH HER PHONE AND SEND IT BACK TO ME.
BIP! BIP! BOOP!
THERE'S YOUR ANSWER!
OH.
WHAT'S WRONG?
MAKING MULTIPLE TRIPS TO THE HARDWARE STORE IS PART OF THE FUN.
SCOTT and BORGMAN

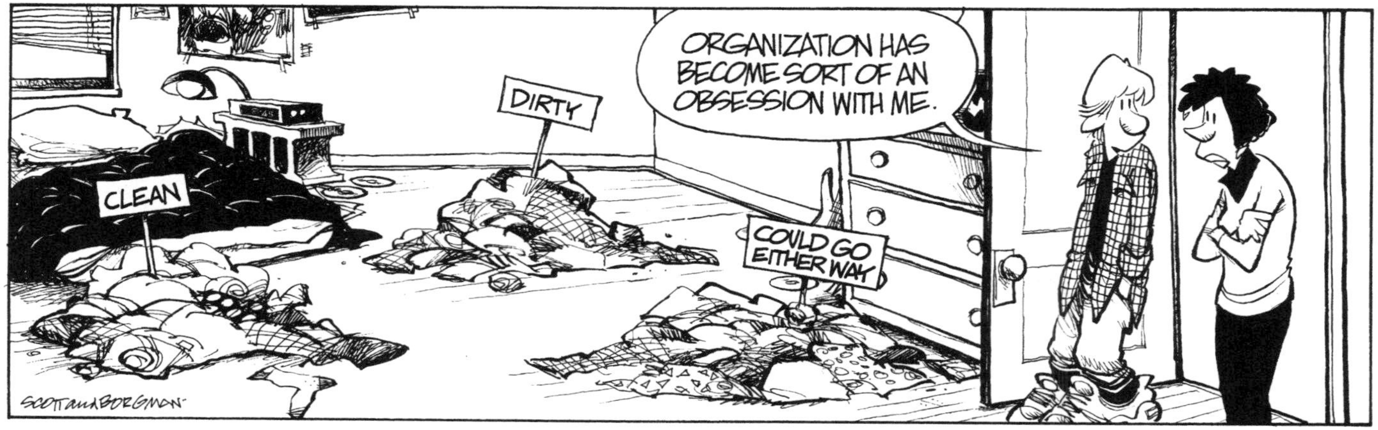
DIRTY
CLEAN
COULD GO EITHER WAY
ORGANIZATION HAS BECOME SORT OF AN OBSESSION WITH ME.
SCOTT and BORGMAN

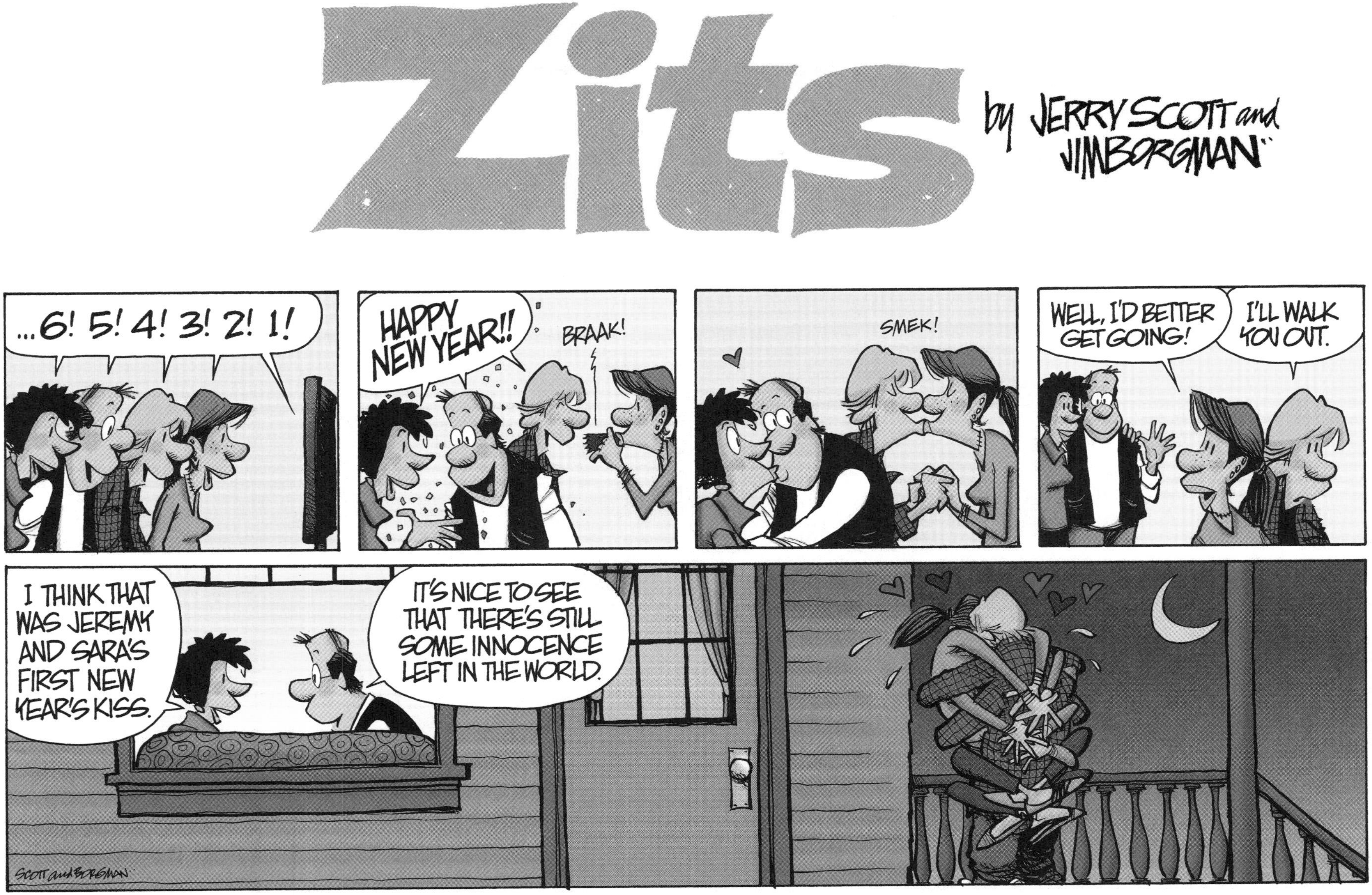
Zits
by JERRY SCOTT and JIM BORGMAN
...6! 5! 4! 3! 2! 1!
HAPPY NEW YEAR!!
BRAAK!
SMEK!
WELL, I'D BETTER GET GOING!
I'LL WALK YOU OUT.
I THINK THAT WAS JEREMY AND SARA'S FIRST NEW YEAR'S KISS.
IT'S NICE TO SEE THAT THERE'S STILL SOME INNOCENCE LEFT IN THE WORLD.
SCOTT and BORGMAN

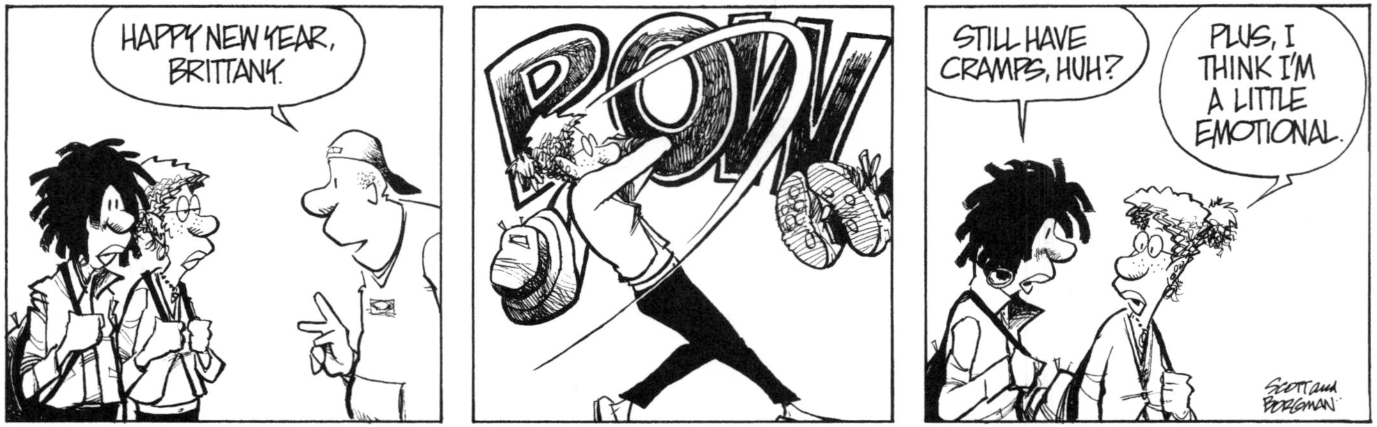
HAPPY NEW YEAR, BRITTANY.
POW
STILL HAVE CRAMPS, HUH?
PLUS, I THINK I'M A LITTLE EMOTIONAL.
SCOTT AND BORGMAN

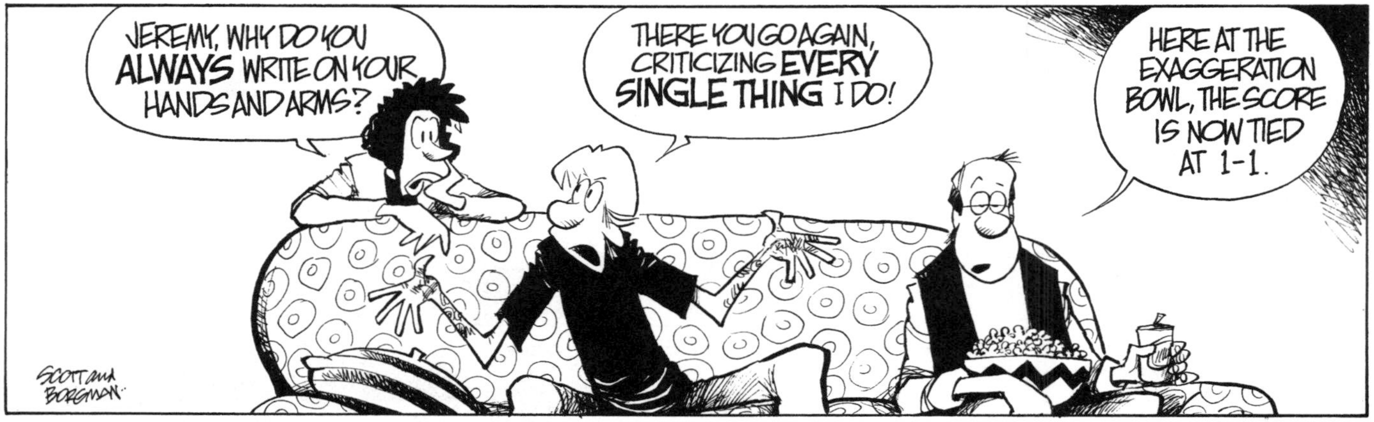
JEREMY, WHY DO YOU **ALWAYS** WRITE ON YOUR HANDS AND ARMS?
THERE YOU GO AGAIN, CRITICIZING **EVERY SINGLE THING** I DO!
HERE AT THE EXAGGERATION BOWL, THE SCORE IS NOW TIED AT 1-1.
SCOTT AND BORGMAN

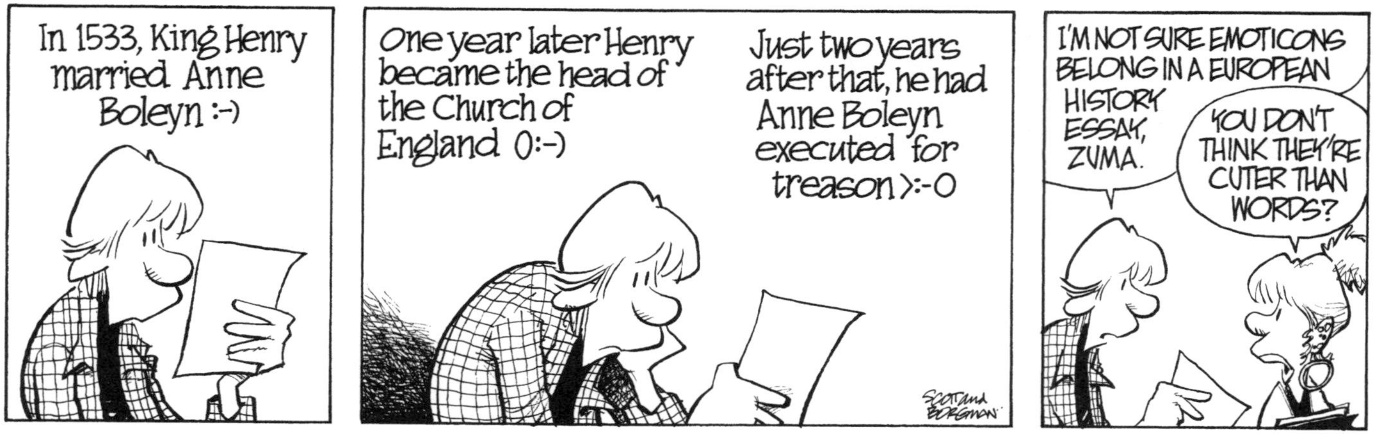
In 1533, King Henry married Anne Boleyn :-)
One year later Henry became the head of the Church of England ():-)
Just two years after that, he had Anne Boleyn executed for treason >:-O
SCOTT AND BORGMAN
I'M NOT SURE EMOTICONS BELONG IN A EUROPEAN HISTORY ESSAY, ZUMA.
YOU DON'T THINK THEY'RE CUTER THAN WORDS?

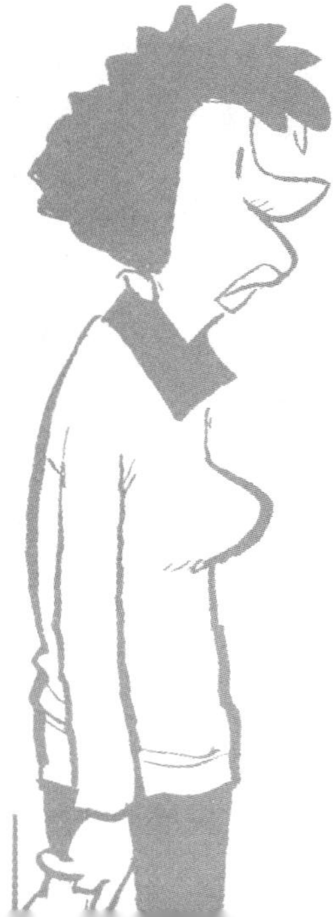

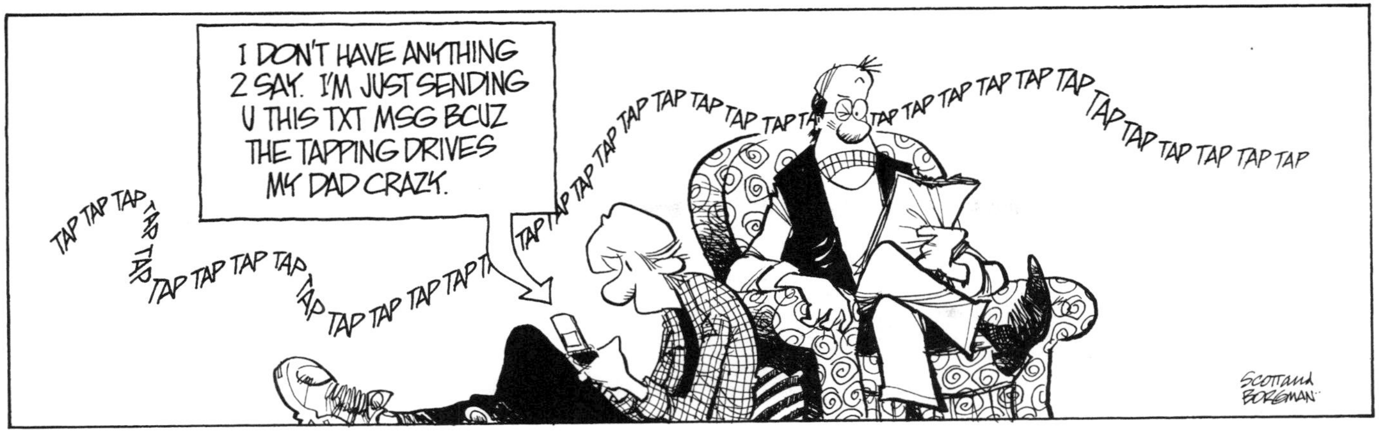
I DON'T HAVE ANYTHING 2 SAY. I'M JUST SENDING U THIS TXT MSG BCUZ THE TAPPING DRIVES MY DAD CRAZY.
TAP TAP TAP

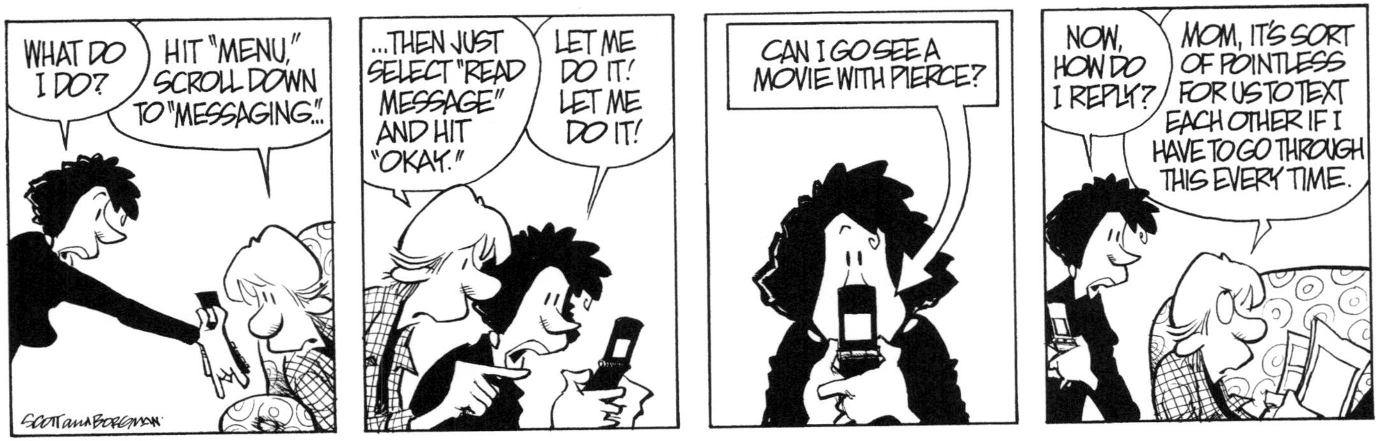
WHAT DO I DO?
HIT "MENU," SCROLL DOWN TO "MESSAGING"...
...THEN JUST SELECT "READ MESSAGE" AND HIT "OKAY."
LET ME DO IT! LET ME DO IT!
CAN I GO SEE A MOVIE WITH PIERCE?
NOW, HOW DO I REPLY?
MOM, IT'S SORT OF POINTLESS FOR US TO TEXT EACH OTHER IF I HAVE TO GO THROUGH THIS EVERY TIME.

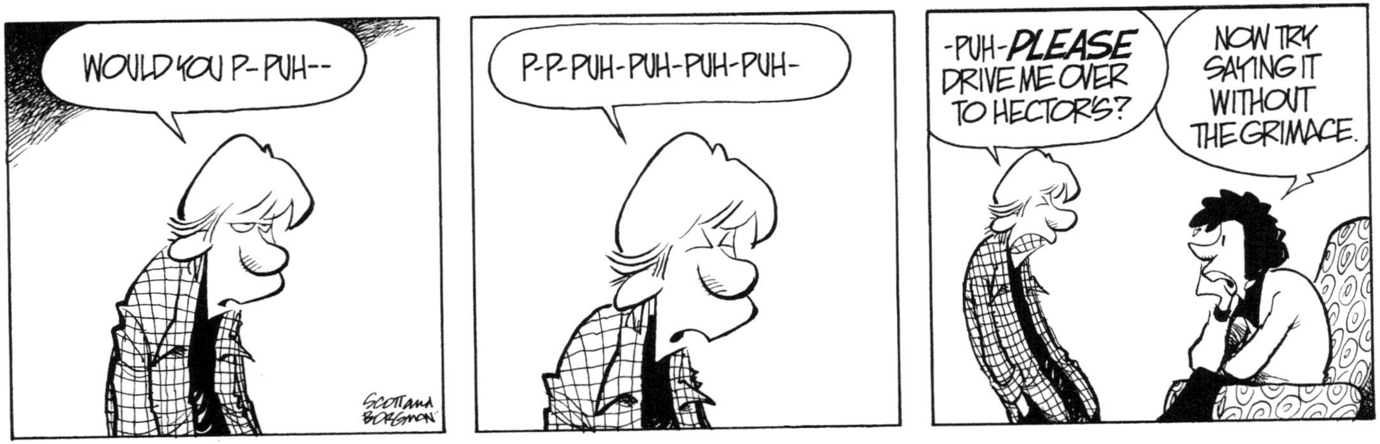
WOULD YOU P-PUH--
P-P-PUH-PUH-PUH-PUH-
-PUH-**PLEASE** DRIVE ME OVER TO HECTOR'S?
NOW TRY SAYING IT WITHOUT THE GRIMACE.

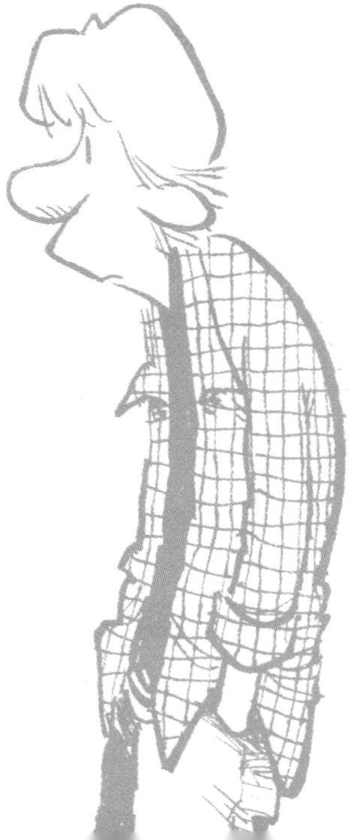

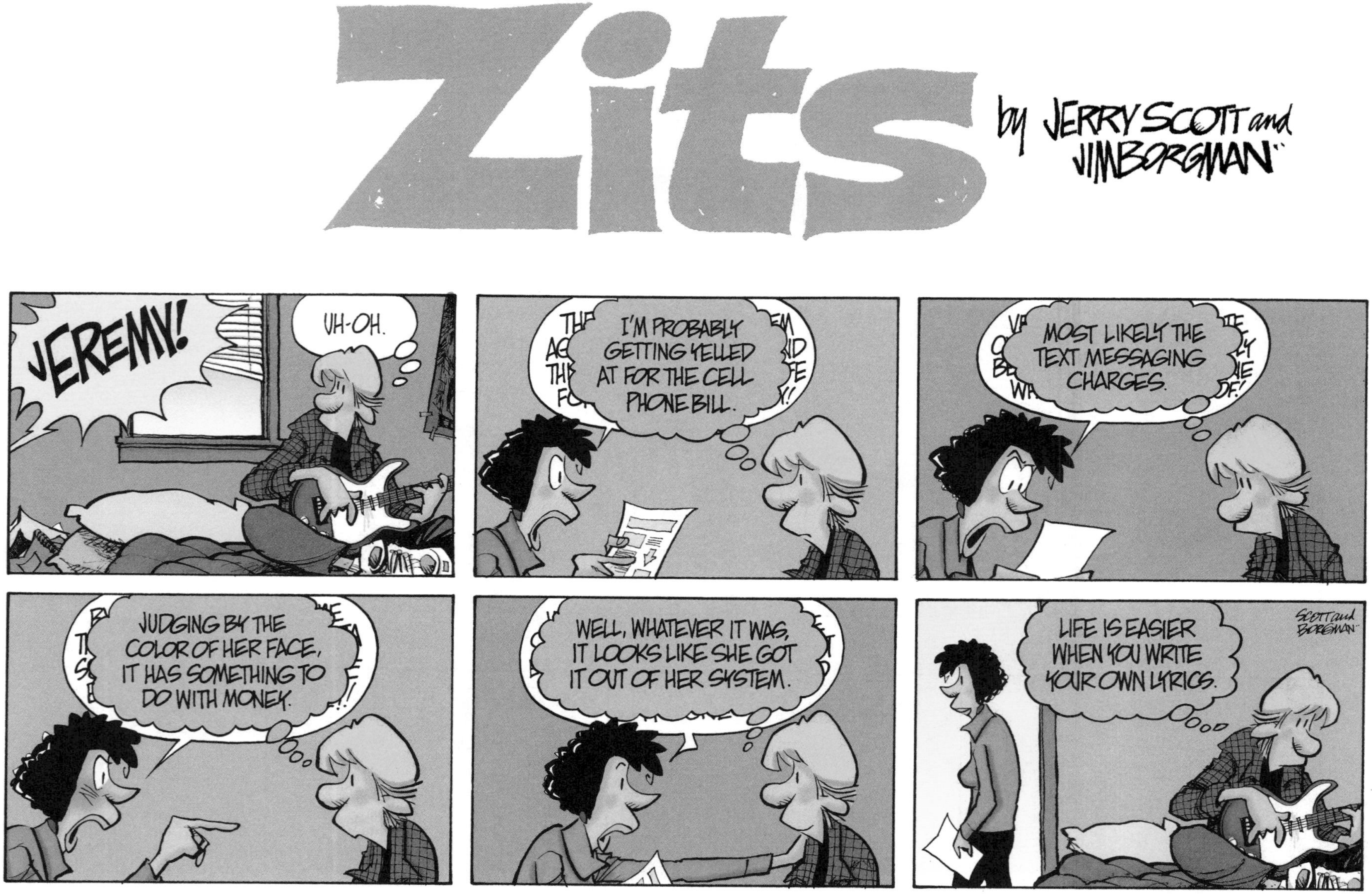
Zits
by JERRY SCOTT and JIM BORGMAN
JEREMY!
UH-OH.
I'M PROBABLY GETTING YELLED AT FOR THE CELL PHONE BILL.
MOST LIKELY THE TEXT MESSAGING CHARGES.
JUDGING BY THE COLOR OF HER FACE, IT HAS SOMETHING TO DO WITH MONEY.
WELL, WHATEVER IT WAS, IT LOOKS LIKE SHE GOT IT OUT OF HER SYSTEM.
SCOTT and BORGMAN
LIFE IS EASIER WHEN YOU WRITE YOUR OWN LYRICS.

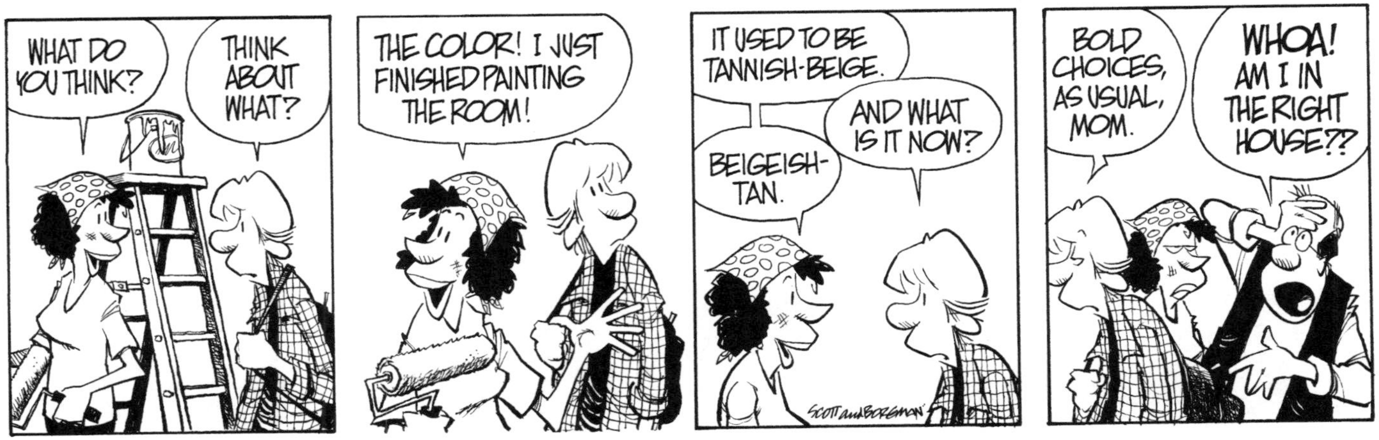
WHAT DO YOU THINK?
THINK ABOUT WHAT?
THE COLOR! I JUST FINISHED PAINTING THE ROOM!
IT USED TO BE TANNISH-BEIGE.
AND WHAT IS IT NOW?
BEIGEISH-TAN.
BOLD CHOICES, AS USUAL, MOM.
WHOA! AM I IN THE RIGHT HOUSE??

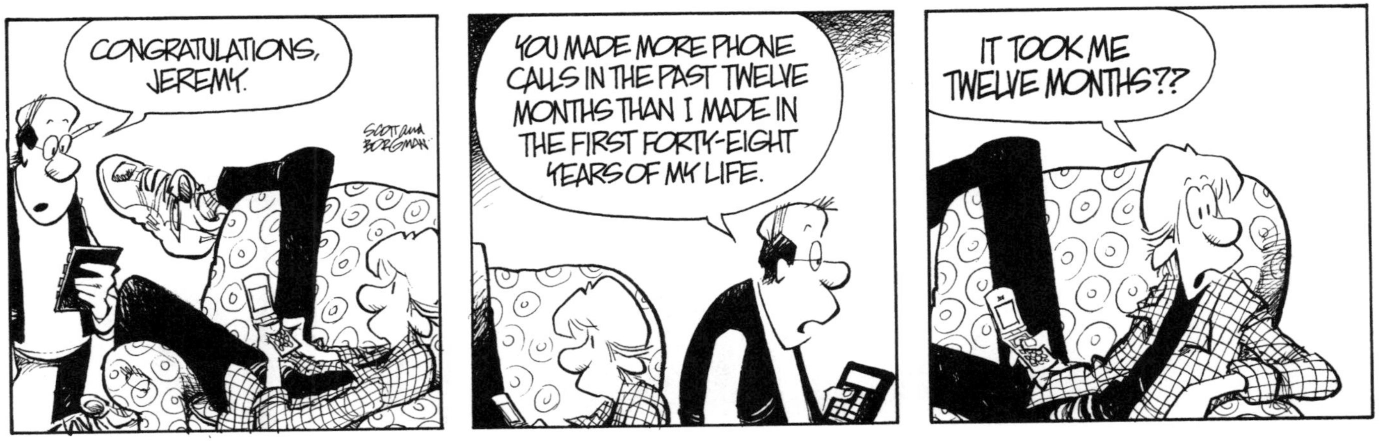
CONGRATULATIONS, JEREMY.
YOU MADE MORE PHONE CALLS IN THE PAST TWELVE MONTHS THAN I MADE IN THE FIRST FORTY-EIGHT YEARS OF MY LIFE.
IT TOOK ME TWELVE MONTHS??

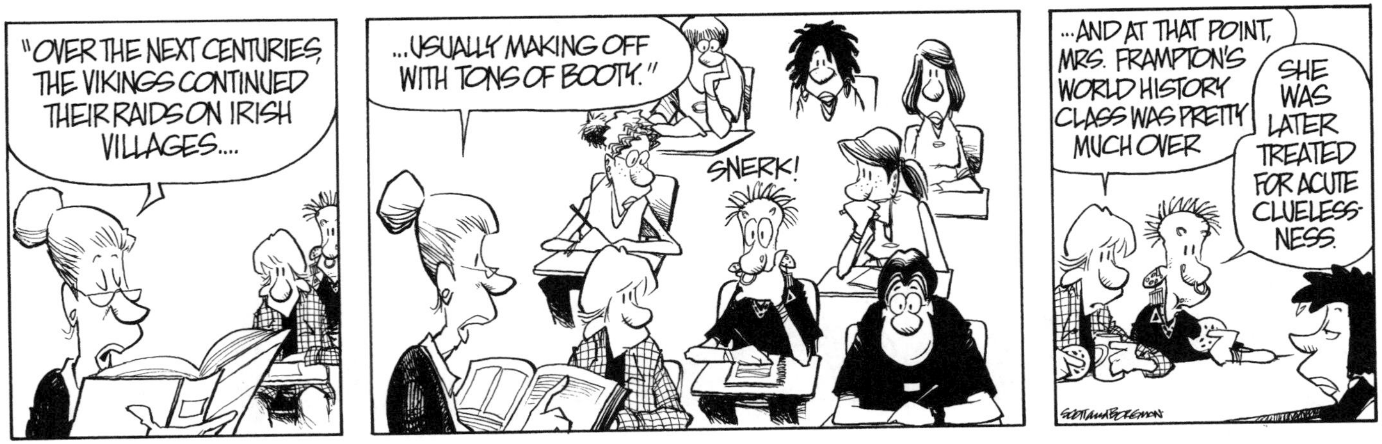
"OVER THE NEXT CENTURIES, THE VIKINGS CONTINUED THEIR RAIDS ON IRISH VILLAGES....
...USUALLY MAKING OFF WITH TONS OF BOOTY."
SNERK!
...AND AT THAT POINT, MRS. FRAMPTON'S WORLD HISTORY CLASS WAS PRETTY MUCH OVER
SHE WAS LATER TREATED FOR ACUTE CLUELESS-NESS.

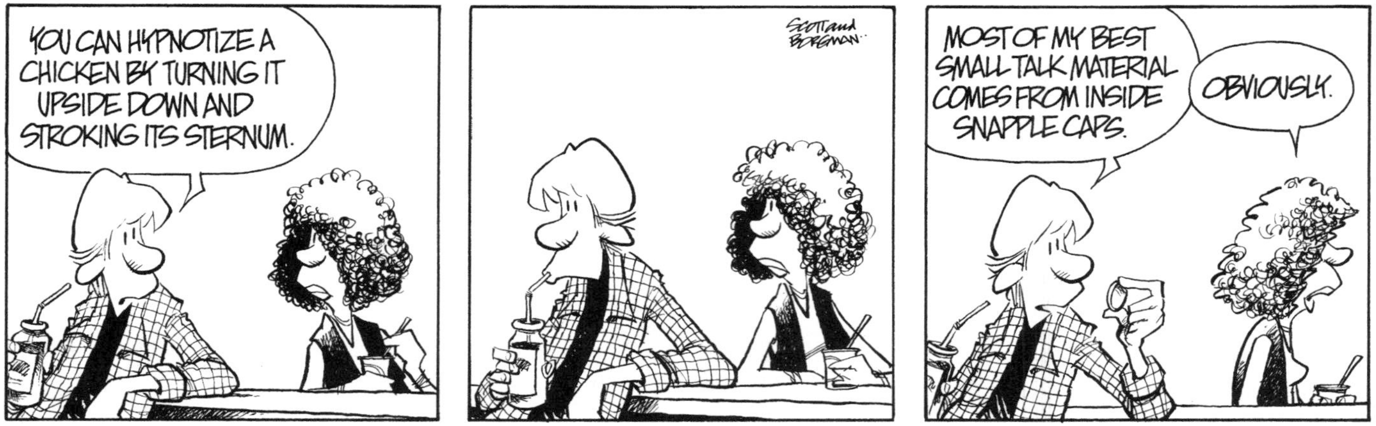
YOU CAN HYPNOTIZE A CHICKEN BY TURNING IT UPSIDE DOWN AND STROKING ITS STERNUM.
MOST OF MY BEST SMALL-TALK MATERIAL COMES FROM INSIDE SNAPPLE CAPS.
OBVIOUSLY.

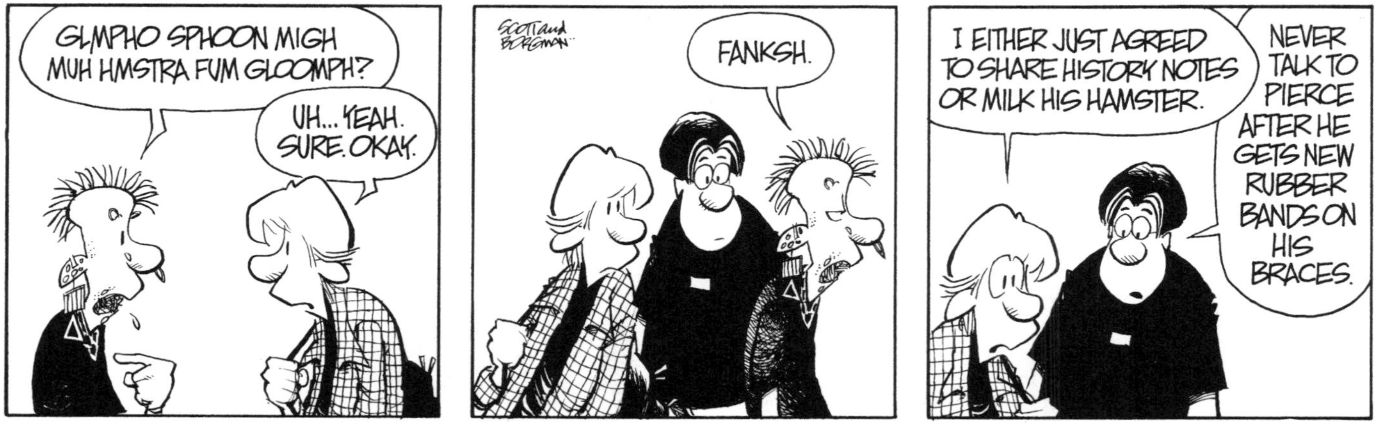
GLMPHO SPHOON MIGH MUH HMSTRA FUM GLOOMPH?
UH... YEAH. SURE. OKAY.
FANKSH.
I EITHER JUST AGREED TO SHARE HISTORY NOTES OR MILK HIS HAMSTER.
NEVER TALK TO PIERCE AFTER HE GETS NEW RUBBER BANDS ON HIS BRACES.

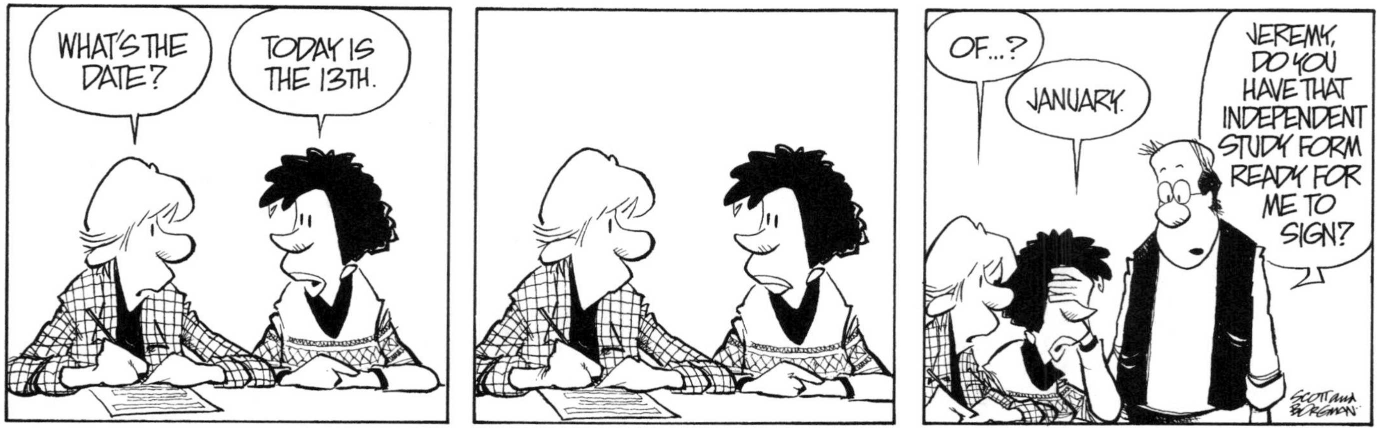
WHAT'S THE DATE?
TODAY IS THE 13TH.
OF...?
JANUARY.
JEREMY, DO YOU HAVE THAT INDEPENDENT STUDY FORM READY FOR ME TO SIGN?

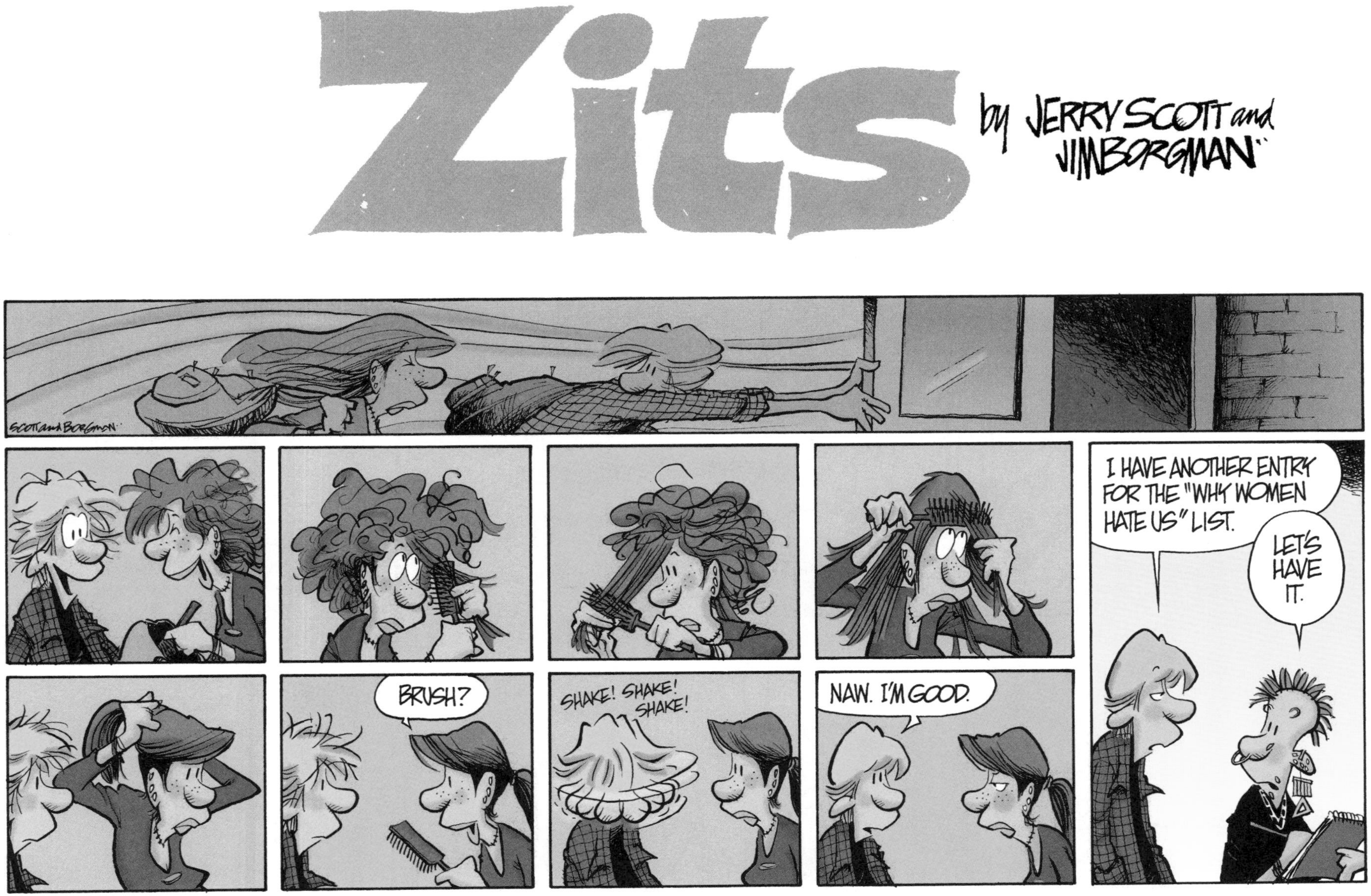
Zits
by JERRY SCOTT and JIM BORGMAN
SCOTT and BORGMAN
BRUSH?
SHAKE! SHAKE! SHAKE!
NAW. I'M GOOD.
I HAVE ANOTHER ENTRY FOR THE "WHY WOMEN HATE US" LIST.
LET'S HAVE IT.

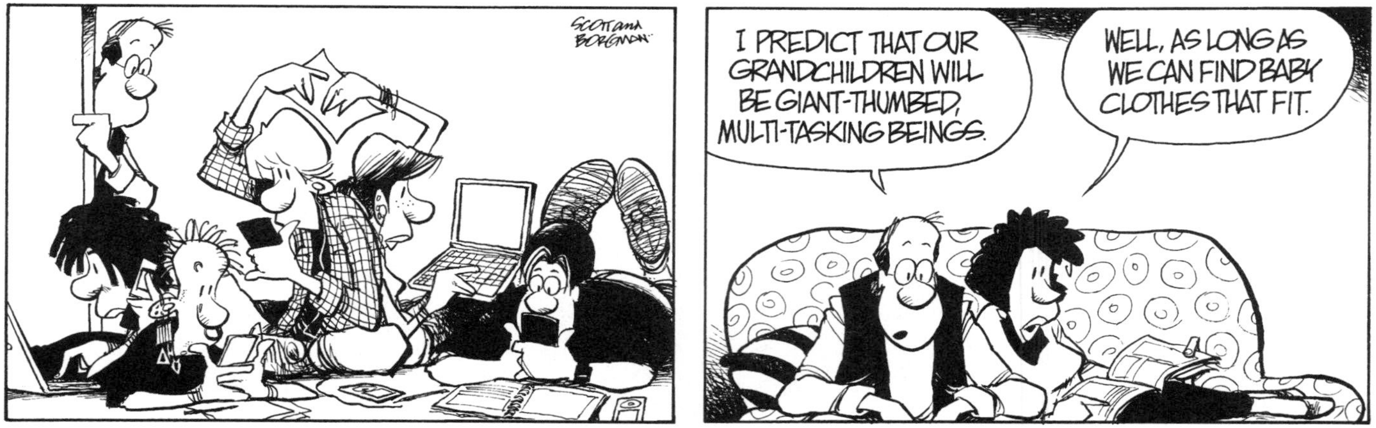
I PREDICT THAT OUR GRANDCHILDREN WILL BE GIANT-THUMBED, MULTI-TASKING BEINGS.
WELL, AS LONG AS WE CAN FIND BABY CLOTHES THAT FIT.

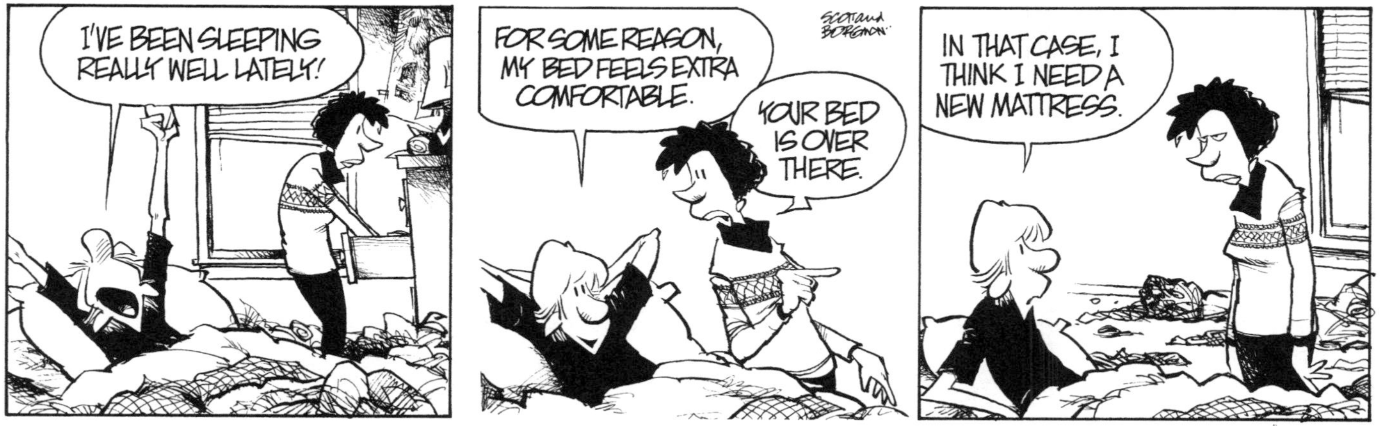
I'VE BEEN SLEEPING REALLY WELL LATELY!
FOR SOME REASON, MY BED FEELS EXTRA COMFORTABLE.
YOUR BED IS OVER THERE.
IN THAT CASE, I THINK I NEED A NEW MATTRESS.

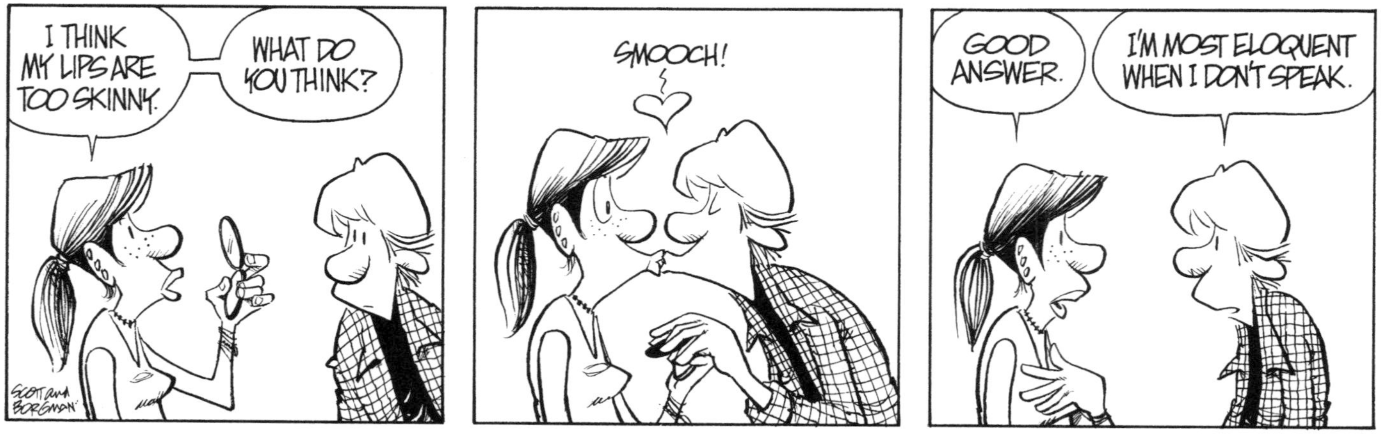
I THINK MY LIPS ARE TOO SKINNY.
WHAT DO YOU THINK?
SMOOCH!
GOOD ANSWER.
I'M MOST ELOQUENT WHEN I DON'T SPEAK.

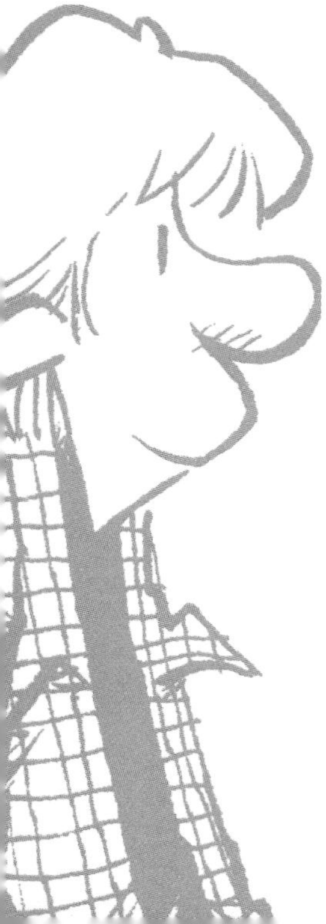

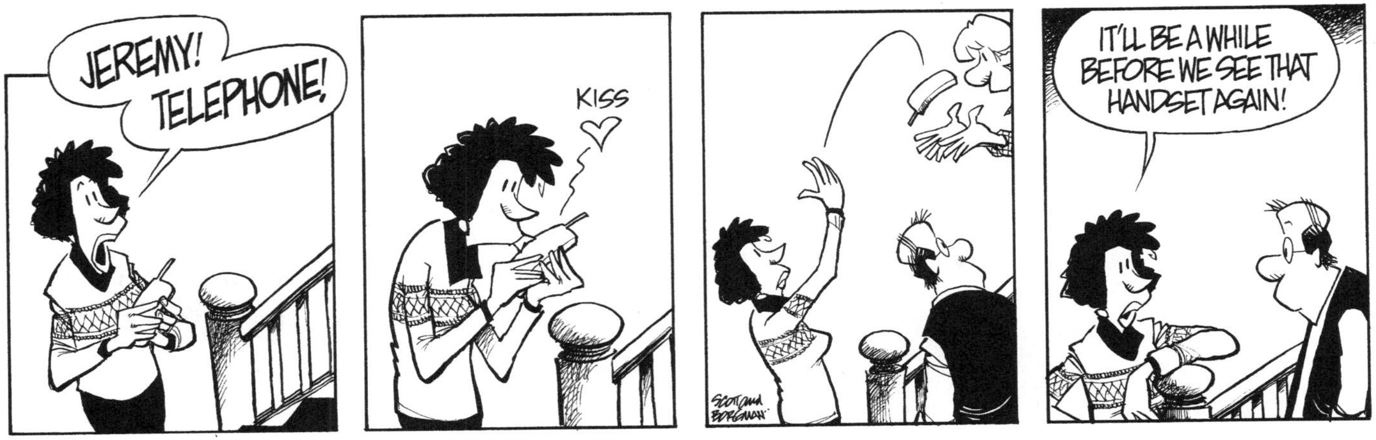
JEREMY! TELEPHONE!
KISS
IT'LL BE A WHILE BEFORE WE SEE THAT HANDSET AGAIN!

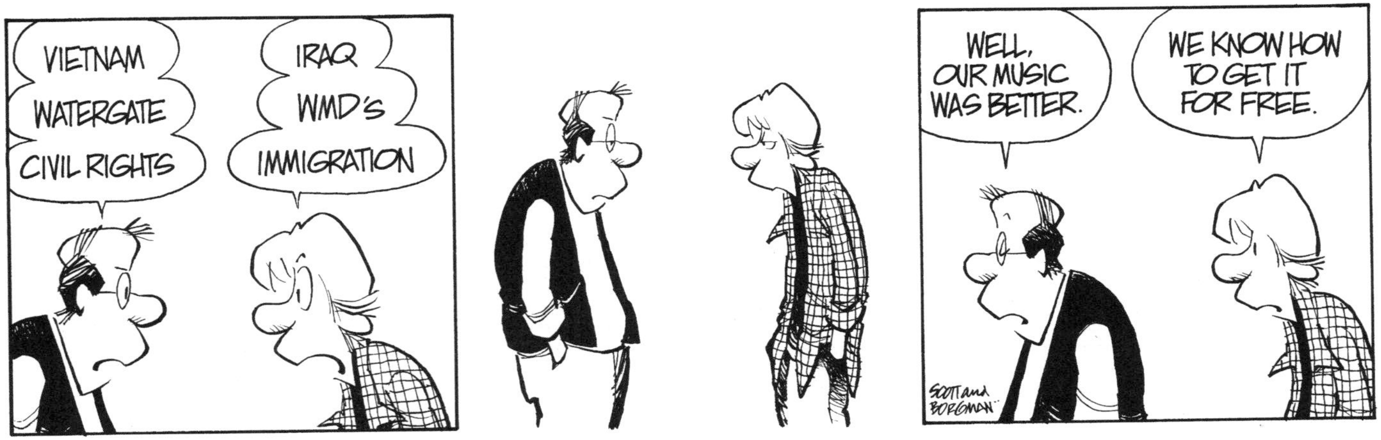
VIETNAM
WATERGATE
CIVIL RIGHTS
IRAQ
WMD's
IMMIGRATION
WELL, OUR MUSIC WAS BETTER.
WE KNOW HOW TO GET IT FOR FREE.

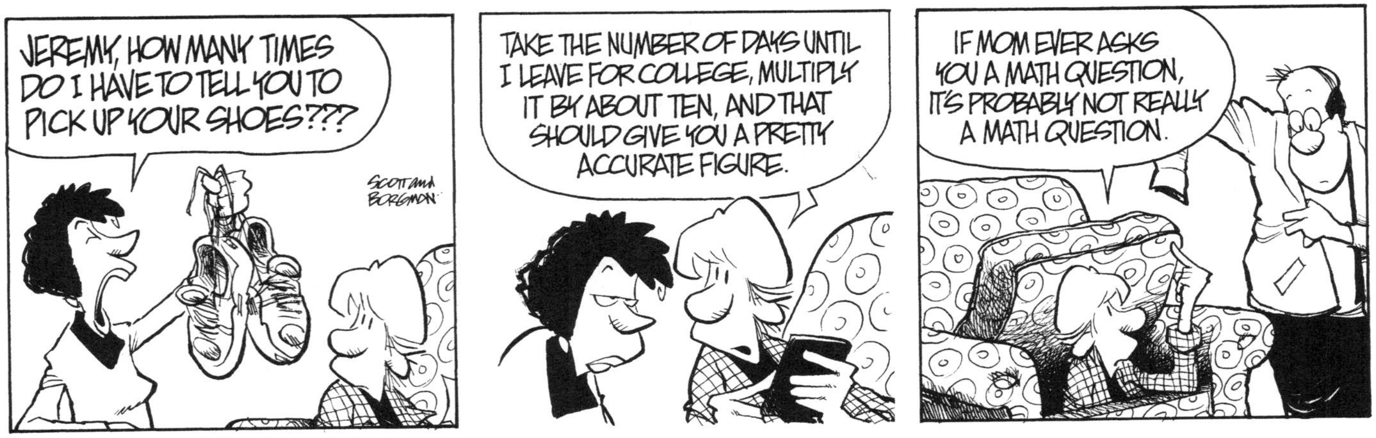
JEREMY, HOW MANY TIMES DO I HAVE TO TELL YOU TO PICK UP YOUR SHOES???
TAKE THE NUMBER OF DAYS UNTIL I LEAVE FOR COLLEGE, MULTIPLY IT BY ABOUT TEN, AND THAT SHOULD GIVE YOU A PRETTY ACCURATE FIGURE.
IF MOM EVER ASKS YOU A MATH QUESTION, IT'S PROBABLY NOT REALLY A MATH QUESTION.

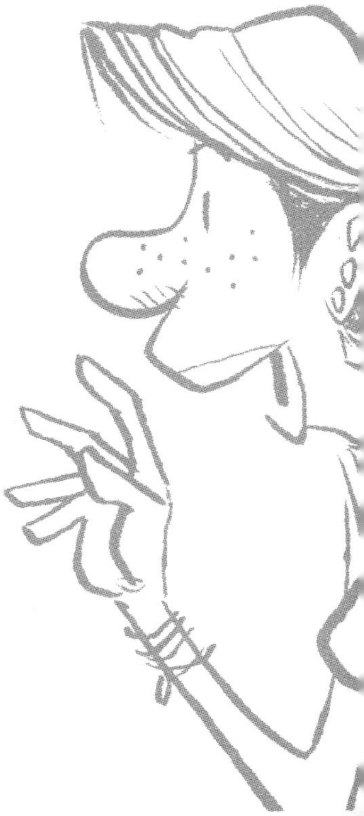

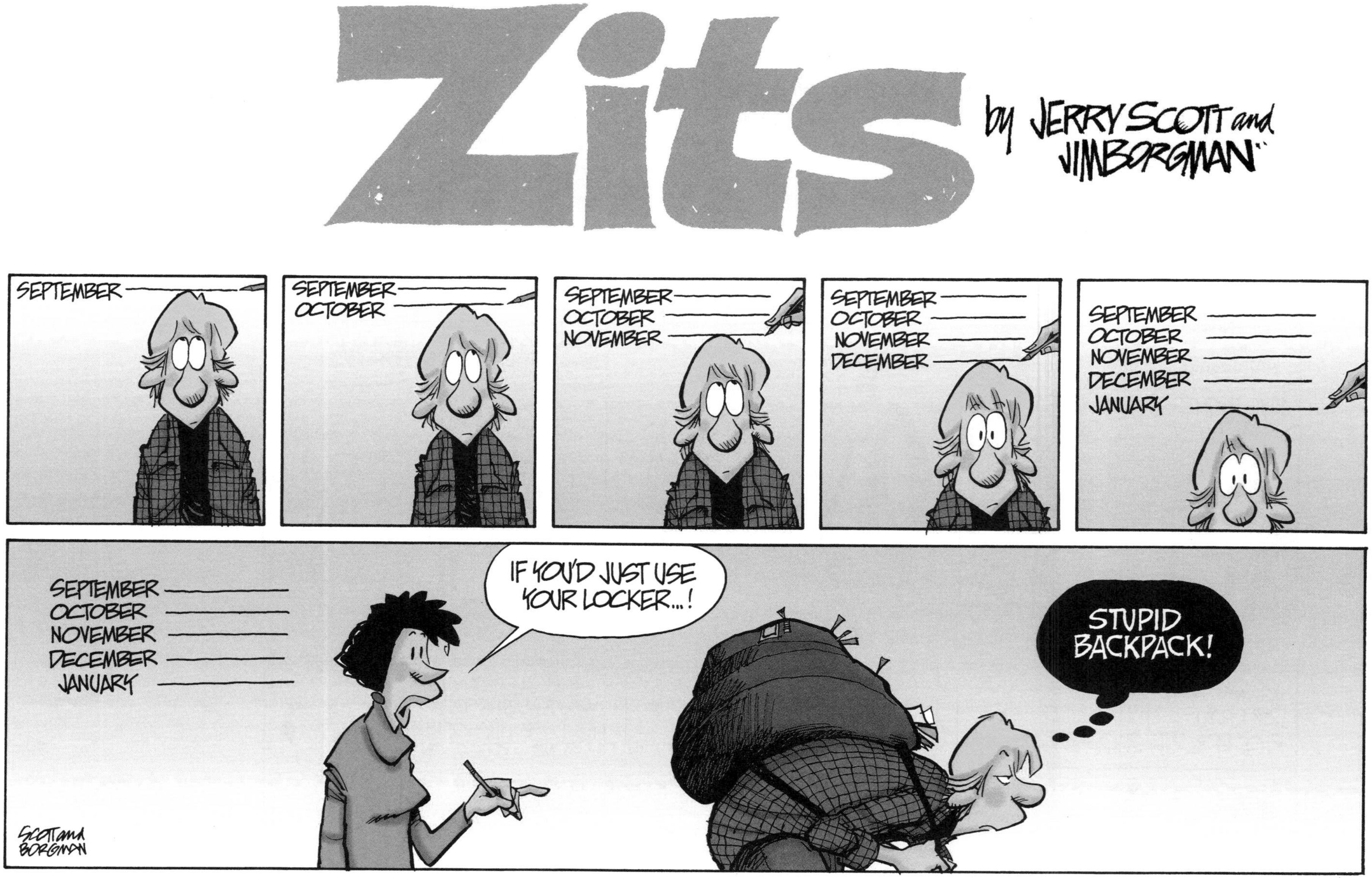
Zits
by JERRY SCOTT and JIM BORGMAN
SEPTEMBER
SEPTEMBER
OCTOBER
SEPTEMBER
OCTOBER
NOVEMBER
SEPTEMBER
OCTOBER
NOVEMBER
DECEMBER
SEPTEMBER
OCTOBER
NOVEMBER
DECEMBER
JANUARY
SEPTEMBER
OCTOBER
NOVEMBER
DECEMBER
JANUARY
IF YOU'D JUST USE YOUR LOCKER...!
STUPID BACKPACK!
SCOTT and BORGMAN

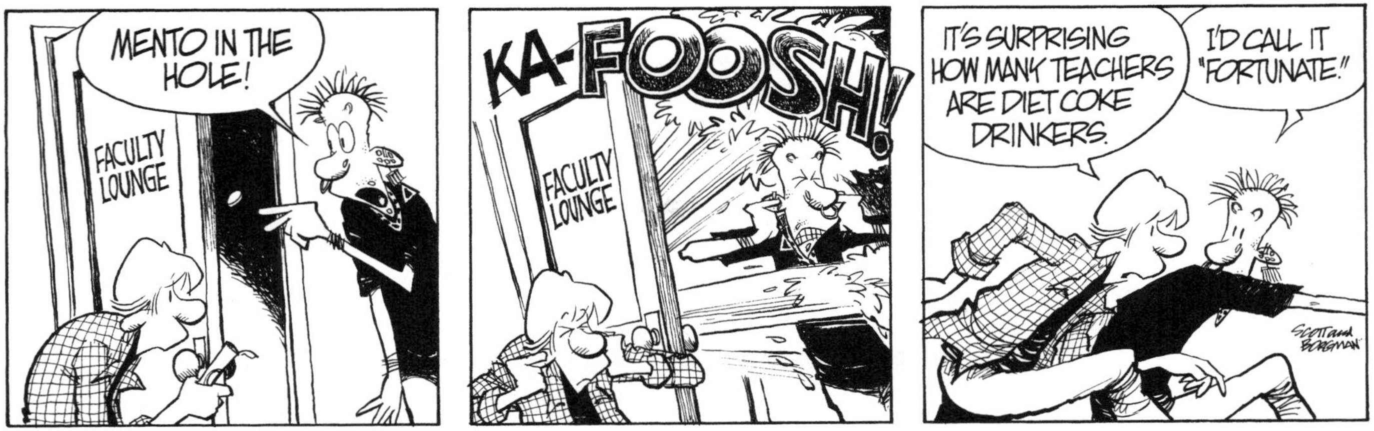
MENTO IN THE HOLE!
FACULTY LOUNGE
KA-FOOSH!
FACULTY LOUNGE
IT'S SURPRISING HOW MANY TEACHERS ARE DIET COKE DRINKERS.
I'D CALL IT "FORTUNATE."

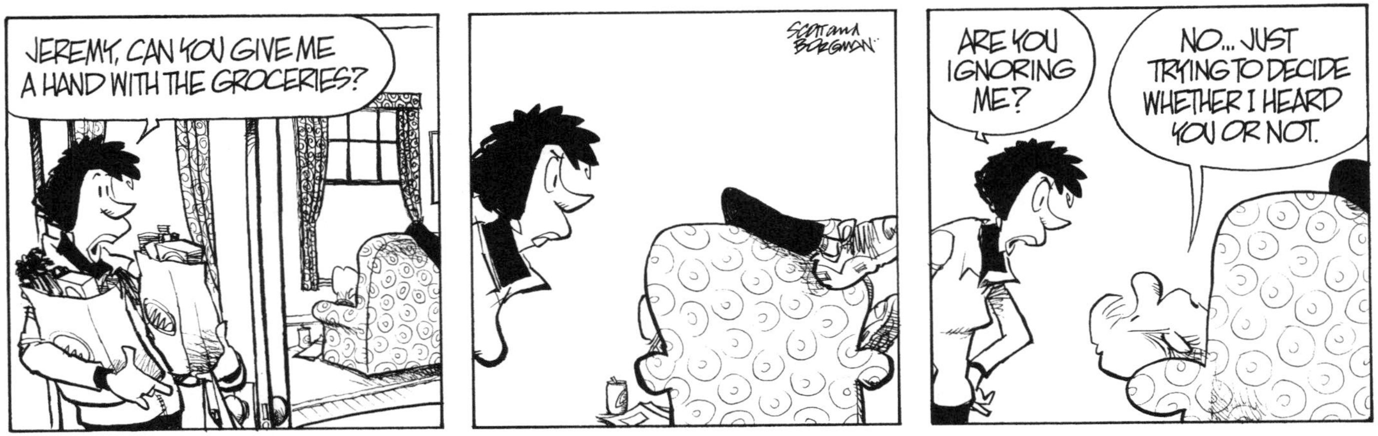
JEREMY, CAN YOU GIVE ME A HAND WITH THE GROCERIES?
ARE YOU IGNORING ME?
NO... JUST TRYING TO DECIDE WHETHER I HEARD YOU OR NOT.

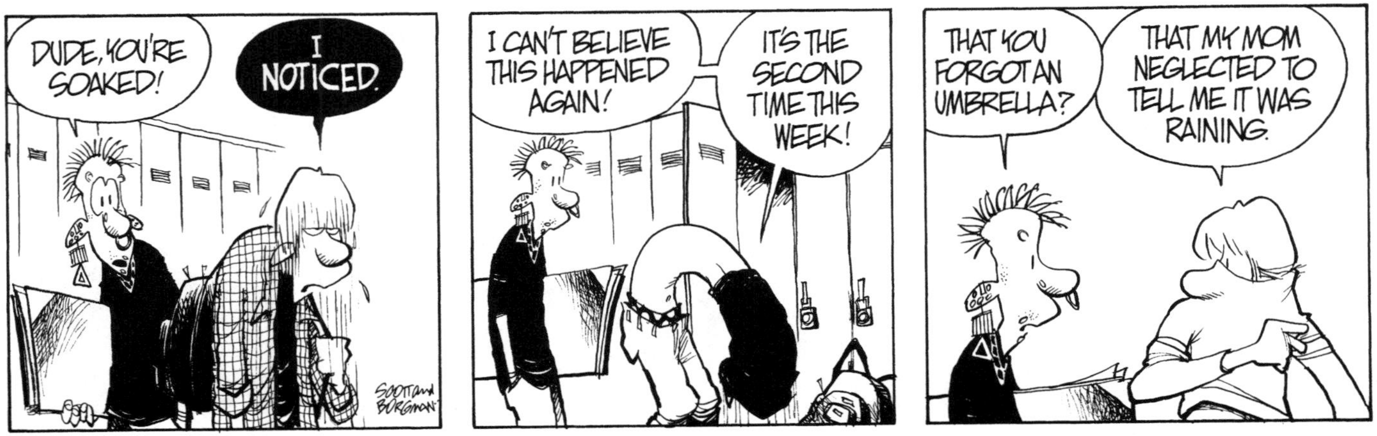
DUDE, YOU'RE SOAKED!
I NOTICED.
I CAN'T BELIEVE THIS HAPPENED AGAIN!
IT'S THE SECOND TIME THIS WEEK!
THAT YOU FORGOT AN UMBRELLA?
THAT MY MOM NEGLECTED TO TELL ME IT WAS RAINING.

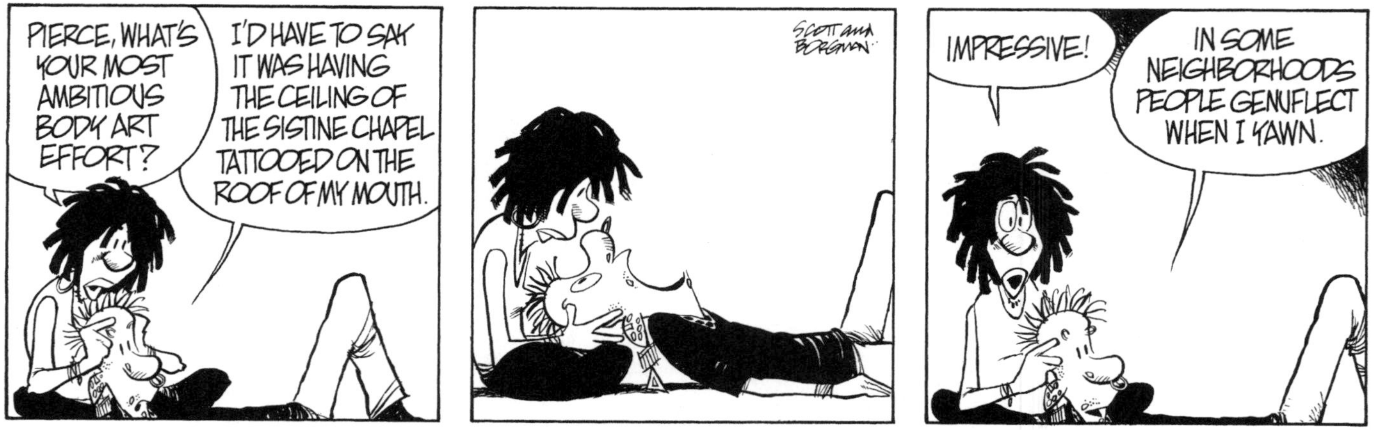
PIERCE, WHAT'S YOUR MOST AMBITIOUS BODY ART EFFORT?
I'D HAVE TO SAY IT WAS HAVING THE CEILING OF THE SISTINE CHAPEL TATTOOED ON THE ROOF OF MY MOUTH.
IMPRESSIVE!
IN SOME NEIGHBORHOODS PEOPLE GENUFLECT WHEN I YAWN.

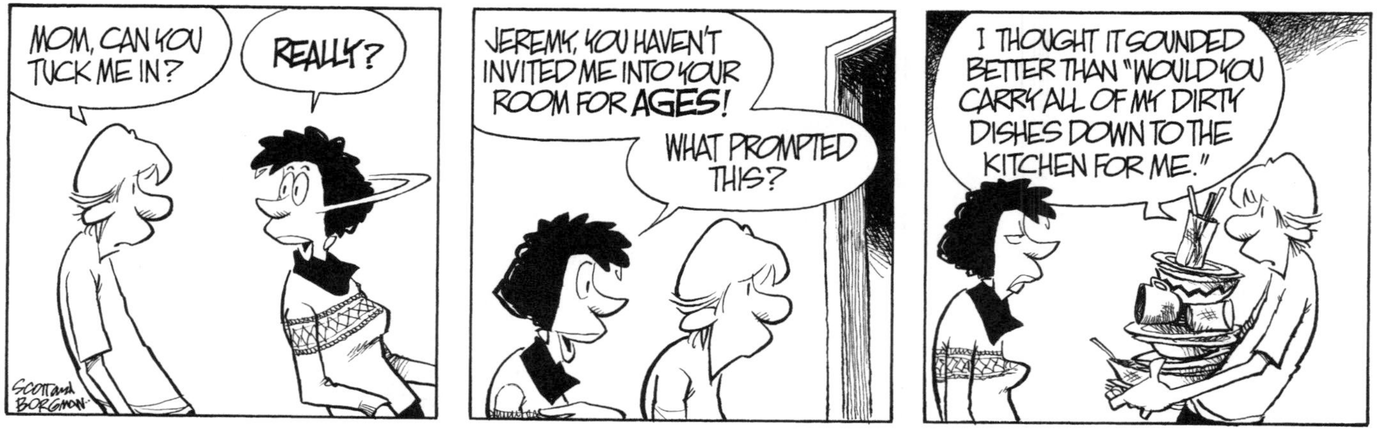
MOM, CAN YOU TUCK ME IN?
REALLY?
JEREMY, YOU HAVEN'T INVITED ME INTO YOUR ROOM FOR **AGES**!
WHAT PROMPTED THIS?
I THOUGHT IT SOUNDED BETTER THAN "WOULD YOU CARRY ALL OF MY DIRTY DISHES DOWN TO THE KITCHEN FOR ME."

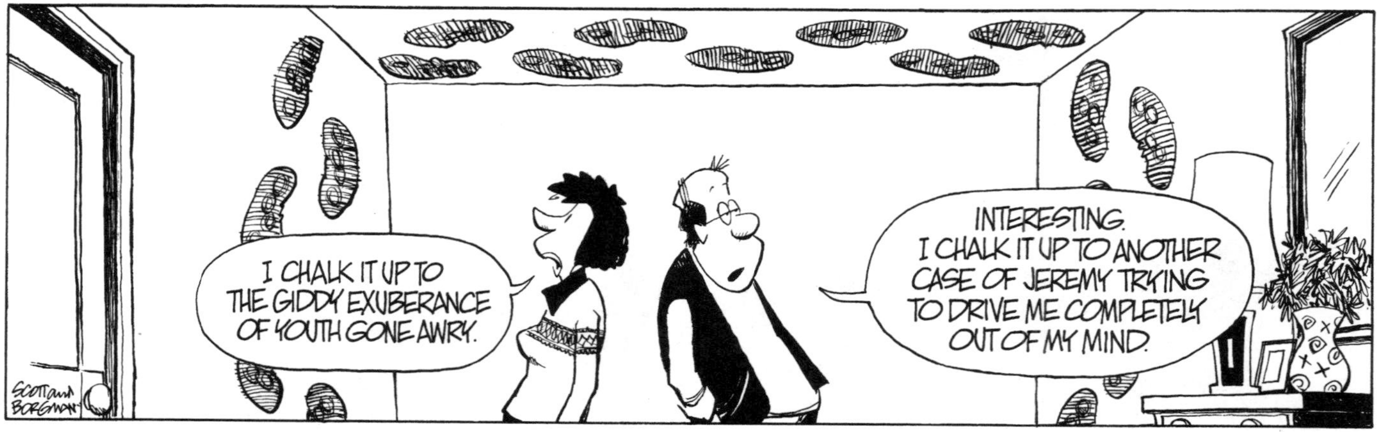
I CHALK IT UP TO THE GIDDY EXUBERANCE OF YOUTH GONE AWRY.
INTERESTING. I CHALK IT UP TO ANOTHER CASE OF JEREMY TRYING TO DRIVE ME COMPLETELY OUT OF MY MIND.

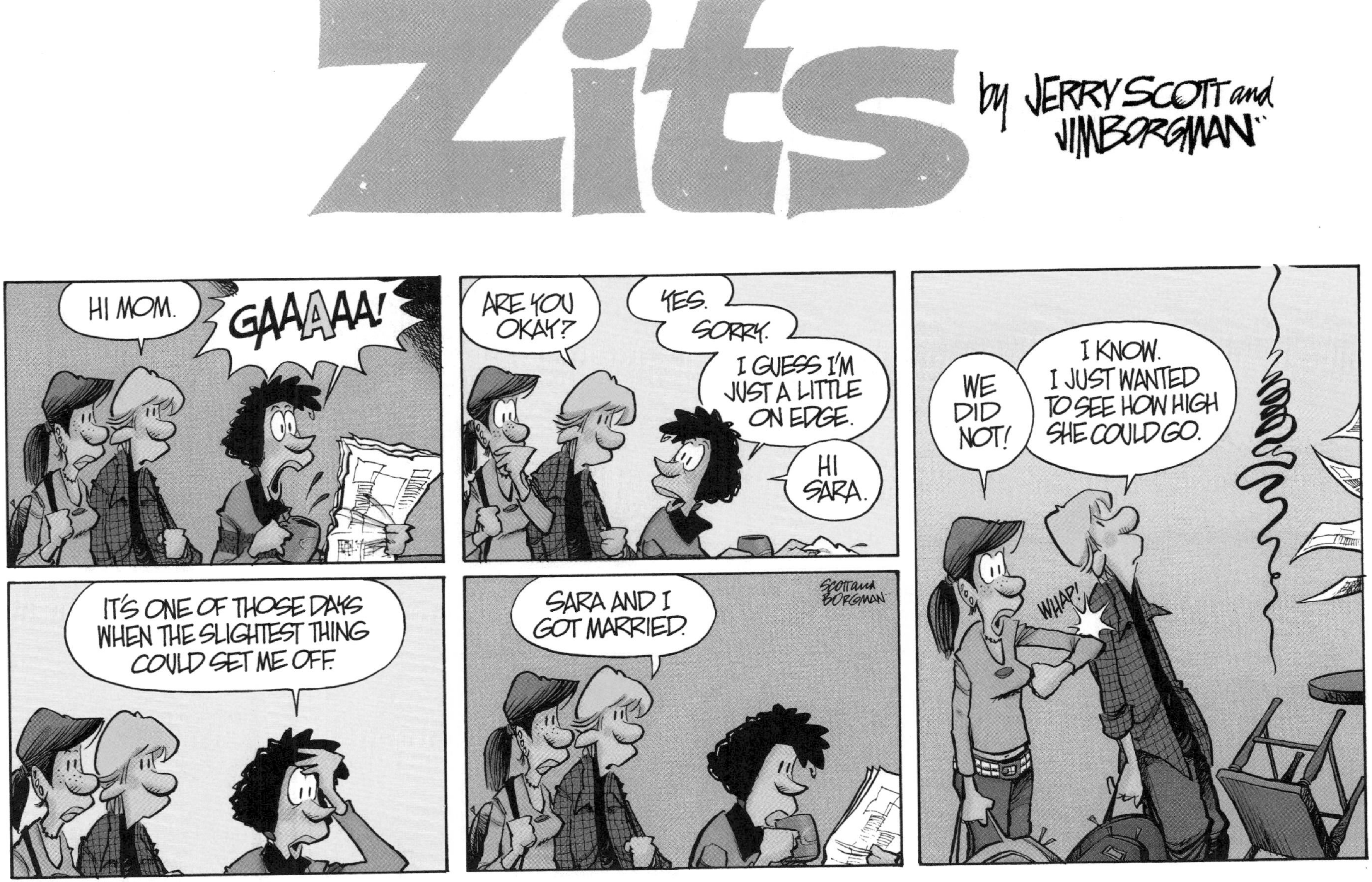
Zits
by JERRY SCOTT and JIM BORGMAN
HI MOM.
GAAAAA!
ARE YOU OKAY?
YES.
SORRY.
I GUESS I'M JUST A LITTLE ON EDGE.
HI SARA.
IT'S ONE OF THOSE DAYS WHEN THE SLIGHTEST THING COULD SET ME OFF.
SARA AND I GOT MARRIED.
SCOTT and BORGMAN
WE DID NOT!
I KNOW. I JUST WANTED TO SEE HOW HIGH SHE COULD GO.
WHAP!

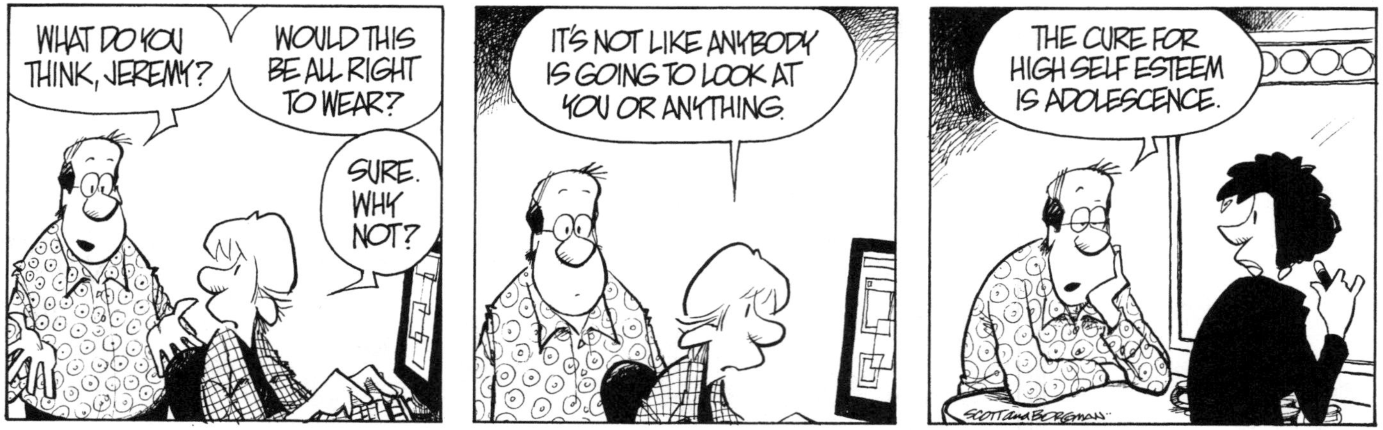
WHAT DO YOU THINK, JEREMY?
WOULD THIS BE ALL RIGHT TO WEAR?
SURE. WHY NOT?
IT'S NOT LIKE ANYBODY IS GOING TO LOOK AT YOU OR ANYTHING.
THE CURE FOR HIGH SELF ESTEEM IS ADOLESCENCE.

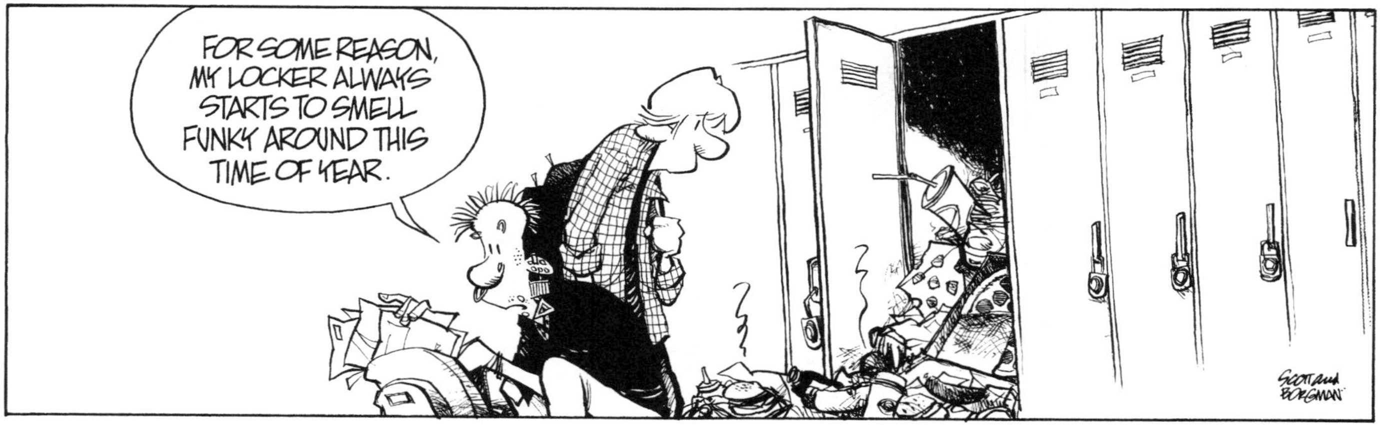
FOR SOME REASON, MY LOCKER ALWAYS STARTS TO SMELL FUNKY AROUND THIS TIME OF YEAR.

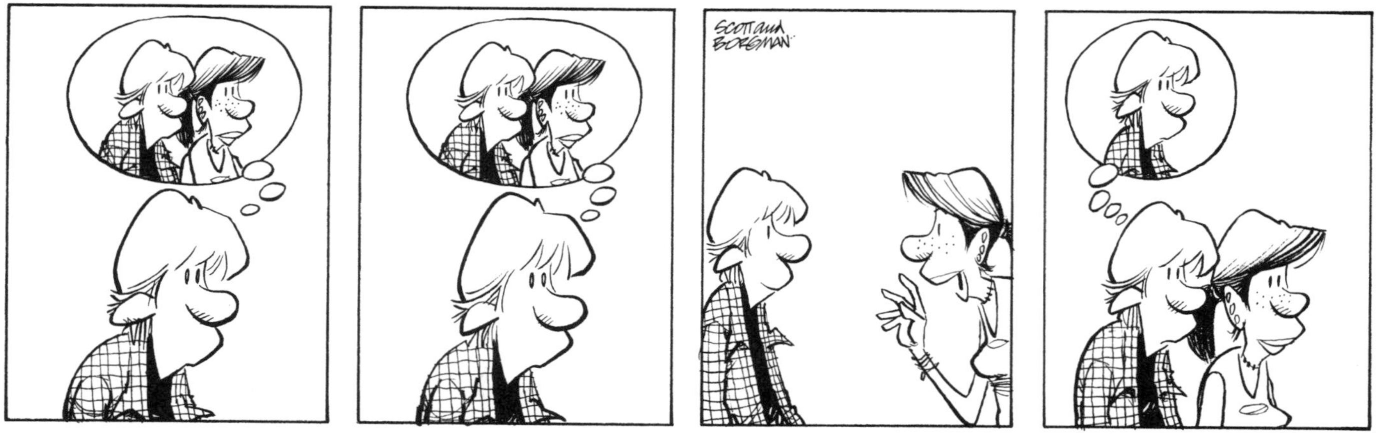

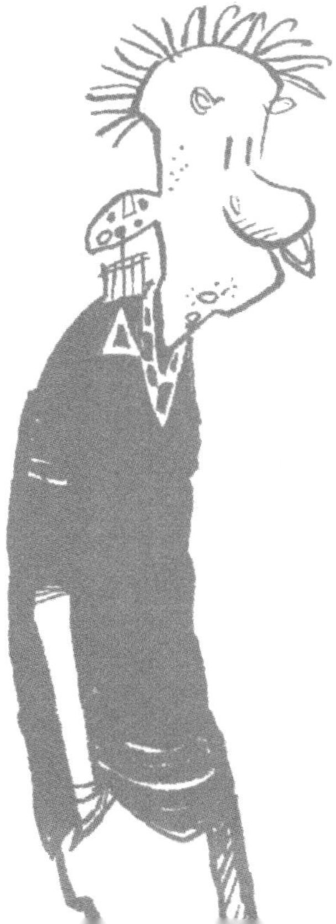

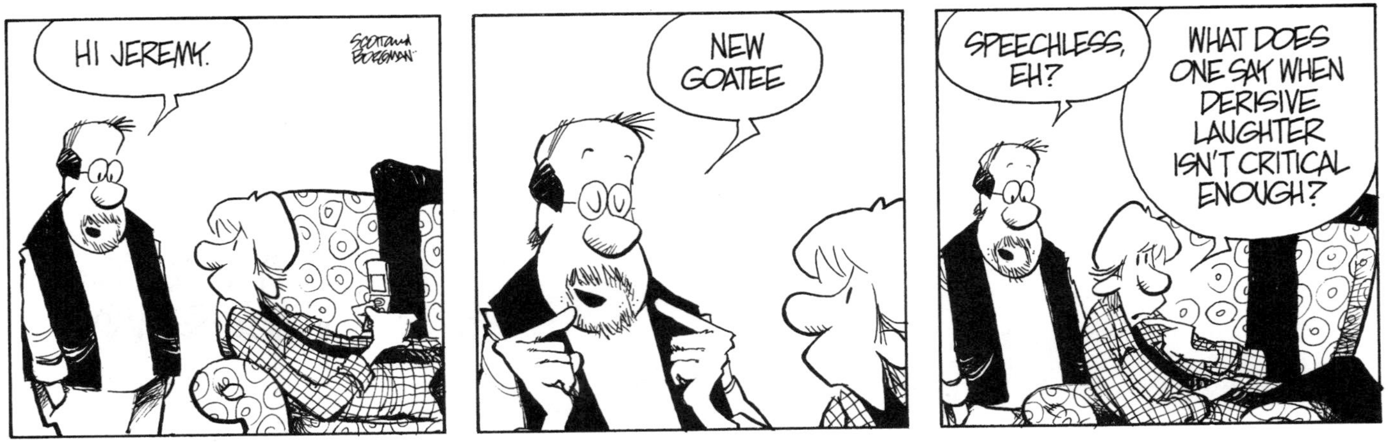
HI JEREMY.
NEW GOATEE
SPEECHLESS, EH?
WHAT DOES ONE SAY WHEN DERISIVE LAUGHTER ISN'T CRITICAL ENOUGH?

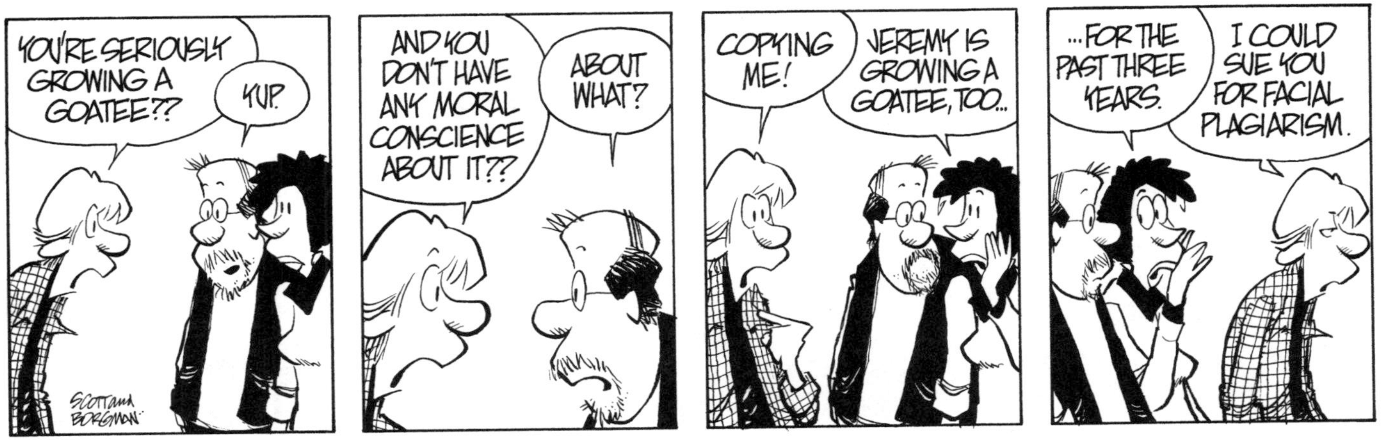
YOU'RE SERIOUSLY GROWING A GOATEE??
YUP.
AND YOU DON'T HAVE ANY MORAL CONSCIENCE ABOUT IT??
ABOUT WHAT?
COPYING ME!
JEREMY IS GROWING A GOATEE, TOO...
...FOR THE PAST THREE YEARS.
I COULD SUE YOU FOR FACIAL PLAGIARISM.

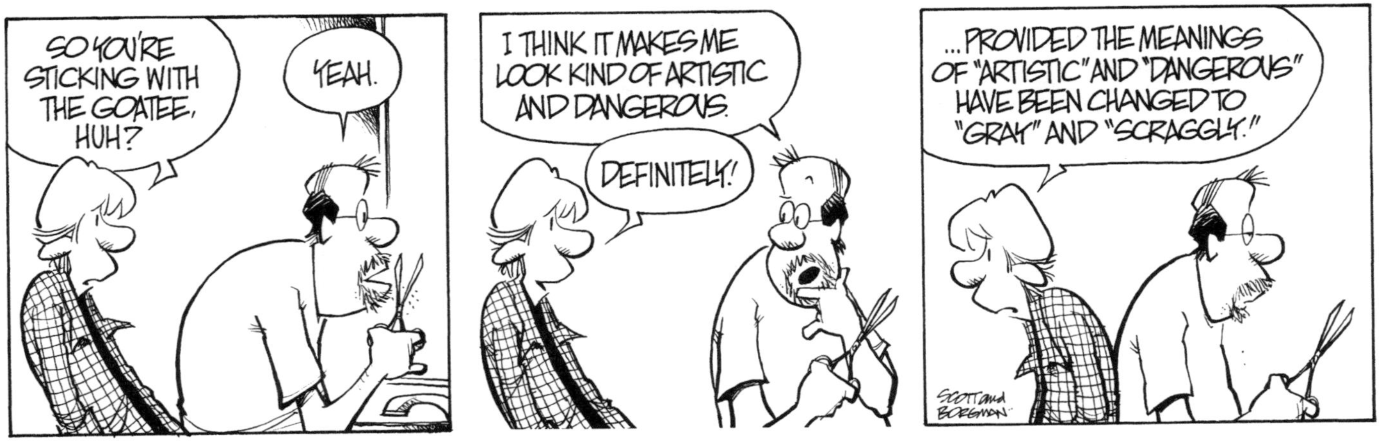
SO YOU'RE STICKING WITH THE GOATEE, HUH?
YEAH.
I THINK IT MAKES ME LOOK KIND OF ARTISTIC AND DANGEROUS.
DEFINITELY!
...PROVIDED THE MEANINGS OF "ARTISTIC" AND "DANGEROUS" HAVE BEEN CHANGED TO "GRAY" AND "SCRAGGLY."

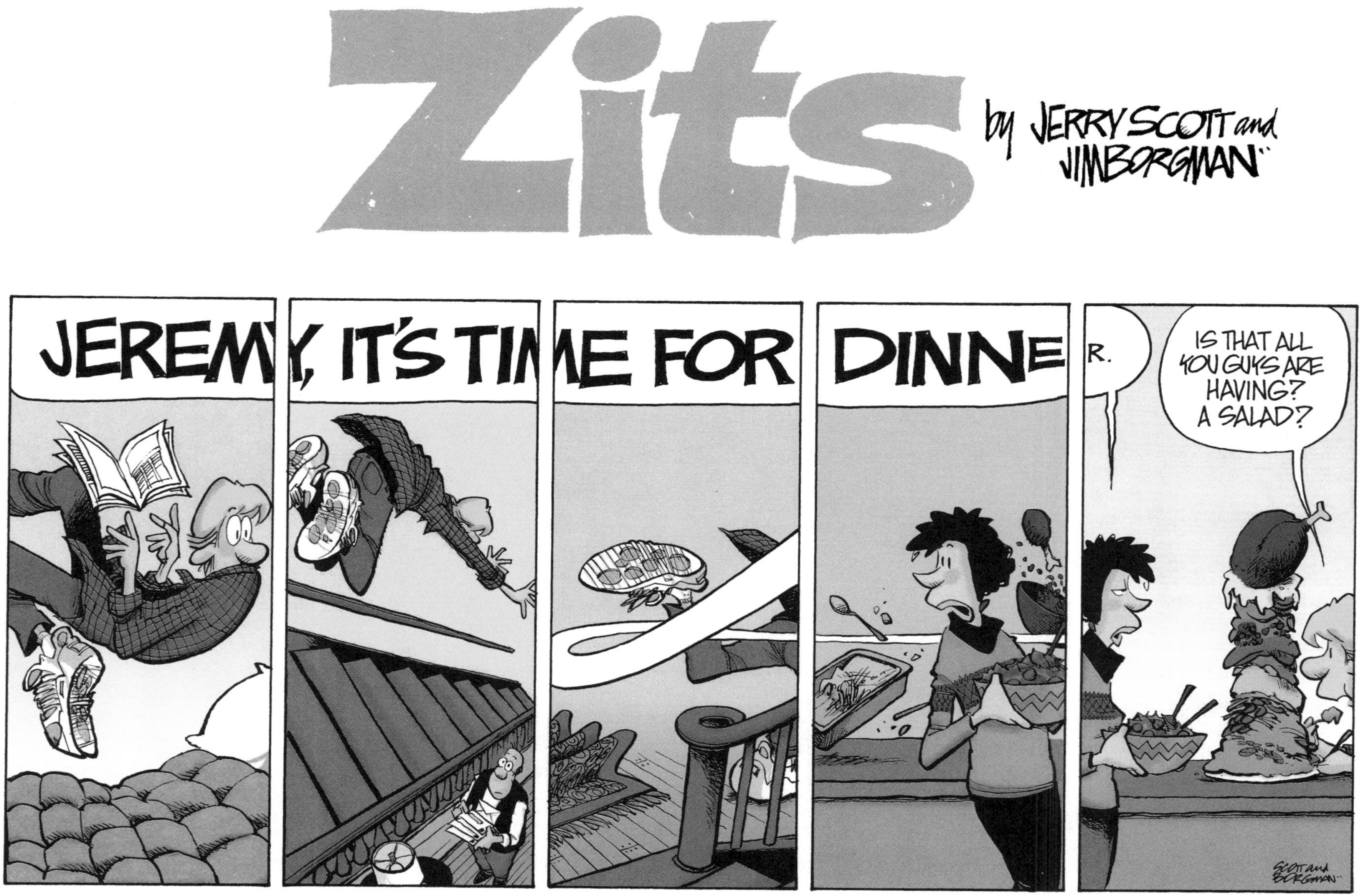
Zits
by JERRY SCOTT and JIM BORGMAN
JEREMY, IT'S TIME FOR DINNER.
IS THAT ALL YOU GUYS ARE HAVING? A SALAD?
SCOTT AND BORGMAN

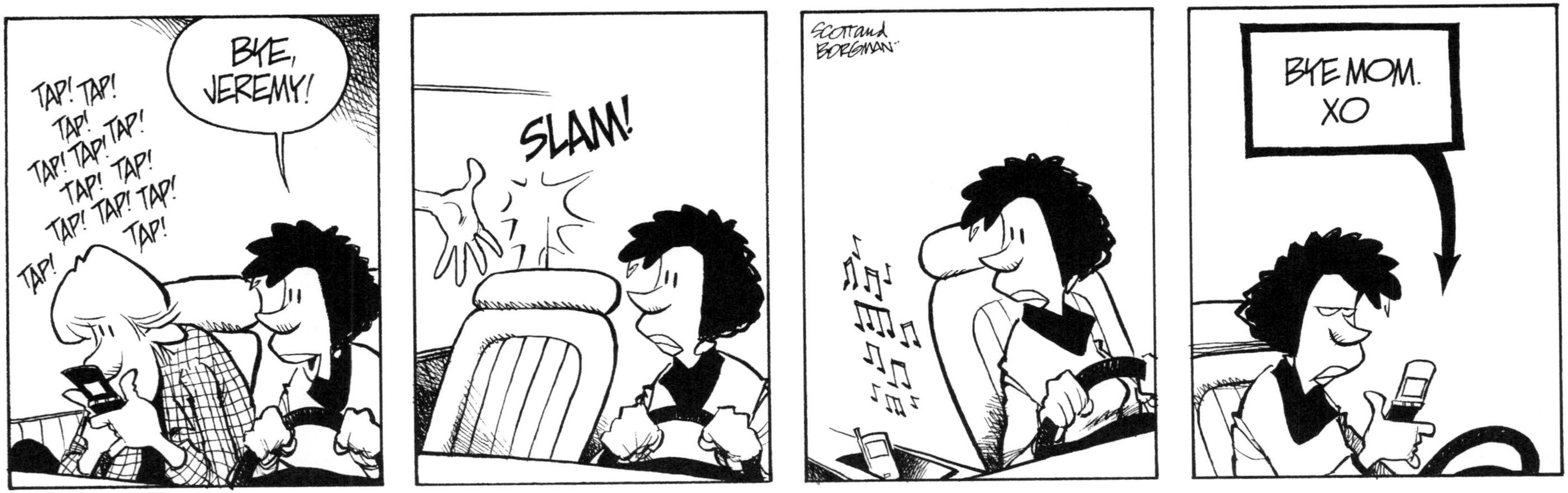
SCOTT and BORGMAN
TAP! TAP! TAP! TAP! TAP! TAP! TAP! TAP! TAP! TAP! TAP! TAP! TAP!
BYE, JEREMY!
SLAM!
BYE MOM. XO

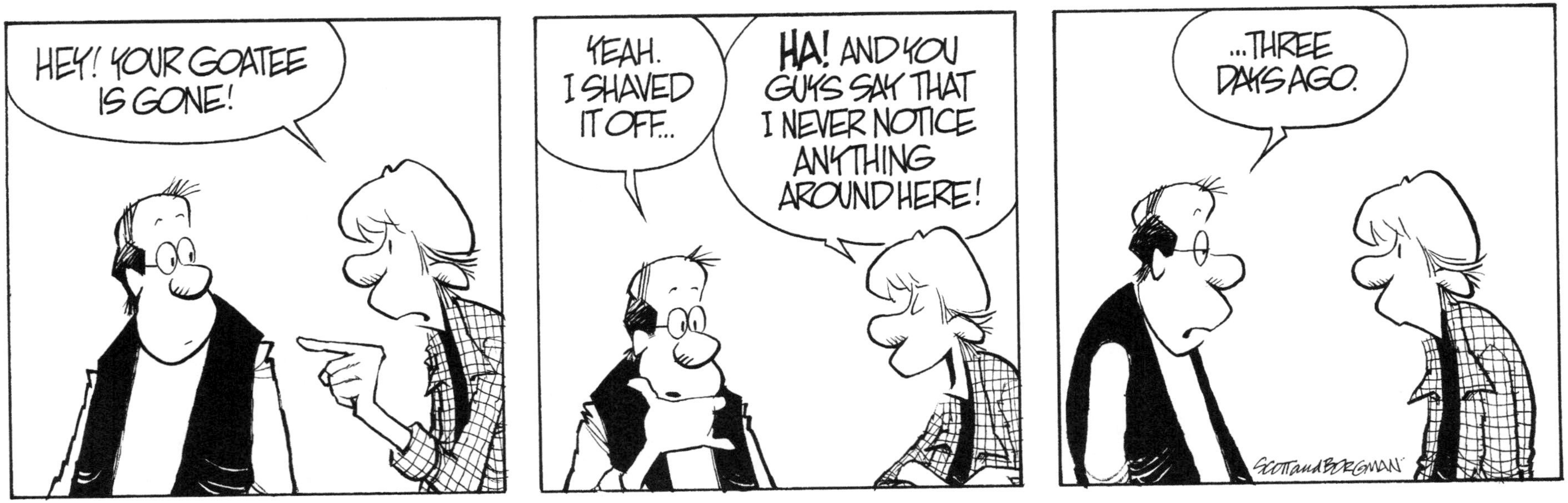
HEY! YOUR GOATEE IS GONE!
YEAH. I SHAVED IT OFF...
HA! AND YOU GUYS SAY THAT I NEVER NOTICE ANYTHING AROUND HERE!
...THREE DAYS AGO.
SCOTT and BORGMAN

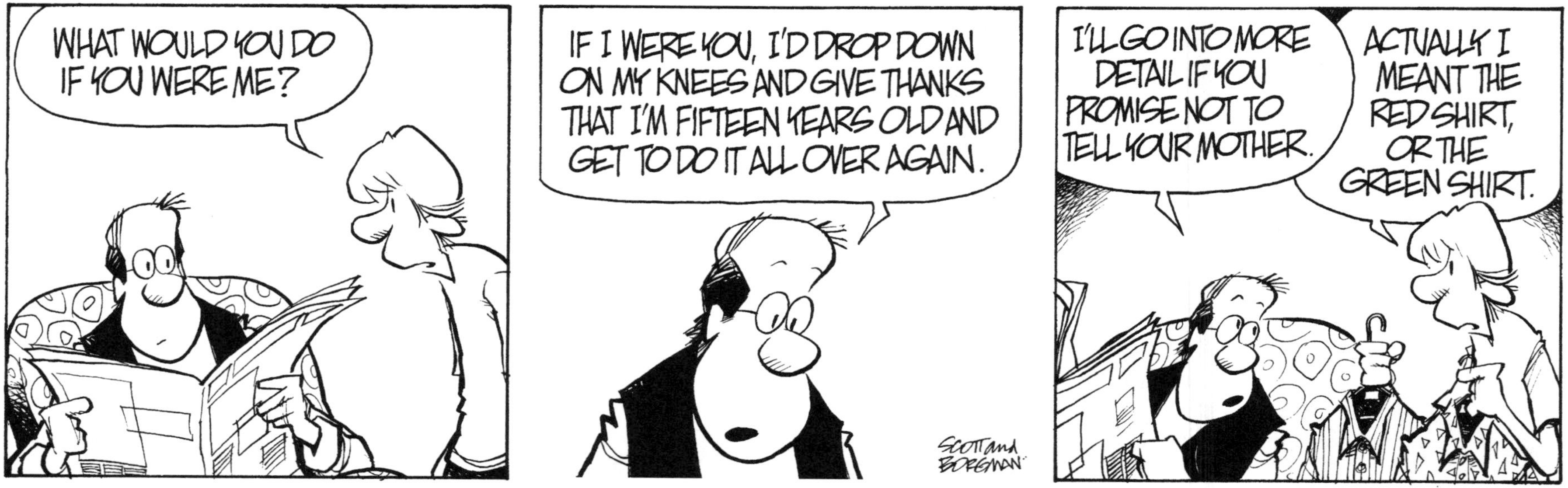
WHAT WOULD YOU DO IF YOU WERE ME?
IF I WERE YOU, I'D DROP DOWN ON MY KNEES AND GIVE THANKS THAT I'M FIFTEEN YEARS OLD AND GET TO DO IT ALL OVER AGAIN.
SCOTT and BORGMAN
I'LL GO INTO MORE DETAIL IF YOU PROMISE NOT TO TELL YOUR MOTHER.
ACTUALLY I MEANT THE RED SHIRT, OR THE GREEN SHIRT.

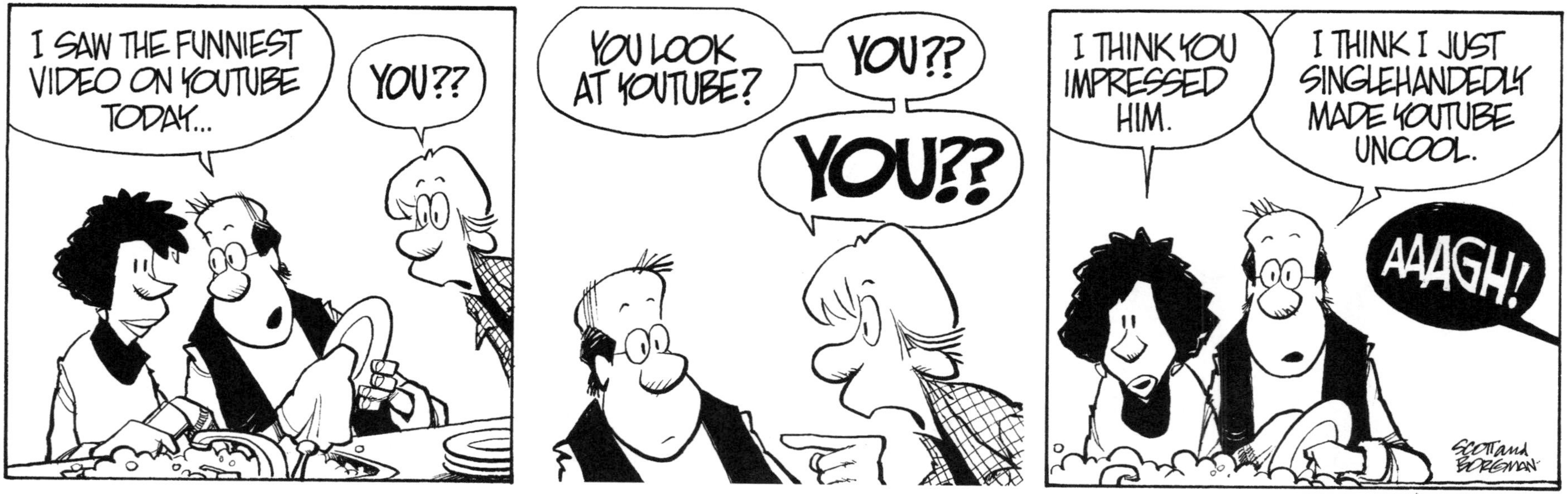
I SAW THE FUNNIEST VIDEO ON YOUTUBE TODAY...
YOU??
YOU LOOK AT YOUTUBE?
YOU??
YOU??
I THINK YOU IMPRESSED HIM.
I THINK I JUST SINGLEHANDEDLY MADE YOUTUBE UNCOOL.
AAAGH!
SCOTT and BORGMAN

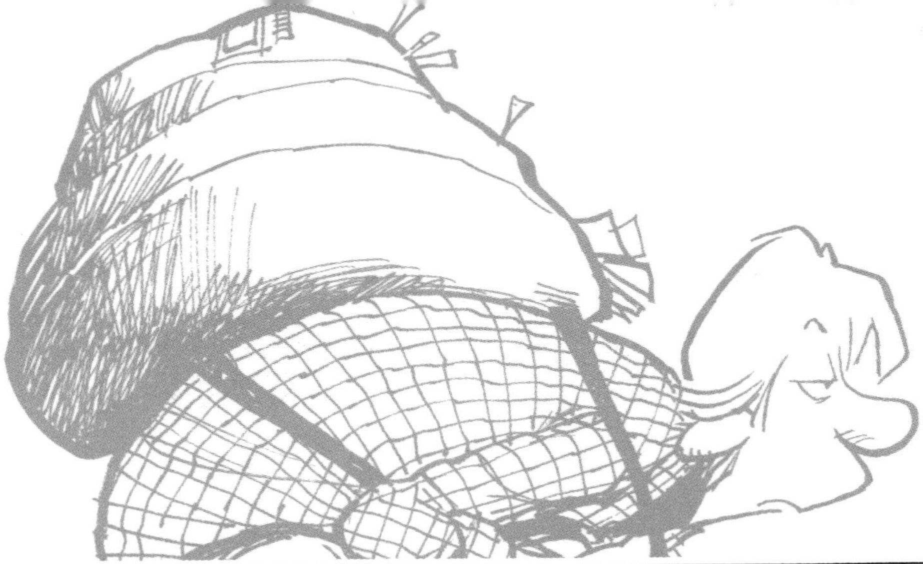

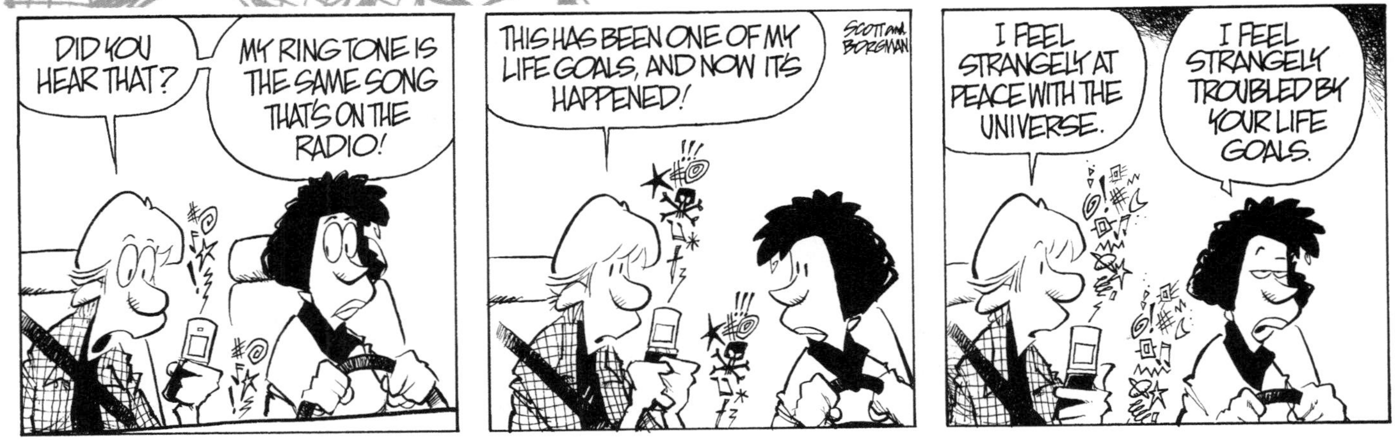

DID YOU HEAR THAT?
MY RING TONE IS THE SAME SONG THAT'S ON THE RADIO!
THIS HAS BEEN ONE OF MY LIFE GOALS, AND NOW IT'S HAPPENED!
SCOTT and BORGMAN
I FEEL STRANGELY AT PEACE WITH THE UNIVERSE.
I FEEL STRANGELY TROUBLED BY YOUR LIFE GOALS.

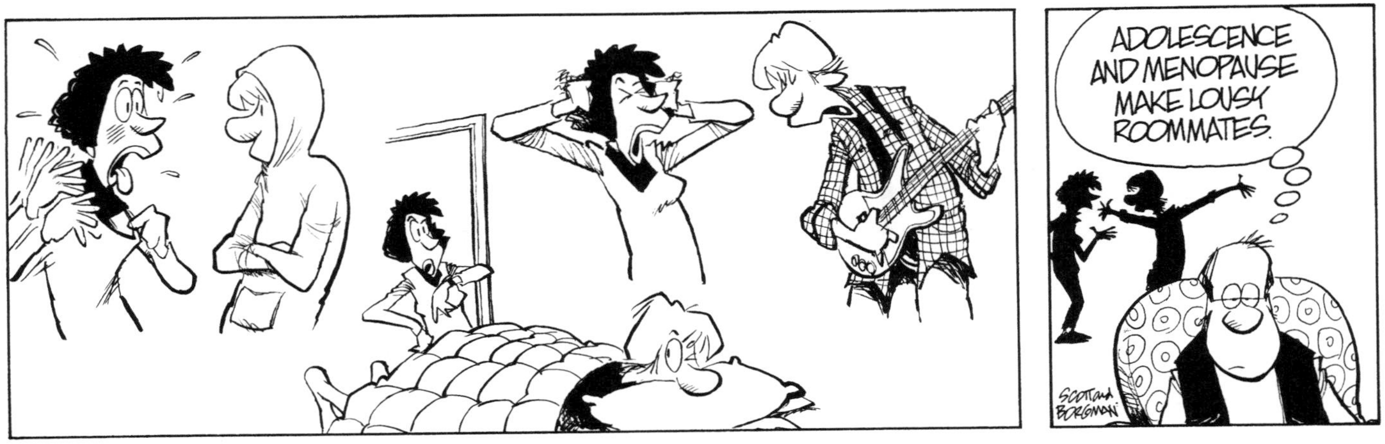

ADOLESCENCE AND MENOPAUSE MAKE LOUSY ROOMMATES.
SCOTT and BORGMAN

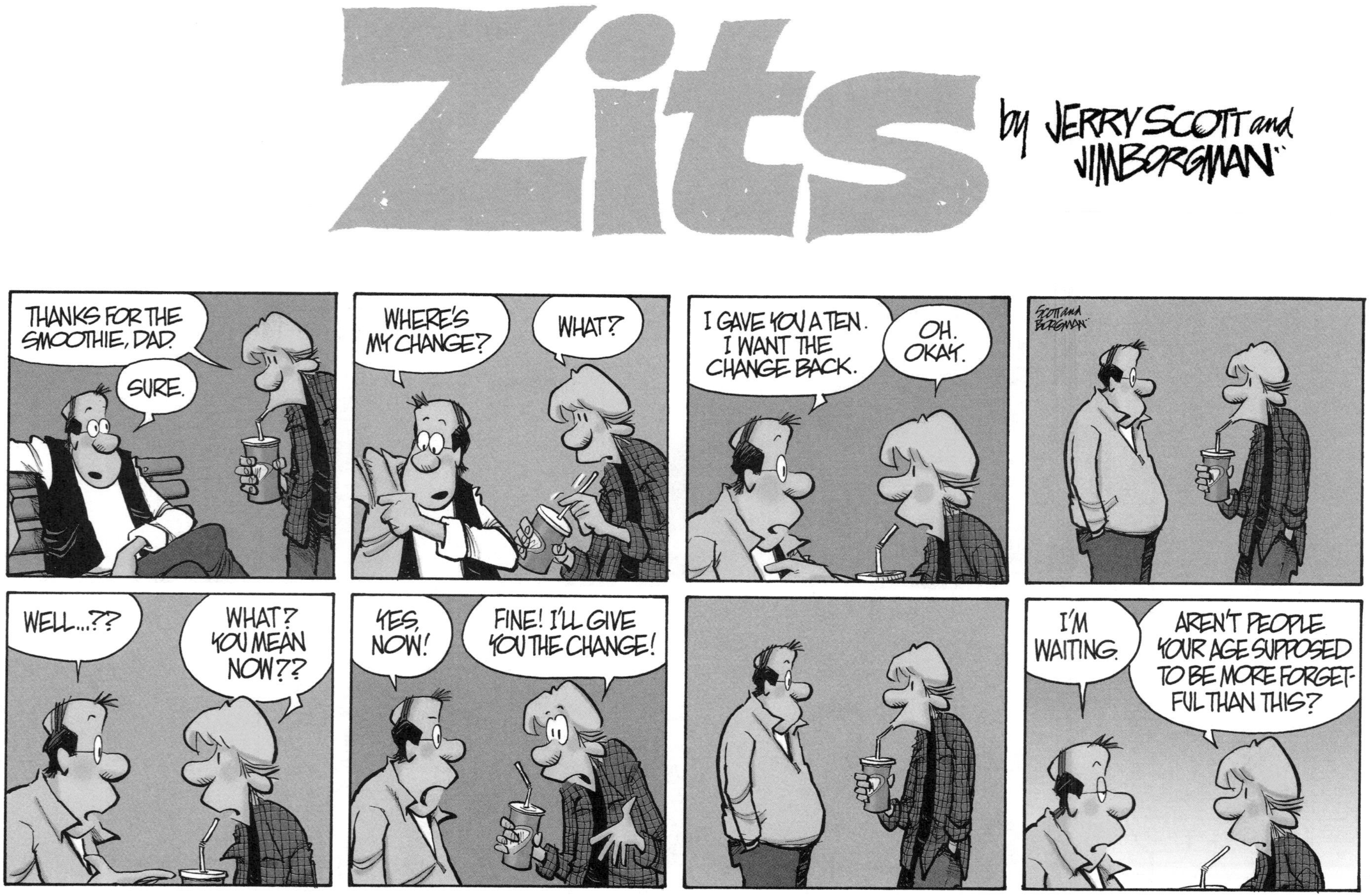
Zits
by JERRY SCOTT and JIM BORGMAN
THANKS FOR THE SMOOTHIE, DAD.
SURE.
WHERE'S MY CHANGE?
WHAT?
I GAVE YOU A TEN. I WANT THE CHANGE BACK.
OH. OKAY.
SCOTT and BORGMAN
WELL...??
WHAT? YOU MEAN NOW??
YES, NOW!
FINE! I'LL GIVE YOU THE CHANGE!
I'M WAITING.
AREN'T PEOPLE YOUR AGE SUPPOSED TO BE MORE FORGET-FUL THAN THIS?

Zits

by JERRY SCOTT and JIM BORGMAN

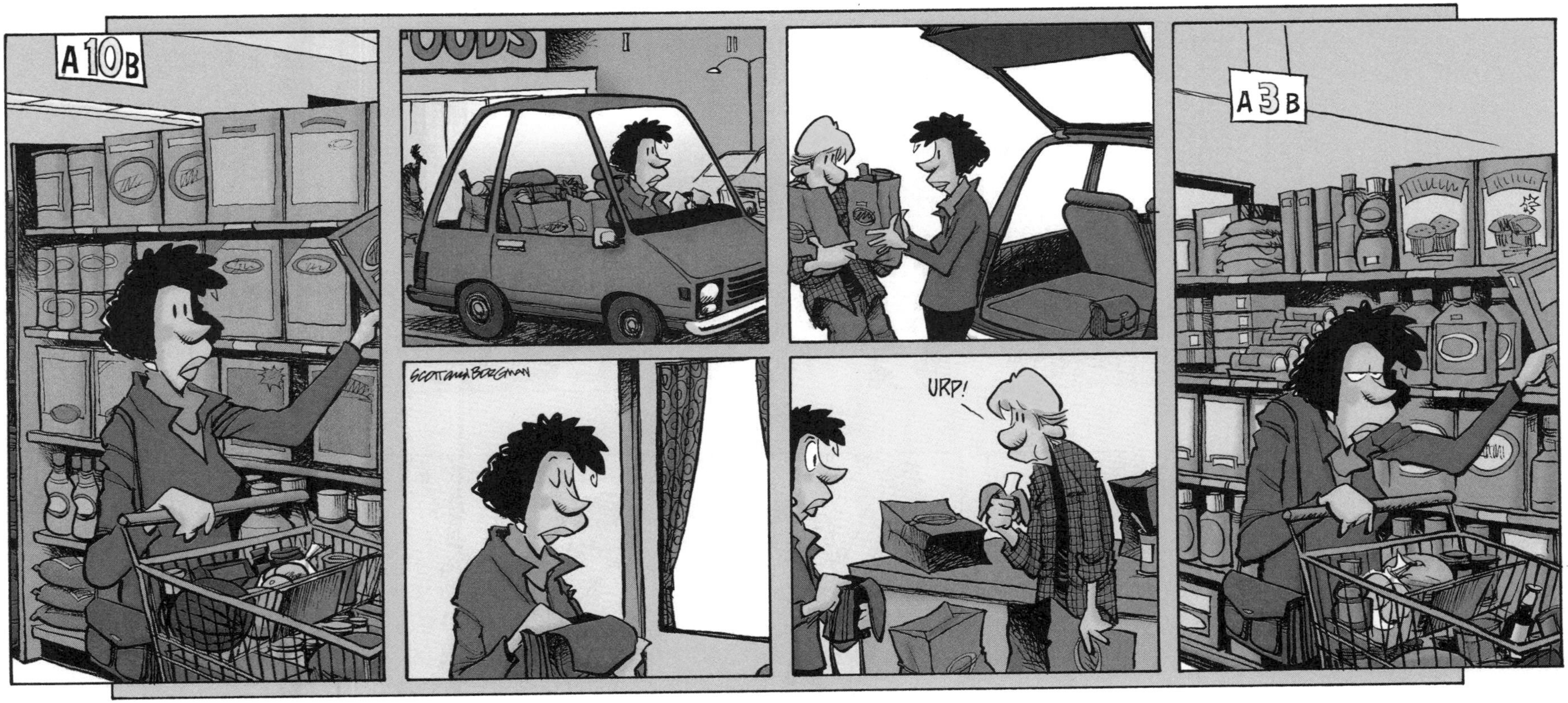
A 10 B
SCOTT and BORGMAN
URP!
A 3 B

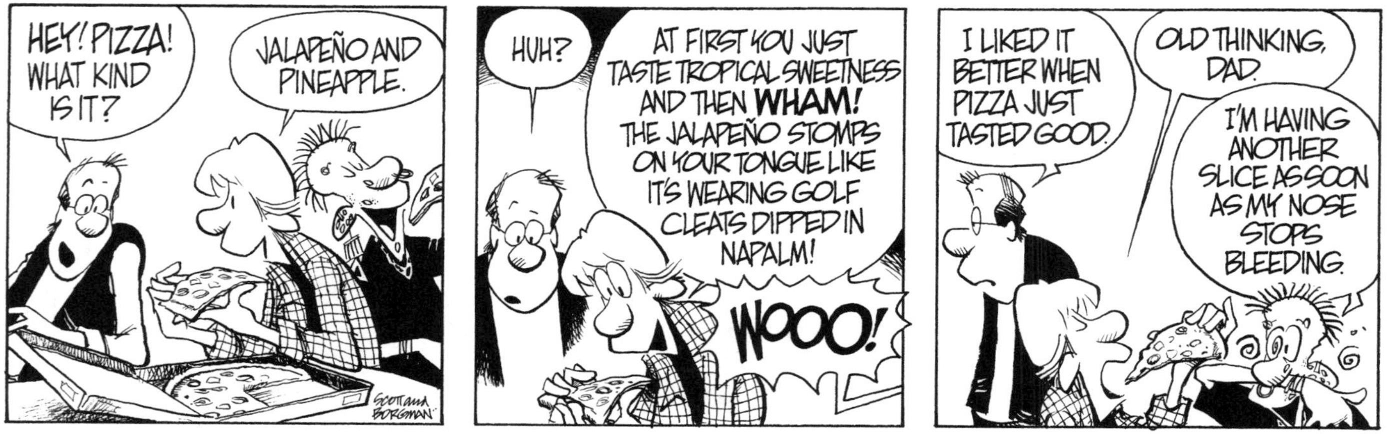
HEY! PIZZA! WHAT KIND IS IT?
JALAPEÑO AND PINEAPPLE.
HUH?
AT FIRST YOU JUST TASTE TROPICAL SWEETNESS AND THEN **WHAM!** THE JALAPEÑO STOMPS ON YOUR TONGUE LIKE IT'S WEARING GOLF CLEATS DIPPED IN NAPALM!
WOOO!
I LIKED IT BETTER WHEN PIZZA JUST TASTED GOOD.
OLD THINKING, DAD.
I'M HAVING ANOTHER SLICE AS SOON AS MY NOSE STOPS BLEEDING.

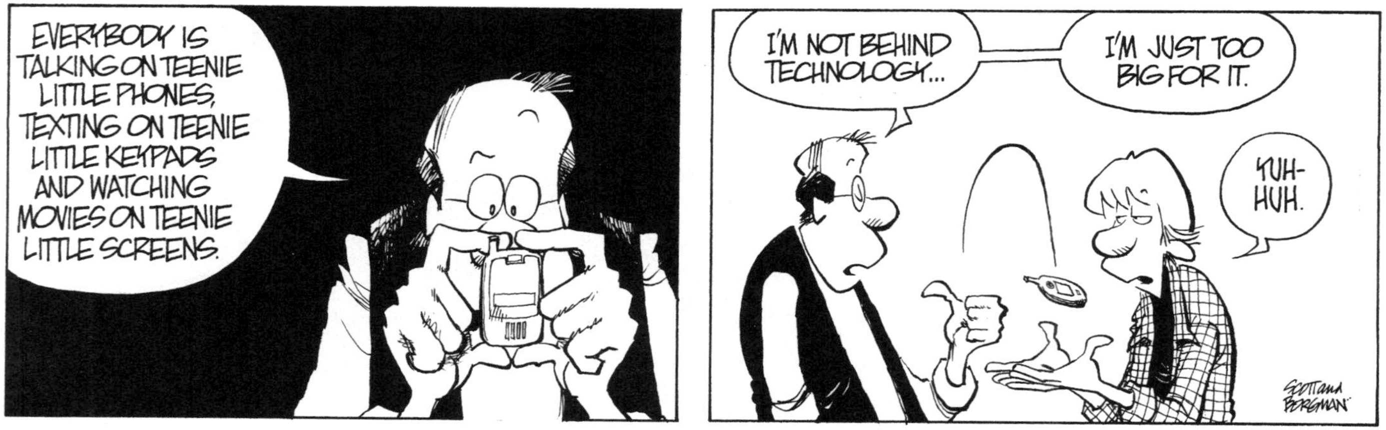
EVERYBODY IS TALKING ON TEENIE LITTLE PHONES, TEXTING ON TEENIE LITTLE KEYPADS AND WATCHING MOVIES ON TEENIE LITTLE SCREENS.
I'M NOT BEHIND TECHNOLOGY...
I'M JUST TOO BIG FOR IT.
YUH-HUH.

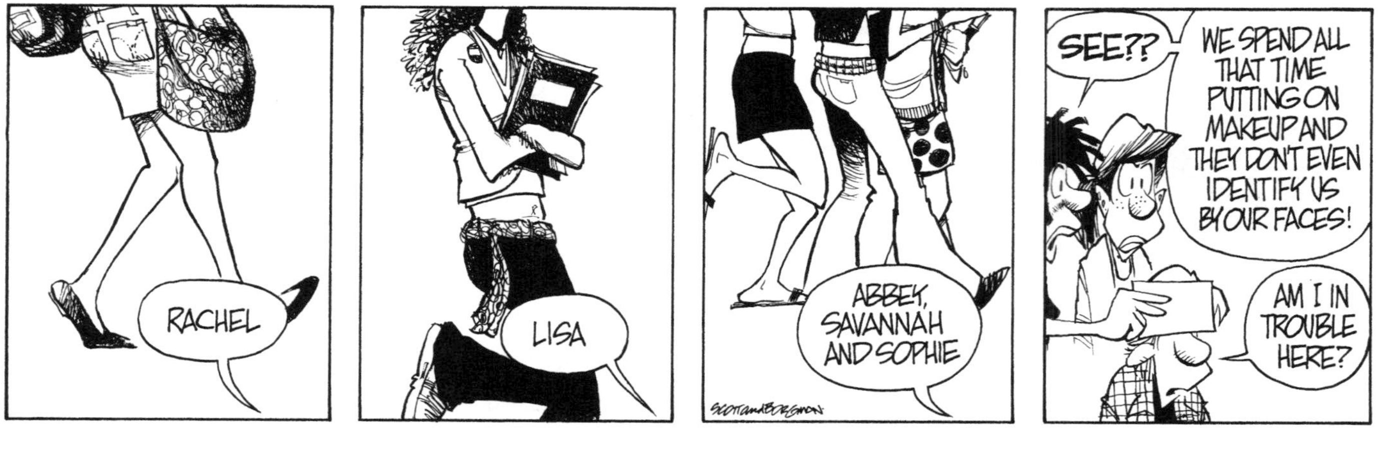
RACHEL
LISA
ABBEY, SAVANNAH AND SOPHIE
SEE??
WE SPEND ALL THAT TIME PUTTING ON MAKEUP AND THEY DON'T EVEN IDENTIFY US BY OUR FACES!
AM I IN TROUBLE HERE?

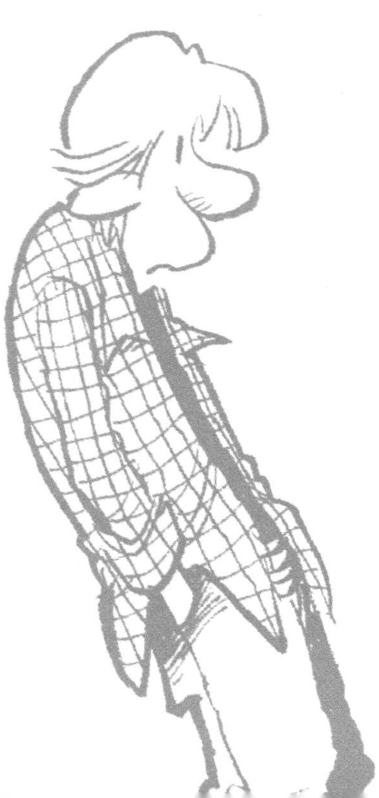

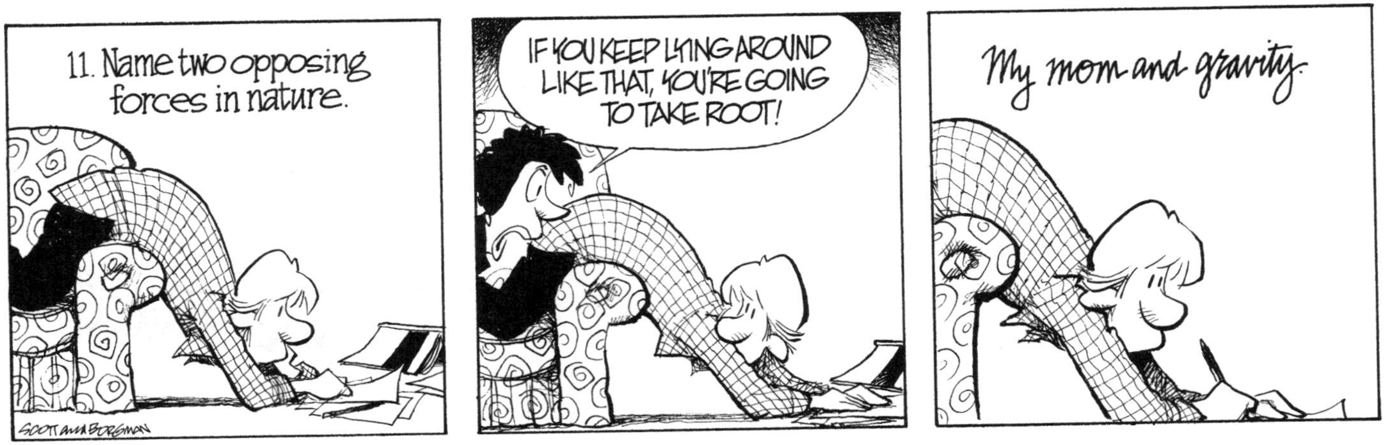
11. Name two opposing forces in nature.
IF YOU KEEP LYING AROUND LIKE THAT, YOU'RE GOING TO TAKE ROOT!
My mom and gravity.

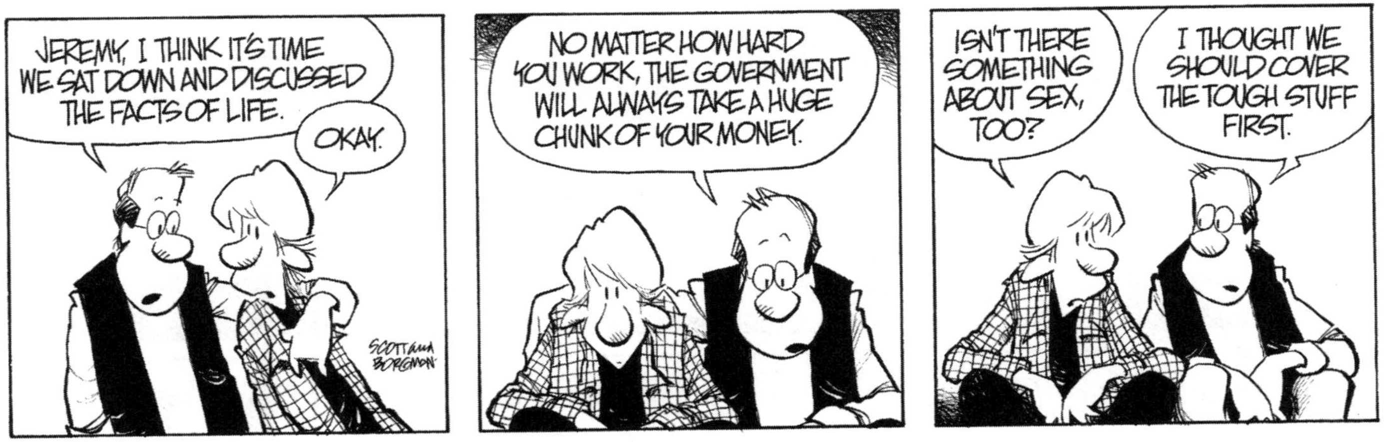
JEREMY, I THINK IT'S TIME WE SAT DOWN AND DISCUSSED THE FACTS OF LIFE.
OKAY.
NO MATTER HOW HARD YOU WORK, THE GOVERNMENT WILL ALWAYS TAKE A HUGE CHUNK OF YOUR MONEY.
ISN'T THERE SOMETHING ABOUT SEX, TOO?
I THOUGHT WE SHOULD COVER THE TOUGH STUFF FIRST.

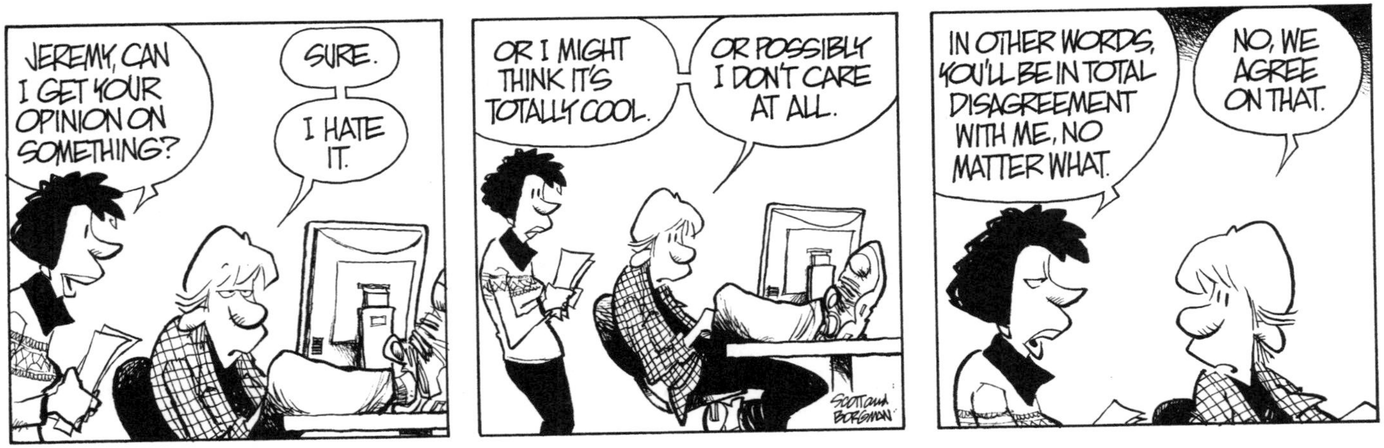
JEREMY, CAN I GET YOUR OPINION ON SOMETHING?
SURE.
I HATE IT.
OR I MIGHT THINK IT'S TOTALLY COOL.
OR POSSIBLY I DON'T CARE AT ALL.
IN OTHER WORDS, YOU'LL BE IN TOTAL DISAGREEMENT WITH ME, NO MATTER WHAT.
NO, WE AGREE ON THAT.

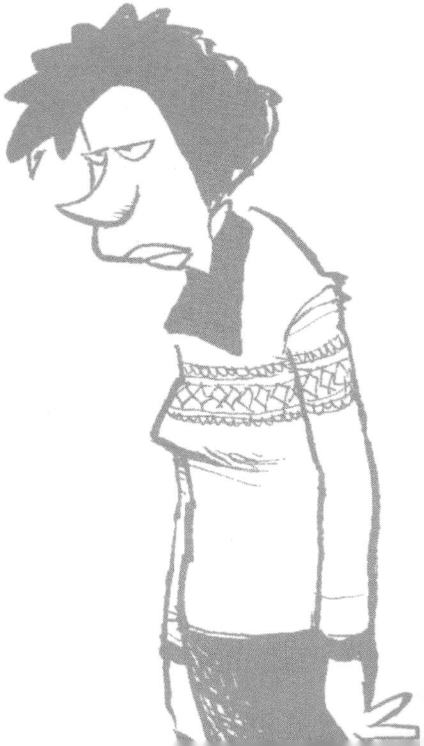

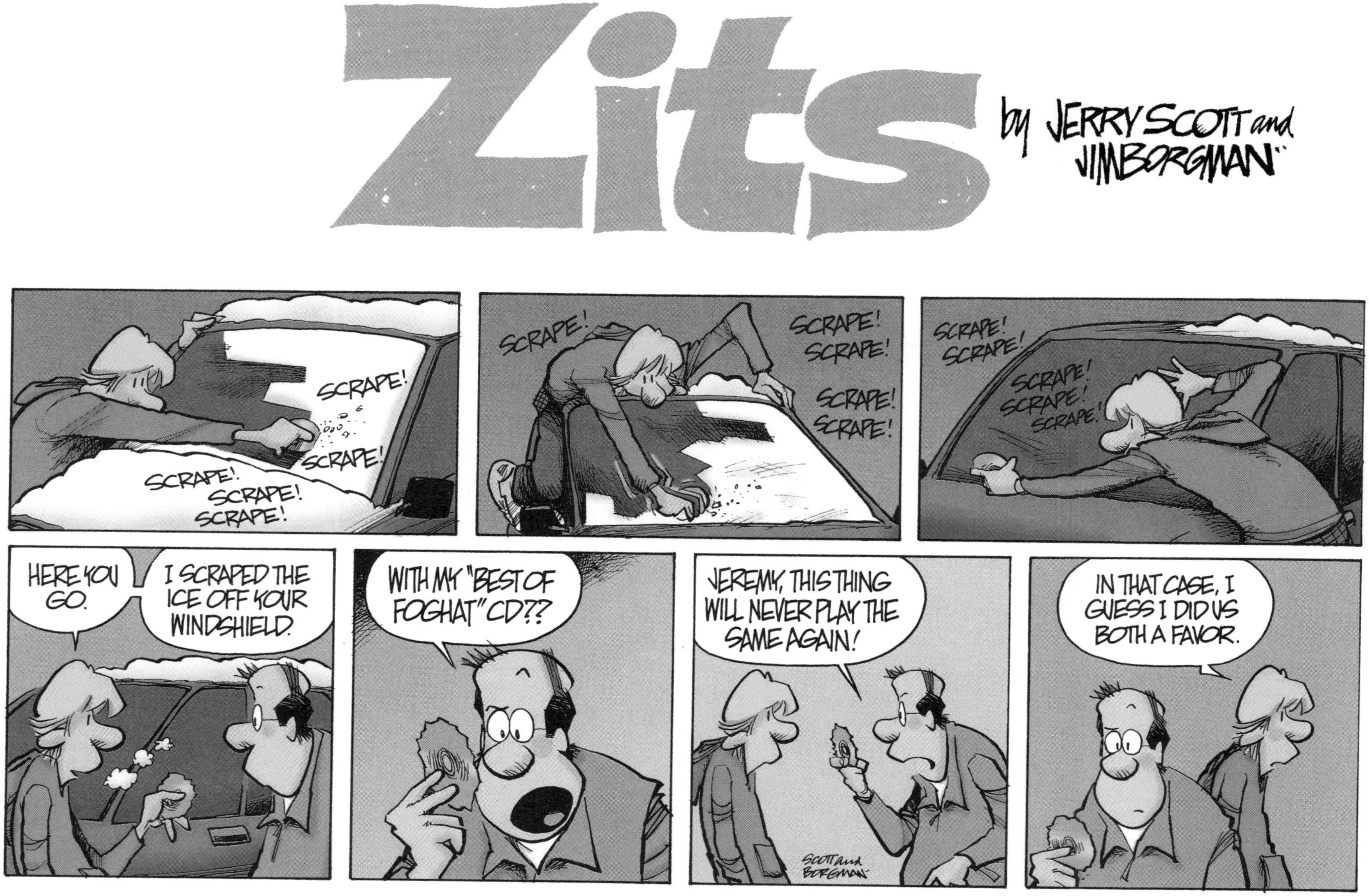
Zits
by JERRY SCOTT and JIM BORGMAN
SCRAPE!
SCRAPE!
SCRAPE! SCRAPE! SCRAPE!
SCRAPE!
SCRAPE! SCRAPE!
SCRAPE! SCRAPE!
SCRAPE! SCRAPE!
SCRAPE! SCRAPE! SCRAPE!
HERE YOU GO.
I SCRAPED THE ICE OFF YOUR WINDSHIELD.
WITH MY "BEST OF FOGHAT" CD??
JEREMY, THIS THING WILL NEVER PLAY THE SAME AGAIN!
SCOTT and BORGMAN
IN THAT CASE, I GUESS I DID US BOTH A FAVOR.

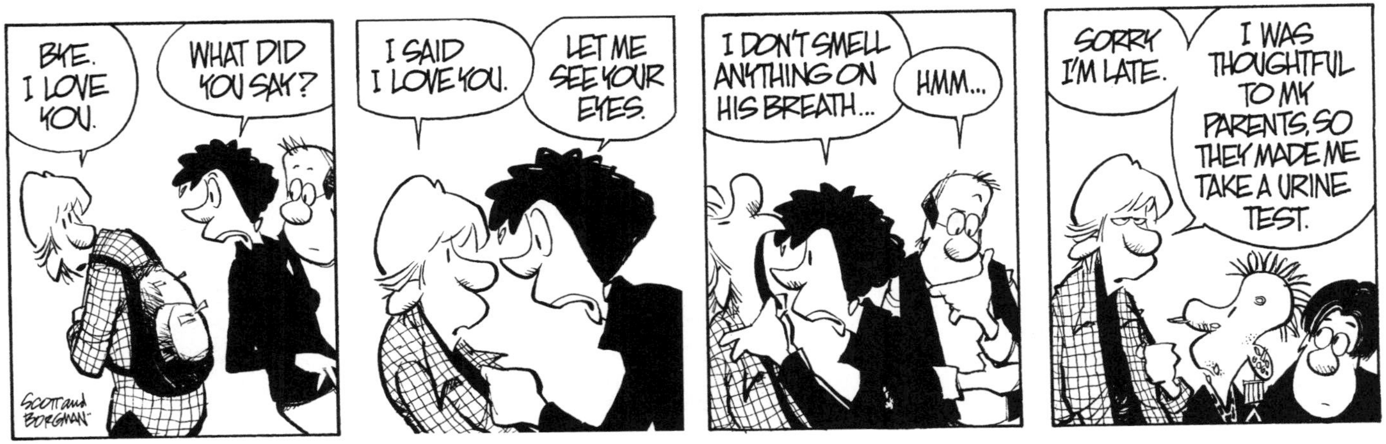
BYE. I LOVE YOU.
WHAT DID YOU SAY?
I SAID I LOVE YOU.
LET ME SEE YOUR EYES.
I DON'T SMELL ANYTHING ON HIS BREATH...
HMM...
SORRY I'M LATE.
I WAS THOUGHTFUL TO MY PARENTS, SO THEY MADE ME TAKE A URINE TEST.

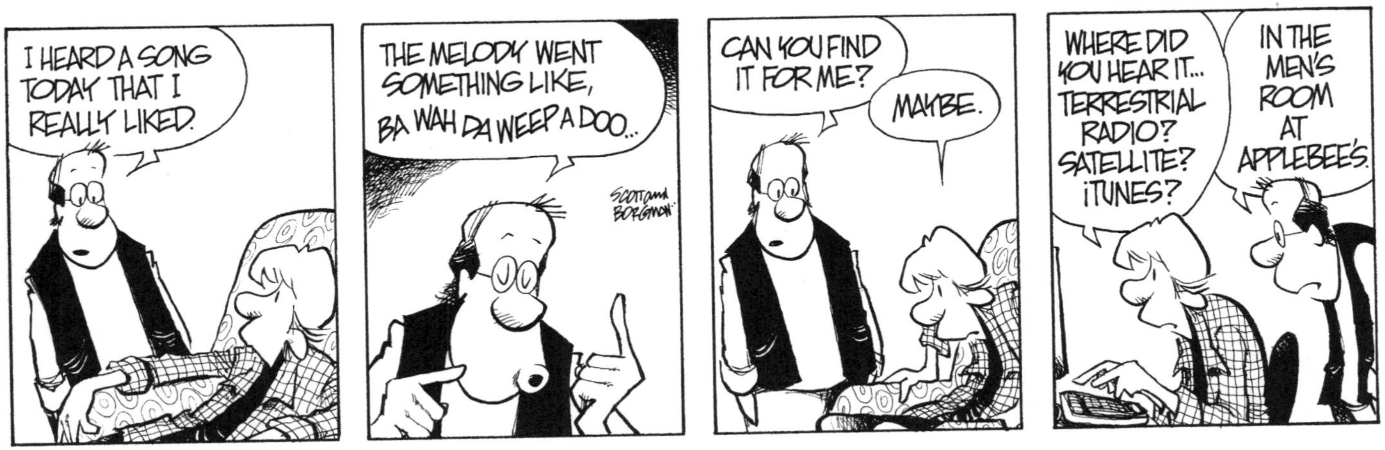
I HEARD A SONG TODAY THAT I REALLY LIKED.
THE MELODY WENT SOMETHING LIKE, BA WAH DA WEEP A DOO...
CAN YOU FIND IT FOR ME?
MAYBE.
WHERE DID YOU HEAR IT... TERRESTRIAL RADIO? SATELLITE? iTUNES?
IN THE MEN'S ROOM AT APPLEBEE'S.

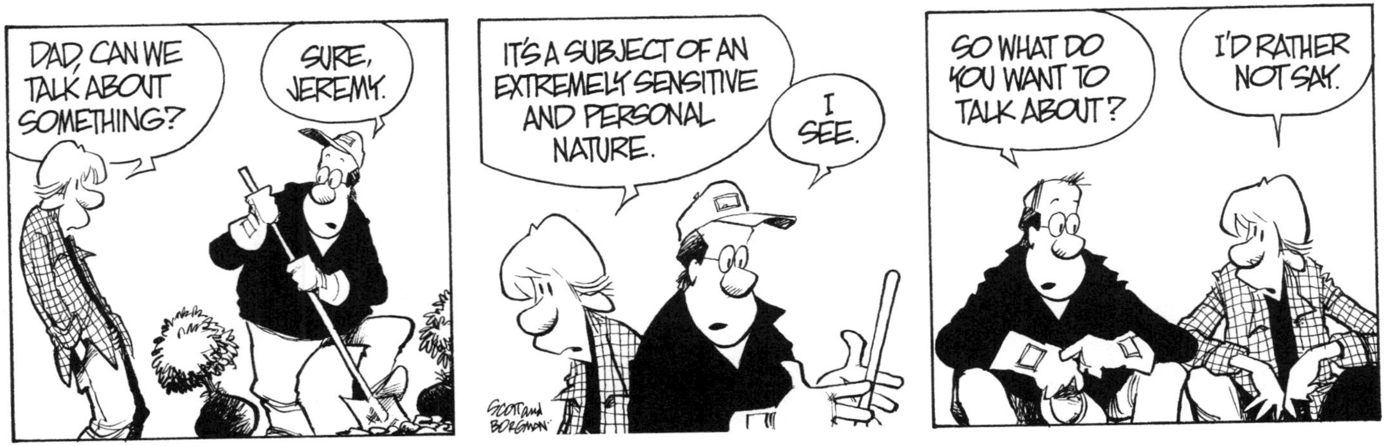
DAD, CAN WE TALK ABOUT SOMETHING?
SURE, JEREMY.
IT'S A SUBJECT OF AN EXTREMELY SENSITIVE AND PERSONAL NATURE.
I SEE.
SO WHAT DO YOU WANT TO TALK ABOUT?
I'D RATHER NOT SAY.

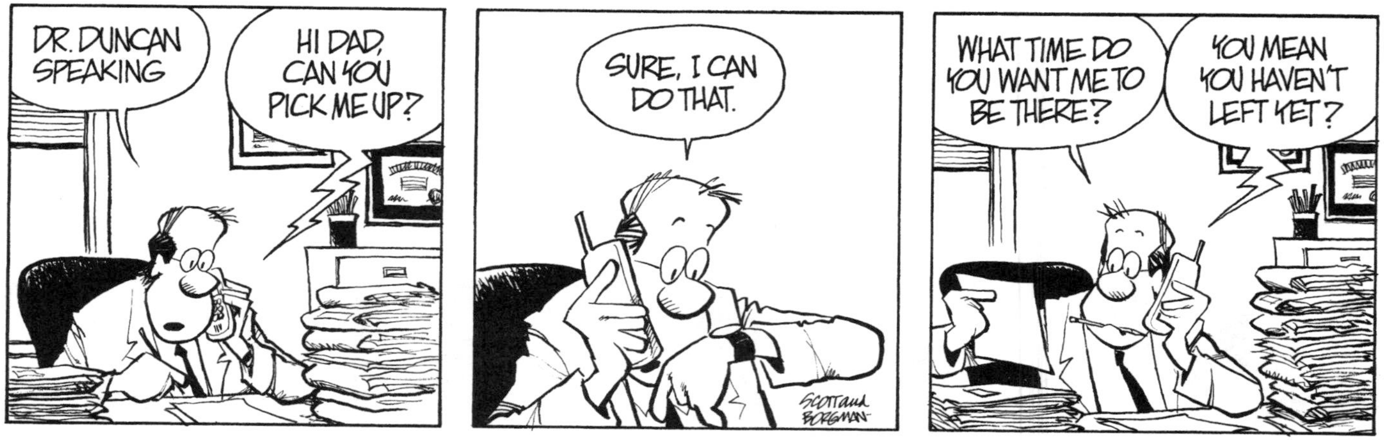
DR. DUNCAN SPEAKING
HI DAD, CAN YOU PICK ME UP?
SURE, I CAN DO THAT.
WHAT TIME DO YOU WANT ME TO BE THERE?
YOU MEAN YOU HAVEN'T LEFT YET?

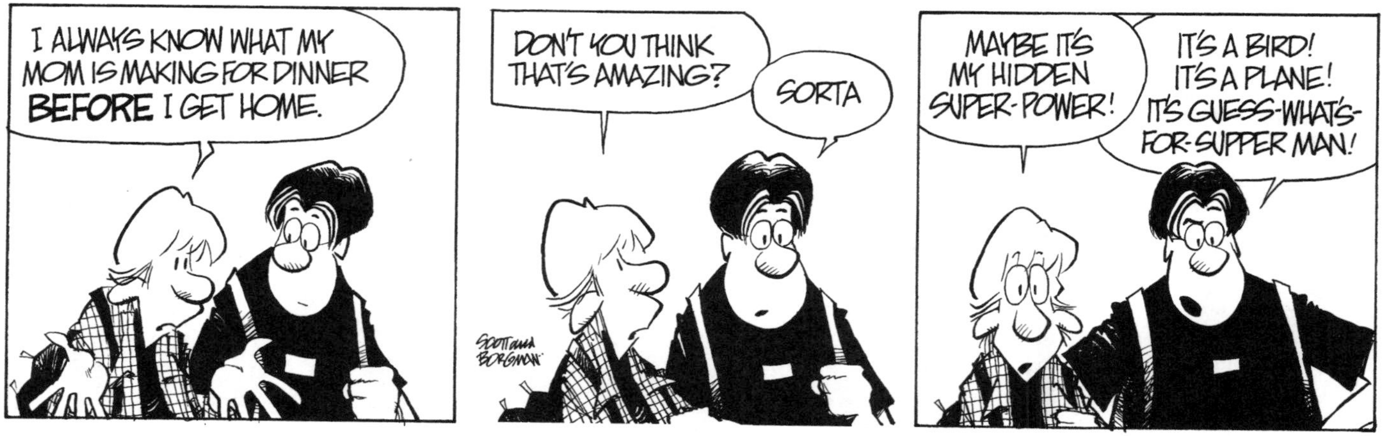
I ALWAYS KNOW WHAT MY MOM IS MAKING FOR DINNER **BEFORE** I GET HOME.
DON'T YOU THINK THAT'S AMAZING?
SORTA
MAYBE IT'S MY HIDDEN SUPER-POWER!
IT'S A BIRD! IT'S A PLANE! IT'S GUESS-WHAT'S-FOR-SUPPER MAN!

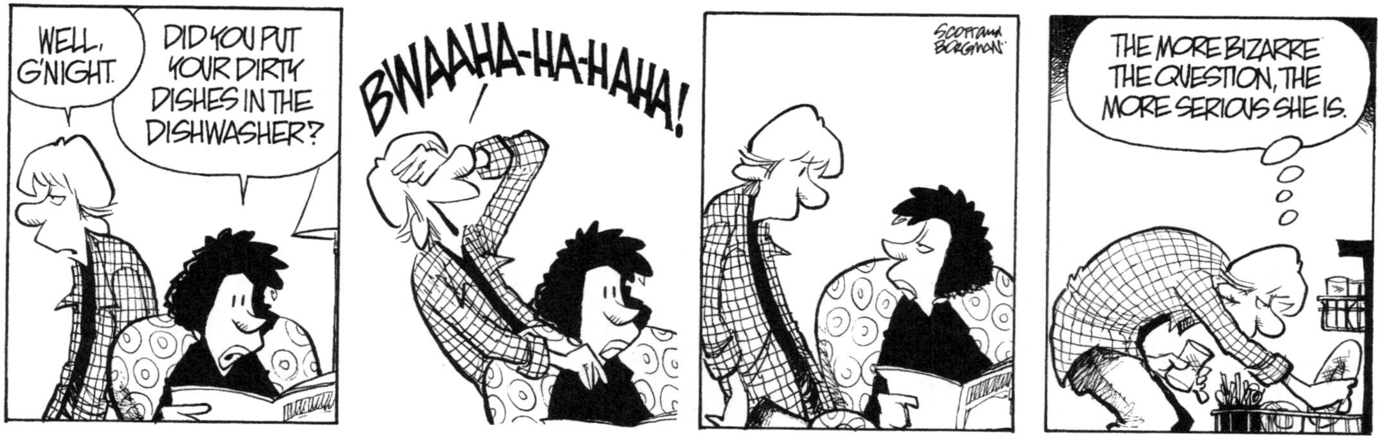
WELL, G'NIGHT.
DID YOU PUT YOUR DIRTY DISHES IN THE DISHWASHER?
BWAAHA-HA-HAHA!
THE MORE BIZARRE THE QUESTION, THE MORE SERIOUS SHE IS.

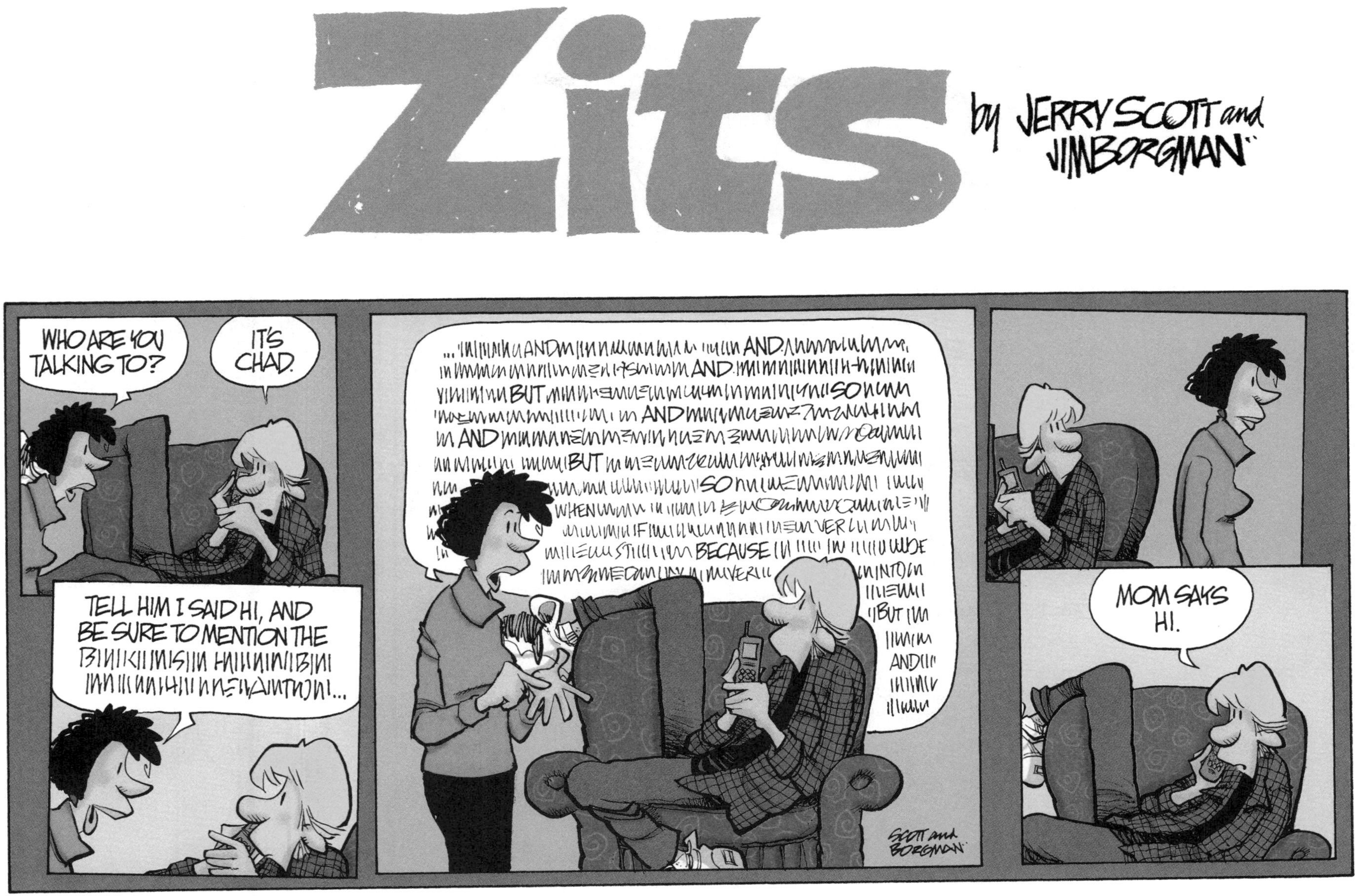
Zits
by JERRY SCOTT and JIM BORGMAN
WHO ARE YOU TALKING TO?
IT'S CHAD.
TELL HIM I SAID HI, AND BE SURE TO MENTION THE ...
AND
AND
BUT
SO
AND
AND
BUT
SO
WHEN
IF
VER
BECAUSE
INTO
BUT
AND
MOM SAYS HI.
SCOTT and BORGMAN

WHAT'S THAT NOISE? JEREMY, ARE YOU TEXTING UNDER THE TABLE?
UM... YEAH.
TAP TAP TAP TAP TAP TAP TAP TAP TAP TAP TAP

WHY WOULD YOU SIT THERE AND SEND MESSAGES TO YOUR FRIENDS INSTEAD OF TALKING TO US?
I DUNNO...

SCOTTAND BORGMAN
...I GUESS MY THUMBS HAVE MORE TO SAY THAN MY MOUTH.

LISTEN TO YOUR MOTHER.
BUT DAD, WHY CAN'T I EAT WITH THIS HAND AND TEXT WITH THIS HAND? IT'S EFFICIENT!

WHO DOES ONE THING AT A TIME ANYMORE?
HUH??
WHO??

YOU'RE TALKING TO A GUY WHO FEELS RUSHED IF HE CUTS HIS PORK CHOP AND CHEWS HIS PEAS AT THE SAME TIME.
OKAY, BESIDES YOU! NOBODY, THAT'S WHO!
SCOTTAND BORGMAN

TEXTING AT THE DINNER TABLE IS JUST PLAIN RUDE!
IN YOUR OPINION.

THE WAY I SEE IT, I'M HAVING DINNER WITH MY PARENTS AND STAYING CONNECTED AT THE SAME TIME.
SCOTTAND BORGMAN

TEXTING IS THE WAY MY GENERATION SHARES URGENT NEWS AND EVENTS.

"I 8 2 MUCH 2 DAY"
SOME MORE URGENT THAN OTHERS.

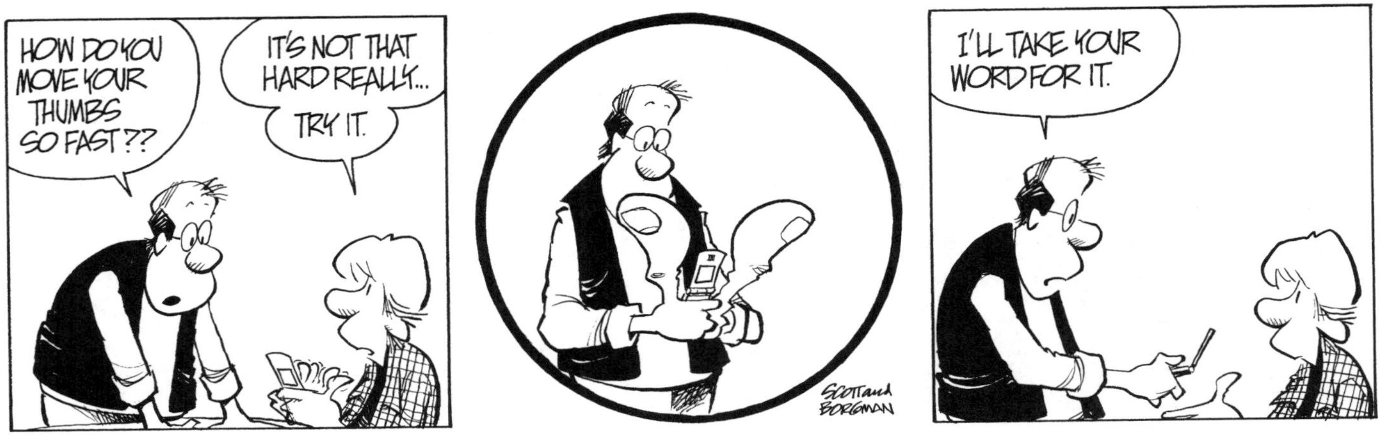
HOW DO YOU MOVE YOUR THUMBS SO FAST??
IT'S NOT THAT HARD REALLY...
TRY IT.
I'LL TAKE YOUR WORD FOR IT.
SCOTT and BORGMAN

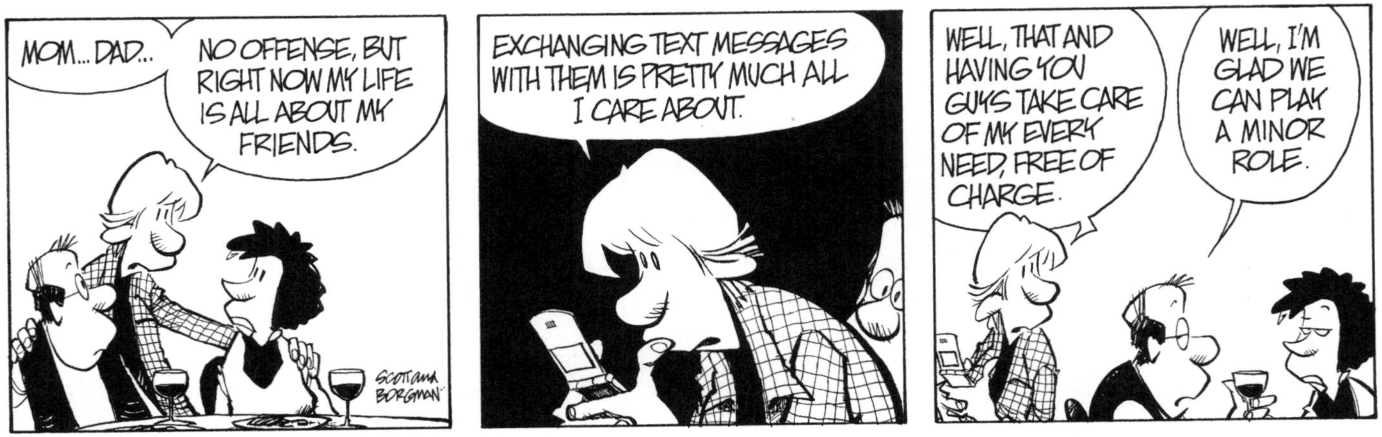
MOM... DAD...
NO OFFENSE, BUT RIGHT NOW MY LIFE IS ALL ABOUT MY FRIENDS.
EXCHANGING TEXT MESSAGES WITH THEM IS PRETTY MUCH ALL I CARE ABOUT.
WELL, THAT AND HAVING YOU GUYS TAKE CARE OF MY EVERY NEED, FREE OF CHARGE.
WELL, I'M GLAD WE CAN PLAY A MINOR ROLE.
SCOTT and BORGMAN

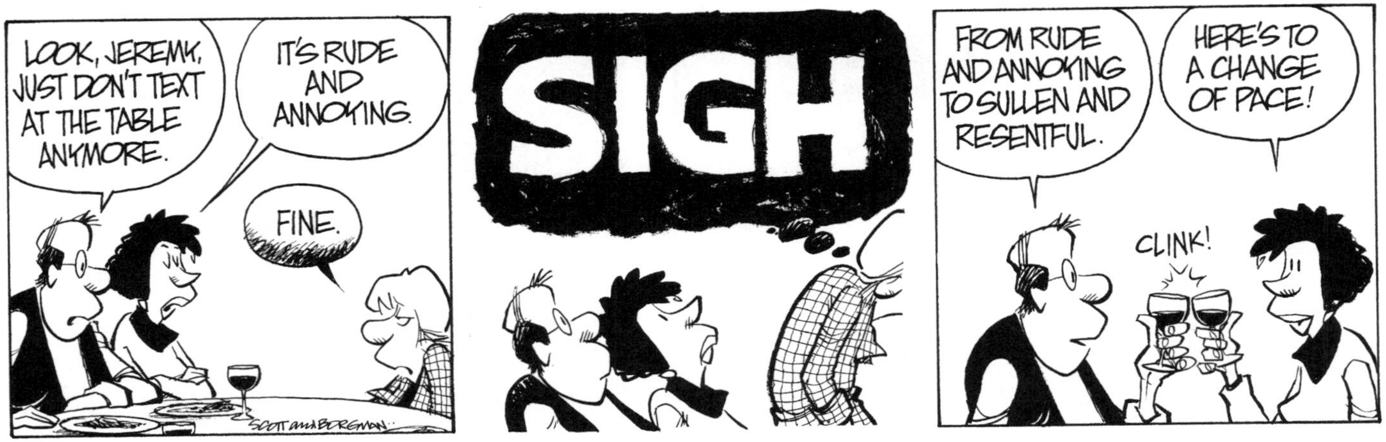
LOOK, JEREMY, JUST DON'T TEXT AT THE TABLE ANYMORE.
IT'S RUDE AND ANNOYING.
FINE.
SIGH
FROM RUDE AND ANNOYING TO SULLEN AND RESENTFUL.
HERE'S TO A CHANGE OF PACE!
CLINK!
SCOTT and BORGMAN

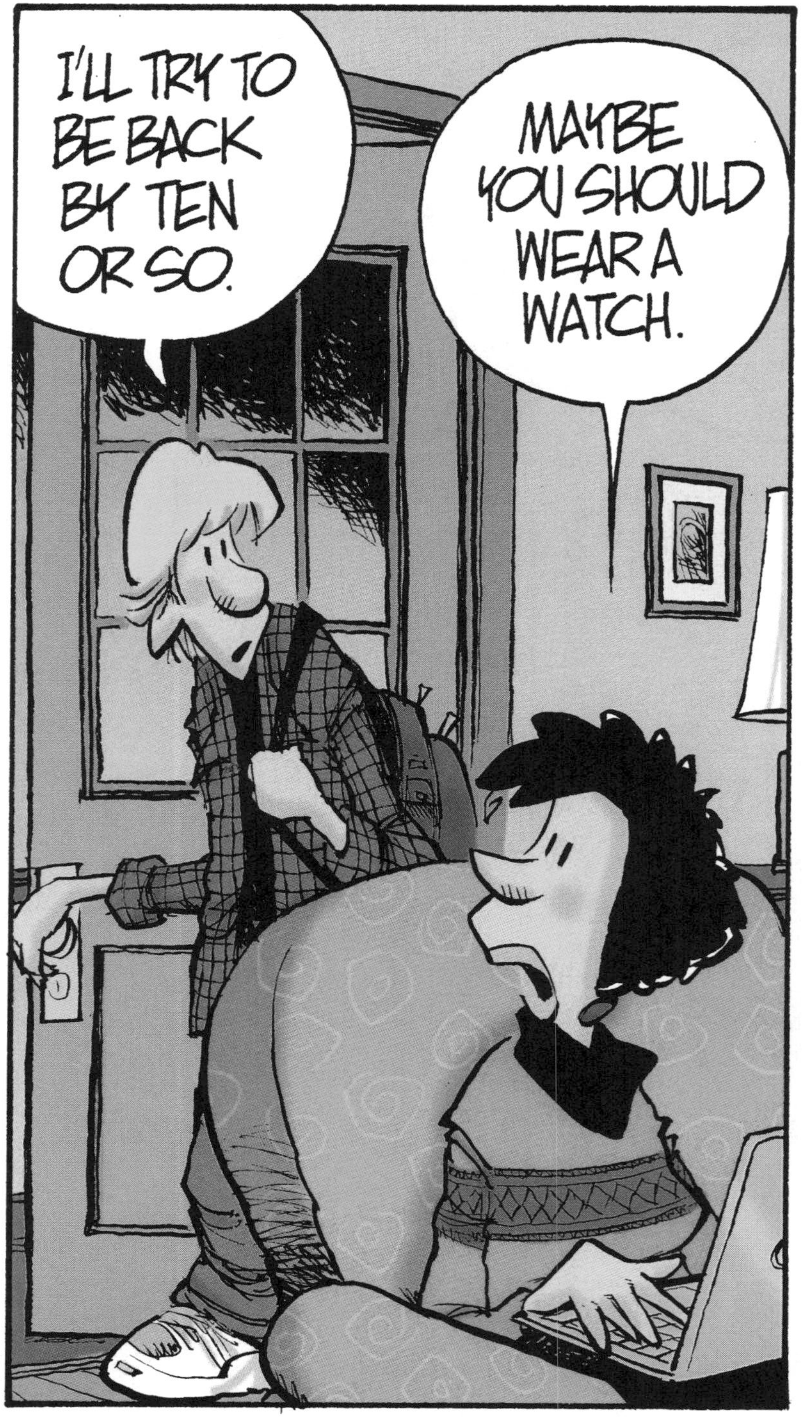
I'LL TRY TO BE BACK BY TEN OR SO.
MAYBE YOU SHOULD WEAR A WATCH.

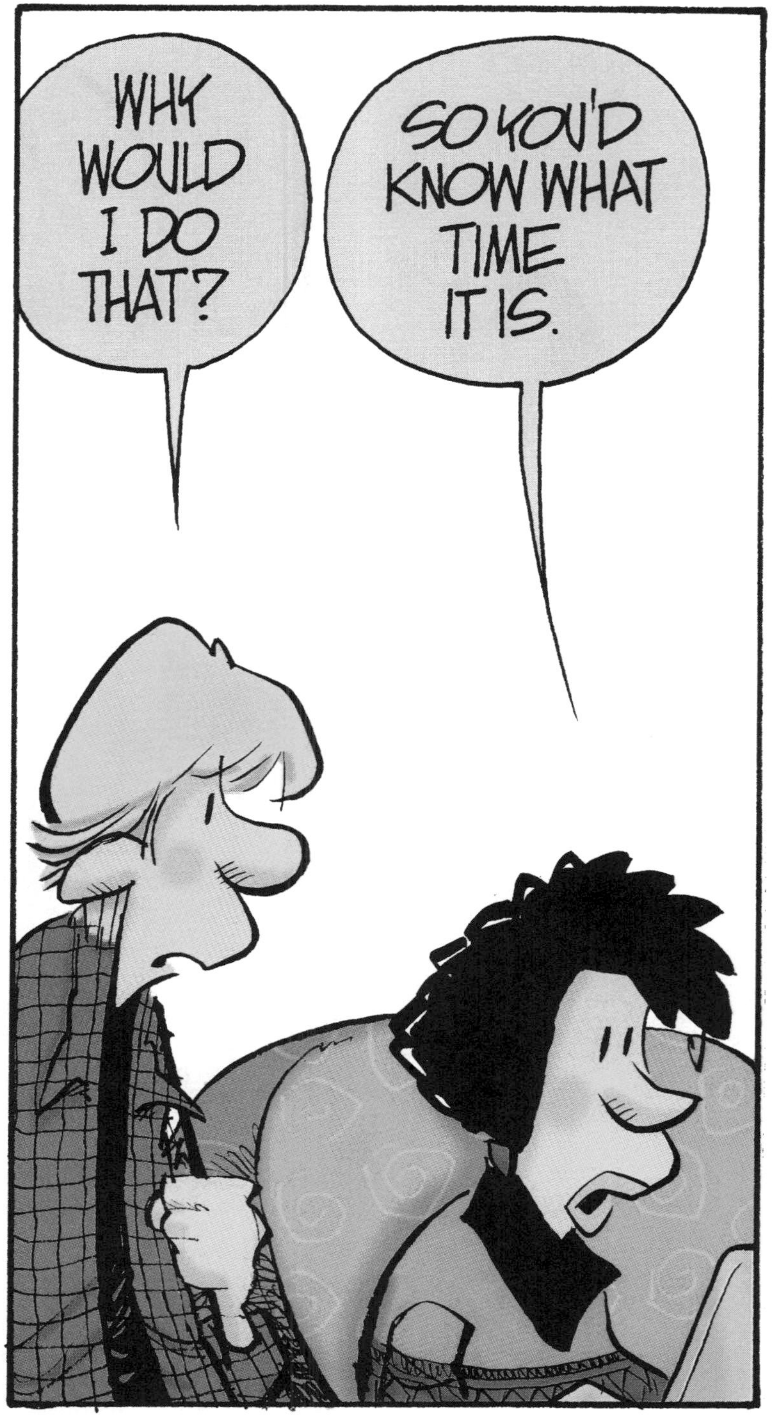
WHY WOULD I DO THAT?
SO YOU'D KNOW WHAT TIME IT IS.

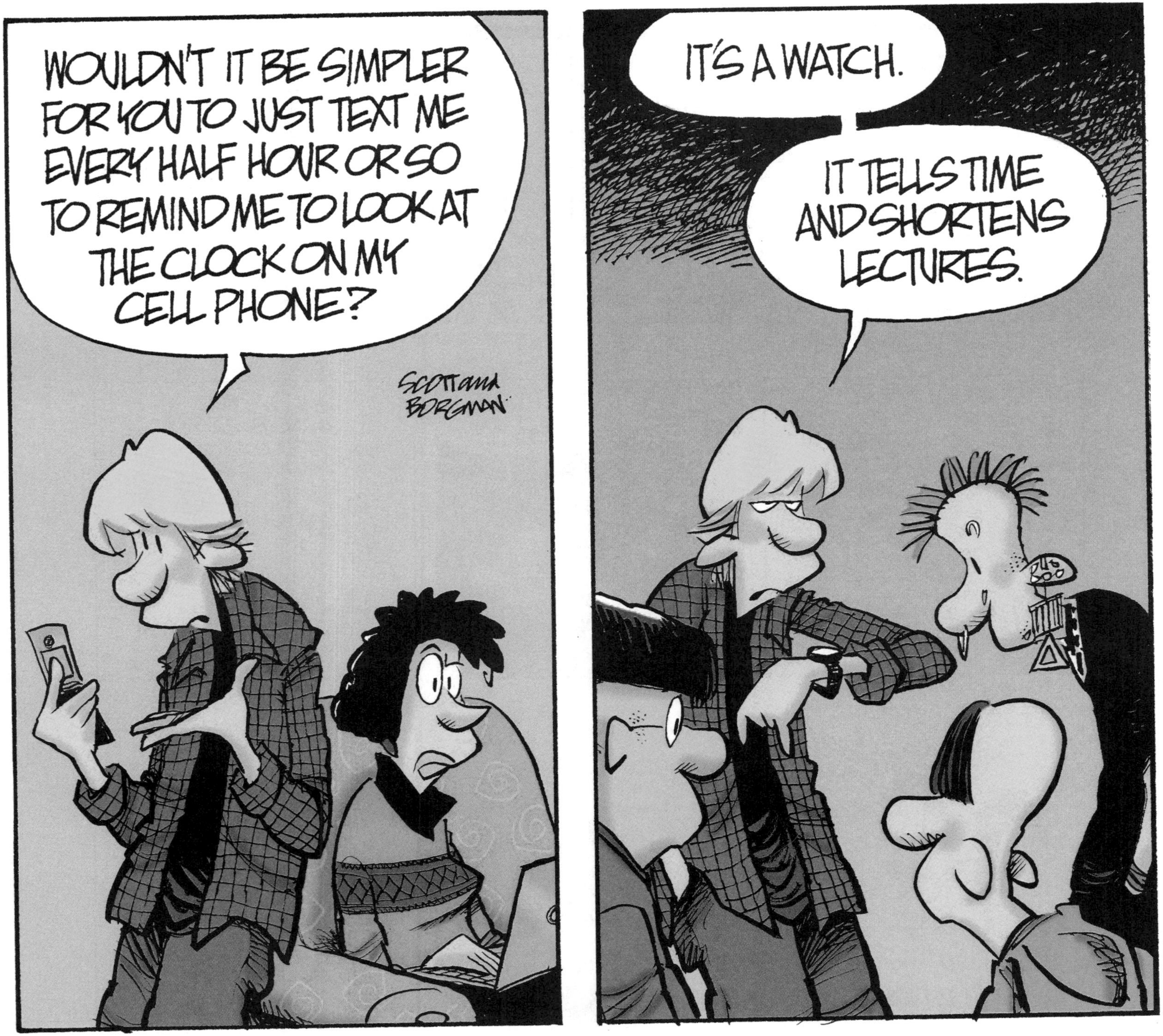
WOULDN'T IT BE SIMPLER FOR YOU TO JUST TEXT ME EVERY HALF HOUR OR SO TO REMIND ME TO LOOK AT THE CLOCK ON MY CELL PHONE?
SCOTT and BORGMAN
IT'S A WATCH.
IT TELLS TIME AND SHORTENS LECTURES.

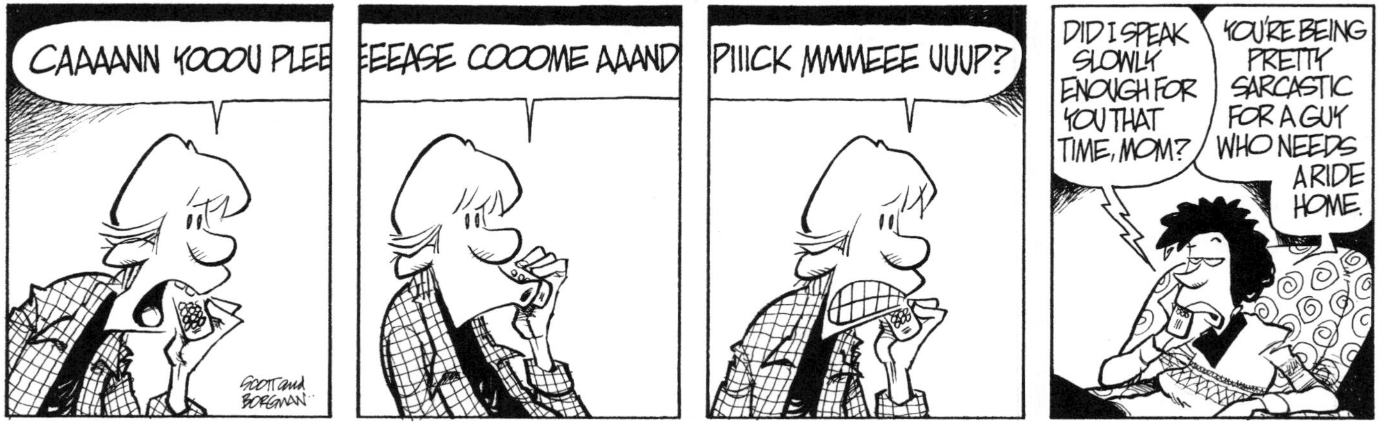
CAAAANN YOOOU PLEE
EEEASE COOOME AAAND
PIIICK MMMEEE UUUP?
DID I SPEAK SLOWLY ENOUGH FOR YOU THAT TIME, MOM?
YOU'RE BEING PRETTY SARCASTIC FOR A GUY WHO NEEDS A RIDE HOME.
SCOTT and BORGMAN

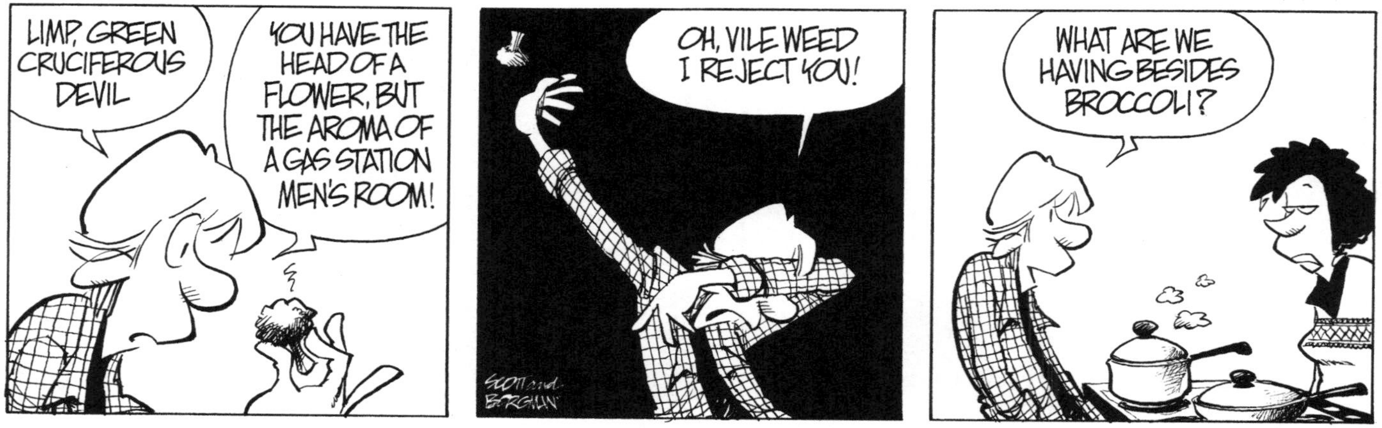
LIMP, GREEN CRUCIFEROUS DEVIL
YOU HAVE THE HEAD OF A FLOWER, BUT THE AROMA OF A GAS STATION MEN'S ROOM!
OH, VILE WEED I REJECT YOU!
WHAT ARE WE HAVING BESIDES BROCCOLI?
SCOTT and BORGMAN

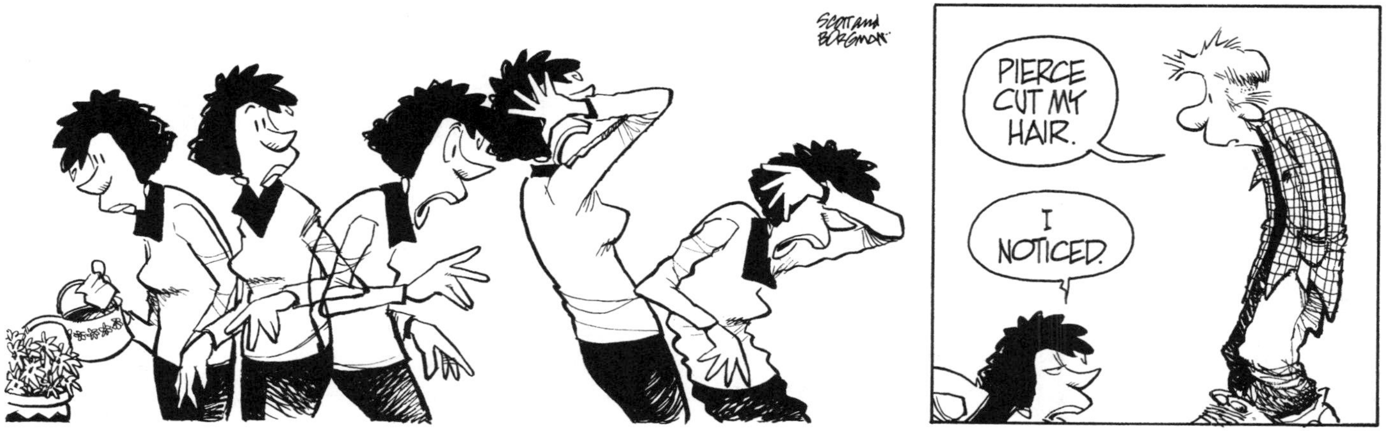
SCOTT and BORGMAN
PIERCE CUT MY HAIR.
I NOTICED.

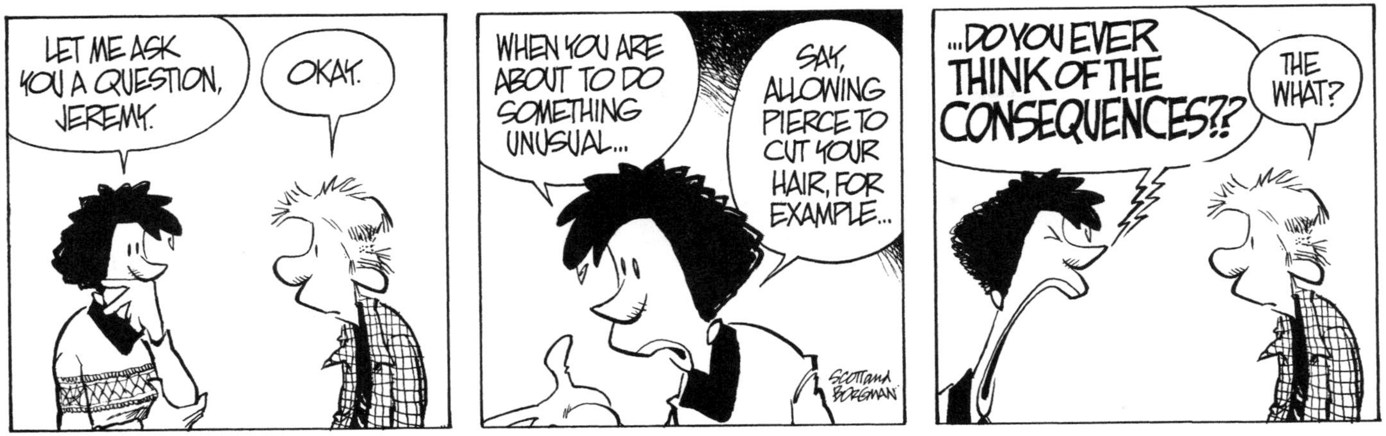
LET ME ASK YOU A QUESTION, JEREMY.
OKAY.
WHEN YOU ARE ABOUT TO DO SOMETHING UNUSUAL...
SAY, ALLOWING PIERCE TO CUT YOUR HAIR, FOR EXAMPLE...
...DO YOU EVER THINK OF THE CONSEQUENCES??
THE WHAT?

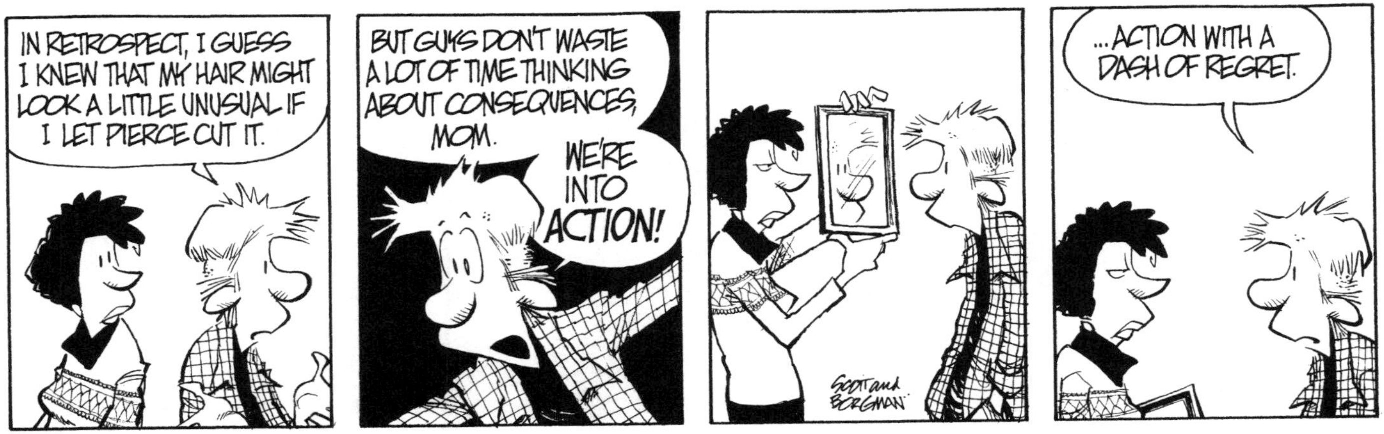
IN RETROSPECT, I GUESS I KNEW THAT MY HAIR MIGHT LOOK A LITTLE UNUSUAL IF I LET PIERCE CUT IT.
BUT GUYS DON'T WASTE A LOT OF TIME THINKING ABOUT CONSEQUENCES, MOM.
WE'RE INTO ACTION!
...ACTION WITH A DASH OF REGRET.

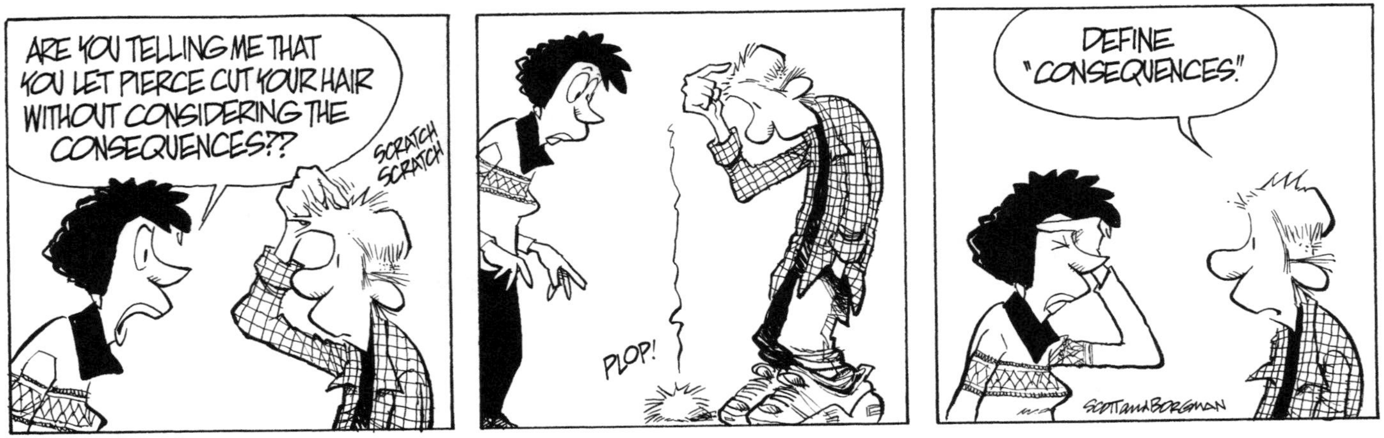
ARE YOU TELLING ME THAT YOU LET PIERCE CUT YOUR HAIR WITHOUT CONSIDERING THE CONSEQUENCES??
SCRATCH SCRATCH
PLOP!
DEFINE "CONSEQUENCES."

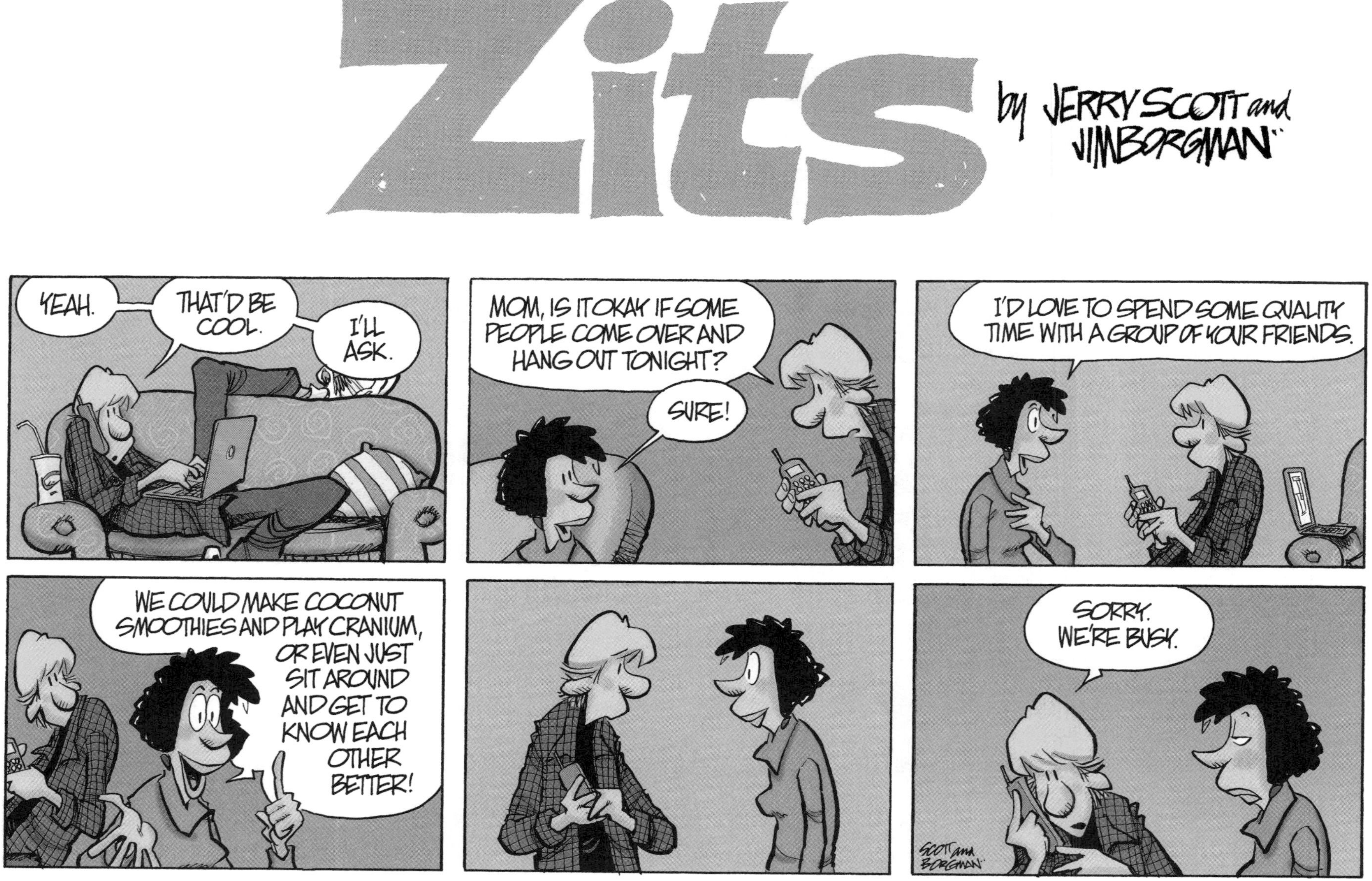
Zits
by JERRY SCOTT and JIM BORGMAN
YEAH.
THAT'D BE COOL.
I'LL ASK.
MOM, IS IT OKAY IF SOME PEOPLE COME OVER AND HANG OUT TONIGHT?
SURE!
I'D LOVE TO SPEND SOME QUALITY TIME WITH A GROUP OF YOUR FRIENDS.
WE COULD MAKE COCONUT SMOOTHIES AND PLAY CRANIUM, OR EVEN JUST SIT AROUND AND GET TO KNOW EACH OTHER BETTER!
SORRY. WE'RE BUSY.
SCOTT and BORGMAN

PSSSSSSSSHHHHHHHH!

SCOTT and BORGMAN

ONE OF US OUGHT TO DO SOMETHING ABOUT JEREMY WEARING SO MUCH BODY SPRAY.

ONE OF US IS.

YES, MOM.

I WILL TAKE THE TRASH CANS OUT TO THE CURB TONIGHT.

SCOTT and BORGMAN

SO, THAT'S A PROMISE?

THINK OF IT MORE AS A NON-BINDING RESOLUTION.

TWO SCOOPS OF PROTEIN POWDER IN A GLASS OF SOY MILK

SCOTT and BORGMAN

WITH A CHOCOLATE SYRUP CHASER.

HOW'S THE NEW HEALTHY EATING THING WORKING OUT FOR YOU?

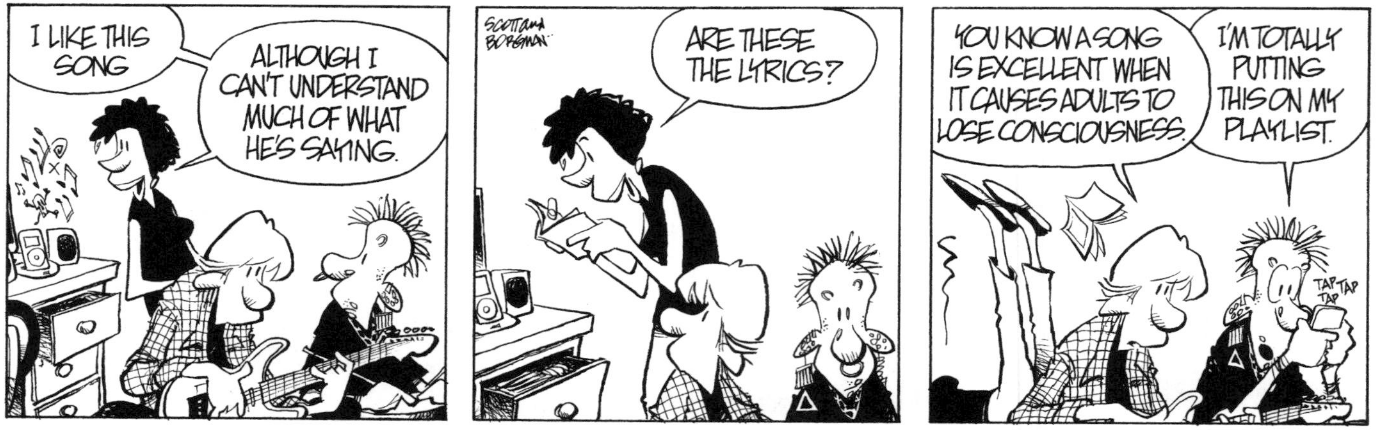
I LIKE THIS SONG
ALTHOUGH I CAN'T UNDERSTAND MUCH OF WHAT HE'S SAYING.
ARE THESE THE LYRICS?
YOU KNOW A SONG IS EXCELLENT WHEN IT CAUSES ADULTS TO LOSE CONSCIOUSNESS.
I'M TOTALLY PUTTING THIS ON MY PLAYLIST.
TAP TAP TAP

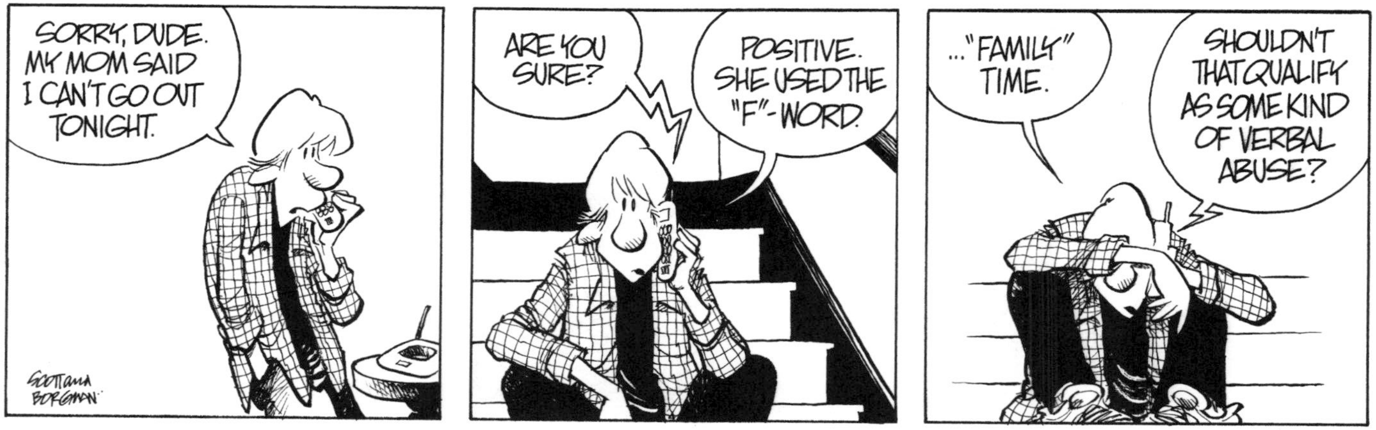
SORRY, DUDE. MY MOM SAID I CAN'T GO OUT TONIGHT.
ARE YOU SURE?
POSITIVE. SHE USED THE "F"-WORD.
..."FAMILY" TIME.
SHOULDN'T THAT QUALIFY AS SOME KIND OF VERBAL ABUSE?

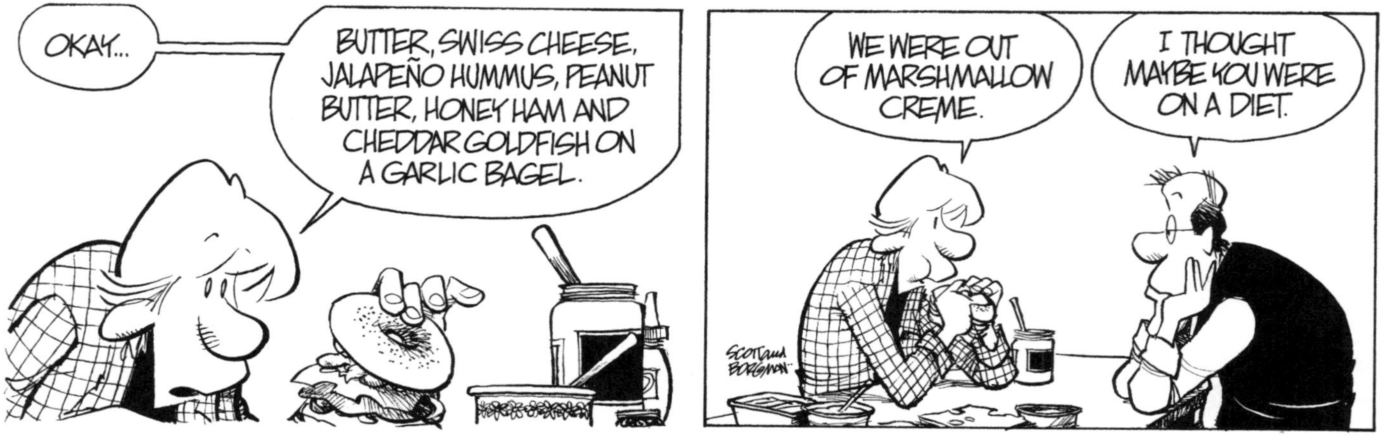
OKAY...
BUTTER, SWISS CHEESE, JALAPEÑO HUMMUS, PEANUT BUTTER, HONEY HAM AND CHEDDAR GOLDFISH ON A GARLIC BAGEL.
WE WERE OUT OF MARSHMALLOW CREME.
I THOUGHT MAYBE YOU WERE ON A DIET.

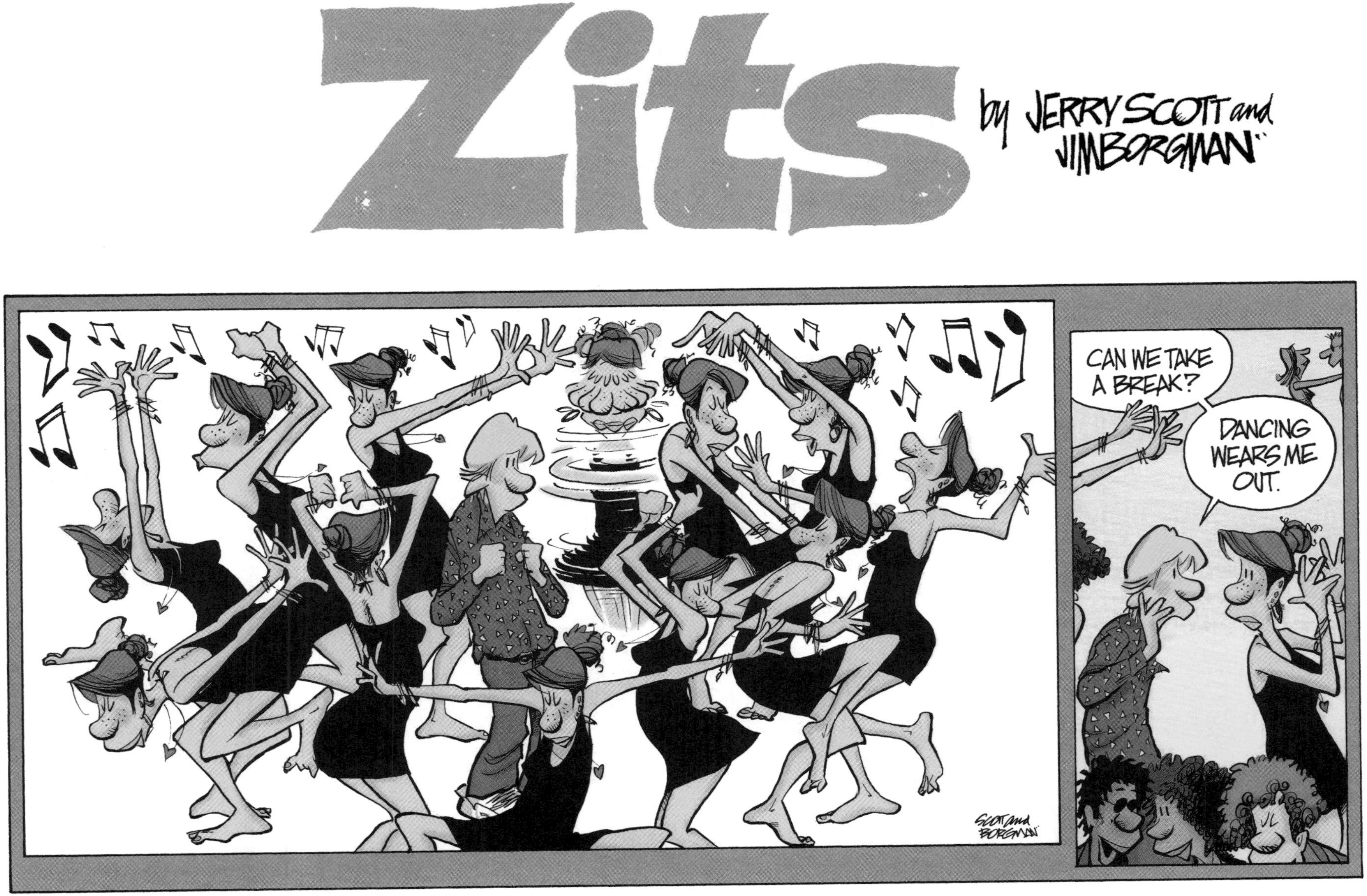
Zits
by JERRY SCOTT and JIM BORGMAN
SCOTT and BORGMAN
CAN WE TAKE A BREAK?
DANCING WEARS ME OUT.

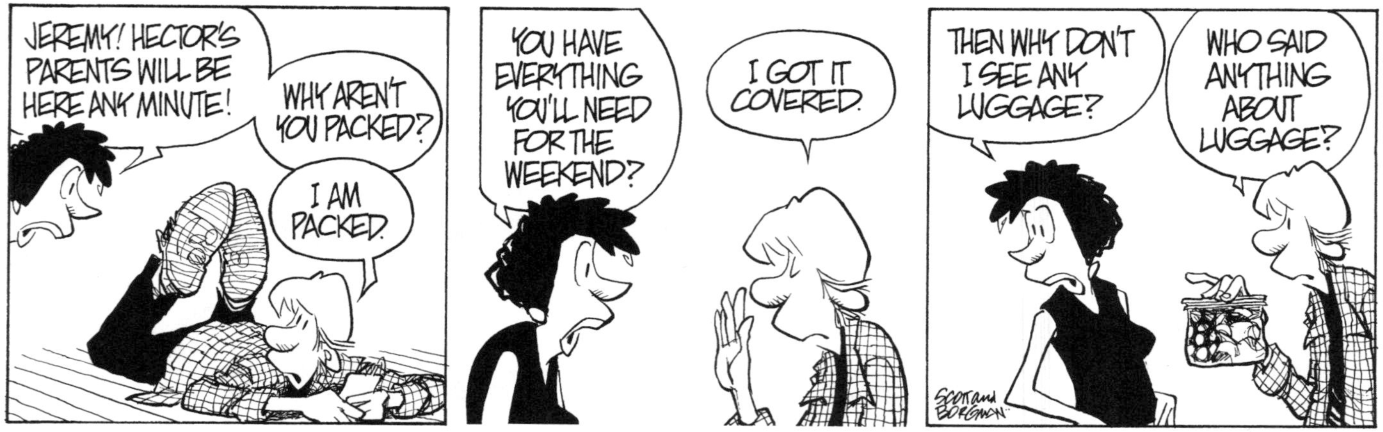
JEREMY! HECTOR'S PARENTS WILL BE HERE ANY MINUTE!
WHY AREN'T YOU PACKED?
I AM PACKED.
YOU HAVE EVERYTHING YOU'LL NEED FOR THE WEEKEND?
I GOT IT COVERED.
THEN WHY DON'T I SEE ANY LUGGAGE?
WHO SAID ANYTHING ABOUT LUGGAGE?
SCOTT and BORGMAN

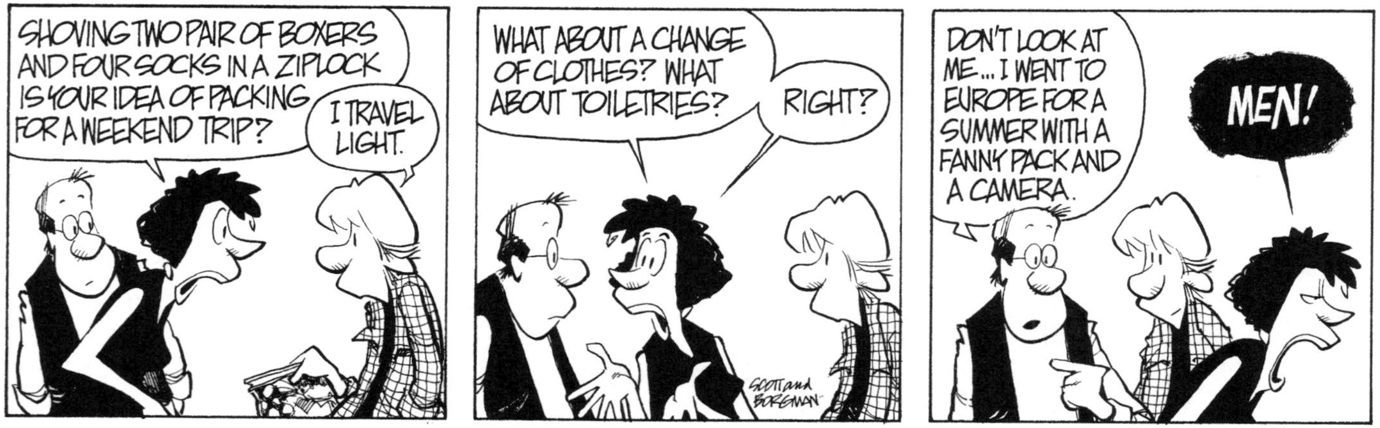
SHOVING TWO PAIR OF BOXERS AND FOUR SOCKS IN A ZIPLOCK IS YOUR IDEA OF PACKING FOR A WEEKEND TRIP?
I TRAVEL LIGHT.
WHAT ABOUT A CHANGE OF CLOTHES? WHAT ABOUT TOILETRIES?
RIGHT?
SCOTT and BORGMAN
DON'T LOOK AT ME... I WENT TO EUROPE FOR A SUMMER WITH A FANNY PACK AND A CAMERA.
MEN!

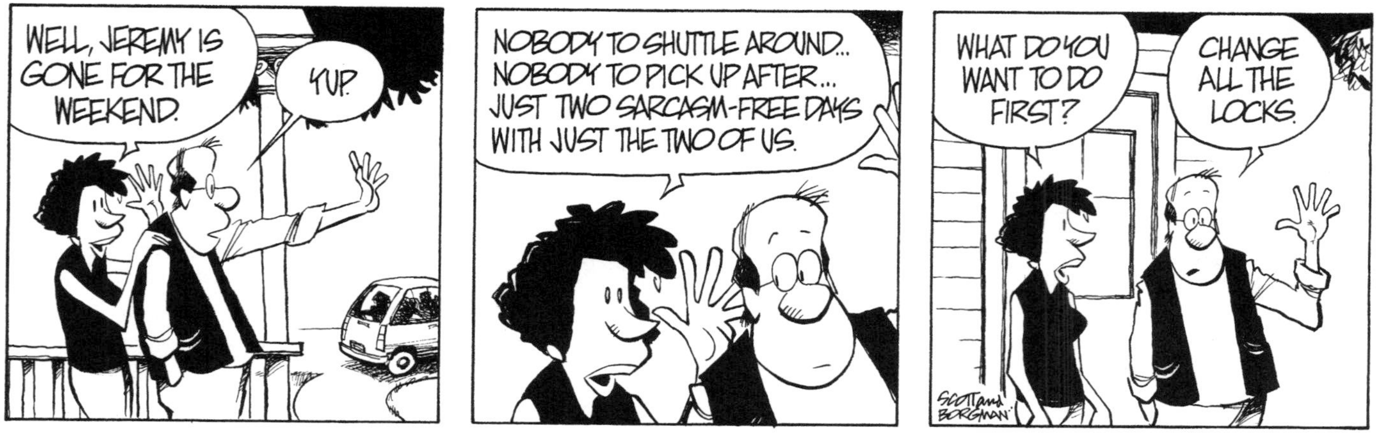
WELL, JEREMY IS GONE FOR THE WEEKEND.
YUP.
NOBODY TO SHUTTLE AROUND... NOBODY TO PICK UP AFTER... JUST TWO SARCASM-FREE DAYS WITH JUST THE TWO OF US.
WHAT DO YOU WANT TO DO FIRST?
CHANGE ALL THE LOCKS.
SCOTT and BORGMAN

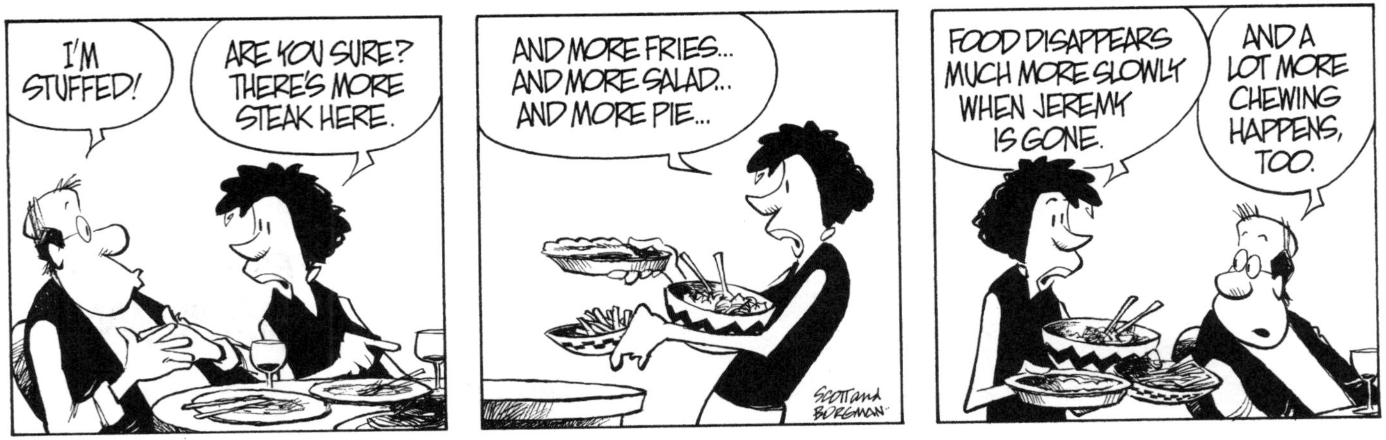
I'M STUFFED!
ARE YOU SURE? THERE'S MORE STEAK HERE.
AND MORE FRIES... AND MORE SALAD... AND MORE PIE...
FOOD DISAPPEARS MUCH MORE SLOWLY WHEN JEREMY IS GONE.
AND A LOT MORE CHEWING HAPPENS, TOO.
SCOTT and BORGMAN

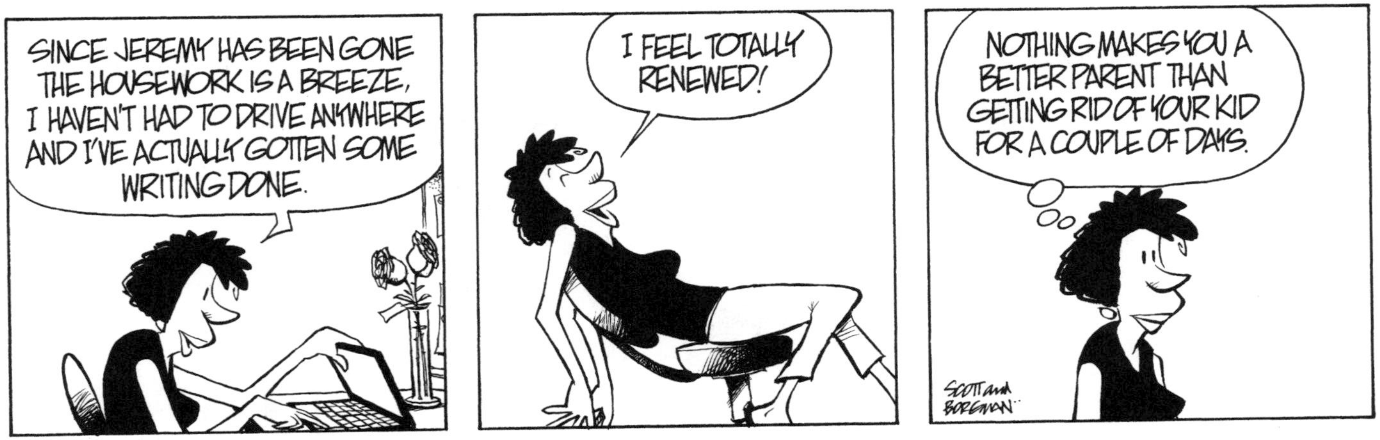
SINCE JEREMY HAS BEEN GONE THE HOUSEWORK IS A BREEZE, I HAVEN'T HAD TO DRIVE ANYWHERE AND I'VE ACTUALLY GOTTEN SOME WRITING DONE.
I FEEL TOTALLY RENEWED!
NOTHING MAKES YOU A BETTER PARENT THAN GETTING RID OF YOUR KID FOR A COUPLE OF DAYS.
SCOTT and BORGMAN

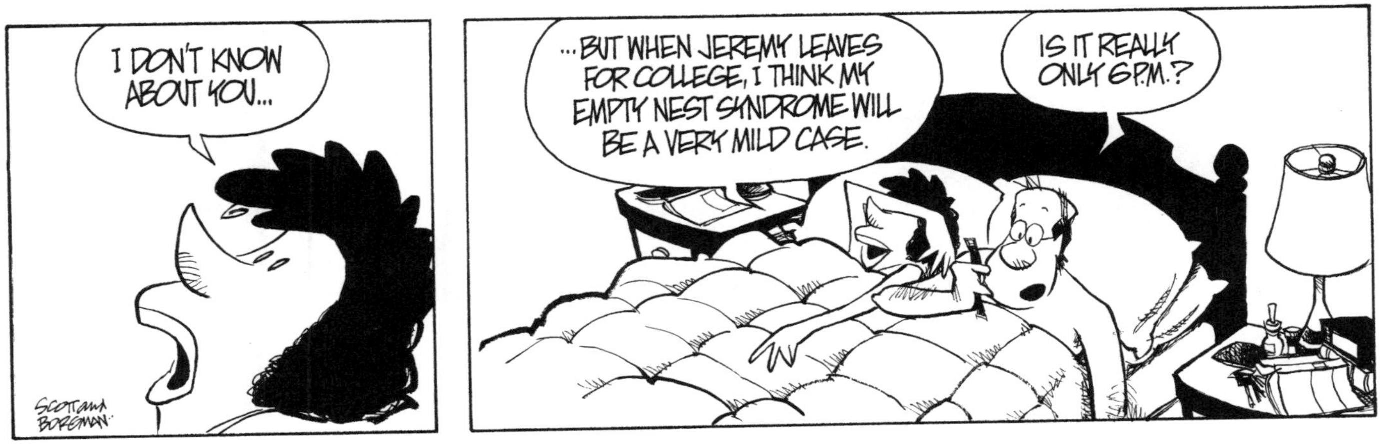
I DON'T KNOW ABOUT YOU...
...BUT WHEN JEREMY LEAVES FOR COLLEGE, I THINK MY EMPTY NEST SYNDROME WILL BE A VERY MILD CASE.
IS IT REALLY ONLY 6 P.M.?
SCOTT and BORGMAN

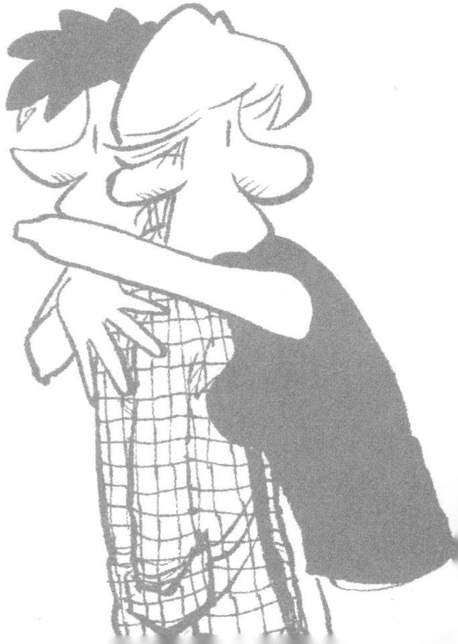

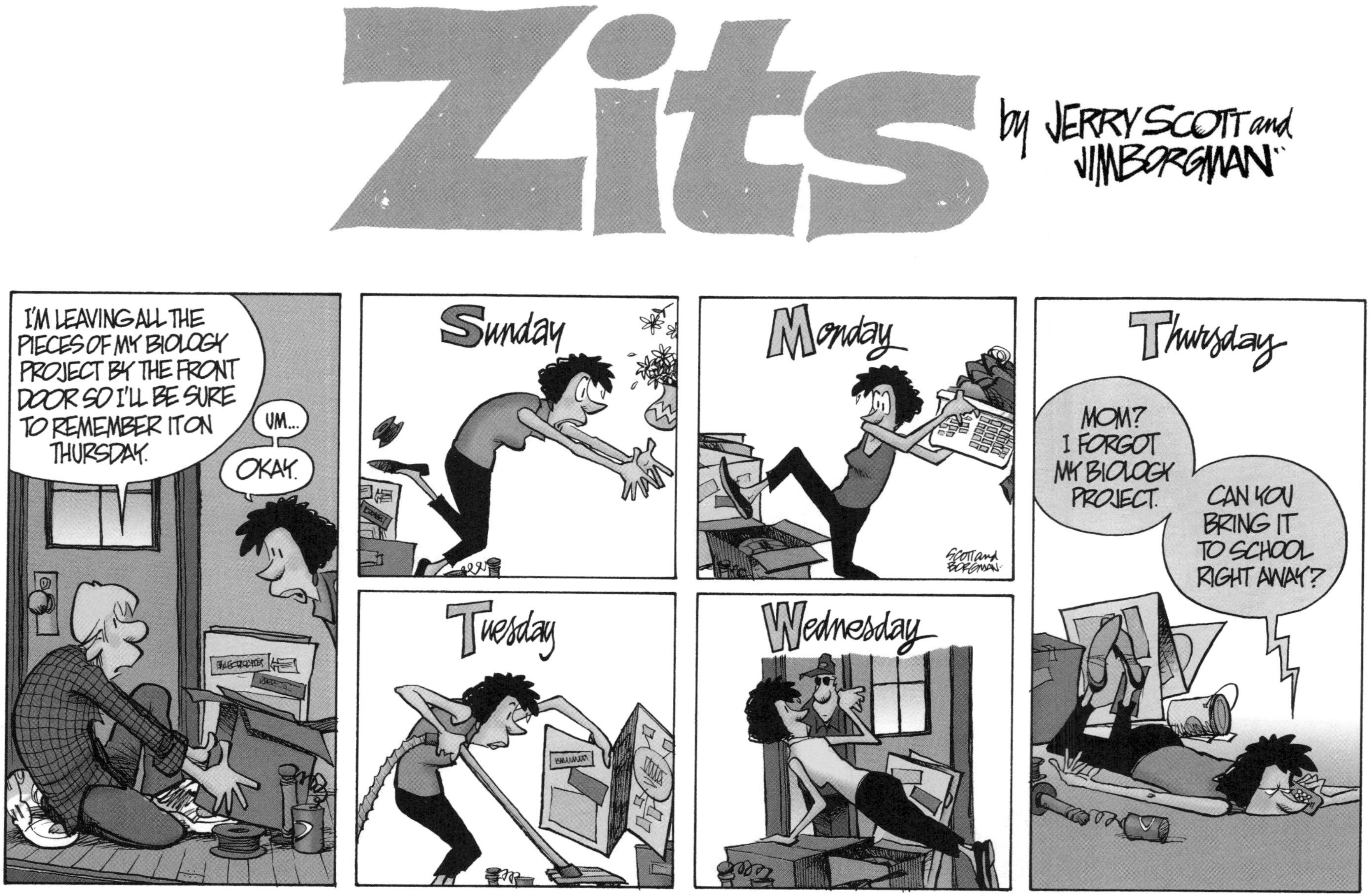
Zits
by JERRY SCOTT and JIM BORGMAN
I'M LEAVING ALL THE PIECES OF MY BIOLOGY PROJECT BY THE FRONT DOOR SO I'LL BE SURE TO REMEMBER IT ON THURSDAY.
UM...
OKAY.
Sunday
Monday
SCOTT and BORGMAN
Tuesday
Wednesday
Thursday
MOM? I FORGOT MY BIOLOGY PROJECT.
CAN YOU BRING IT TO SCHOOL RIGHT AWAY?

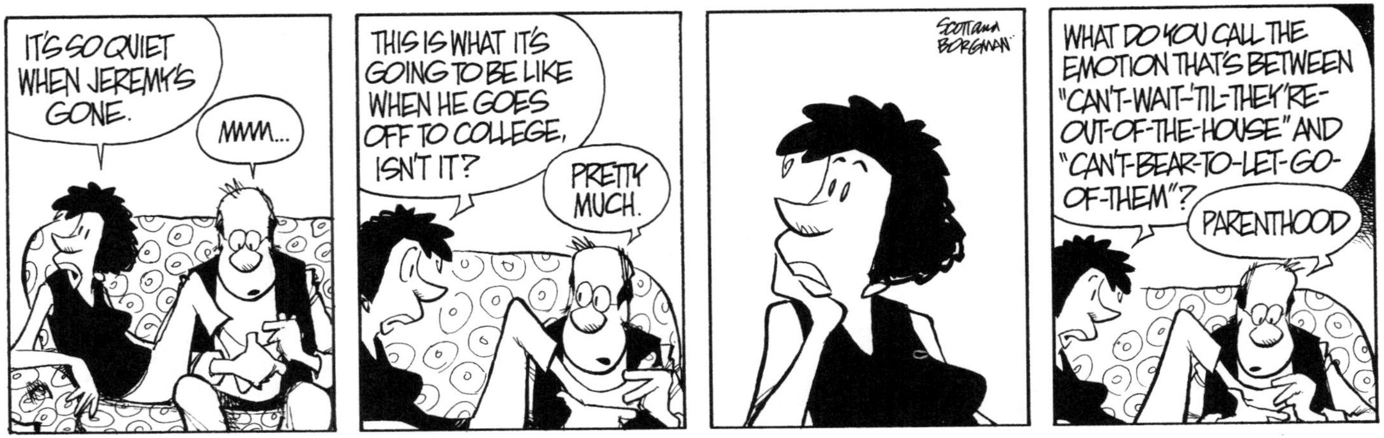
IT'S SO QUIET WHEN JEREMY'S GONE.
MMM...
THIS IS WHAT IT'S GOING TO BE LIKE WHEN HE GOES OFF TO COLLEGE, ISN'T IT?
PRETTY MUCH.
WHAT DO YOU CALL THE EMOTION THAT'S BETWEEN "CAN'T-WAIT-'TIL-THEY'RE-OUT-OF-THE-HOUSE" AND "CAN'T-BEAR-TO-LET-GO-OF-THEM"?
PARENTHOOD

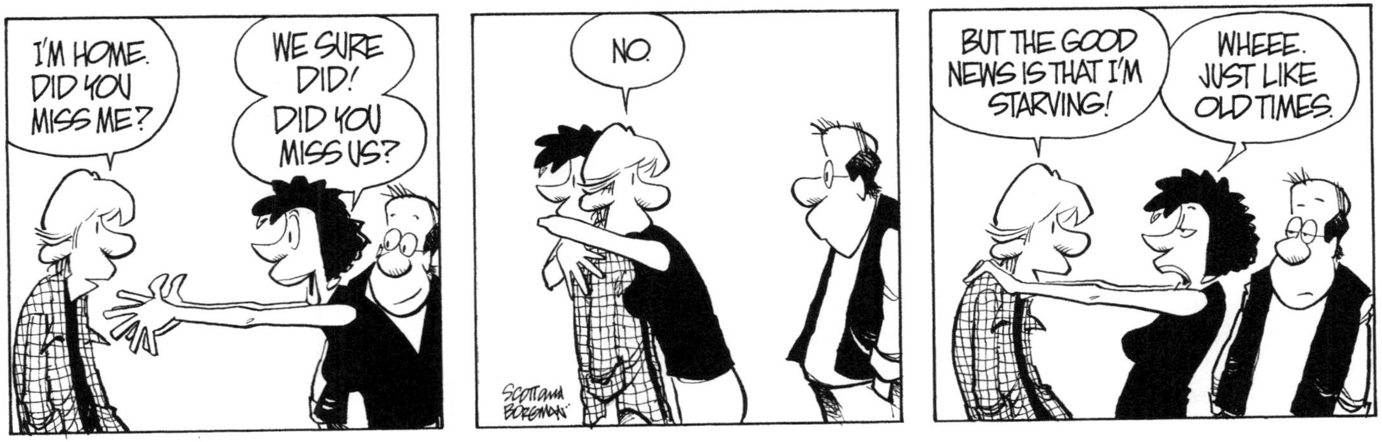
I'M HOME. DID YOU MISS ME?
WE SURE DID!
DID YOU MISS US?
NO.
BUT THE GOOD NEWS IS THAT I'M STARVING!
WHEEE. JUST LIKE OLD TIMES.

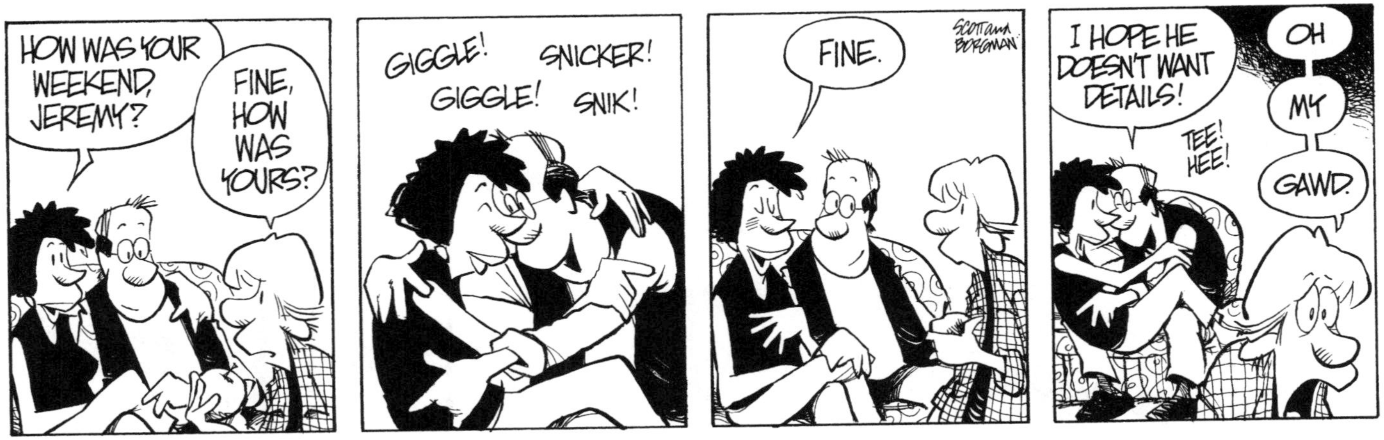
HOW WAS YOUR WEEKEND, JEREMY?
FINE, HOW WAS YOURS?
GIGGLE!
SNICKER!
GIGGLE!
SNIK!
FINE.
I HOPE HE DOESN'T WANT DETAILS!
TEE! HEE!
OH
MY
GAWD.

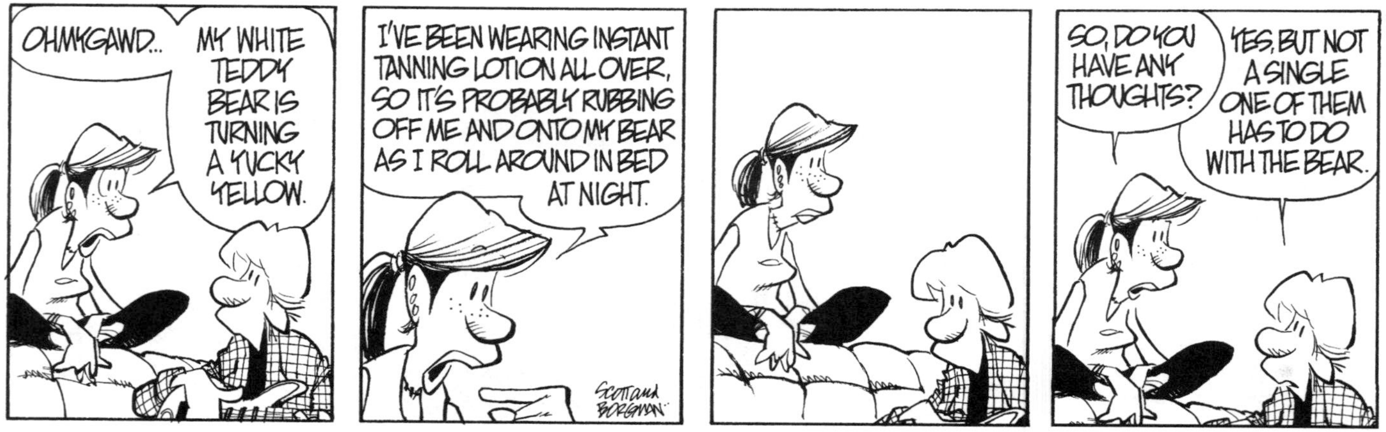
OHMYGAWD...
MY WHITE TEDDY BEAR IS TURNING A YUCKY YELLOW.
I'VE BEEN WEARING INSTANT TANNING LOTION ALL OVER, SO IT'S PROBABLY RUBBING OFF ME AND ONTO MY BEAR AS I ROLL AROUND IN BED AT NIGHT.
SCOTT and BORGMAN
SO, DO YOU HAVE ANY THOUGHTS?
YES, BUT NOT A SINGLE ONE OF THEM HAS TO DO WITH THE BEAR.

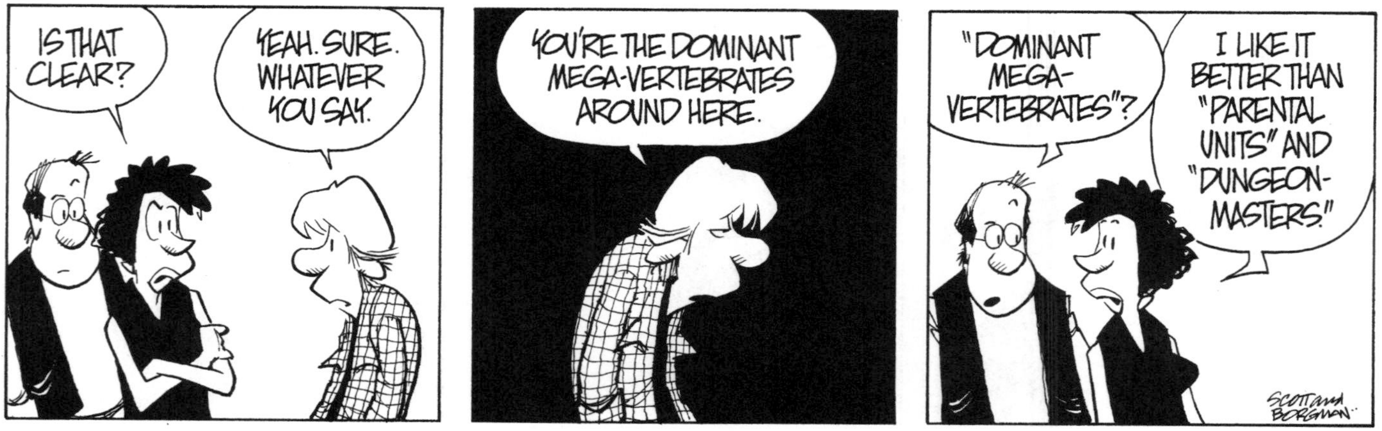
IS THAT CLEAR?
YEAH. SURE. WHATEVER YOU SAY.
YOU'RE THE DOMINANT MEGA-VERTEBRATES AROUND HERE.
"DOMINANT MEGA-VERTEBRATES"?
I LIKE IT BETTER THAN "PARENTAL UNITS" AND "DUNGEON-MASTERS."
SCOTT and BORGMAN

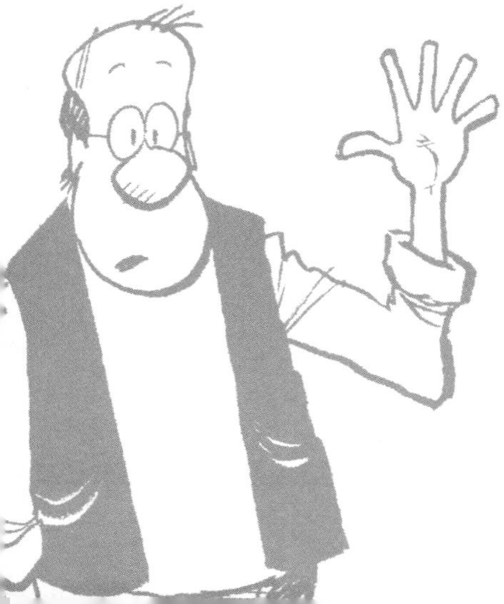

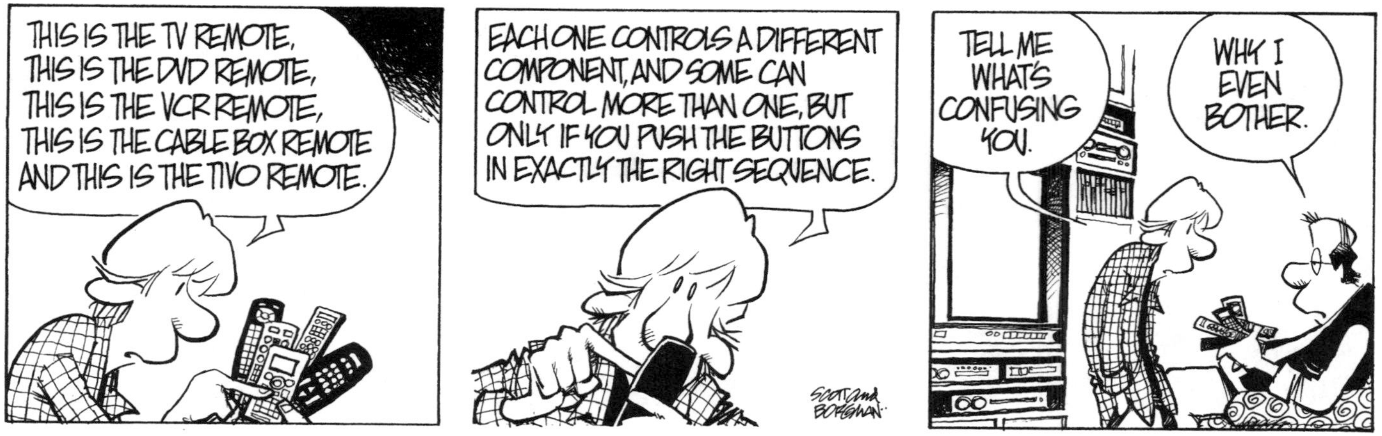
THIS IS THE TV REMOTE, THIS IS THE DVD REMOTE, THIS IS THE VCR REMOTE, THIS IS THE CABLE BOX REMOTE AND THIS IS THE TIVO REMOTE.
EACH ONE CONTROLS A DIFFERENT COMPONENT, AND SOME CAN CONTROL MORE THAN ONE, BUT ONLY IF YOU PUSH THE BUTTONS IN EXACTLY THE RIGHT SEQUENCE.
SCOTT and BORGMAN
TELL ME WHAT'S CONFUSING YOU.
WHY I EVEN BOTHER.

Zits

by JERRY SCOTT and JIM BORGMAN

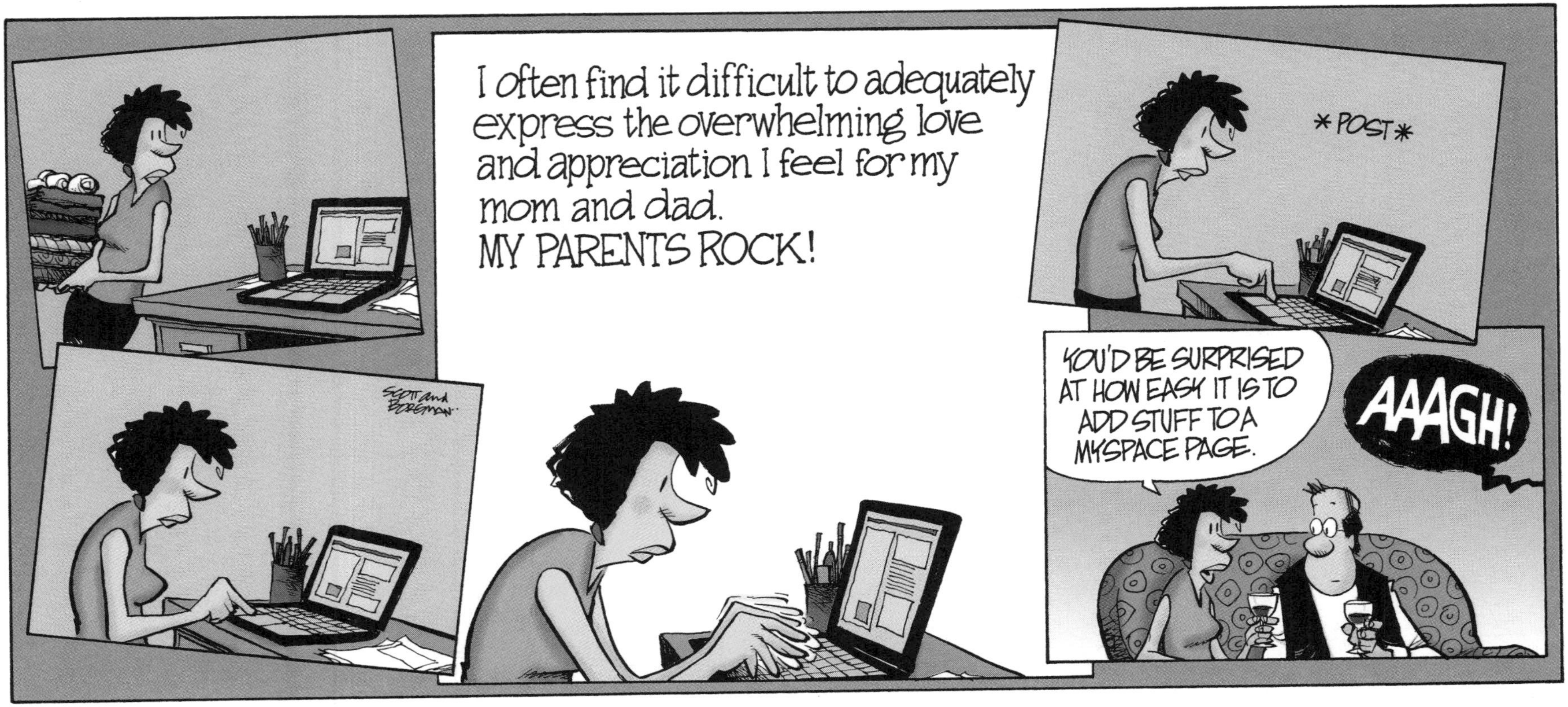
I often find it difficult to adequately express the overwhelming love and appreciation I feel for my mom and dad.
MY PARENTS ROCK!
POST
YOU'D BE SURPRISED AT HOW EASY IT IS TO ADD STUFF TO A MYSPACE PAGE.
AAAGH!

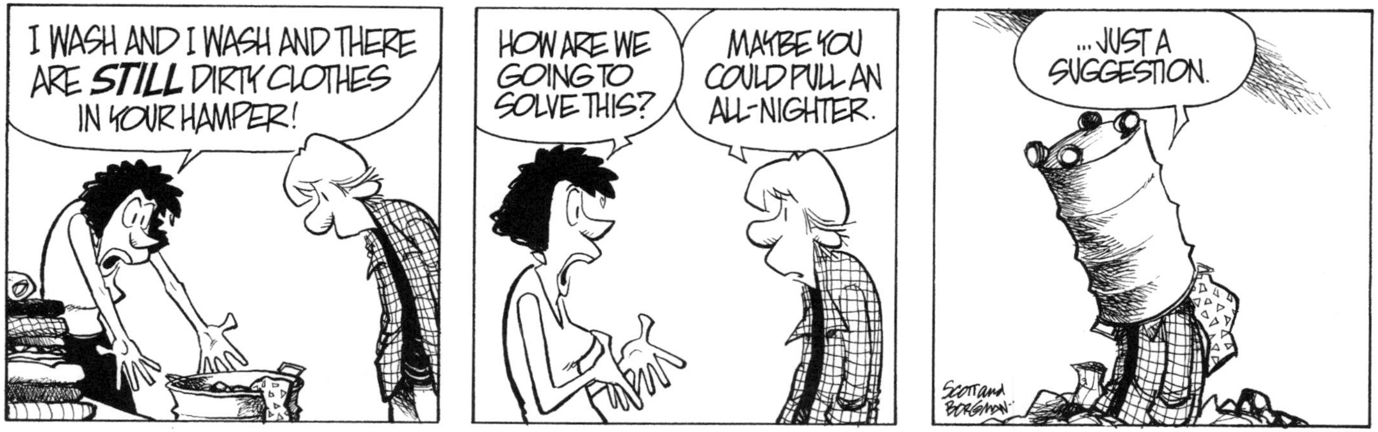
I WASH AND I WASH AND THERE ARE **STILL** DIRTY CLOTHES IN YOUR HAMPER!
HOW ARE WE GOING TO SOLVE THIS?
MAYBE YOU COULD PULL AN ALL-NIGHTER.
...JUST A SUGGESTION.
SCOTT and BORGMAN

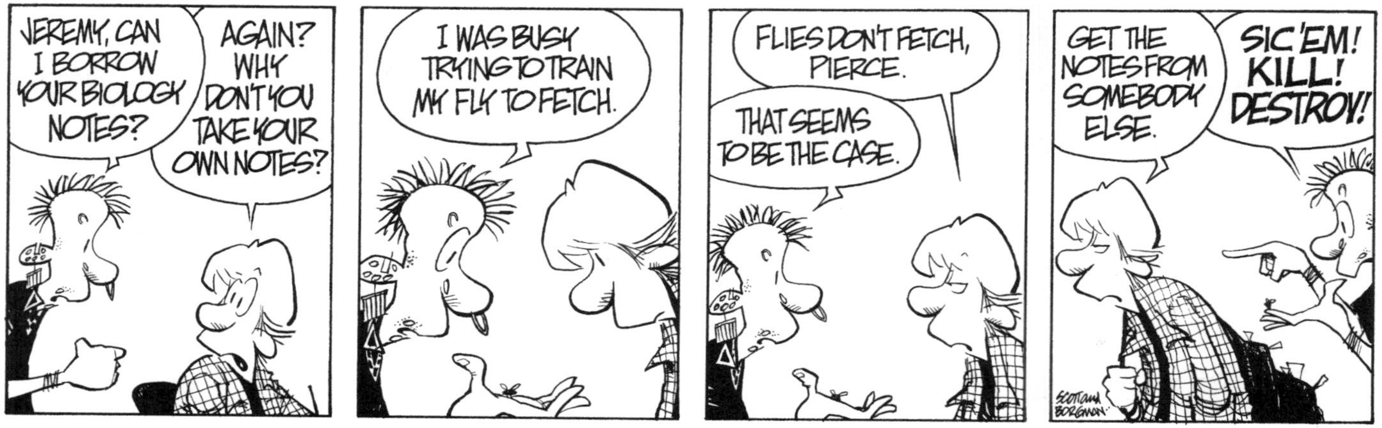
JEREMY, CAN I BORROW YOUR BIOLOGY NOTES?
AGAIN? WHY DON'T YOU TAKE YOUR OWN NOTES?
I WAS BUSY TRYING TO TRAIN MY FLY TO FETCH.
FLIES DON'T FETCH, PIERCE.
THAT SEEMS TO BE THE CASE.
GET THE NOTES FROM SOMEBODY ELSE.
SIC 'EM! **KILL! DESTROY!**
SCOTT and BORGMAN

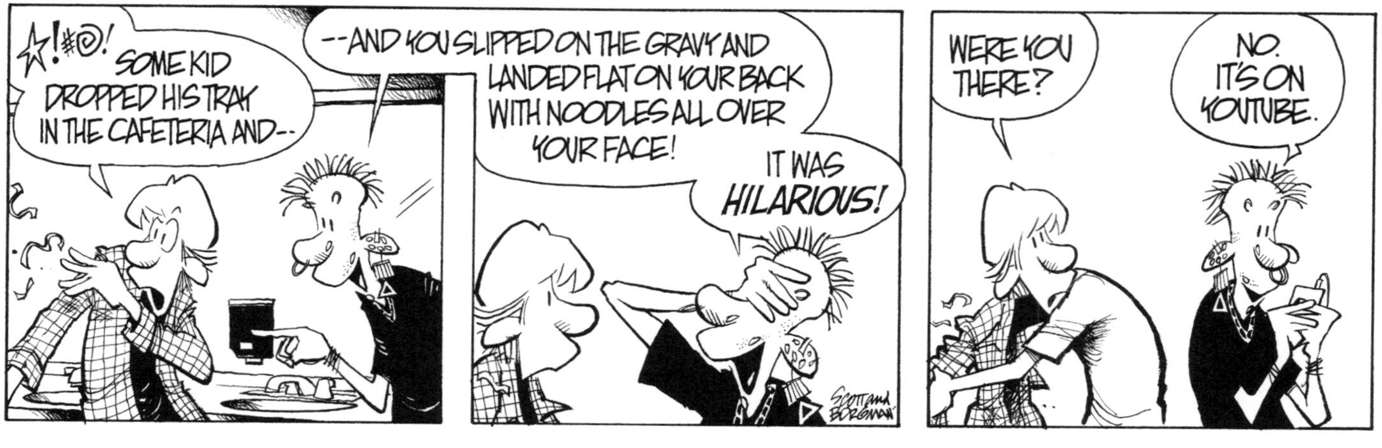
☆!#@! SOME KID DROPPED HIS TRAY IN THE CAFETERIA AND--
--AND YOU SLIPPED ON THE GRAVY AND LANDED FLAT ON YOUR BACK WITH NOODLES ALL OVER YOUR FACE!
IT WAS **HILARIOUS!**
SCOTT and BORGMAN
WERE YOU THERE?
NO. IT'S ON YOUTUBE.

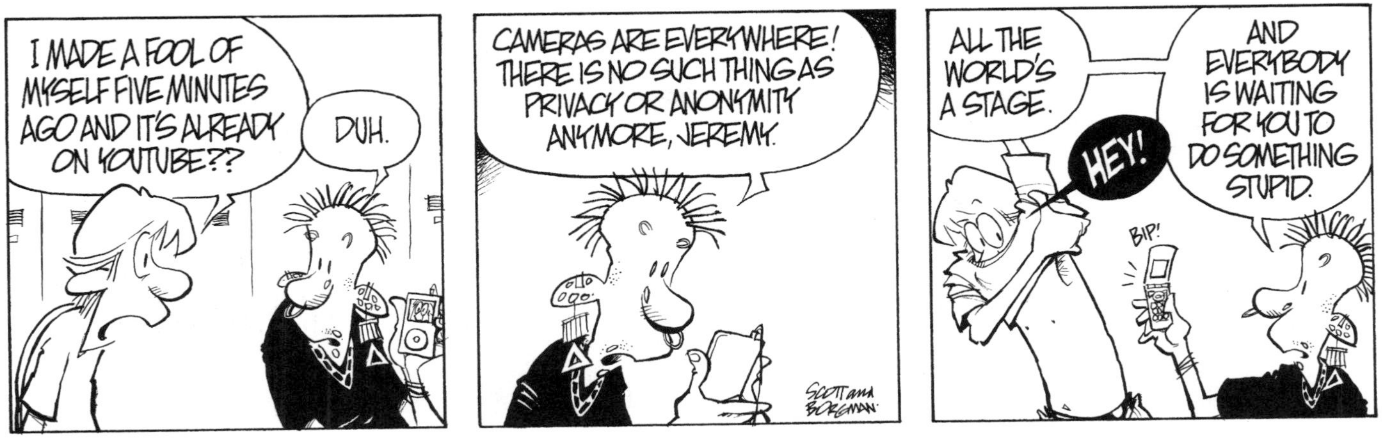
I MADE A FOOL OF MYSELF FIVE MINUTES AGO AND IT'S ALREADY ON YOUTUBE??
DUH.
CAMERAS ARE EVERYWHERE! THERE IS NO SUCH THING AS PRIVACY OR ANONYMITY ANYMORE, JEREMY.
SCOTT and BORGMAN
ALL THE WORLD'S A STAGE.
AND EVERYBODY IS WAITING FOR YOU TO DO SOMETHING STUPID.
HEY!
BIP!

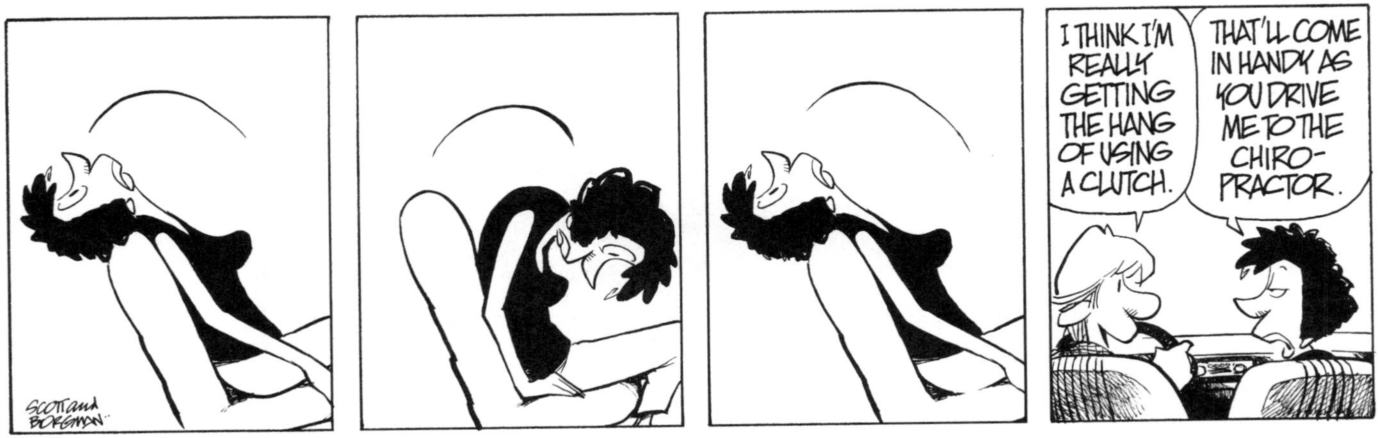
SCOTT and BORGMAN
I THINK I'M REALLY GETTING THE HANG OF USING A CLUTCH.
THAT'LL COME IN HANDY AS YOU DRIVE ME TO THE CHIRO-PRACTOR.

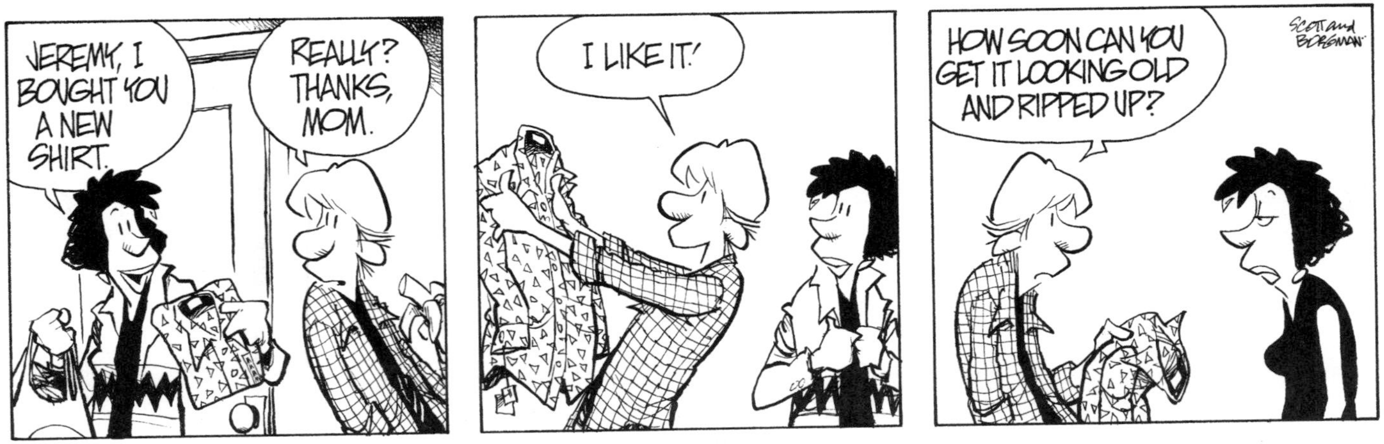
JEREMY, I BOUGHT YOU A NEW SHIRT.
REALLY? THANKS, MOM.
I LIKE IT!
HOW SOON CAN YOU GET IT LOOKING OLD AND RIPPED UP?
SCOTT and BORGMAN

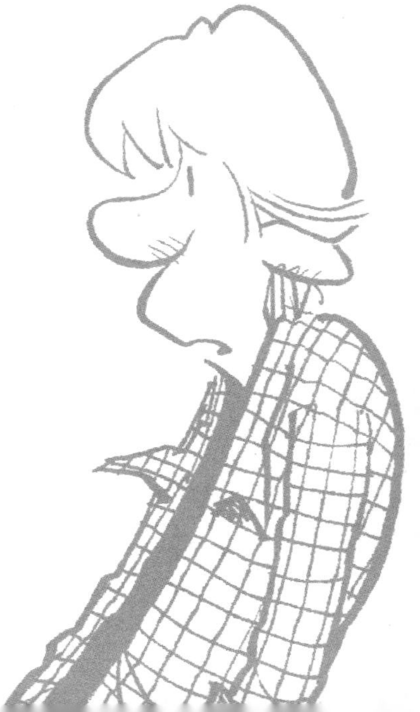

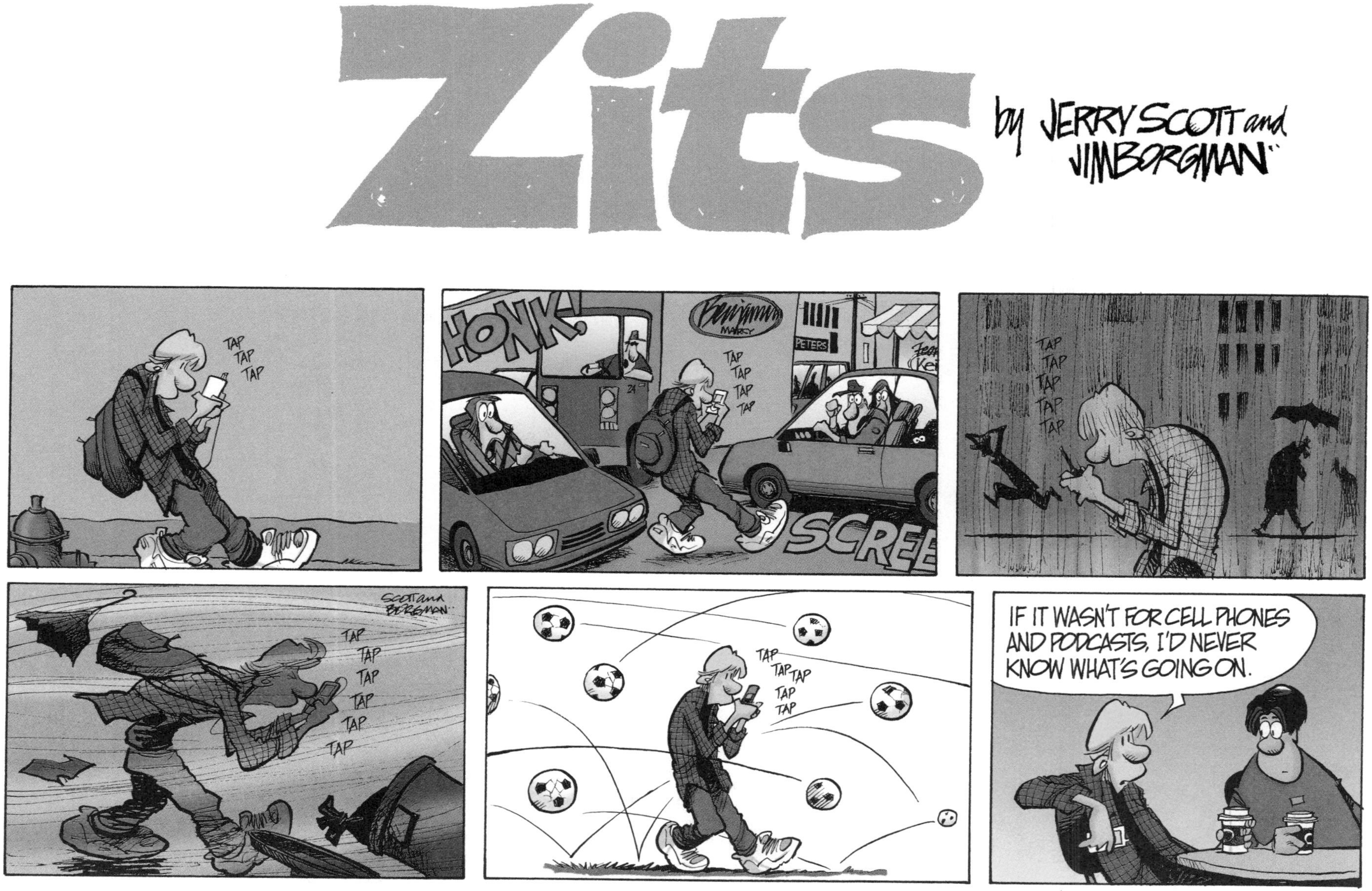
Zits
by JERRY SCOTT and JIM BORGMAN
TAP TAP TAP
HONK!
PETERS
TAP TAP TAP TAP
SCREE
TAP TAP TAP TAP TAP
SCOTT and BORGMAN
TAP TAP TAP TAP TAP TAP
TAP TAP TAP TAP TAP
IF IT WASN'T FOR CELL PHONES AND PODCASTS, I'D NEVER KNOW WHAT'S GOING ON.

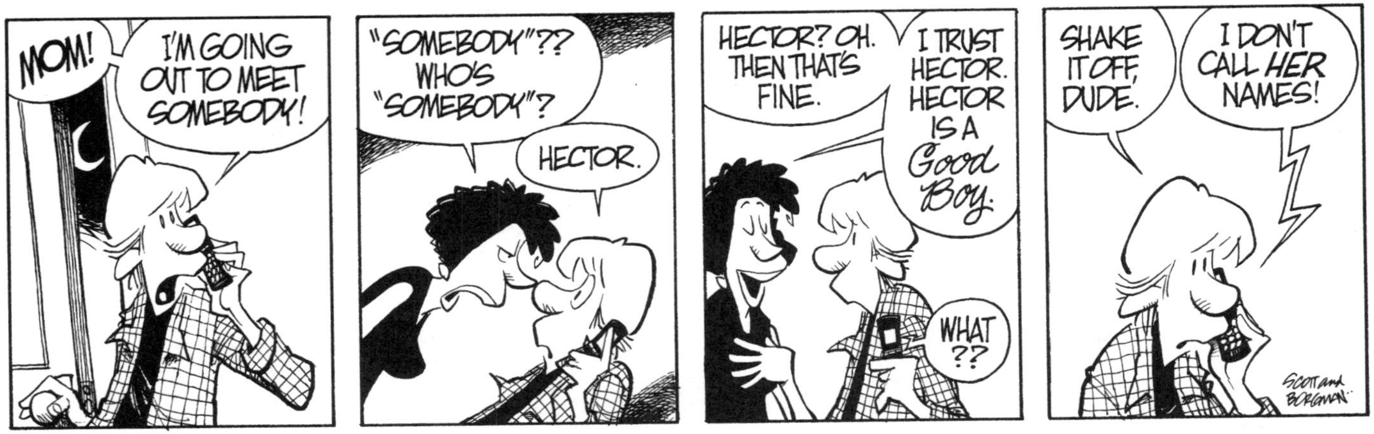
MOM!
I'M GOING OUT TO MEET SOMEBODY!
"SOMEBODY"?? WHO'S "SOMEBODY"?
HECTOR.
HECTOR? OH. THEN THAT'S FINE.
I TRUST HECTOR. HECTOR IS A Good Boy.
WHAT ??
SHAKE IT OFF, DUDE.
I DON'T CALL HER NAMES!
SCOTT and BORGMAN

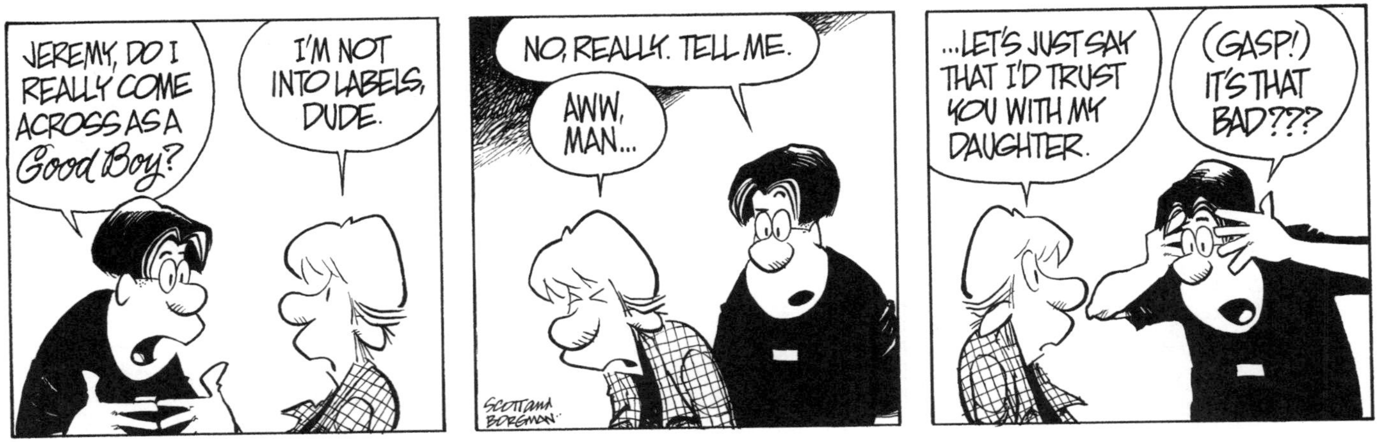
JEREMY, DO I REALLY COME ACROSS AS A Good Boy?
I'M NOT INTO LABELS, DUDE.
NO, REALLY. TELL ME.
AWW, MAN...
SCOTT and BORGMAN
...LET'S JUST SAY THAT I'D TRUST YOU WITH MY DAUGHTER.
(GASP!) IT'S THAT BAD???

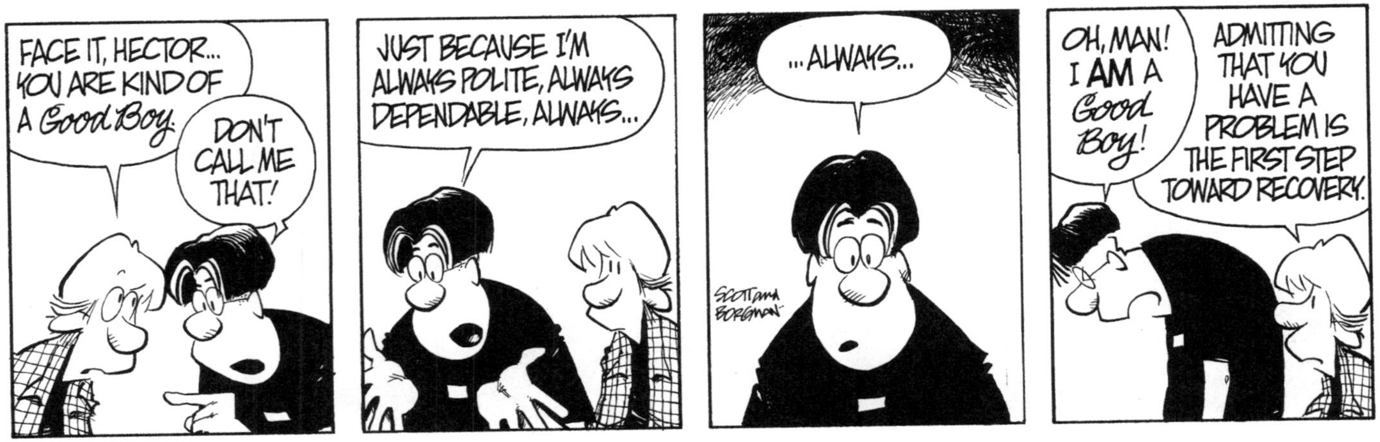
FACE IT, HECTOR... YOU ARE KIND OF A Good Boy.
DON'T CALL ME THAT!
JUST BECAUSE I'M ALWAYS POLITE, ALWAYS DEPENDABLE, ALWAYS...
...ALWAYS...
SCOTT and BORGMAN
OH, MAN! I AM A Good Boy!
ADMITTING THAT YOU HAVE A PROBLEM IS THE FIRST STEP TOWARD RECOVERY.

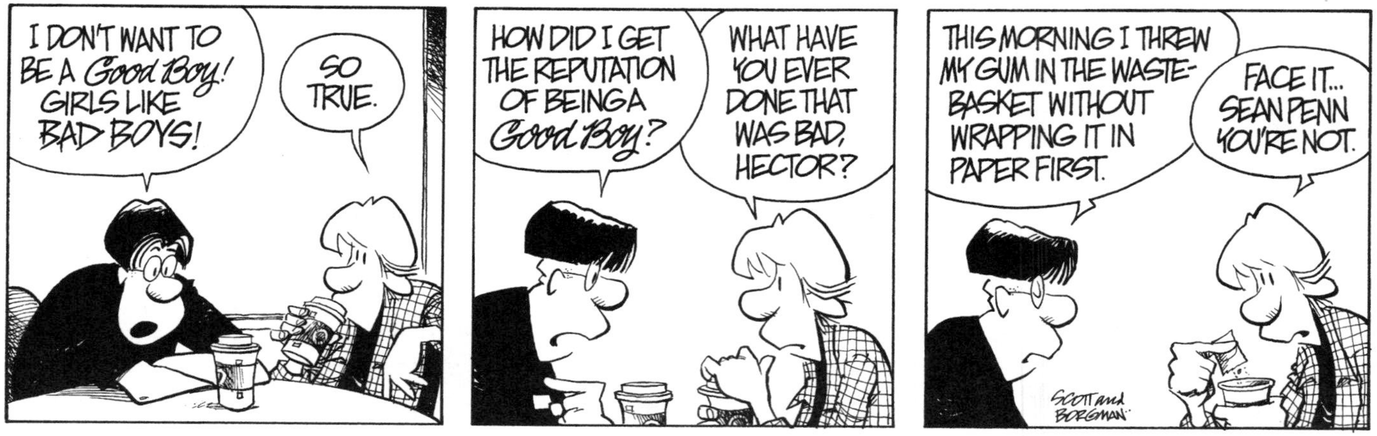
I DON'T WANT TO BE A Good Boy! GIRLS LIKE BAD BOYS!
SO TRUE.
HOW DID I GET THE REPUTATION OF BEING A Good Boy?
WHAT HAVE YOU EVER DONE THAT WAS BAD, HECTOR?
THIS MORNING I THREW MY GUM IN THE WASTE-BASKET WITHOUT WRAPPING IT IN PAPER FIRST.
FACE IT... SEAN PENN YOU'RE NOT.
SCOTT and BORGMAN

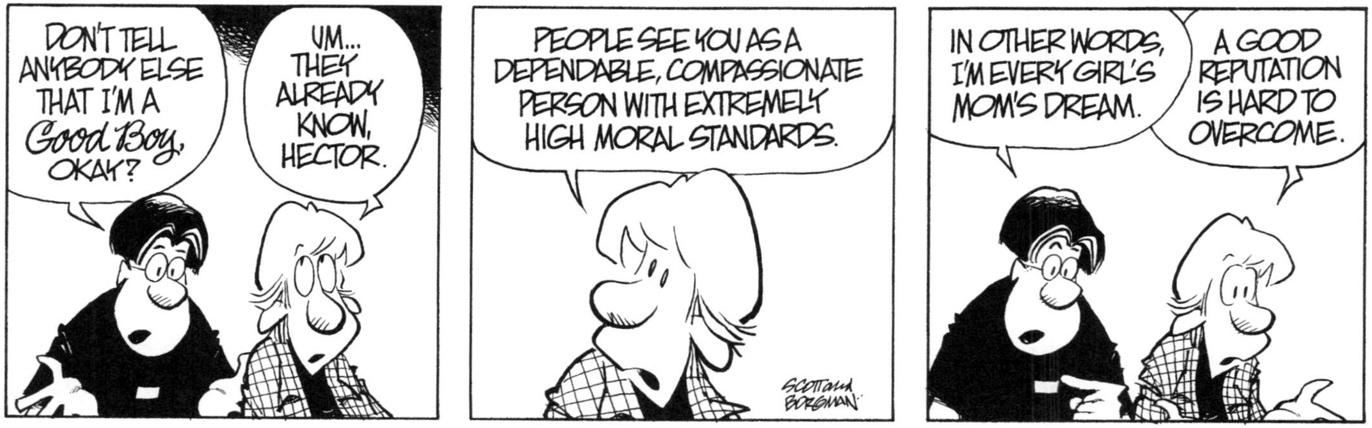
DON'T TELL ANYBODY ELSE THAT I'M A Good Boy, OKAY?
UM... THEY ALREADY KNOW, HECTOR.
PEOPLE SEE YOU AS A DEPENDABLE, COMPASSIONATE PERSON WITH EXTREMELY HIGH MORAL STANDARDS.
SCOTT and BORGMAN
IN OTHER WORDS, I'M EVERY GIRL'S MOM'S DREAM.
A GOOD REPUTATION IS HARD TO OVERCOME.

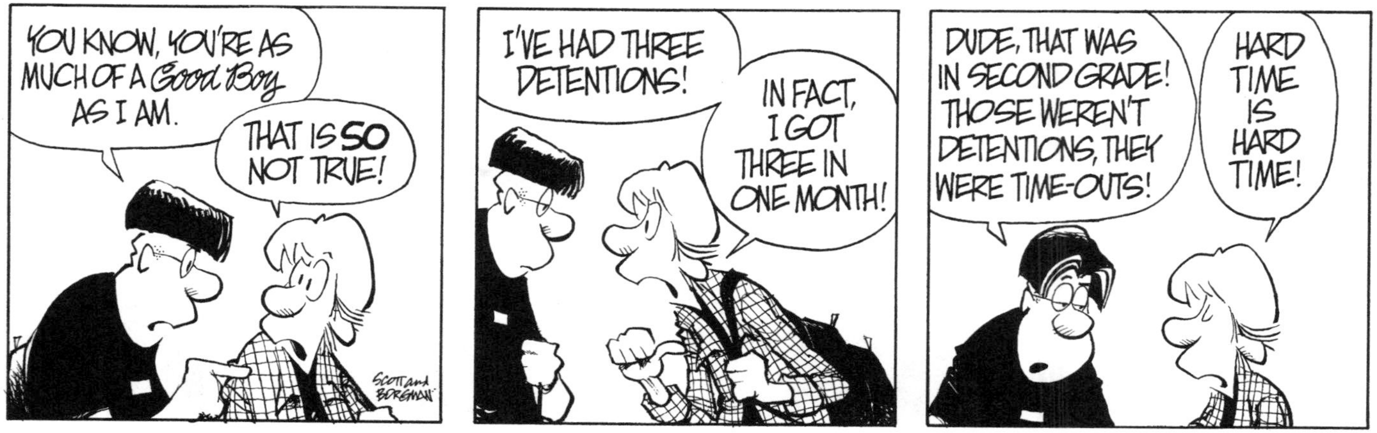
YOU KNOW, YOU'RE AS MUCH OF A Good Boy AS I AM.
THAT IS SO NOT TRUE!
SCOTT and BORGMAN
I'VE HAD THREE DETENTIONS!
IN FACT, I GOT THREE IN ONE MONTH!
DUDE, THAT WAS IN SECOND GRADE! THOSE WEREN'T DETENTIONS, THEY WERE TIME-OUTS!
HARD TIME IS HARD TIME!

Zits

by JERRY SCOTT and JIM BORGMAN

WE DID IT!
YEAH!
FLICK!
SCOTT and BORGMAN
WHAT EVER HAPPENED TO THE HIGH-FIVE?

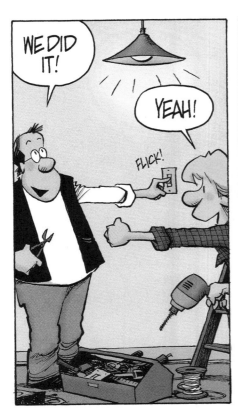

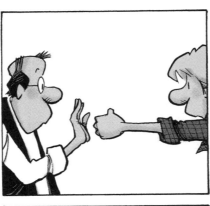

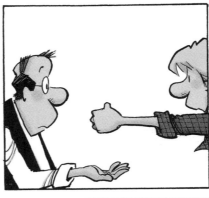

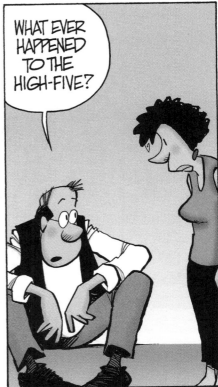

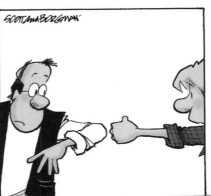

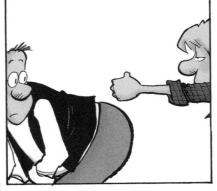

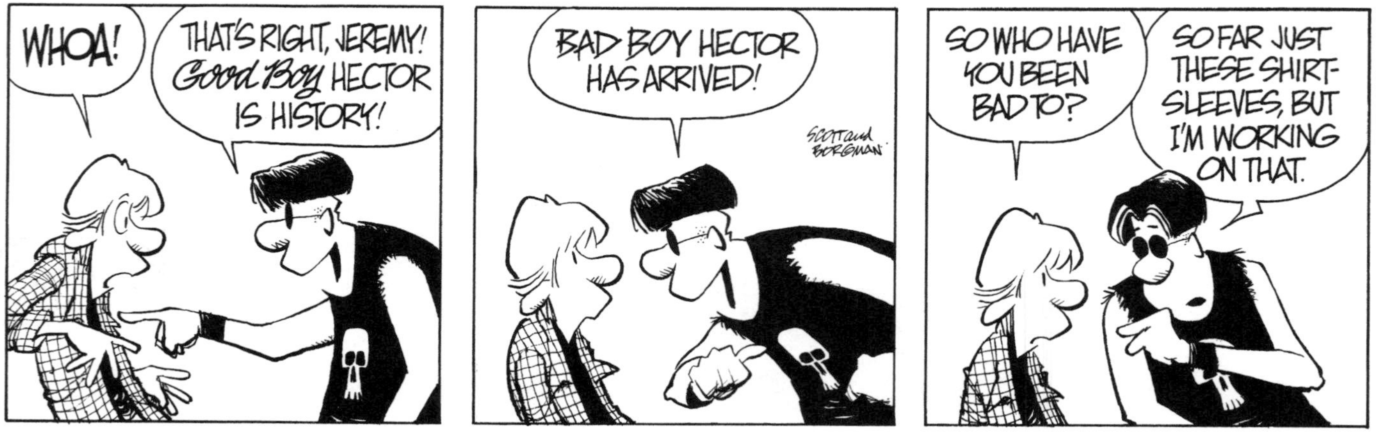
WHOA!
THAT'S RIGHT, JEREMY! Good Boy HECTOR IS HISTORY!
BAD BOY HECTOR HAS ARRIVED!
SCOTT and BORGMAN
SO WHO HAVE YOU BEEN BAD TO?
SO FAR JUST THESE SHIRT-SLEEVES, BUT I'M WORKING ON THAT.

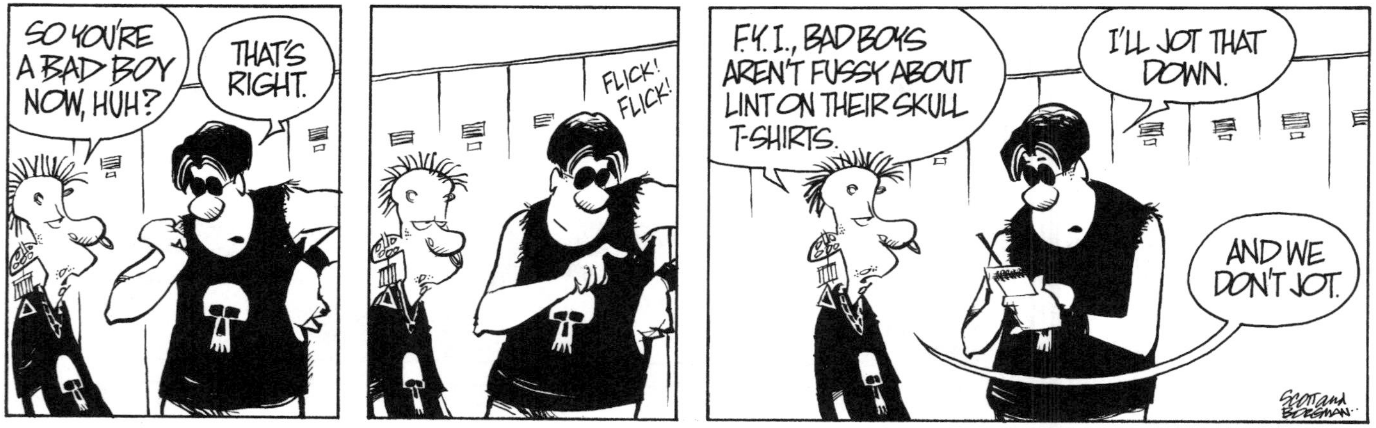
SO YOU'RE A BAD BOY NOW, HUH?
THAT'S RIGHT.
FLICK! FLICK!
F.Y.I., BAD BOYS AREN'T FUSSY ABOUT LINT ON THEIR SKULL T-SHIRTS.
I'LL JOT THAT DOWN.
AND WE DON'T JOT.
SCOTT and BORGMAN

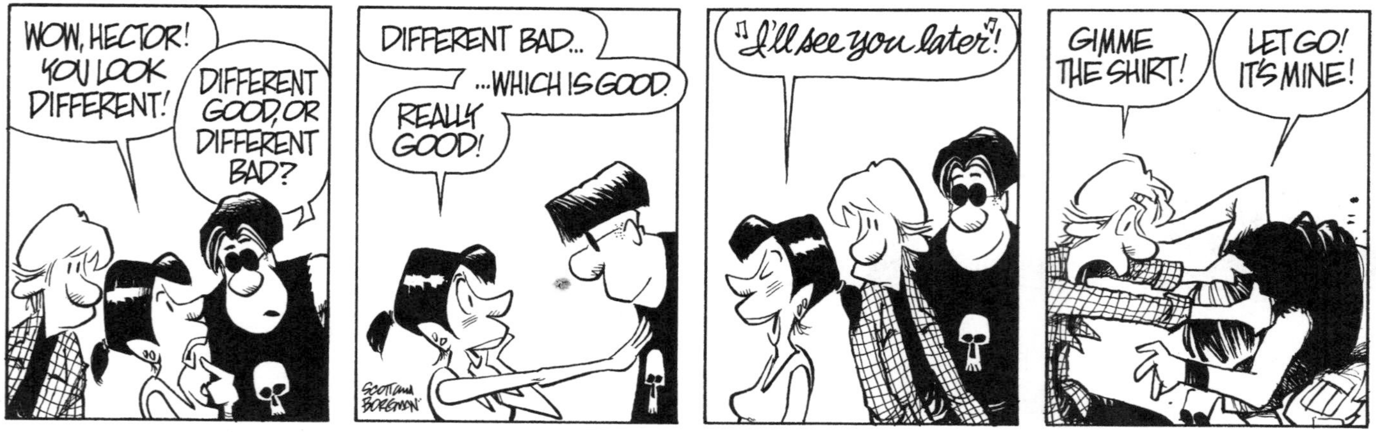
WOW, HECTOR! YOU LOOK DIFFERENT!
DIFFERENT GOOD, OR DIFFERENT BAD?
DIFFERENT BAD...
...WHICH IS GOOD.
REALLY GOOD!
SCOTT and BORGMAN
♫ I'll see you later! ♫
GIMME THE SHIRT!
LET GO! IT'S MINE!

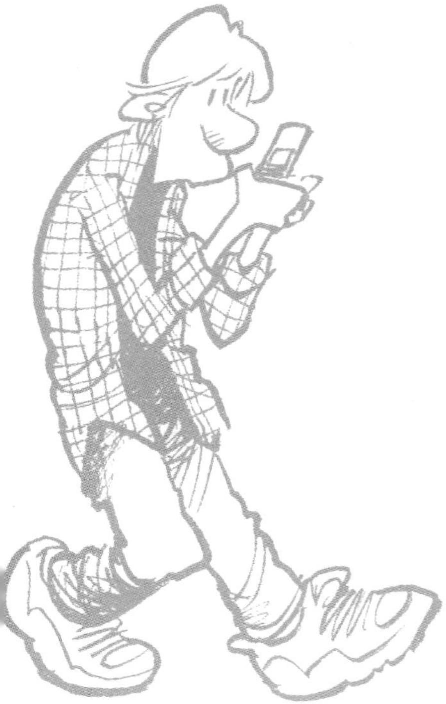

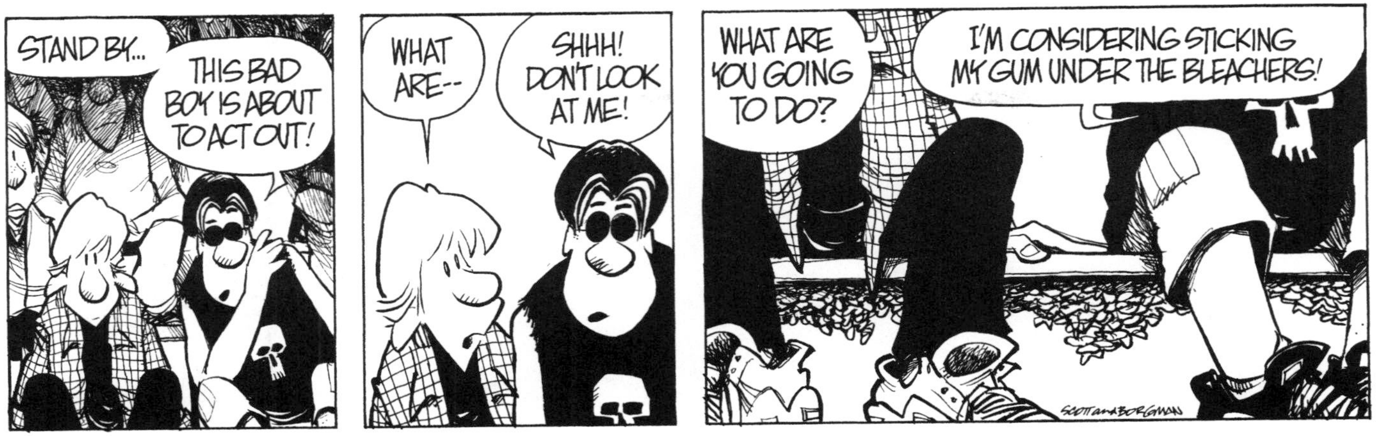
STAND BY...
THIS BAD BOY IS ABOUT TO ACT OUT!
WHAT ARE--
SHHH! DON'T LOOK AT ME!
WHAT ARE YOU GOING TO DO?
I'M CONSIDERING STICKING MY GUM UNDER THE BLEACHERS!

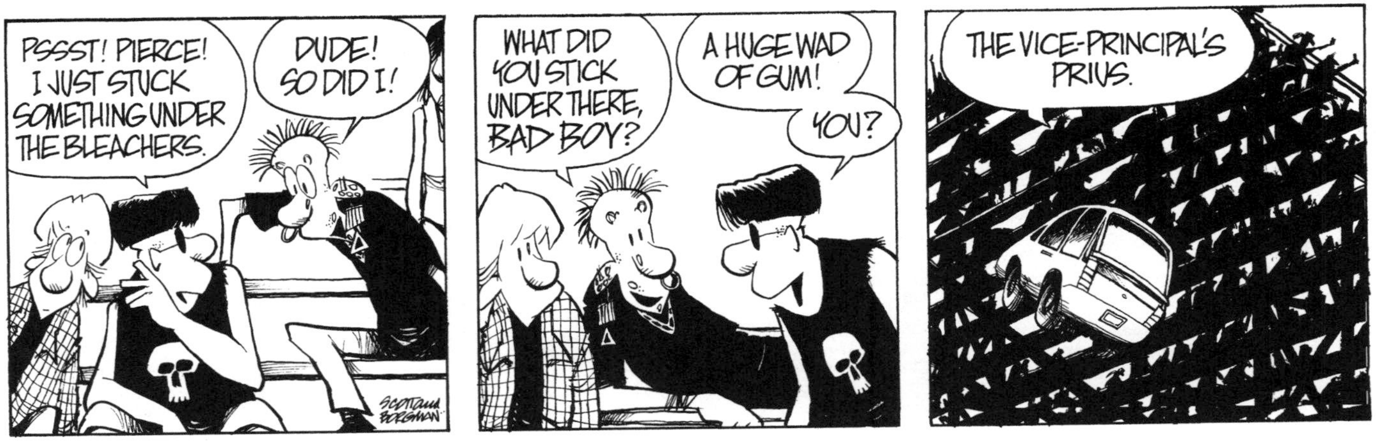
PSSST! PIERCE! I JUST STUCK SOMETHING UNDER THE BLEACHERS.
DUDE! SO DID I!
WHAT DID YOU STICK UNDER THERE, BAD BOY?
A HUGE WAD OF GUM!
YOU?
THE VICE-PRINCIPAL'S PRIUS.

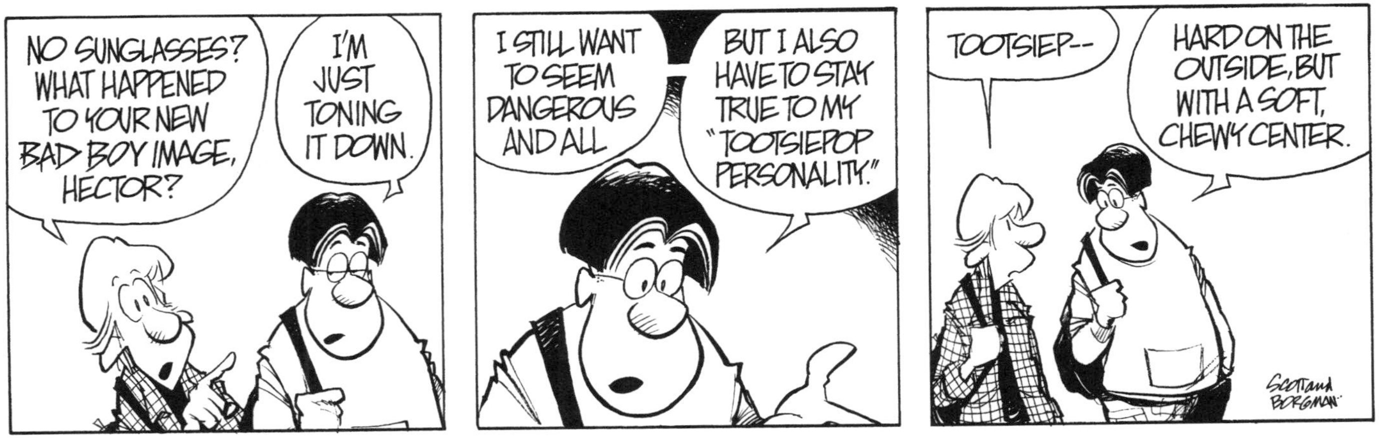
NO SUNGLASSES? WHAT HAPPENED TO YOUR NEW BAD BOY IMAGE, HECTOR?
I'M JUST TONING IT DOWN.
I STILL WANT TO SEEM DANGEROUS AND ALL
BUT I ALSO HAVE TO STAY TRUE TO MY "TOOTSIEPOP PERSONALITY."
TOOTSIEP--
HARD ON THE OUTSIDE, BUT WITH A SOFT, CHEWY CENTER.

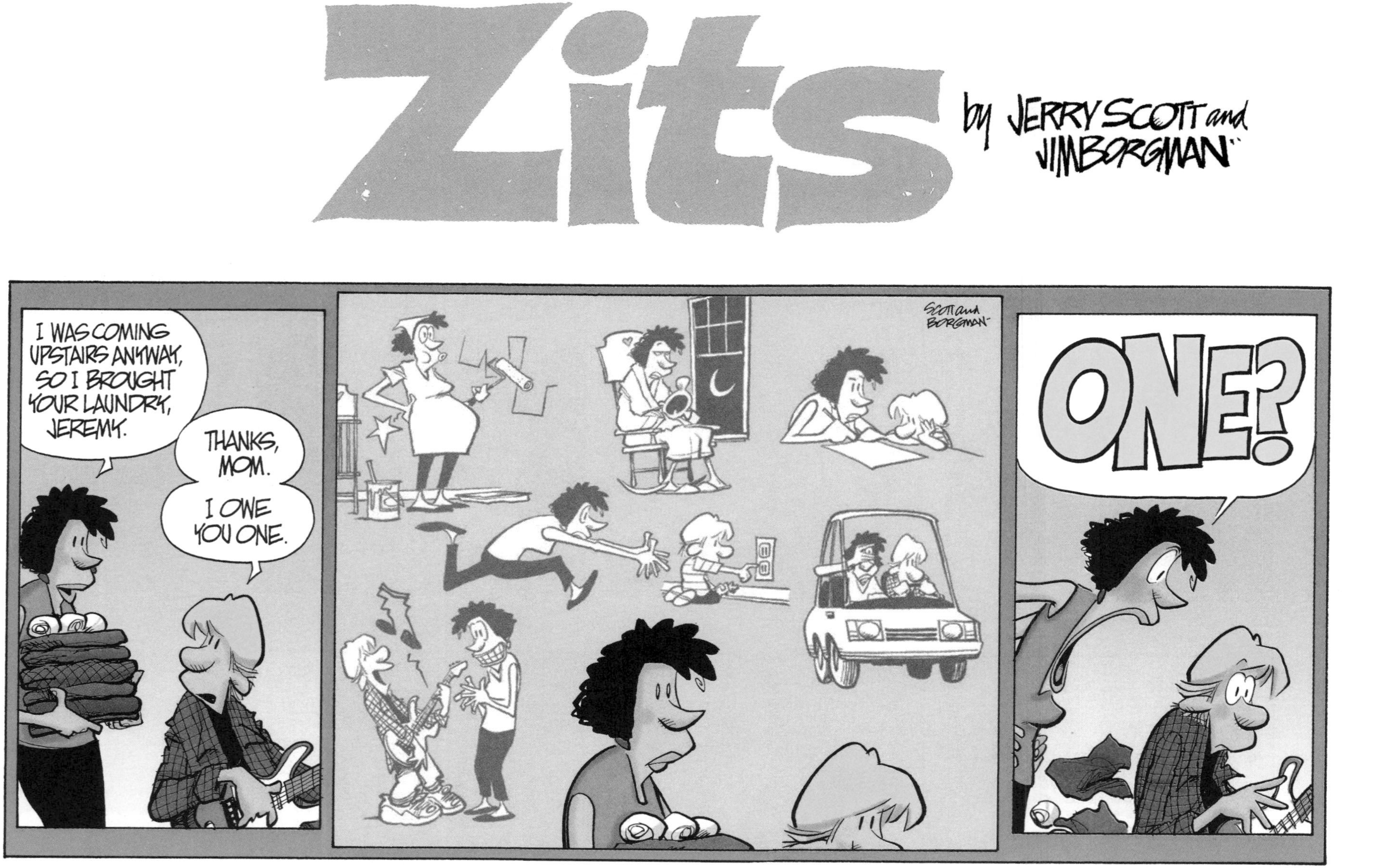
Zits
by JERRY SCOTT and JIM BORGMAN
I WAS COMING UPSTAIRS ANYWAY, SO I BROUGHT YOUR LAUNDRY, JEREMY.
THANKS, MOM.
I OWE YOU ONE.
SCOTT and BORGMAN
ONE?

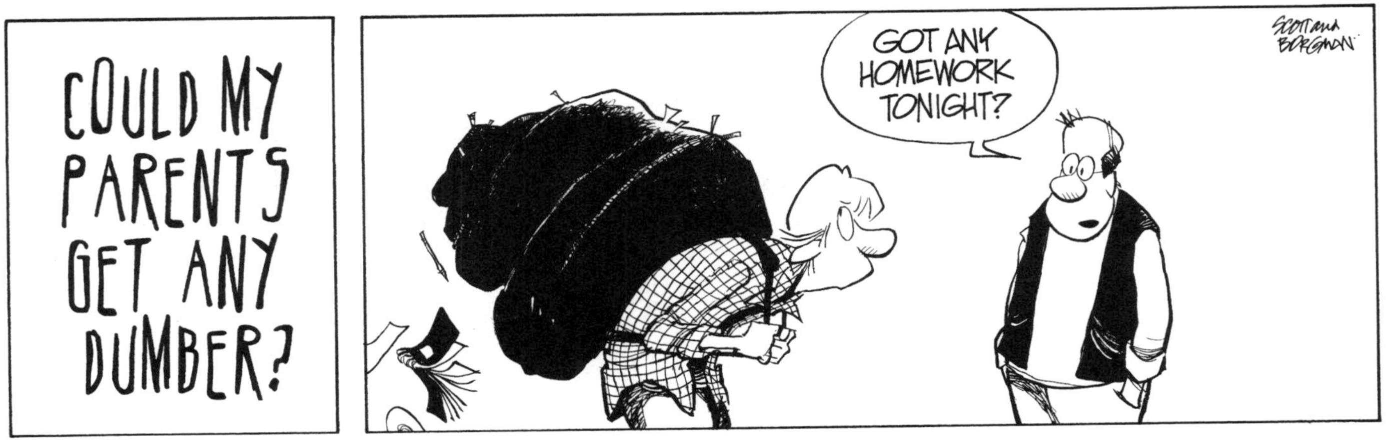
COULD MY PARENTS GET ANY DUMBER?
GOT ANY HOMEWORK TONIGHT?
SCOTT and BORGMAN

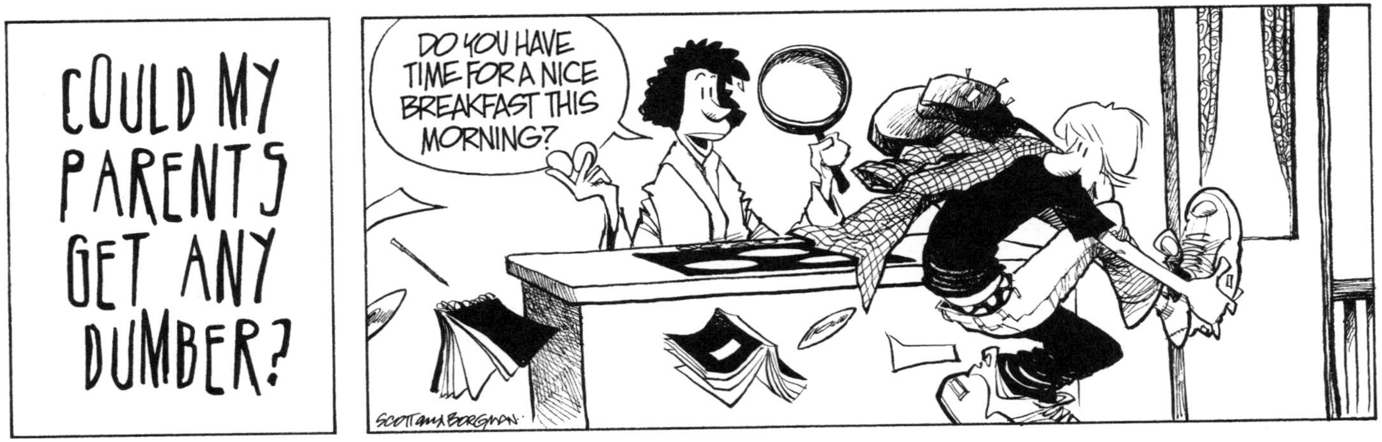
COULD MY PARENTS GET ANY DUMBER?
DO YOU HAVE TIME FOR A NICE BREAKFAST THIS MORNING?
SCOTT and BORGMAN

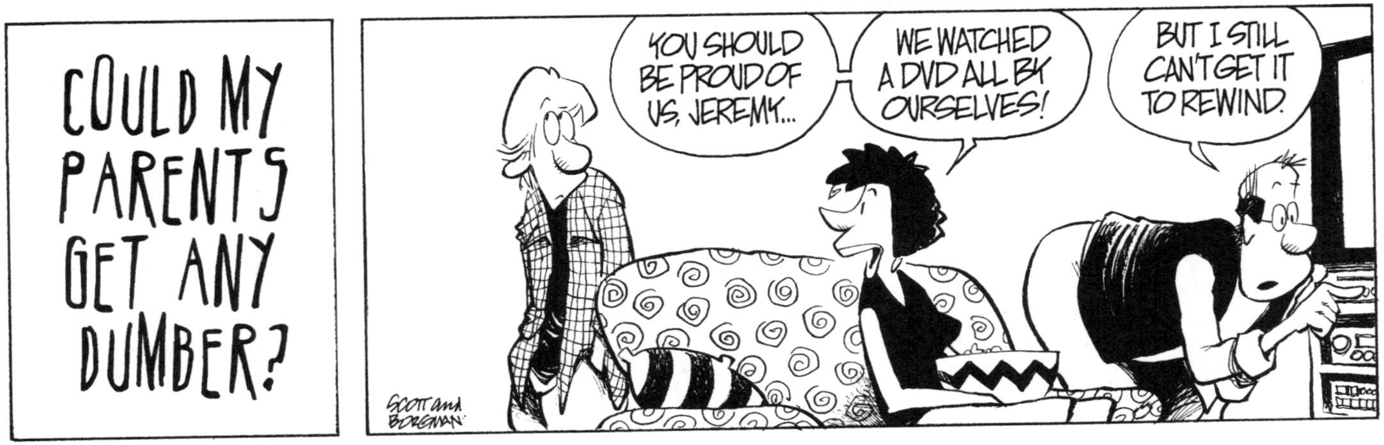
COULD MY PARENTS GET ANY DUMBER?
YOU SHOULD BE PROUD OF US, JEREMY...
WE WATCHED A DVD ALL BY OURSELVES!
BUT I STILL CAN'T GET IT TO REWIND.
SCOTT and BORGMAN

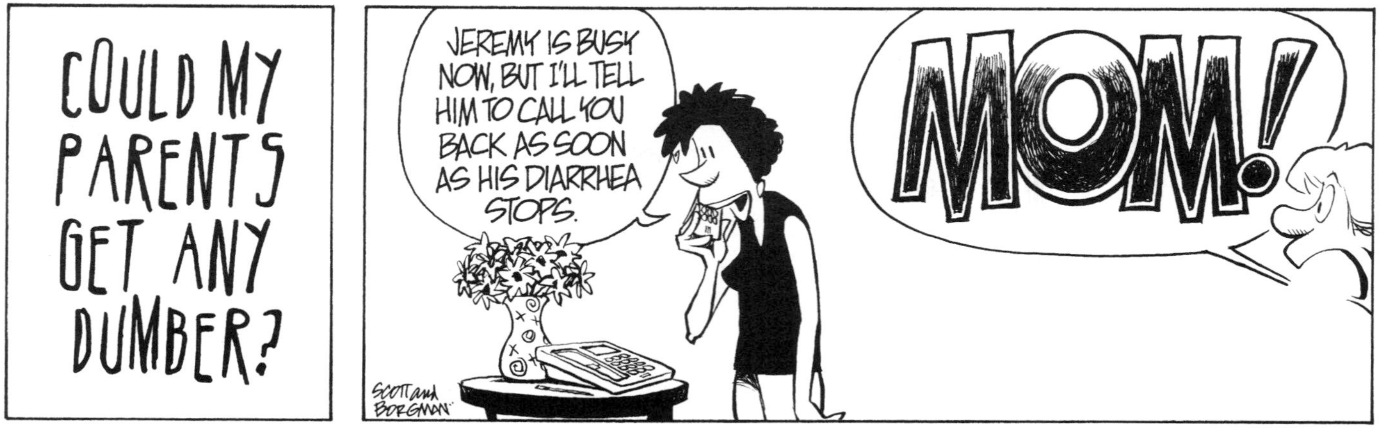
COULD MY PARENTS GET ANY DUMBER?
JEREMY IS BUSY NOW, BUT I'LL TELL HIM TO CALL YOU BACK AS SOON AS HIS DIARRHEA STOPS.
MOM!
SCOTT and BORGMAN

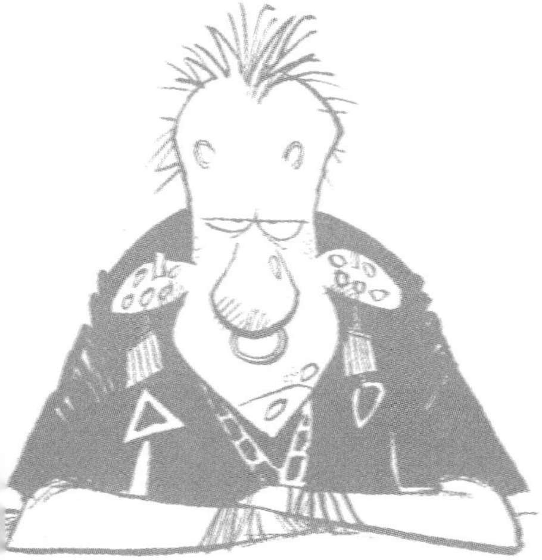

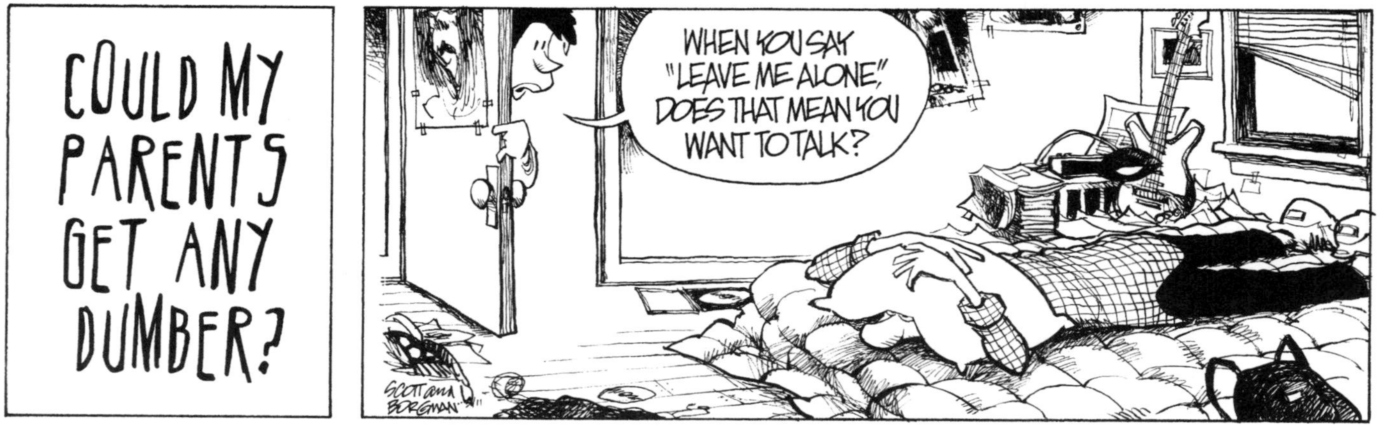
COULD MY PARENTS GET ANY DUMBER?
WHEN YOU SAY "LEAVE ME ALONE," DOES THAT MEAN YOU WANT TO TALK?
SCOTT and BORGMAN

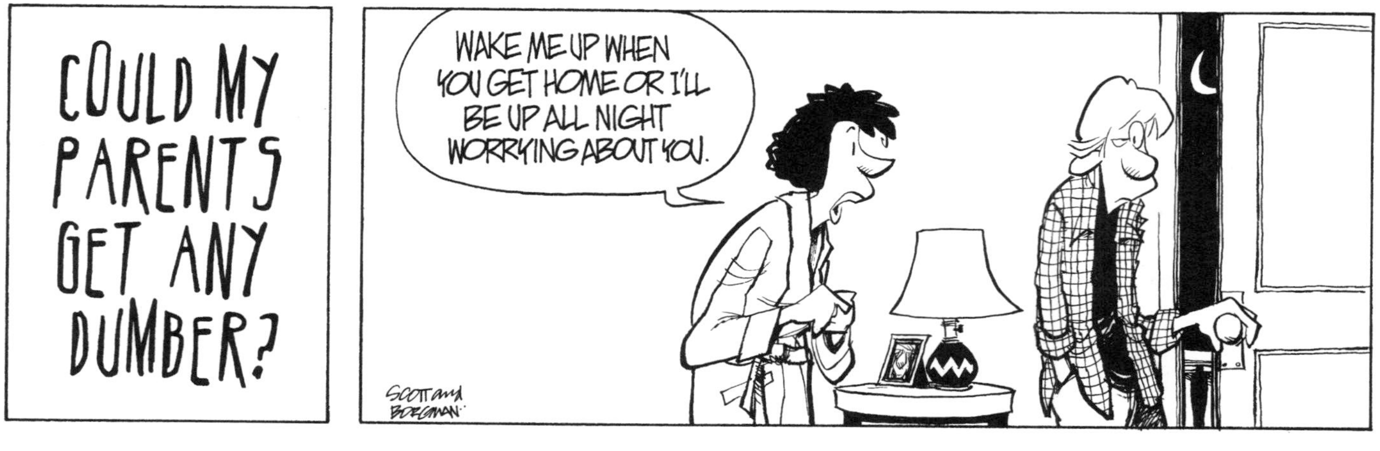
COULD MY PARENTS GET ANY DUMBER?
WAKE ME UP WHEN YOU GET HOME OR I'LL BE UP ALL NIGHT WORRYING ABOUT YOU.
SCOTT and BORGMAN

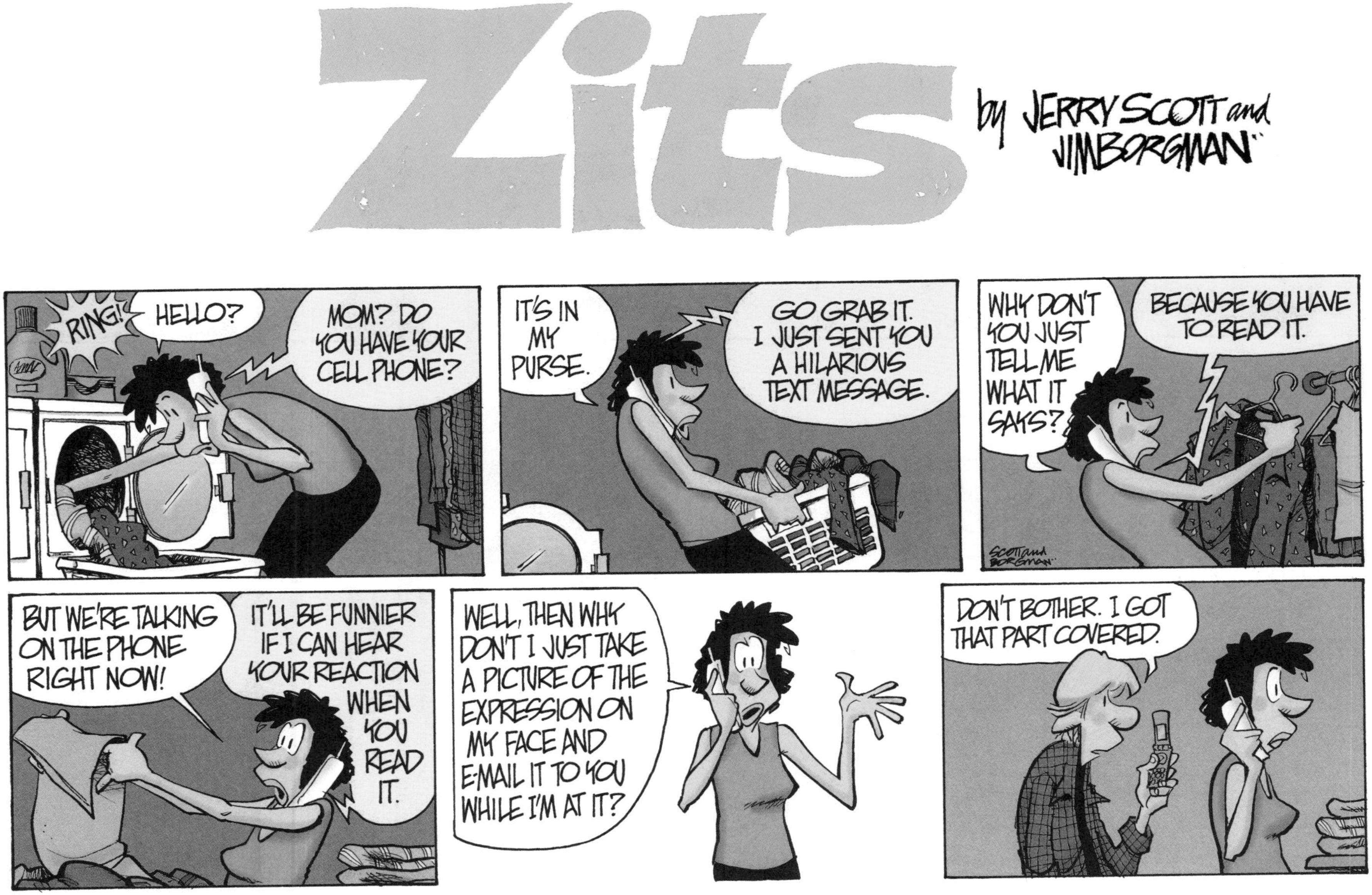
Zits
by JERRY SCOTT and JIM BORGMAN
RING!
HELLO?
MOM? DO YOU HAVE YOUR CELL PHONE?
IT'S IN MY PURSE.
GO GRAB IT. I JUST SENT YOU A HILARIOUS TEXT MESSAGE.
WHY DON'T YOU JUST TELL ME WHAT IT SAYS?
BECAUSE YOU HAVE TO READ IT.
BUT WE'RE TALKING ON THE PHONE RIGHT NOW!
IT'LL BE FUNNIER IF I CAN HEAR YOUR REACTION WHEN YOU READ IT.
WELL, THEN WHY DON'T I JUST TAKE A PICTURE OF THE EXPRESSION ON MY FACE AND E-MAIL IT TO YOU WHILE I'M AT IT?
DON'T BOTHER. I GOT THAT PART COVERED.

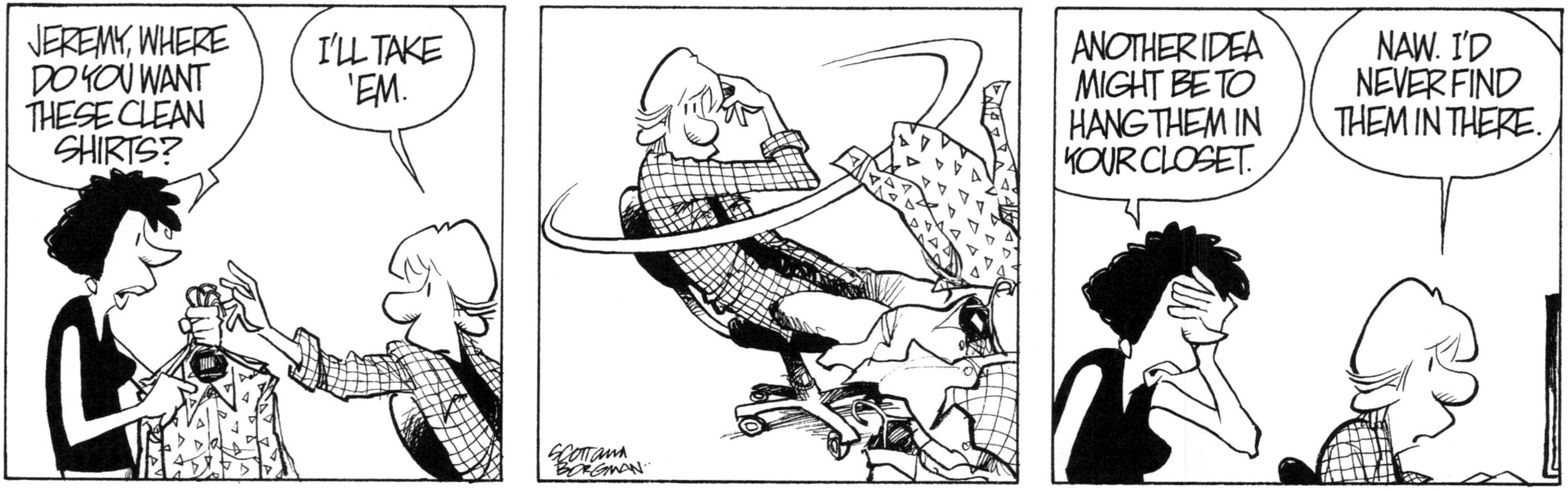
JEREMY, WHERE DO YOU WANT THESE CLEAN SHIRTS?
I'LL TAKE 'EM.
SCOTT and BORGMAN
ANOTHER IDEA MIGHT BE TO HANG THEM IN YOUR CLOSET.
NAW. I'D NEVER FIND THEM IN THERE.

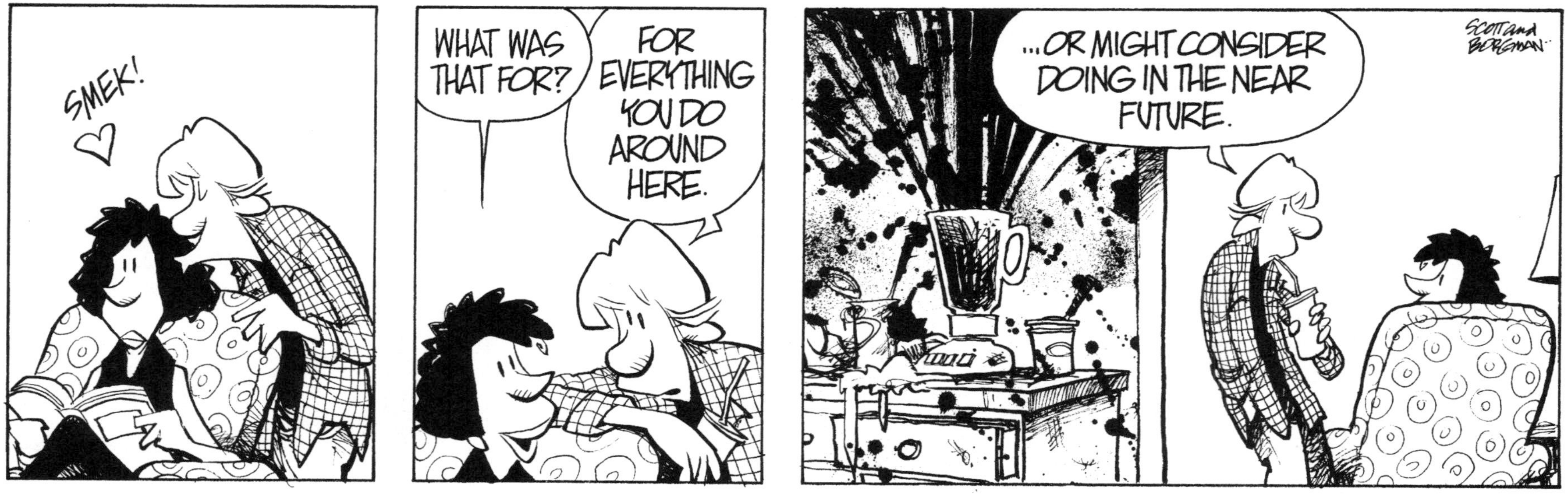
SMEK!
WHAT WAS THAT FOR?
FOR EVERYTHING YOU DO AROUND HERE.
...OR MIGHT CONSIDER DOING IN THE NEAR FUTURE.
SCOTT and BORGMAN

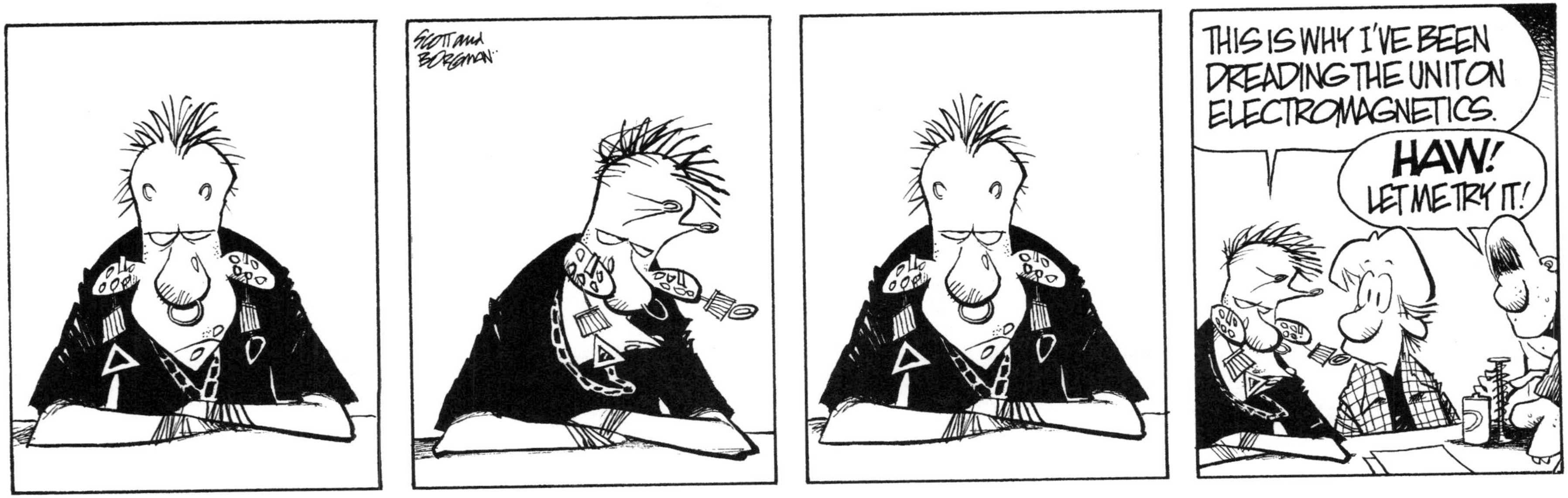
SCOTT and BORGMAN
THIS IS WHY I'VE BEEN DREADING THE UNIT ON ELECTROMAGNETICS.
HAW! LET ME TRY IT!

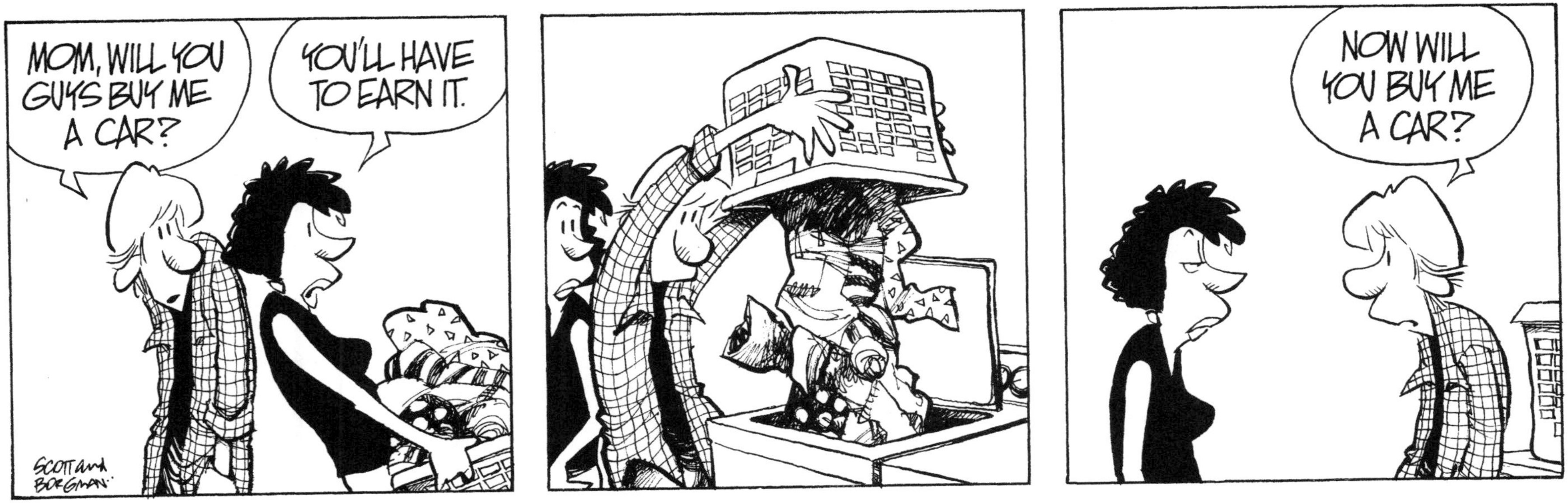
MOM, WILL YOU GUYS BUY ME A CAR?
YOU'LL HAVE TO EARN IT.
SCOTT and BORGMAN
NOW WILL YOU BUY ME A CAR?

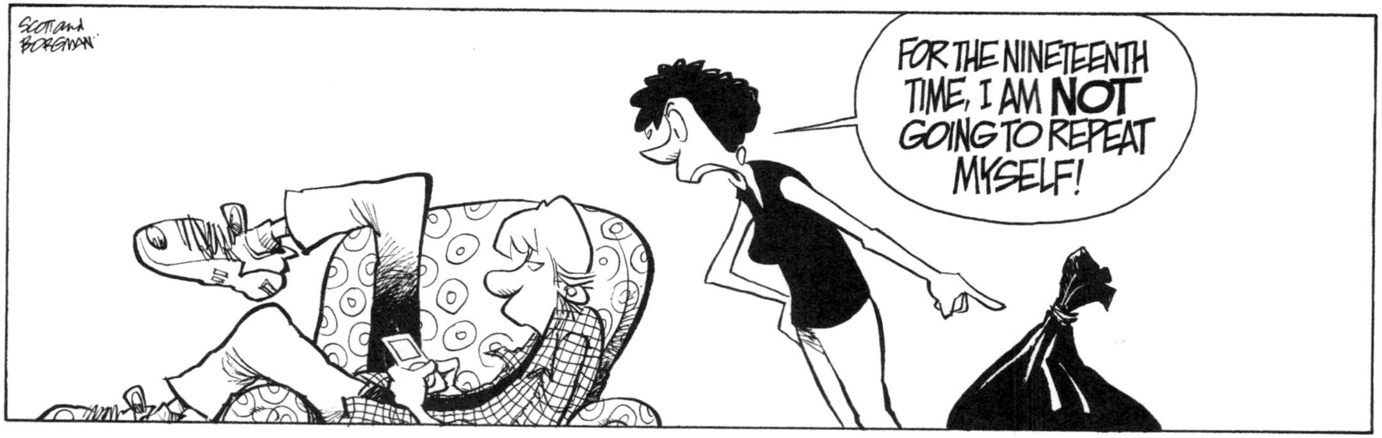
SCOTT and BORGMAN
FOR THE NINETEENTH TIME, I AM **NOT** GOING TO REPEAT MYSELF!

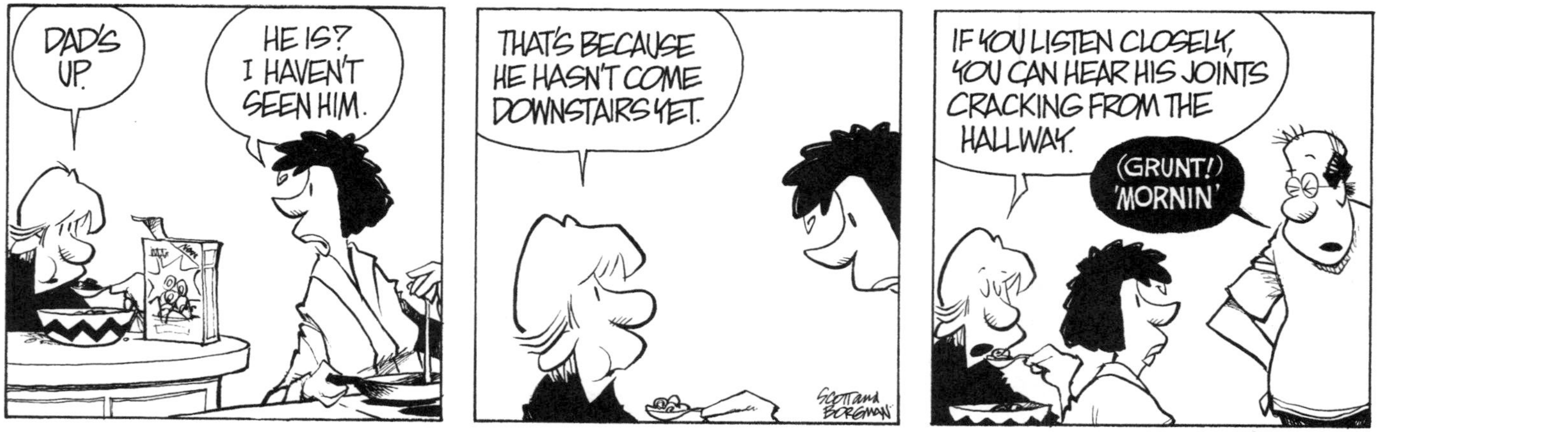
DAD'S UP.
HE IS? I HAVEN'T SEEN HIM.
THAT'S BECAUSE HE HASN'T COME DOWNSTAIRS YET.
SCOTT and BORGMAN
IF YOU LISTEN CLOSELY, YOU CAN HEAR HIS JOINTS CRACKING FROM THE HALLWAY.
(GRUNT!) 'MORNIN'

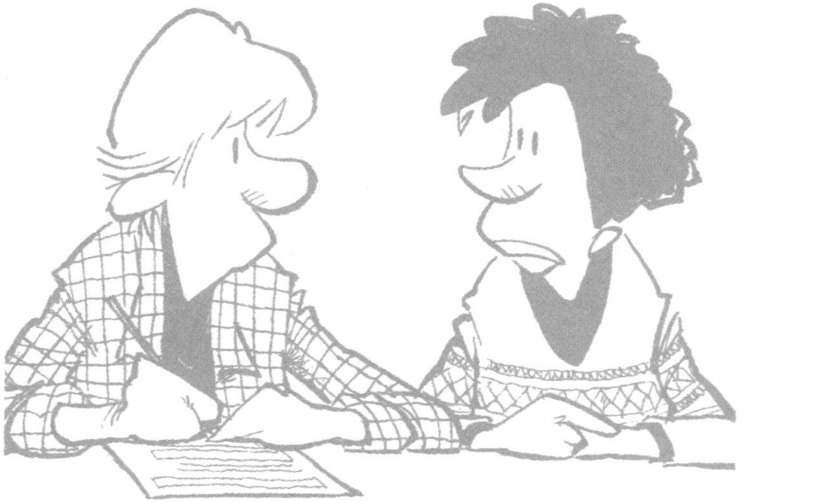

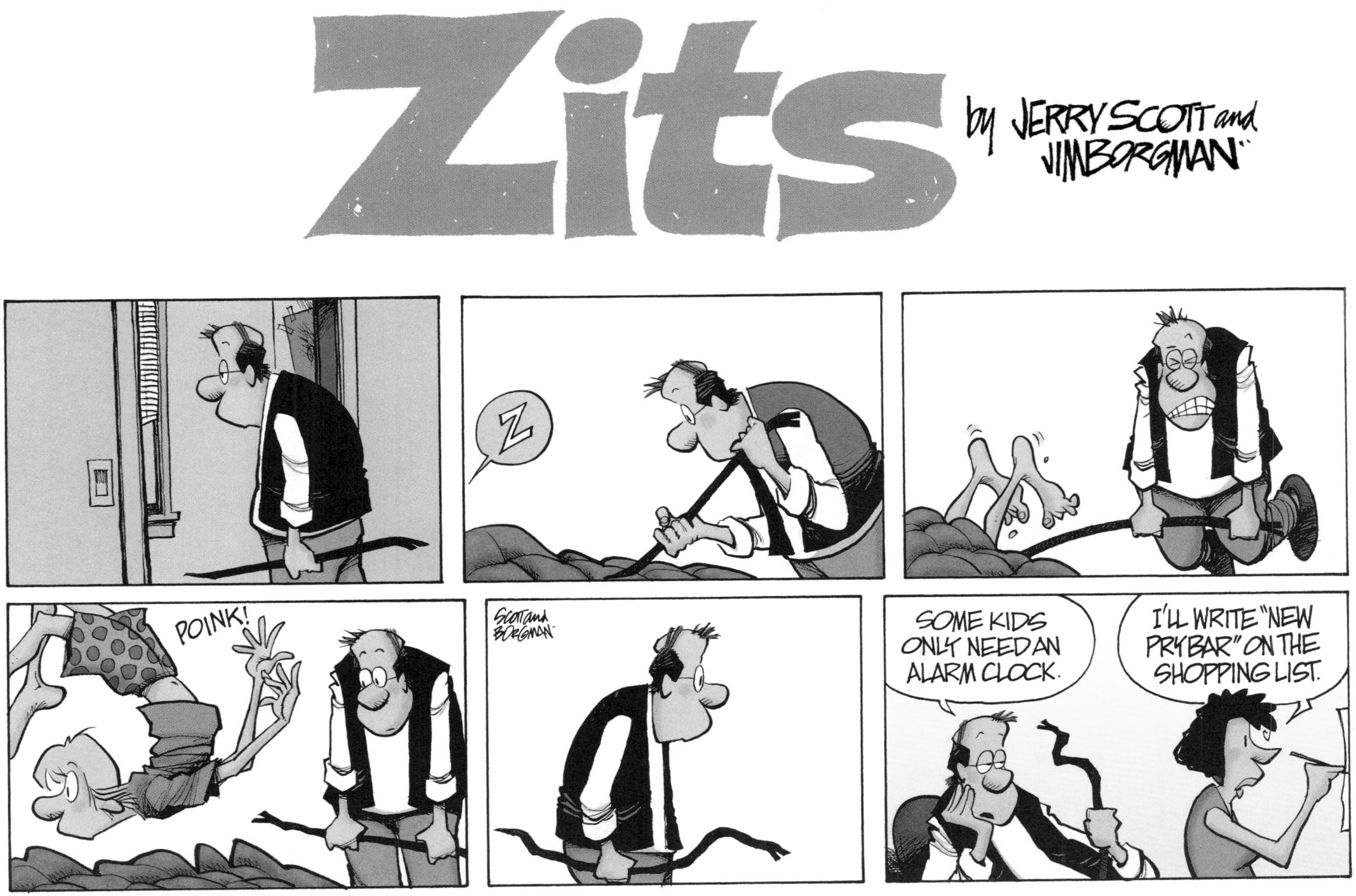
Zits
by JERRY SCOTT and JIM BORGMAN
Z
POINK!
SCOTT and BORGMAN
SOME KIDS ONLY NEED AN ALARM CLOCK.
I'LL WRITE "NEW PRYBAR" ON THE SHOPPING LIST.

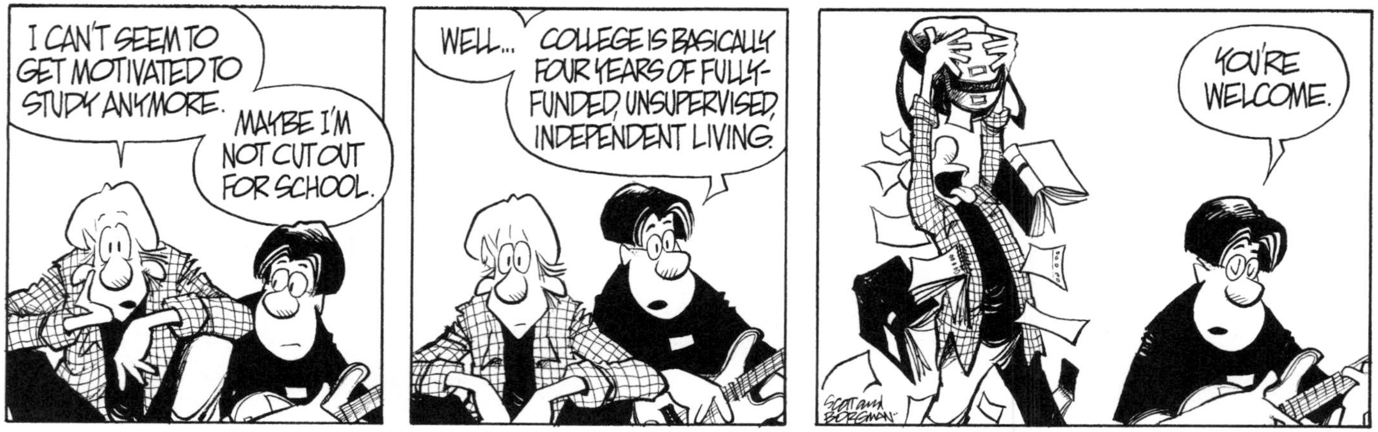
I CAN'T SEEM TO GET MOTIVATED TO STUDY ANYMORE.
MAYBE I'M NOT CUT OUT FOR SCHOOL.
WELL...
COLLEGE IS BASICALLY FOUR YEARS OF FULLY-FUNDED, UNSUPERVISED, INDEPENDENT LIVING.
YOU'RE WELCOME.

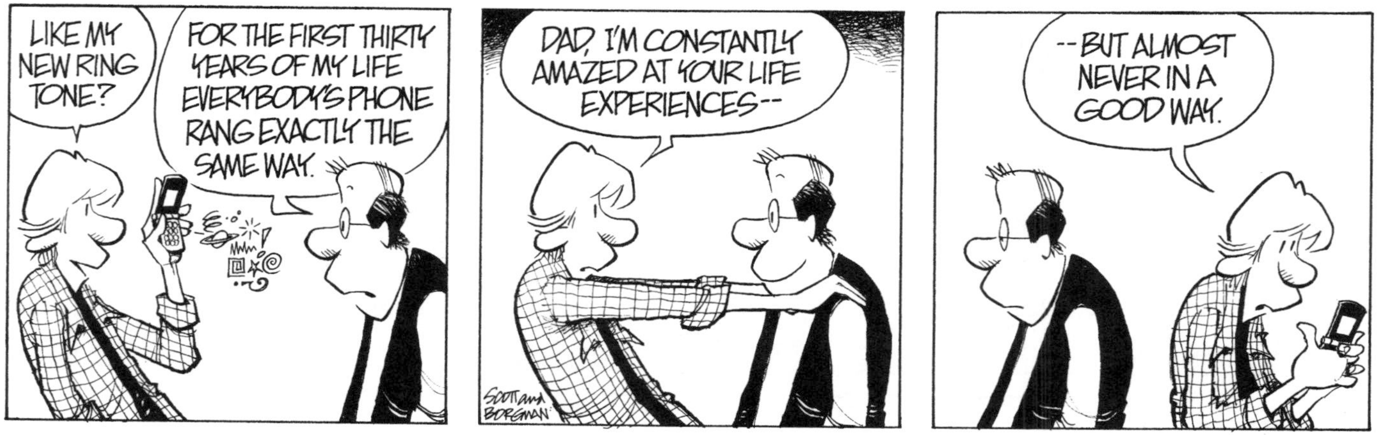
LIKE MY NEW RING TONE?
FOR THE FIRST THIRTY YEARS OF MY LIFE EVERYBODY'S PHONE RANG EXACTLY THE SAME WAY.
DAD, I'M CONSTANTLY AMAZED AT YOUR LIFE EXPERIENCES--
--BUT ALMOST NEVER IN A GOOD WAY.

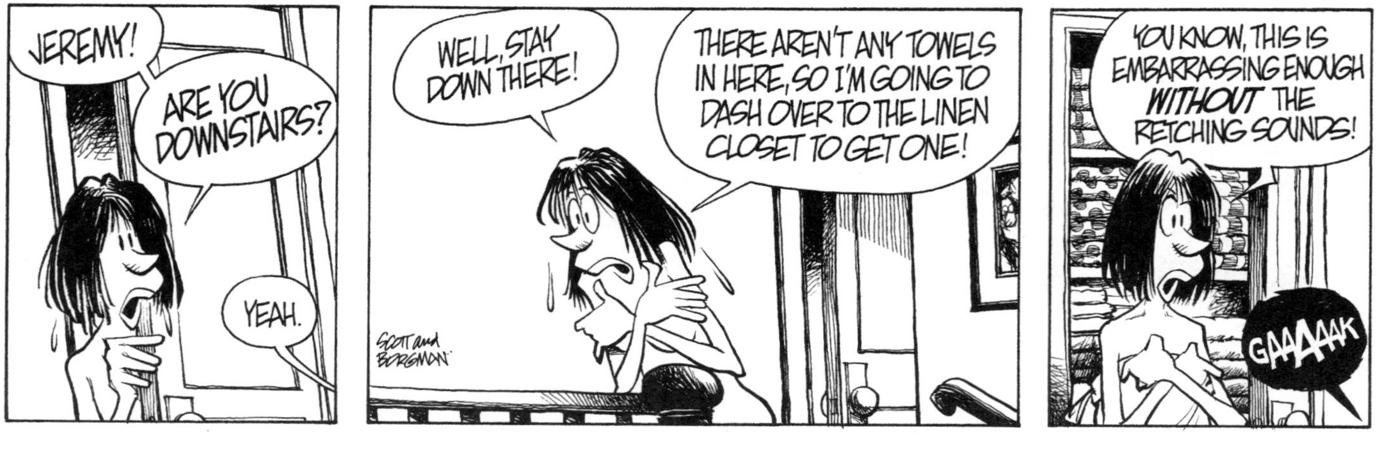
JEREMY!
ARE YOU DOWNSTAIRS?
YEAH.
WELL, STAY DOWN THERE!
THERE AREN'T ANY TOWELS IN HERE, SO I'M GOING TO DASH OVER TO THE LINEN CLOSET TO GET ONE!
YOU KNOW, THIS IS EMBARRASSING ENOUGH *WITHOUT* THE RETCHING SOUNDS!
GAAAAAK

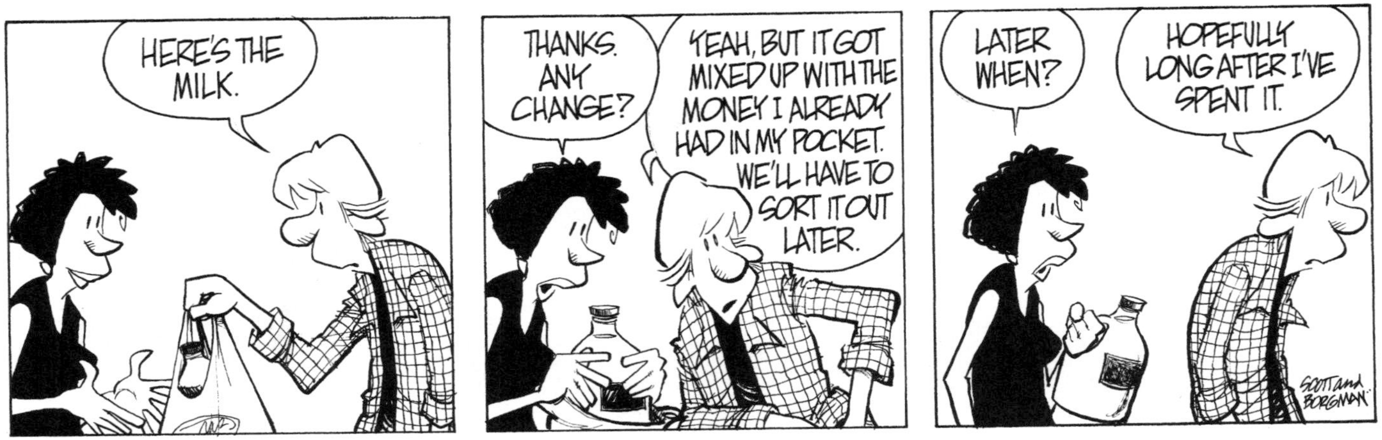
HERE'S THE MILK.
THANKS. ANY CHANGE?
YEAH, BUT IT GOT MIXED UP WITH THE MONEY I ALREADY HAD IN MY POCKET. WE'LL HAVE TO SORT IT OUT LATER.
LATER WHEN?
HOPEFULLY LONG AFTER I'VE SPENT IT.
SCOTT and BORGMAN

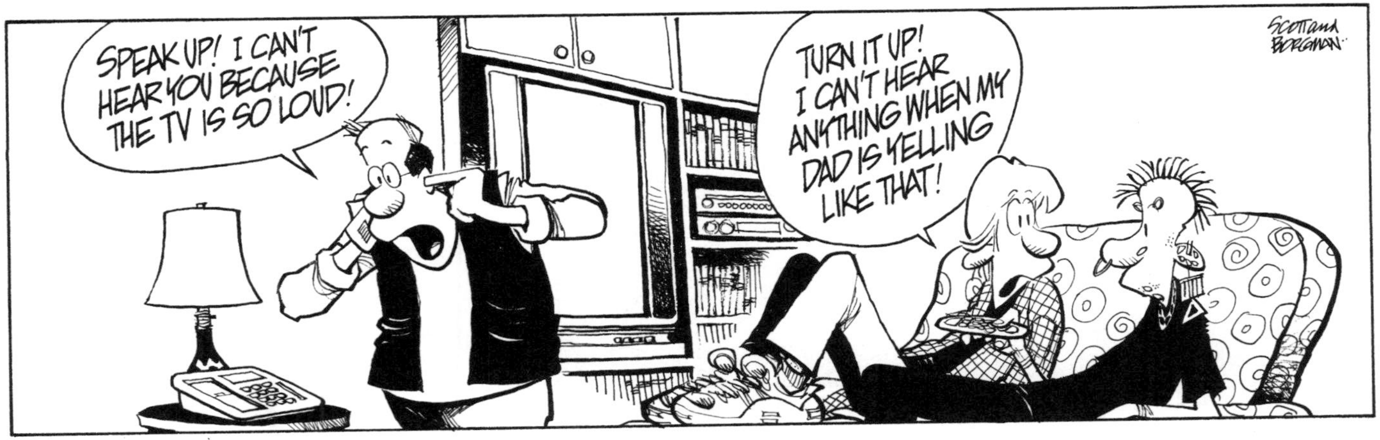
SPEAK UP! I CAN'T HEAR YOU BECAUSE THE TV IS SO LOUD!
TURN IT UP! I CAN'T HEAR ANYTHING WHEN MY DAD IS YELLING LIKE THAT!
SCOTT and BORGMAN

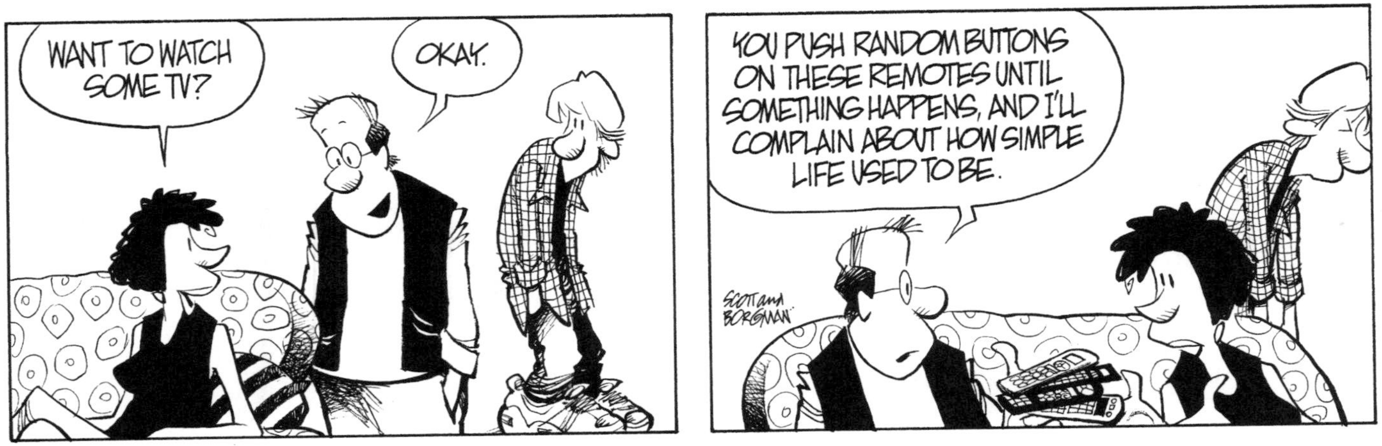
WANT TO WATCH SOME TV?
OKAY.
YOU PUSH RANDOM BUTTONS ON THESE REMOTES UNTIL SOMETHING HAPPENS, AND I'LL COMPLAIN ABOUT HOW SIMPLE LIFE USED TO BE.
SCOTT and BORGMAN

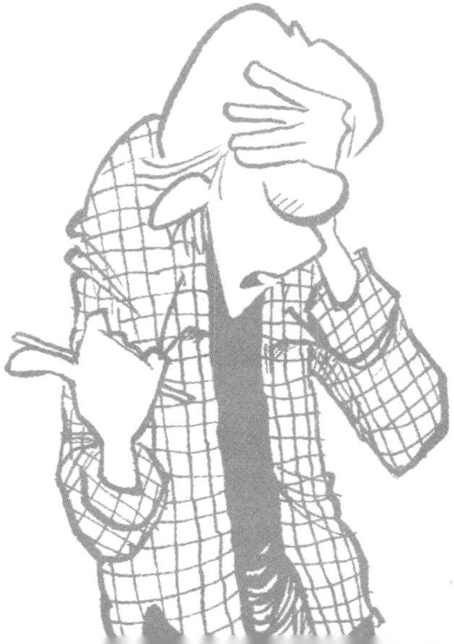

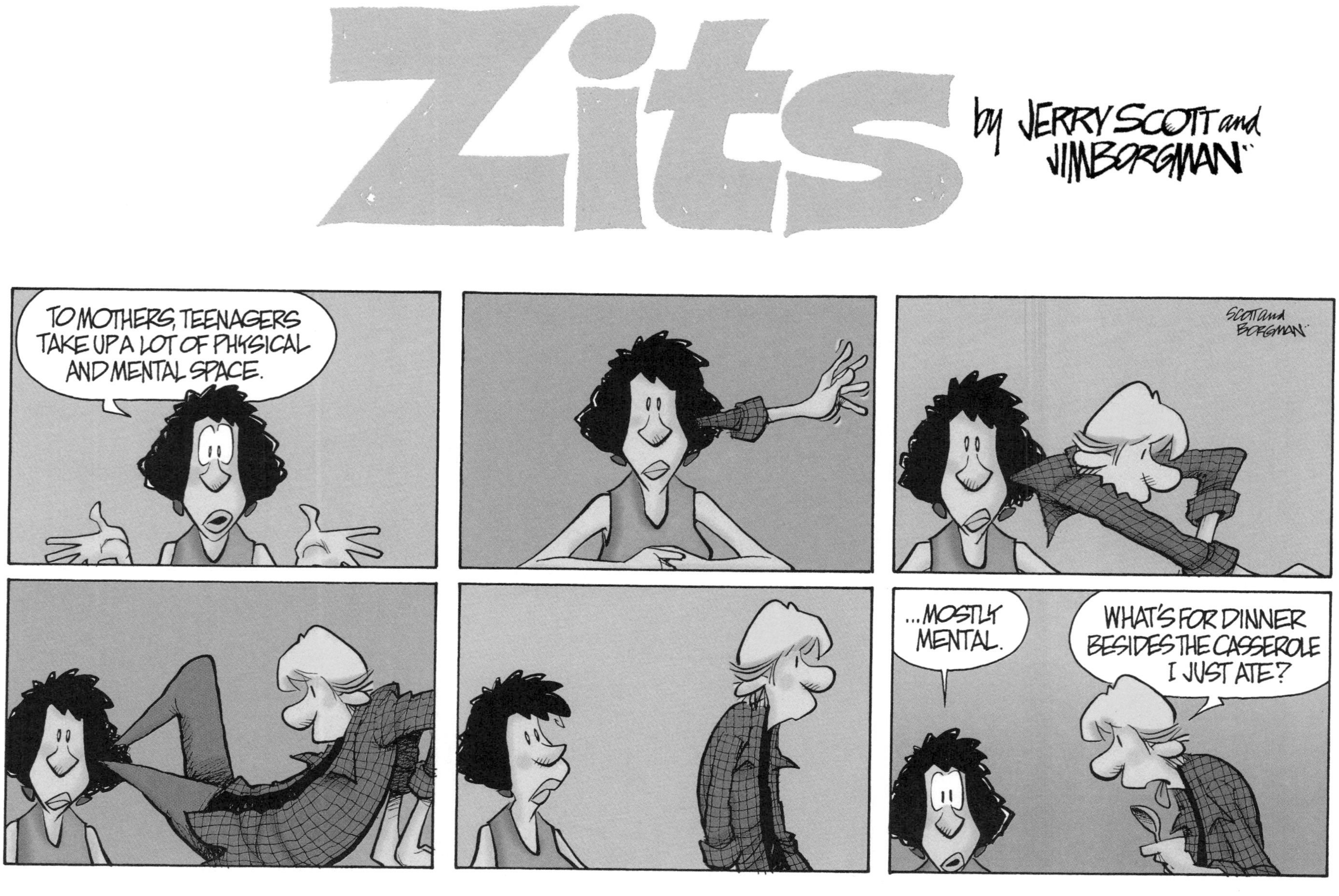
Zits
by JERRY SCOTT and JIM BORGMAN
TO MOTHERS, TEENAGERS TAKE UP A LOT OF PHYSICAL AND MENTAL SPACE.
SCOTT and BORGMAN
...MOSTLY MENTAL.
WHAT'S FOR DINNER BESIDES THE CASSEROLE I JUST ATE?

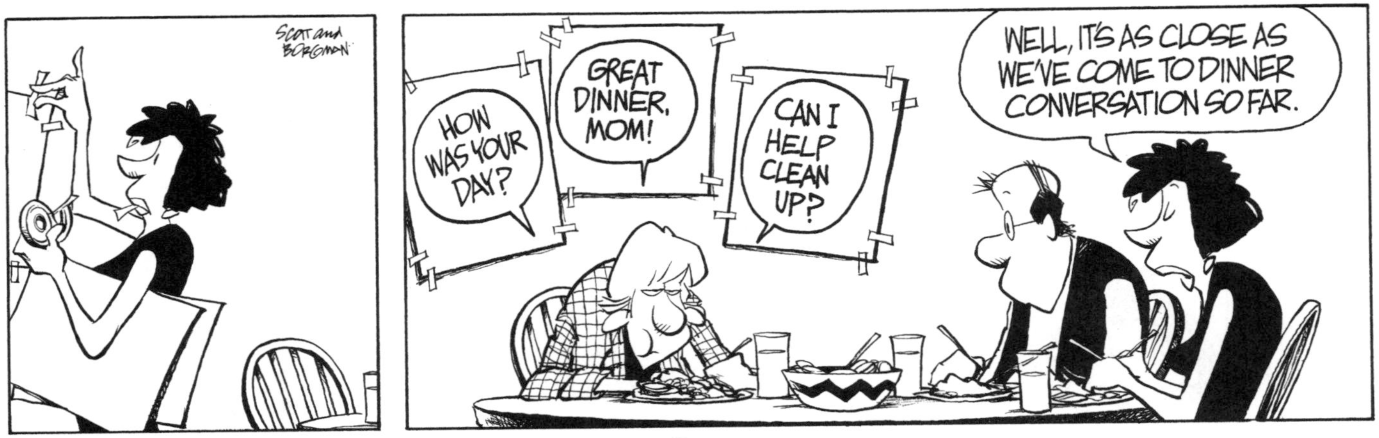
SCOTT and BORGMAN
HOW WAS YOUR DAY?
GREAT DINNER, MOM!
CAN I HELP CLEAN UP?
WELL, IT'S AS CLOSE AS WE'VE COME TO DINNER CONVERSATION SO FAR.

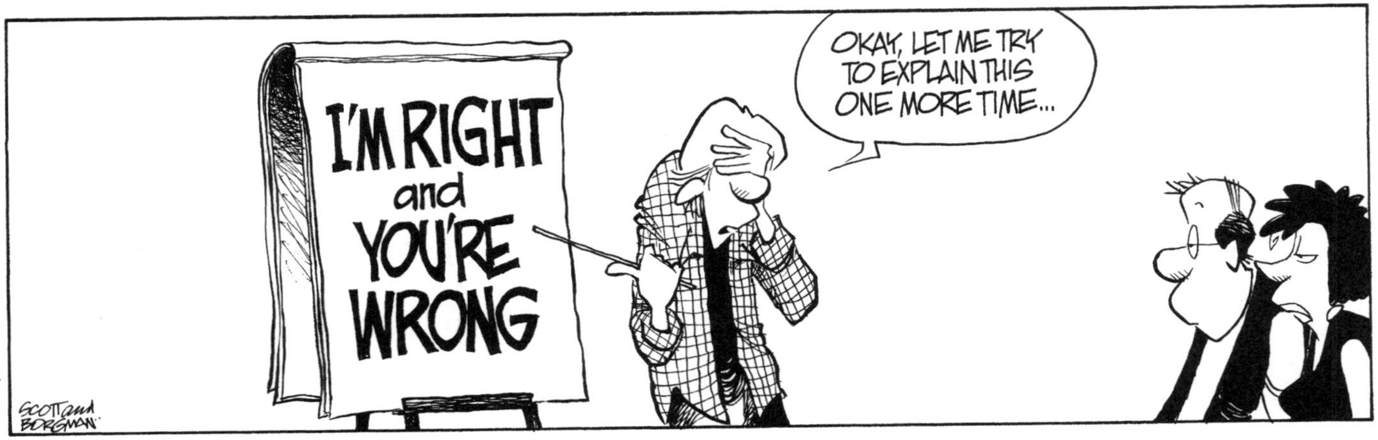
I'M RIGHT and YOU'RE WRONG
OKAY, LET ME TRY TO EXPLAIN THIS ONE MORE TIME...
SCOTT and BORGMAN

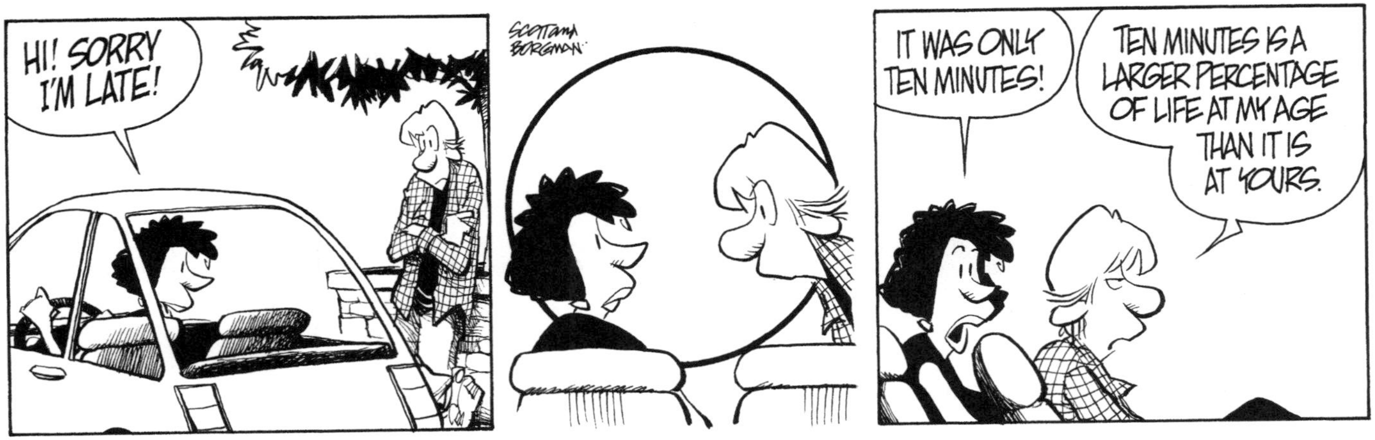
HI! SORRY I'M LATE!
SCOTT and BORGMAN
IT WAS ONLY TEN MINUTES!
TEN MINUTES IS A LARGER PERCENTAGE OF LIFE AT MY AGE THAN IT IS AT YOURS.

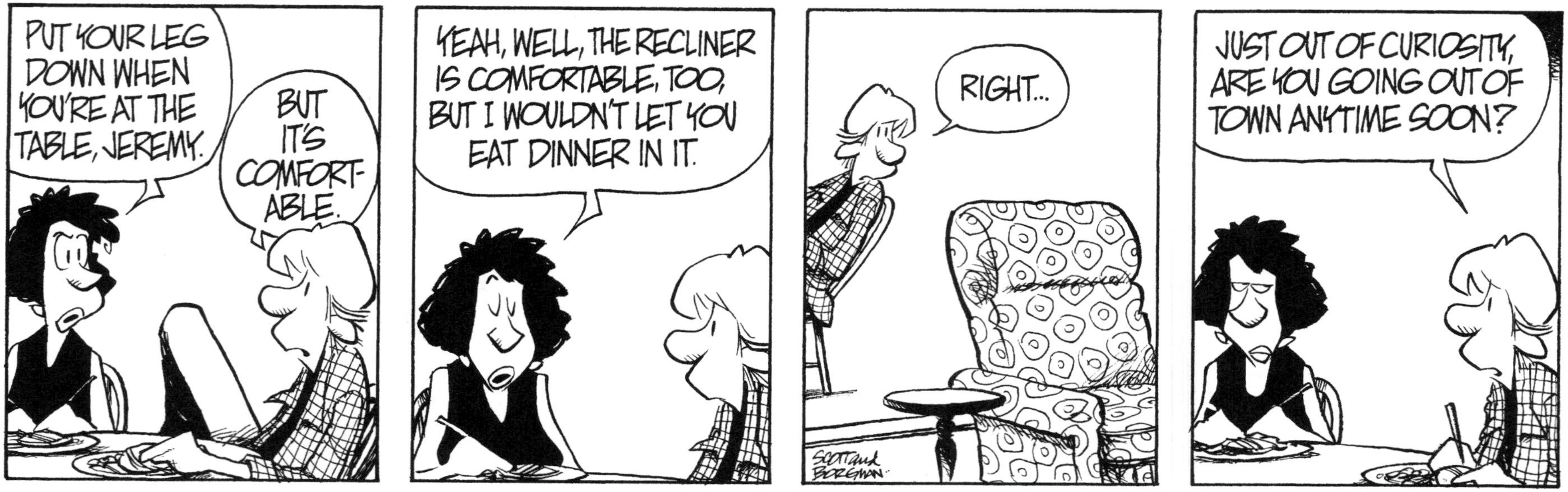
PUT YOUR LEG DOWN WHEN YOU'RE AT THE TABLE, JEREMY.
BUT IT'S COMFORTABLE.
YEAH, WELL, THE RECLINER IS COMFORTABLE, TOO, BUT I WOULDN'T LET YOU EAT DINNER IN IT.
RIGHT...
SCOTT and BORGMAN
JUST OUT OF CURIOSITY, ARE YOU GOING OUT OF TOWN ANYTIME SOON?

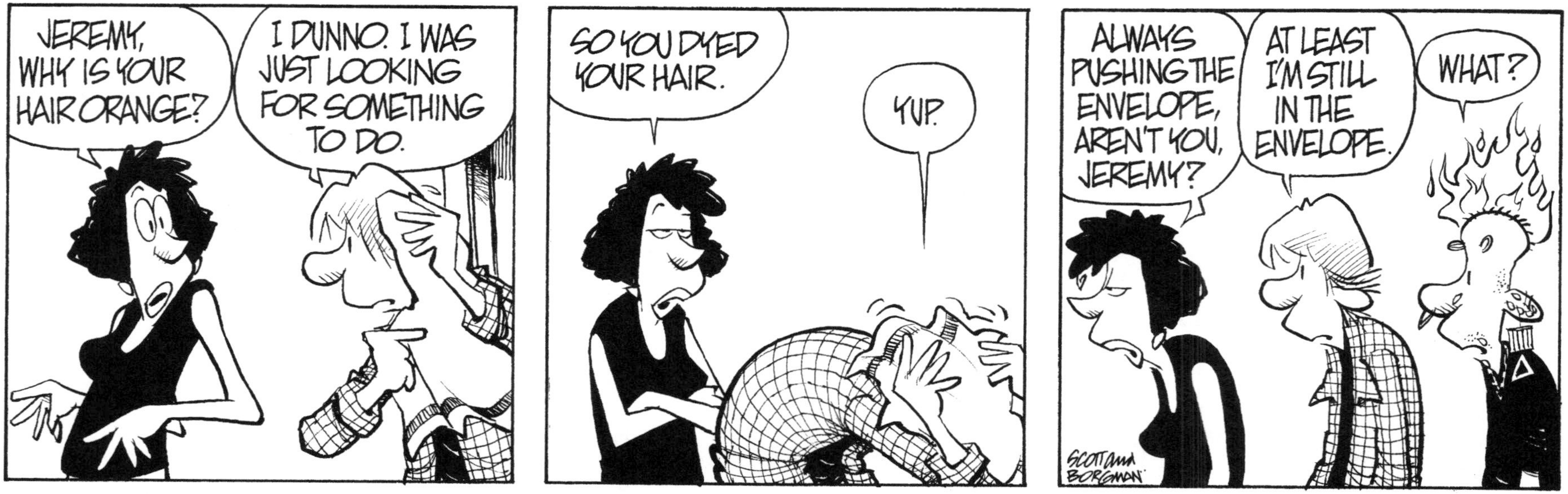
JEREMY, WHY IS YOUR HAIR ORANGE?
I DUNNO. I WAS JUST LOOKING FOR SOMETHING TO DO.
SO YOU DYED YOUR HAIR.
YUP.
ALWAYS PUSHING THE ENVELOPE, AREN'T YOU, JEREMY?
AT LEAST I'M STILL IN THE ENVELOPE.
WHAT?
SCOTT and BORGMAN

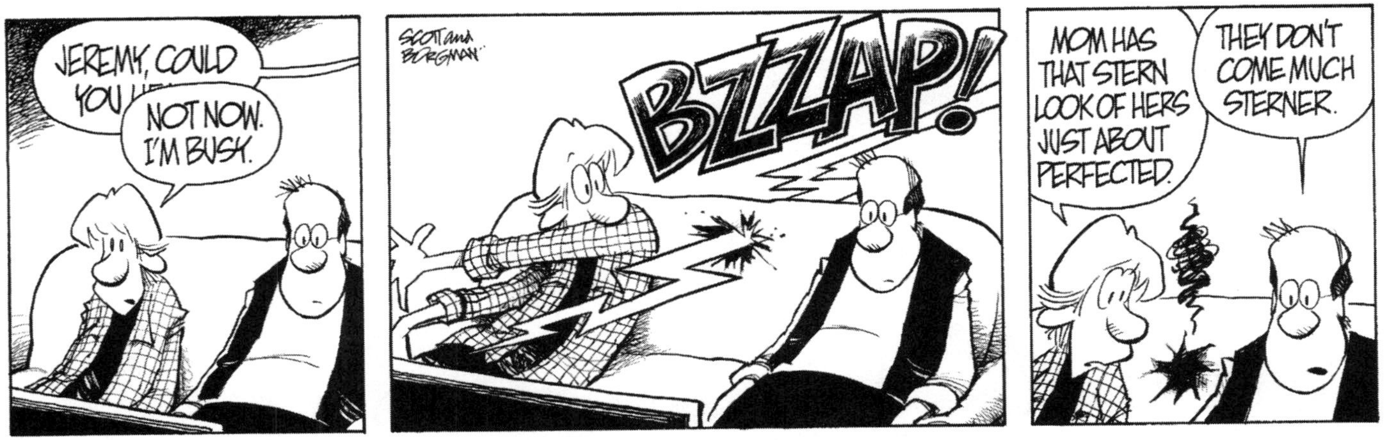
JEREMY, COULD YOU
NOT NOW. I'M BUSY.
SCOTT and BORGMAN
BZZAP!
MOM HAS THAT STERN LOOK OF HERS JUST ABOUT PERFECTED.
THEY DON'T COME MUCH STERNER.

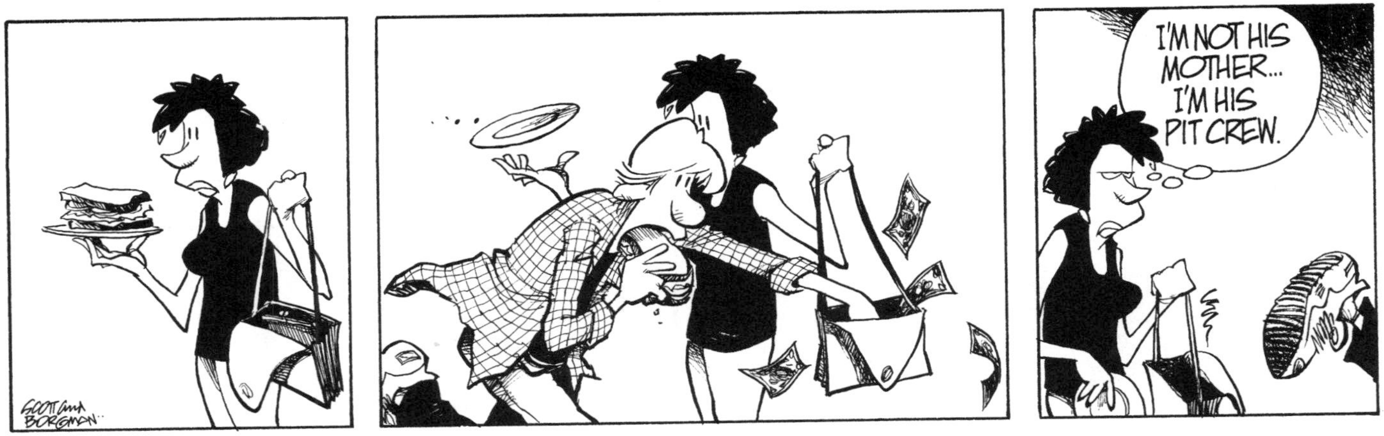
SCOTT and BORGMAN
I'M NOT HIS MOTHER... I'M HIS PIT CREW.

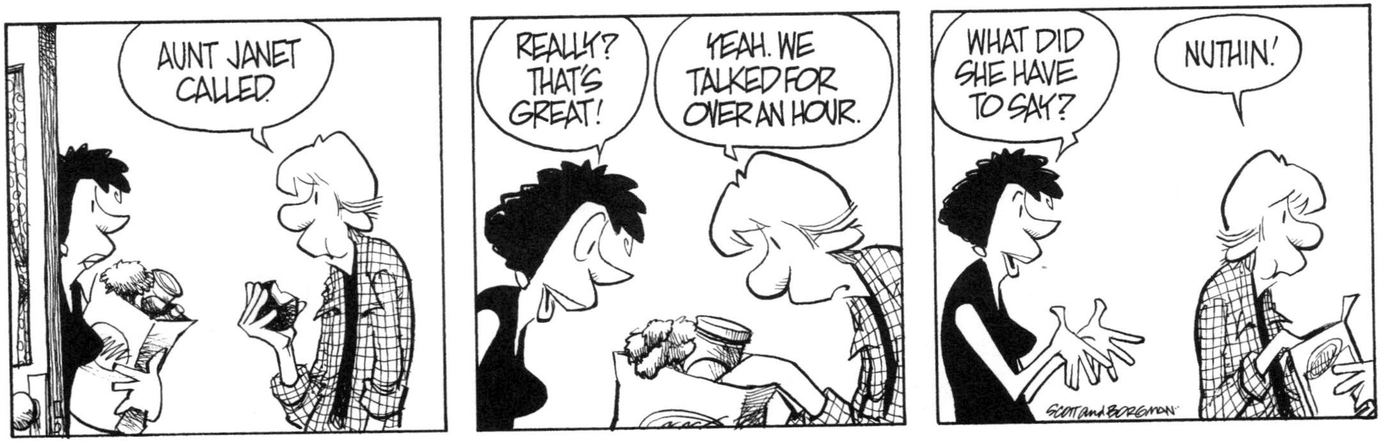
AUNT JANET CALLED.
REALLY? THAT'S GREAT!
YEAH. WE TALKED FOR OVER AN HOUR.
WHAT DID SHE HAVE TO SAY?
NUTHIN'.
SCOTT and BORGMAN

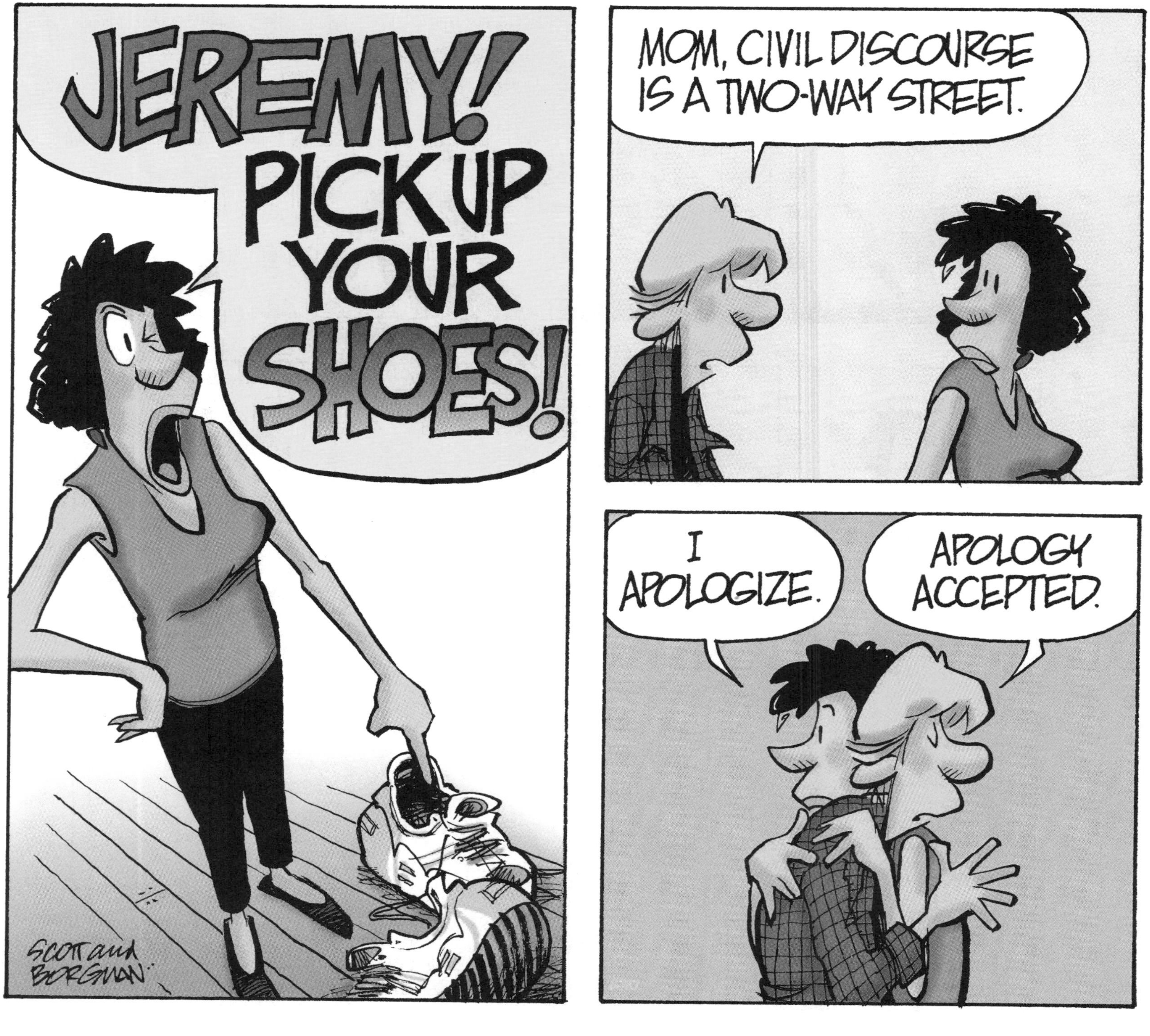
JEREMY! PICK UP YOUR SHOES!
SCOTT AND BORGMAN
MOM, CIVIL DISCOURSE IS A TWO-WAY STREET.
I APOLOGIZE.
APOLOGY ACCEPTED.

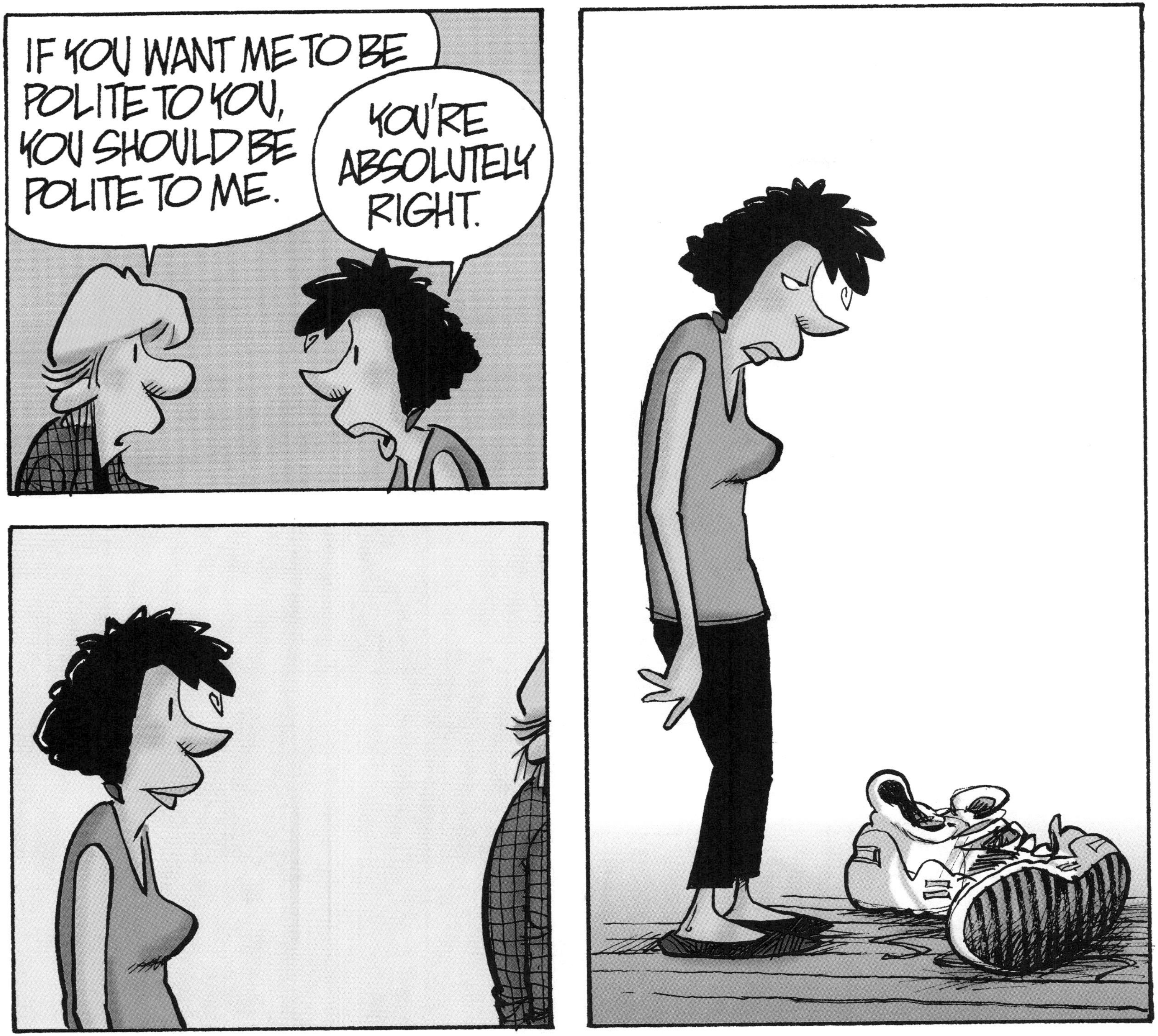

IF YOU WANT ME TO BE POLITE TO YOU, YOU SHOULD BE POLITE TO ME.
YOU'RE ABSOLUTELY RIGHT.

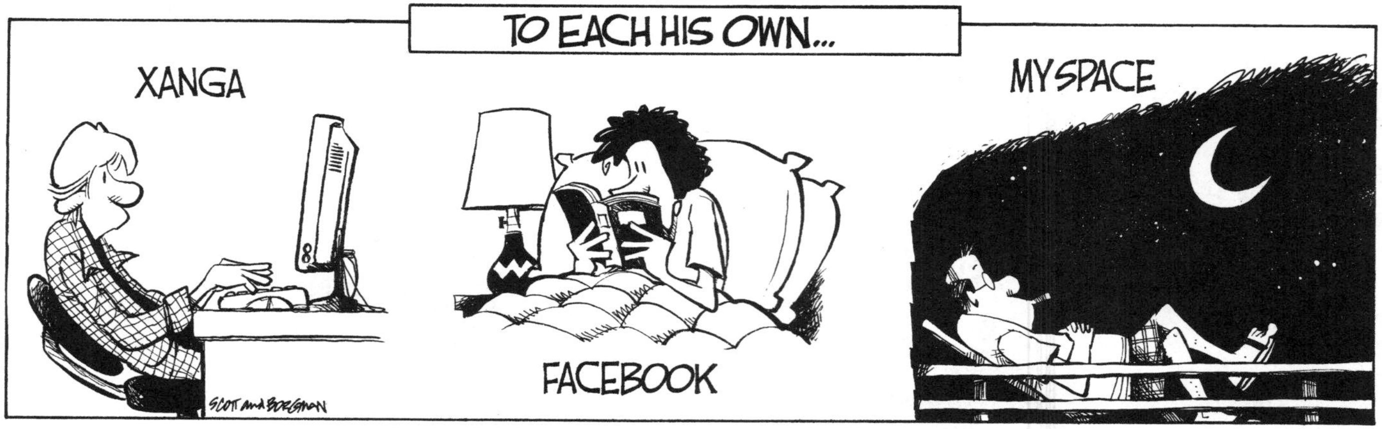
TO EACH HIS OWN...
XANGA
FACEBOOK
MYSPACE
SCOTT and BORGMAN

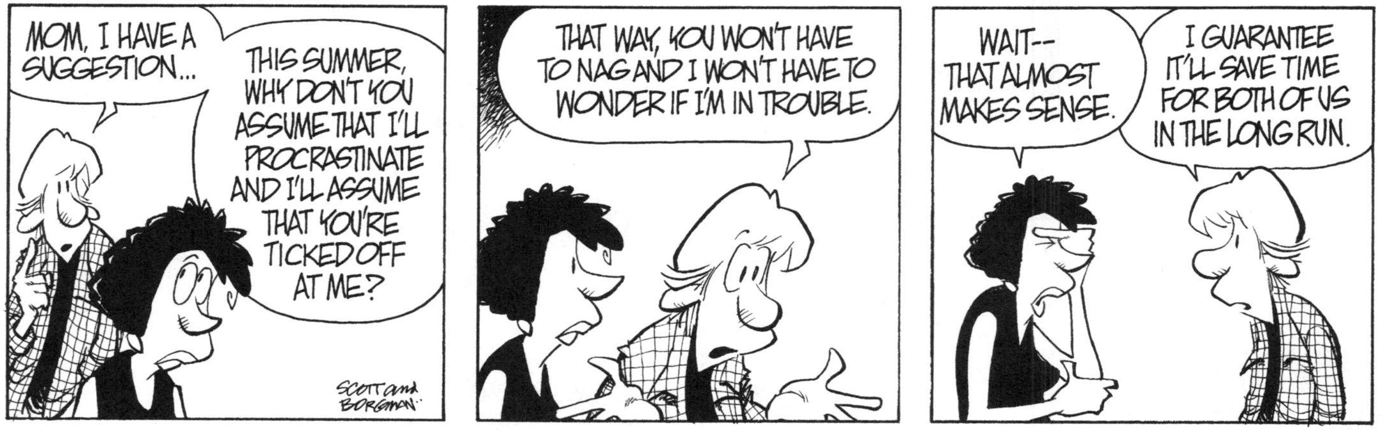
MOM, I HAVE A SUGGESTION...
THIS SUMMER, WHY DON'T YOU ASSUME THAT I'LL PROCRASTINATE AND I'LL ASSUME THAT YOU'RE TICKED OFF AT ME?
SCOTT and BORGMAN
THAT WAY, YOU WON'T HAVE TO NAG AND I WON'T HAVE TO WONDER IF I'M IN TROUBLE.
WAIT-- THAT ALMOST MAKES SENSE.
I GUARANTEE IT'LL SAVE TIME FOR BOTH OF US IN THE LONG RUN.

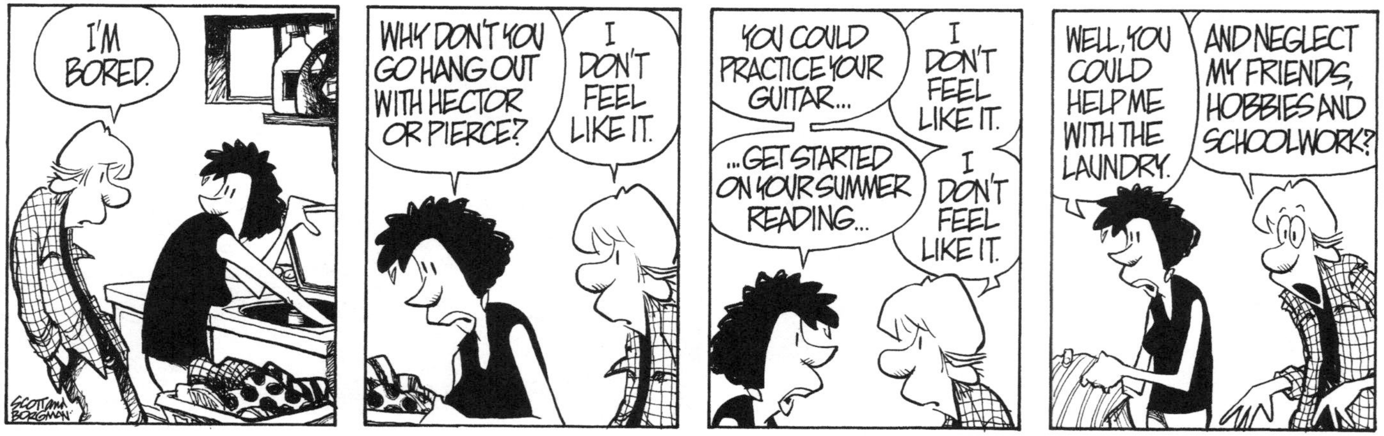
I'M BORED.
SCOTT and BORGMAN
WHY DON'T YOU GO HANG OUT WITH HECTOR OR PIERCE?
I DON'T FEEL LIKE IT.
YOU COULD PRACTICE YOUR GUITAR...
I DON'T FEEL LIKE IT.
...GET STARTED ON YOUR SUMMER READING...
I DON'T FEEL LIKE IT.
WELL, YOU COULD HELP ME WITH THE LAUNDRY.
AND NEGLECT MY FRIENDS, HOBBIES AND SCHOOLWORK?

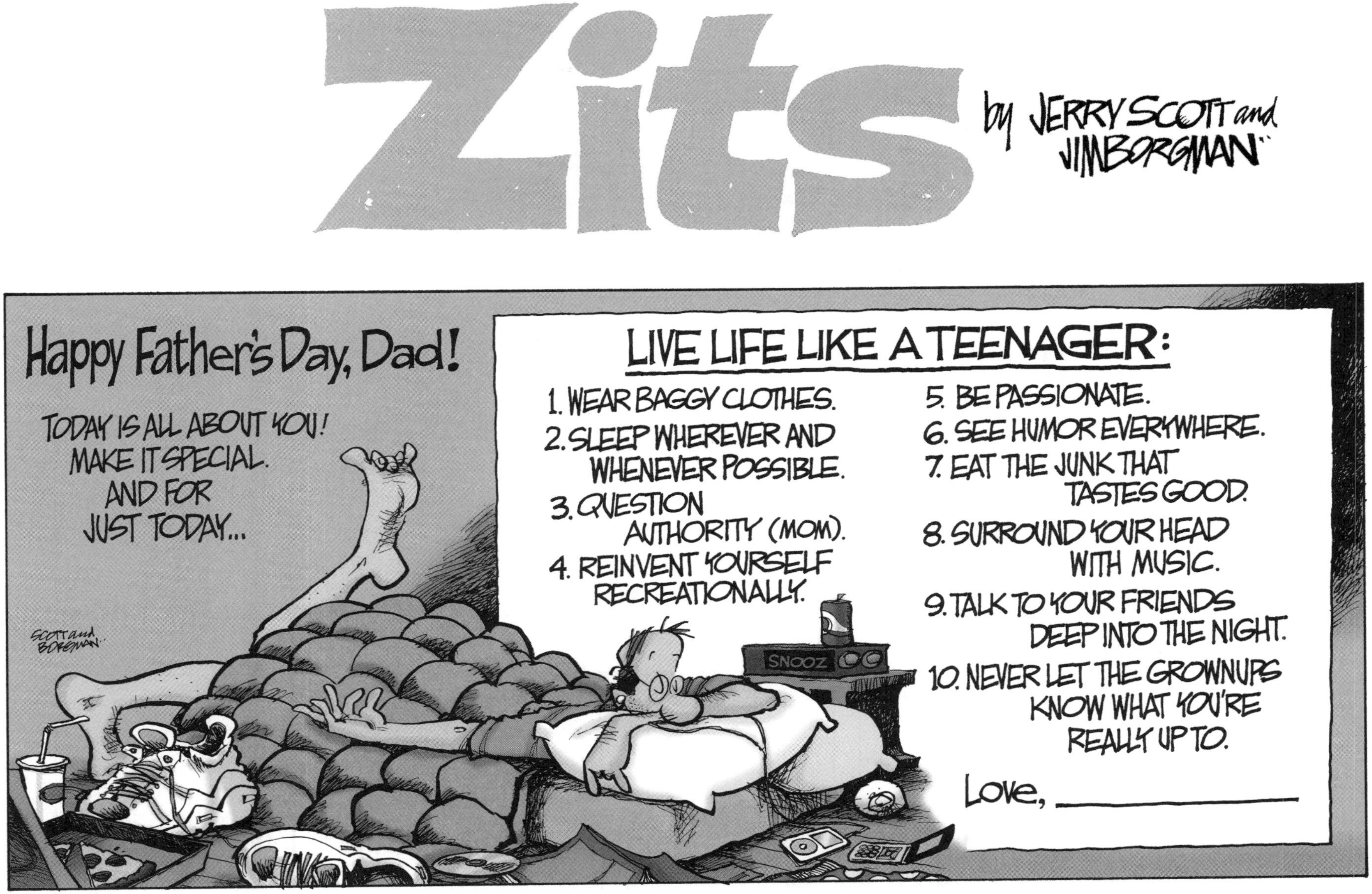
Zits
by JERRY SCOTT and JIM BORGMAN
Happy Father's Day, Dad!
TODAY IS ALL ABOUT YOU! MAKE IT SPECIAL. AND FOR JUST TODAY...
LIVE LIFE LIKE A TEENAGER:
1. WEAR BAGGY CLOTHES.
2. SLEEP WHEREVER AND WHENEVER POSSIBLE.
3. QUESTION AUTHORITY (MOM).
4. REINVENT YOURSELF RECREATIONALLY.
5. BE PASSIONATE.
6. SEE HUMOR EVERYWHERE.
7. EAT THE JUNK THAT TASTES GOOD.
8. SURROUND YOUR HEAD WITH MUSIC.
9. TALK TO YOUR FRIENDS DEEP INTO THE NIGHT.
10. NEVER LET THE GROWNUPS KNOW WHAT YOU'RE REALLY UP TO.
Love, ____________
SNOOZ
SCOTT and BORGMAN

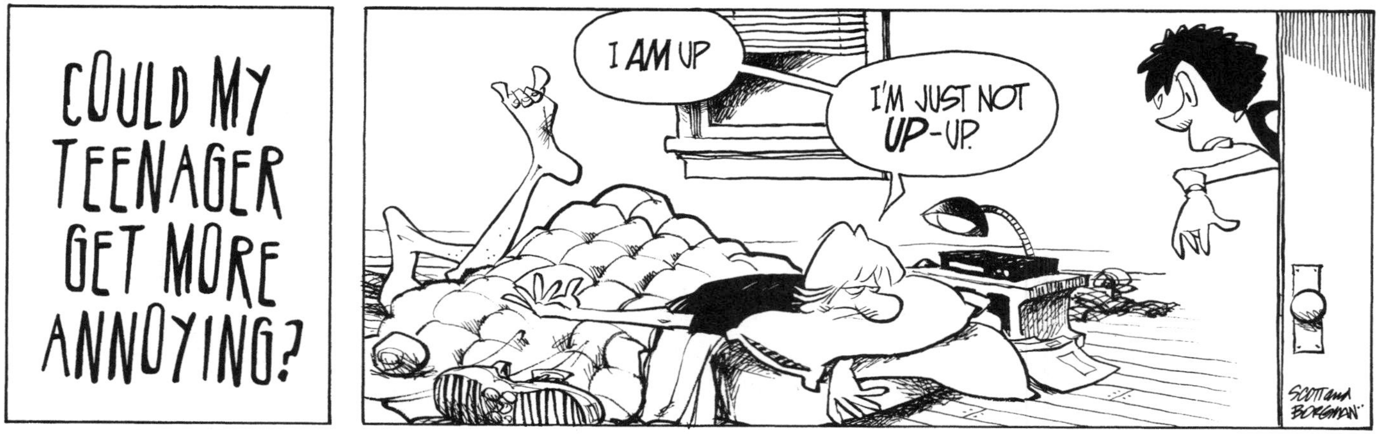
COULD MY TEENAGER GET MORE ANNOYING?
I AM UP
I'M JUST NOT UP-UP.
SCOTT and BORGMAN

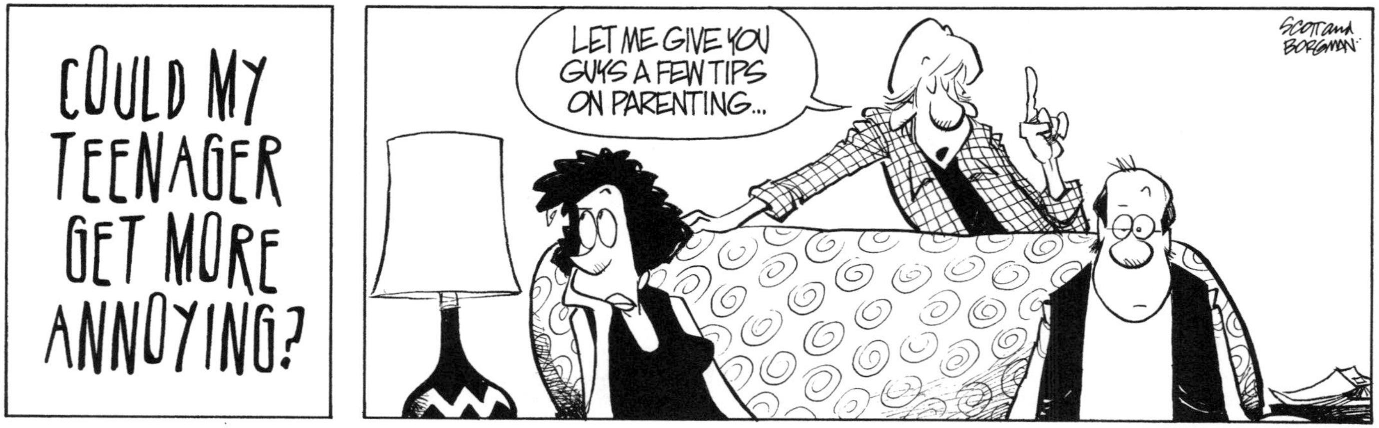
COULD MY TEENAGER GET MORE ANNOYING?
LET ME GIVE YOU GUYS A FEW TIPS ON PARENTING...
SCOTT and BORGMAN

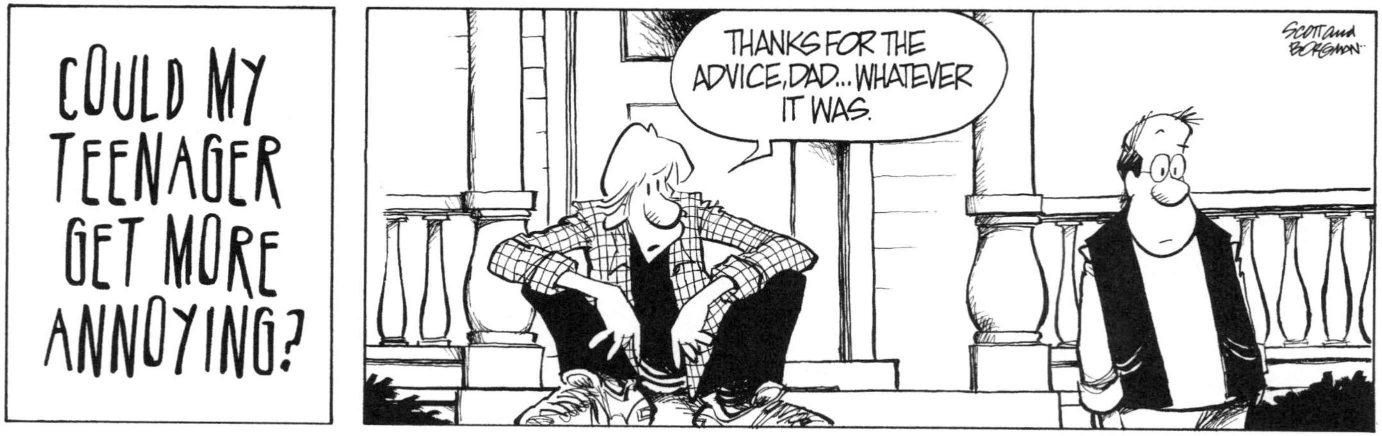
COULD MY TEENAGER GET MORE ANNOYING?
THANKS FOR THE ADVICE, DAD... WHATEVER IT WAS.
SCOTT and BORGMAN

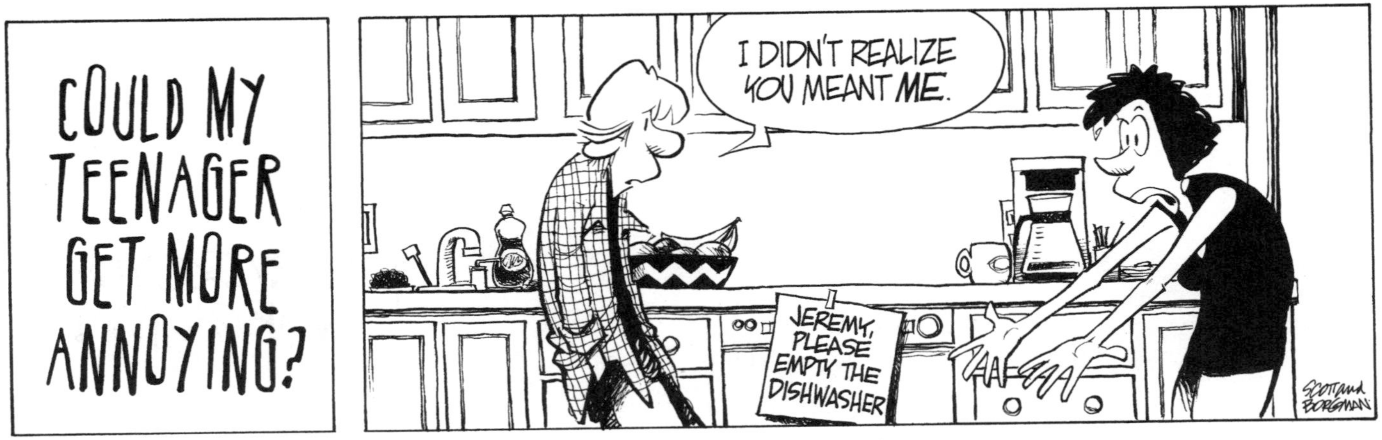
COULD MY TEENAGER GET MORE ANNOYING?
I DIDN'T REALIZE YOU MEANT ME.
JEREMY, PLEASE EMPTY THE DISHWASHER
SCOTT and BORGMAN

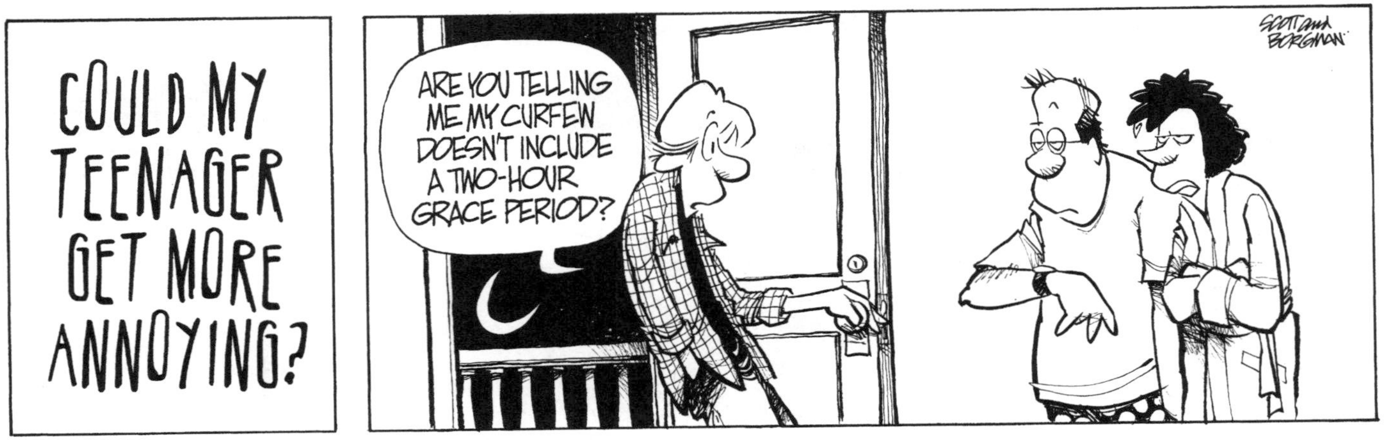
COULD MY TEENAGER GET MORE ANNOYING?
ARE YOU TELLING ME MY CURFEW DOESN'T INCLUDE A TWO-HOUR GRACE PERIOD?
SCOTT and BORGMAN

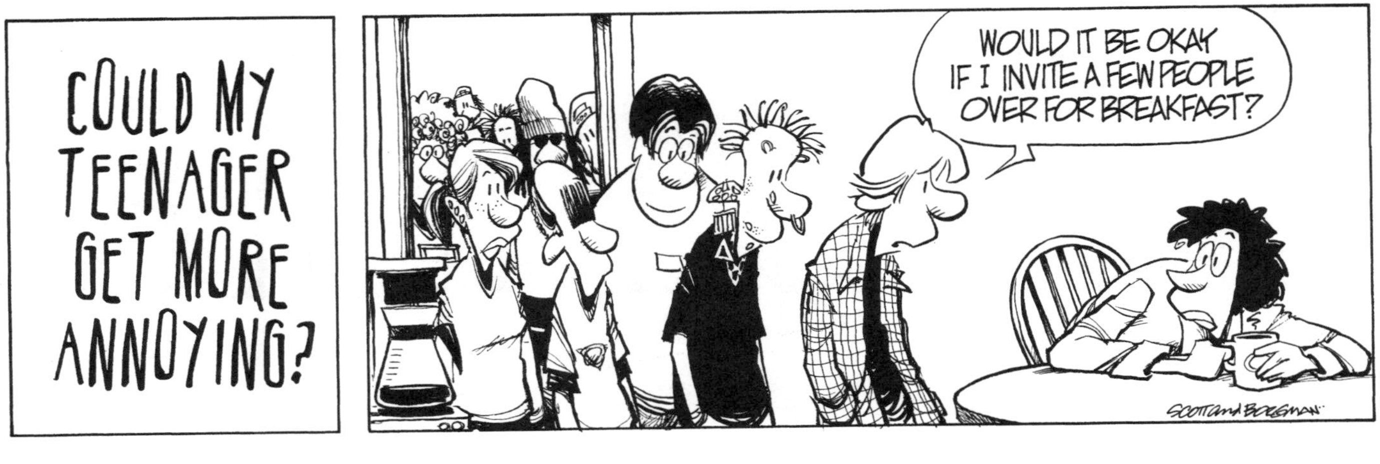
COULD MY TEENAGER GET MORE ANNOYING?
WOULD IT BE OKAY IF I INVITE A FEW PEOPLE OVER FOR BREAKFAST?
SCOTT and BORGMAN

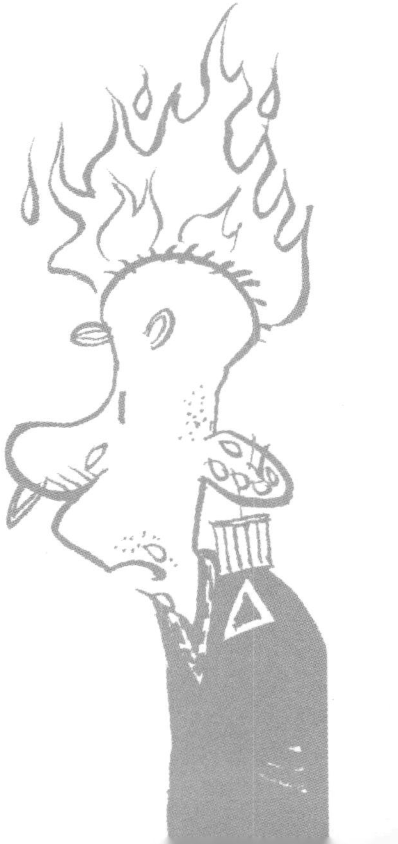

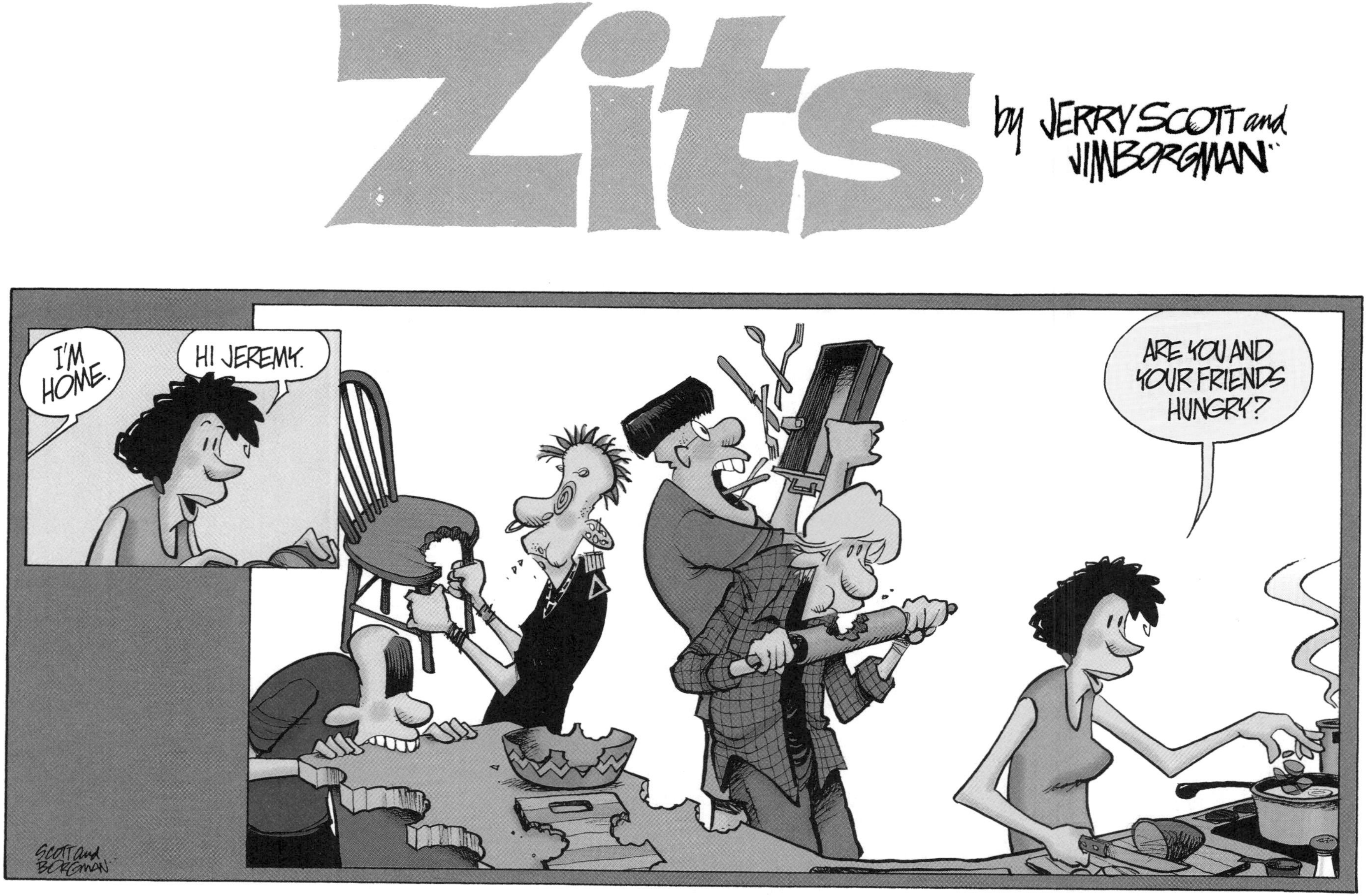
Zits
by JERRY SCOTT and JIM BORGMAN
I'M HOME.
HI JEREMY.
ARE YOU AND YOUR FRIENDS HUNGRY?
SCOTT and BORGMAN

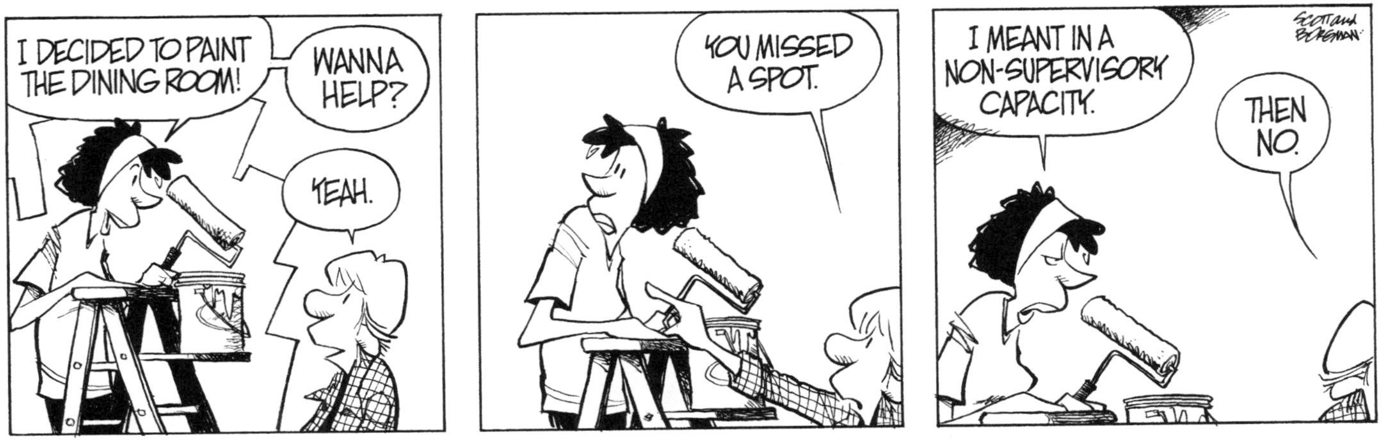
I DECIDED TO PAINT THE DINING ROOM!
WANNA HELP?
YEAH.
YOU MISSED A SPOT.
I MEANT IN A NON-SUPERVISORY CAPACITY.
THEN NO.
SCOTT and BORGMAN

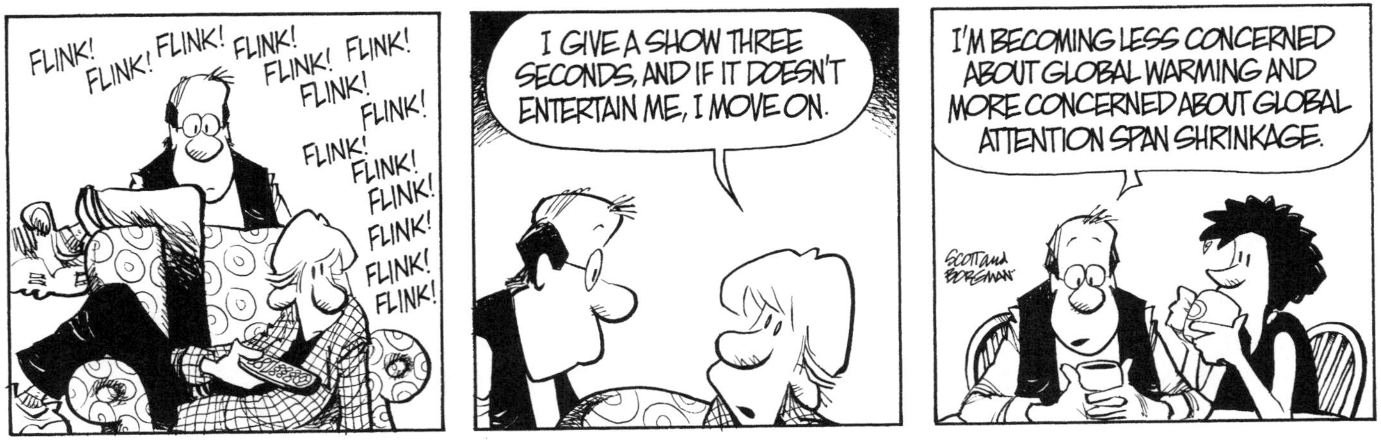
FLINK! FLINK! FLINK! FLINK! FLINK! FLINK! FLINK! FLINK! FLINK! FLINK! FLINK! FLINK! FLINK! FLINK! FLINK!
I GIVE A SHOW THREE SECONDS, AND IF IT DOESN'T ENTERTAIN ME, I MOVE ON.
I'M BECOMING LESS CONCERNED ABOUT GLOBAL WARMING AND MORE CONCERNED ABOUT GLOBAL ATTENTION SPAN SHRINKAGE.
SCOTT and BORGMAN

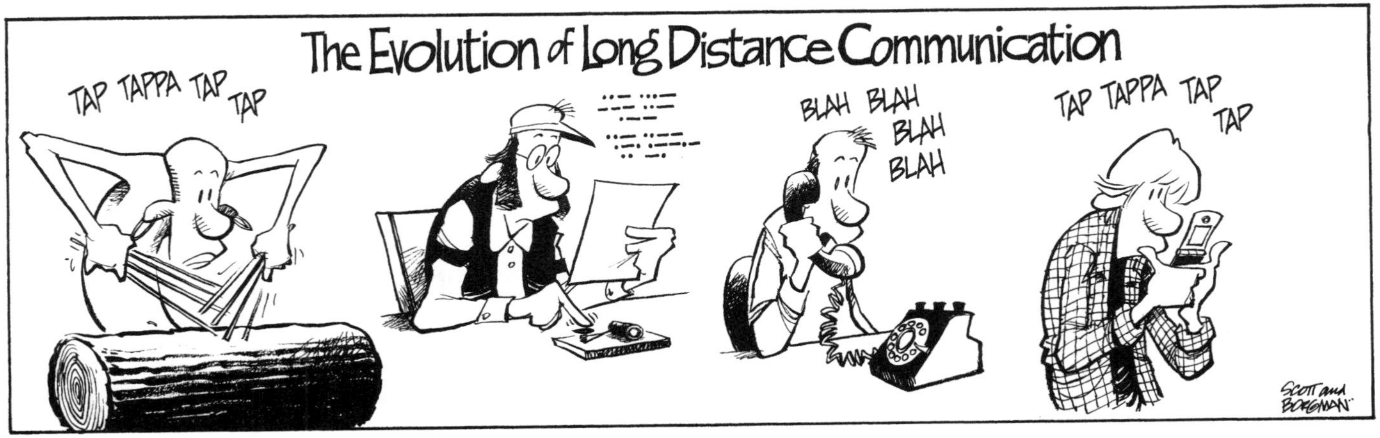
The Evolution of Long Distance Communication
TAP TAPPA TAP TAP
BLAH BLAH BLAH BLAH
TAP TAPPA TAP TAP
SCOTT and BORGMAN

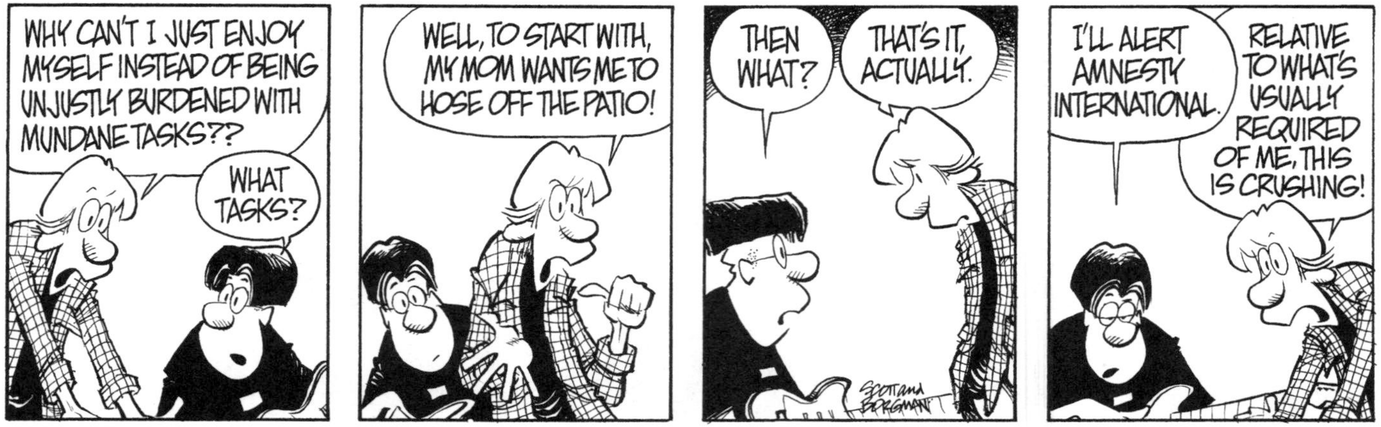
WHY CAN'T I JUST ENJOY MYSELF INSTEAD OF BEING UNJUSTLY BURDENED WITH MUNDANE TASKS??
WHAT TASKS?
WELL, TO START WITH, MY MOM WANTS ME TO HOSE OFF THE PATIO!
THEN WHAT?
THAT'S IT, ACTUALLY.
I'LL ALERT AMNESTY INTERNATIONAL.
RELATIVE TO WHAT'S USUALLY REQUIRED OF ME, THIS IS CRUSHING!

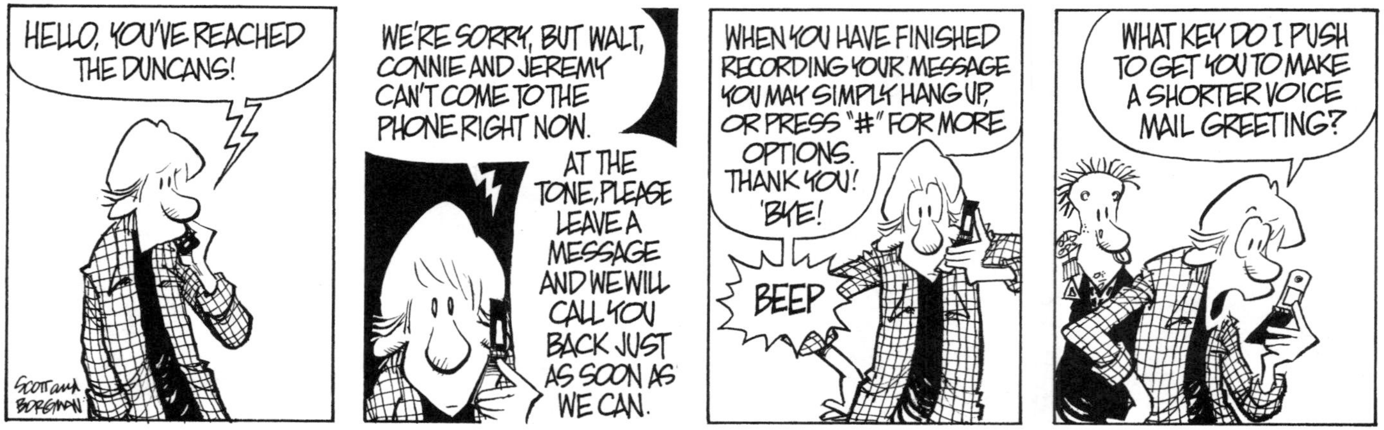
HELLO, YOU'VE REACHED THE DUNCANS!
WE'RE SORRY, BUT WALT, CONNIE AND JEREMY CAN'T COME TO THE PHONE RIGHT NOW.
AT THE TONE, PLEASE LEAVE A MESSAGE AND WE WILL CALL YOU BACK JUST AS SOON AS WE CAN.
WHEN YOU HAVE FINISHED RECORDING YOUR MESSAGE YOU MAY SIMPLY HANG UP, OR PRESS "#" FOR MORE OPTIONS. THANK YOU! 'BYE!
BEEP
WHAT KEY DO I PUSH TO GET YOU TO MAKE A SHORTER VOICE MAIL GREETING?

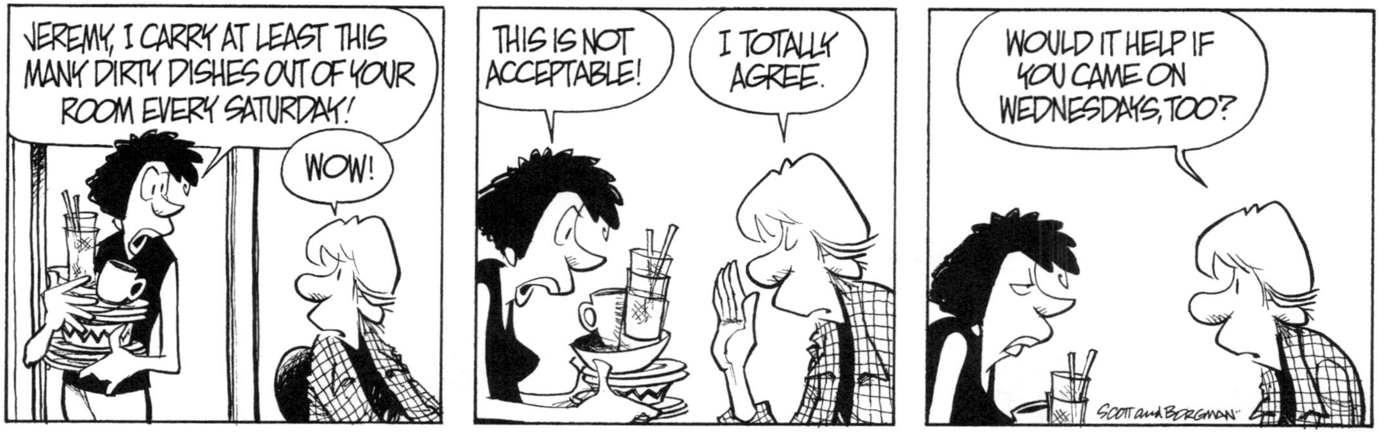
JEREMY, I CARRY AT LEAST THIS MANY DIRTY DISHES OUT OF YOUR ROOM EVERY SATURDAY!
WOW!
THIS IS NOT ACCEPTABLE!
I TOTALLY AGREE.
WOULD IT HELP IF YOU CAME ON WEDNESDAYS, TOO?

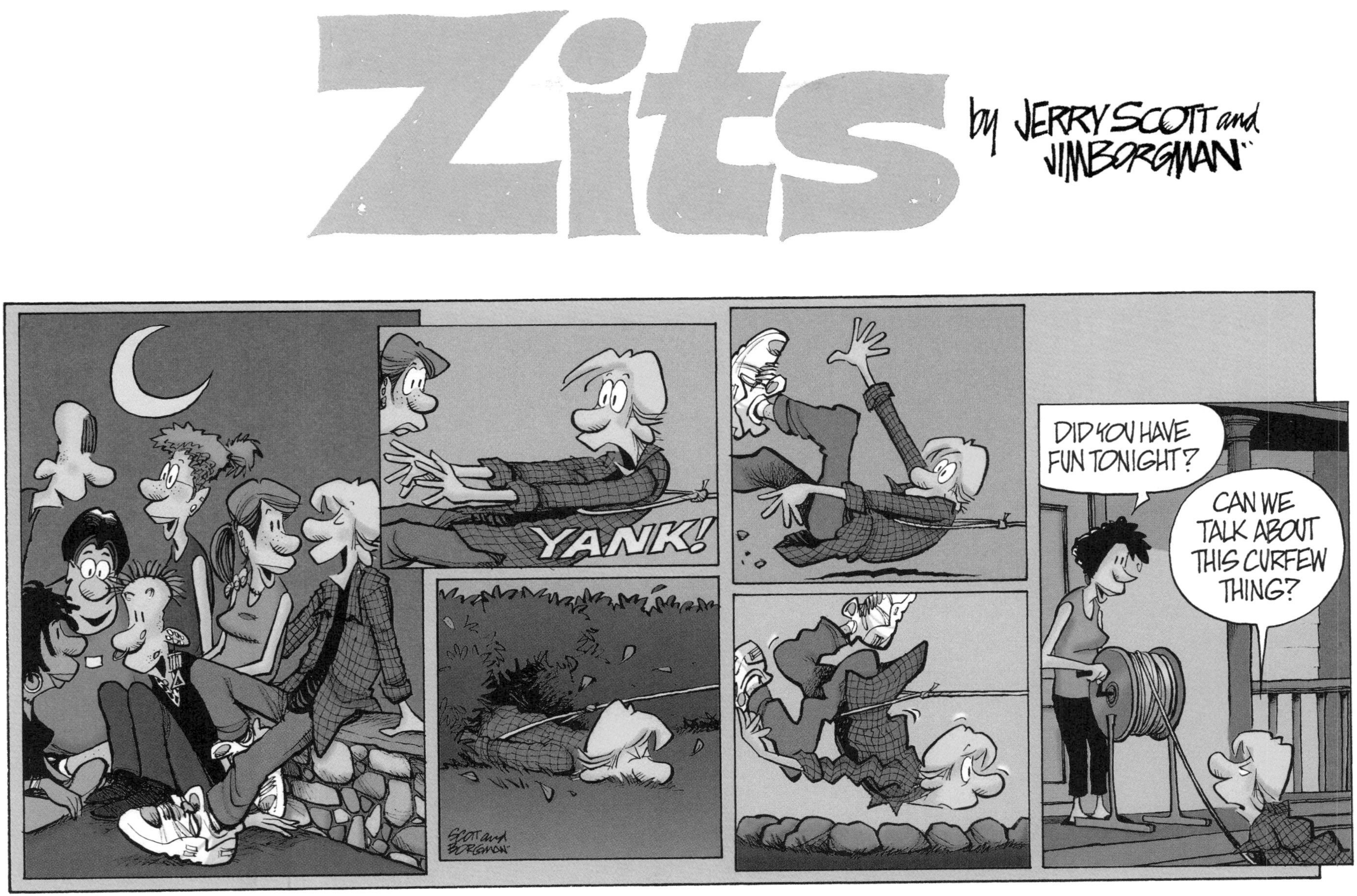
Zits
by JERRY SCOTT and JIM BORGMAN
YANK!
SCOTT and BORGMAN
DID YOU HAVE FUN TONIGHT?
CAN WE TALK ABOUT THIS CURFEW THING?

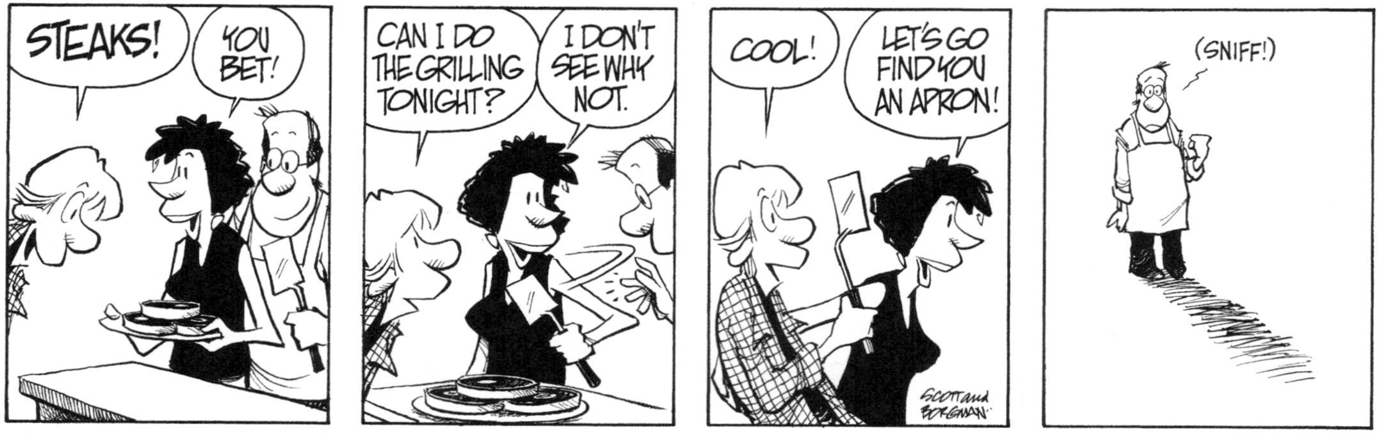
STEAKS!
YOU BET!
CAN I DO THE GRILLING TONIGHT?
I DON'T SEE WHY NOT.
COOL!
LET'S GO FIND YOU AN APRON!
SCOTT and BORGMAN
(SNIFF!)

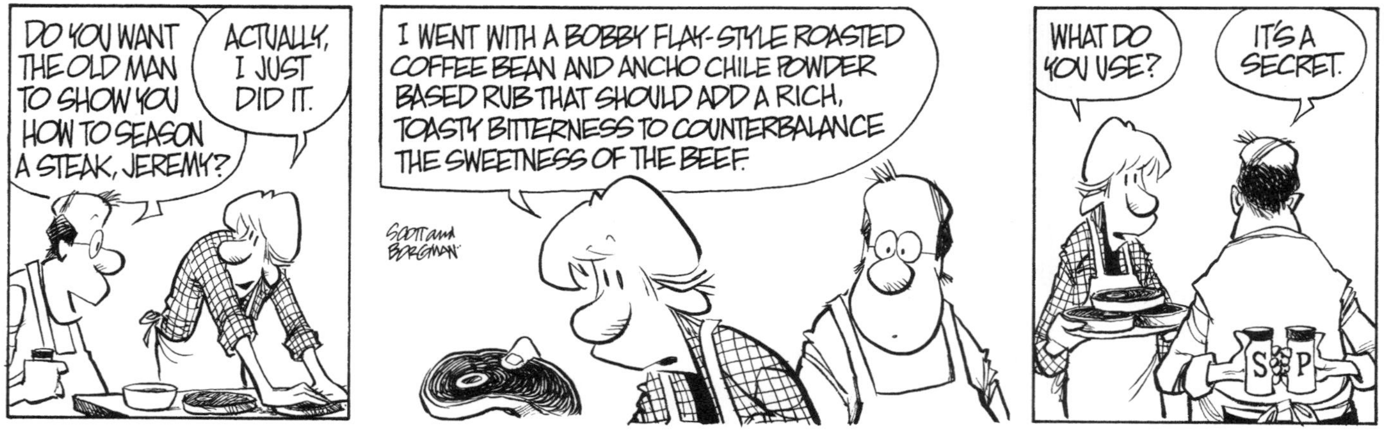
DO YOU WANT THE OLD MAN TO SHOW YOU HOW TO SEASON A STEAK, JEREMY?
ACTUALLY, I JUST DID IT.
I WENT WITH A BOBBY FLAY-STYLE ROASTED COFFEE BEAN AND ANCHO CHILE POWDER BASED RUB THAT SHOULD ADD A RICH, TOASTY BITTERNESS TO COUNTERBALANCE THE SWEETNESS OF THE BEEF.
SCOTT and BORGMAN
WHAT DO YOU USE?
IT'S A SECRET.
S
P

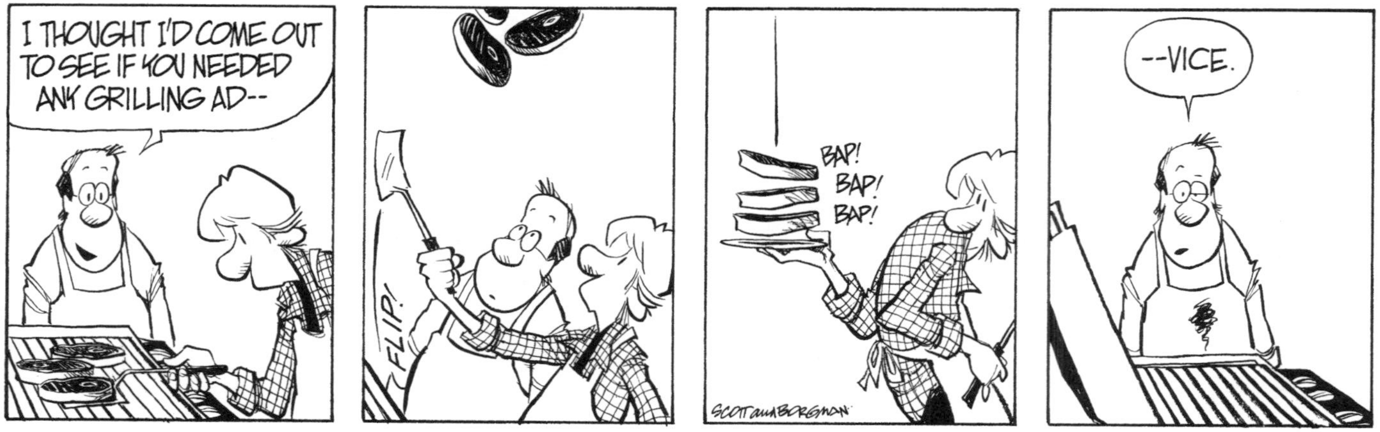
I THOUGHT I'D COME OUT TO SEE IF YOU NEEDED ANY GRILLING AD--
FLIP!
BAP! BAP! BAP!
SCOTT and BORGMAN
--VICE.

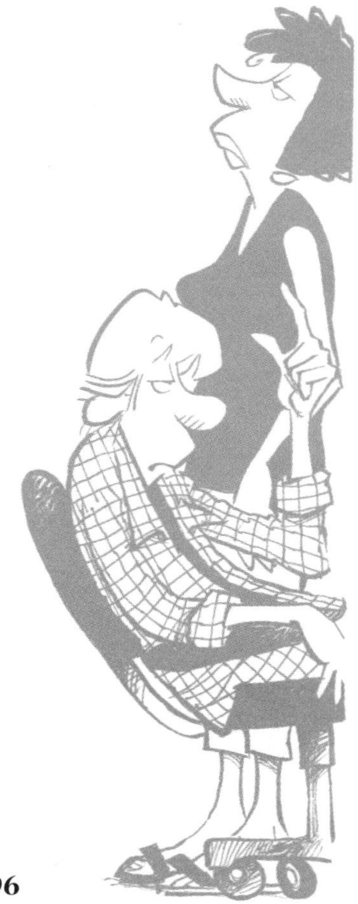

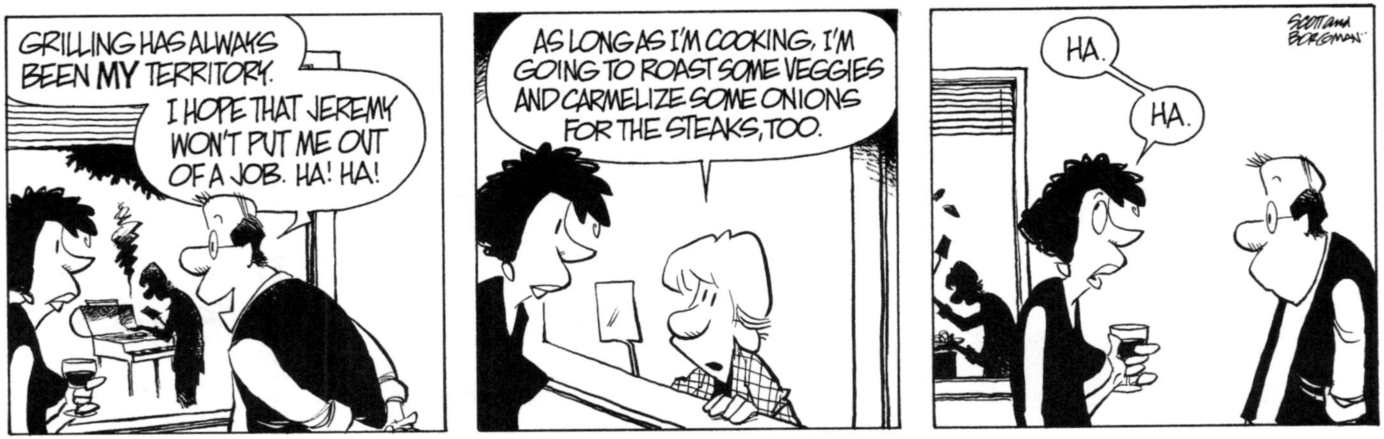
GRILLING HAS ALWAYS BEEN **MY** TERRITORY.
I HOPE THAT JEREMY WON'T PUT ME OUT OF A JOB. HA! HA!
AS LONG AS I'M COOKING, I'M GOING TO ROAST SOME VEGGIES AND CARMELIZE SOME ONIONS FOR THE STEAKS, TOO.
HA.
HA.

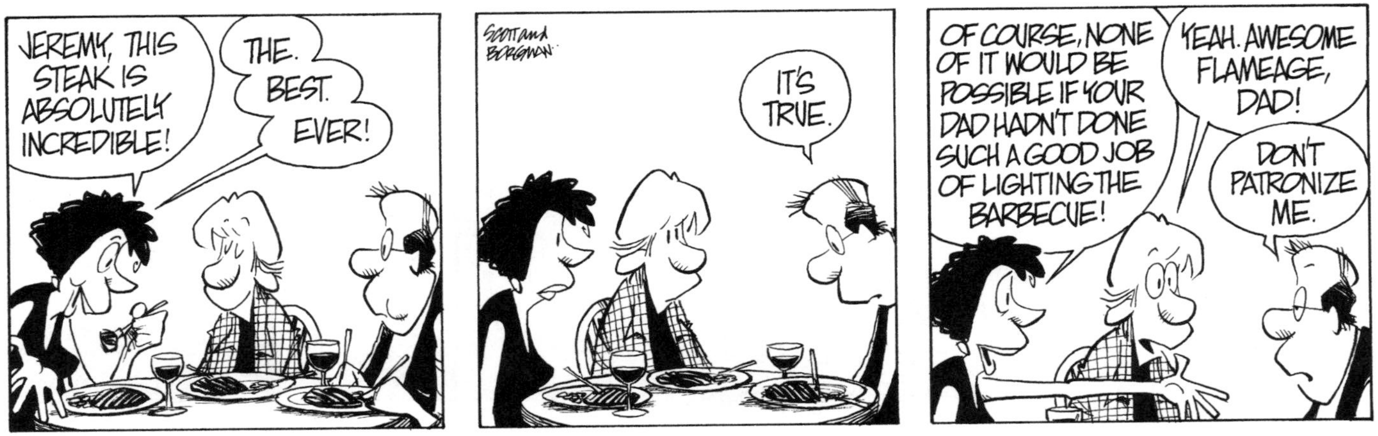
JEREMY, THIS STEAK IS ABSOLUTELY INCREDIBLE!
THE. BEST. EVER!
IT'S TRUE.
OF COURSE, NONE OF IT WOULD BE POSSIBLE IF YOUR DAD HADN'T DONE SUCH A GOOD JOB OF LIGHTING THE BARBECUE!
YEAH. AWESOME FLAMEAGE, DAD!
DON'T PATRONIZE ME.

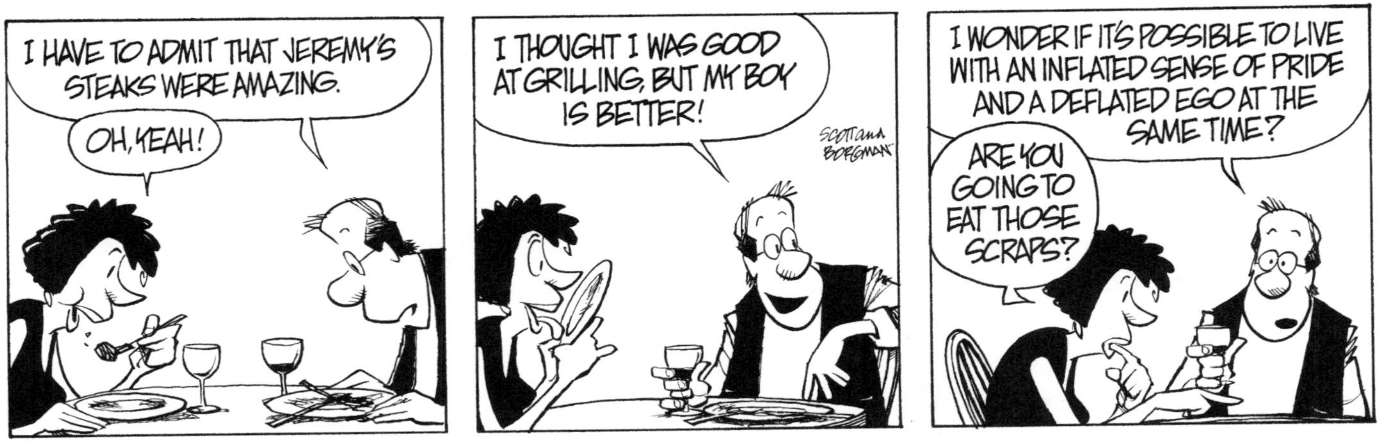
I HAVE TO ADMIT THAT JEREMY'S STEAKS WERE AMAZING.
OH, YEAH!
I THOUGHT I WAS GOOD AT GRILLING, BUT MY BOY IS BETTER!
I WONDER IF IT'S POSSIBLE TO LIVE WITH AN INFLATED SENSE OF PRIDE AND A DEFLATED EGO AT THE SAME TIME?
ARE YOU GOING TO EAT THOSE SCRAPS?

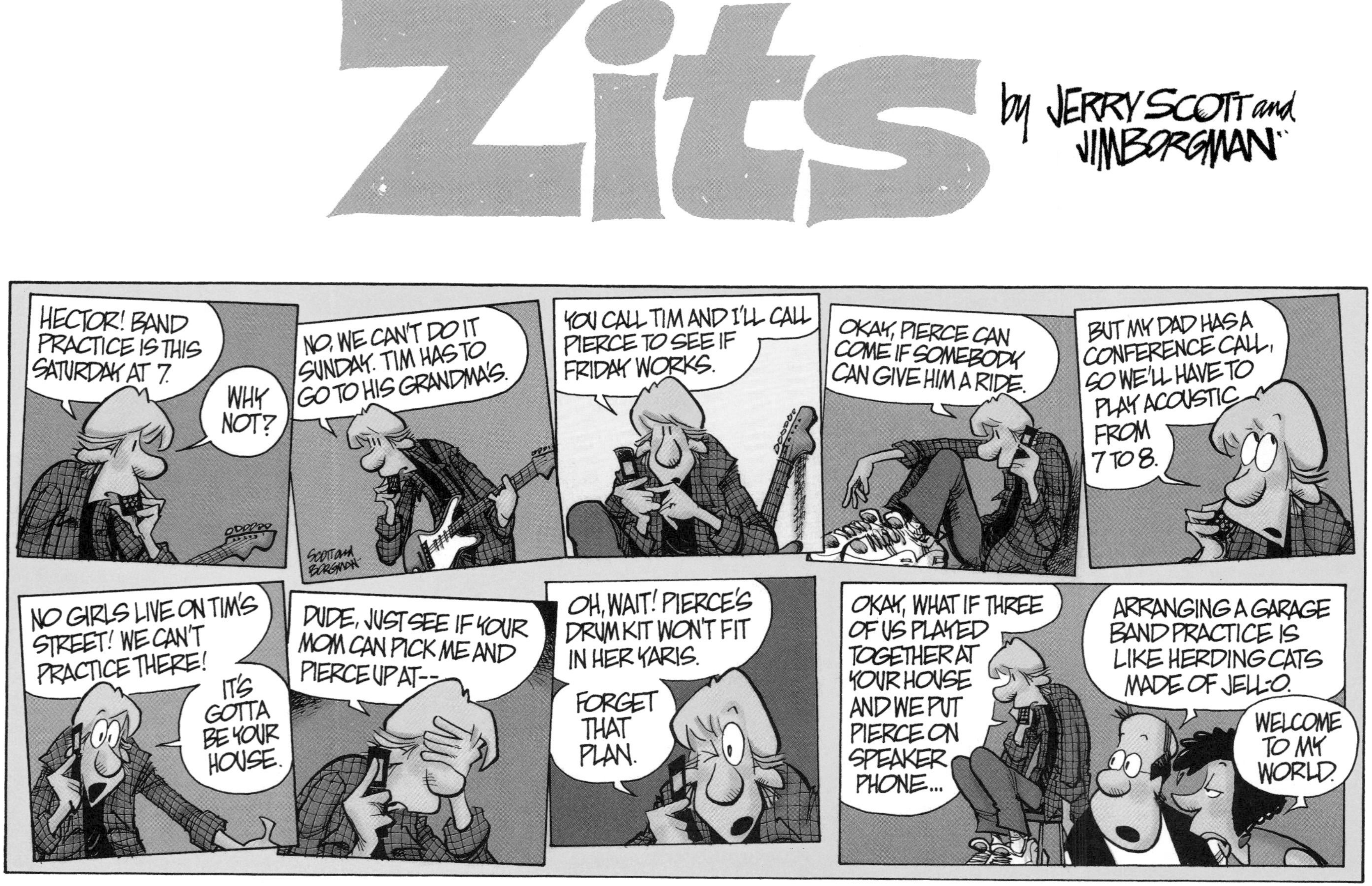
Zits
by JERRY SCOTT and JIM BORGMAN
HECTOR! BAND PRACTICE IS THIS SATURDAY AT 7.
WHY NOT?
NO, WE CAN'T DO IT SUNDAY. TIM HAS TO GO TO HIS GRANDMA'S.
SCOTT and BORGMAN
YOU CALL TIM AND I'LL CALL PIERCE TO SEE IF FRIDAY WORKS.
OKAY, PIERCE CAN COME IF SOMEBODY CAN GIVE HIM A RIDE.
BUT MY DAD HAS A CONFERENCE CALL, SO WE'LL HAVE TO PLAY ACOUSTIC FROM 7 TO 8.
NO GIRLS LIVE ON TIM'S STREET! WE CAN'T PRACTICE THERE!
IT'S GOTTA BE YOUR HOUSE.
DUDE, JUST SEE IF YOUR MOM CAN PICK ME AND PIERCE UP AT--
OH, WAIT! PIERCE'S DRUM KIT WON'T FIT IN HER YARIS.
FORGET THAT PLAN.
OKAY, WHAT IF THREE OF US PLAYED TOGETHER AT YOUR HOUSE AND WE PUT PIERCE ON SPEAKER PHONE...
ARRANGING A GARAGE BAND PRACTICE IS LIKE HERDING CATS MADE OF JELL-O.
WELCOME TO MY WORLD.

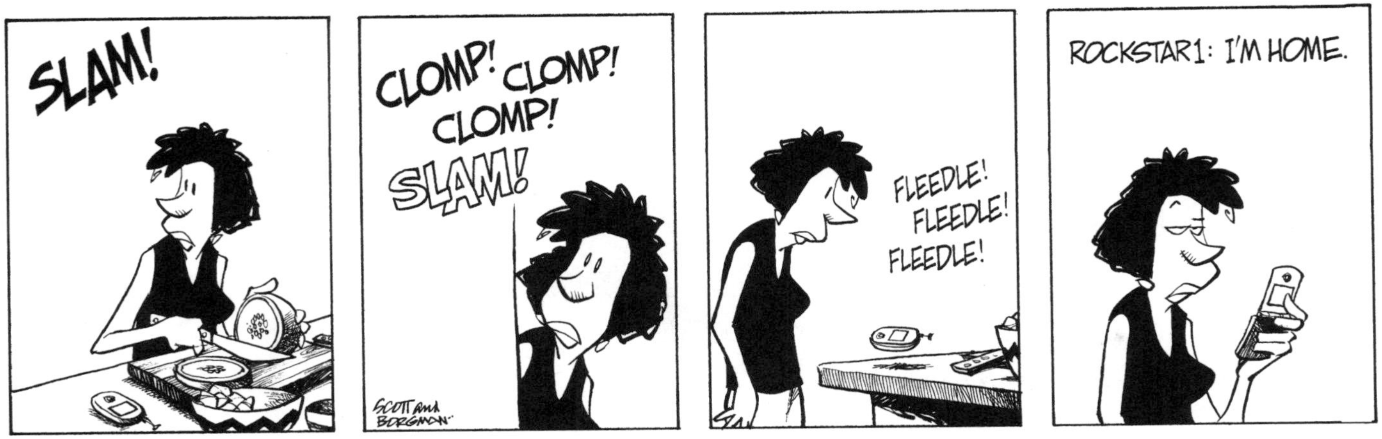
SLAM!
CLOMP! CLOMP!
CLOMP!
SLAM!
SCOTT and BORGMAN
FLEEDLE!
FLEEDLE!
FLEEDLE!
ROCKSTAR1: I'M HOME.

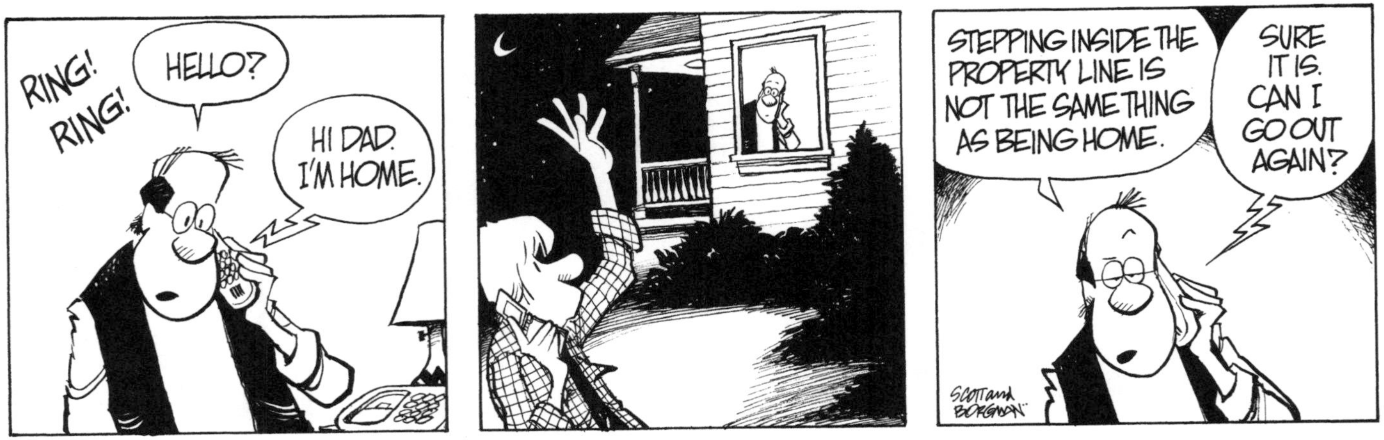
RING!
RING!
HELLO?
HI DAD. I'M HOME.
STEPPING INSIDE THE PROPERTY LINE IS NOT THE SAME THING AS BEING HOME.
SURE IT IS. CAN I GO OUT AGAIN?
SCOTT and BORGMAN

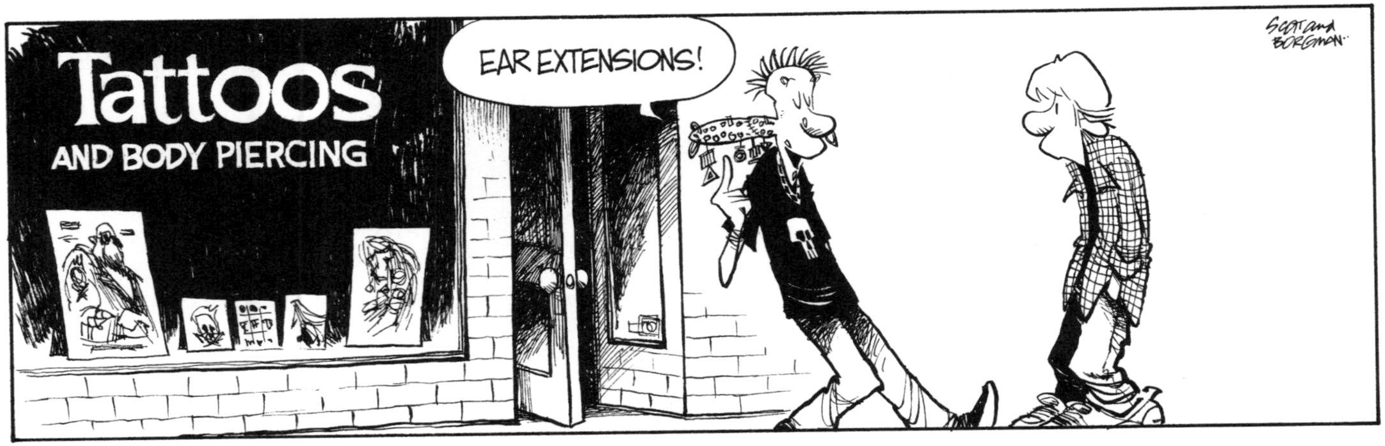
Tattoos
AND BODY PIERCING
EAR EXTENSIONS!
SCOTT and BORGMAN

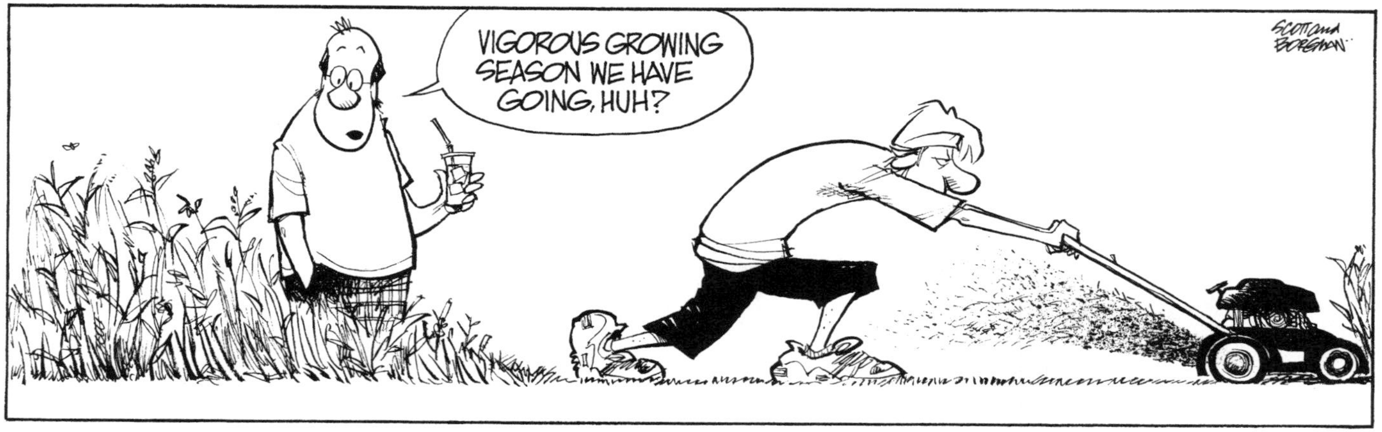
VIGOROUS GROWING SEASON WE HAVE GOING, HUH?

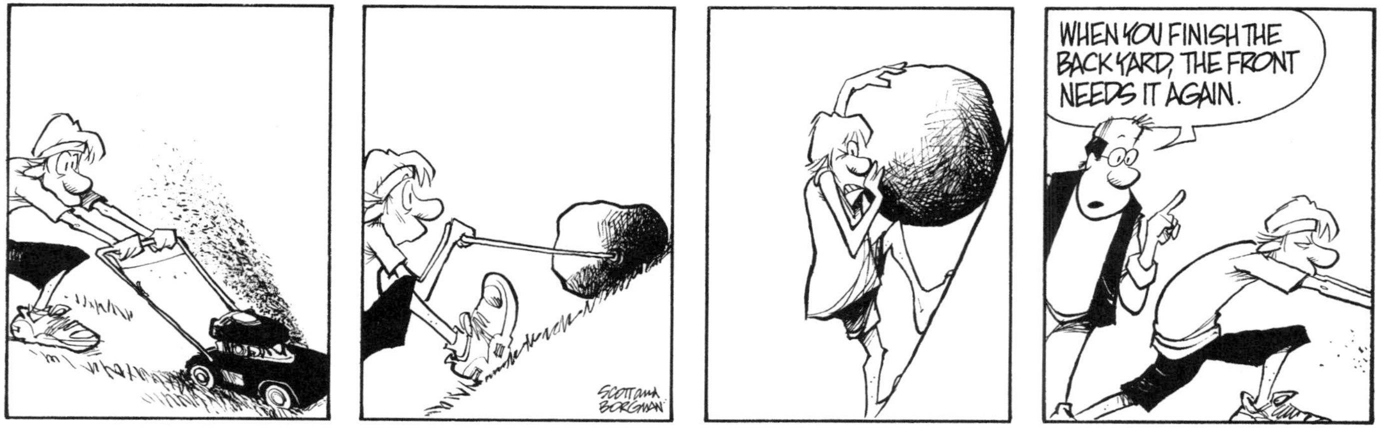
WHEN YOU FINISH THE BACK YARD, THE FRONT NEEDS IT AGAIN.

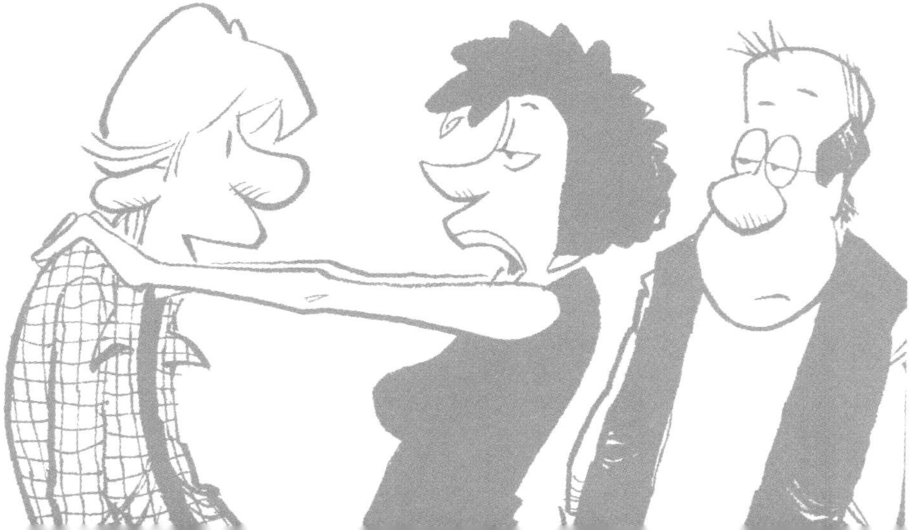

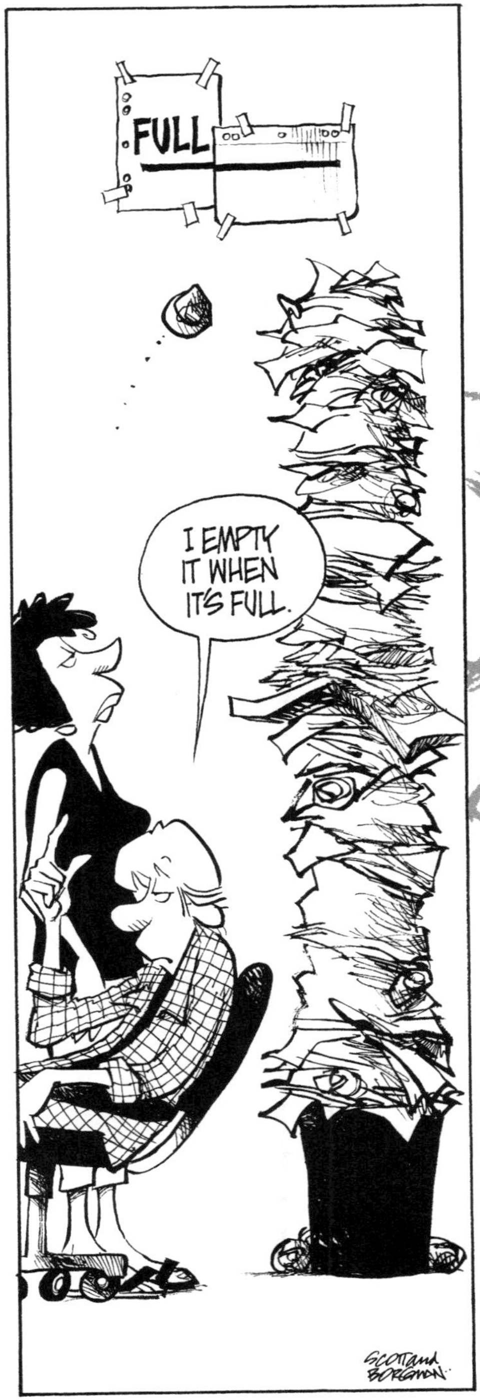
FULL
I EMPTY IT WHEN IT'S FULL.

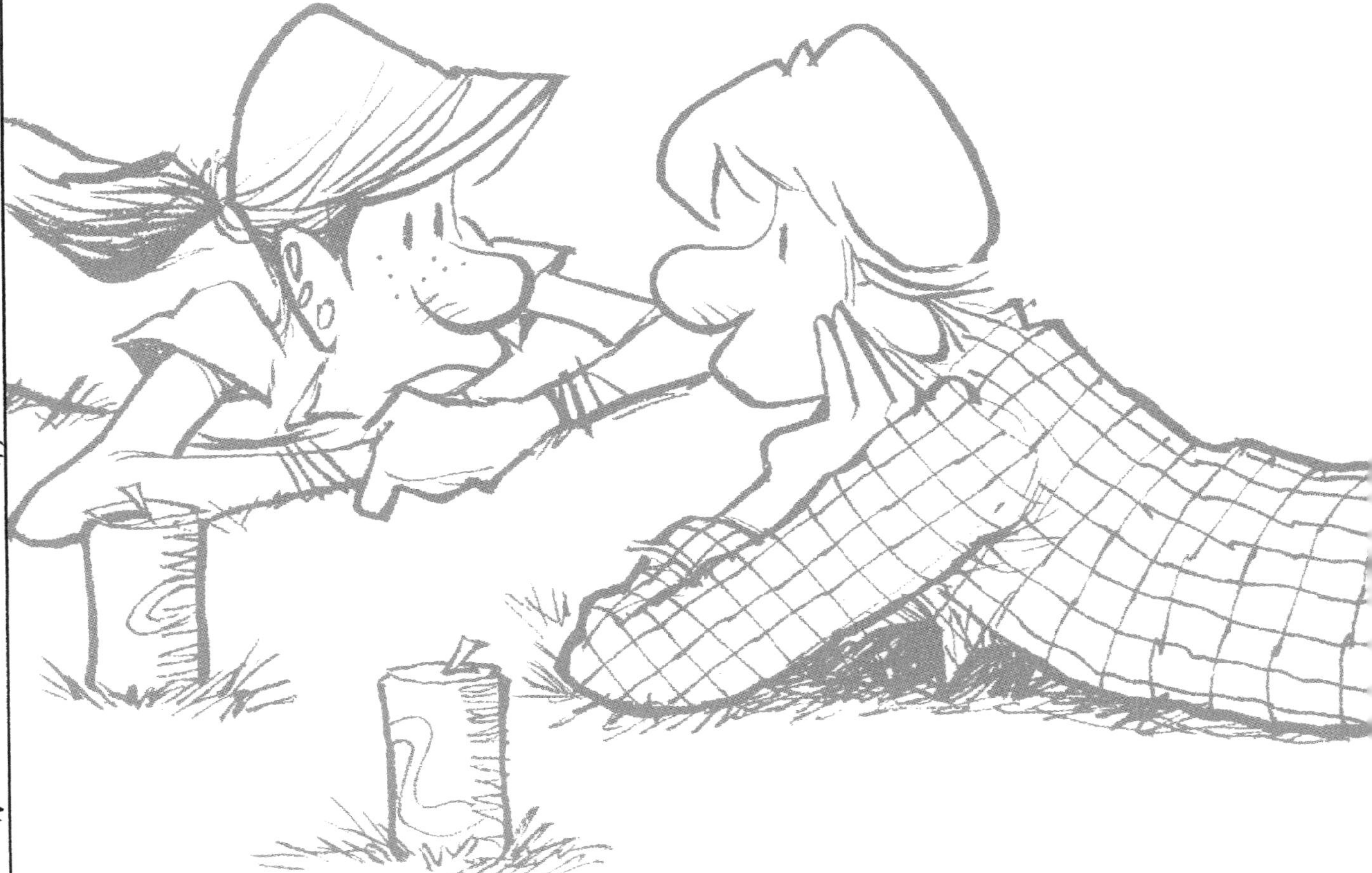

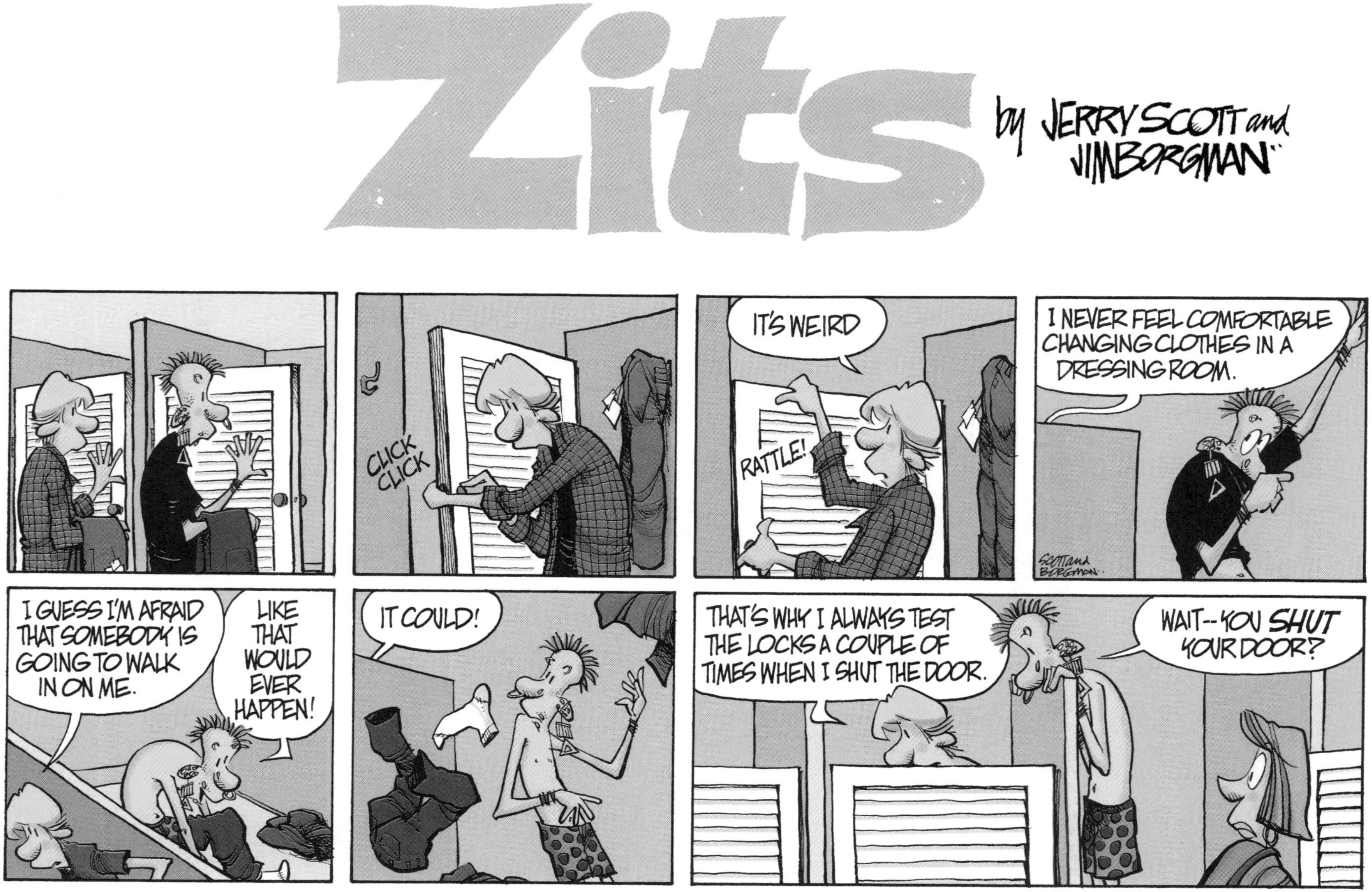
Zits
by JERRY SCOTT and JIM BORGMAN
CLICK CLICK
IT'S WEIRD
RATTLE!
I NEVER FEEL COMFORTABLE CHANGING CLOTHES IN A DRESSING ROOM.
SCOTT and BORGMAN
I GUESS I'M AFRAID THAT SOMEBODY IS GOING TO WALK IN ON ME.
LIKE THAT WOULD EVER HAPPEN!
IT COULD!
THAT'S WHY I ALWAYS TEST THE LOCKS A COUPLE OF TIMES WHEN I SHUT THE DOOR.
WAIT--YOU SHUT YOUR DOOR?

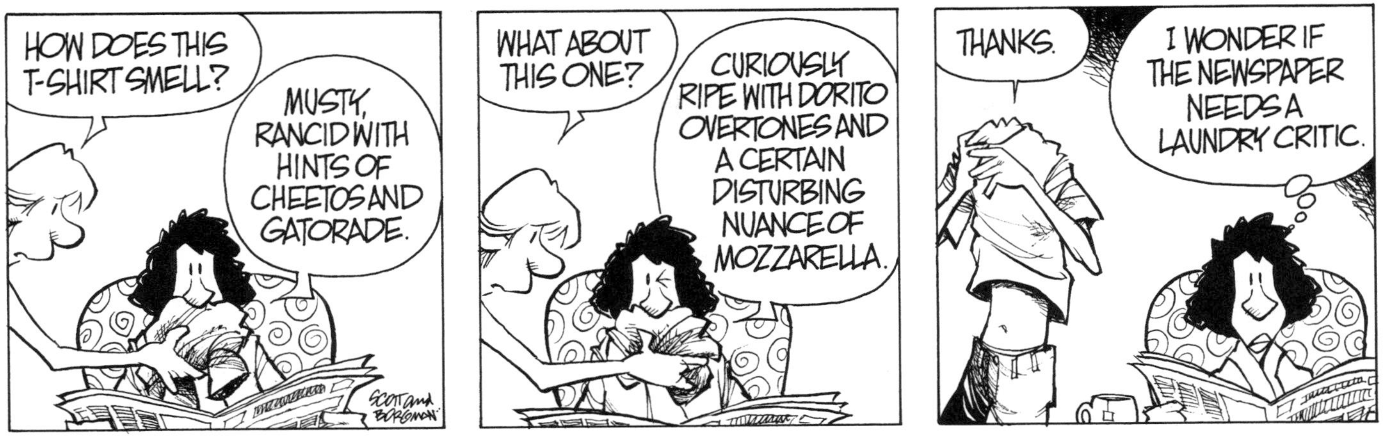
HOW DOES THIS T-SHIRT SMELL?
MUSTY, RANCID WITH HINTS OF CHEETOS AND GATORADE.
WHAT ABOUT THIS ONE?
CURIOUSLY RIPE WITH DORITO OVERTONES AND A CERTAIN DISTURBING NUANCE OF MOZZARELLA.
THANKS.
I WONDER IF THE NEWSPAPER NEEDS A LAUNDRY CRITIC.

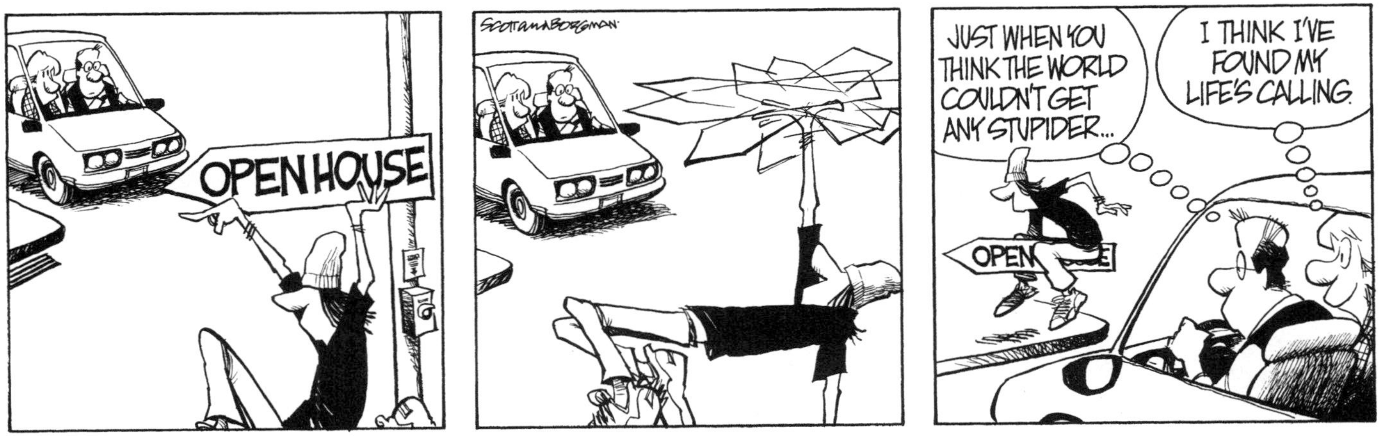
OPEN HOUSE
JUST WHEN YOU THINK THE WORLD COULDN'T GET ANY STUPIDER...
I THINK I'VE FOUND MY LIFE'S CALLING.

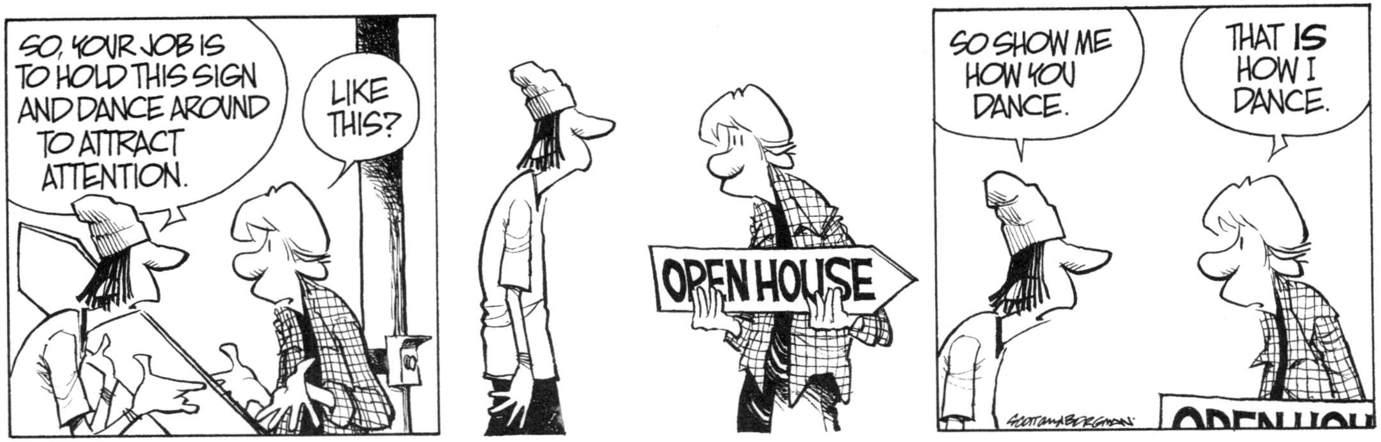
SO, YOUR JOB IS TO HOLD THIS SIGN AND DANCE AROUND TO ATTRACT ATTENTION.
LIKE THIS?
OPEN HOUSE
SO SHOW ME HOW YOU DANCE.
THAT **IS** HOW I DANCE.

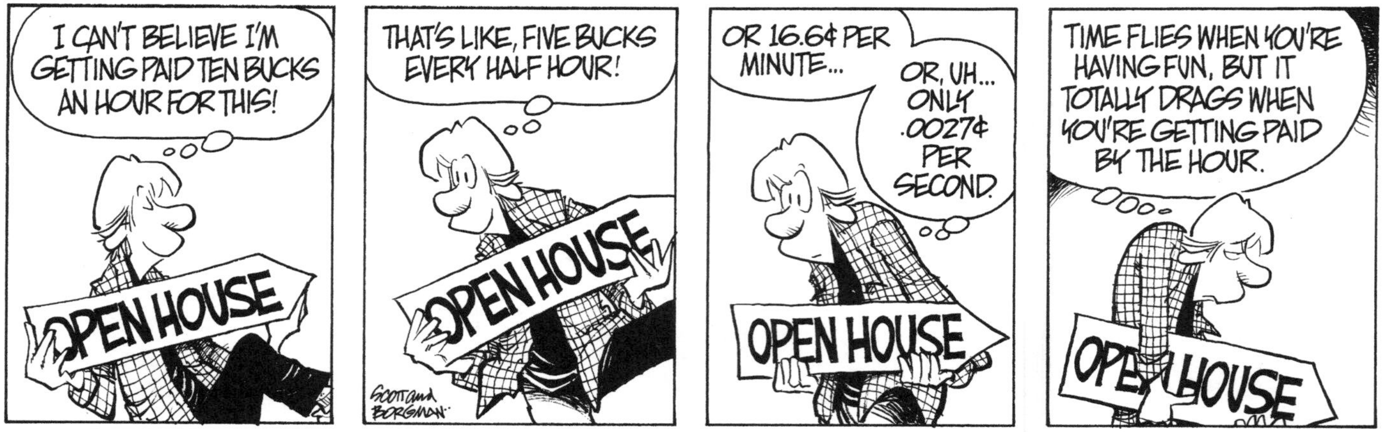
I CAN'T BELIEVE I'M GETTING PAID TEN BUCKS AN HOUR FOR THIS!
OPEN HOUSE
THAT'S LIKE, FIVE BUCKS EVERY HALF HOUR!
OPEN HOUSE
OR 16.6¢ PER MINUTE...
OR, UH... ONLY .0027¢ PER SECOND.
OPEN HOUSE
TIME FLIES WHEN YOU'RE HAVING FUN, BUT IT TOTALLY DRAGS WHEN YOU'RE GETTING PAID BY THE HOUR.
OPEN HOUSE

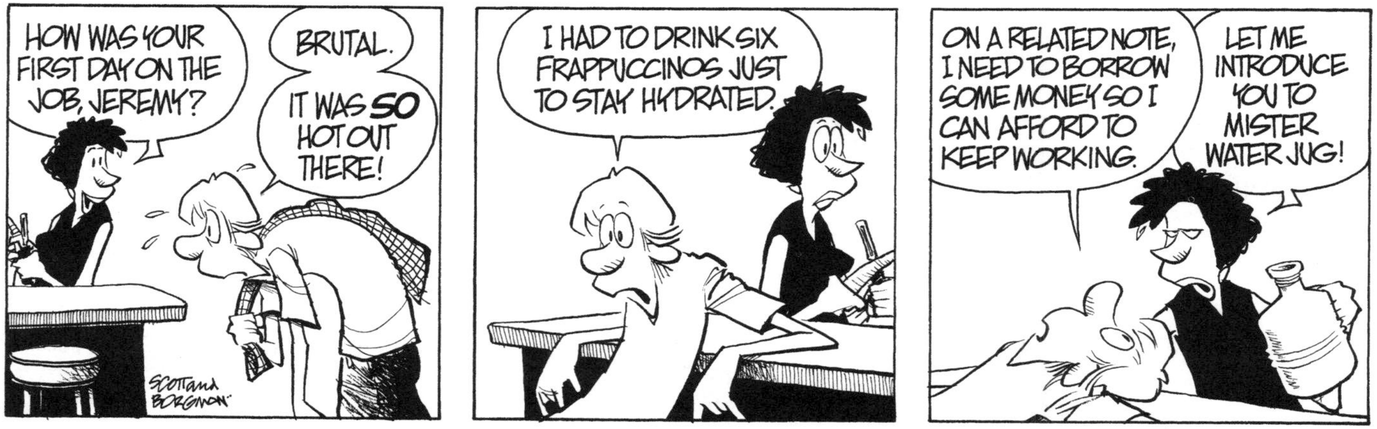
HOW WAS YOUR FIRST DAY ON THE JOB, JEREMY?
BRUTAL.
IT WAS **SO** HOT OUT THERE!
I HAD TO DRINK SIX FRAPPUCCINOS JUST TO STAY HYDRATED.
ON A RELATED NOTE, I NEED TO BORROW SOME MONEY SO I CAN AFFORD TO KEEP WORKING.
LET ME INTRODUCE YOU TO MISTER WATER JUG!

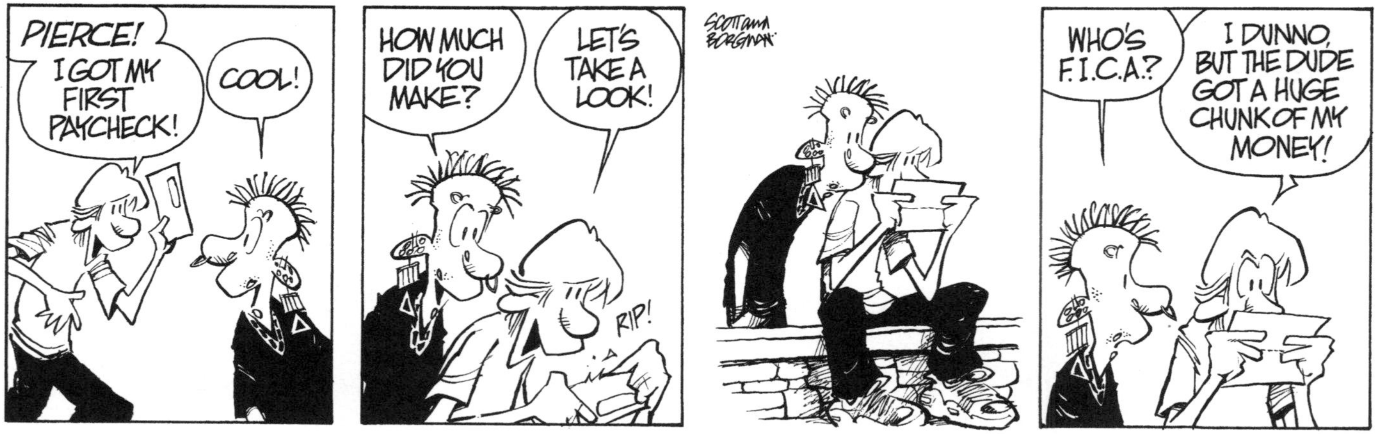
PIERCE! I GOT MY FIRST PAYCHECK!
COOL!
HOW MUCH DID YOU MAKE?
LET'S TAKE A LOOK!
RIP!
WHO'S F.I.C.A.?
I DUNNO, BUT THE DUDE GOT A HUGE CHUNK OF MY MONEY!

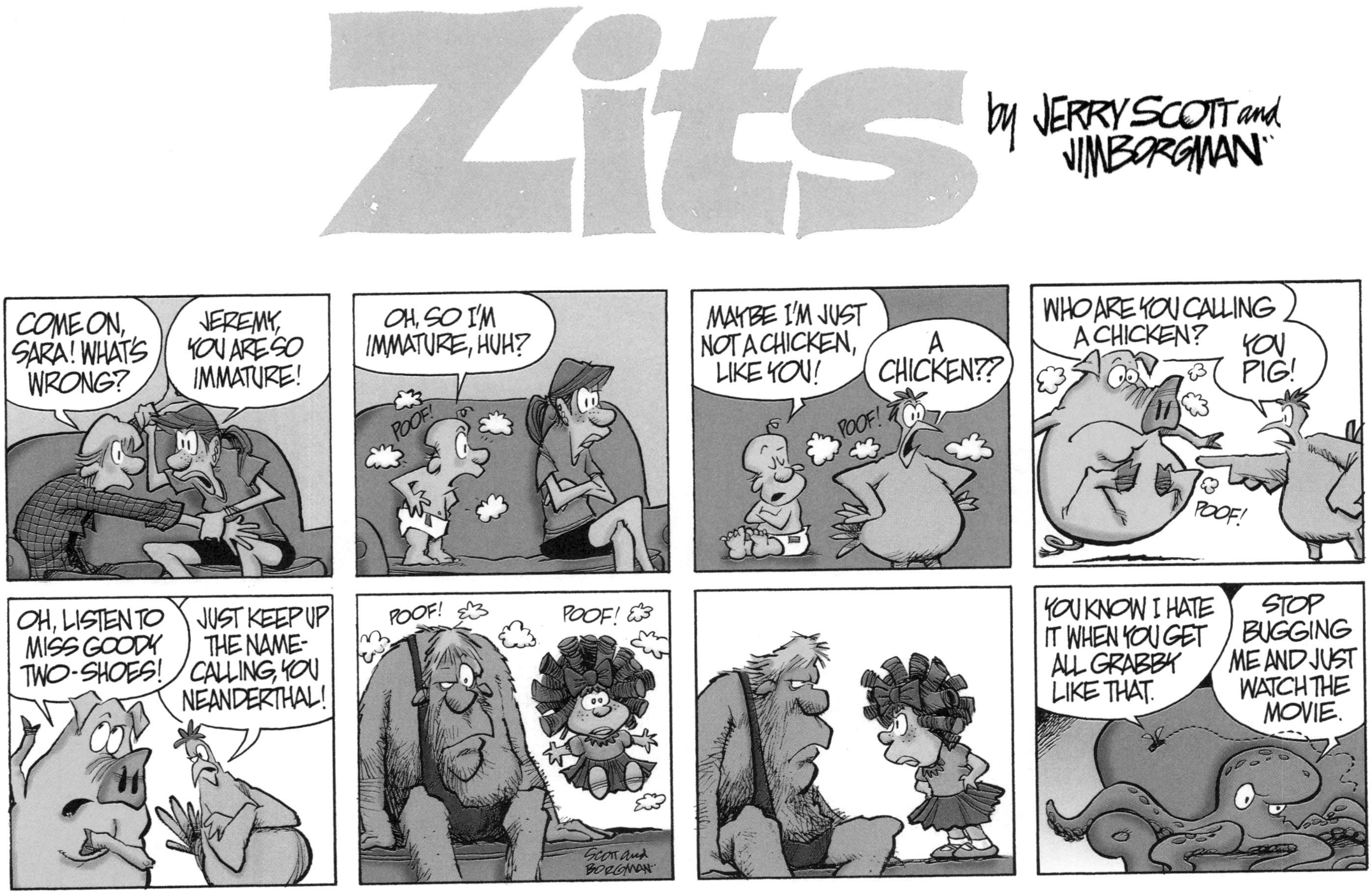
Zits
by JERRY SCOTT and JIM BORGMAN
COME ON, SARA! WHAT'S WRONG?
JEREMY, YOU ARE SO IMMATURE!
POOF!
OH, SO I'M IMMATURE, HUH?
MAYBE I'M JUST NOT A CHICKEN, LIKE YOU!
POOF!
A CHICKEN??
WHO ARE YOU CALLING A CHICKEN?
YOU PIG!
POOF!
OH, LISTEN TO MISS GOODY TWO-SHOES!
JUST KEEP UP THE NAME-CALLING, YOU NEANDERTHAL!
POOF!
POOF!
SCOTT and BORGMAN
YOU KNOW I HATE IT WHEN YOU GET ALL GRABBY LIKE THAT.
STOP BUGGING ME AND JUST WATCH THE MOVIE.

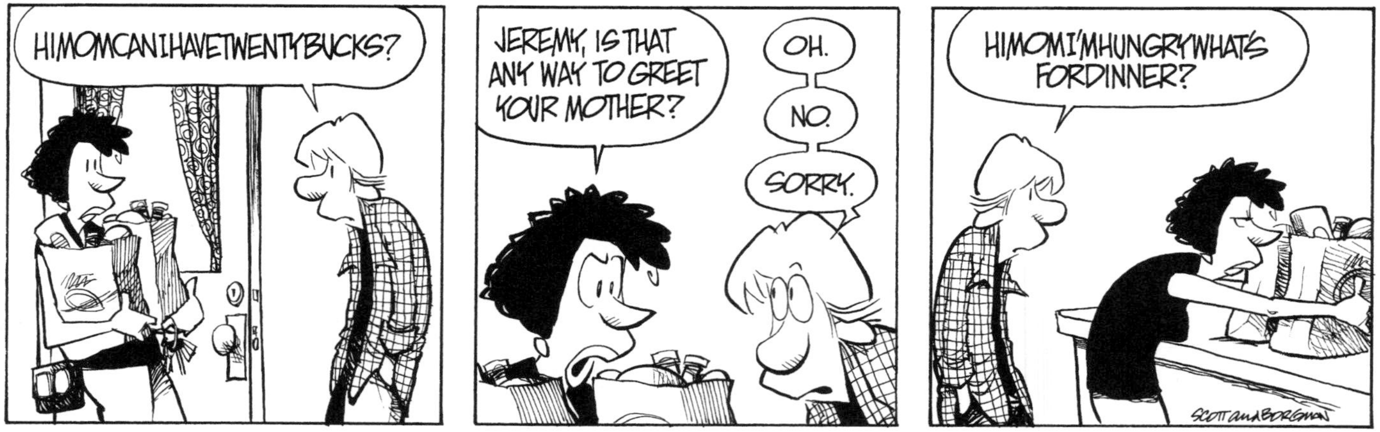
HIMOMCANIHAVETWENTYBUCKS?
JEREMY, IS THAT ANY WAY TO GREET YOUR MOTHER?
OH.
NO.
SORRY.
HIMOMI'MHUNGRYWHAT'S FORDINNER?

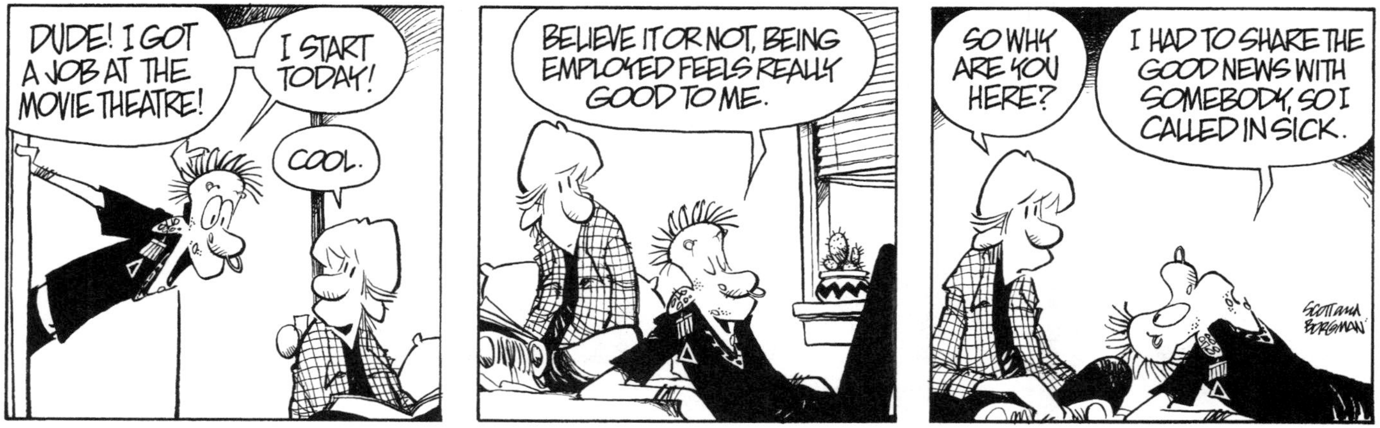
DUDE! I GOT A JOB AT THE MOVIE THEATRE!
I START TODAY!
COOL.
BELIEVE IT OR NOT, BEING EMPLOYED FEELS REALLY GOOD TO ME.
SO WHY ARE YOU HERE?
I HAD TO SHARE THE GOOD NEWS WITH SOMEBODY, SO I CALLED IN SICK.

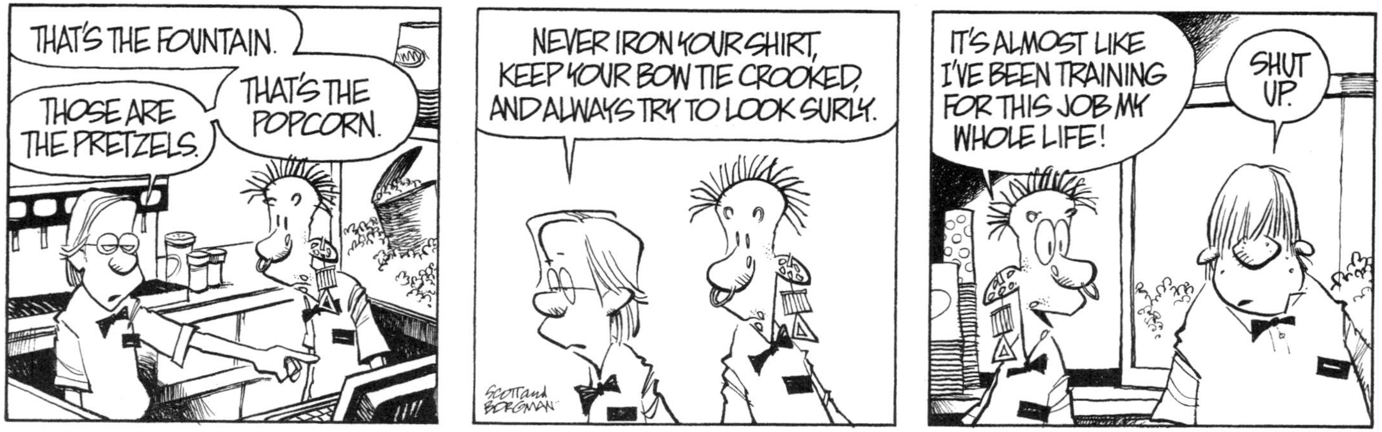
THAT'S THE FOUNTAIN.
THOSE ARE THE PRETZELS.
THAT'S THE POPCORN.
NEVER IRON YOUR SHIRT, KEEP YOUR BOW TIE CROOKED, AND ALWAYS TRY TO LOOK SURLY.
IT'S ALMOST LIKE I'VE BEEN TRAINING FOR THIS JOB MY WHOLE LIFE!
SHUT UP.

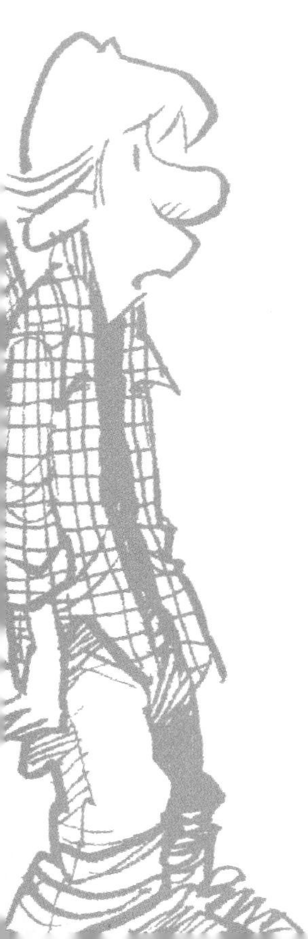

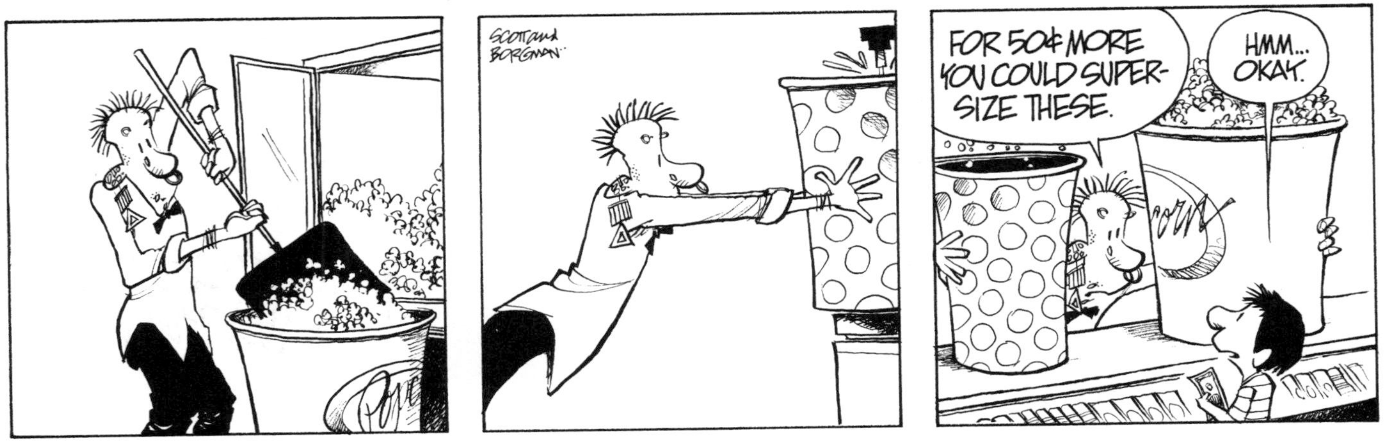
SCOTT and BORGMAN
FOR 50¢ MORE YOU COULD SUPER-SIZE THESE.
HMM... OKAY.

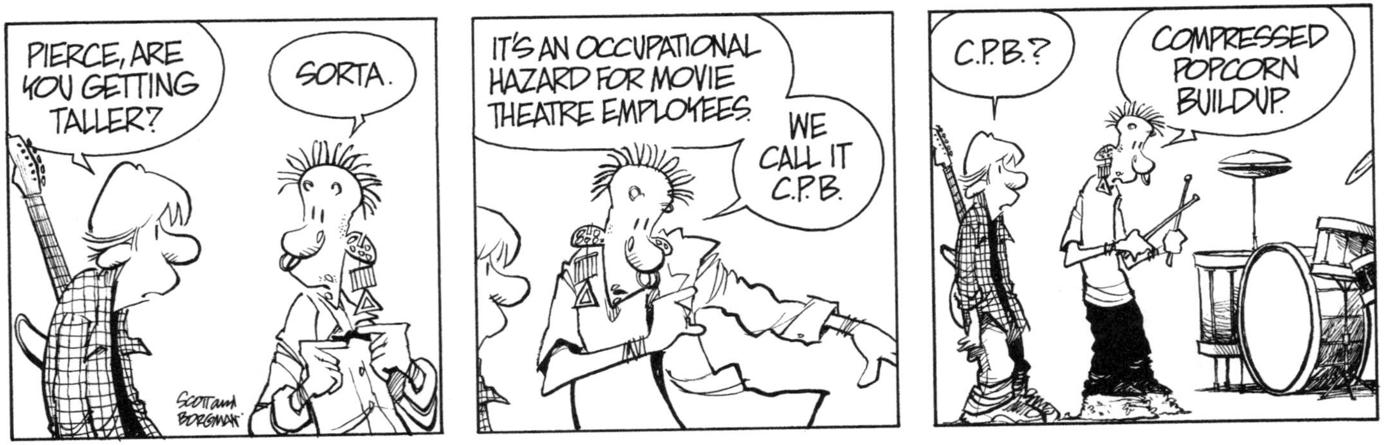
PIERCE, ARE YOU GETTING TALLER?
SORTA.
SCOTT and BORGMAN
IT'S AN OCCUPATIONAL HAZARD FOR MOVIE THEATRE EMPLOYEES.
WE CALL IT C.P.B.
C.P.B.?
COMPRESSED POPCORN BUILDUP.

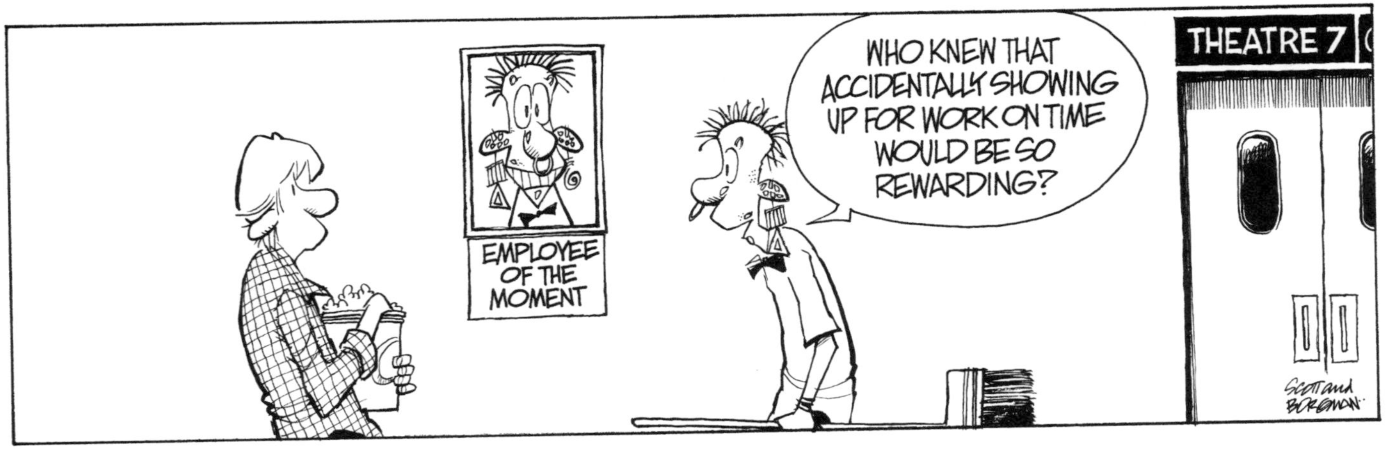
EMPLOYEE OF THE MOMENT
WHO KNEW THAT ACCIDENTALLY SHOWING UP FOR WORK ON TIME WOULD BE SO REWARDING?
THEATRE 7
SCOTT and BORGMAN

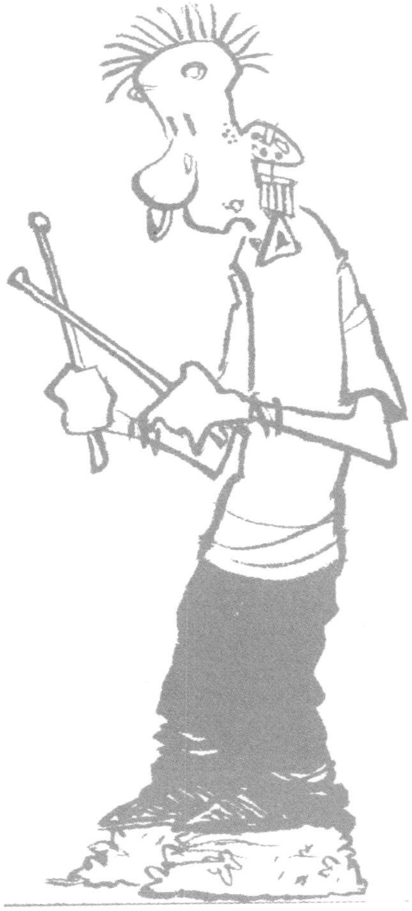

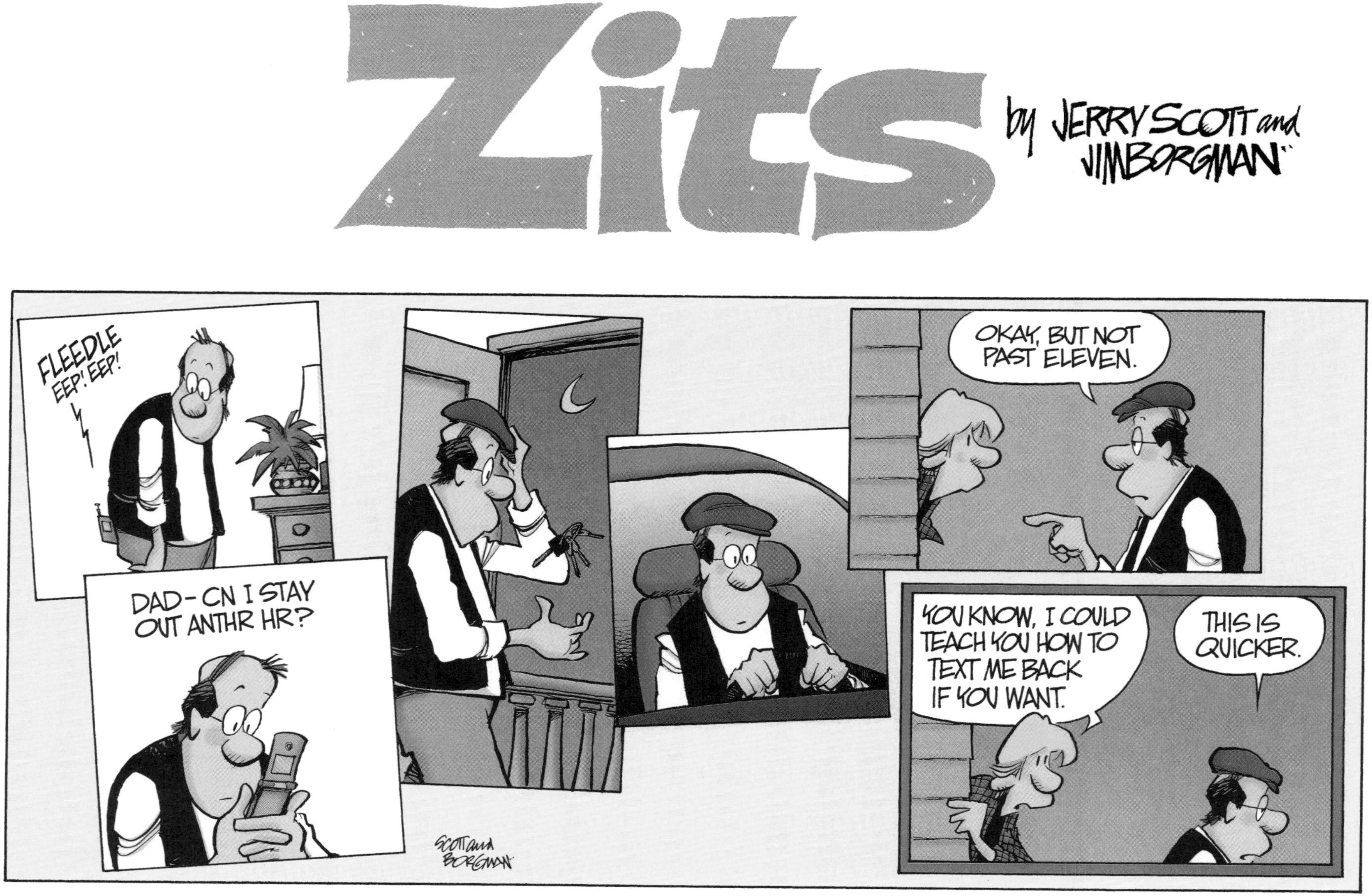
Zits
by JERRY SCOTT and JIM BORGMAN
FLEEDLE EEP! EEP!
DAD- CN I STAY OUT ANTHR HR?
OKAY, BUT NOT PAST ELEVEN.
YOU KNOW, I COULD TEACH YOU HOW TO TEXT ME BACK IF YOU WANT.
THIS IS QUICKER.
SCOTT and BORGMAN

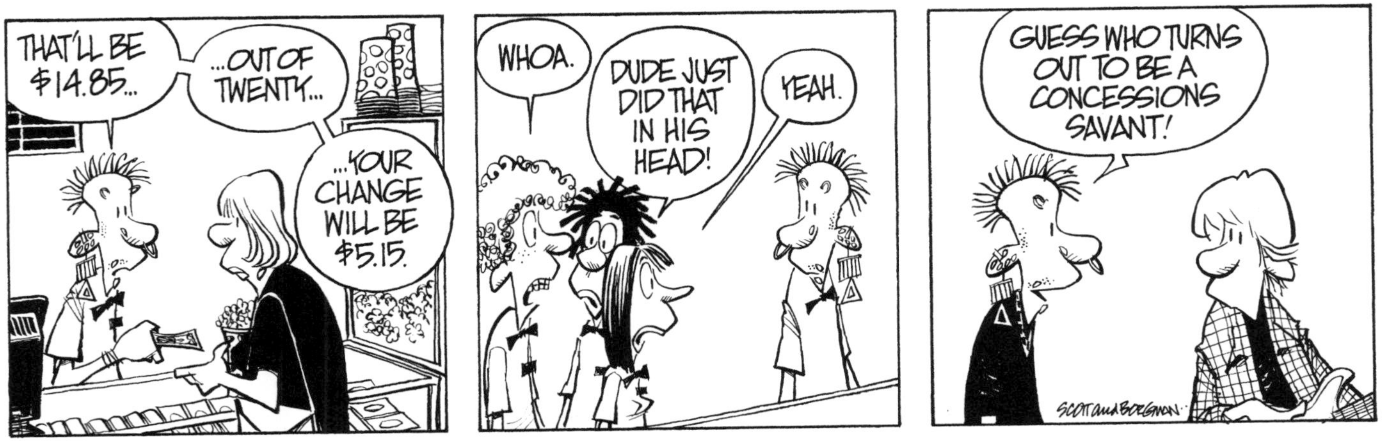
THAT'LL BE $14.85...
...OUT OF TWENTY...
...YOUR CHANGE WILL BE $5.15.
WHOA.
DUDE JUST DID THAT IN HIS HEAD!
YEAH.
GUESS WHO TURNS OUT TO BE A CONCESSIONS SAVANT!

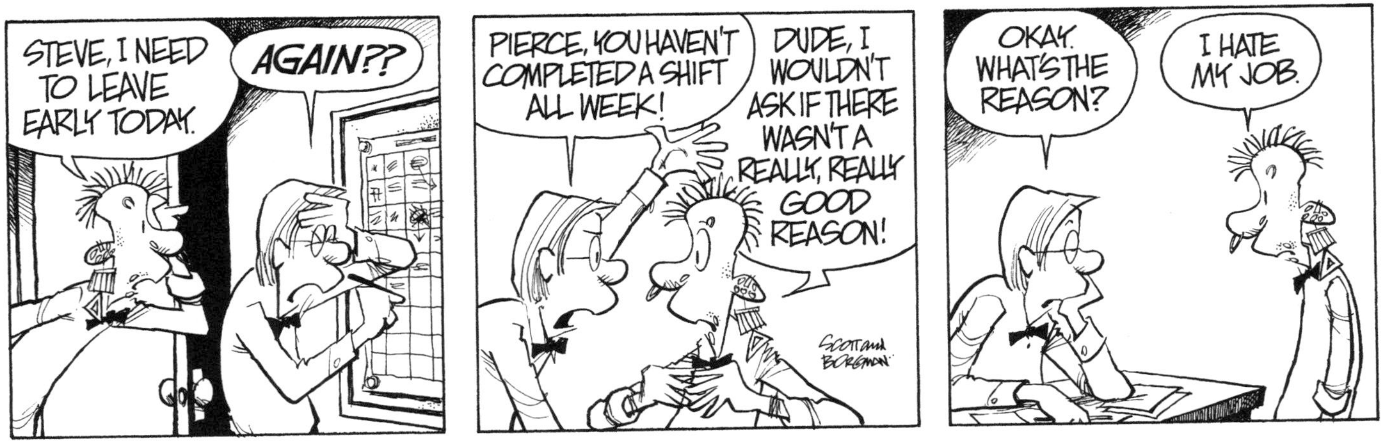
STEVE, I NEED TO LEAVE EARLY TODAY.
AGAIN??
PIERCE, YOU HAVEN'T COMPLETED A SHIFT ALL WEEK!
DUDE, I WOULDN'T ASK IF THERE WASN'T A REALLY, REALLY GOOD REASON!
OKAY. WHAT'S THE REASON?
I HATE MY JOB.

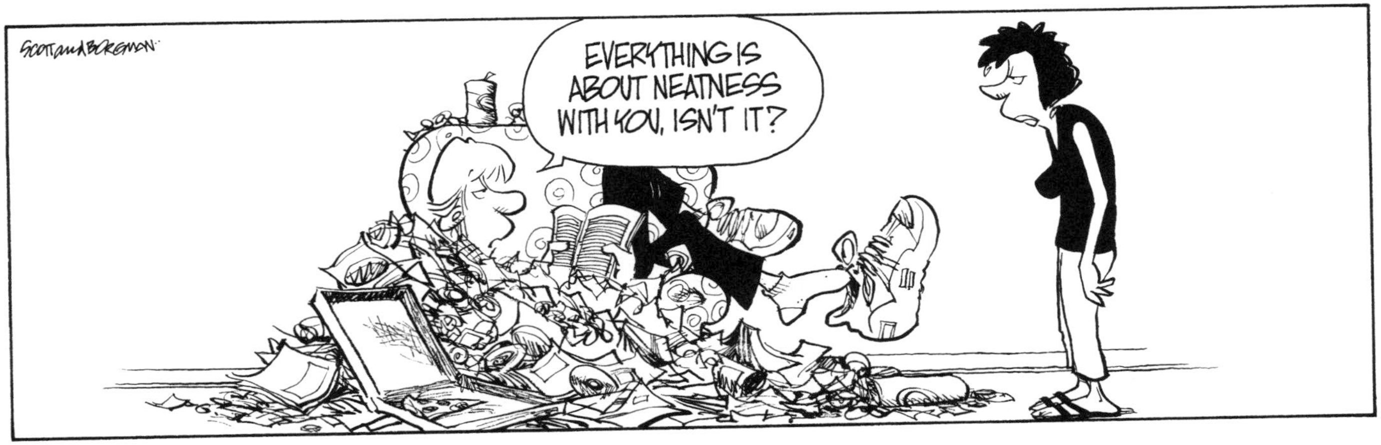
EVERYTHING IS ABOUT NEATNESS WITH YOU, ISN'T IT?

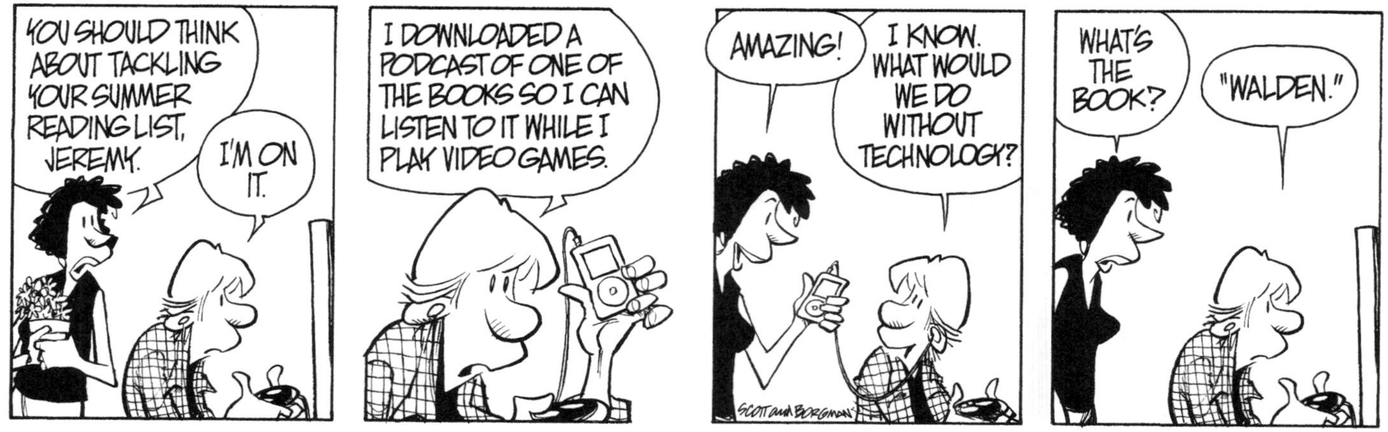
YOU SHOULD THINK ABOUT TACKLING YOUR SUMMER READING LIST, JEREMY.
I'M ON IT.
I DOWNLOADED A PODCAST OF ONE OF THE BOOKS SO I CAN LISTEN TO IT WHILE I PLAY VIDEO GAMES.
AMAZING!
I KNOW. WHAT WOULD WE DO WITHOUT TECHNOLOGY?
WHAT'S THE BOOK?
"WALDEN."

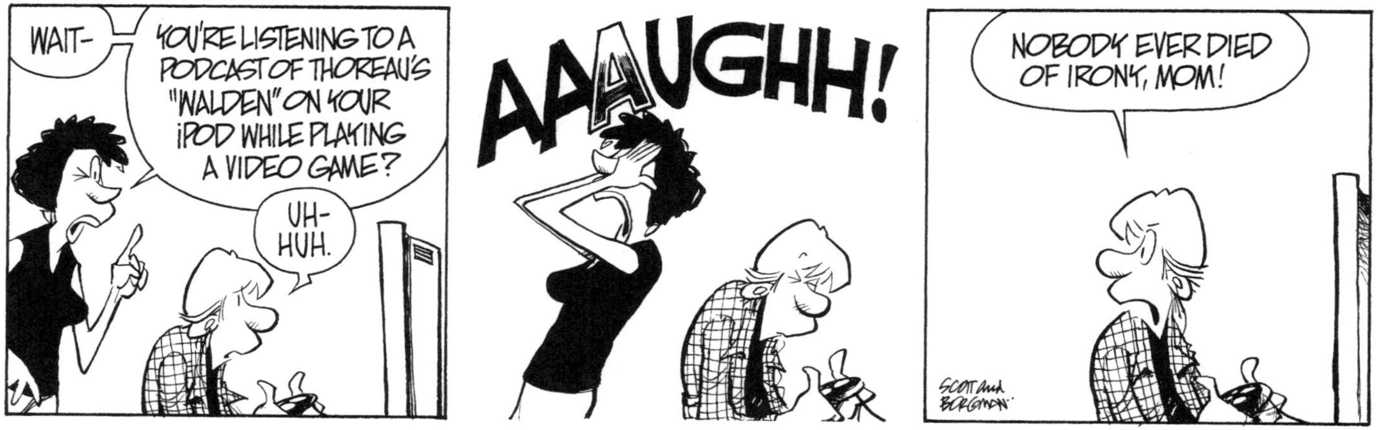
WAIT-
YOU'RE LISTENING TO A PODCAST OF THOREAU'S "WALDEN" ON YOUR iPOD WHILE PLAYING A VIDEO GAME?
UH-HUH.
AAAUGHH!
NOBODY EVER DIED OF IRONY, MOM!

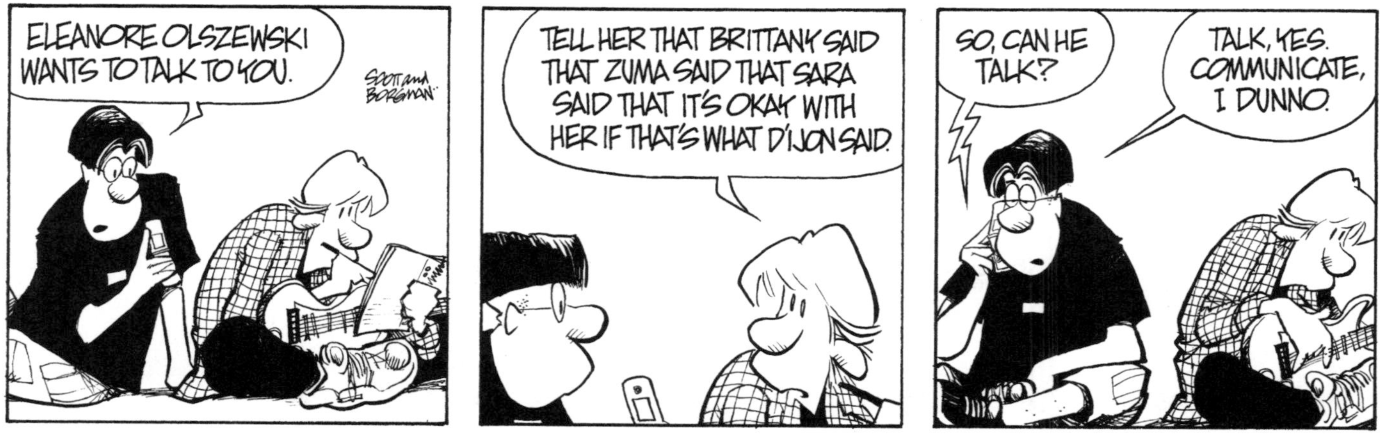
ELEANORE OLSZEWSKI WANTS TO TALK TO YOU.
TELL HER THAT BRITTANY SAID THAT ZUMA SAID THAT SARA SAID THAT IT'S OKAY WITH HER IF THAT'S WHAT D'JON SAID.
SO, CAN HE TALK?
TALK, YES. COMMUNICATE, I DUNNO.

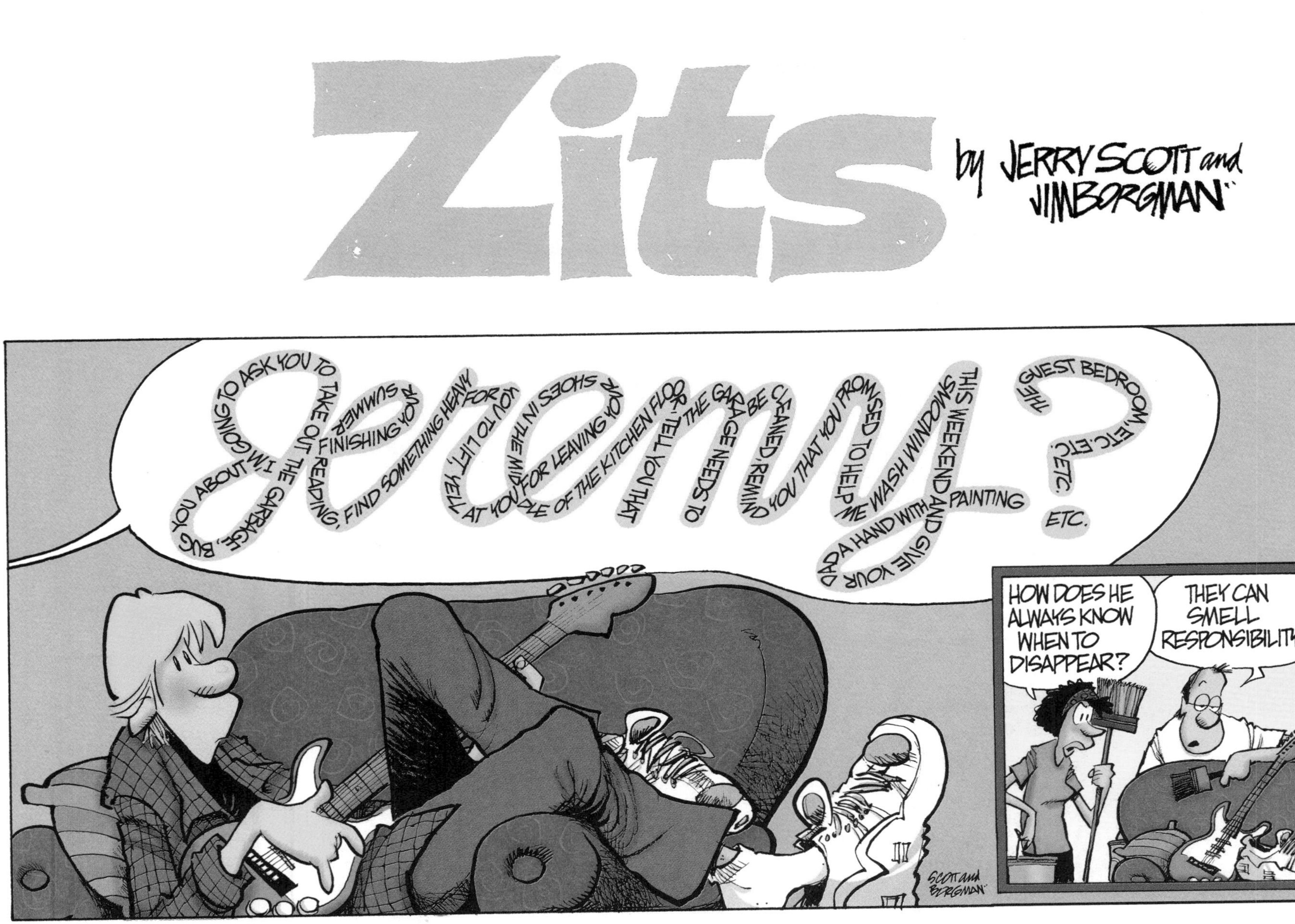
Zits
by JERRY SCOTT and JIM BORGMAN
Jeremy?
I'M GOING TO ASK YOU TO TAKE OUT THE GARBAGE, BUG YOU ABOUT FINISHING YOUR SUMMER READING, FIND SOMETHING HEAVY FOR YOU TO LIFT, YELL AT YOU FOR LEAVING YOUR SHOES IN THE MIDDLE OF THE KITCHEN FLOOR, TELL YOU THAT THE GARAGE NEEDS TO BE CLEANED, REMIND YOU THAT YOU PROMISED TO HELP ME WASH WINDOWS THIS WEEKEND AND GIVE YOUR DAD A HAND WITH PAINTING THE GUEST BEDROOM, ETC. ETC. ETC. ETC.
HOW DOES HE ALWAYS KNOW WHEN TO DISAPPEAR?
THEY CAN SMELL RESPONSIBILITY.
SCOTT AND BORGMAN

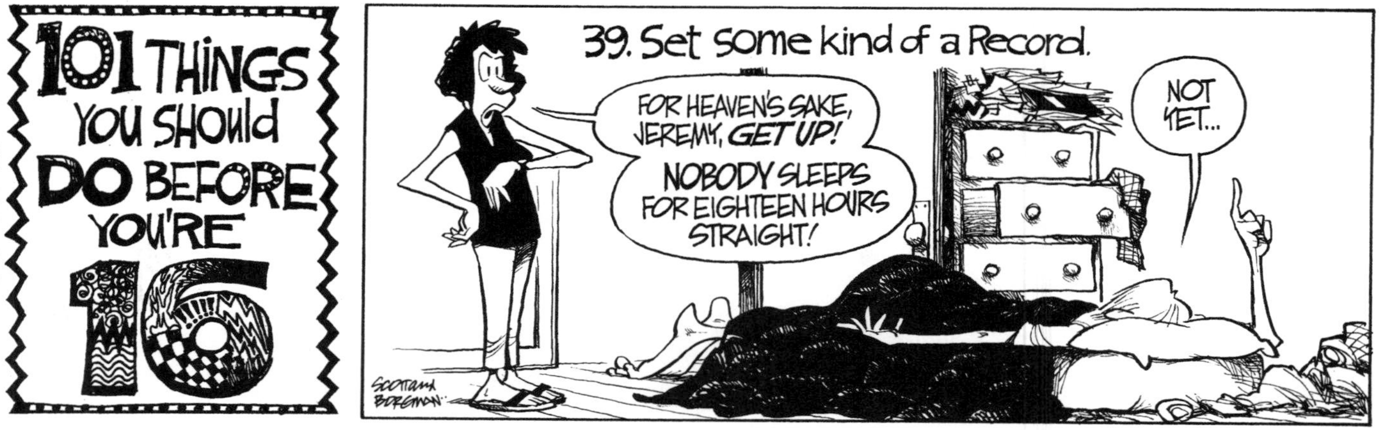
101 THINGS YOU SHOULD DO BEFORE YOU'RE 16
39. Set some kind of a Record.
FOR HEAVEN'S SAKE, JEREMY, GET UP!
NOBODY SLEEPS FOR EIGHTEEN HOURS STRAIGHT!
NOT YET...
SCOTT and BORGMAN

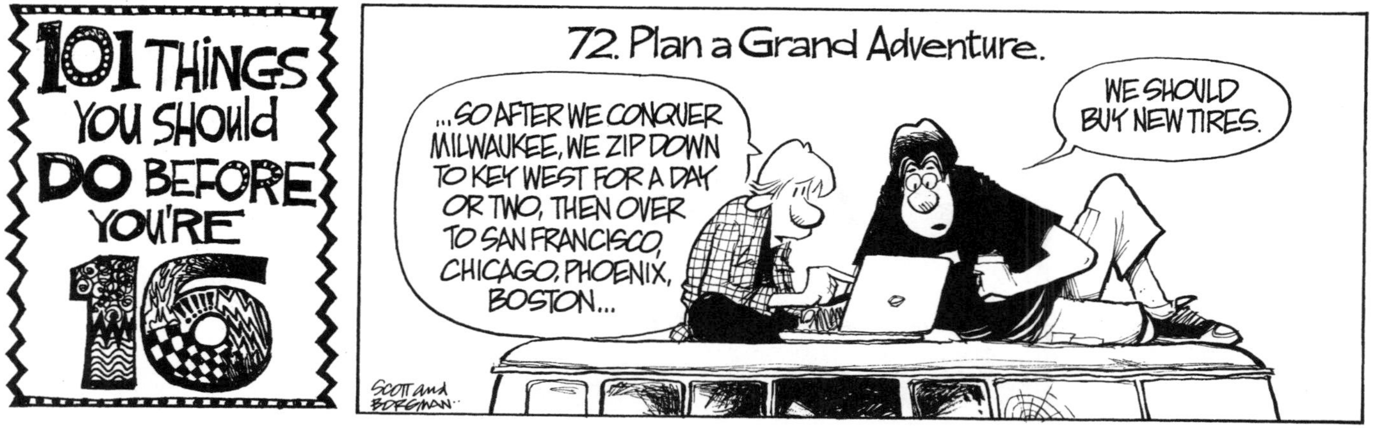
101 THINGS YOU SHOULD DO BEFORE YOU'RE 16
72. Plan a Grand Adventure.
...SO AFTER WE CONQUER MILWAUKEE, WE ZIP DOWN TO KEY WEST FOR A DAY OR TWO, THEN OVER TO SAN FRANCISCO, CHICAGO, PHOENIX, BOSTON...
WE SHOULD BUY NEW TIRES.
SCOTT and BORGMAN

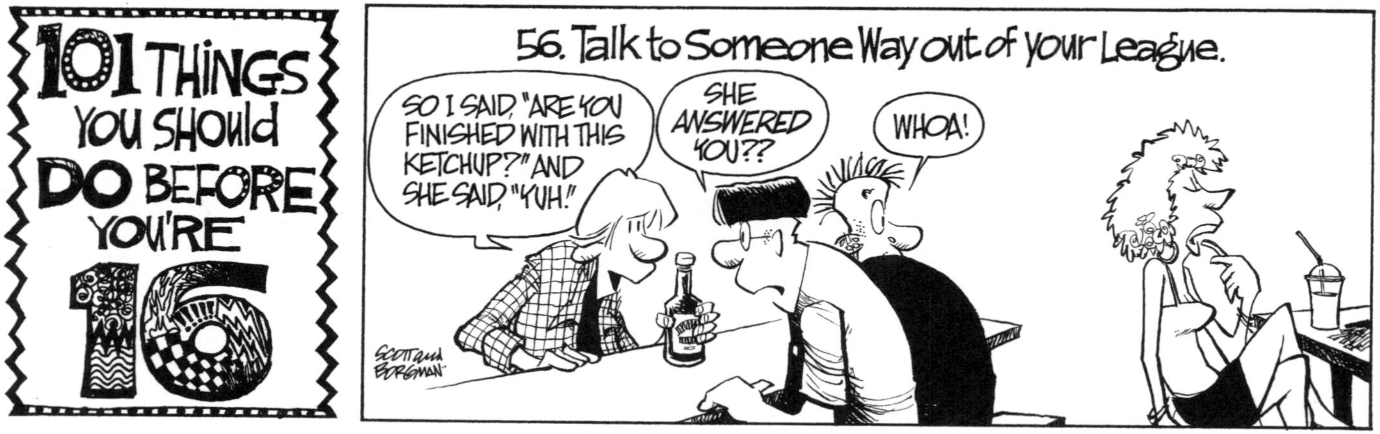
101 THINGS YOU SHOULD DO BEFORE YOU'RE 16
56. Talk to Someone Way out of your League.
SO I SAID, "ARE YOU FINISHED WITH THIS KETCHUP?" AND SHE SAID, "YUH."
SHE ANSWERED YOU??
WHOA!
SCOTT and BORGMAN

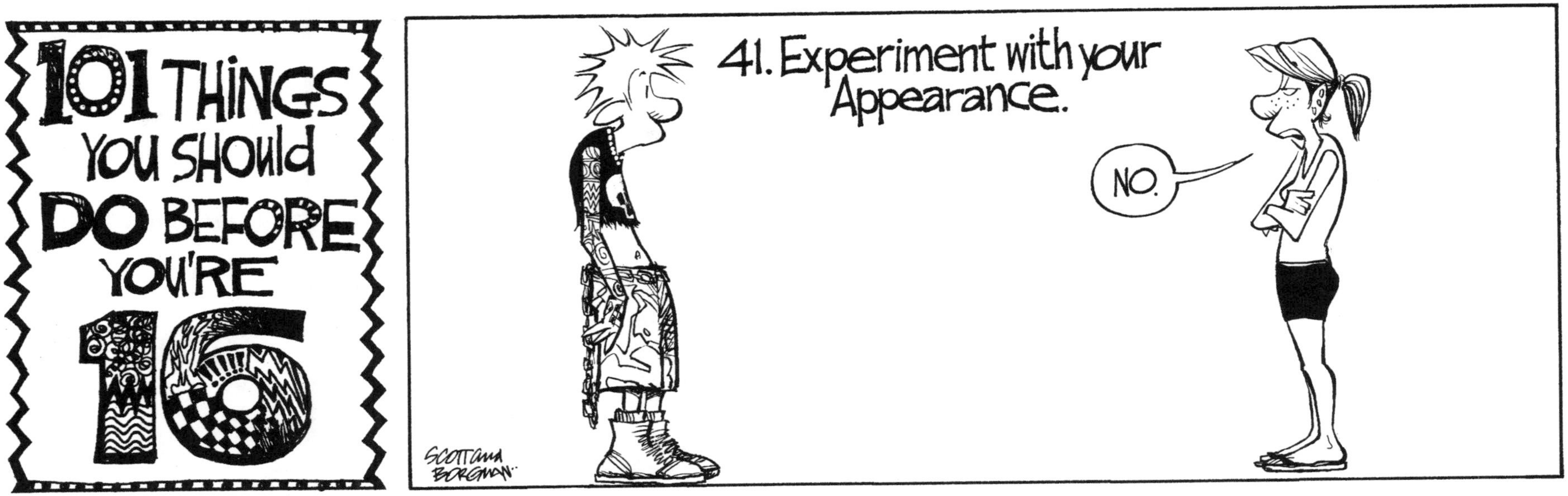
101 THINGS YOU SHOULD DO BEFORE YOU'RE 16
41. Experiment with your Appearance.
NO.

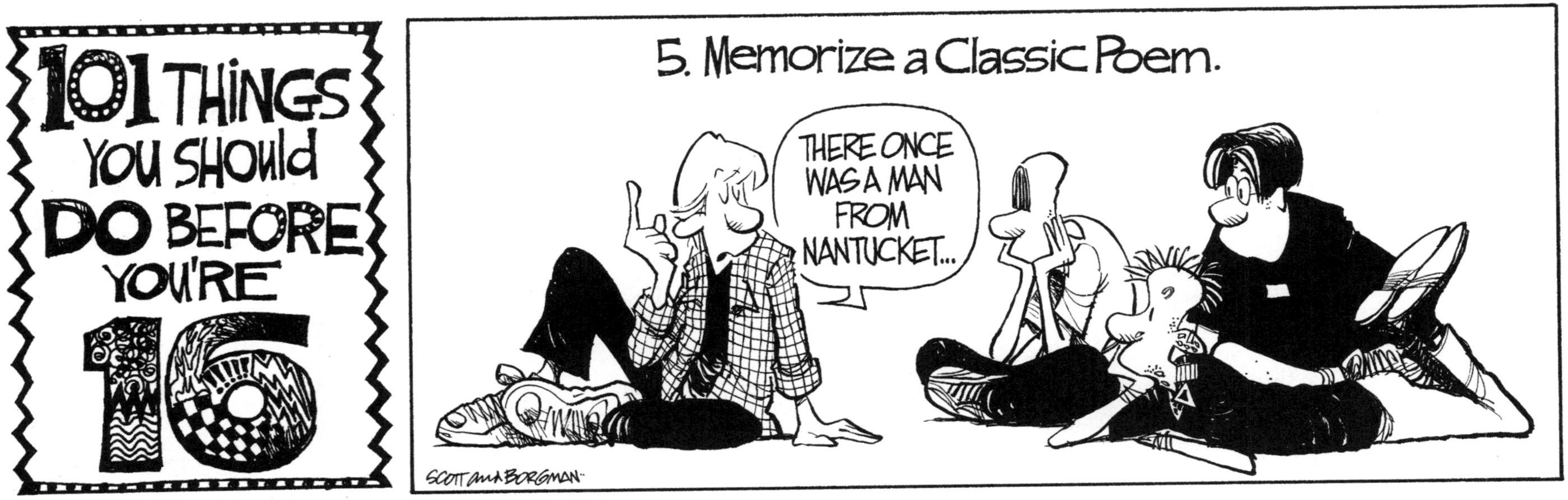
101 THINGS YOU SHOULD DO BEFORE YOU'RE 16
5. Memorize a Classic Poem.
THERE ONCE WAS A MAN FROM NANTUCKET...

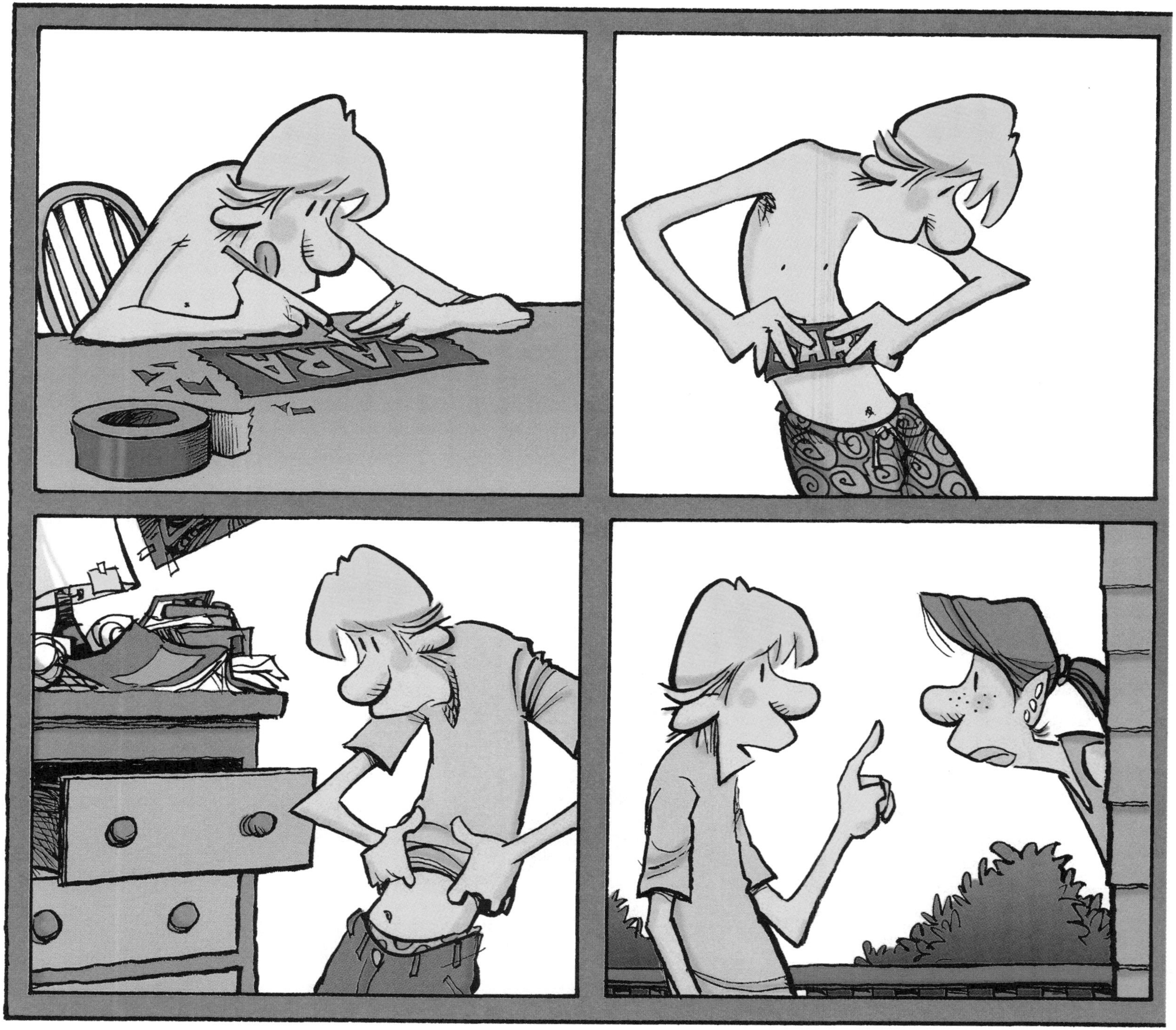

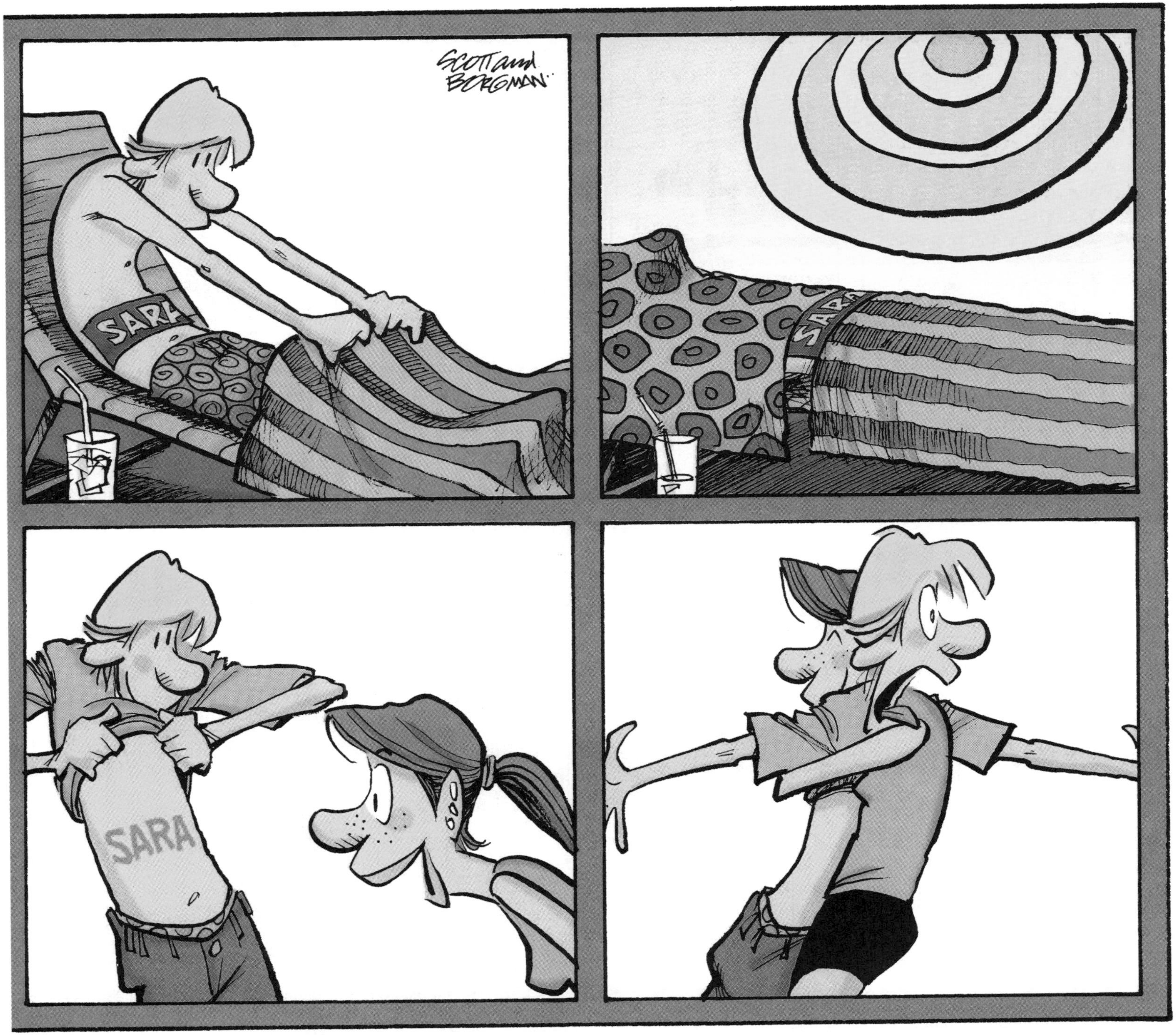
SCOTT and BORGMAN
SARA
SARA
SARA

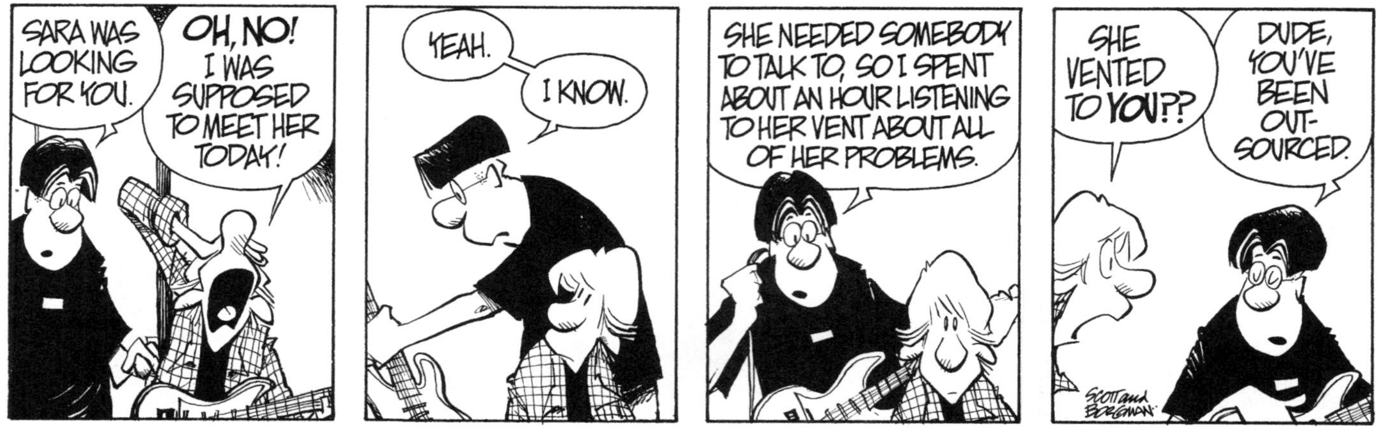
SARA WAS LOOKING FOR YOU.
OH, NO! I WAS SUPPOSED TO MEET HER TODAY!
YEAH.
I KNOW.
SHE NEEDED SOMEBODY TO TALK TO, SO I SPENT ABOUT AN HOUR LISTENING TO HER VENT ABOUT ALL OF HER PROBLEMS.
SHE VENTED TO YOU??
DUDE, YOU'VE BEEN OUT-SOURCED.

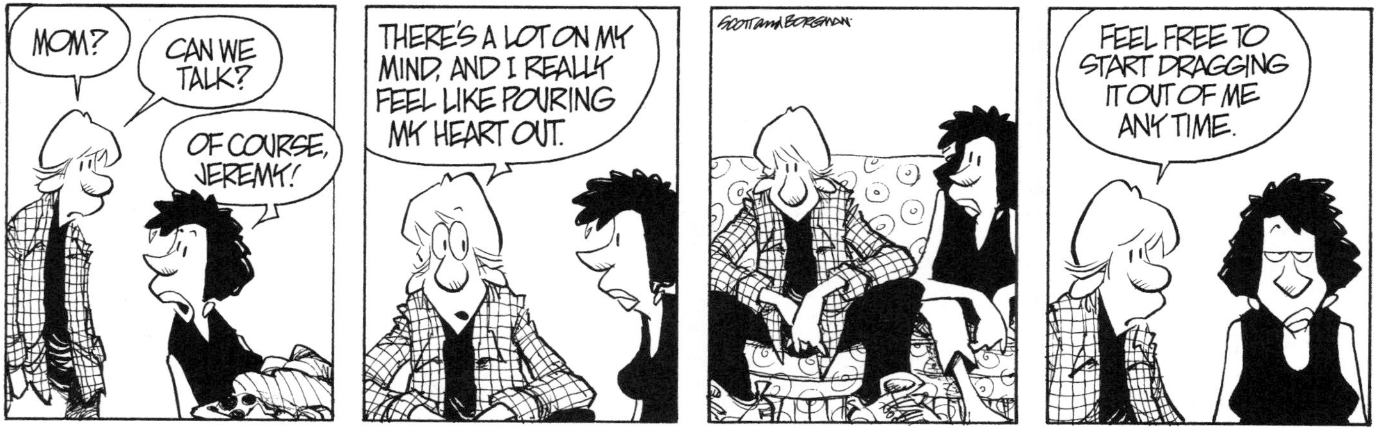
MOM?
CAN WE TALK?
OF COURSE, JEREMY!
THERE'S A LOT ON MY MIND, AND I REALLY FEEL LIKE POURING MY HEART OUT.
FEEL FREE TO START DRAGGING IT OUT OF ME ANY TIME.

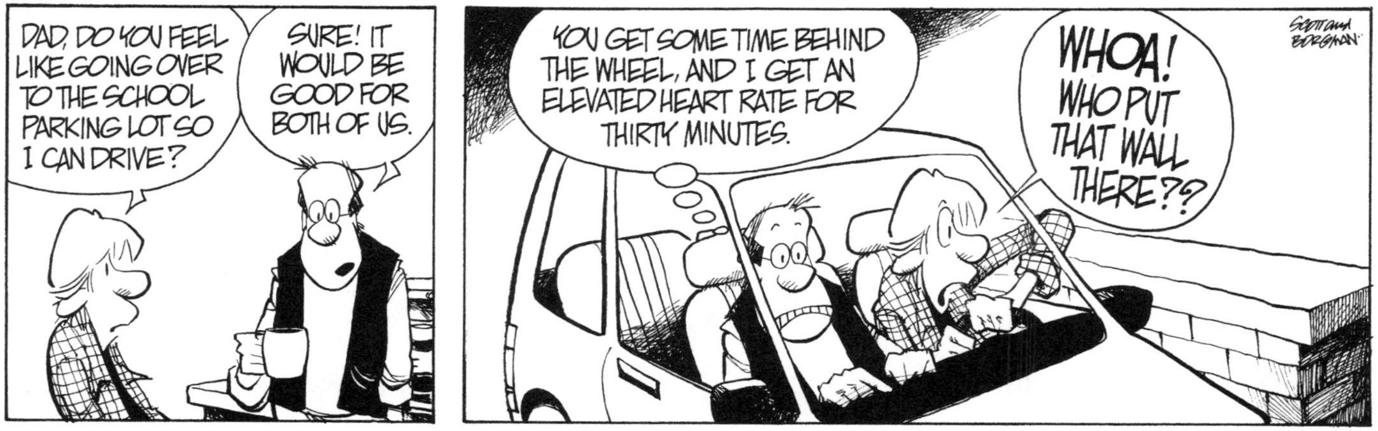
DAD, DO YOU FEEL LIKE GOING OVER TO THE SCHOOL PARKING LOT SO I CAN DRIVE?
SURE! IT WOULD BE GOOD FOR BOTH OF US.
YOU GET SOME TIME BEHIND THE WHEEL, AND I GET AN ELEVATED HEART RATE FOR THIRTY MINUTES.
WHOA! WHO PUT THAT WALL THERE??

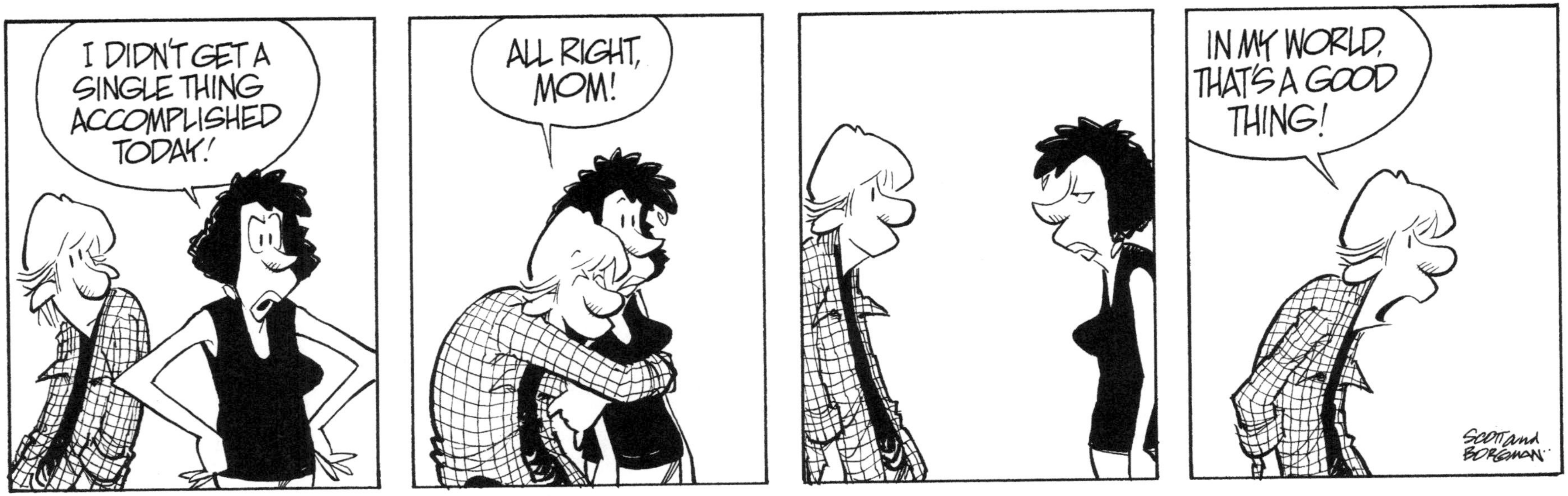
I DIDN'T GET A SINGLE THING ACCOMPLISHED TODAY!
ALL RIGHT, MOM!
IN MY WORLD, THAT'S A GOOD THING!
SCOTT and BORGMAN

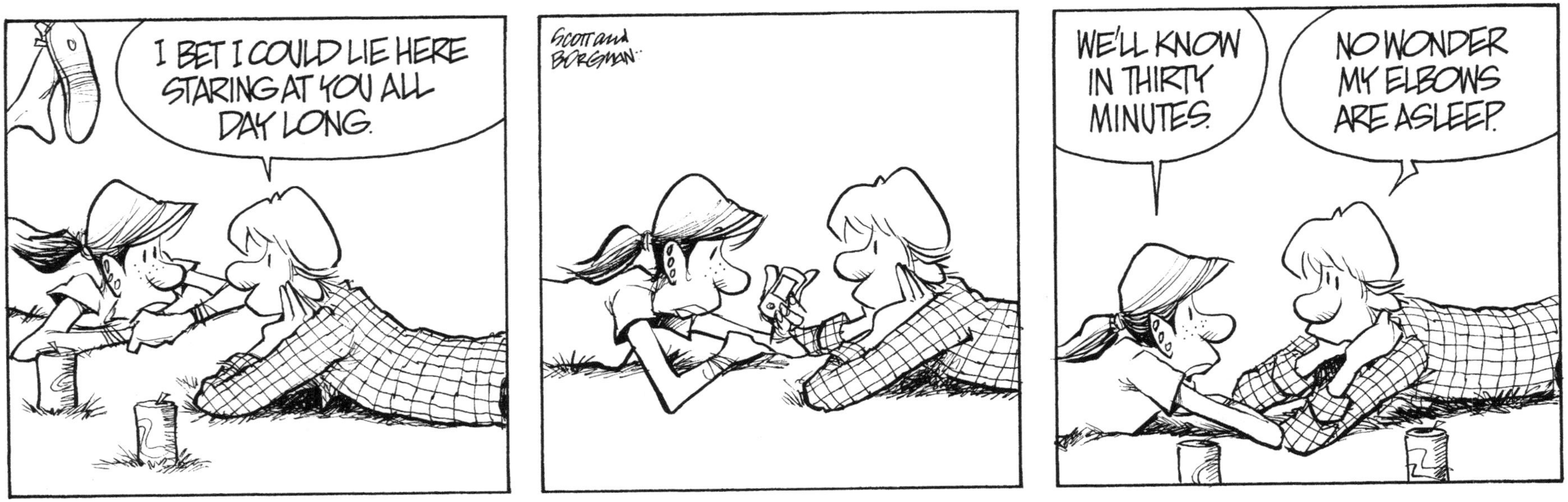
I BET I COULD LIE HERE STARING AT YOU ALL DAY LONG.
SCOTT and BORGMAN
WE'LL KNOW IN THIRTY MINUTES.
NO WONDER MY ELBOWS ARE ASLEEP.

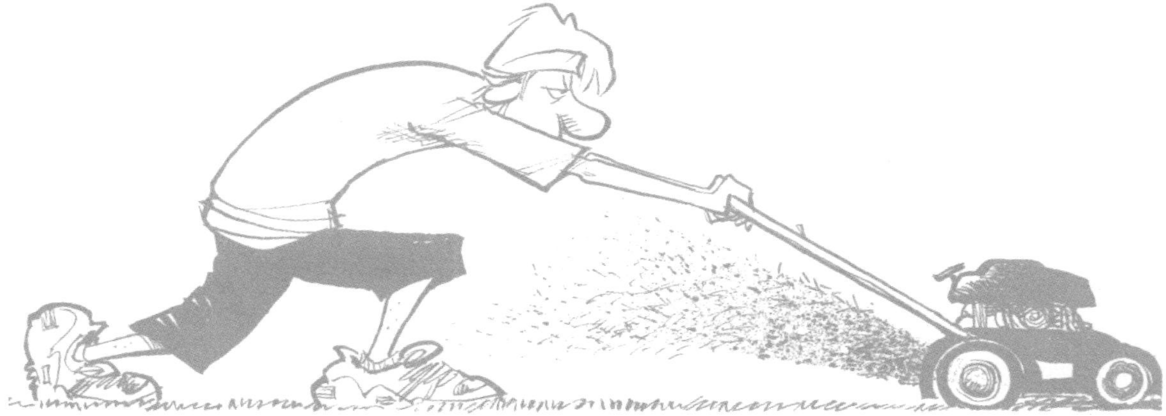

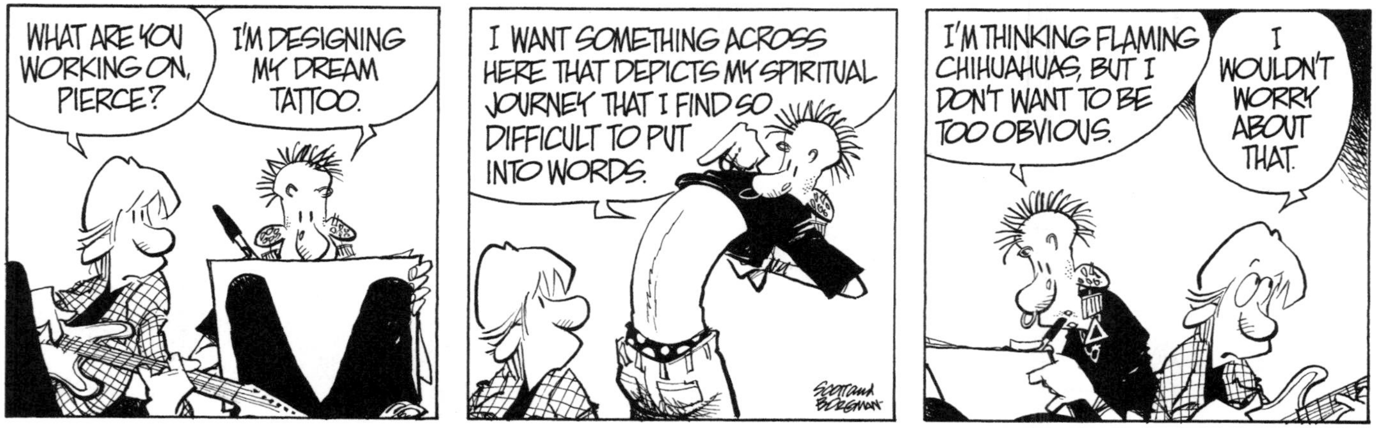

WHAT ARE YOU WORKING ON, PIERCE?
I'M DESIGNING MY DREAM TATTOO.
I WANT SOMETHING ACROSS HERE THAT DEPICTS MY SPIRITUAL JOURNEY THAT I FIND SO DIFFICULT TO PUT INTO WORDS.
I'M THINKING FLAMING CHIHUAHUAS, BUT I DON'T WANT TO BE TOO OBVIOUS.
I WOULDN'T WORRY ABOUT THAT.

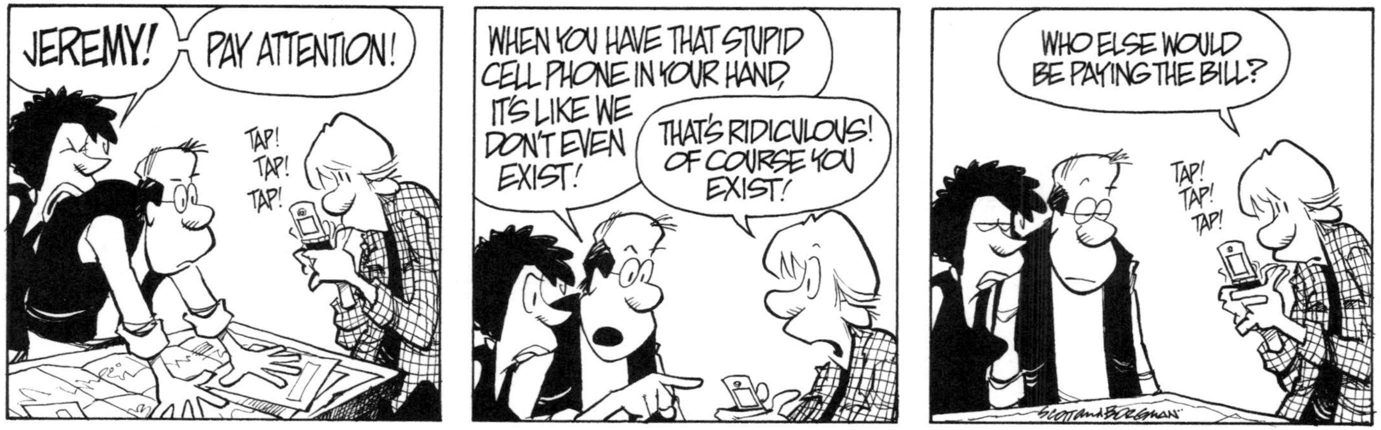

JEREMY!
PAY ATTENTION!
TAP! TAP! TAP!
WHEN YOU HAVE THAT STUPID CELL PHONE IN YOUR HAND, IT'S LIKE WE DON'T EVEN EXIST!
THAT'S RIDICULOUS! OF COURSE YOU EXIST!
WHO ELSE WOULD BE PAYING THE BILL?
TAP! TAP! TAP!

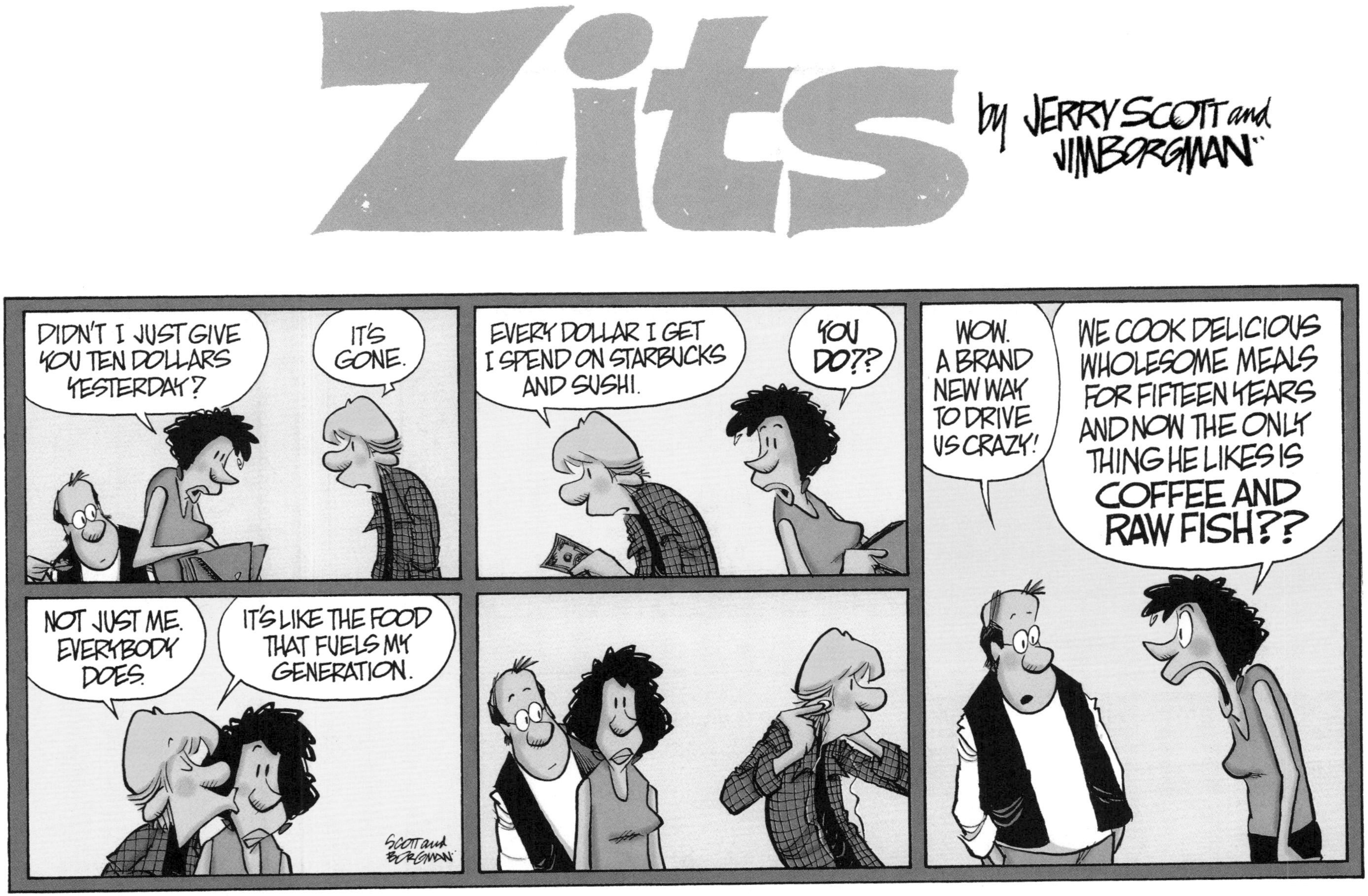
Zits
by JERRY SCOTT and JIM BORGMAN
DIDN'T I JUST GIVE YOU TEN DOLLARS YESTERDAY?
IT'S GONE.
EVERY DOLLAR I GET I SPEND ON STARBUCKS AND SUSHI.
YOU DO??
NOT JUST ME. EVERYBODY DOES.
IT'S LIKE THE FOOD THAT FUELS MY GENERATION.
WOW. A BRAND NEW WAY TO DRIVE US CRAZY!
WE COOK DELICIOUS WHOLESOME MEALS FOR FIFTEEN YEARS AND NOW THE ONLY THING HE LIKES IS COFFEE AND RAW FISH??
SCOTT and BORGMAN

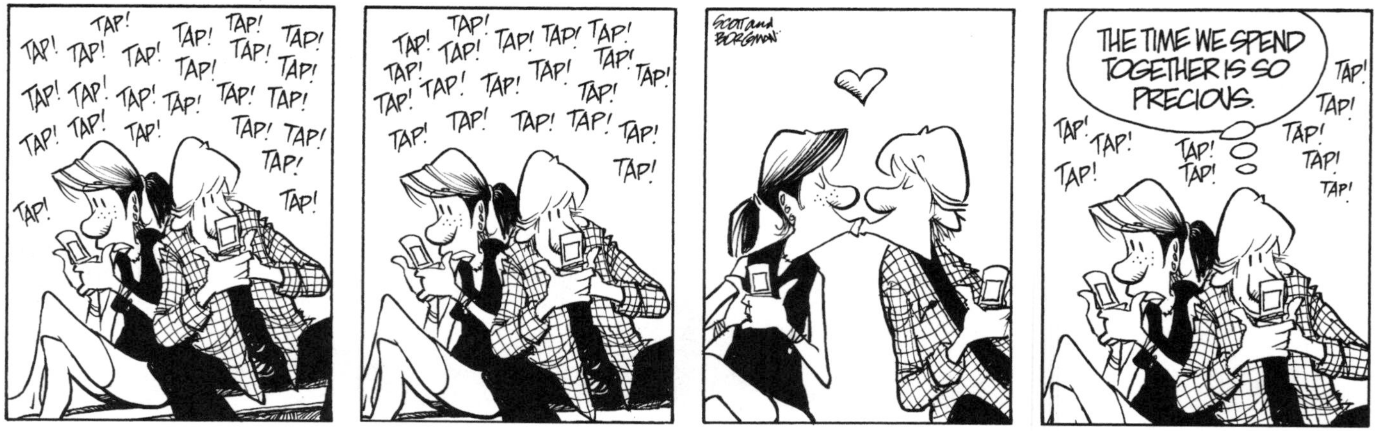
TAP!
TAP!
SCOTT and BORGMAN
THE TIME WE SPEND TOGETHER IS SO PRECIOUS.
TAP!

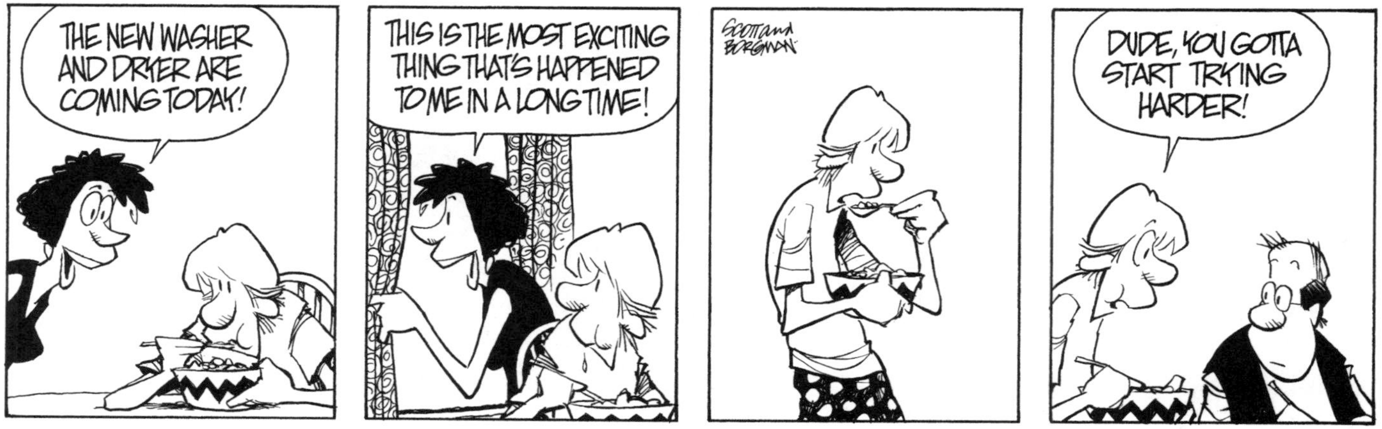
THE NEW WASHER AND DRYER ARE COMING TODAY!
THIS IS THE MOST EXCITING THING THAT'S HAPPENED TO ME IN A LONG TIME!
SCOTT and BORGMAN
DUDE, YOU GOTTA START TRYING HARDER!

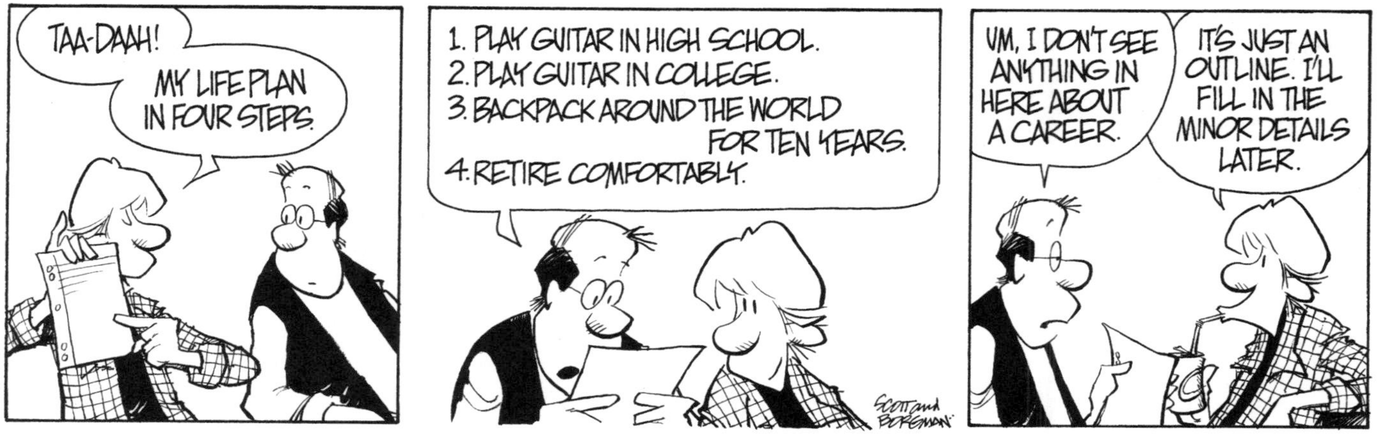
TAA-DAAH!
MY LIFE PLAN IN FOUR STEPS.
1. PLAY GUITAR IN HIGH SCHOOL.
2. PLAY GUITAR IN COLLEGE.
3. BACKPACK AROUND THE WORLD FOR TEN YEARS.
4. RETIRE COMFORTABLY.
SCOTT and BORGMAN
UM, I DON'T SEE ANYTHING IN HERE ABOUT A CAREER.
IT'S JUST AN OUTLINE. I'LL FILL IN THE MINOR DETAILS LATER.

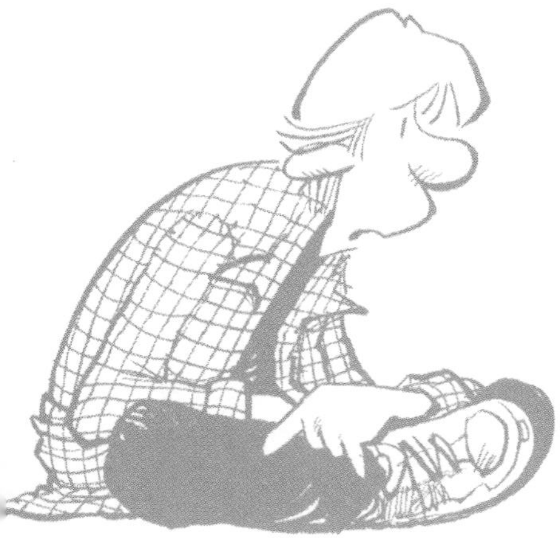

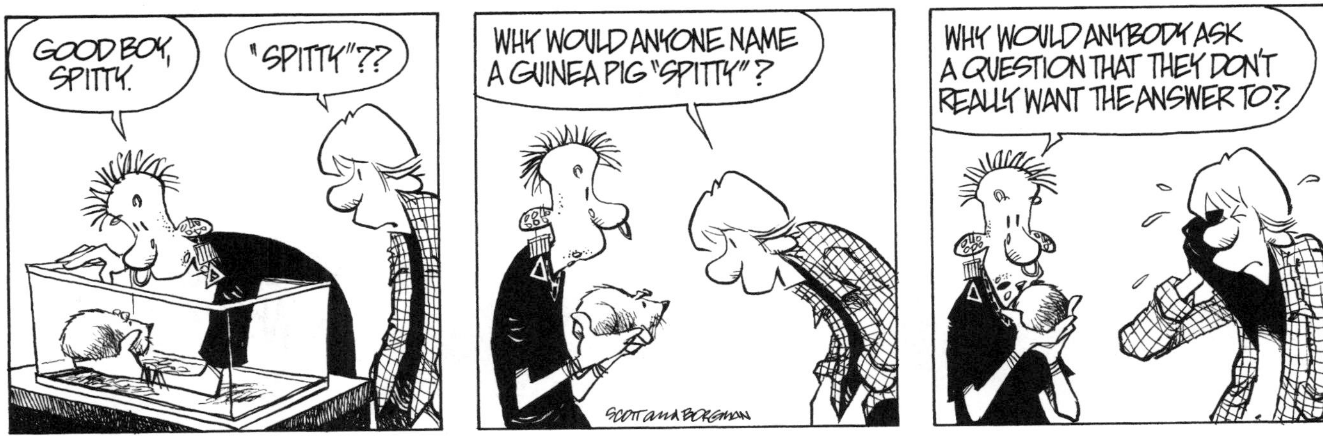
GOOD BOY, SPITTY.
"SPITTY"??
WHY WOULD ANYONE NAME A GUINEA PIG "SPITTY"?
WHY WOULD ANYBODY ASK A QUESTION THAT THEY DON'T REALLY WANT THE ANSWER TO?

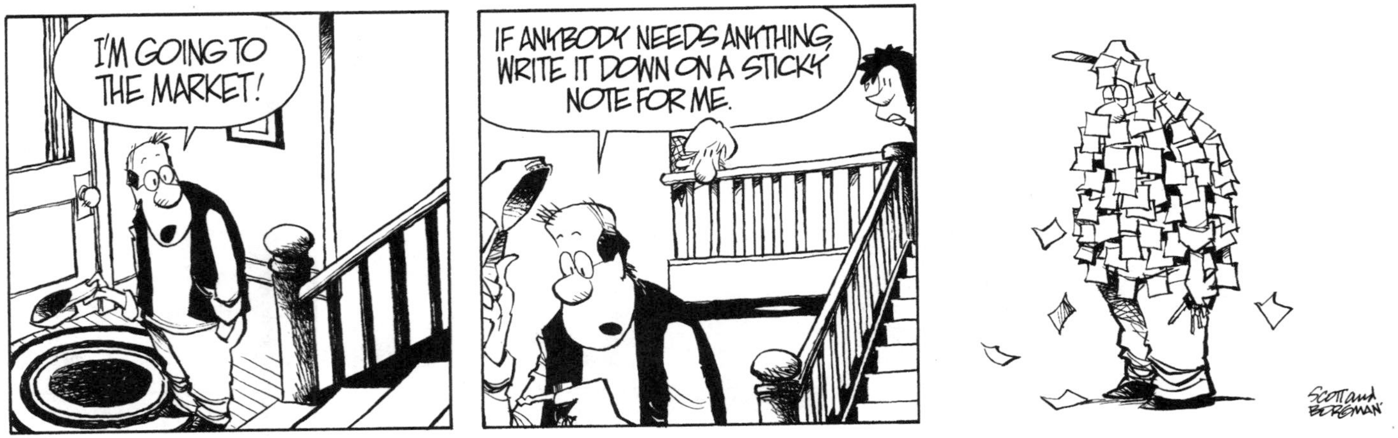
I'M GOING TO THE MARKET!
IF ANYBODY NEEDS ANYTHING, WRITE IT DOWN ON A STICKY NOTE FOR ME.

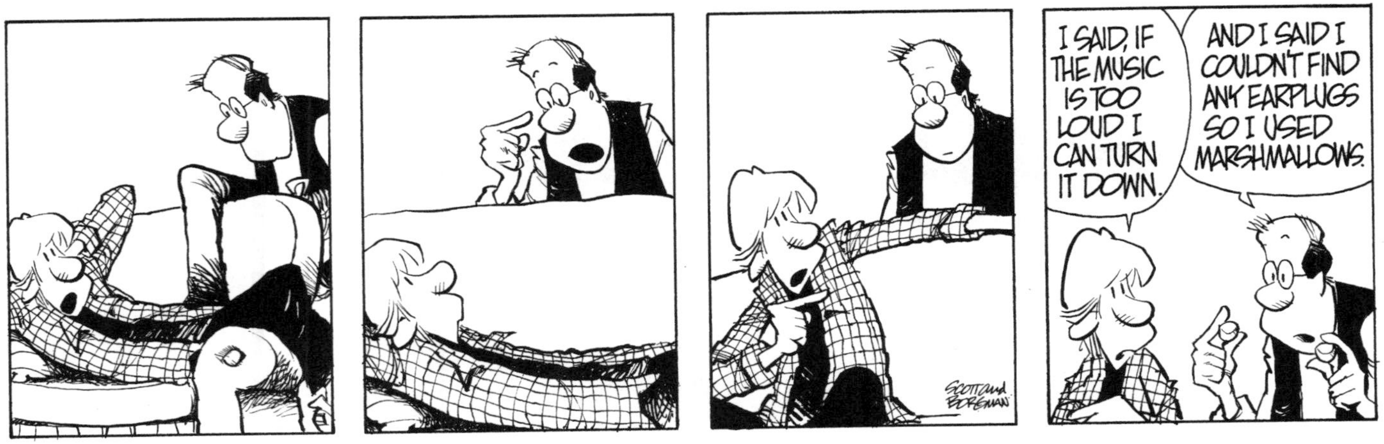
I SAID, IF THE MUSIC IS TOO LOUD I CAN TURN IT DOWN.
AND I SAID I COULDN'T FIND ANY EARPLUGS SO I USED MARSHMALLOWS.

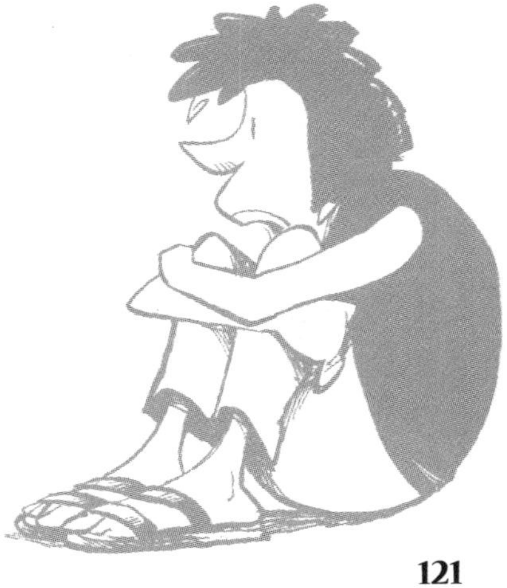

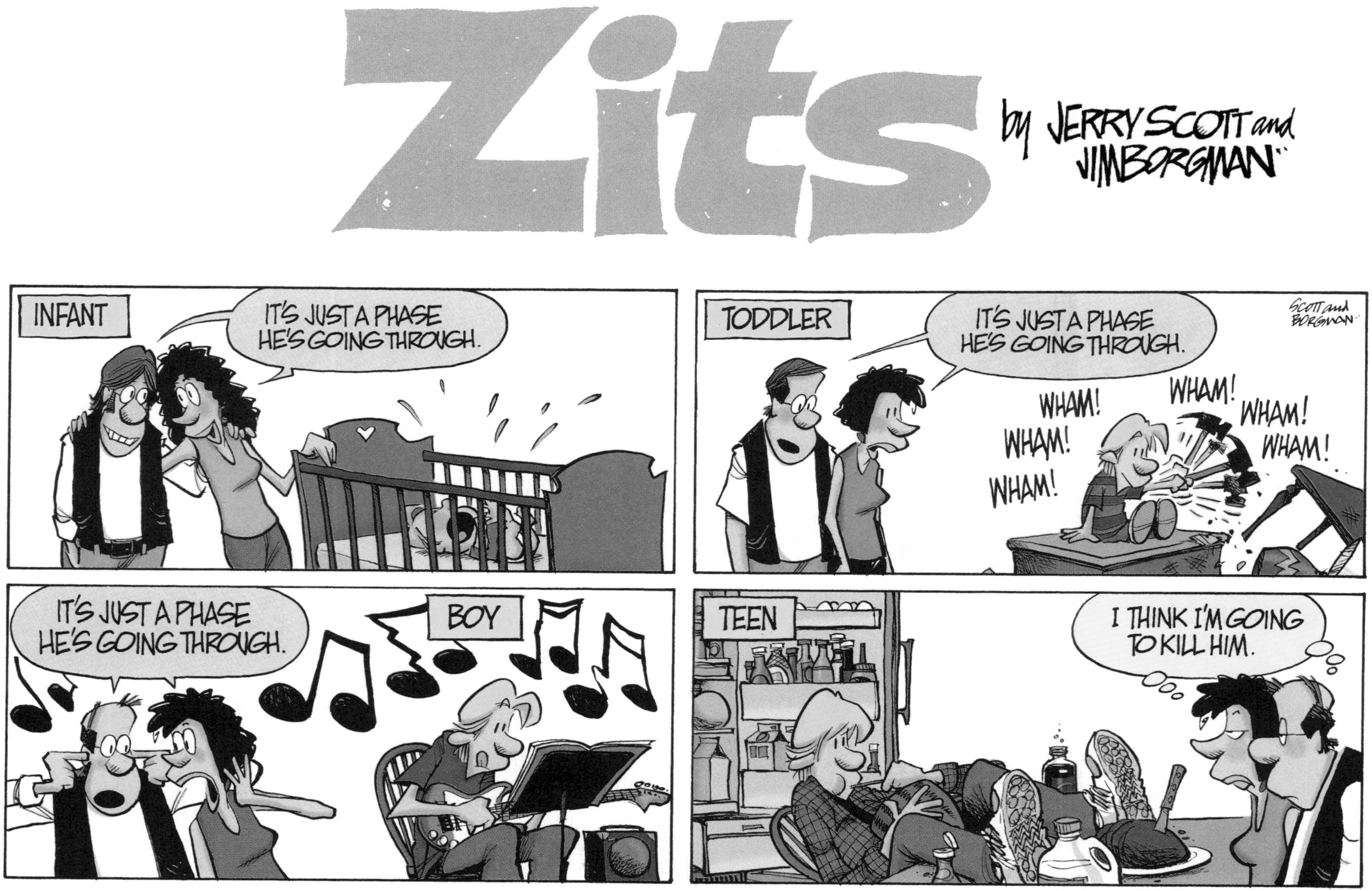
Zits
by JERRY SCOTT and JIM BORGMAN
INFANT
IT'S JUST A PHASE HE'S GOING THROUGH.
TODDLER
SCOTT and BORGMAN
IT'S JUST A PHASE HE'S GOING THROUGH.
WHAM!
WHAM!
WHAM!
WHAM!
WHAM!
WHAM!
IT'S JUST A PHASE HE'S GOING THROUGH.
BOY
TEEN
I THINK I'M GOING TO KILL HIM.

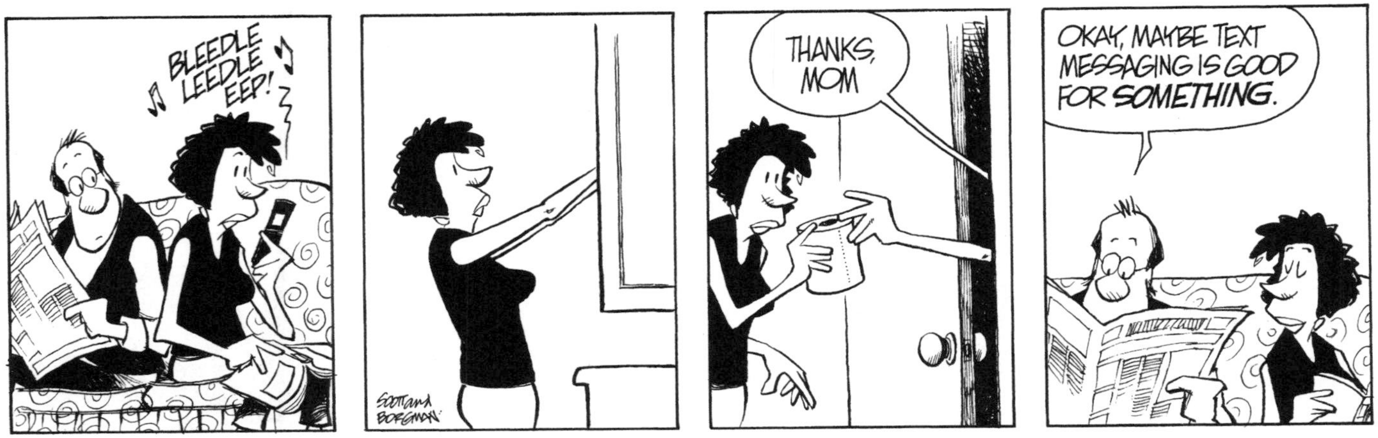
BLEEDLE LEEDLE EEP!
THANKS, MOM
OKAY, MAYBE TEXT MESSAGING IS GOOD FOR **SOMETHING**.

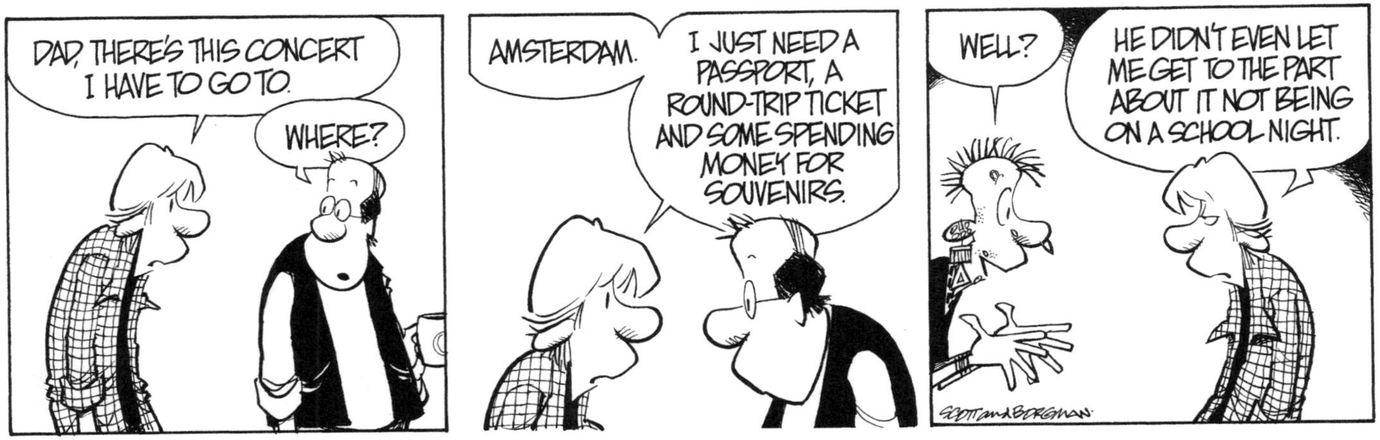
DAD, THERE'S THIS CONCERT I HAVE TO GO TO.
WHERE?
AMSTERDAM.
I JUST NEED A PASSPORT, A ROUND-TRIP TICKET AND SOME SPENDING MONEY FOR SOUVENIRS.
WELL?
HE DIDN'T EVEN LET ME GET TO THE PART ABOUT IT NOT BEING ON A SCHOOL NIGHT.

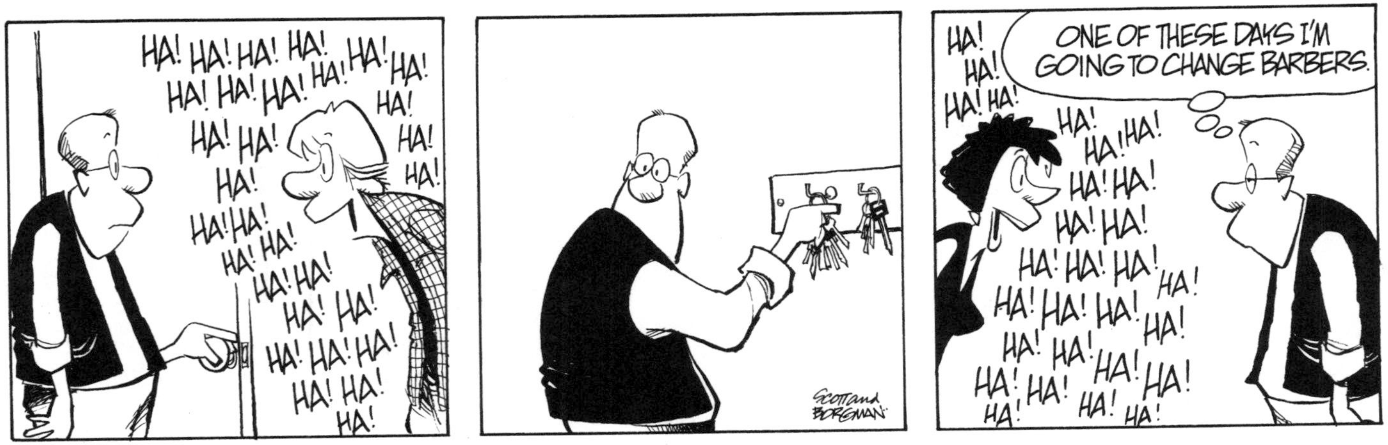
HA! HA! HA! HA! HA! HA! HA! HA! HA! HA! HA! HA! HA! HA! HA! HA! HA! HA! HA! HA! HA! HA! HA! HA! HA! HA! HA! HA! HA! HA! HA! HA! HA! HA!
HA! HA! HA! HA!
ONE OF THESE DAYS I'M GOING TO CHANGE BARBERS.
HA! HA! HA! HA! HA! HA! HA! HA! HA! HA! HA! HA! HA! HA! HA! HA! HA! HA! HA! HA! HA! HA! HA! HA! HA! HA!

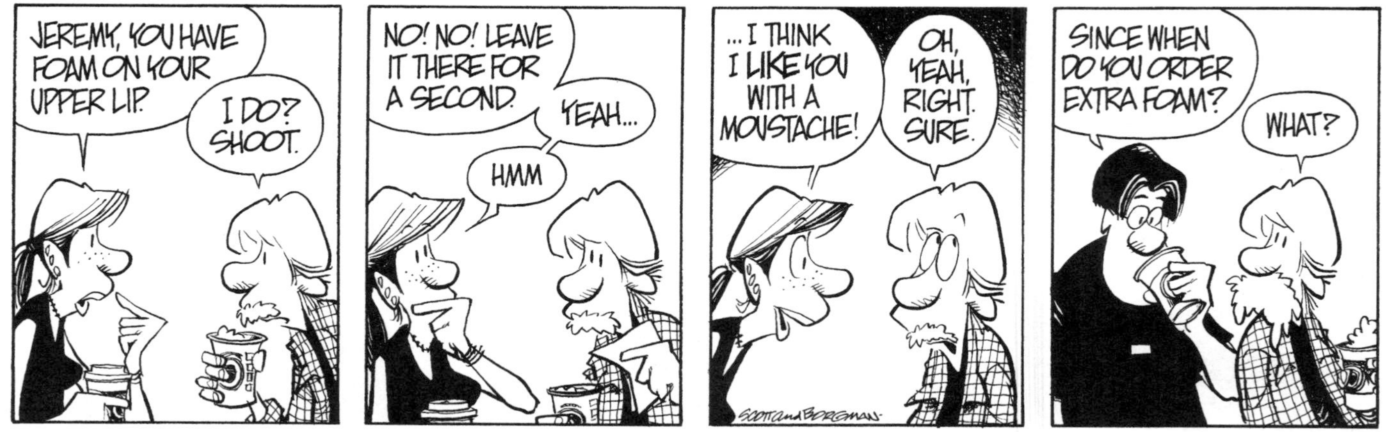
JEREMY, YOU HAVE FOAM ON YOUR UPPER LIP.
I DO? SHOOT.
NO! NO! LEAVE IT THERE FOR A SECOND.
YEAH...
HMM
...I THINK I **LIKE** YOU WITH A MOUSTACHE!
OH, YEAH, RIGHT. SURE.
SCOTT and BORGMAN
SINCE WHEN DO YOU ORDER EXTRA FOAM?
WHAT?

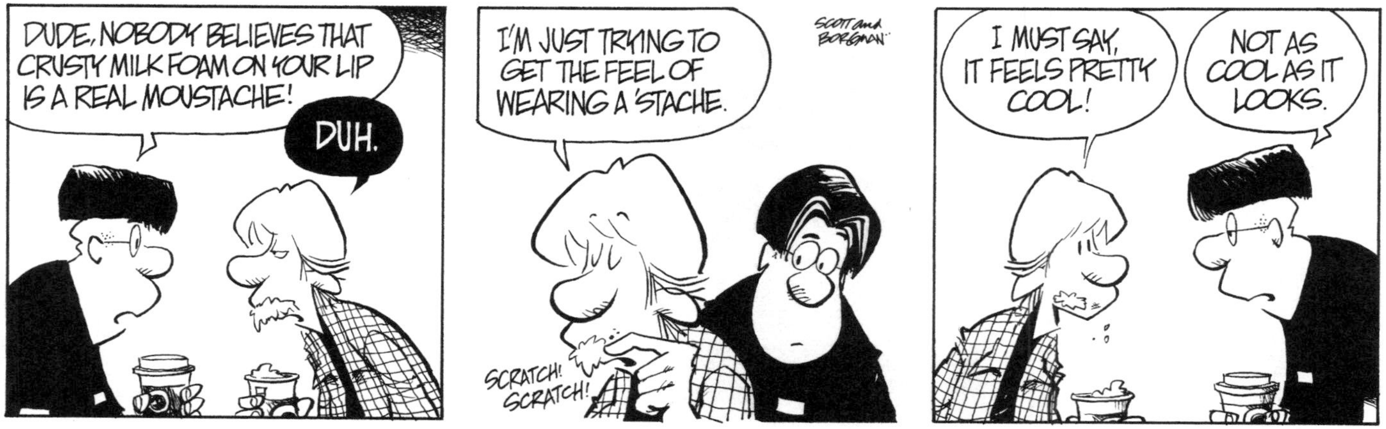
DUDE, NOBODY BELIEVES THAT CRUSTY MILK FOAM ON YOUR LIP IS A REAL MOUSTACHE!
DUH.
I'M JUST TRYING TO GET THE FEEL OF WEARING A 'STACHE.
SCRATCH! SCRATCH!
SCOTT and BORGMAN
I MUST SAY, IT FEELS PRETTY COOL!
NOT AS COOL AS IT LOOKS.

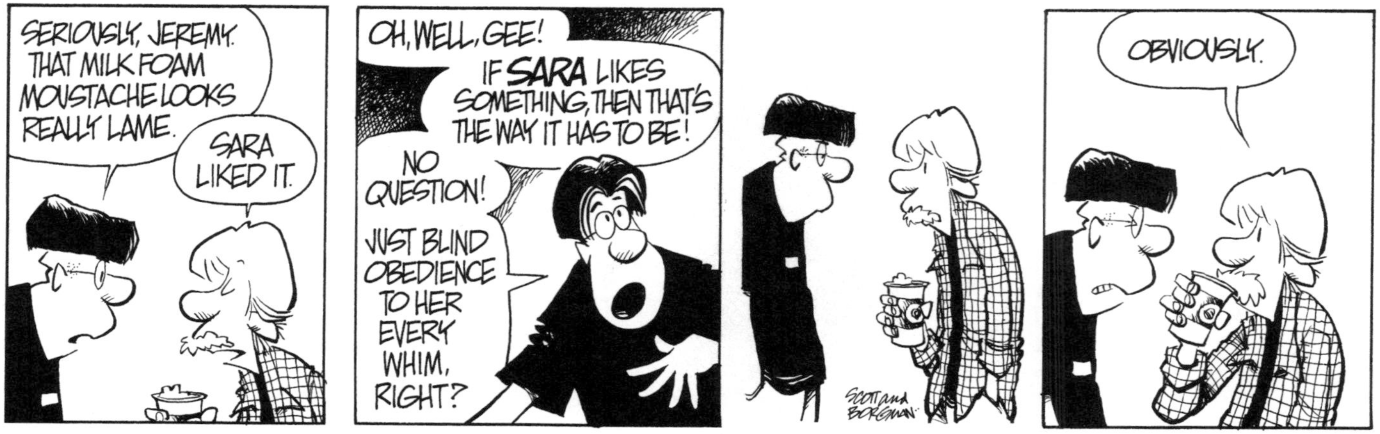
SERIOUSLY, JEREMY. THAT MILK FOAM MOUSTACHE LOOKS REALLY LAME.
SARA LIKED IT.
OH, WELL, GEE!
IF **SARA** LIKES SOMETHING, THEN THAT'S THE WAY IT HAS TO BE!
NO QUESTION!
JUST BLIND OBEDIENCE TO HER EVERY WHIM, RIGHT?
SCOTT and BORGMAN
OBVIOUSLY.

Zits

by JERRY SCOTT and JIM BORGMAN

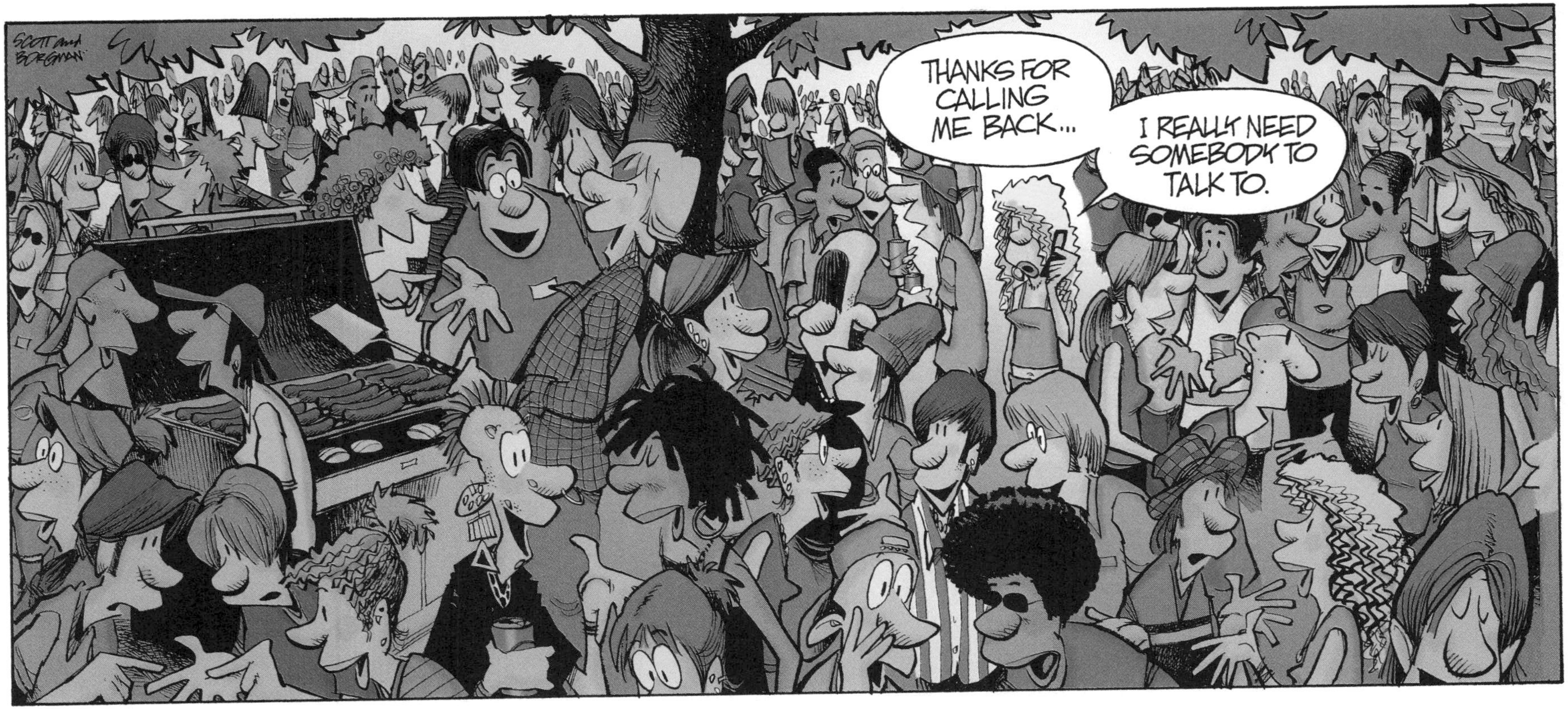
SCOTT and BORGMAN
THANKS FOR CALLING ME BACK...
I REALLY NEED SOMEBODY TO TALK TO.

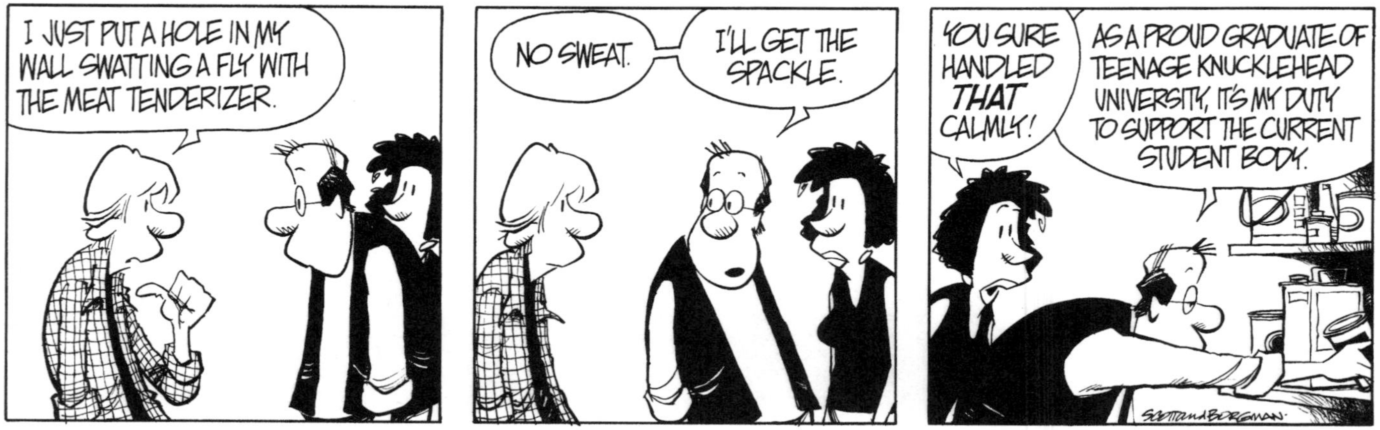
I JUST PUT A HOLE IN MY WALL SWATTING A FLY WITH THE MEAT TENDERIZER.
NO SWEAT.
I'LL GET THE SPACKLE.
YOU SURE HANDLED THAT CALMLY!
AS A PROUD GRADUATE OF TEENAGE KNUCKLEHEAD UNIVERSITY, IT'S MY DUTY TO SUPPORT THE CURRENT STUDENT BODY.

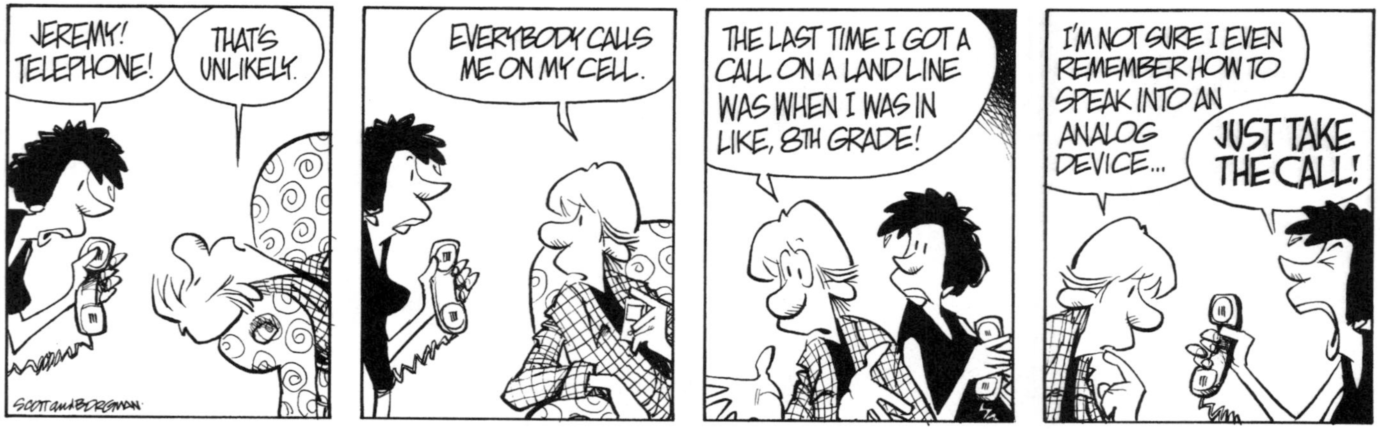
JEREMY! TELEPHONE!
THAT'S UNLIKELY.
EVERYBODY CALLS ME ON MY CELL.
THE LAST TIME I GOT A CALL ON A LAND LINE WAS WHEN I WAS IN LIKE, 8TH GRADE!
I'M NOT SURE I EVEN REMEMBER HOW TO SPEAK INTO AN ANALOG DEVICE...
JUST TAKE THE CALL!

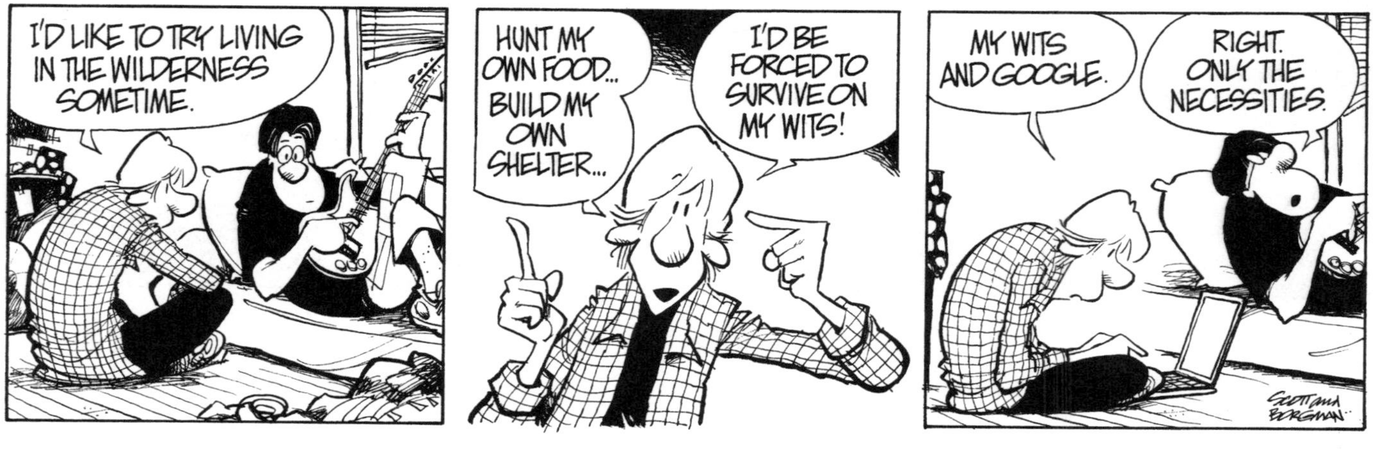
I'D LIKE TO TRY LIVING IN THE WILDERNESS SOMETIME.
HUNT MY OWN FOOD... BUILD MY OWN SHELTER...
I'D BE FORCED TO SURVIVE ON MY WITS!
MY WITS AND GOOGLE.
RIGHT. ONLY THE NECESSITIES.

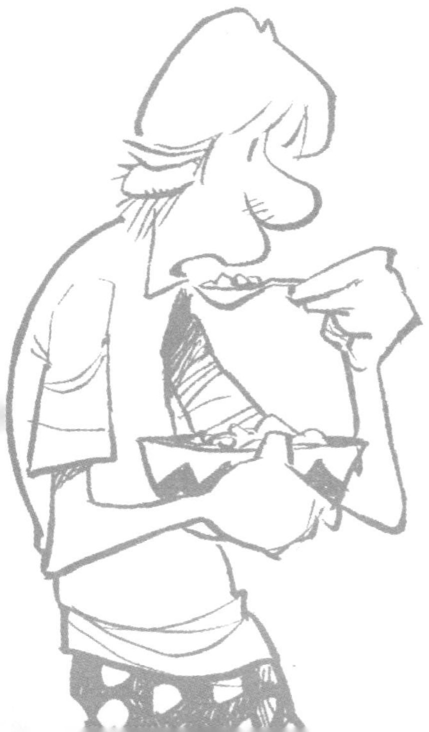

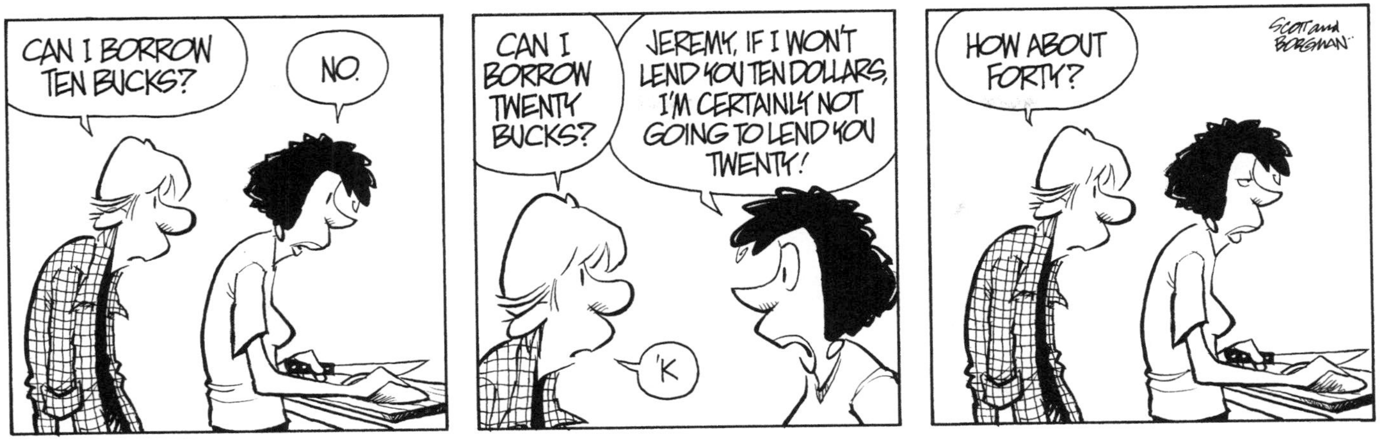
CAN I BORROW TEN BUCKS?
NO.
CAN I BORROW TWENTY BUCKS?
JEREMY, IF I WON'T LEND YOU TEN DOLLARS, I'M CERTAINLY NOT GOING TO LEND YOU TWENTY!
'K
HOW ABOUT FORTY?
SCOTT and BORGMAN

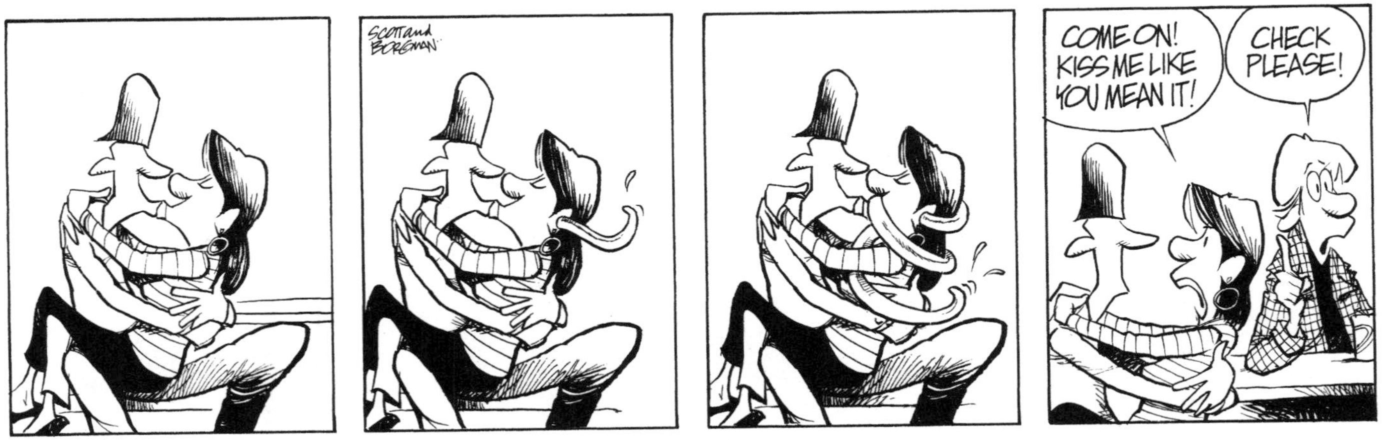
SCOTT and BORGMAN
COME ON! KISS ME LIKE YOU MEAN IT!
CHECK PLEASE!

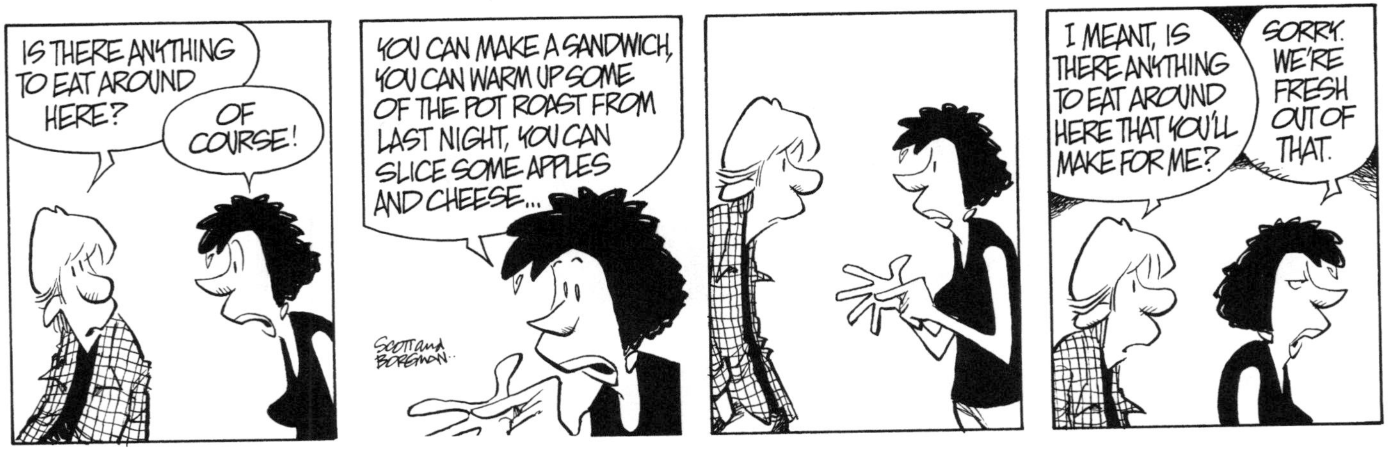
IS THERE ANYTHING TO EAT AROUND HERE?
OF COURSE!
YOU CAN MAKE A SANDWICH, YOU CAN WARM UP SOME OF THE POT ROAST FROM LAST NIGHT, YOU CAN SLICE SOME APPLES AND CHEESE...
SCOTT and BORGMAN
I MEANT, IS THERE ANYTHING TO EAT AROUND HERE THAT YOU'LL MAKE FOR ME?
SORRY. WE'RE FRESH OUT OF THAT.

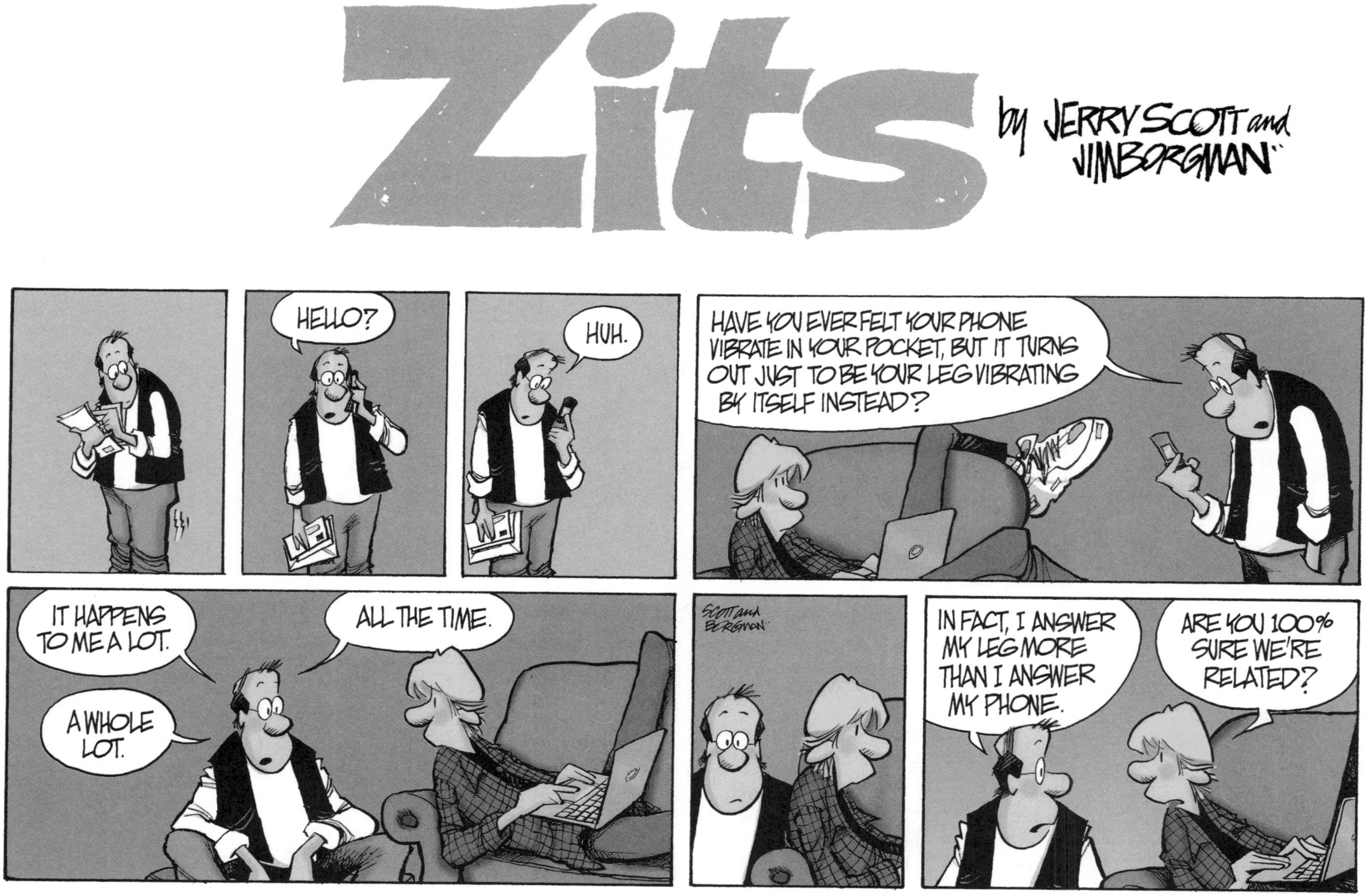
Zits
by JERRY SCOTT and JIM BORGMAN
HELLO?
HUH.
HAVE YOU EVER FELT YOUR PHONE VIBRATE IN YOUR POCKET, BUT IT TURNS OUT JUST TO BE YOUR LEG VIBRATING BY ITSELF INSTEAD?
IT HAPPENS TO ME A LOT.
A WHOLE LOT.
ALL THE TIME.
SCOTT and BORGMAN
IN FACT, I ANSWER MY LEG MORE THAN I ANSWER MY PHONE.
ARE YOU 100% SURE WE'RE RELATED?

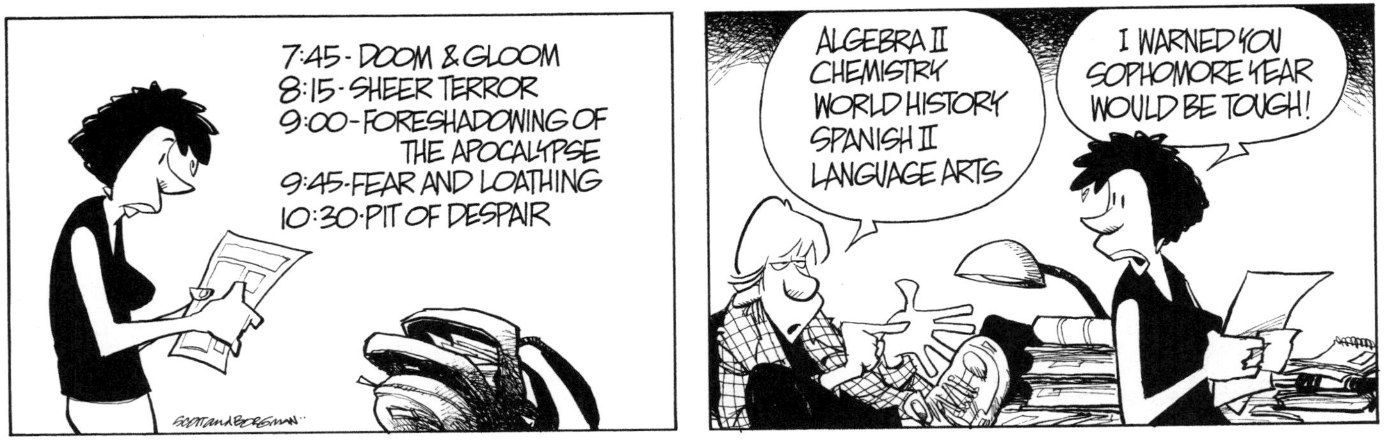
7:45 - DOOM & GLOOM
8:15 - SHEER TERROR
9:00 - FORESHADOWING OF THE APOCALYPSE
9:45 - FEAR AND LOATHING
10:30 - PIT OF DESPAIR
ALGEBRA II CHEMISTRY WORLD HISTORY SPANISH II LANGUAGE ARTS
I WARNED YOU SOPHOMORE YEAR WOULD BE TOUGH!

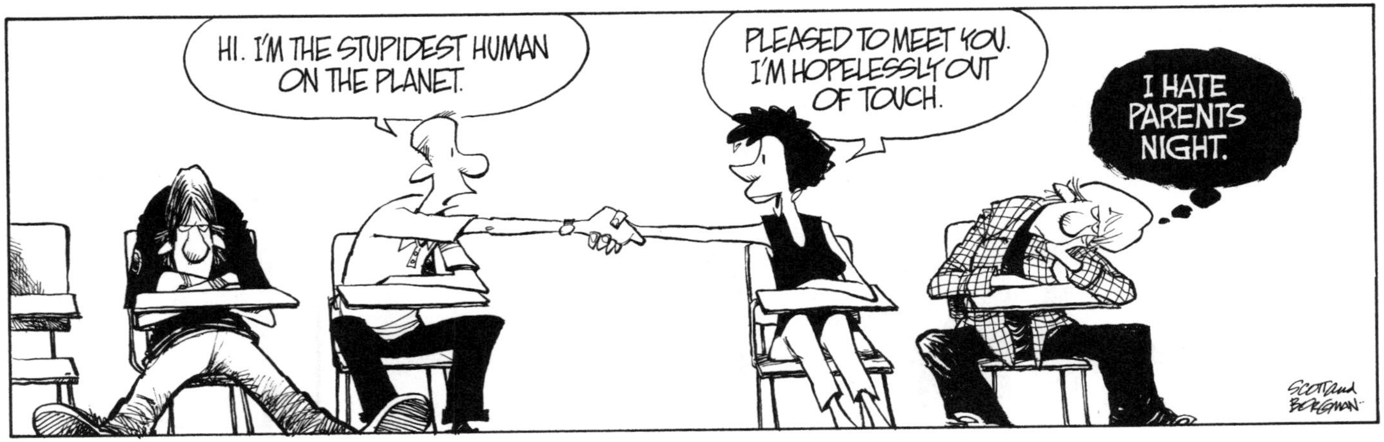
HI. I'M THE STUPIDEST HUMAN ON THE PLANET.
PLEASED TO MEET YOU. I'M HOPELESSLY OUT OF TOUCH.
I HATE PARENTS NIGHT.

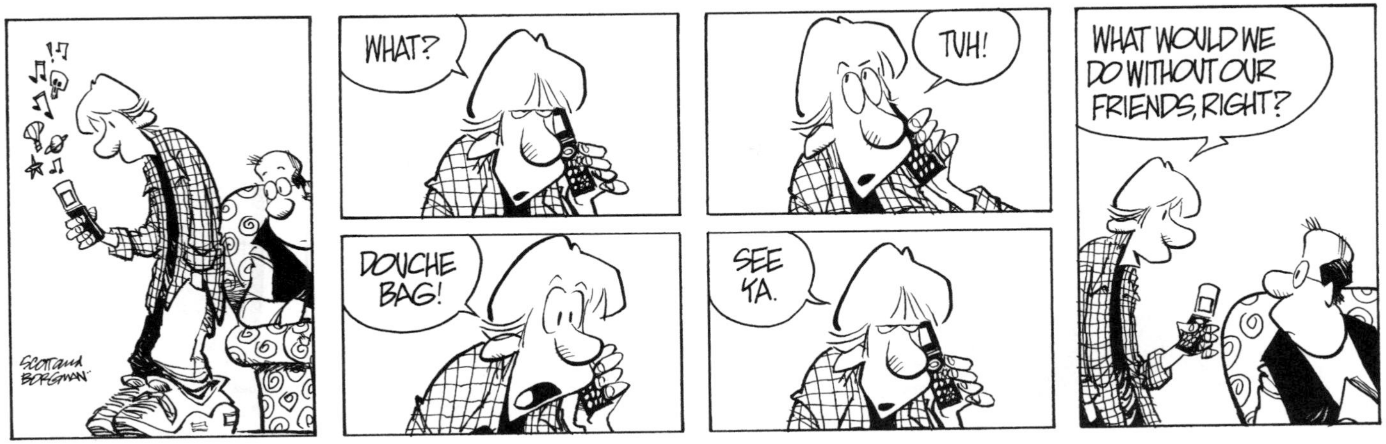
WHAT?
DOUCHE BAG!
TUH!
SEE YA.
WHAT WOULD WE DO WITHOUT OUR FRIENDS, RIGHT?

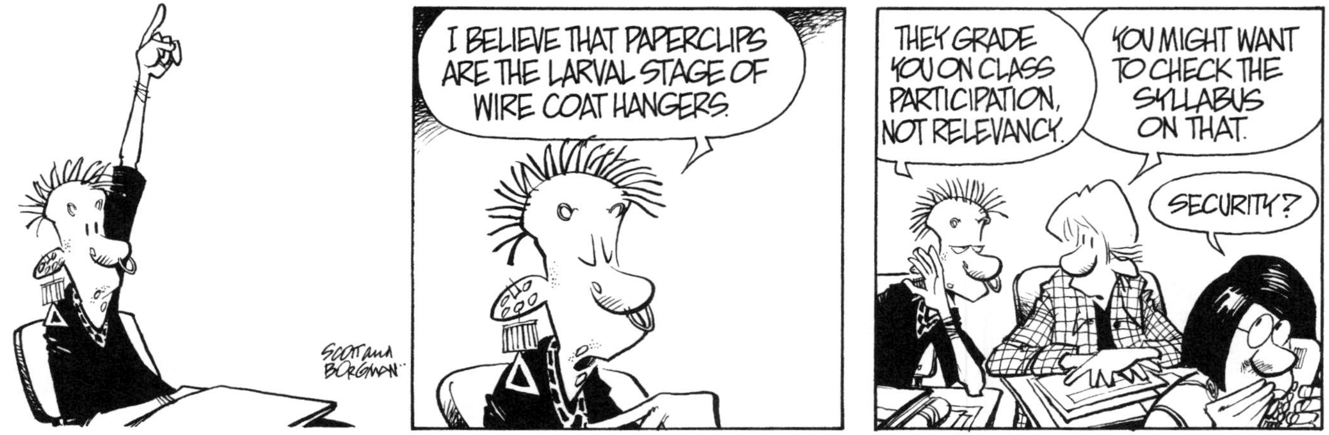
I BELIEVE THAT PAPERCLIPS ARE THE LARVAL STAGE OF WIRE COAT HANGERS.
THEY GRADE YOU ON CLASS PARTICIPATION, NOT RELEVANCY.
YOU MIGHT WANT TO CHECK THE SYLLABUS ON THAT.
SECURITY?

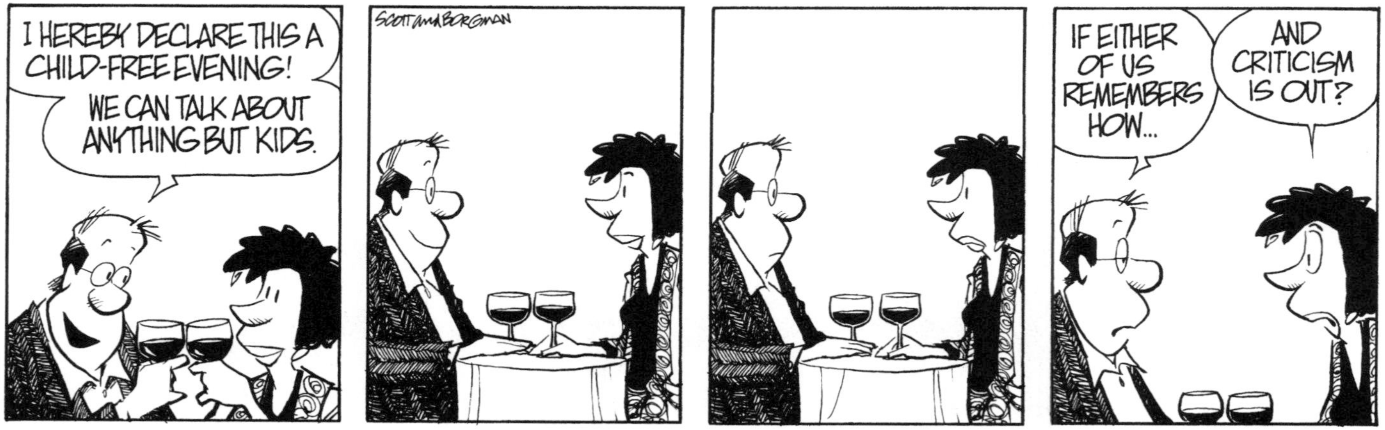
I HEREBY DECLARE THIS A CHILD-FREE EVENING!
WE CAN TALK ABOUT ANYTHING BUT KIDS.
IF EITHER OF US REMEMBERS HOW...
AND CRITICISM IS OUT?

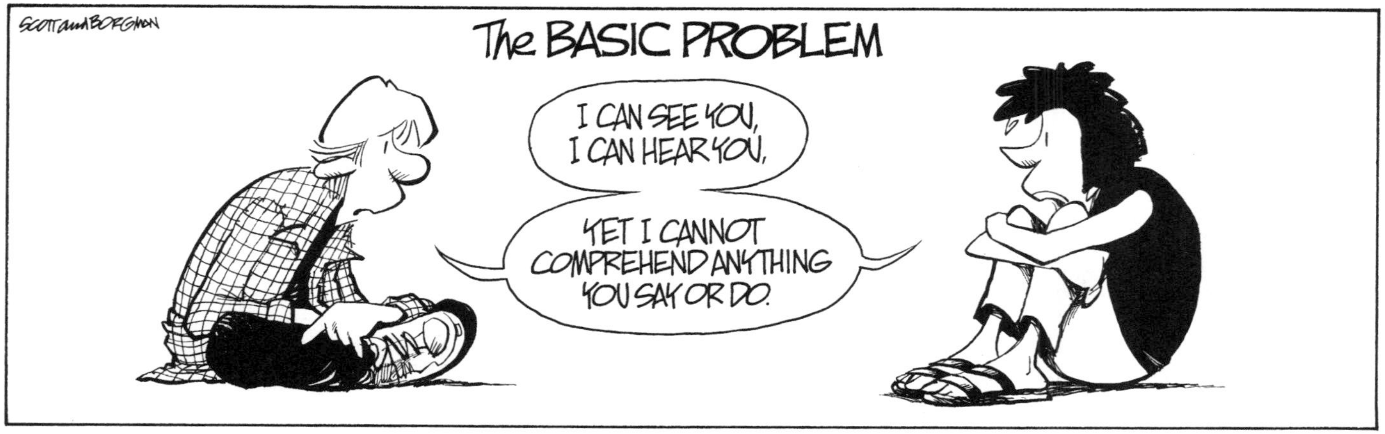
The BASIC PROBLEM
I CAN SEE YOU, I CAN HEAR YOU,
YET I CANNOT COMPREHEND ANYTHING YOU SAY OR DO.

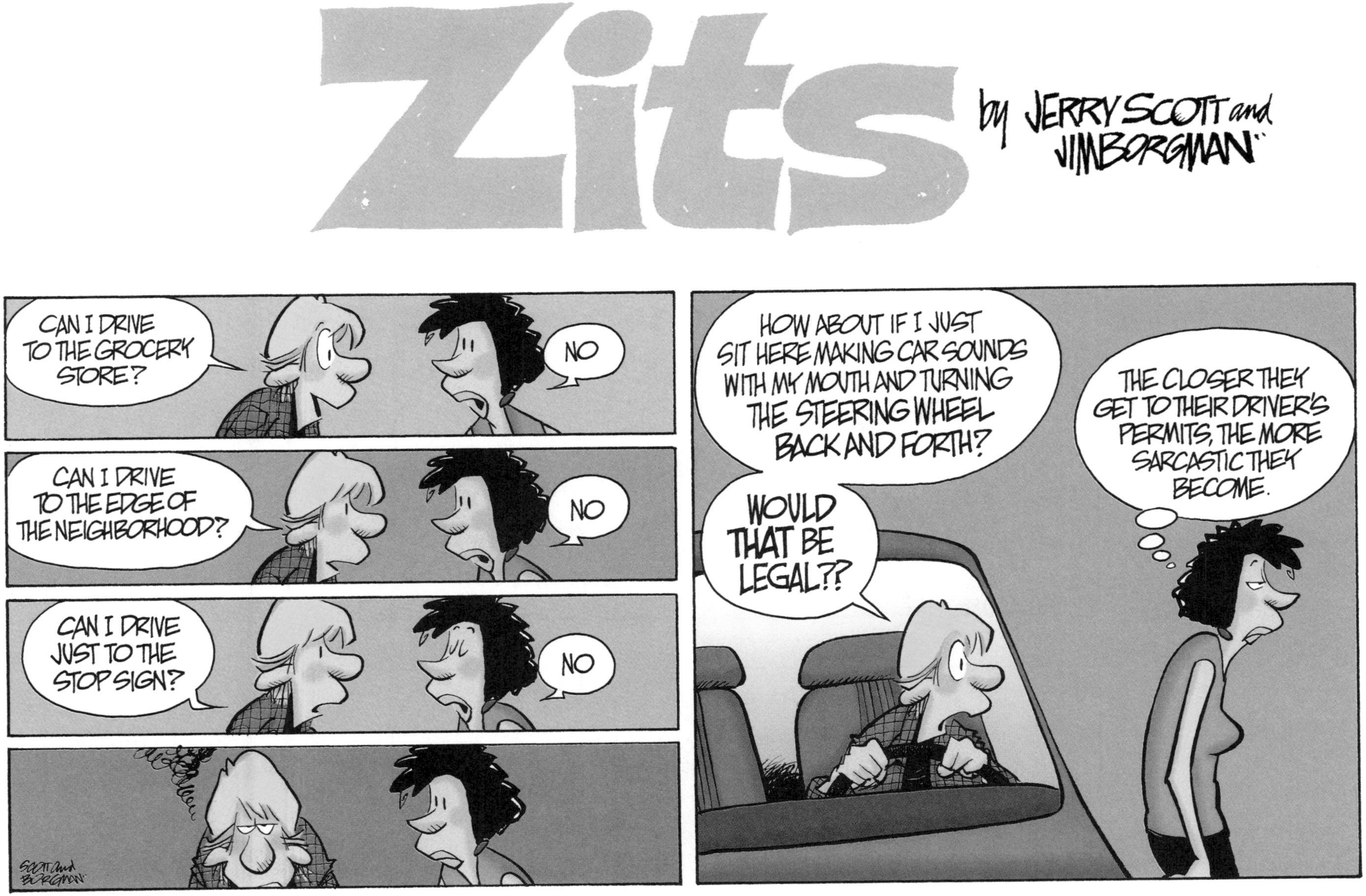
Zits
by JERRY SCOTT and JIM BORGMAN
CAN I DRIVE TO THE GROCERY STORE?
NO
CAN I DRIVE TO THE EDGE OF THE NEIGHBORHOOD?
NO
CAN I DRIVE JUST TO THE STOP SIGN?
NO
SCOTT and BORGMAN
HOW ABOUT IF I JUST SIT HERE MAKING CAR SOUNDS WITH MY MOUTH AND TURNING THE STEERING WHEEL BACK AND FORTH?
WOULD THAT BE LEGAL??
THE CLOSER THEY GET TO THEIR DRIVER'S PERMITS, THE MORE SARCASTIC THEY BECOME.

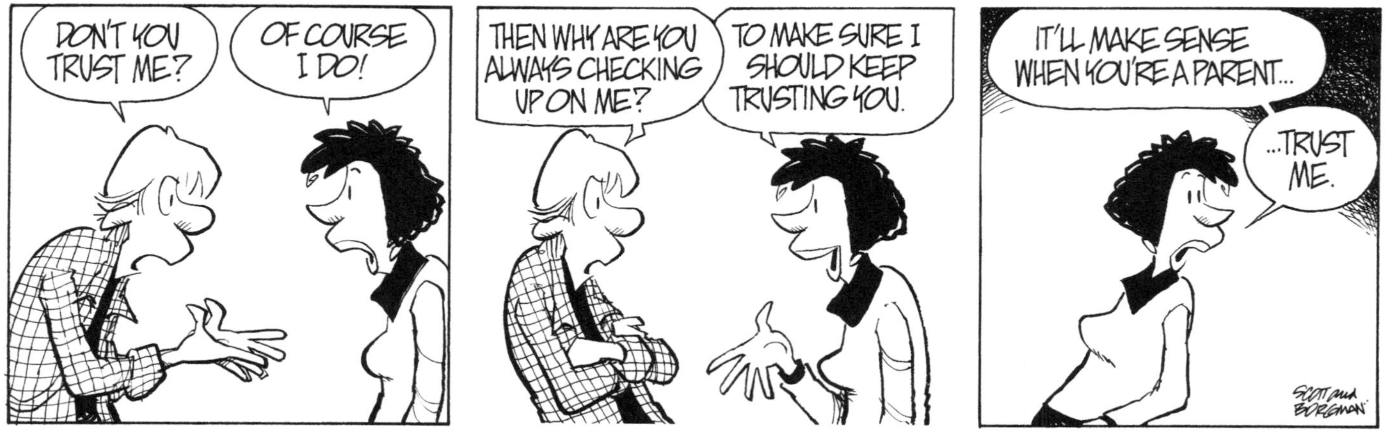
DON'T YOU TRUST ME?
OF COURSE I DO!
THEN WHY ARE YOU ALWAYS CHECKING UP ON ME?
TO MAKE SURE I SHOULD KEEP TRUSTING YOU.
IT'LL MAKE SENSE WHEN YOU'RE A PARENT...
...TRUST ME.
SCOTT and BORGMAN

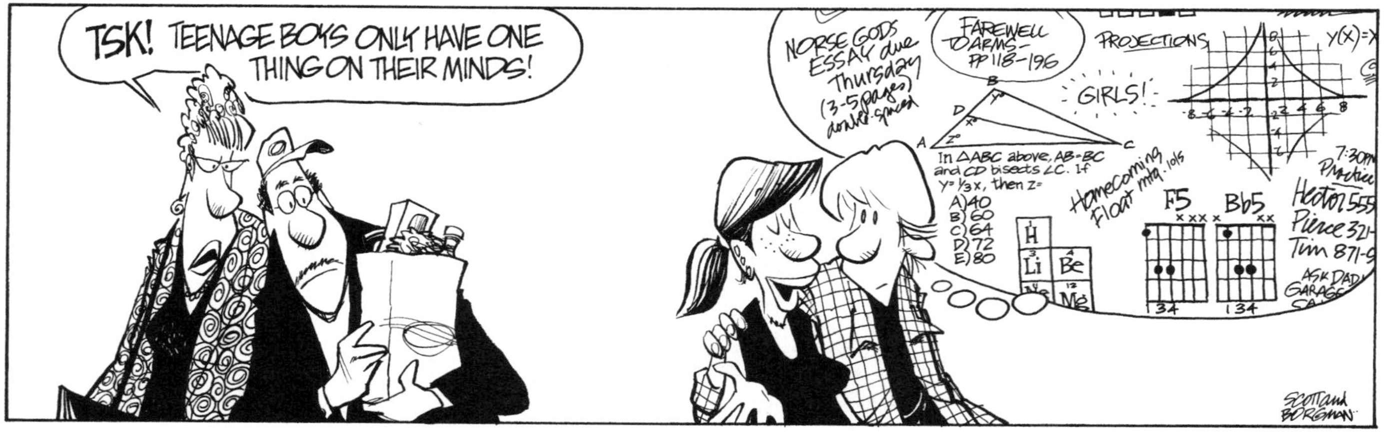
TSK! TEENAGE BOYS ONLY HAVE ONE THING ON THEIR MINDS!
NORSE GODS ESSAY due Thursday (3-5 pages) double-spaced
FAREWELL TO ARMS - PP 118-196
PROJECTIONS
GIRLS!
In △ABC above, AB=BC and CD bisects ∠C. If y=1/3x, then z=
A) 40
B) 60
C) 64
D) 72
E) 80
Homecoming Float mtg. 10/15
F5
Bb5
7:30PM Practice
SCOTT and BORGMAN

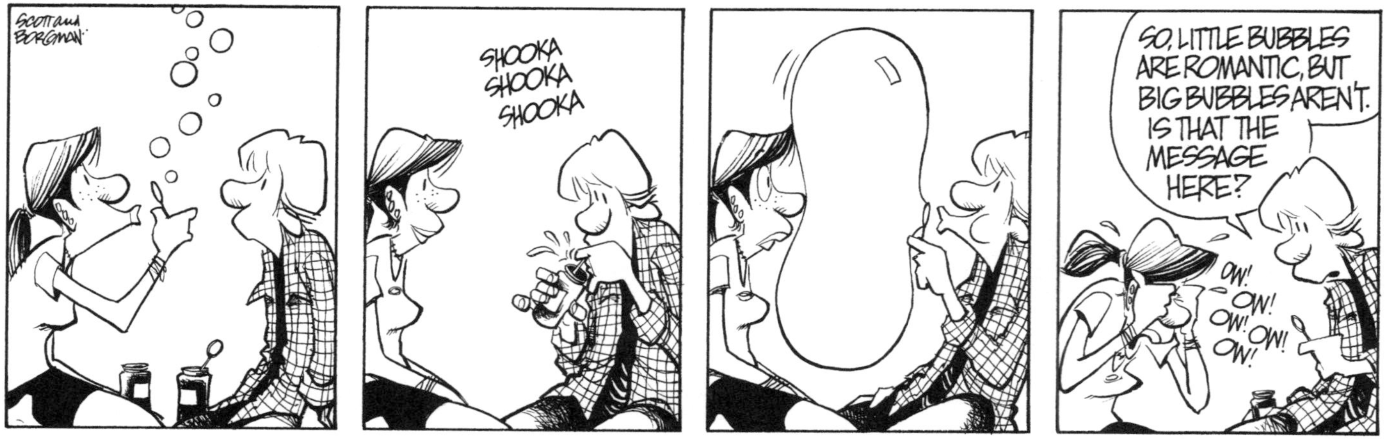
SCOTT and BORGMAN
SHOOKA SHOOKA SHOOKA
SO, LITTLE BUBBLES ARE ROMANTIC, BUT BIG BUBBLES AREN'T. IS THAT THE MESSAGE HERE?
OW! OW! OW! OW! OW!

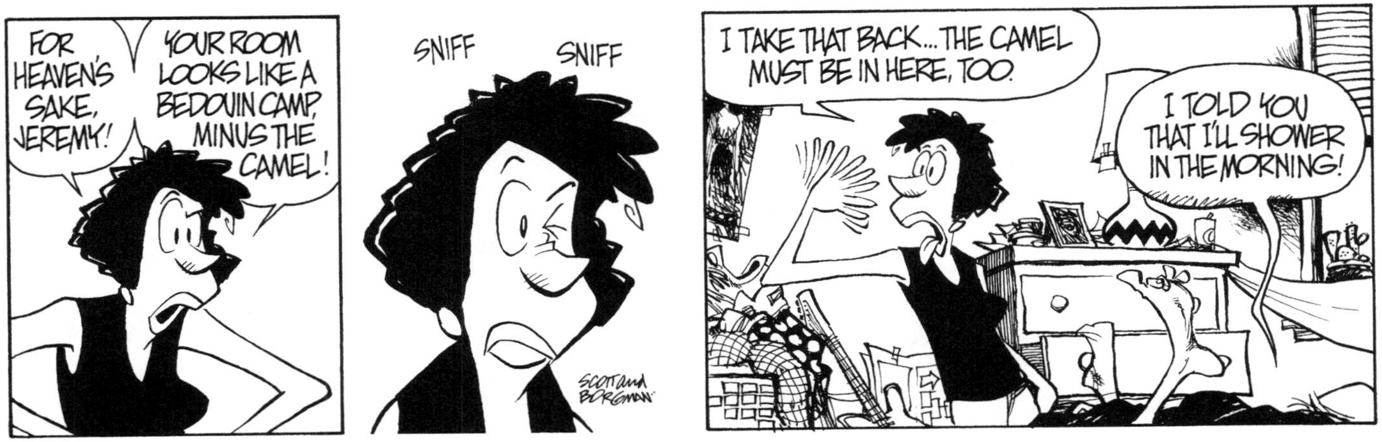
FOR HEAVEN'S SAKE, JEREMY!
YOUR ROOM LOOKS LIKE A BEDOUIN CAMP, MINUS THE CAMEL!
SNIFF
SNIFF
SCOTT and BORGMAN
I TAKE THAT BACK... THE CAMEL MUST BE IN HERE, TOO.
I TOLD YOU THAT I'LL SHOWER IN THE MORNING!

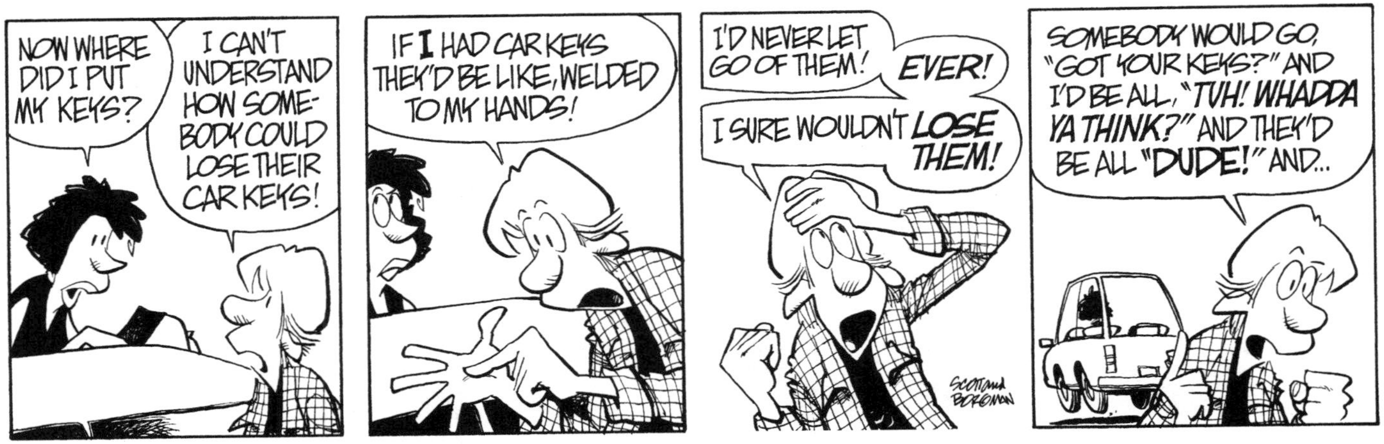
NOW WHERE DID I PUT MY KEYS?
I CAN'T UNDERSTAND HOW SOMEBODY COULD LOSE THEIR CAR KEYS!
IF I HAD CAR KEYS THEY'D BE LIKE, WELDED TO MY HANDS!
I'D NEVER LET GO OF THEM!
EVER!
I SURE WOULDN'T LOSE THEM!
SCOTT and BORGMAN
SOMEBODY WOULD GO, "GOT YOUR KEYS?" AND I'D BE ALL, "TUH! WHADDA YA THINK?" AND THEY'D BE ALL "DUDE!" AND...

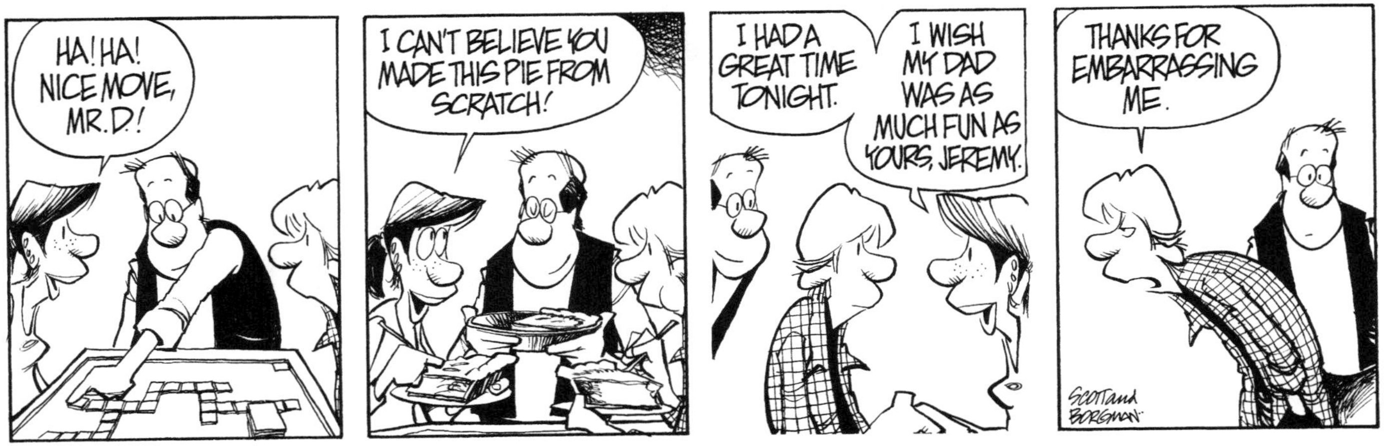
HA! HA! NICE MOVE, MR. D!
I CAN'T BELIEVE YOU MADE THIS PIE FROM SCRATCH!
I HAD A GREAT TIME TONIGHT.
I WISH MY DAD WAS AS MUCH FUN AS YOURS, JEREMY.
THANKS FOR EMBARRASSING ME.
SCOTT and BORGMAN

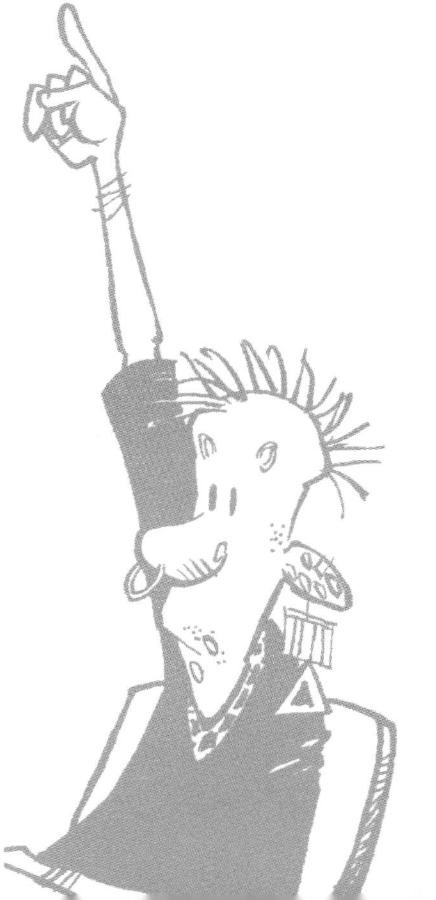

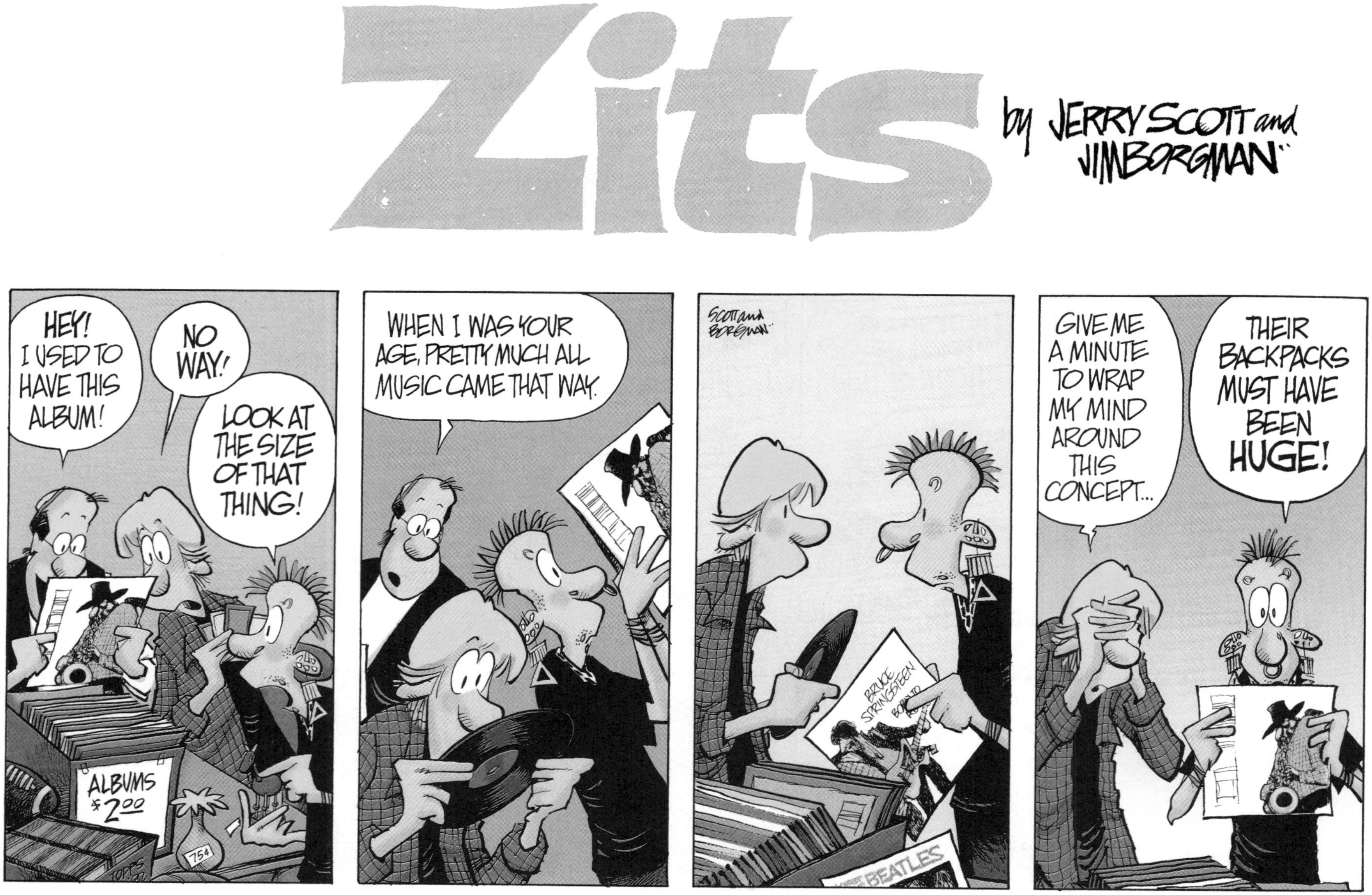
Zits
by JERRY SCOTT and JIM BORGMAN
HEY! I USED TO HAVE THIS ALBUM!
NO WAY!
LOOK AT THE SIZE OF THAT THING!
ALBUMS $2.00
75¢
WHEN I WAS YOUR AGE, PRETTY MUCH ALL MUSIC CAME THAT WAY.
SCOTT and BORGMAN
BRUCE SPRINGSTEEN
BEATLES
GIVE ME A MINUTE TO WRAP MY MIND AROUND THIS CONCEPT...
THEIR BACKPACKS MUST HAVE BEEN HUGE!

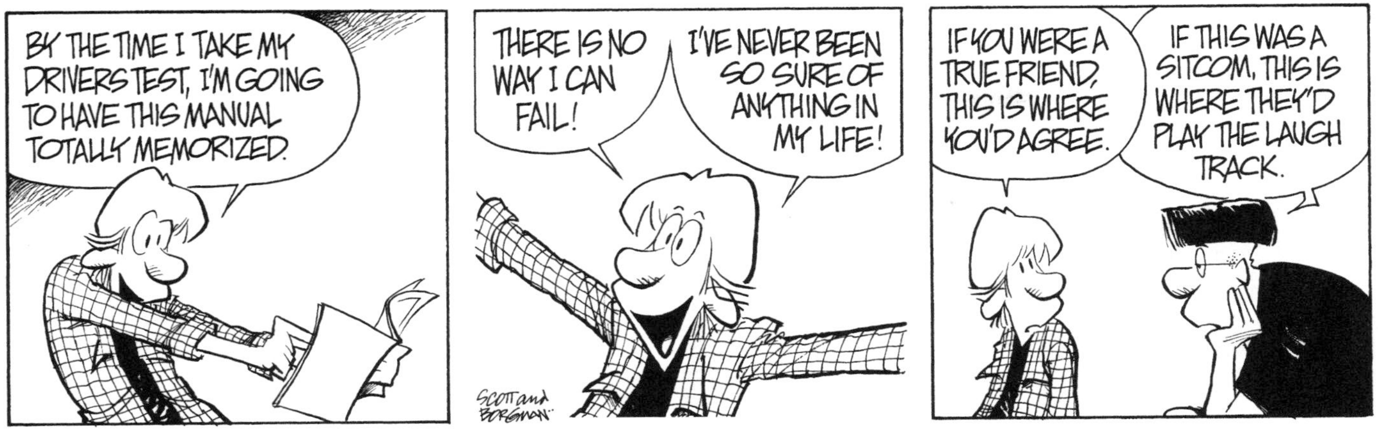
BY THE TIME I TAKE MY DRIVERS TEST, I'M GOING TO HAVE THIS MANUAL TOTALLY MEMORIZED.
THERE IS NO WAY I CAN FAIL!
I'VE NEVER BEEN SO SURE OF ANYTHING IN MY LIFE!
SCOTT and BORGMAN
IF YOU WERE A TRUE FRIEND, THIS IS WHERE YOU'D AGREE.
IF THIS WAS A SITCOM, THIS IS WHERE THEY'D PLAY THE LAUGH TRACK.

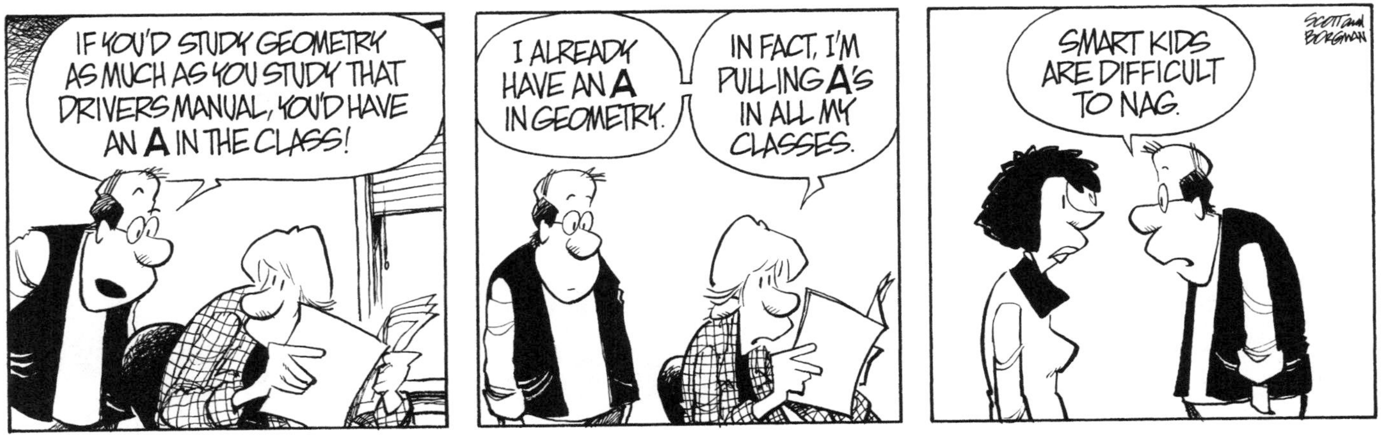
IF YOU'D STUDY GEOMETRY AS MUCH AS YOU STUDY THAT DRIVERS MANUAL, YOU'D HAVE AN A IN THE CLASS!
I ALREADY HAVE AN A IN GEOMETRY.
IN FACT, I'M PULLING A'S IN ALL MY CLASSES.
SCOTT and BORGMAN
SMART KIDS ARE DIFFICULT TO NAG.

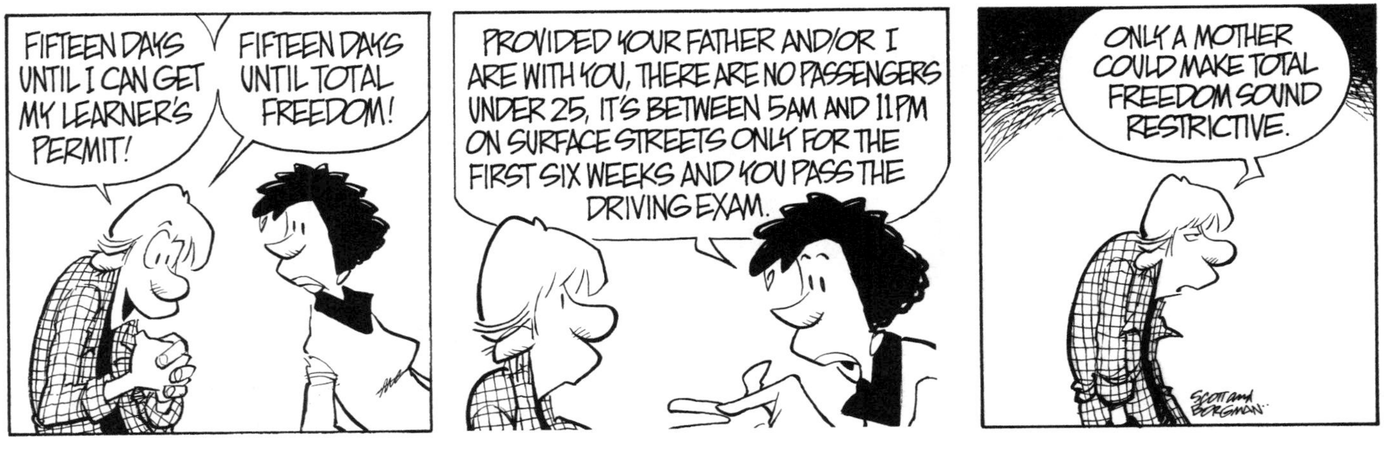
FIFTEEN DAYS UNTIL I CAN GET MY LEARNER'S PERMIT!
FIFTEEN DAYS UNTIL TOTAL FREEDOM!
PROVIDED YOUR FATHER AND/OR I ARE WITH YOU, THERE ARE NO PASSENGERS UNDER 25, IT'S BETWEEN 5AM AND 11PM ON SURFACE STREETS ONLY FOR THE FIRST SIX WEEKS AND YOU PASS THE DRIVING EXAM.
ONLY A MOTHER COULD MAKE TOTAL FREEDOM SOUND RESTRICTIVE.
SCOTT and BORGMAN

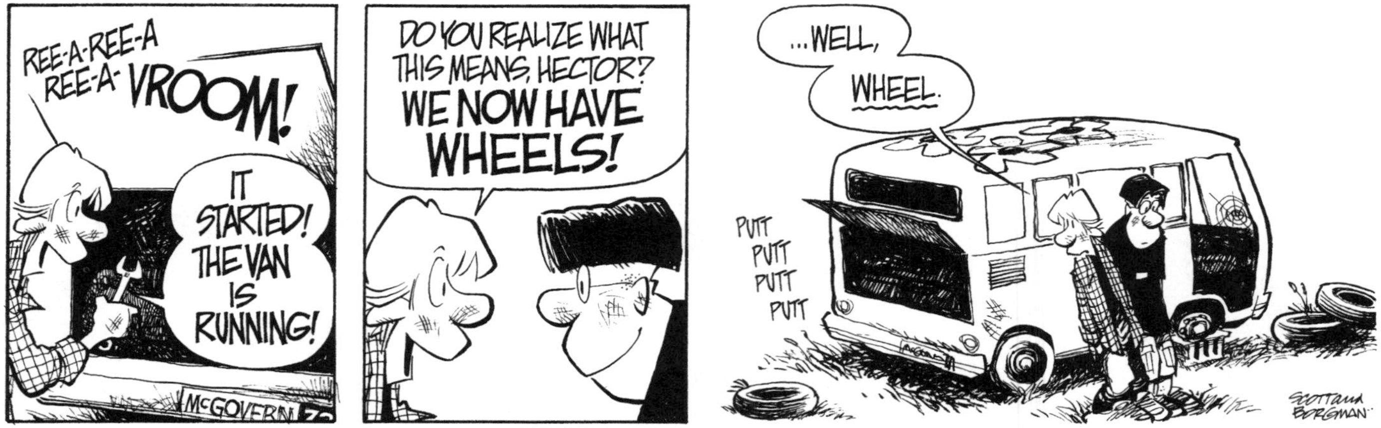
REE-A-REE-A REE-A-REE-A VROOM!
IT STARTED! THE VAN IS RUNNING!
McGOVERN
DO YOU REALIZE WHAT THIS MEANS, HECTOR? WE NOW HAVE WHEELS!
...WELL,
WHEEL.
PUTT PUTT PUTT PUTT
SCOTT and BORGMAN

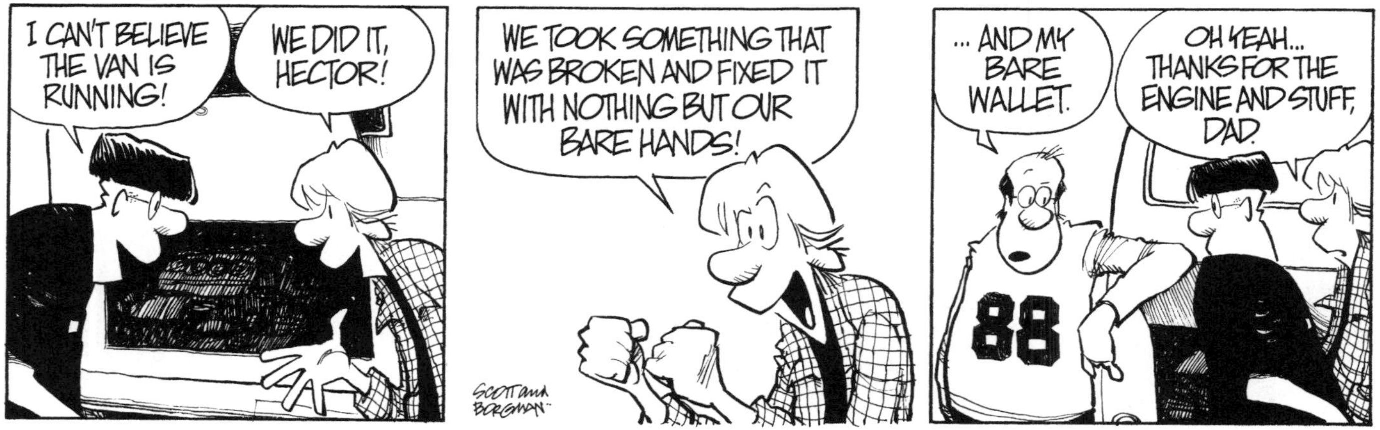
I CAN'T BELIEVE THE VAN IS RUNNING!
WE DID IT, HECTOR!
SCOTT and BORGMAN
WE TOOK SOMETHING THAT WAS BROKEN AND FIXED IT WITH NOTHING BUT OUR BARE HANDS!
... AND MY BARE WALLET.
OH YEAH... THANKS FOR THE ENGINE AND STUFF, DAD.
88

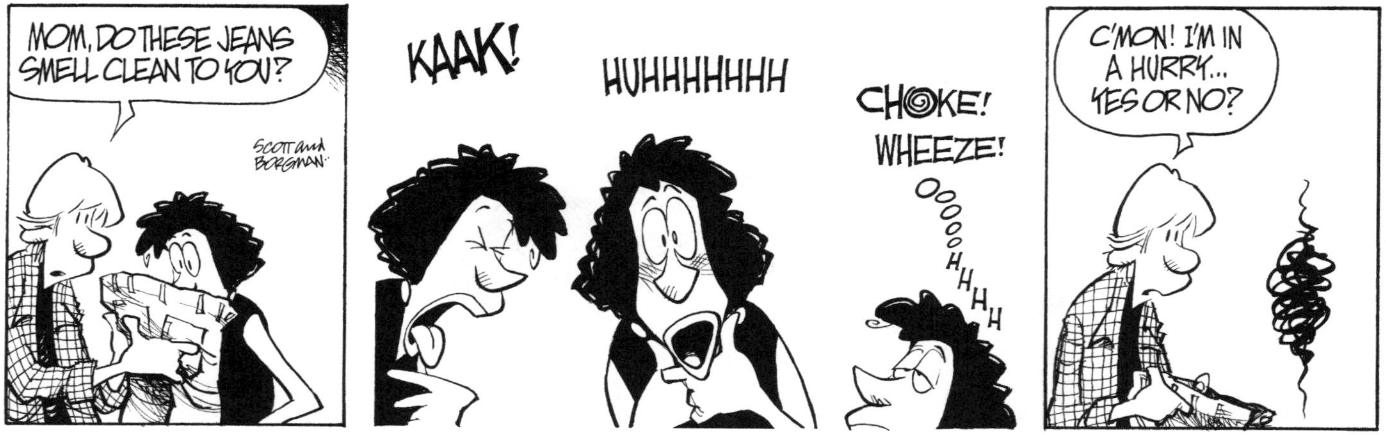
MOM, DO THESE JEANS SMELL CLEAN TO YOU?
SCOTT and BORGMAN
KAAK!
HUHHHHHHH
CHOKE!
WHEEZE!
OOOOOHHHHH
C'MON! I'M IN A HURRY... YES OR NO?

Zits

by JERRY SCOTT and JIM BORGMAN

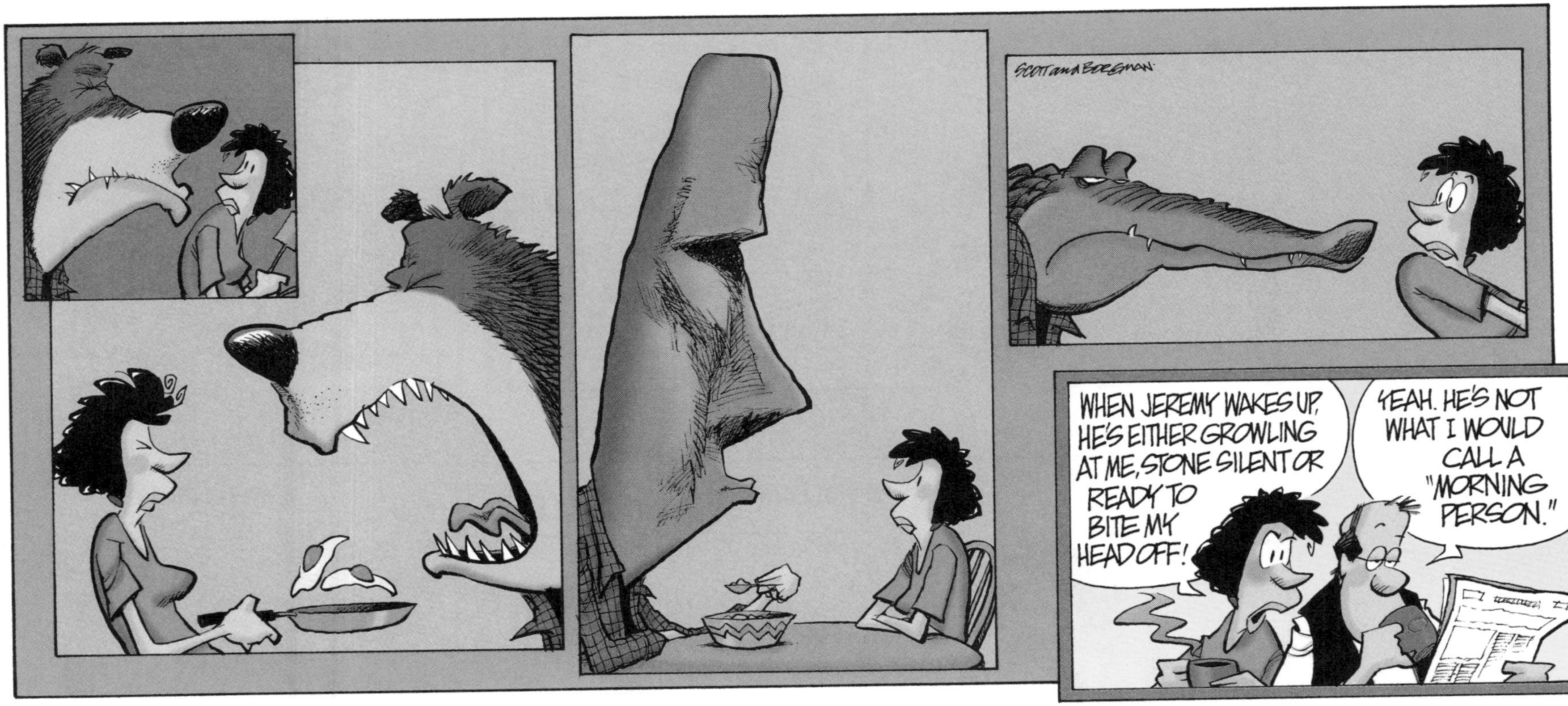
SCOTT and BORGMAN
WHEN JEREMY WAKES UP, HE'S EITHER GROWLING AT ME, STONE SILENT OR READY TO BITE MY HEAD OFF!
YEAH. HE'S NOT WHAT I WOULD CALL A "MORNING PERSON."

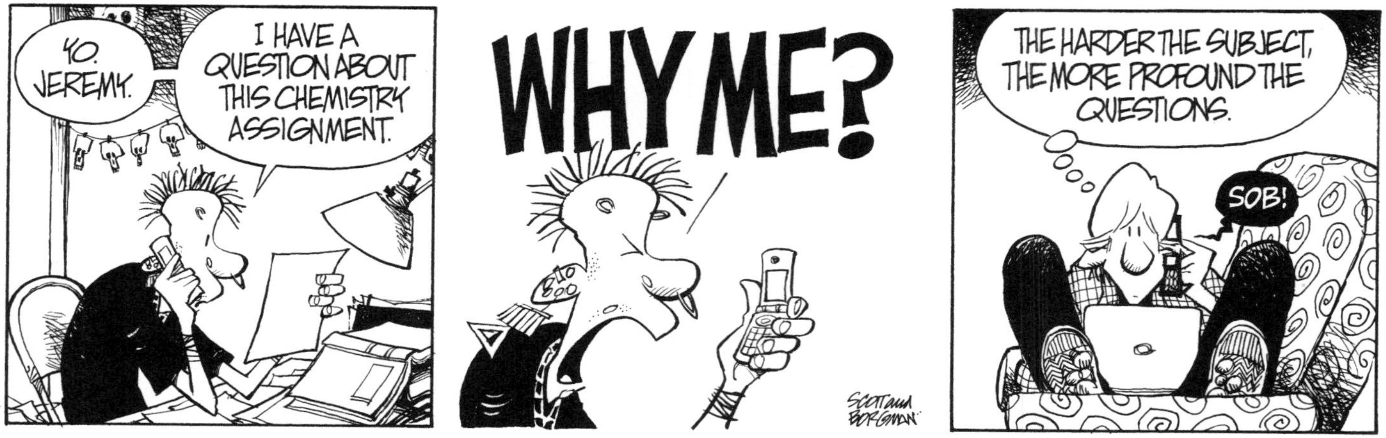
YO. JEREMY.
I HAVE A QUESTION ABOUT THIS CHEMISTRY ASSIGNMENT.
WHY ME?
THE HARDER THE SUBJECT, THE MORE PROFOUND THE QUESTIONS.
SOB!

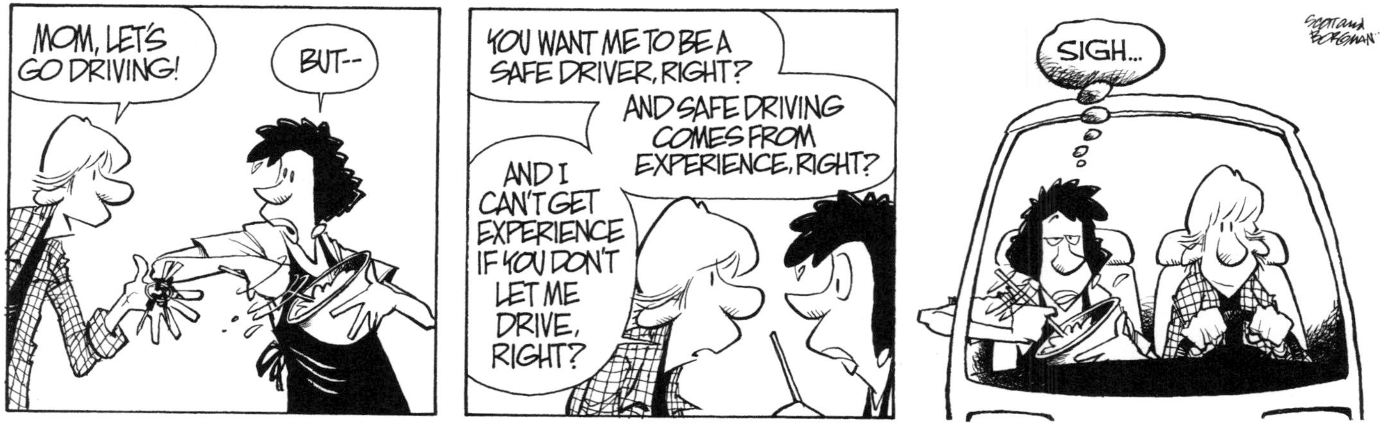
MOM, LET'S GO DRIVING!
BUT--
YOU WANT ME TO BE A SAFE DRIVER, RIGHT?
AND SAFE DRIVING COMES FROM EXPERIENCE, RIGHT?
AND I CAN'T GET EXPERIENCE IF YOU DON'T LET ME DRIVE, RIGHT?
SIGH...

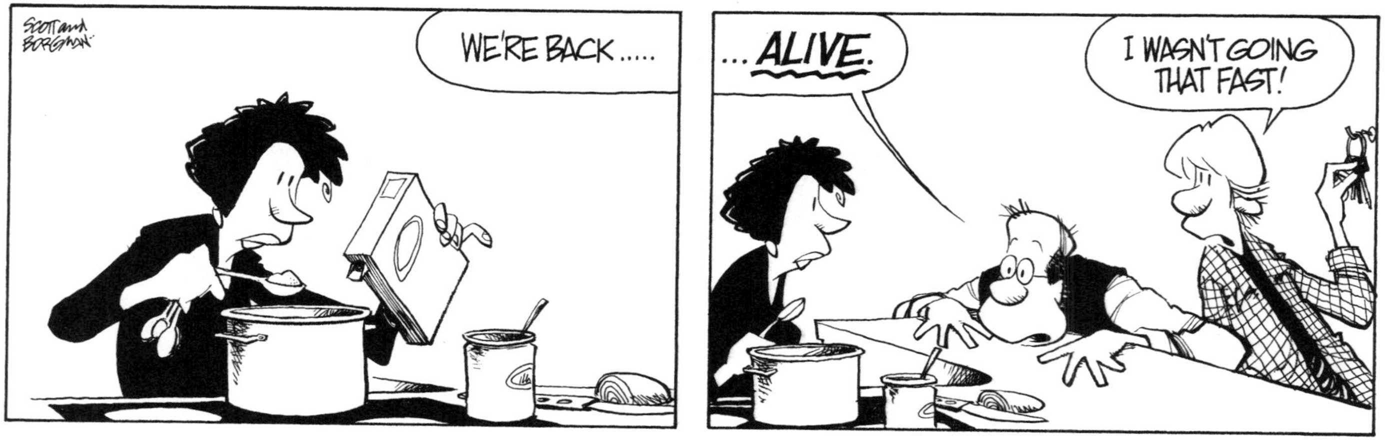
WE'RE BACK.....
...ALIVE.
I WASN'T GOING THAT FAST!

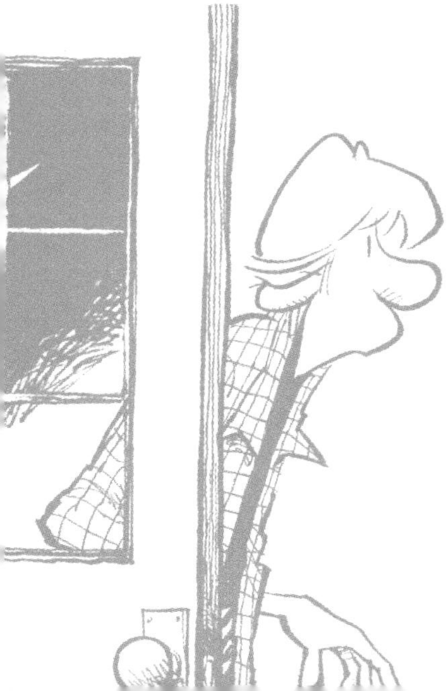

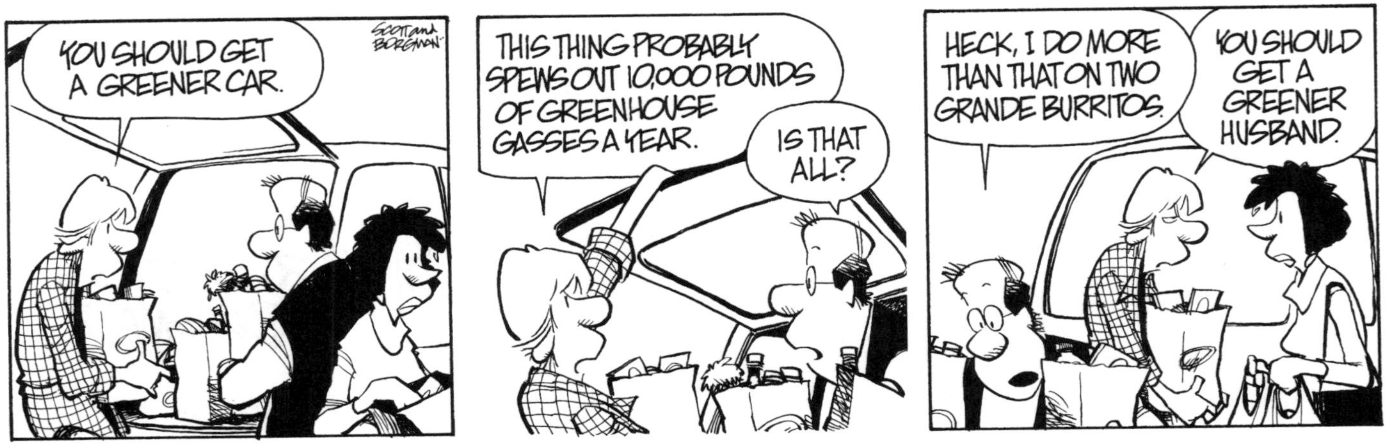
YOU SHOULD GET A GREENER CAR.
THIS THING PROBABLY SPEWS OUT 10,000 POUNDS OF GREENHOUSE GASSES A YEAR.
IS THAT ALL?
HECK, I DO MORE THAN THAT ON TWO GRANDE BURRITOS.
YOU SHOULD GET A GREENER HUSBAND.

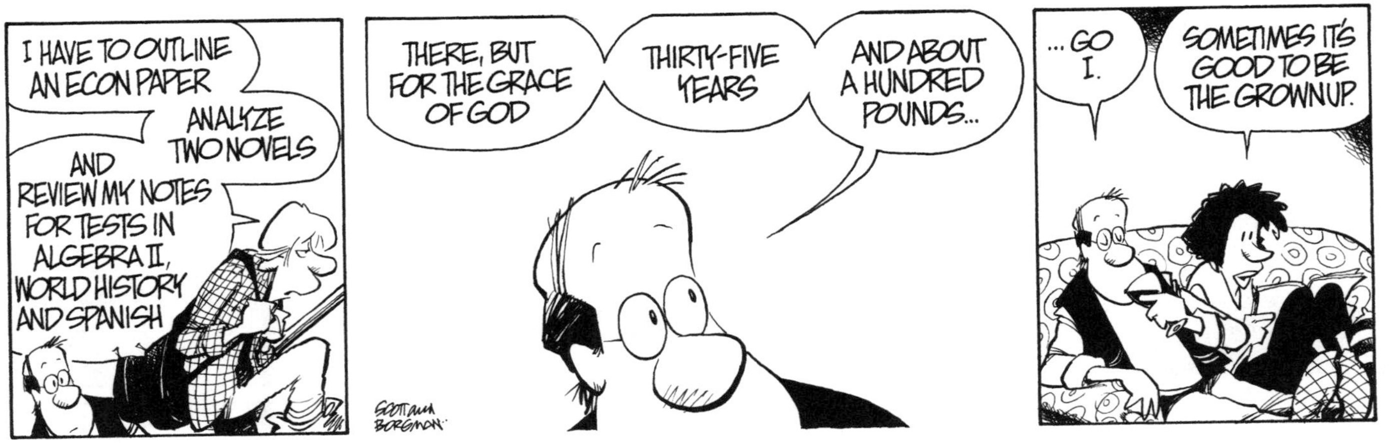
I HAVE TO OUTLINE AN ECON PAPER
ANALYZE TWO NOVELS
AND REVIEW MY NOTES FOR TESTS IN ALGEBRA II, WORLD HISTORY AND SPANISH
THERE, BUT FOR THE GRACE OF GOD
THIRTY-FIVE YEARS
AND ABOUT A HUNDRED POUNDS...
...GO I.
SOMETIMES IT'S GOOD TO BE THE GROWNUP.

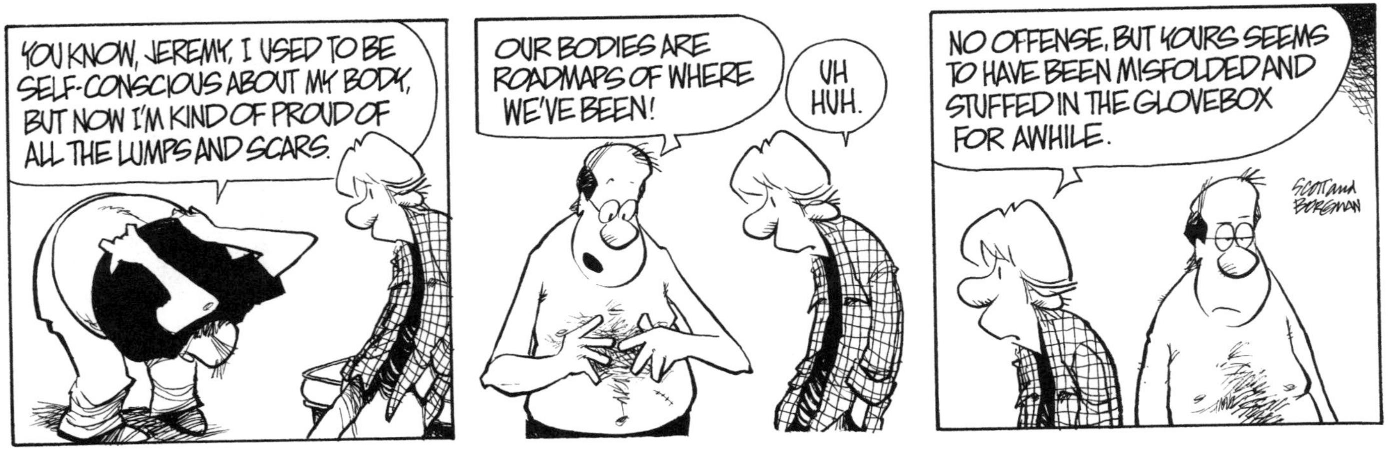
YOU KNOW, JEREMY, I USED TO BE SELF-CONSCIOUS ABOUT MY BODY, BUT NOW I'M KIND OF PROUD OF ALL THE LUMPS AND SCARS.
OUR BODIES ARE ROADMAPS OF WHERE WE'VE BEEN!
UH HUH.
NO OFFENSE, BUT YOURS SEEMS TO HAVE BEEN MISFOLDED AND STUFFED IN THE GLOVEBOX FOR AWHILE.

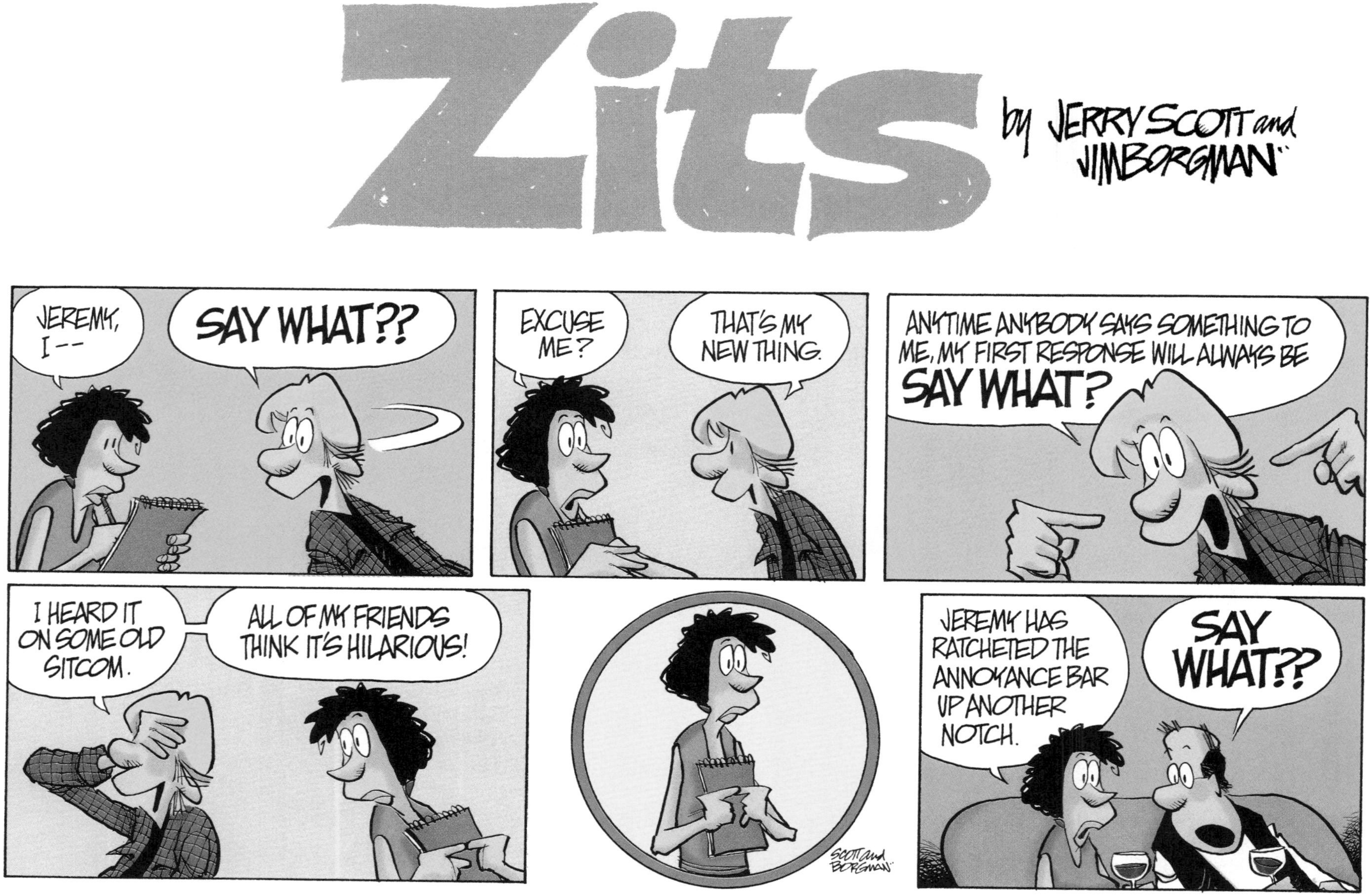
Zits
by JERRY SCOTT and JIM BORGMAN
JEREMY, I --
SAY WHAT??
EXCUSE ME?
THAT'S MY NEW THING.
ANYTIME ANYBODY SAYS SOMETHING TO ME, MY FIRST RESPONSE WILL ALWAYS BE SAY WHAT?
I HEARD IT ON SOME OLD SITCOM.
ALL OF MY FRIENDS THINK IT'S HILARIOUS!
SCOTT and BORGMAN
JEREMY HAS RATCHETED THE ANNOYANCE BAR UP ANOTHER NOTCH.
SAY WHAT??

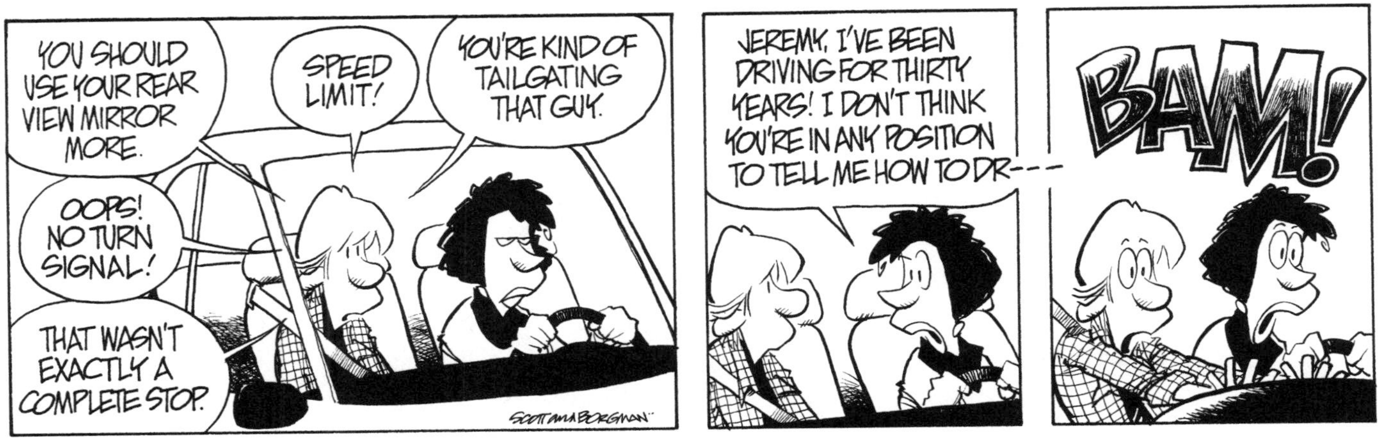
YOU SHOULD USE YOUR REAR VIEW MIRROR MORE.
SPEED LIMIT!
YOU'RE KIND OF TAILGATING THAT GUY.
OOPS! NO TURN SIGNAL!
THAT WASN'T EXACTLY A COMPLETE STOP.
JEREMY, I'VE BEEN DRIVING FOR THIRTY YEARS! I DON'T THINK YOU'RE IN ANY POSITION TO TELL ME HOW TO DR---
BAM!

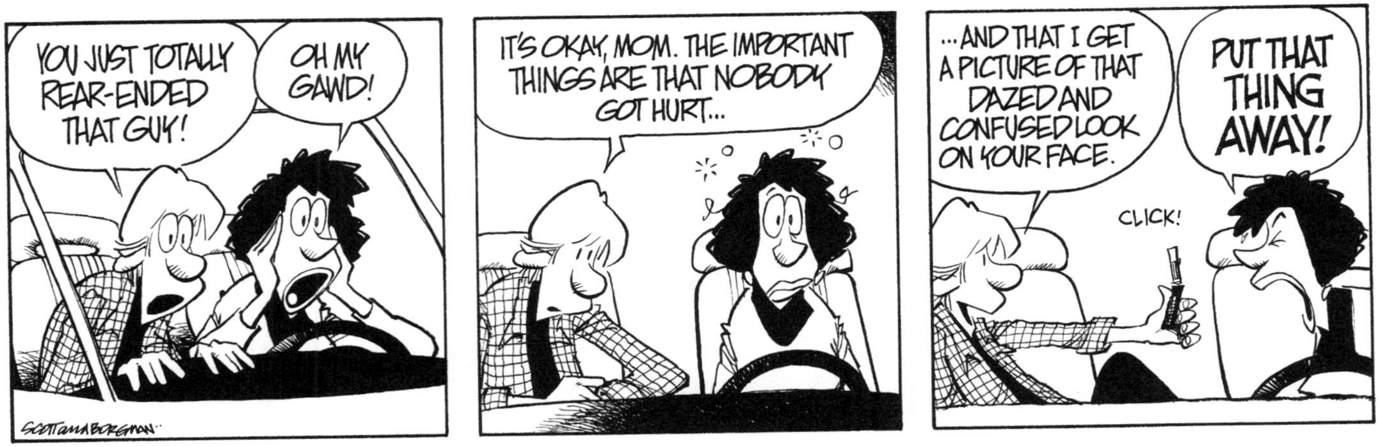
YOU JUST TOTALLY REAR-ENDED THAT GUY!
OH MY GAWD!
IT'S OKAY, MOM. THE IMPORTANT THINGS ARE THAT NOBODY GOT HURT...
...AND THAT I GET A PICTURE OF THAT DAZED AND CONFUSED LOOK ON YOUR FACE.
CLICK!
PUT THAT THING AWAY!

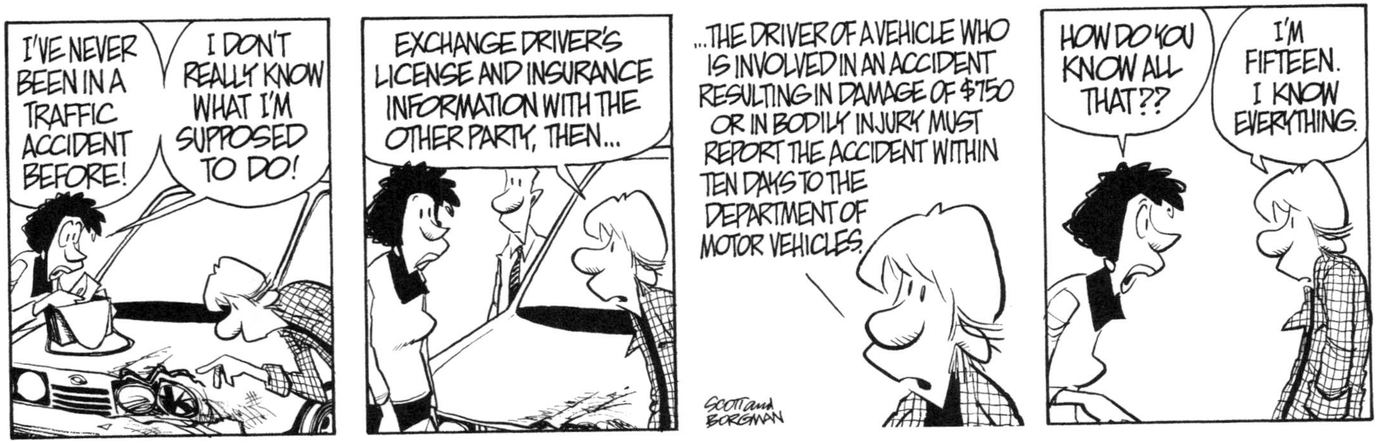
I'VE NEVER BEEN IN A TRAFFIC ACCIDENT BEFORE!
I DON'T REALLY KNOW WHAT I'M SUPPOSED TO DO!
EXCHANGE DRIVER'S LICENSE AND INSURANCE INFORMATION WITH THE OTHER PARTY, THEN...
...THE DRIVER OF A VEHICLE WHO IS INVOLVED IN AN ACCIDENT RESULTING IN DAMAGE OF $750 OR IN BODILY INJURY MUST REPORT THE ACCIDENT WITHIN TEN DAYS TO THE DEPARTMENT OF MOTOR VEHICLES.
HOW DO YOU KNOW ALL THAT??
I'M FIFTEEN. I KNOW EVERYTHING.

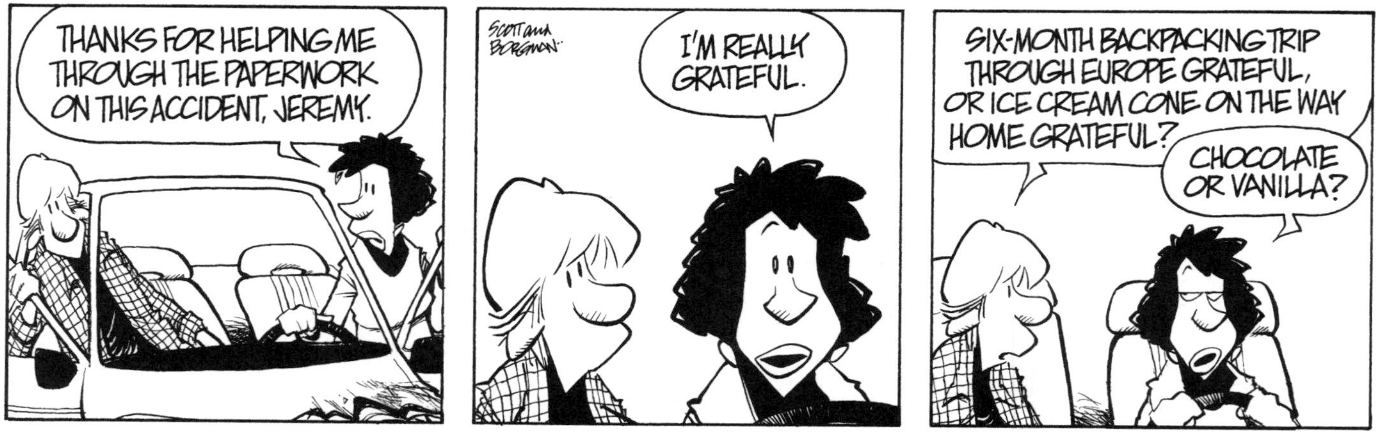
THANKS FOR HELPING ME THROUGH THE PAPERWORK ON THIS ACCIDENT, JEREMY.
SCOTT and BORGMAN
I'M REALLY GRATEFUL.
SIX-MONTH BACKPACKING TRIP THROUGH EUROPE GRATEFUL, OR ICE CREAM CONE ON THE WAY HOME GRATEFUL?
CHOCOLATE OR VANILLA?

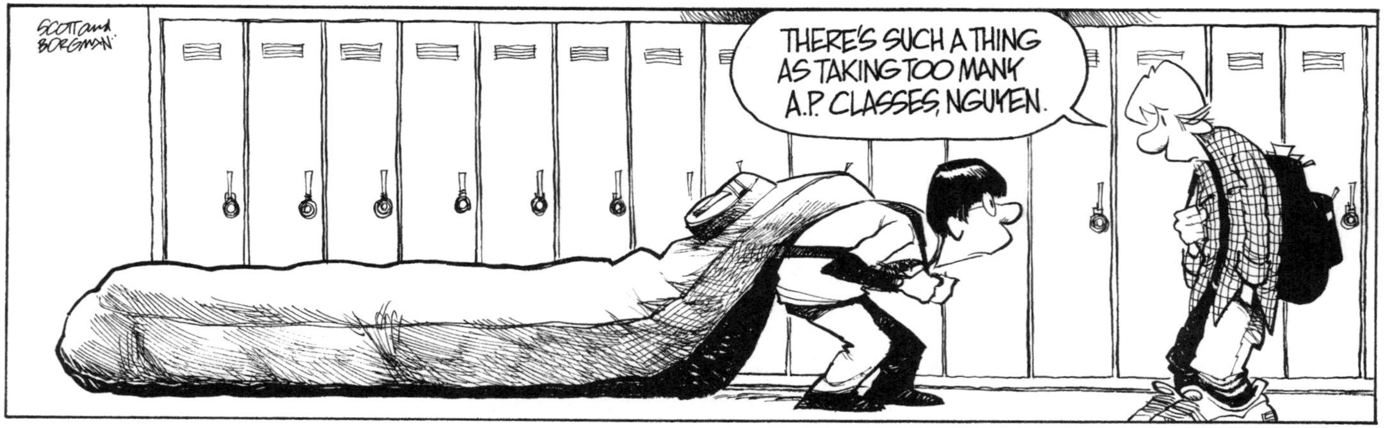
SCOTT and BORGMAN
THERE'S SUCH A THING AS TAKING TOO MANY A.P. CLASSES, NGUYEN.

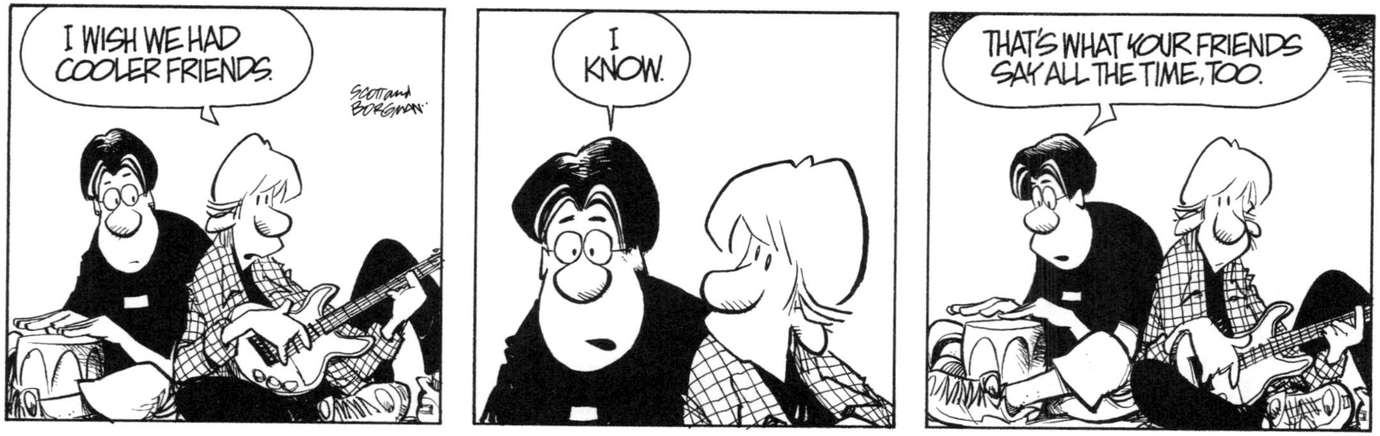
I WISH WE HAD COOLER FRIENDS.
SCOTT and BORGMAN
I KNOW.
THAT'S WHAT YOUR FRIENDS SAY ALL THE TIME, TOO.

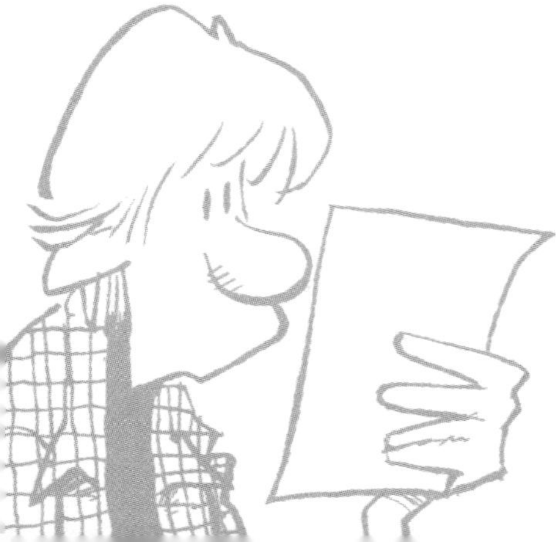

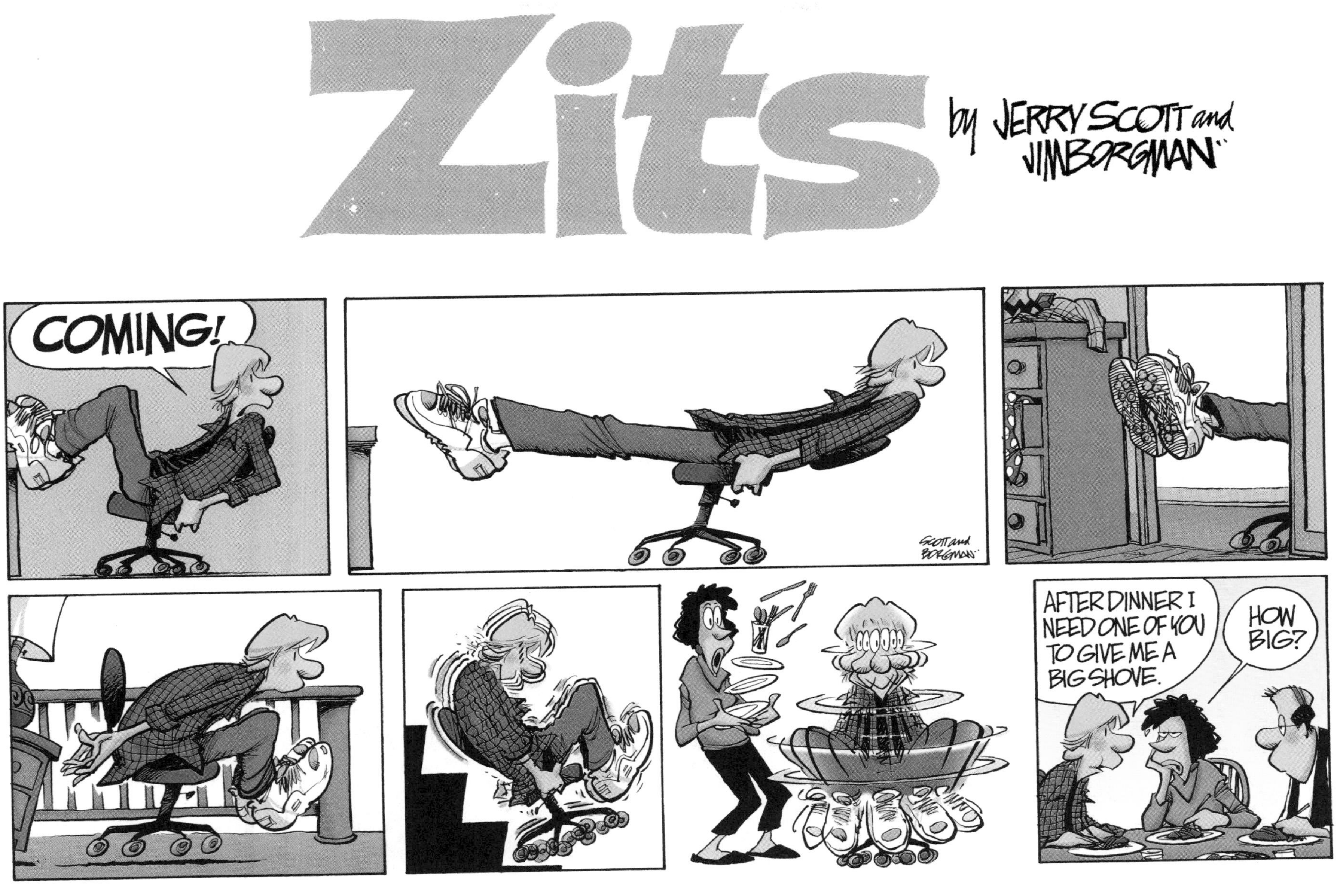
Zits
by JERRY SCOTT and JIM BORGMAN
COMING!
SCOTT and BORGMAN
AFTER DINNER I NEED ONE OF YOU TO GIVE ME A BIG SHOVE.
HOW BIG?

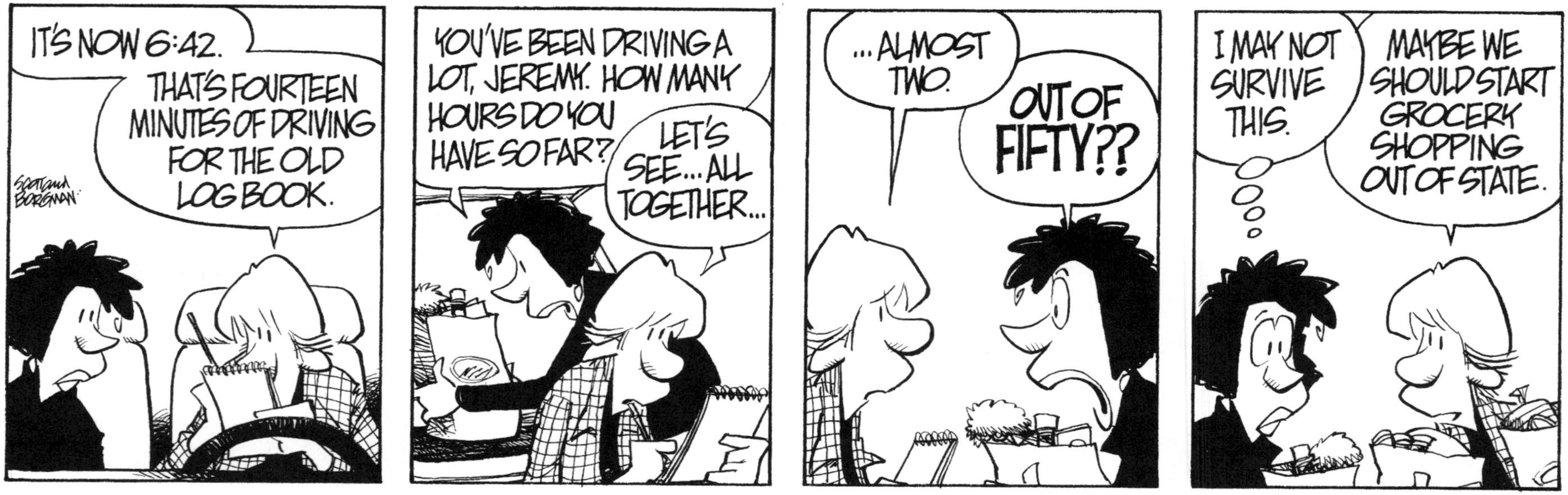
IT'S NOW 6:42.
THAT'S FOURTEEN MINUTES OF DRIVING FOR THE OLD LOG BOOK.
YOU'VE BEEN DRIVING A LOT, JEREMY. HOW MANY HOURS DO YOU HAVE SO FAR?
LET'S SEE... ALL TOGETHER...
...ALMOST TWO.
OUT OF FIFTY??
I MAY NOT SURVIVE THIS.
MAYBE WE SHOULD START GROCERY SHOPPING OUT OF STATE.

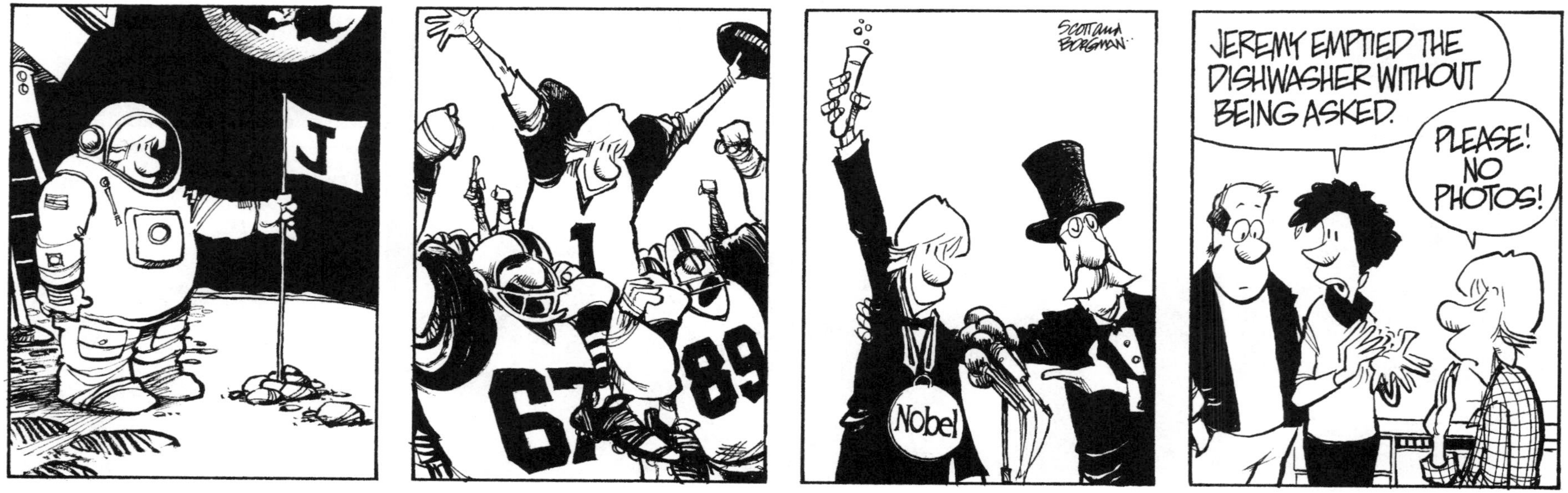
J
1
67
89
Nobel
JEREMY EMPTIED THE DISHWASHER WITHOUT BEING ASKED.
PLEASE! NO PHOTOS!

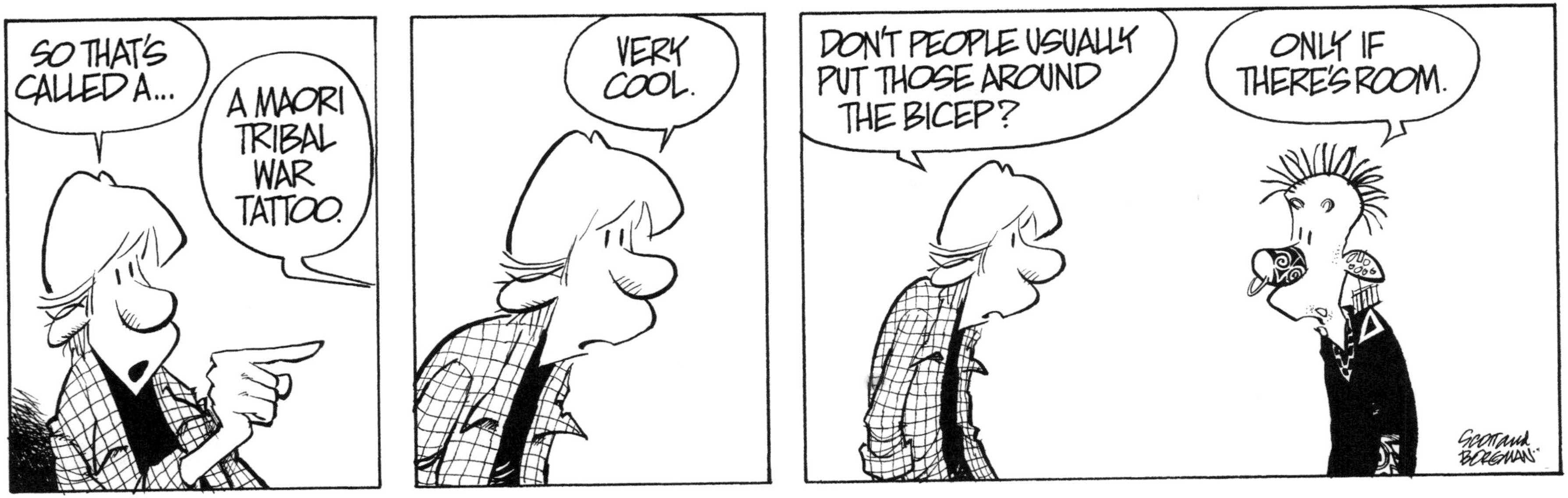
SO THAT'S CALLED A...
A MAORI TRIBAL WAR TATTOO.
VERY COOL.
DON'T PEOPLE USUALLY PUT THOSE AROUND THE BICEP?
ONLY IF THERE'S ROOM.
SCOTT AND BORGMAN

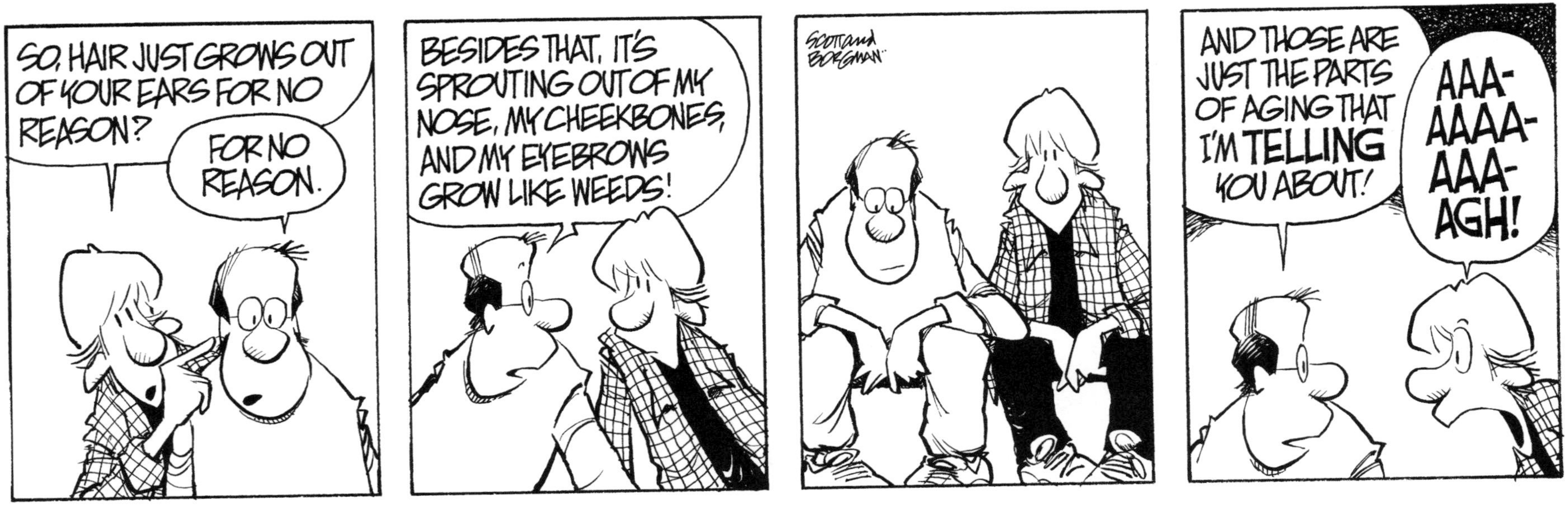
SO, HAIR JUST GROWS OUT OF YOUR EARS FOR NO REASON?
FOR NO REASON.
BESIDES THAT, IT'S SPROUTING OUT OF MY NOSE, MY CHEEKBONES, AND MY EYEBROWS GROW LIKE WEEDS!
SCOTT AND BORGMAN
AND THOSE ARE JUST THE PARTS OF AGING THAT I'M TELLING YOU ABOUT!
AAA-AAAA-AAA-AGH!

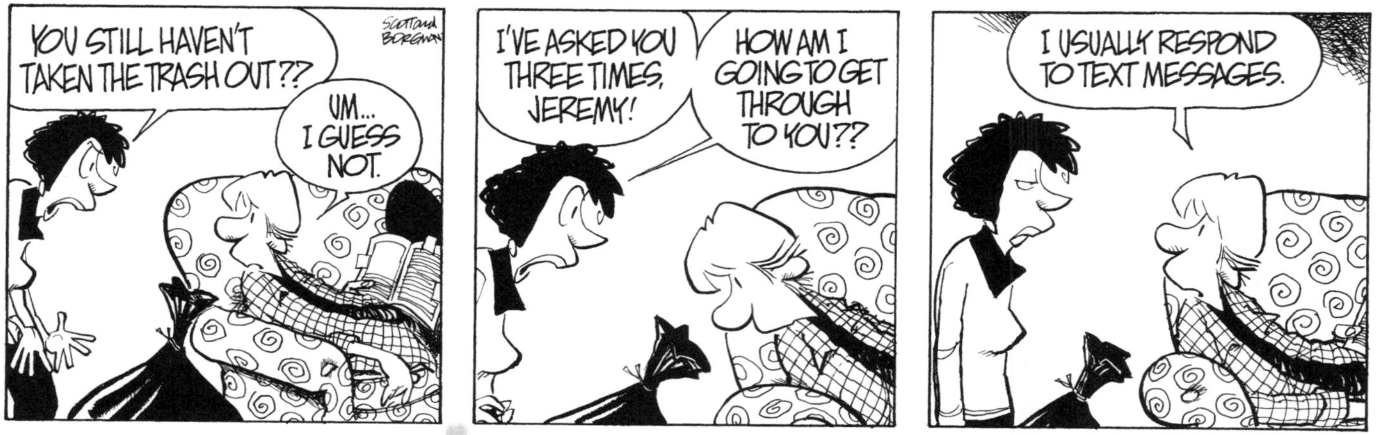
SCOTT and BORGMAN
YOU STILL HAVEN'T TAKEN THE TRASH OUT??
UM... I GUESS NOT.
I'VE ASKED YOU THREE TIMES, JEREMY!
HOW AM I GOING TO GET THROUGH TO YOU??
I USUALLY RESPOND TO TEXT MESSAGES.

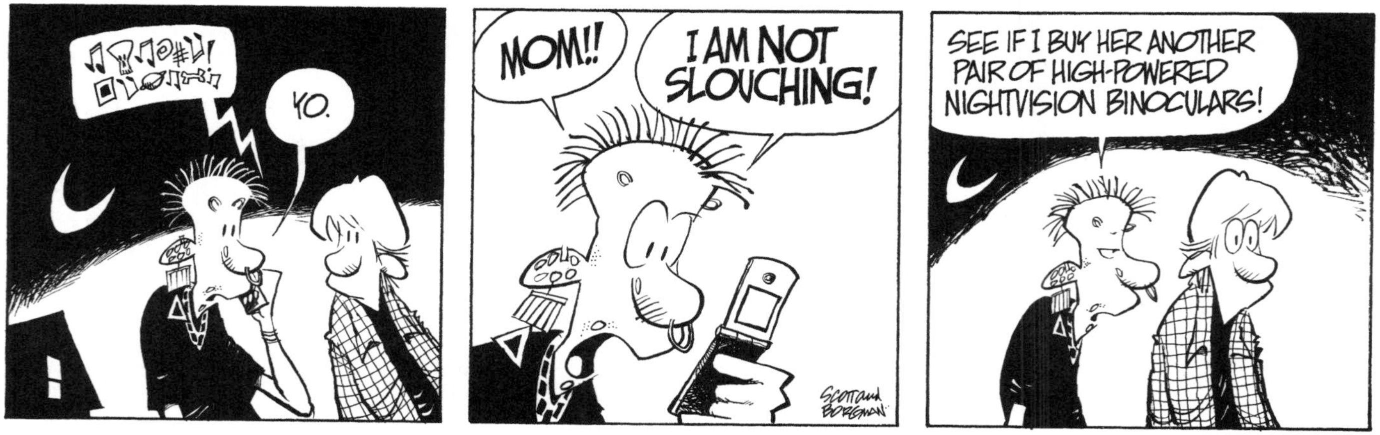
YO.
MOM!!
I AM NOT SLOUCHING!
SCOTT and BORGMAN
SEE IF I BUY HER ANOTHER PAIR OF HIGH-POWERED NIGHTVISION BINOCULARS!

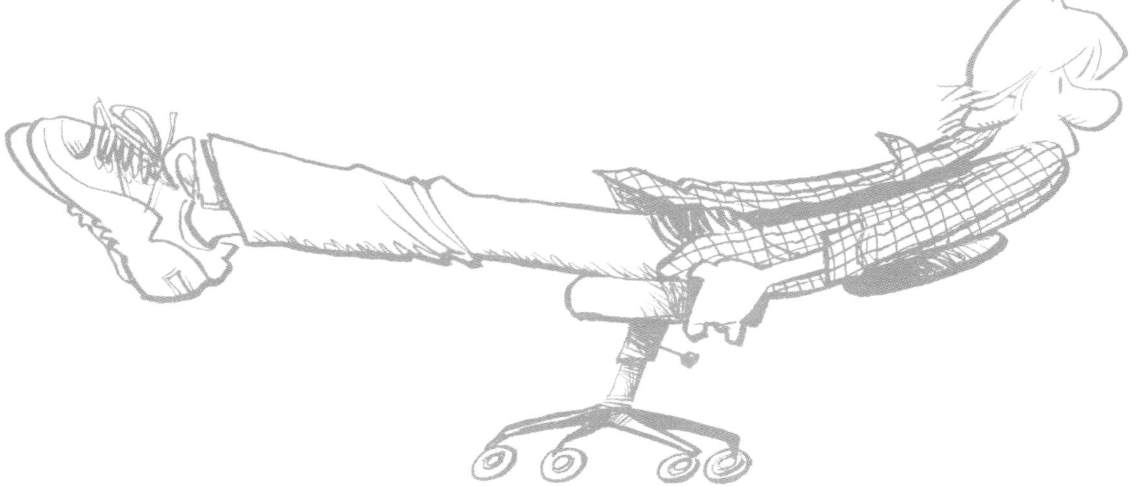

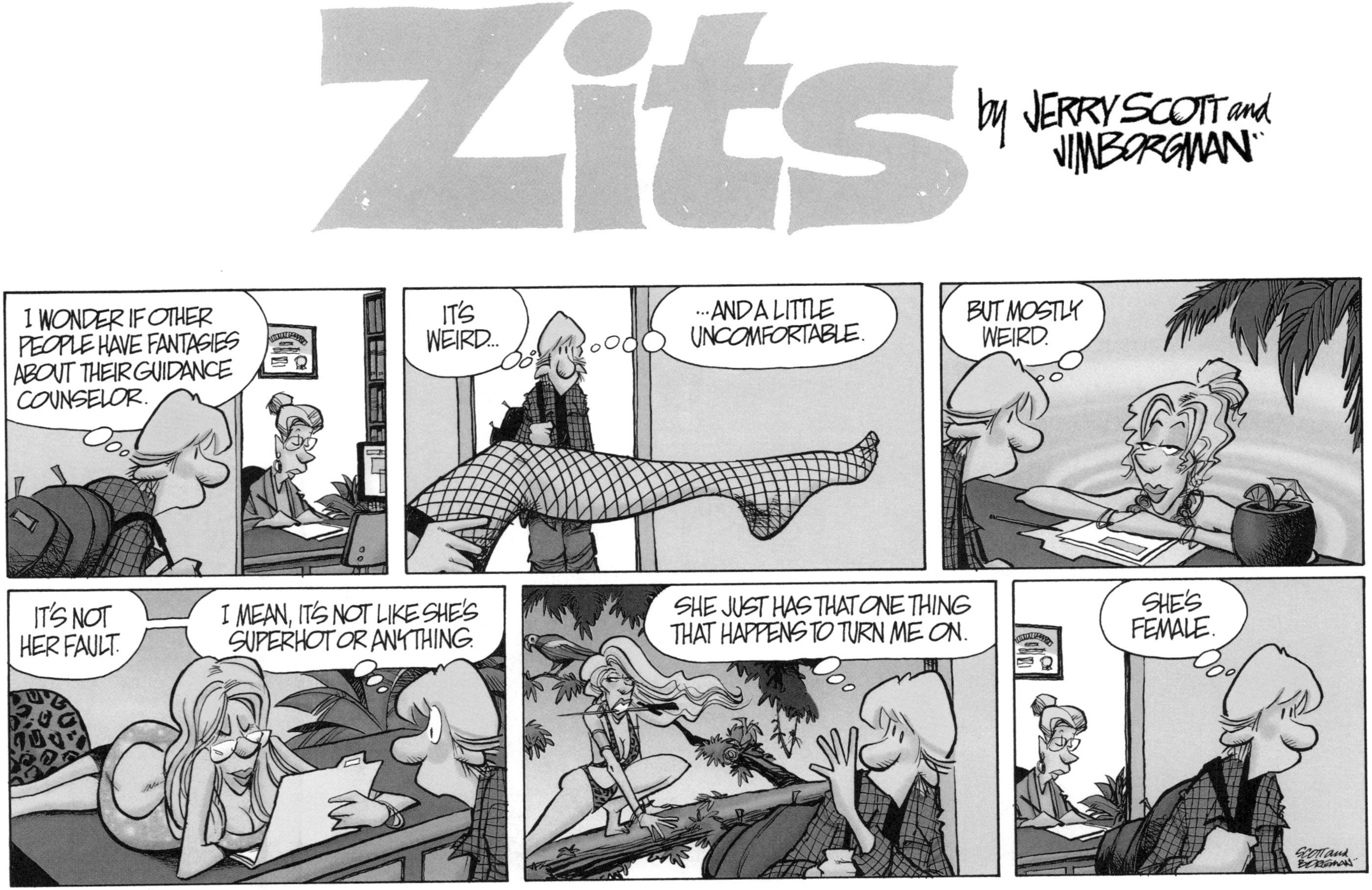
Zits
by JERRY SCOTT and JIM BORGMAN
I WONDER IF OTHER PEOPLE HAVE FANTASIES ABOUT THEIR GUIDANCE COUNSELOR.
IT'S WEIRD...
...AND A LITTLE UNCOMFORTABLE.
BUT MOSTLY WEIRD.
IT'S NOT HER FAULT.
I MEAN, IT'S NOT LIKE SHE'S SUPERHOT OR ANYTHING.
SHE JUST HAS THAT ONE THING THAT HAPPENS TO TURN ME ON.
SHE'S FEMALE.
SCOTT and BORGMAN

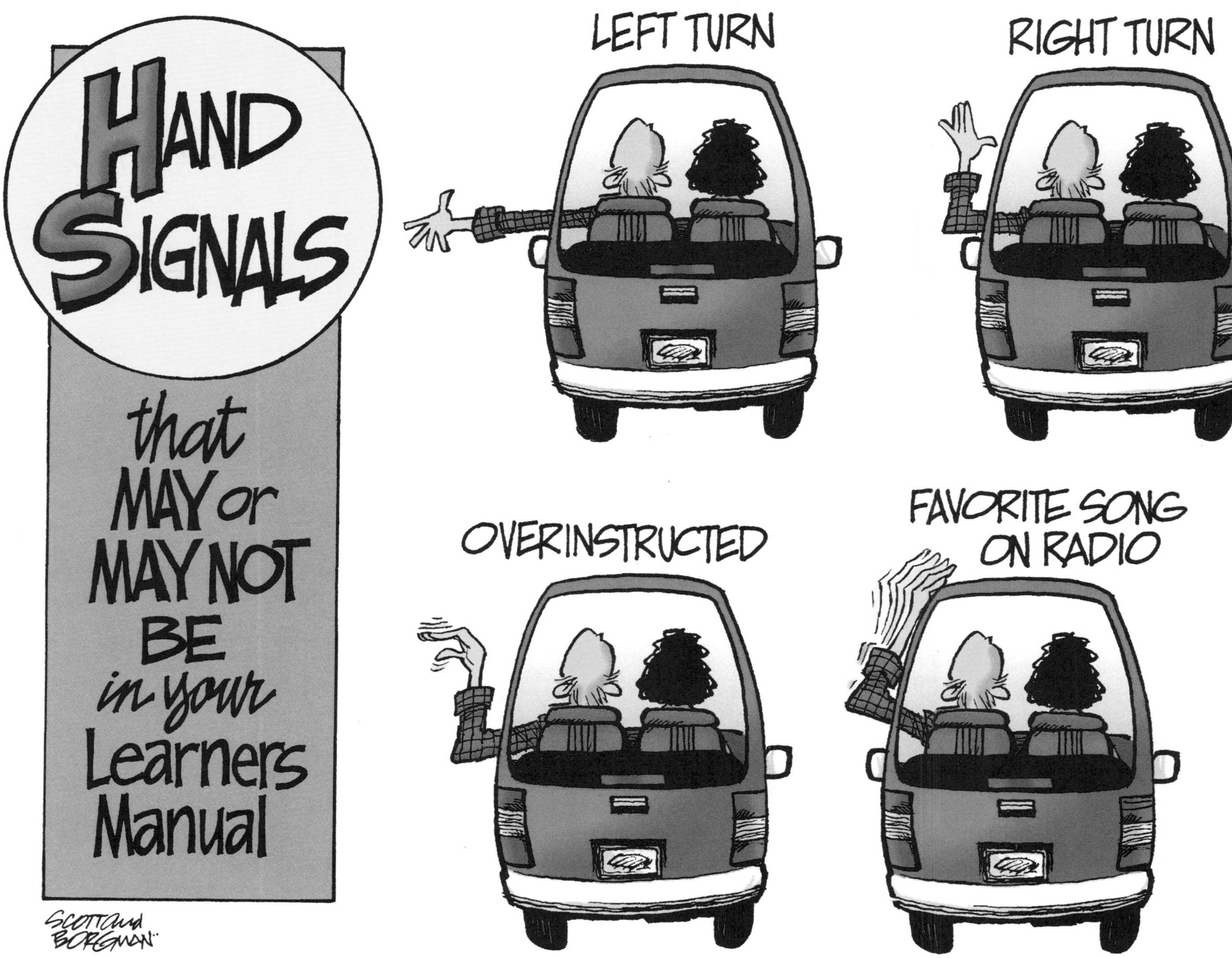
HAND SIGNALS
that MAY or MAY NOT BE in your Learners Manual
LEFT TURN
RIGHT TURN
OVERINSTRUCTED
FAVORITE SONG ON RADIO
SCOTT and BORGMAN

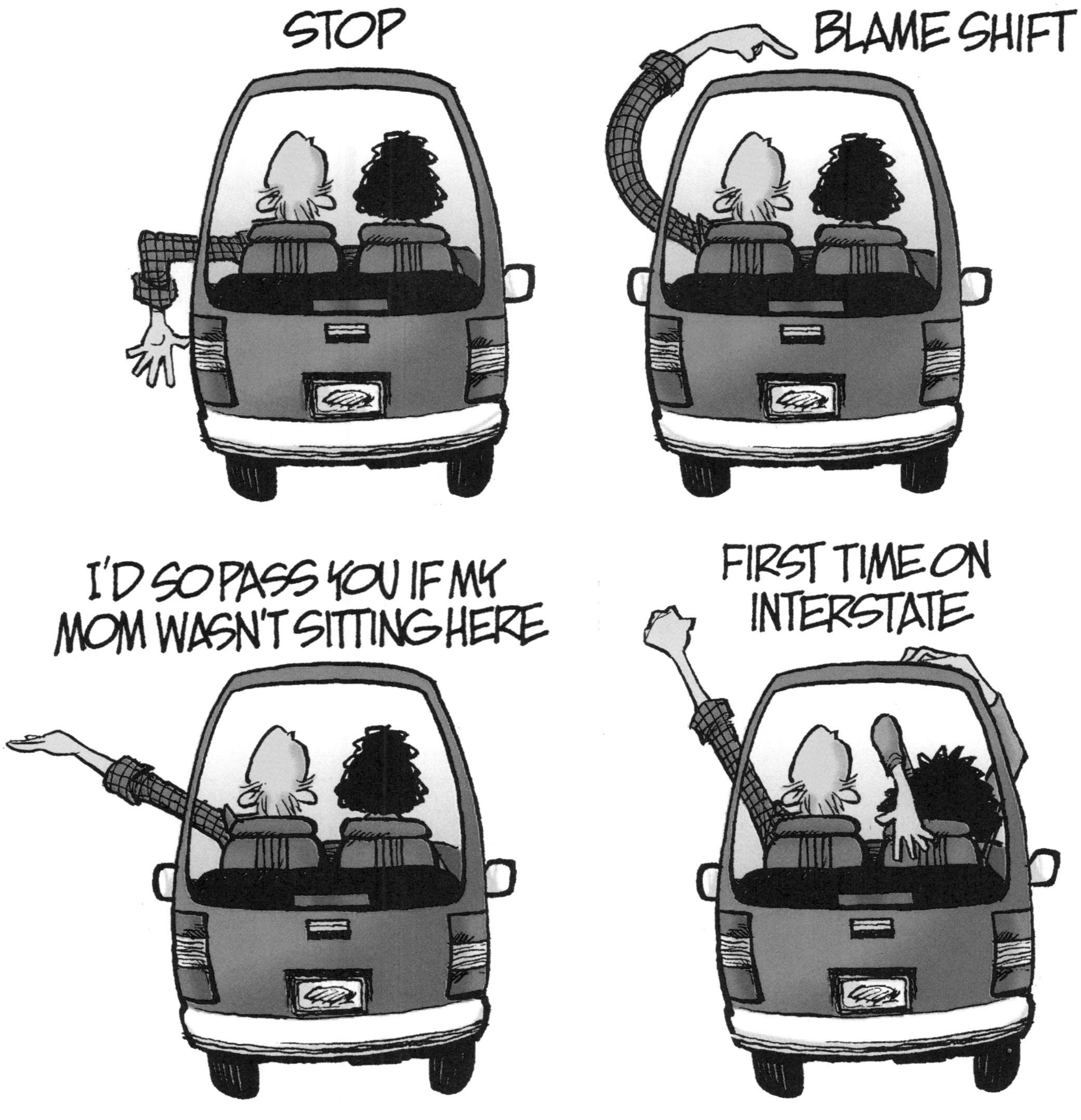
STOP
BLAME SHIFT
I'D SO PASS YOU IF MY MOM WASN'T SITTING HERE
FIRST TIME ON INTERSTATE

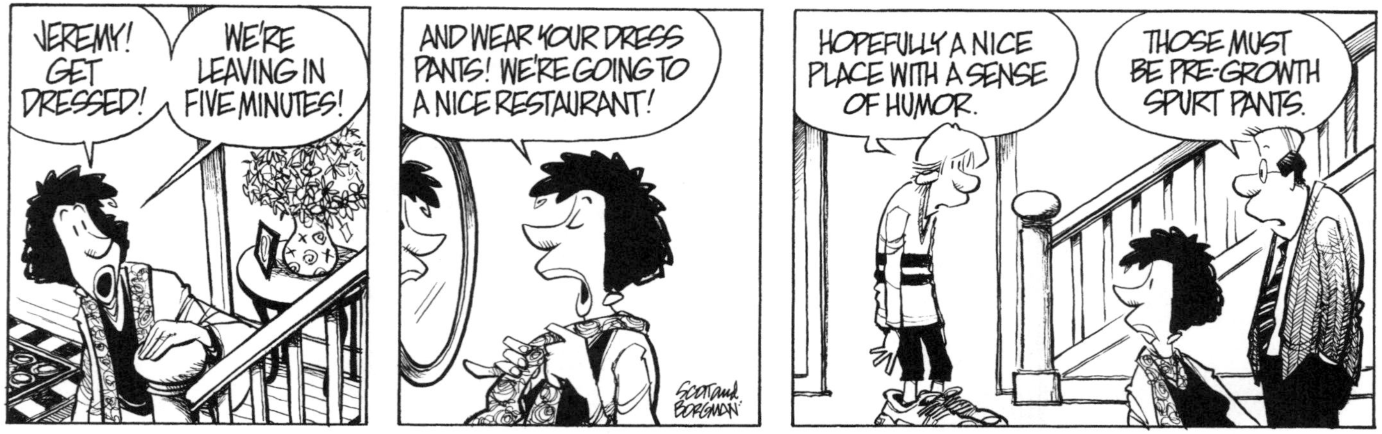
JEREMY! GET DRESSED!
WE'RE LEAVING IN FIVE MINUTES!
AND WEAR YOUR DRESS PANTS! WE'RE GOING TO A NICE RESTAURANT!
HOPEFULLY A NICE PLACE WITH A SENSE OF HUMOR.
THOSE MUST BE PRE-GROWTH SPURT PANTS.

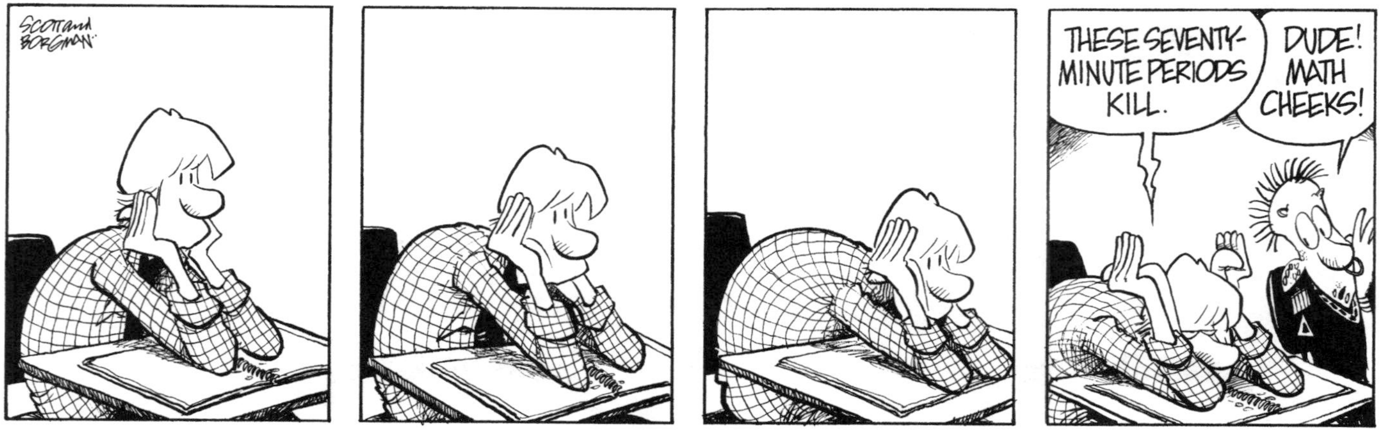
THESE SEVENTY-MINUTE PERIODS KILL.
DUDE! MATH CHEEKS!

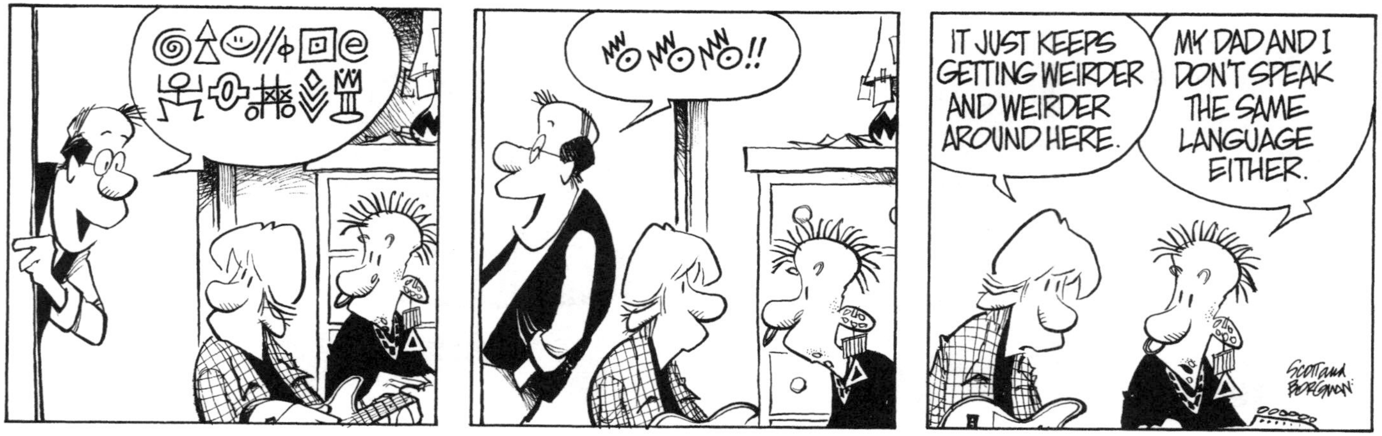
IT JUST KEEPS GETTING WEIRDER AND WEIRDER AROUND HERE.
MY DAD AND I DON'T SPEAK THE SAME LANGUAGE EITHER.

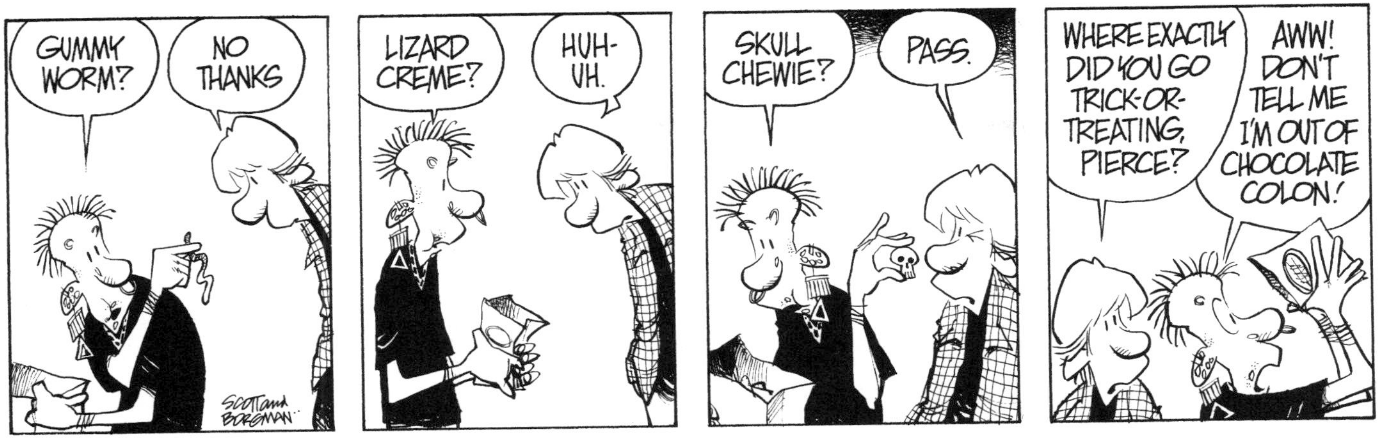
GUMMY WORM?
NO THANKS
SCOTT and BORGMAN
LIZARD CREME?
HUH-UH.
SKULL CHEWIE?
PASS.
WHERE EXACTLY DID YOU GO TRICK-OR-TREATING, PIERCE?
AWW! DON'T TELL ME I'M OUT OF CHOCOLATE COLON!

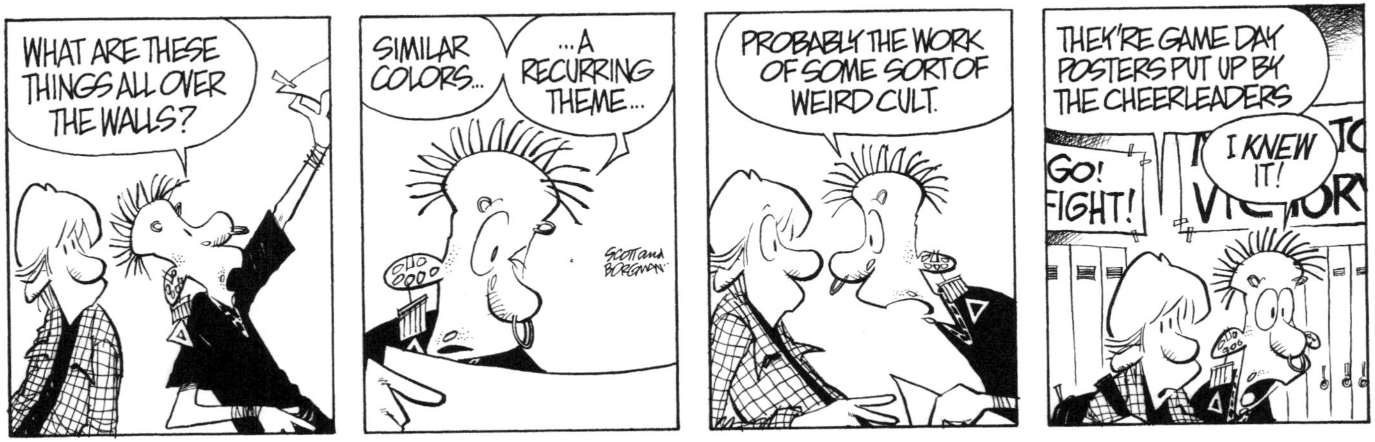
WHAT ARE THESE THINGS ALL OVER THE WALLS?
SIMILAR COLORS...
...A RECURRING THEME...
SCOTT and BORGMAN
PROBABLY THE WORK OF SOME SORT OF WEIRD CULT.
THEY'RE GAME DAY POSTERS PUT UP BY THE CHEERLEADERS
GO! FIGHT!
I KNEW IT!

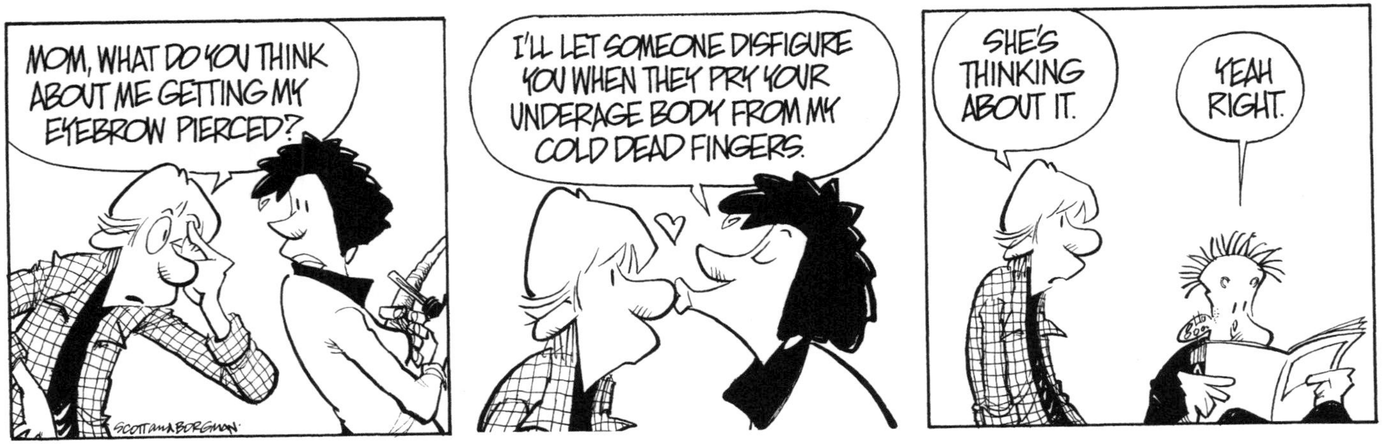
MOM, WHAT DO YOU THINK ABOUT ME GETTING MY EYEBROW PIERCED?
SCOTT and BORGMAN
I'LL LET SOMEONE DISFIGURE YOU WHEN THEY PRY YOUR UNDERAGE BODY FROM MY COLD DEAD FINGERS.
SHE'S THINKING ABOUT IT.
YEAH RIGHT.

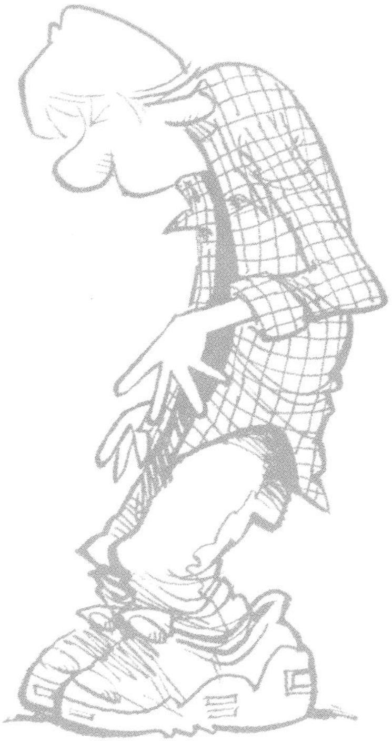

Zits

by JERRY SCOTT and JIM BORGMAN

SCOTT and BORGMAN

Glossary of Grunts

A ZITS PUBLIC SERVICE GUIDE TO INTERPRETING THE LANGUAGE OF THE TEENAGE SPECIES

Unh! (EXASPERATED)
1. A short, pointed sound. "I already knew that!"
2. Duh!

mmnh! (BARELY AUDIBLE)
1. An acknowledgment. "I heard you, now please go away."

uunh! (LOUD AND BREATHY)
1. An expression of global frustration. "Why me?"
2. A surrender. "Fine. Whatever you say."

uhhhhhhhhhhhhhhhhhhh (SHORT GRUNT FOLLOWED BY A LONG WHOOSH OF AIR)
1. Generational disapproval. "I can't believe I share the planet with a being as hopeless as you."

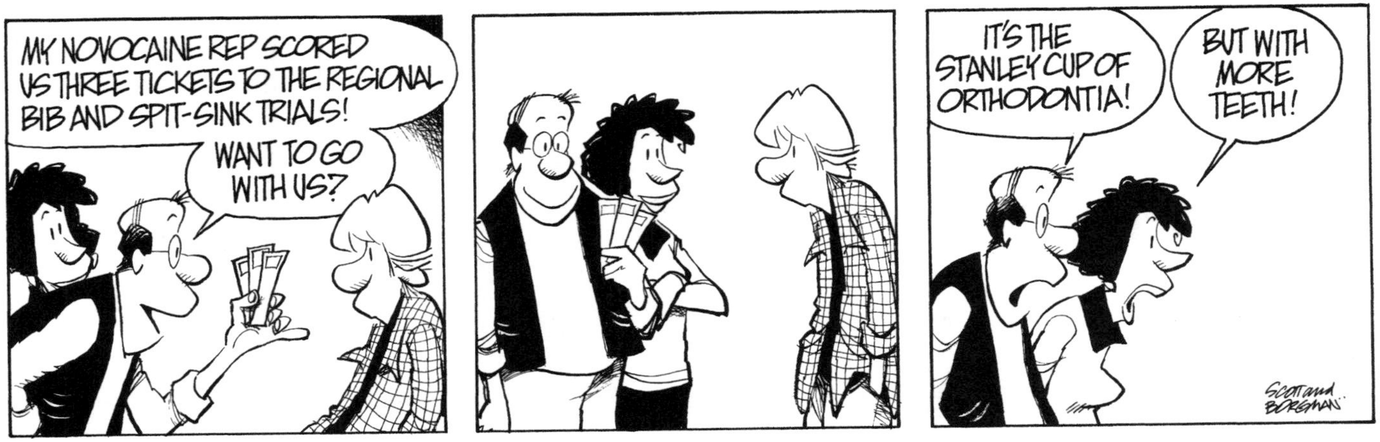
MY NOVOCAINE REP SCORED US THREE TICKETS TO THE REGIONAL BIB AND SPIT-SINK TRIALS!
WANT TO GO WITH US?
IT'S THE STANLEY CUP OF ORTHODONTIA!
BUT WITH MORE TEETH!

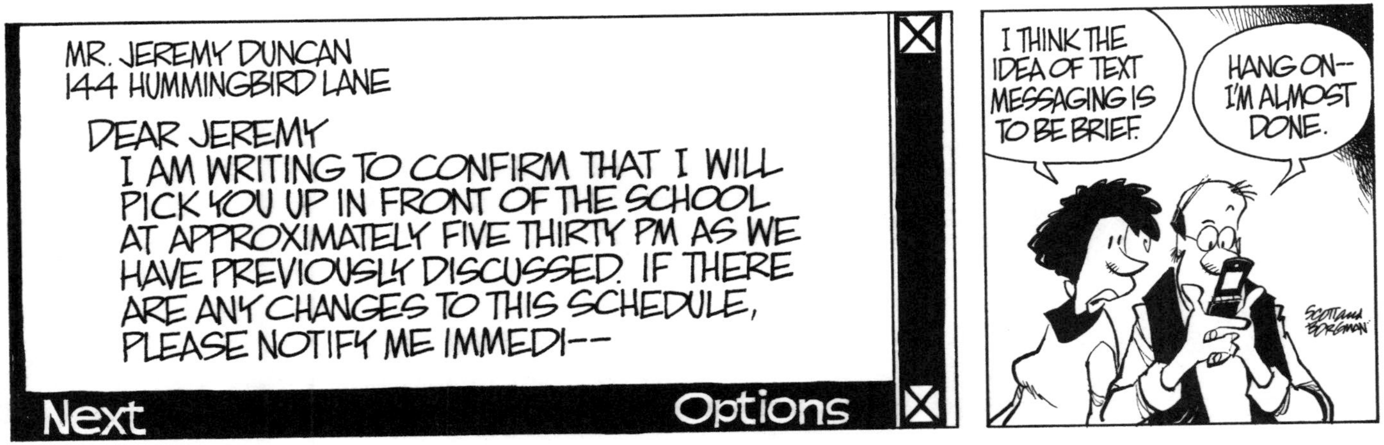
MR. JEREMY DUNCAN
144 HUMMINGBIRD LANE
DEAR JEREMY
I AM WRITING TO CONFIRM THAT I WILL PICK YOU UP IN FRONT OF THE SCHOOL AT APPROXIMATELY FIVE THIRTY PM AS WE HAVE PREVIOUSLY DISCUSSED. IF THERE ARE ANY CHANGES TO THIS SCHEDULE, PLEASE NOTIFY ME IMMEDI--
Next
Options
I THINK THE IDEA OF TEXT MESSAGING IS TO BE BRIEF.
HANG ON-- I'M ALMOST DONE.

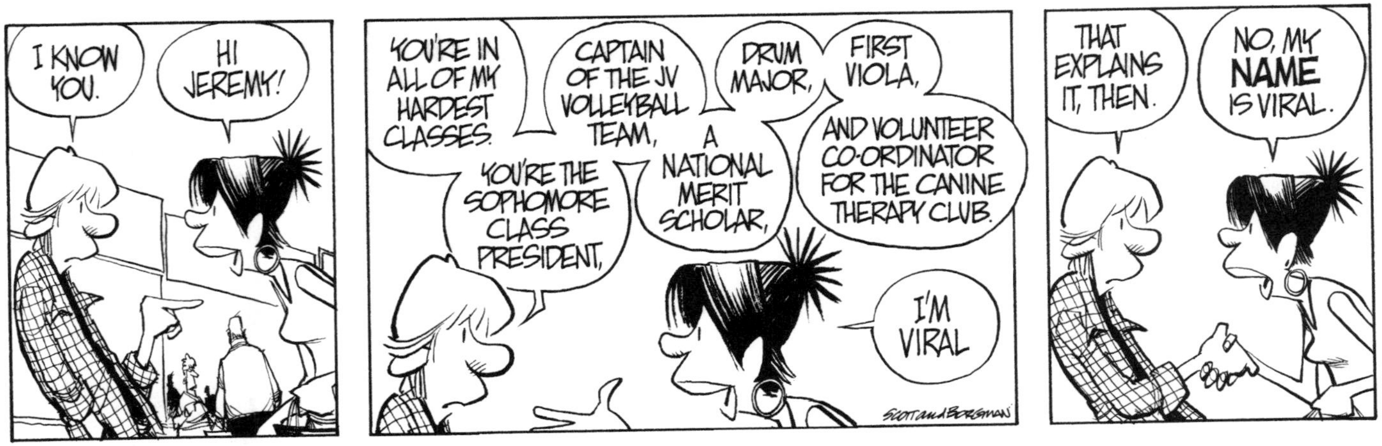
I KNOW YOU.
HI JEREMY!
YOU'RE IN ALL OF MY HARDEST CLASSES.
CAPTAIN OF THE JV VOLLEYBALL TEAM,
DRUM MAJOR,
FIRST VIOLA,
YOU'RE THE SOPHOMORE CLASS PRESIDENT,
A NATIONAL MERIT SCHOLAR,
AND VOLUNTEER CO-ORDINATOR FOR THE CANINE THERAPY CLUB.
I'M VIRAL
THAT EXPLAINS IT, THEN.
NO, MY **NAME** IS VIRAL.

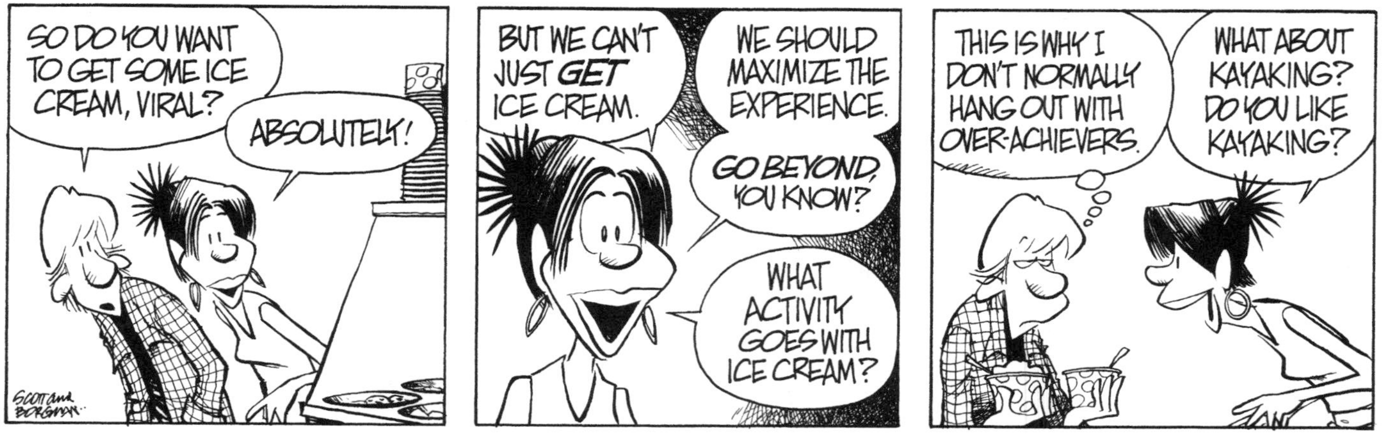

SO DO YOU WANT TO GET SOME ICE CREAM, VIRAL?
ABSOLUTELY!
BUT WE CAN'T JUST **GET** ICE CREAM.
WE SHOULD MAXIMIZE THE EXPERIENCE.
GO BEYOND, YOU KNOW?
WHAT ACTIVITY GOES WITH ICE CREAM?
THIS IS WHY I DON'T NORMALLY HANG OUT WITH OVER-ACHIEVERS.
WHAT ABOUT KAYAKING? DO YOU LIKE KAYAKING?

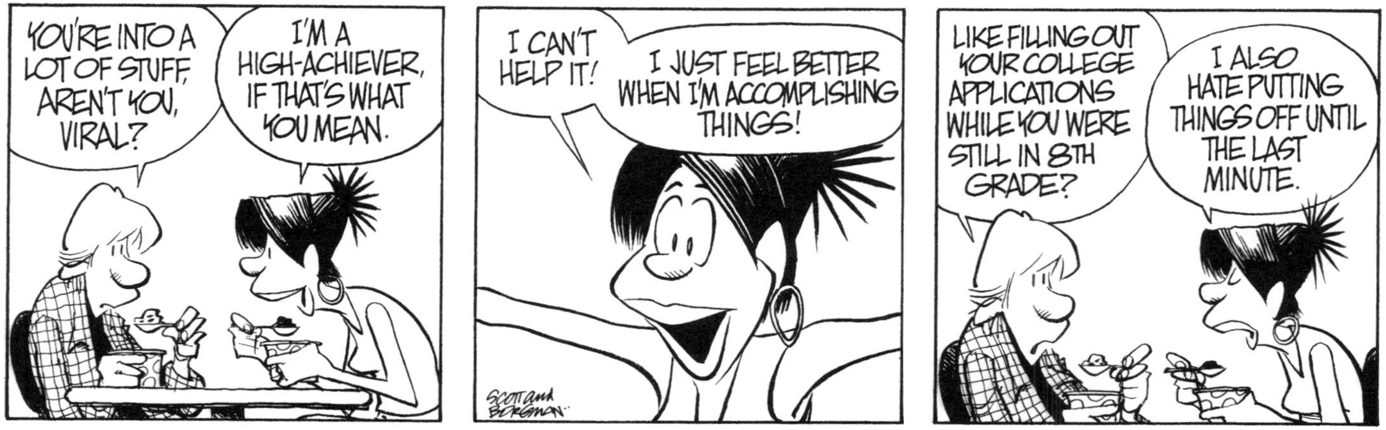

YOU'RE INTO A LOT OF STUFF, AREN'T YOU, VIRAL?
I'M A HIGH-ACHIEVER, IF THAT'S WHAT YOU MEAN.
I CAN'T HELP IT!
I JUST FEEL BETTER WHEN I'M ACCOMPLISHING THINGS!
LIKE FILLING OUT YOUR COLLEGE APPLICATIONS WHILE YOU WERE STILL IN 8TH GRADE?
I ALSO HATE PUTTING THINGS OFF UNTIL THE LAST MINUTE.

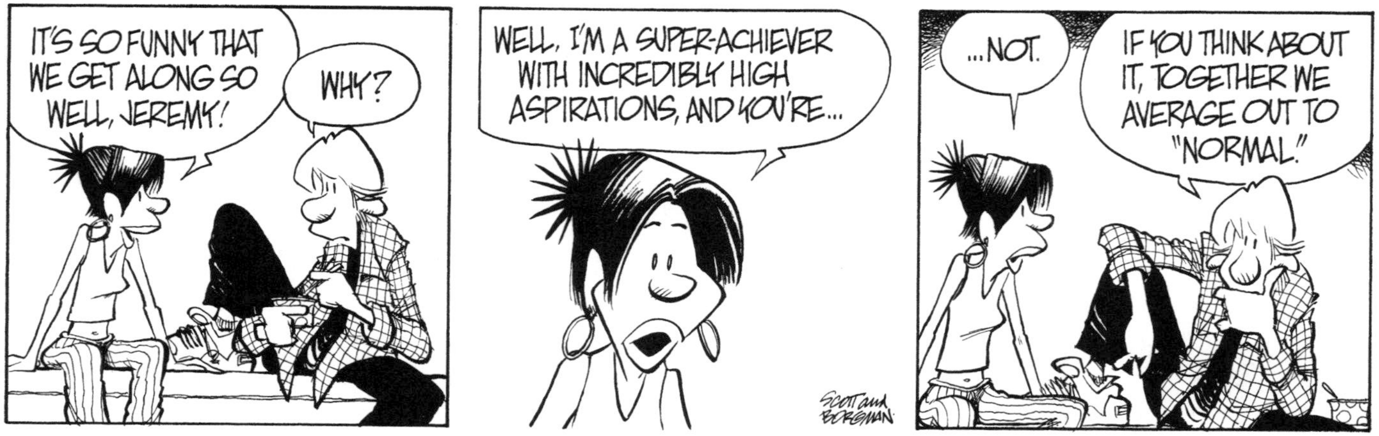

IT'S SO FUNNY THAT WE GET ALONG SO WELL, JEREMY!
WHY?
WELL, I'M A SUPER-ACHIEVER WITH INCREDIBLY HIGH ASPIRATIONS, AND YOU'RE...
...NOT.
IF YOU THINK ABOUT IT, TOGETHER WE AVERAGE OUT TO "NORMAL."

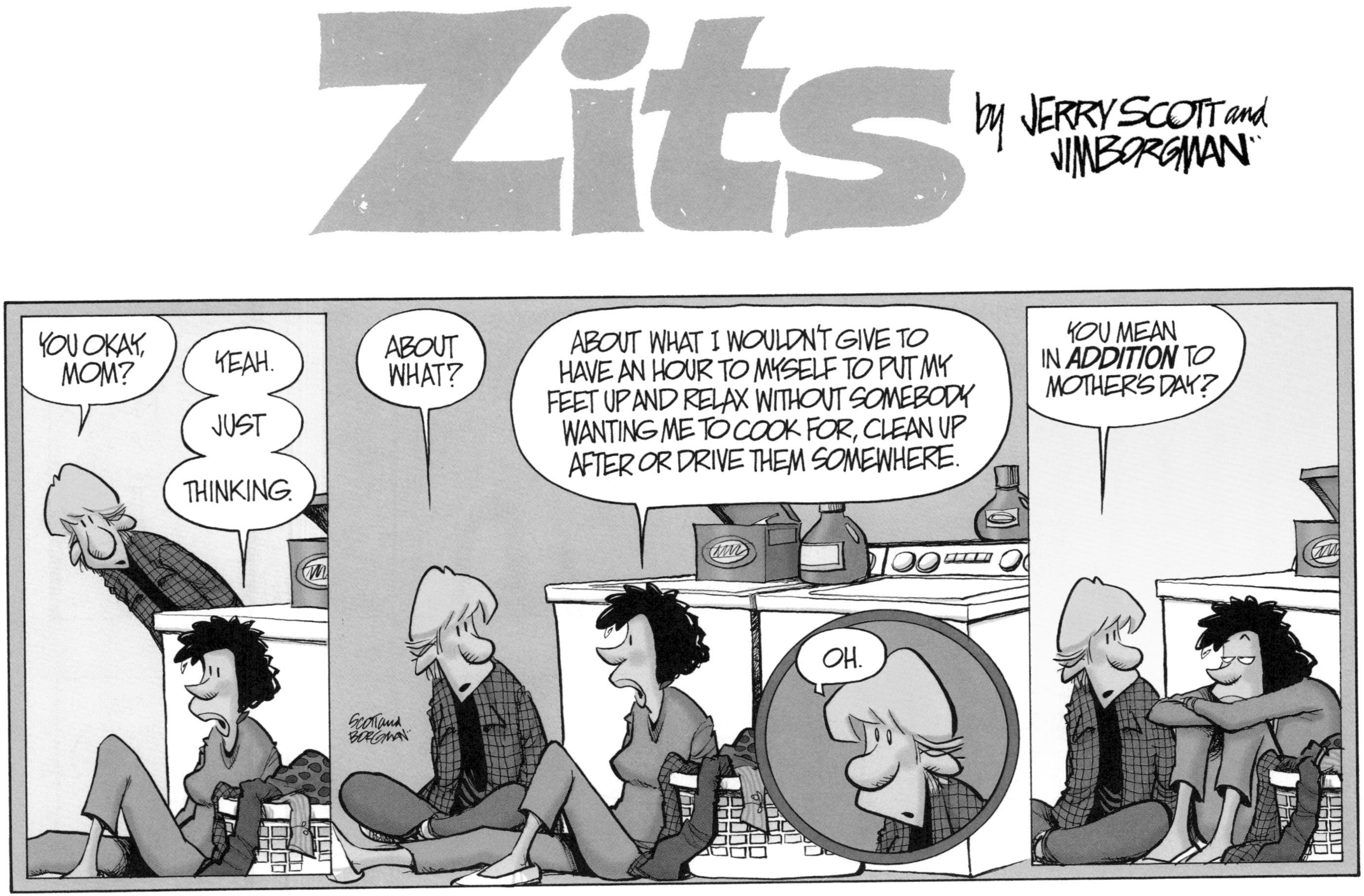

Zits
by JERRY SCOTT and JIM BORGMAN
YOU OKAY, MOM?
YEAH.
JUST
THINKING.
ABOUT WHAT?
ABOUT WHAT I WOULDN'T GIVE TO HAVE AN HOUR TO MYSELF TO PUT MY FEET UP AND RELAX WITHOUT SOMEBODY WANTING ME TO COOK FOR, CLEAN UP AFTER OR DRIVE THEM SOMEWHERE.
OH.
YOU MEAN IN **ADDITION** TO MOTHER'S DAY?

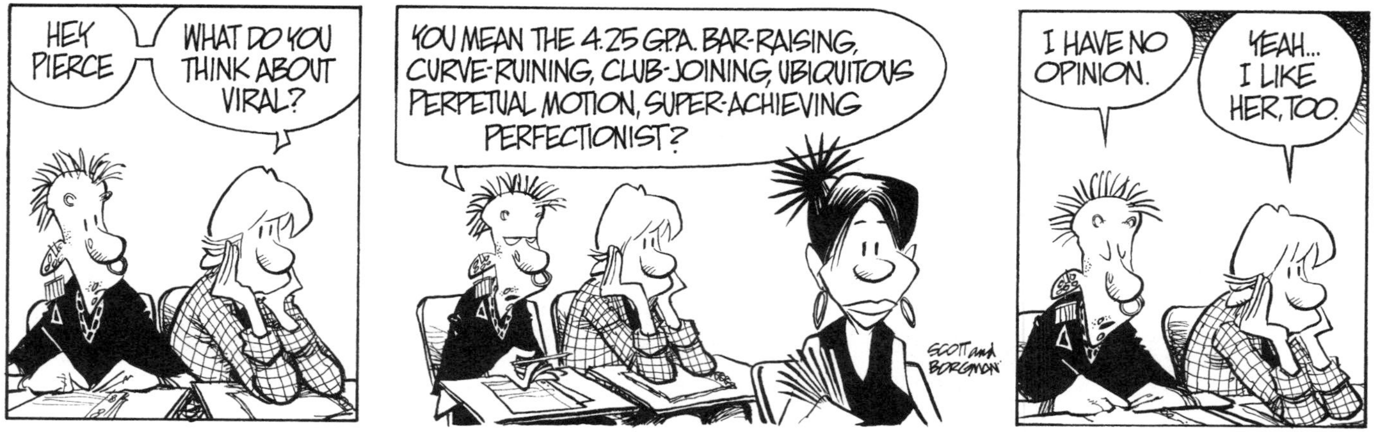
HEY PIERCE
WHAT DO YOU THINK ABOUT VIRAL?
YOU MEAN THE 4.25 G.P.A. BAR-RAISING, CURVE-RUINING, CLUB-JOINING, UBIQUITOUS PERPETUAL MOTION, SUPER-ACHIEVING PERFECTIONIST?
SCOTT and BORGMAN
I HAVE NO OPINION.
YEAH... I LIKE HER, TOO.

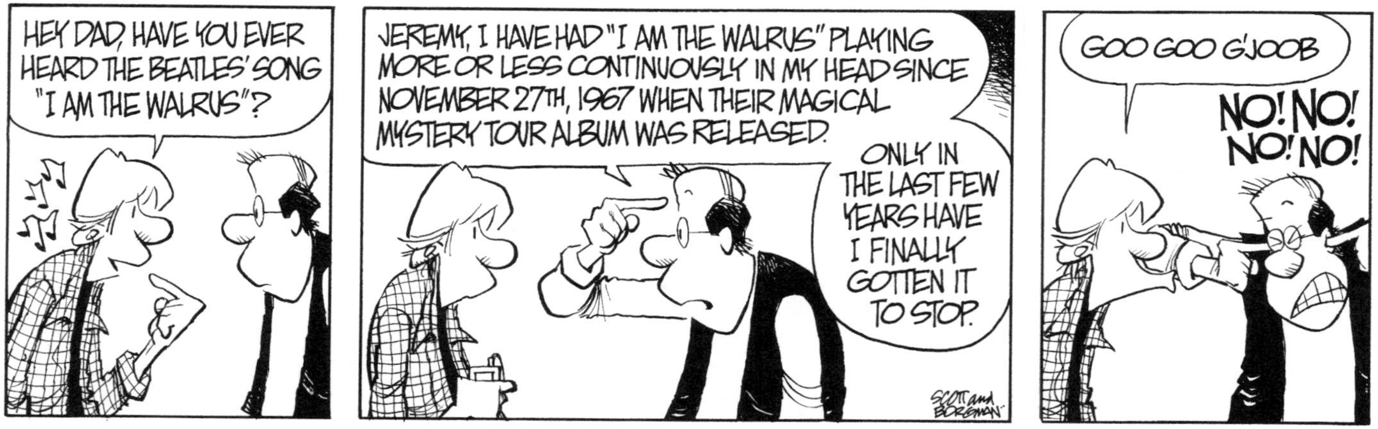
HEY DAD, HAVE YOU EVER HEARD THE BEATLES' SONG "I AM THE WALRUS"?
JEREMY, I HAVE HAD "I AM THE WALRUS" PLAYING MORE OR LESS CONTINUOUSLY IN MY HEAD SINCE NOVEMBER 27TH, 1967 WHEN THEIR MAGICAL MYSTERY TOUR ALBUM WAS RELEASED.
ONLY IN THE LAST FEW YEARS HAVE I FINALLY GOTTEN IT TO STOP.
SCOTT and BORGMAN
GOO GOO G'JOOB
NO! NO! NO! NO!

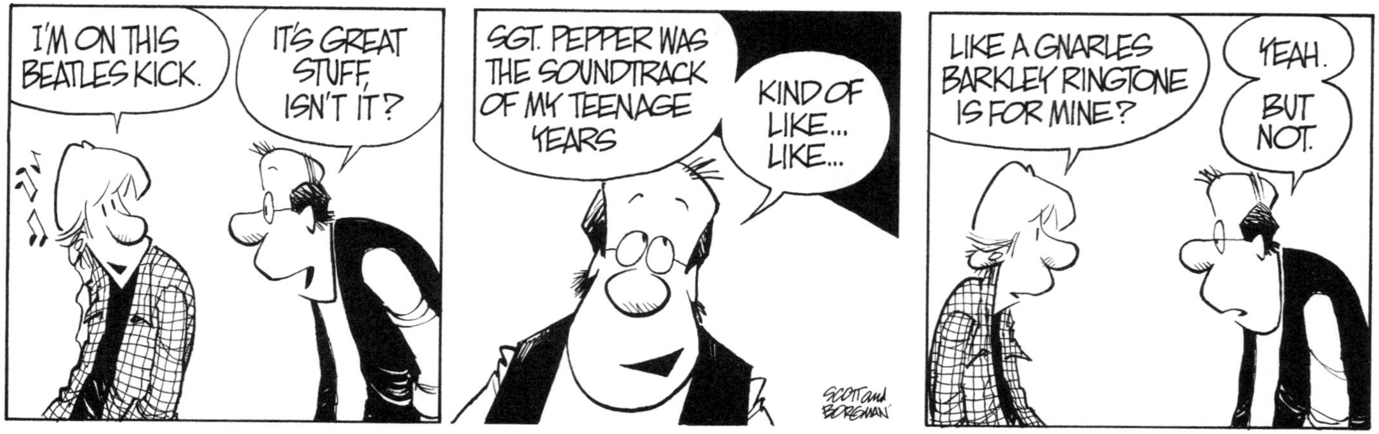
I'M ON THIS BEATLES KICK.
IT'S GREAT STUFF, ISN'T IT?
SGT. PEPPER WAS THE SOUNDTRACK OF MY TEENAGE YEARS
KIND OF LIKE... LIKE...
SCOTT and BORGMAN
LIKE A GNARLES BARKLEY RINGTONE IS FOR MINE?
YEAH.
BUT NOT.

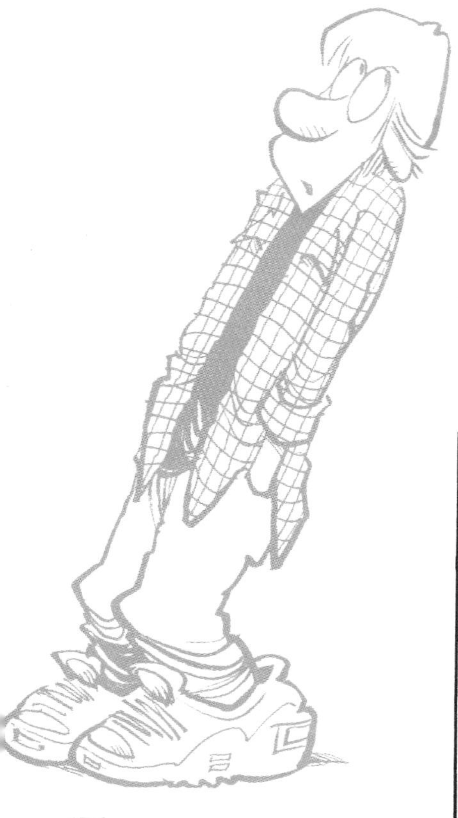

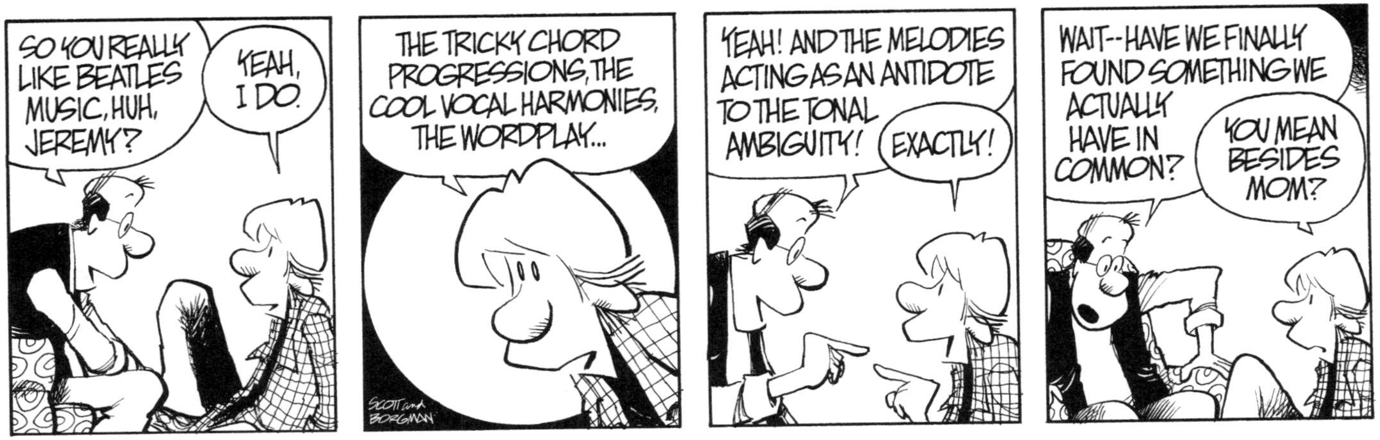
SO YOU REALLY LIKE BEATLES MUSIC, HUH, JEREMY?
YEAH, I DO.
THE TRICKY CHORD PROGRESSIONS, THE COOL VOCAL HARMONIES, THE WORDPLAY...
YEAH! AND THE MELODIES ACTING AS AN ANTIDOTE TO THE TONAL AMBIGUITY!
EXACTLY!
WAIT--HAVE WE FINALLY FOUND SOMETHING WE ACTUALLY HAVE IN COMMON?
YOU MEAN BESIDES MOM?

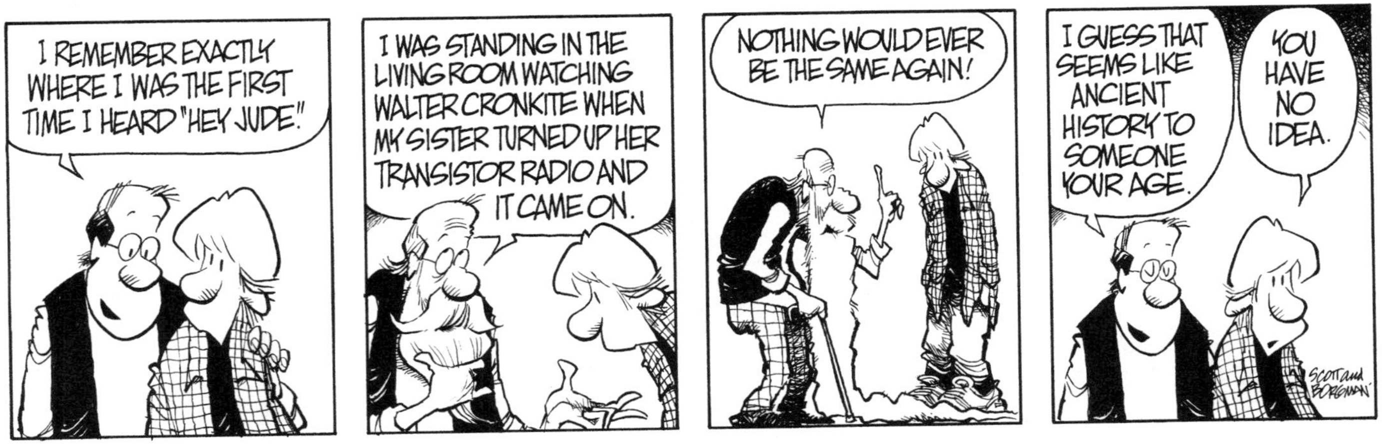
I REMEMBER EXACTLY WHERE I WAS THE FIRST TIME I HEARD "HEY JUDE."
I WAS STANDING IN THE LIVING ROOM WATCHING WALTER CRONKITE WHEN MY SISTER TURNED UP HER TRANSISTOR RADIO AND IT CAME ON.
NOTHING WOULD EVER BE THE SAME AGAIN!
I GUESS THAT SEEMS LIKE ANCIENT HISTORY TO SOMEONE YOUR AGE.
YOU HAVE NO IDEA.

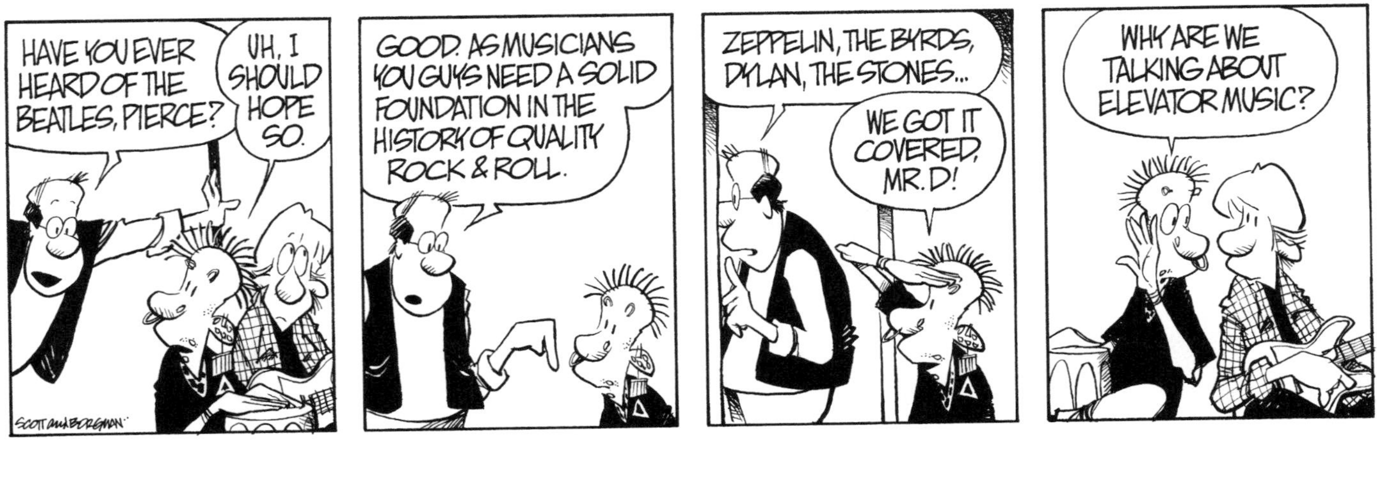
HAVE YOU EVER HEARD OF THE BEATLES, PIERCE?
UH, I SHOULD HOPE SO.
GOOD. AS MUSICIANS YOU GUYS NEED A SOLID FOUNDATION IN THE HISTORY OF QUALITY ROCK & ROLL.
ZEPPELIN, THE BYRDS, DYLAN, THE STONES...
WE GOT IT COVERED, MR. D!
WHY ARE WE TALKING ABOUT ELEVATOR MUSIC?

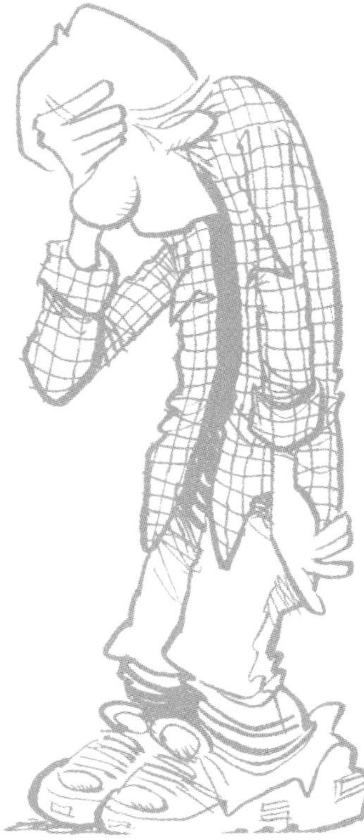

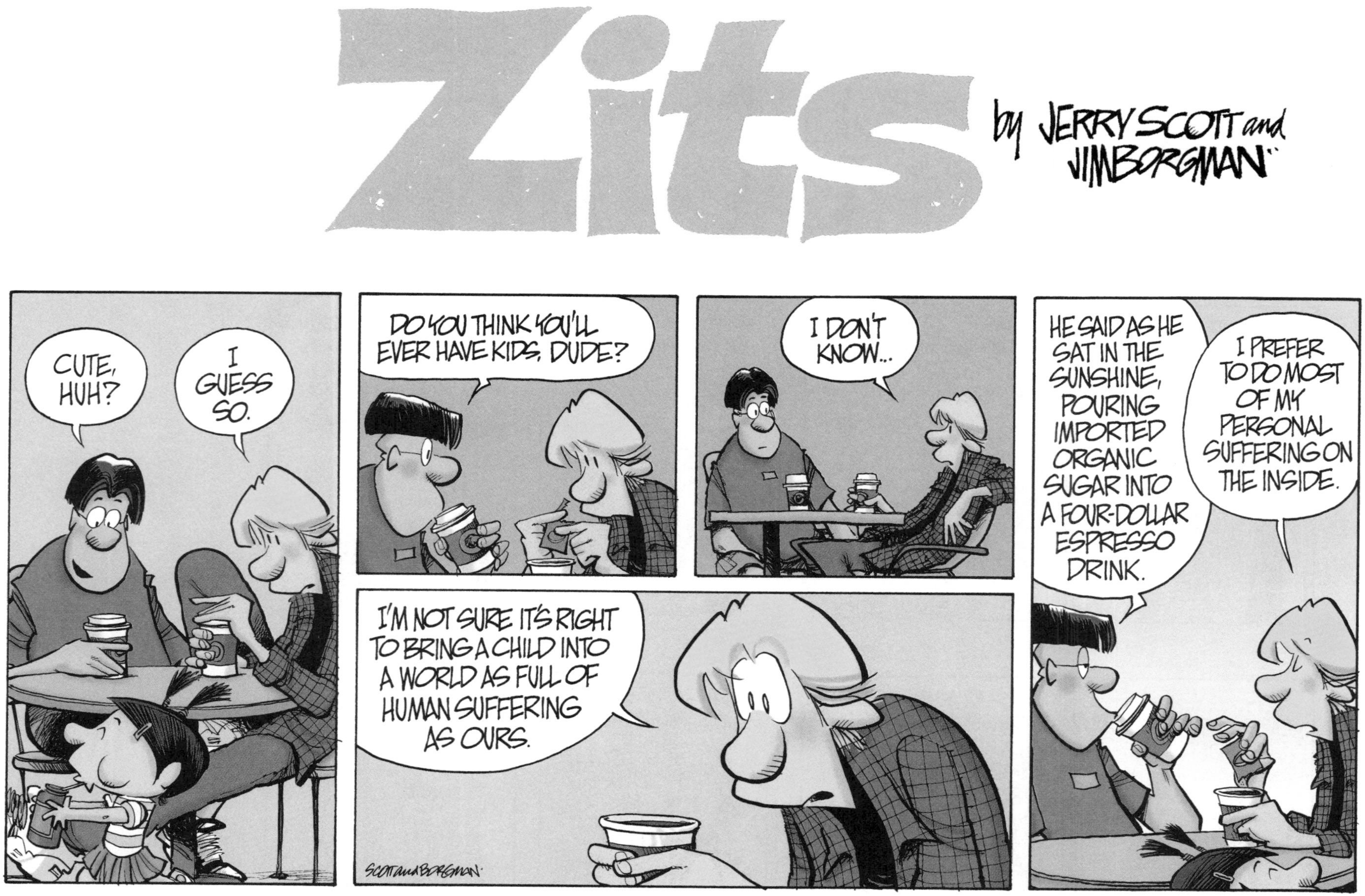
Zits
by JERRY SCOTT and JIM BORGMAN
CUTE, HUH?
I GUESS SO.
DO YOU THINK YOU'LL EVER HAVE KIDS, DUDE?
I DON'T KNOW...
I'M NOT SURE IT'S RIGHT TO BRING A CHILD INTO A WORLD AS FULL OF HUMAN SUFFERING AS OURS.
HE SAID AS HE SAT IN THE SUNSHINE, POURING IMPORTED ORGANIC SUGAR INTO A FOUR-DOLLAR ESPRESSO DRINK.
I PREFER TO DO MOST OF MY PERSONAL SUFFERING ON THE INSIDE.
SCOTT and BORGMAN

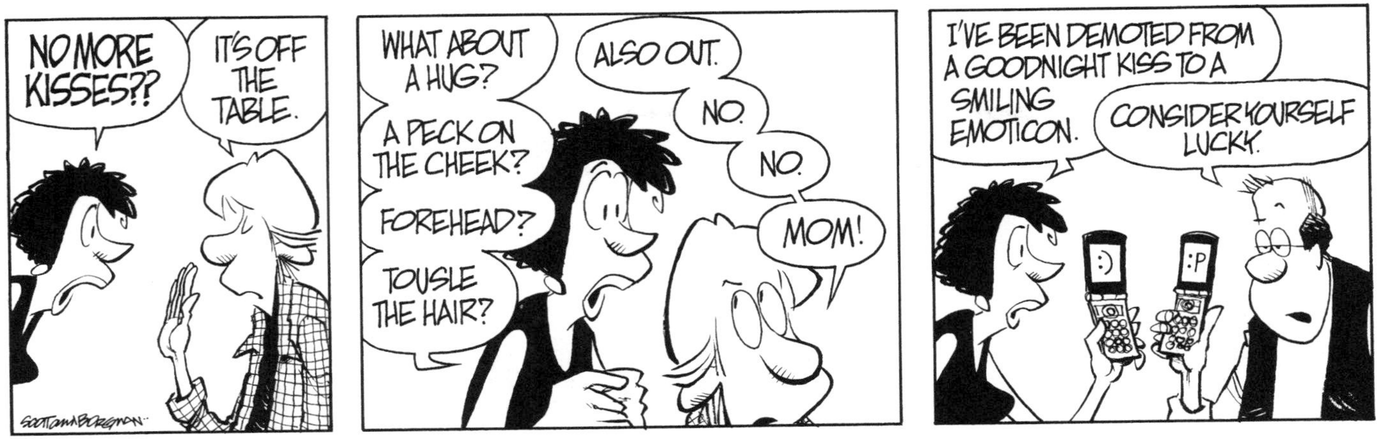
NO MORE KISSES??
IT'S OFF THE TABLE.
WHAT ABOUT A HUG?
ALSO OUT.
A PECK ON THE CHEEK?
NO.
FOREHEAD?
NO.
TOUSLE THE HAIR?
MOM!
I'VE BEEN DEMOTED FROM A GOODNIGHT KISS TO A SMILING EMOTICON.
:)
:P
CONSIDER YOURSELF LUCKY.

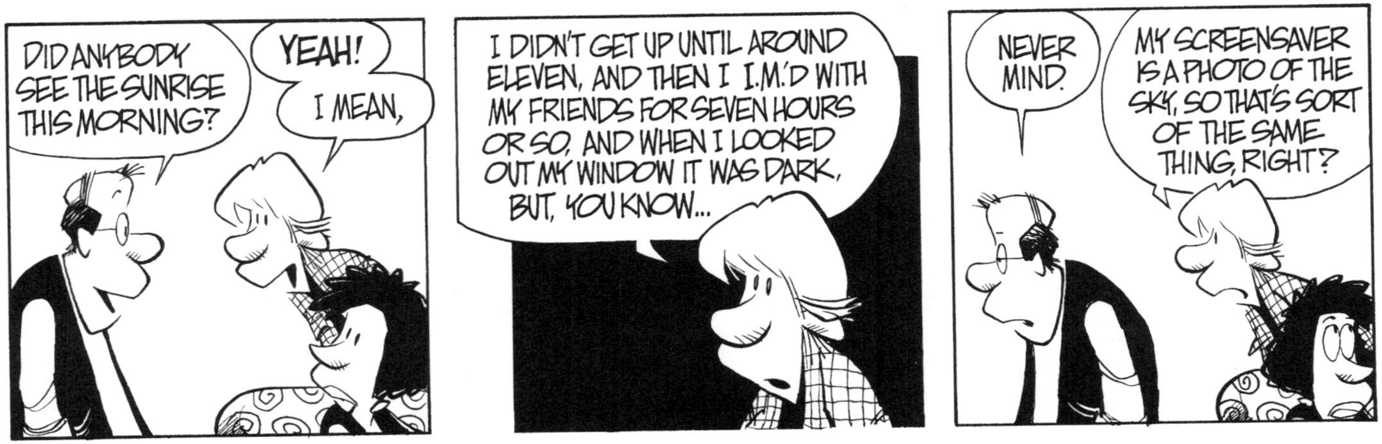
DID ANYBODY SEE THE SUNRISE THIS MORNING?
YEAH!
I MEAN,
I DIDN'T GET UP UNTIL AROUND ELEVEN, AND THEN I I.M.'D WITH MY FRIENDS FOR SEVEN HOURS OR SO, AND WHEN I LOOKED OUT MY WINDOW IT WAS DARK, BUT, YOU KNOW...
NEVER MIND.
MY SCREENSAVER IS A PHOTO OF THE SKY, SO THAT'S SORT OF THE SAME THING, RIGHT?

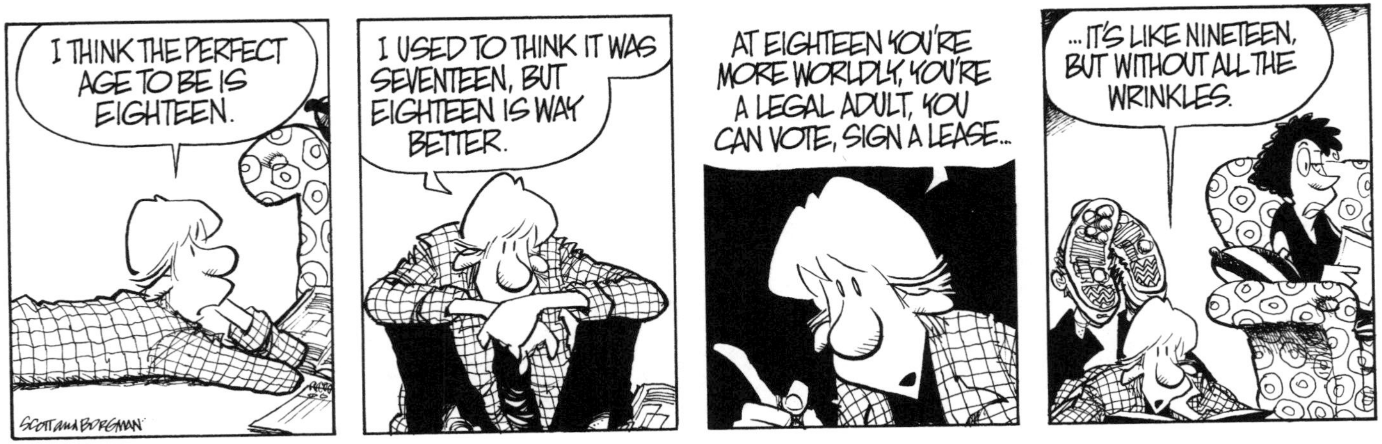
I THINK THE PERFECT AGE TO BE IS EIGHTEEN.
I USED TO THINK IT WAS SEVENTEEN, BUT EIGHTEEN IS WAY BETTER.
AT EIGHTEEN YOU'RE MORE WORLDLY, YOU'RE A LEGAL ADULT, YOU CAN VOTE, SIGN A LEASE...
...IT'S LIKE NINETEEN, BUT WITHOUT ALL THE WRINKLES.

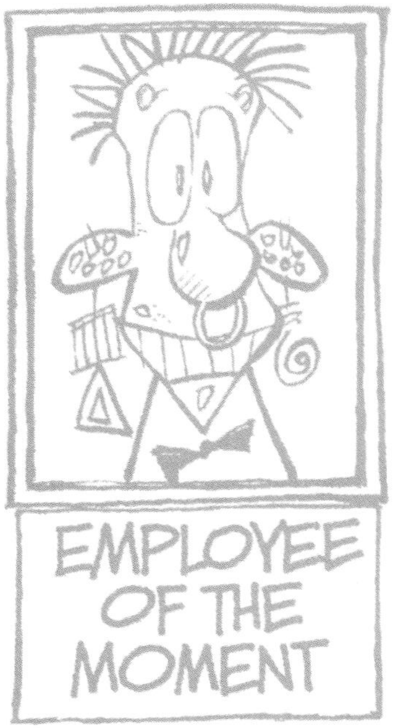
EMPLOYEE OF THE MOMENT

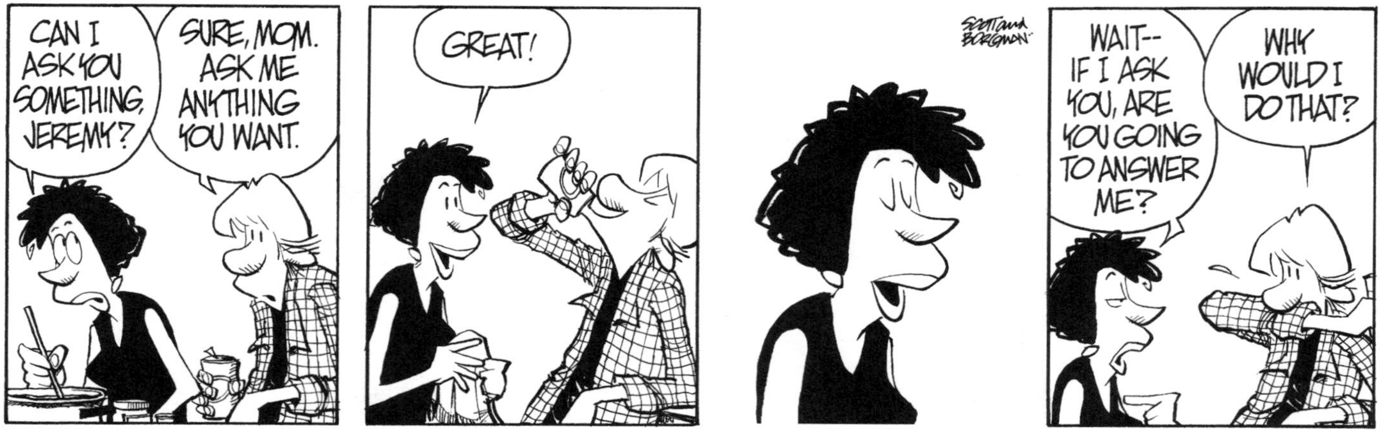
CAN I ASK YOU SOMETHING, JEREMY?
SURE, MOM. ASK ME ANYTHING YOU WANT.
GREAT!
WAIT-- IF I ASK YOU, ARE YOU GOING TO ANSWER ME?
WHY WOULD I DO THAT?

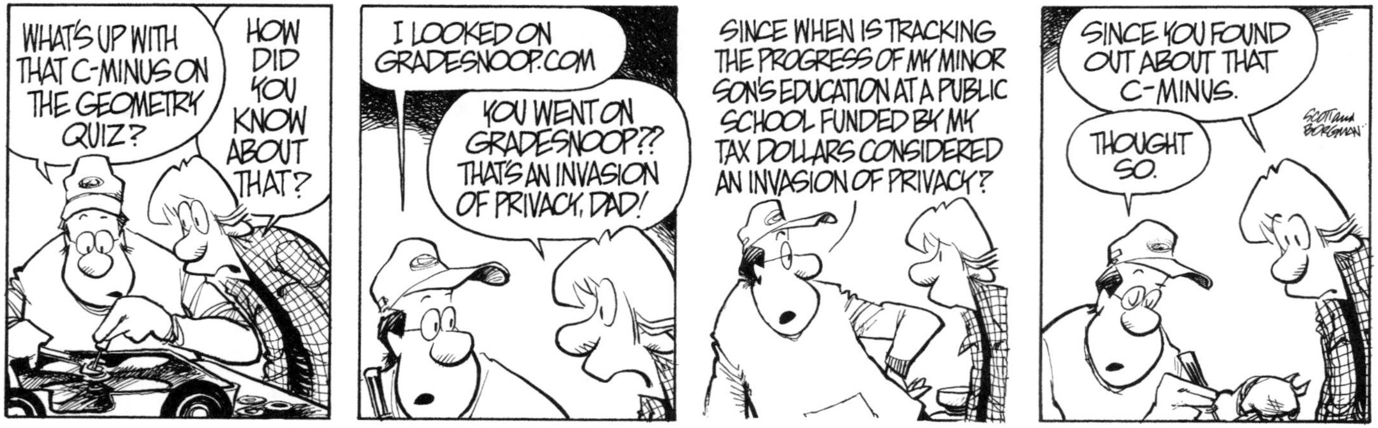
WHAT'S UP WITH THAT C-MINUS ON THE GEOMETRY QUIZ?
HOW DID YOU KNOW ABOUT THAT?
I LOOKED ON GRADESNOOP.COM
YOU WENT ON GRADESNOOP?? THAT'S AN INVASION OF PRIVACY, DAD!
SINCE WHEN IS TRACKING THE PROGRESS OF MY MINOR SON'S EDUCATION AT A PUBLIC SCHOOL FUNDED BY MY TAX DOLLARS CONSIDERED AN INVASION OF PRIVACY?
SINCE YOU FOUND OUT ABOUT THAT C-MINUS.
THOUGHT SO.

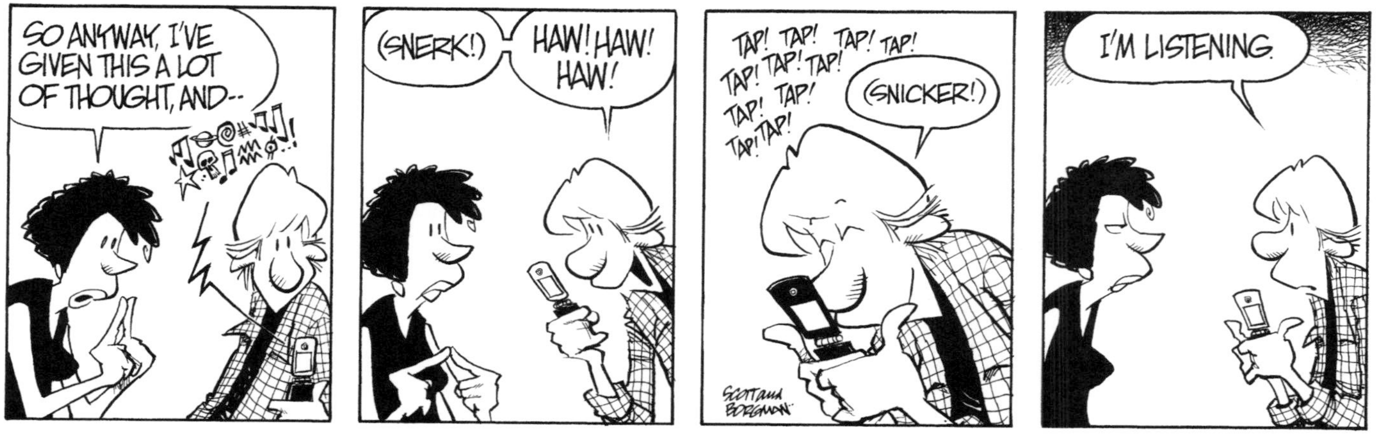
SO ANYWAY, I'VE GIVEN THIS A LOT OF THOUGHT, AND--
(SNERK!)
HAW! HAW! HAW!
TAP! TAP! TAP! TAP! TAP! TAP! TAP! TAP! TAP! TAP! TAP! TAP!
(SNICKER!)
I'M LISTENING.

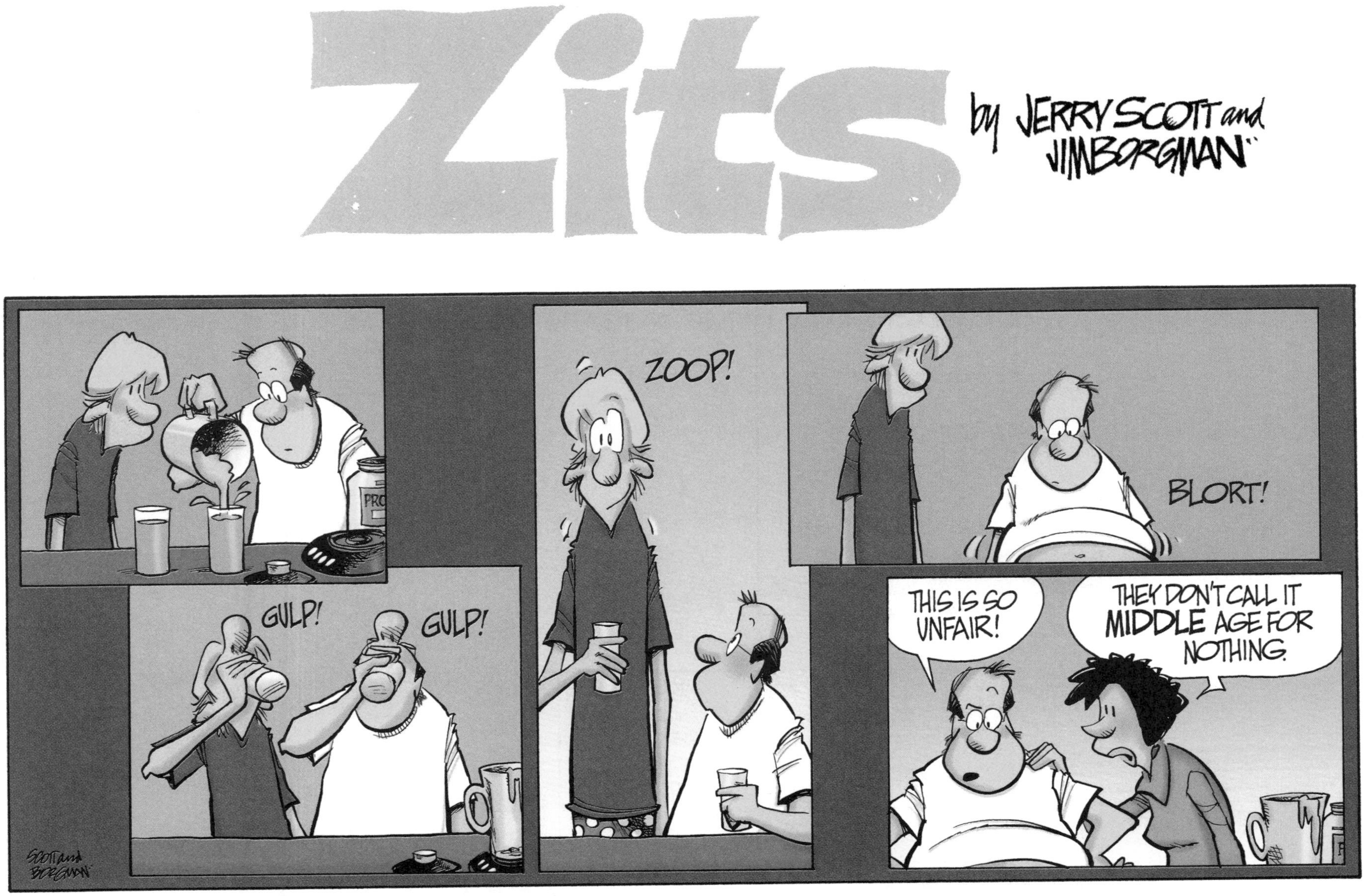
Zits
by JERRY SCOTT and JIM BORGMAN
GULP!
GULP!
SCOTT and BORGMAN
ZOOP!
BLORT!
THIS IS SO UNFAIR!
THEY DON'T CALL IT MIDDLE AGE FOR NOTHING.

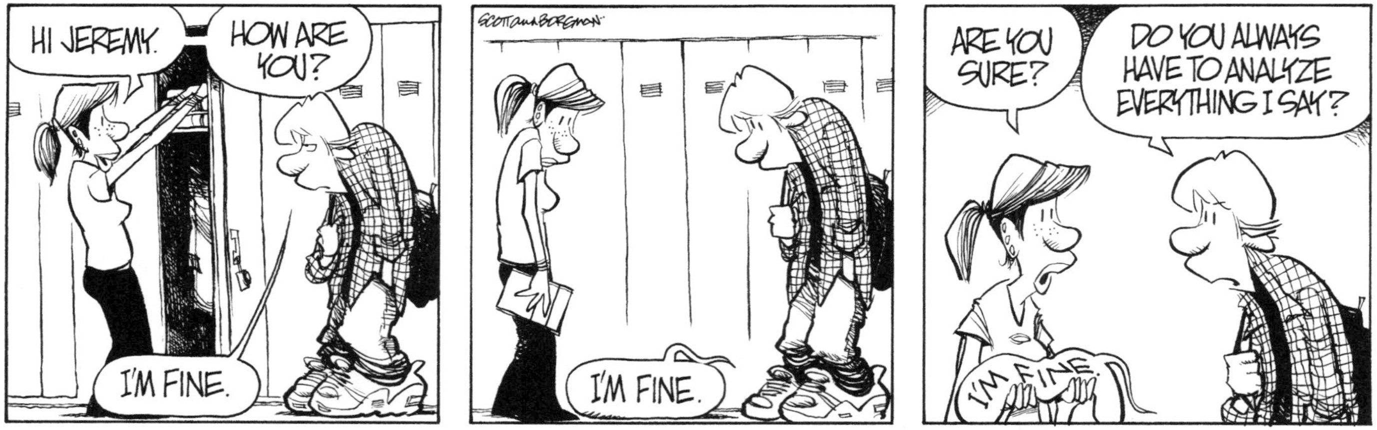
HI JEREMY.
HOW ARE YOU?
I'M FINE.
I'M FINE.
ARE YOU SURE?
DO YOU ALWAYS HAVE TO ANALYZE EVERYTHING I SAY?
I'M FINE.

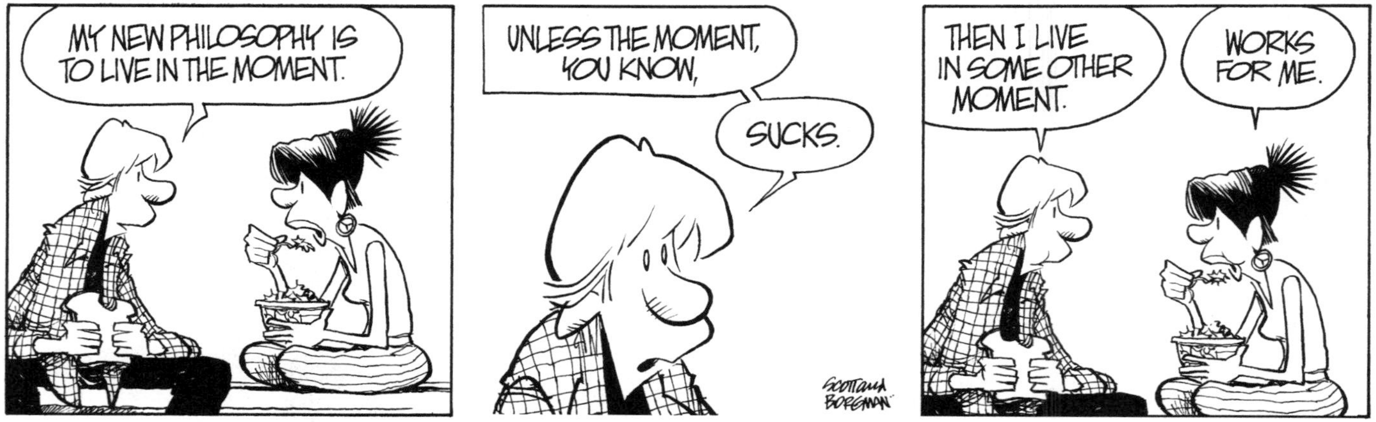
MY NEW PHILOSOPHY IS TO LIVE IN THE MOMENT.
UNLESS THE MOMENT, YOU KNOW,
SUCKS.
THEN I LIVE IN SOME OTHER MOMENT.
WORKS FOR ME.

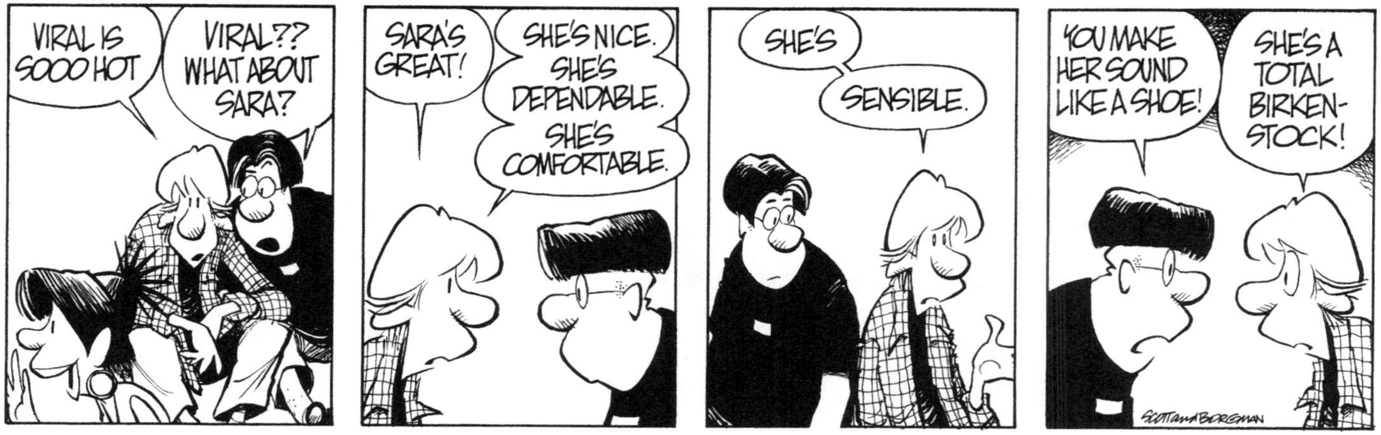
VIRAL IS SOOO HOT
VIRAL?? WHAT ABOUT SARA?
SARA'S GREAT!
SHE'S NICE.
SHE'S DEPENDABLE.
SHE'S COMFORTABLE.
SHE'S
SENSIBLE.
YOU MAKE HER SOUND LIKE A SHOE!
SHE'S A TOTAL BIRKEN-STOCK!

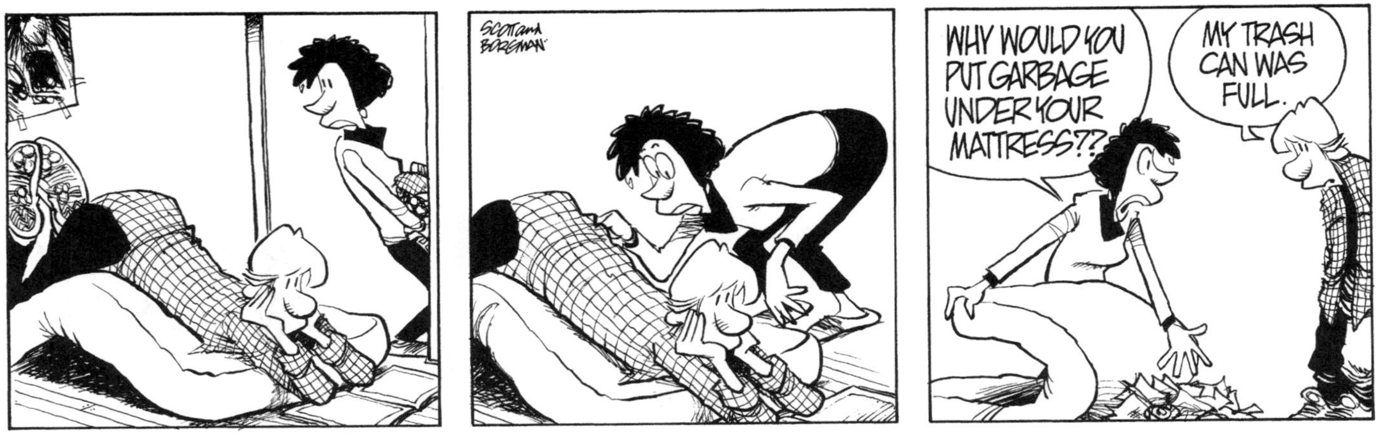
WHY WOULD YOU PUT GARBAGE UNDER YOUR MATTRESS??
MY TRASH CAN WAS FULL.

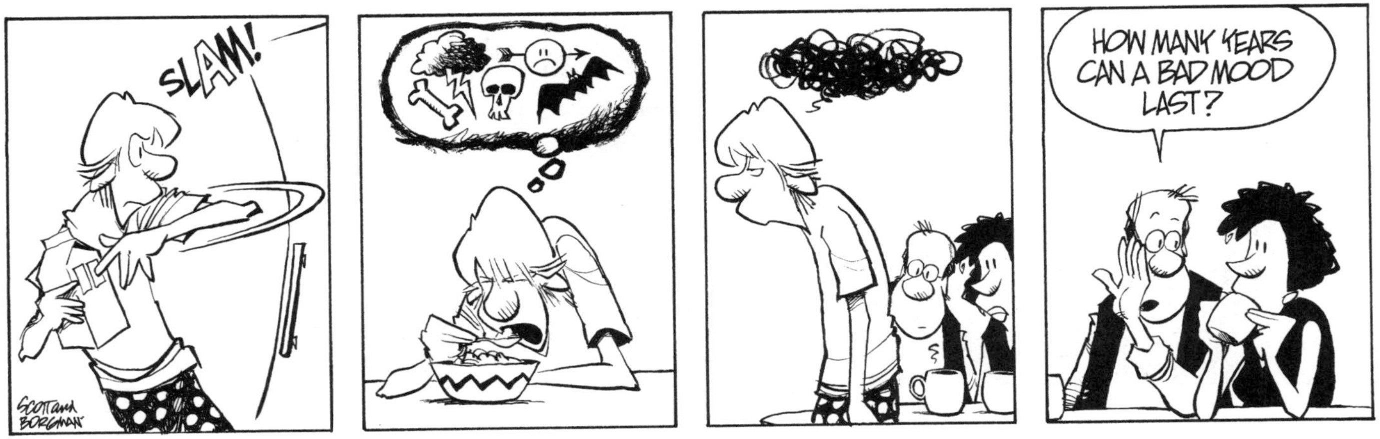
SLAM!
HOW MANY YEARS CAN A BAD MOOD LAST?

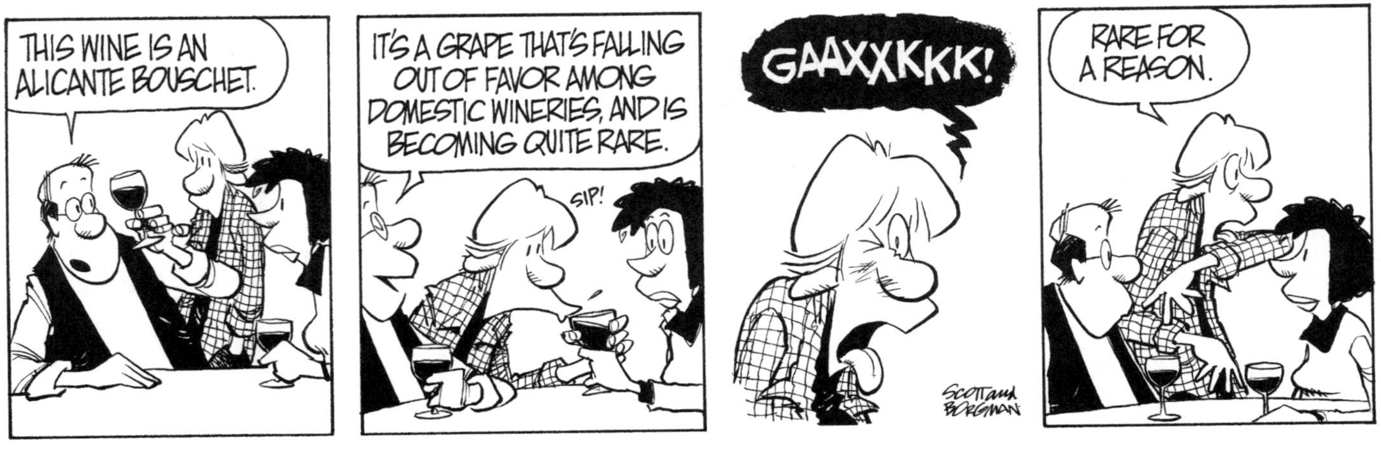
THIS WINE IS AN ALICANTE BOUSCHET.
IT'S A GRAPE THAT'S FALLING OUT OF FAVOR AMONG DOMESTIC WINERIES, AND IS BECOMING QUITE RARE.
SIP!
GAAXXKKK!
RARE FOR A REASON.

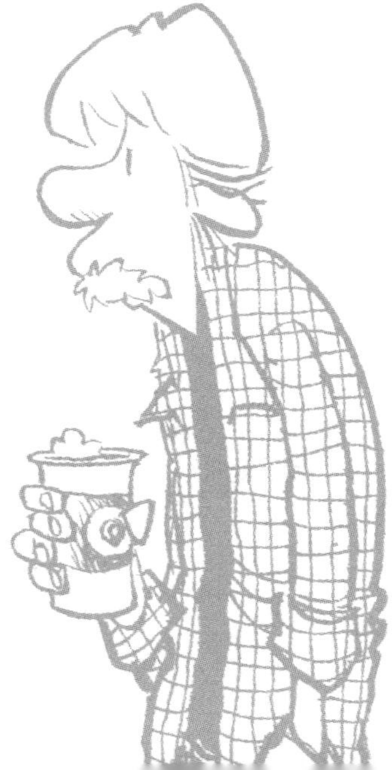

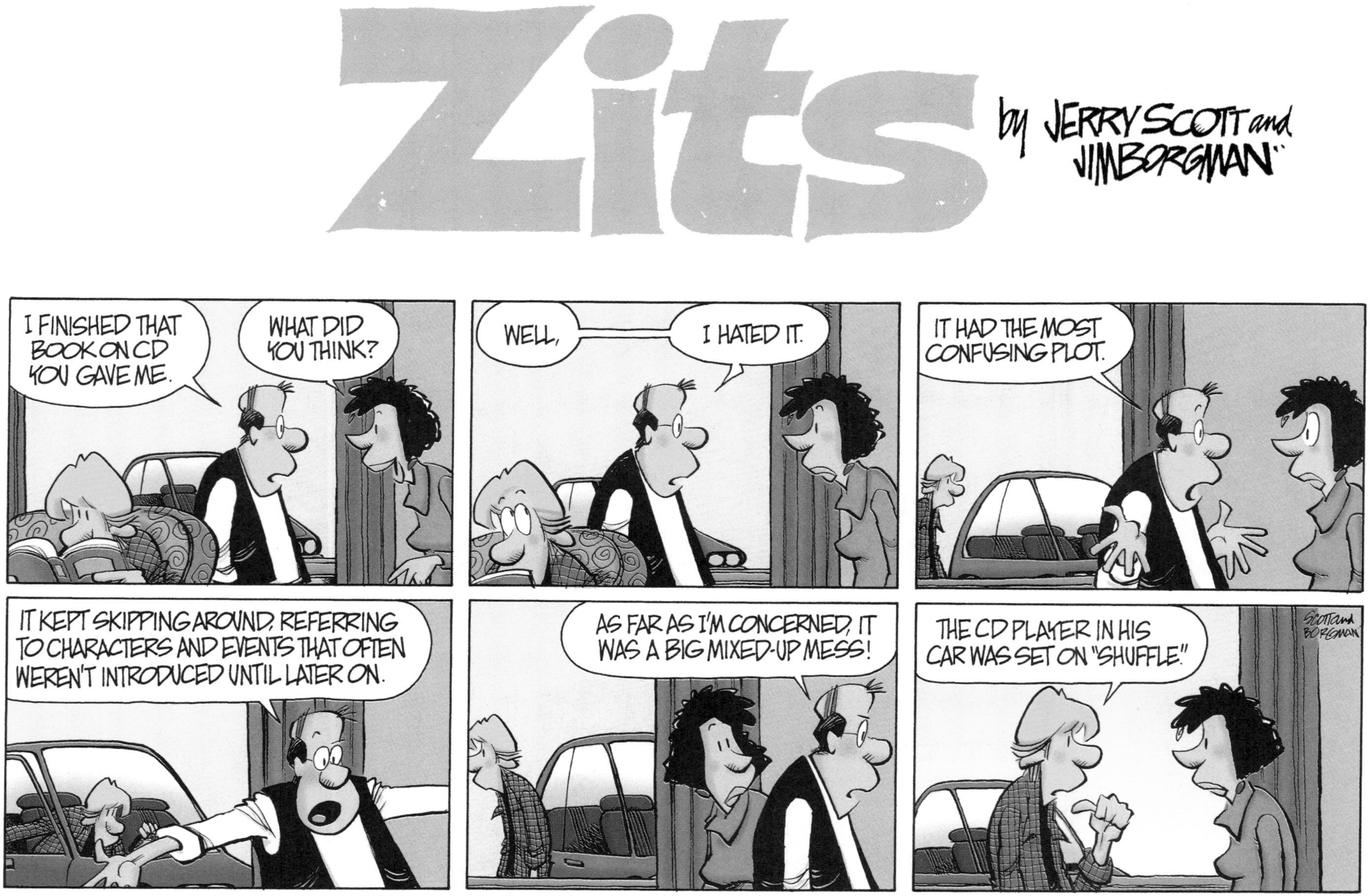
Zits
by JERRY SCOTT and JIM BORGMAN
I FINISHED THAT BOOK ON CD YOU GAVE ME.
WHAT DID YOU THINK?
WELL,
I HATED IT.
IT HAD THE MOST CONFUSING PLOT.
IT KEPT SKIPPING AROUND, REFERRING TO CHARACTERS AND EVENTS THAT OFTEN WEREN'T INTRODUCED UNTIL LATER ON.
AS FAR AS I'M CONCERNED, IT WAS A BIG MIXED-UP MESS!
THE CD PLAYER IN HIS CAR WAS SET ON "SHUFFLE."
SCOTT and BORGMAN

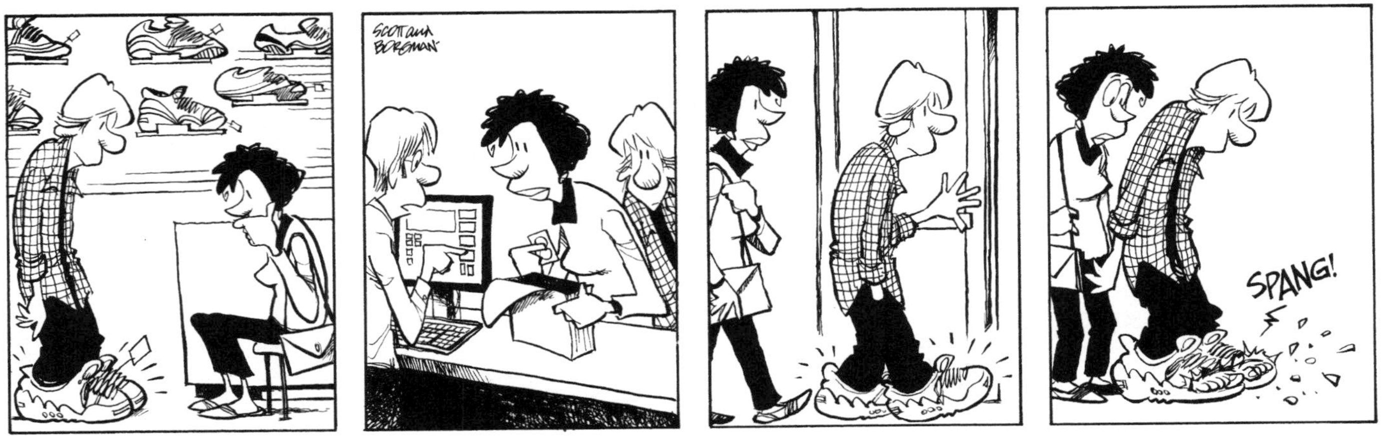
SPANG!

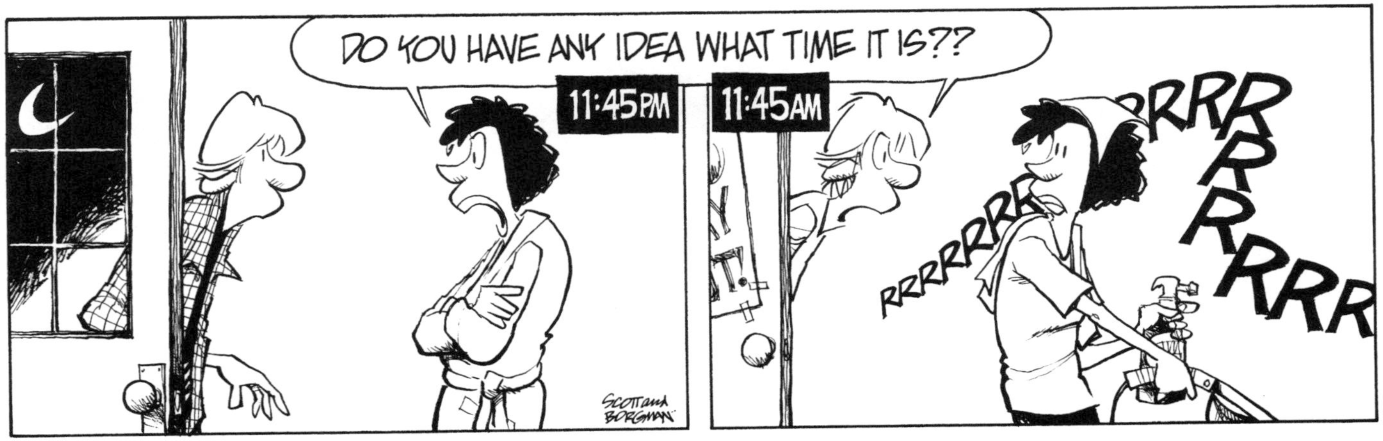
11:45PM
DO YOU HAVE ANY IDEA WHAT TIME IT IS??
11:45AM

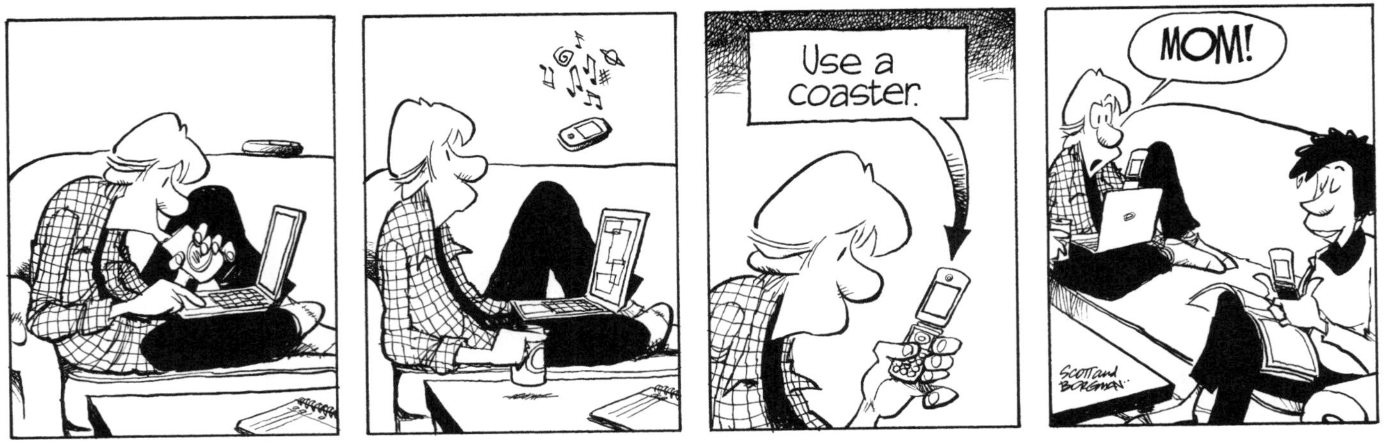
Use a coaster.
MOM!

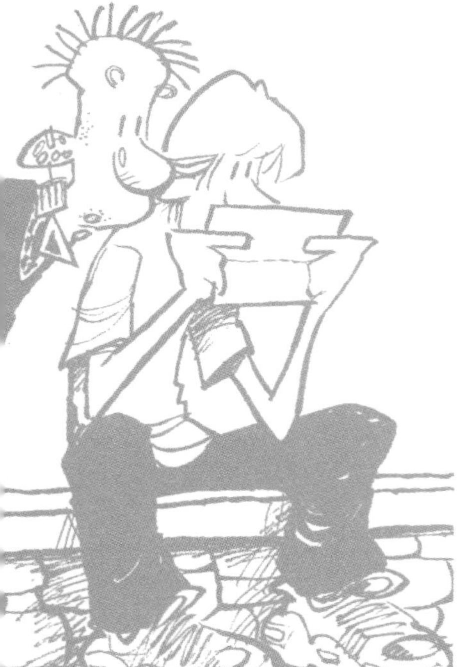

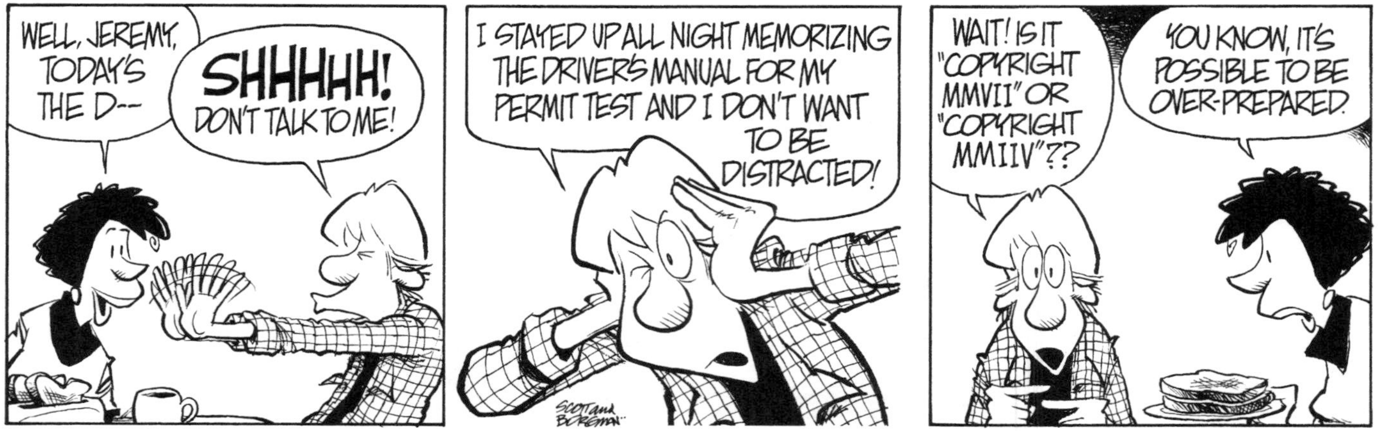
WELL, JEREMY, TODAY'S THE D--
SHHHHH! DON'T TALK TO ME!
I STAYED UP ALL NIGHT MEMORIZING THE DRIVER'S MANUAL FOR MY PERMIT TEST AND I DON'T WANT TO BE DISTRACTED!
WAIT! IS IT "COPYRIGHT MMVII" OR "COPYRIGHT MMIIV"??
YOU KNOW, IT'S POSSIBLE TO BE OVER-PREPARED.

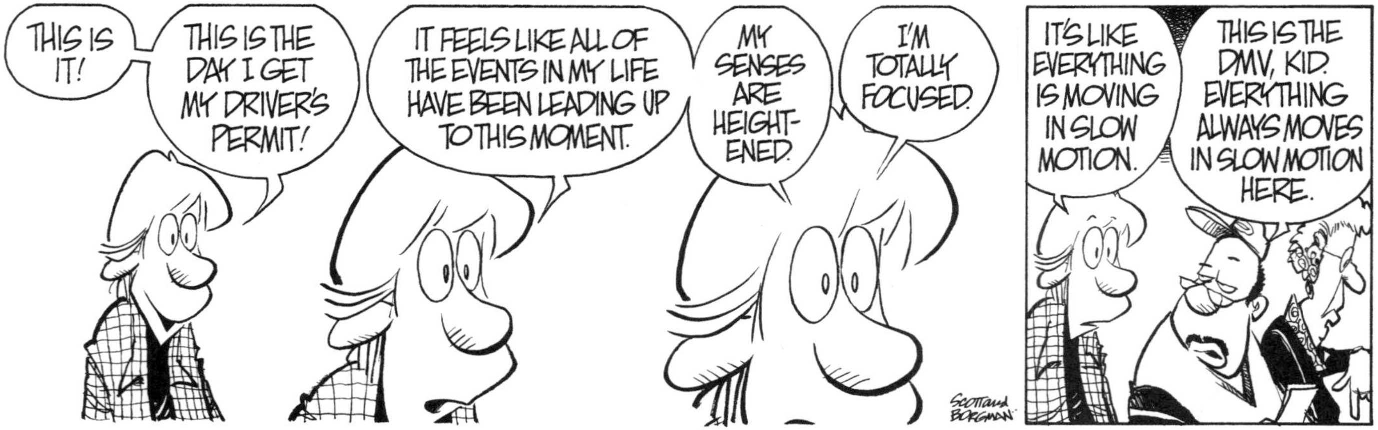
THIS IS IT!
THIS IS THE DAY I GET MY DRIVER'S PERMIT!
IT FEELS LIKE ALL OF THE EVENTS IN MY LIFE HAVE BEEN LEADING UP TO THIS MOMENT.
MY SENSES ARE HEIGHT-ENED.
I'M TOTALLY FOCUSED.
IT'S LIKE EVERYTHING IS MOVING IN SLOW MOTION.
THIS IS THE DMV, KID. EVERYTHING ALWAYS MOVES IN SLOW MOTION HERE.

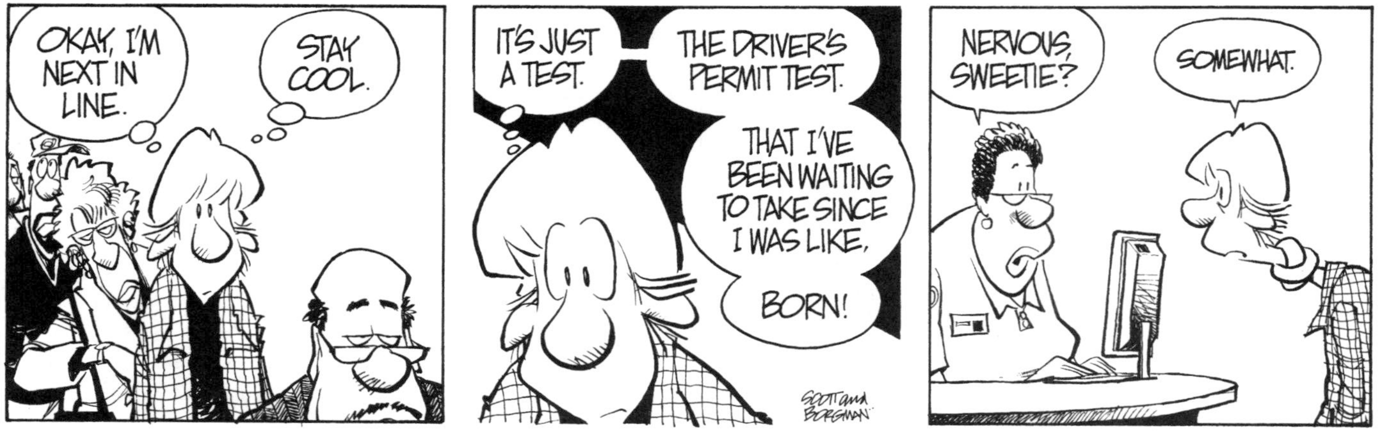
OKAY, I'M NEXT IN LINE.
STAY COOL.
IT'S JUST A TEST.
THE DRIVER'S PERMIT TEST.
THAT I'VE BEEN WAITING TO TAKE SINCE I WAS LIKE,
BORN!
NERVOUS, SWEETIE?
SOMEWHAT.

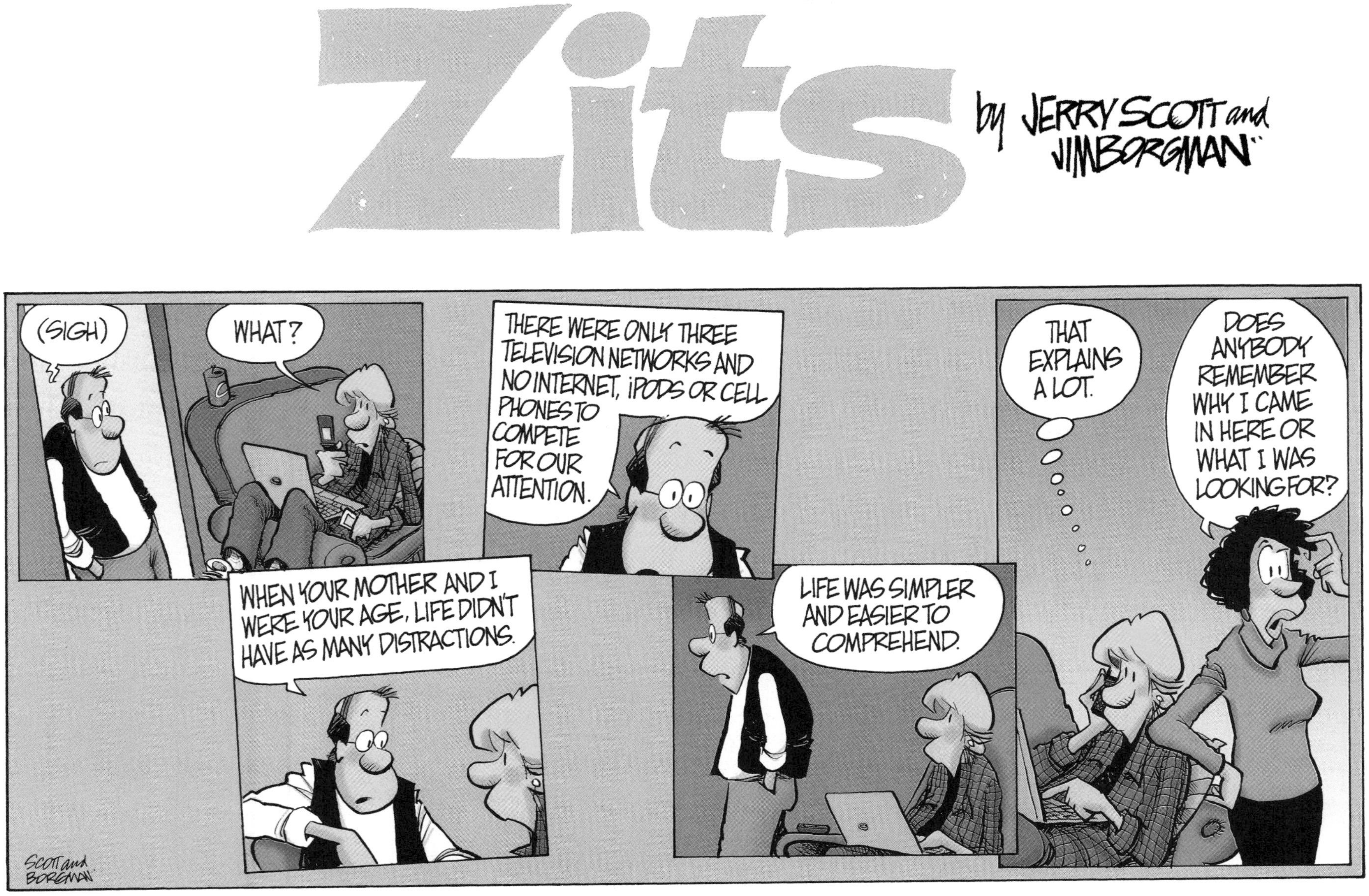
Zits
by JERRY SCOTT and JIM BORGMAN
(SIGH)
WHAT?
WHEN YOUR MOTHER AND I WERE YOUR AGE, LIFE DIDN'T HAVE AS MANY DISTRACTIONS.
THERE WERE ONLY THREE TELEVISION NETWORKS AND NO INTERNET, iPODS OR CELL PHONES TO COMPETE FOR OUR ATTENTION.
LIFE WAS SIMPLER AND EASIER TO COMPREHEND.
THAT EXPLAINS A LOT.
DOES ANYBODY REMEMBER WHY I CAME IN HERE OR WHAT I WAS LOOKING FOR?
SCOTT and BORGMAN

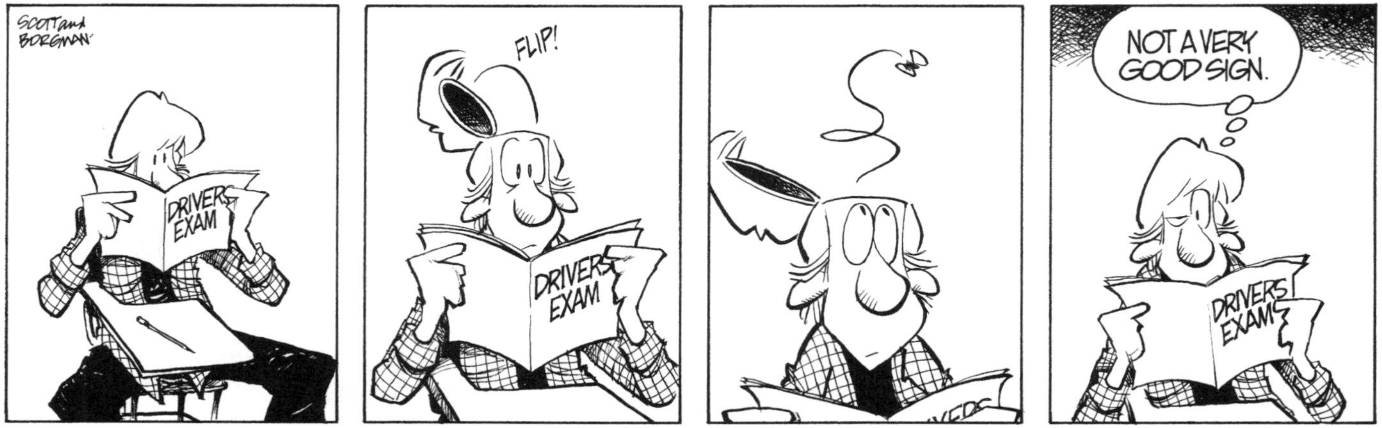
SCOTT and BORGMAN
DRIVERS EXAM
FLIP!
DRIVERS EXAM
NOT A VERY GOOD SIGN.
DRIVERS EXAM

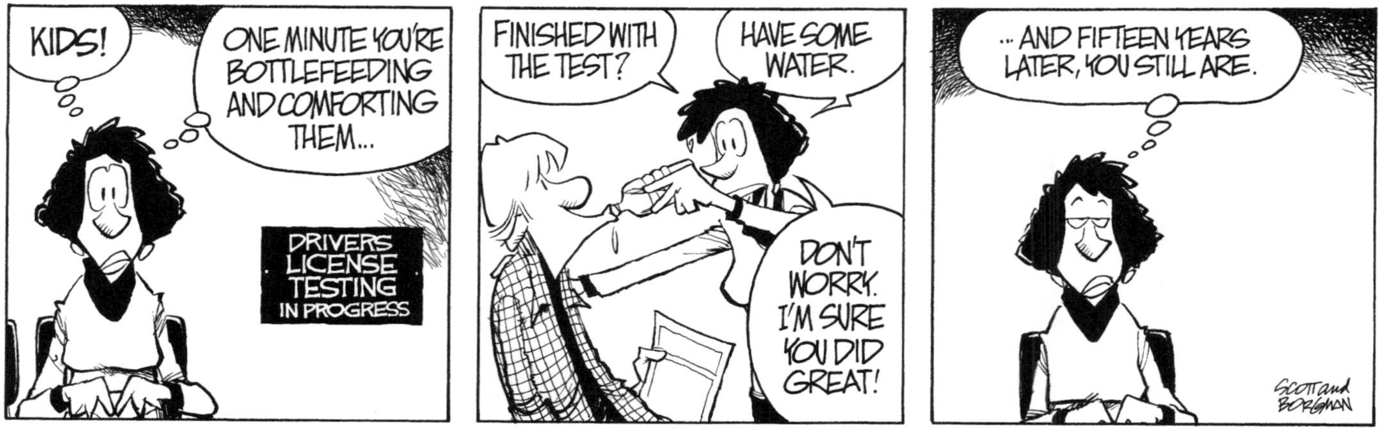
KIDS!
ONE MINUTE YOU'RE BOTTLEFEEDING AND COMFORTING THEM...
DRIVERS LICENSE TESTING IN PROGRESS
FINISHED WITH THE TEST?
HAVE SOME WATER.
DON'T WORRY. I'M SURE YOU DID GREAT!
...AND FIFTEEN YEARS LATER, YOU STILL ARE.
SCOTT and BORGMAN

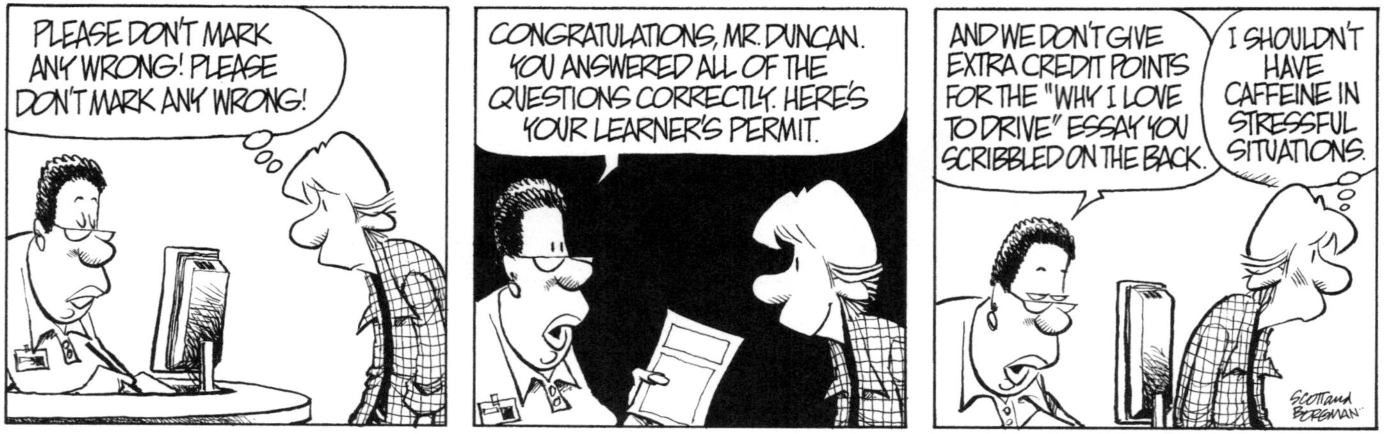
PLEASE DON'T MARK ANY WRONG! PLEASE DON'T MARK ANY WRONG!
CONGRATULATIONS, MR. DUNCAN. YOU ANSWERED ALL OF THE QUESTIONS CORRECTLY. HERE'S YOUR LEARNER'S PERMIT.
AND WE DON'T GIVE EXTRA CREDIT POINTS FOR THE "WHY I LOVE TO DRIVE" ESSAY YOU SCRIBBLED ON THE BACK.
I SHOULDN'T HAVE CAFFEINE IN STRESSFUL SITUATIONS.
SCOTT and BORGMAN

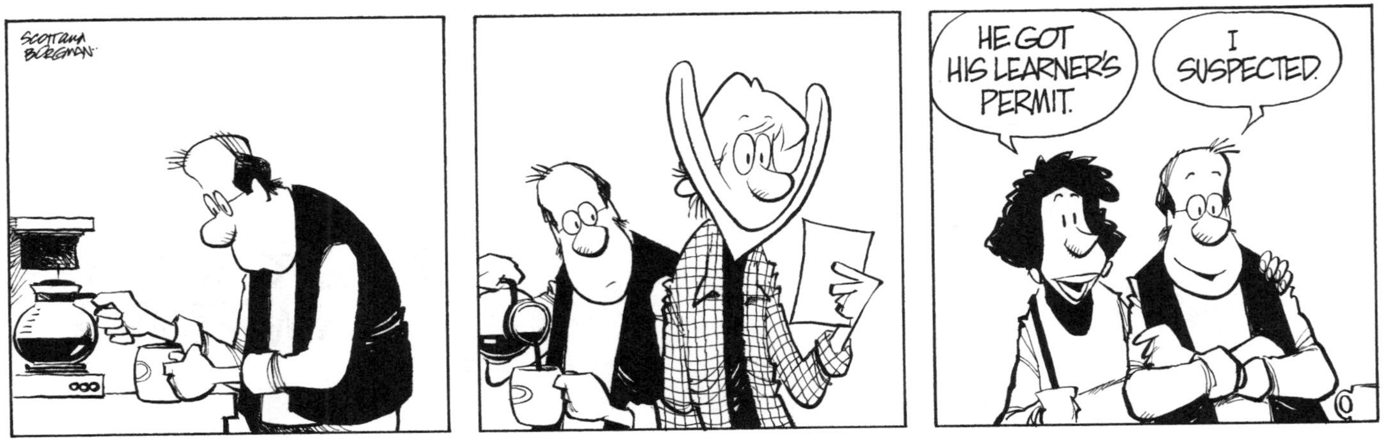
HE GOT HIS LEARNER'S PERMIT.
I SUSPECTED.

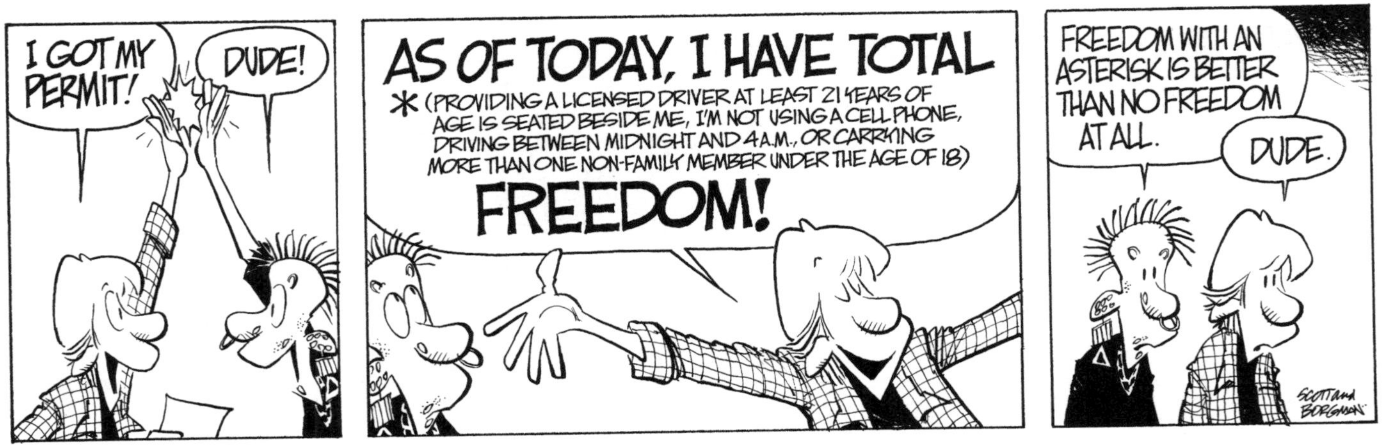
I GOT MY PERMIT!
DUDE!
AS OF TODAY, I HAVE TOTAL
* (PROVIDING A LICENSED DRIVER AT LEAST 21 YEARS OF AGE IS SEATED BESIDE ME, I'M NOT USING A CELL PHONE, DRIVING BETWEEN MIDNIGHT AND 4 A.M., OR CARRYING MORE THAN ONE NON-FAMILY MEMBER UNDER THE AGE OF 18)
FREEDOM!
FREEDOM WITH AN ASTERISK IS BETTER THAN NO FREEDOM AT ALL.
DUDE.

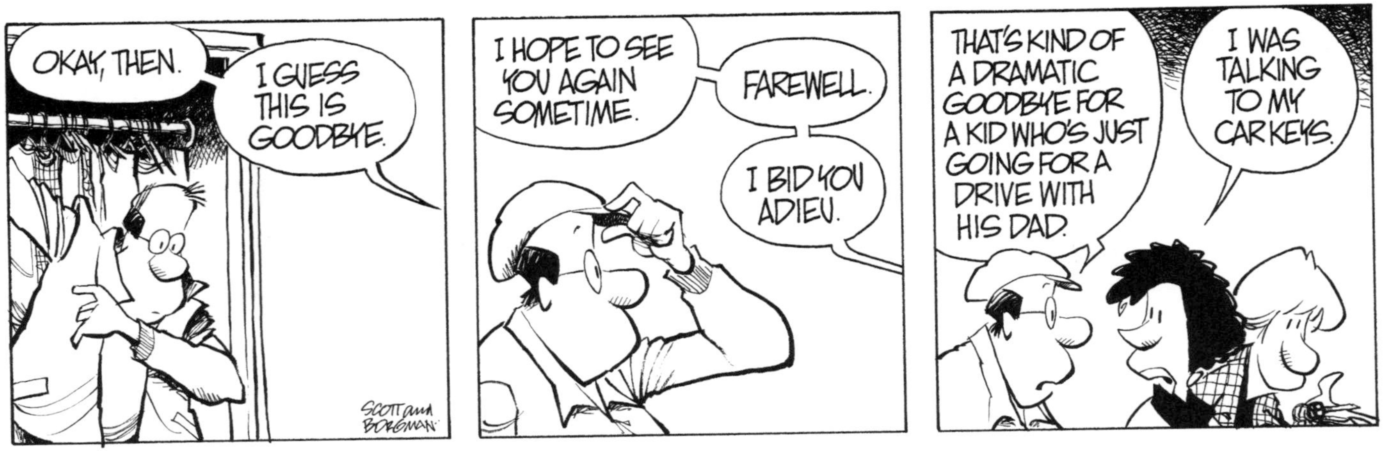
OKAY, THEN.
I GUESS THIS IS GOODBYE.
I HOPE TO SEE YOU AGAIN SOMETIME.
FAREWELL.
I BID YOU ADIEU.
THAT'S KIND OF A DRAMATIC GOODBYE FOR A KID WHO'S JUST GOING FOR A DRIVE WITH HIS DAD.
I WAS TALKING TO MY CAR KEYS.

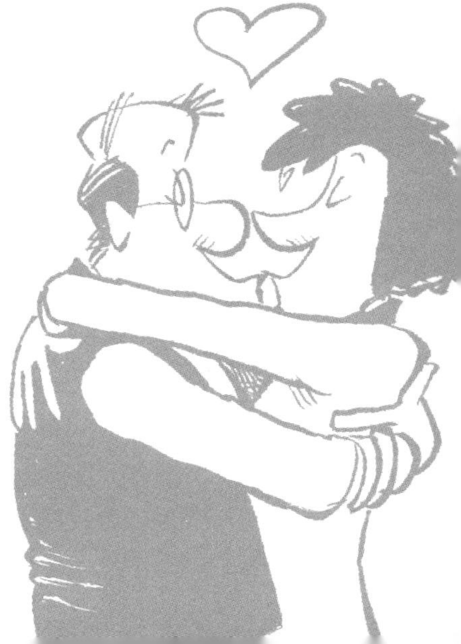

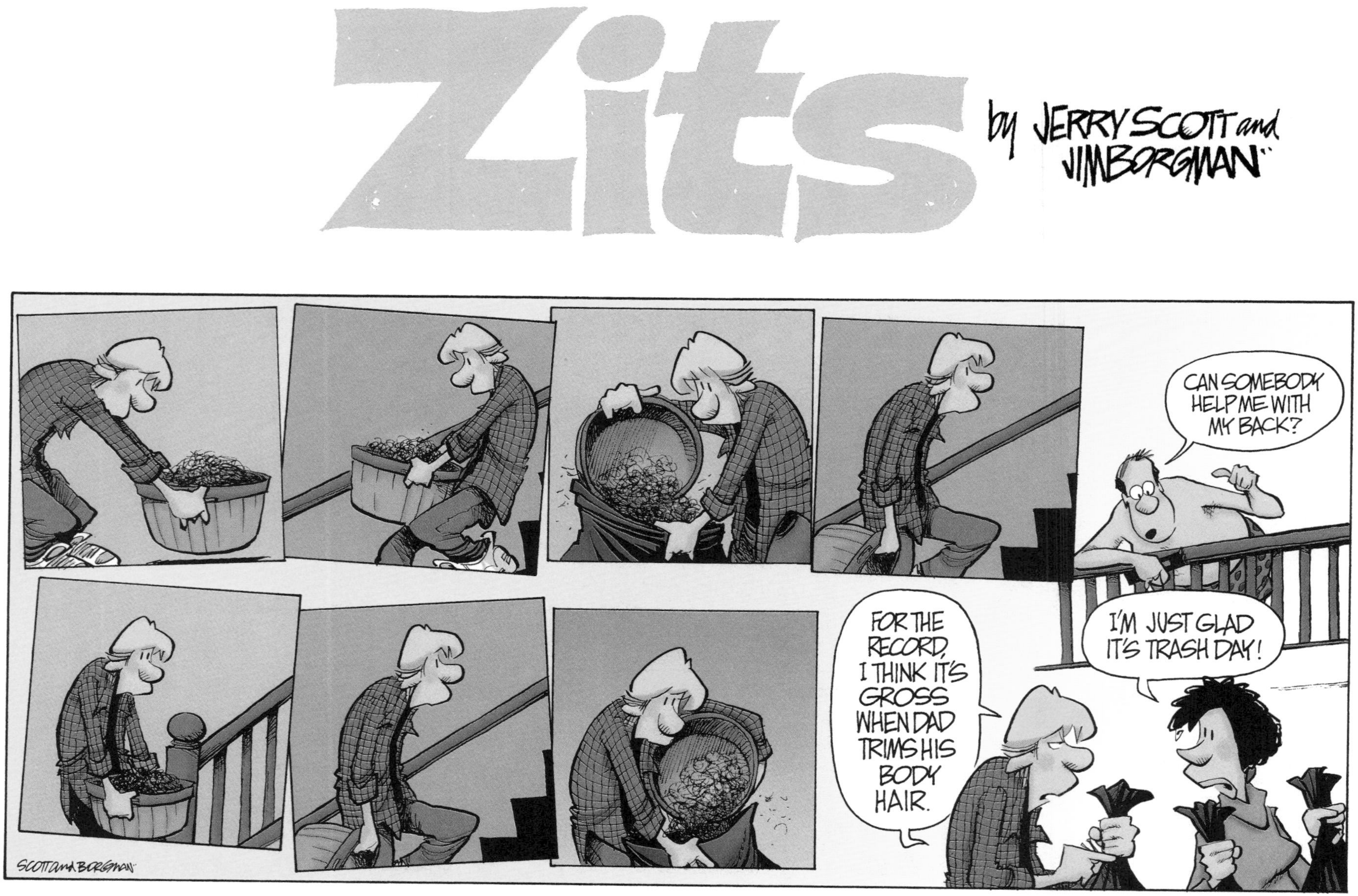
Zits
by JERRY SCOTT and JIM BORGMAN
CAN SOMEBODY HELP ME WITH MY BACK?
FOR THE RECORD, I THINK IT'S GROSS WHEN DAD TRIMS HIS BODY HAIR.
I'M JUST GLAD IT'S TRASH DAY!
SCOTT and BORGMAN

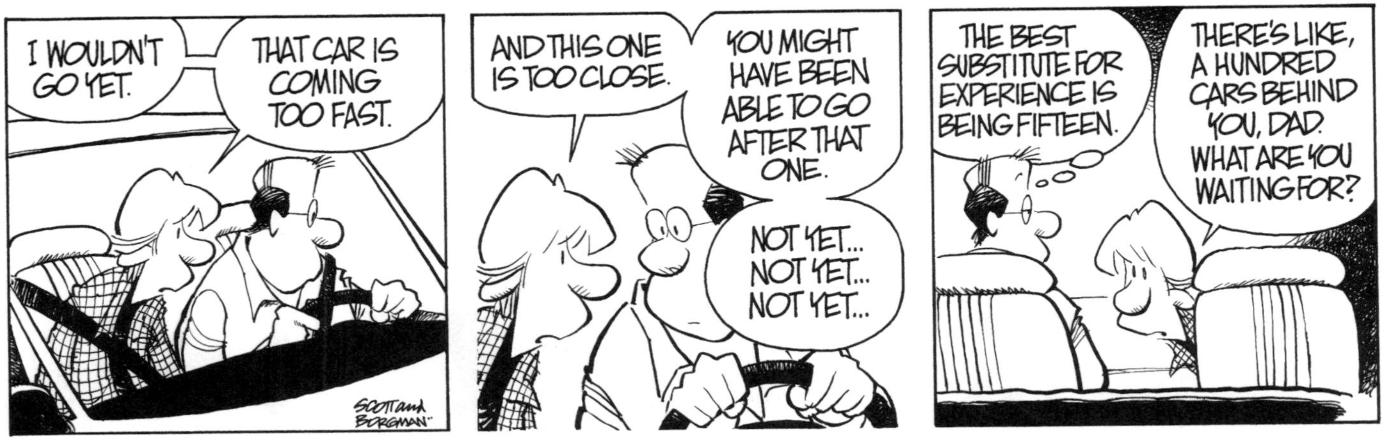
I WOULDN'T GO YET.
THAT CAR IS COMING TOO FAST.
SCOTT AND BORGMAN
AND THIS ONE IS TOO CLOSE.
YOU MIGHT HAVE BEEN ABLE TO GO AFTER THAT ONE.
NOT YET... NOT YET... NOT YET...
THE BEST SUBSTITUTE FOR EXPERIENCE IS BEING FIFTEEN.
THERE'S LIKE, A HUNDRED CARS BEHIND YOU, DAD. WHAT ARE YOU WAITING FOR?

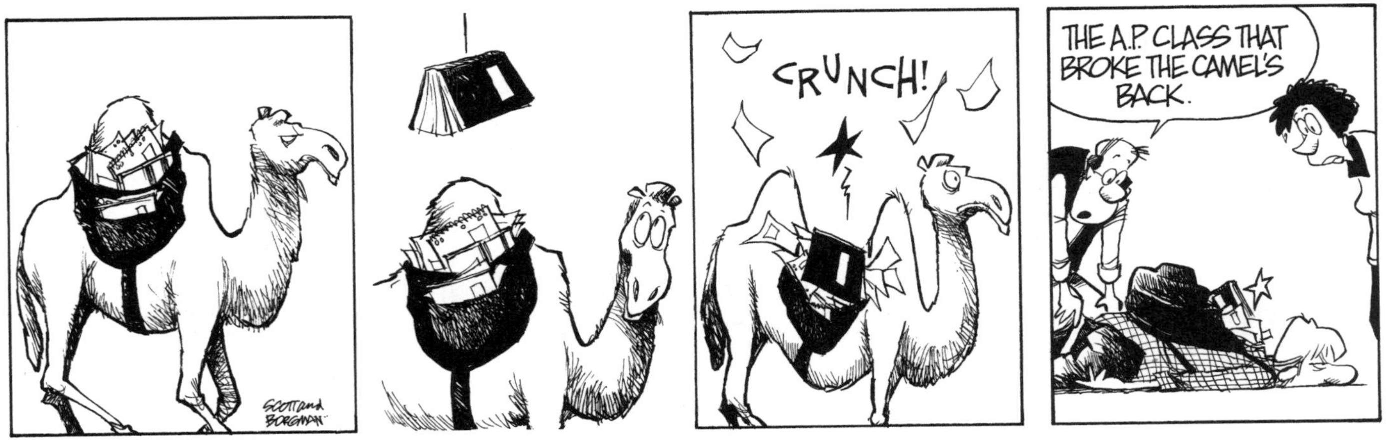
SCOTT AND BORGMAN
CRUNCH!
THE A.P. CLASS THAT BROKE THE CAMEL'S BACK.

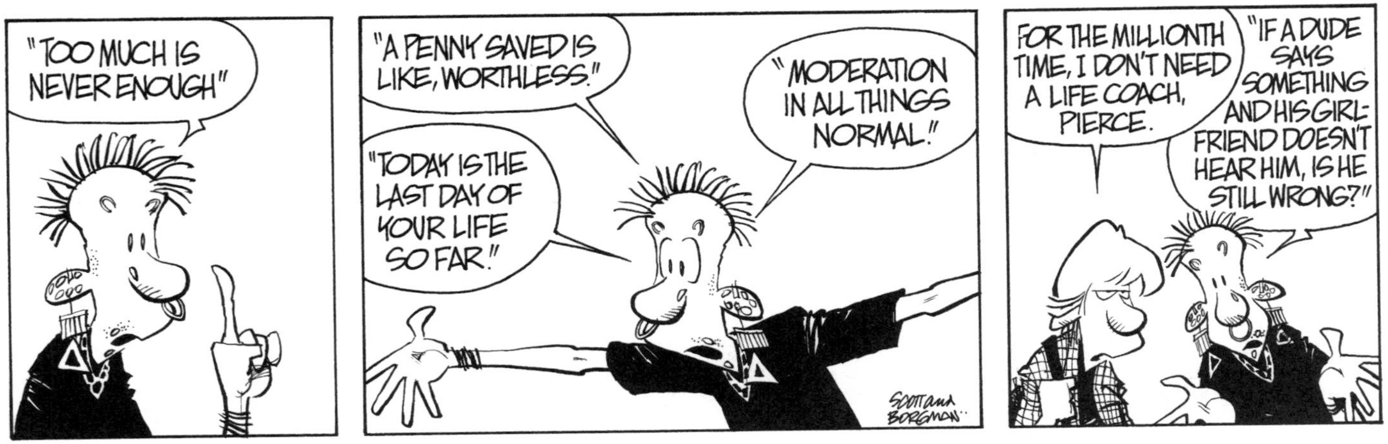
"TOO MUCH IS NEVER ENOUGH"
"A PENNY SAVED IS LIKE, WORTHLESS."
"TODAY IS THE LAST DAY OF YOUR LIFE SO FAR."
"MODERATION IN ALL THINGS NORMAL."
SCOTT AND BORGMAN
FOR THE MILLIONTH TIME, I DON'T NEED A LIFE COACH, PIERCE.
"IF A DUDE SAYS SOMETHING AND HIS GIRLFRIEND DOESN'T HEAR HIM, IS HE STILL WRONG?"

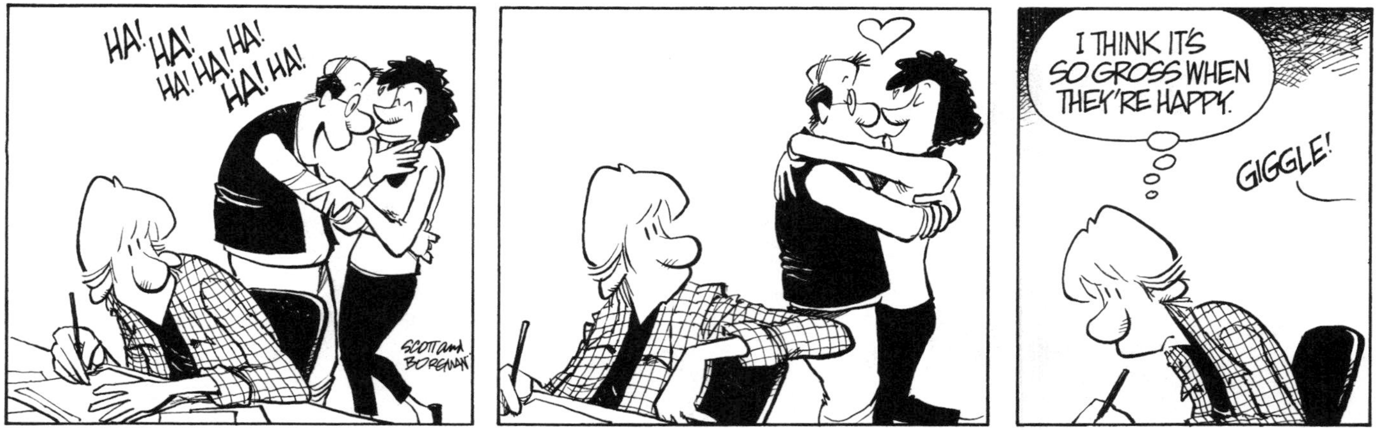
HA! HA! HA! HA! HA! HA! HA! HA!
I THINK IT'S SO GROSS WHEN THEY'RE HAPPY.
GIGGLE!

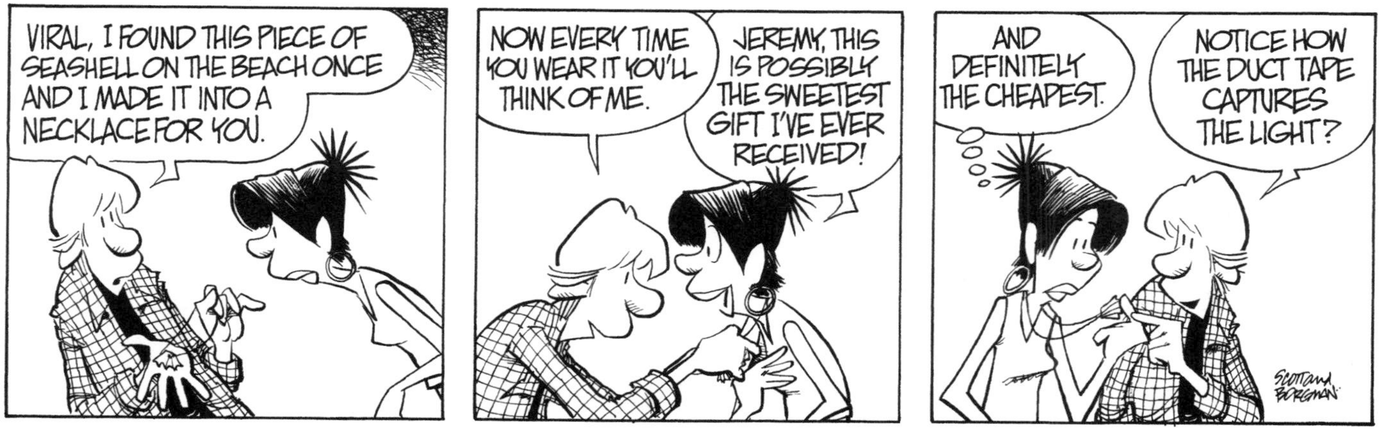
VIRAL, I FOUND THIS PIECE OF SEASHELL ON THE BEACH ONCE AND I MADE IT INTO A NECKLACE FOR YOU.
NOW EVERY TIME YOU WEAR IT YOU'LL THINK OF ME.
JEREMY, THIS IS POSSIBLY THE SWEETEST GIFT I'VE EVER RECEIVED!
AND DEFINITELY THE CHEAPEST.
NOTICE HOW THE DUCT TAPE CAPTURES THE LIGHT?

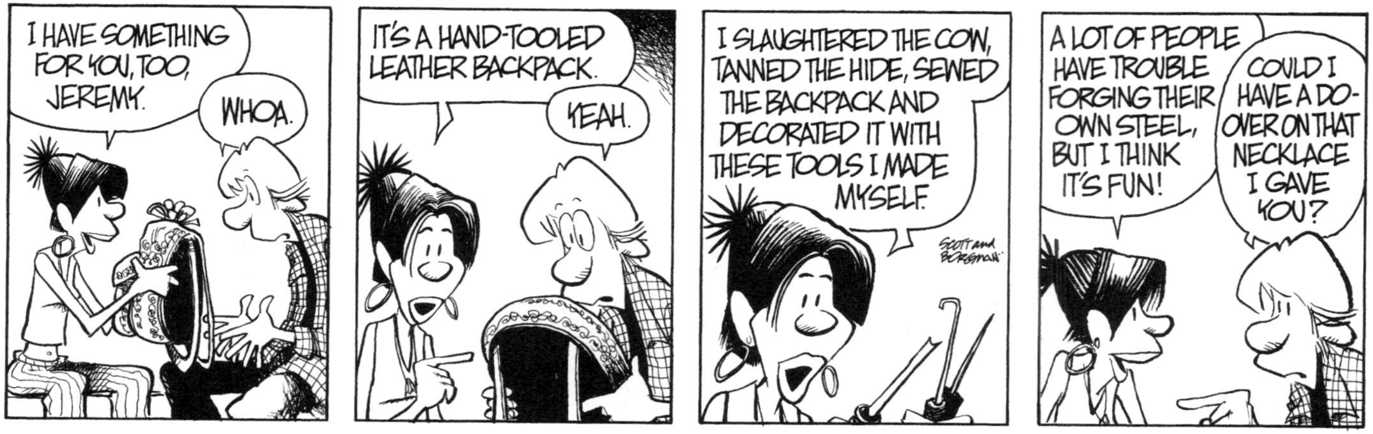
I HAVE SOMETHING FOR YOU, TOO, JEREMY.
WHOA.
IT'S A HAND-TOOLED LEATHER BACKPACK.
YEAH.
I SLAUGHTERED THE COW, TANNED THE HIDE, SEWED THE BACKPACK AND DECORATED IT WITH THESE TOOLS I MADE MYSELF.
A LOT OF PEOPLE HAVE TROUBLE FORGING THEIR OWN STEEL, BUT I THINK IT'S FUN!
COULD I HAVE A DO-OVER ON THAT NECKLACE I GAVE YOU?

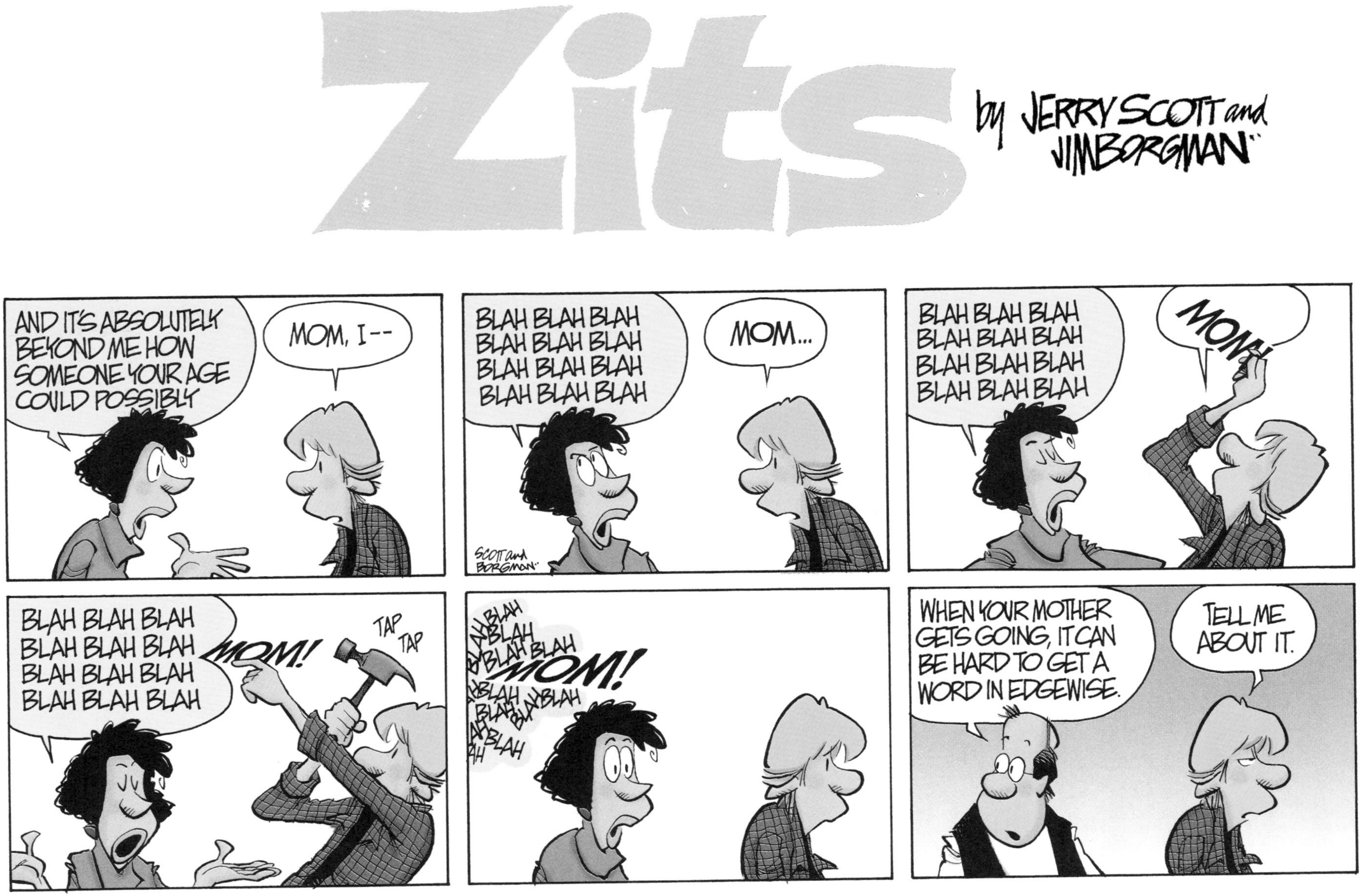
Zits
by JERRY SCOTT and JIM BORGMAN
AND IT'S ABSOLUTELY BEYOND ME HOW SOMEONE YOUR AGE COULD POSSIBLY
MOM, I--
BLAH BLAH BLAH BLAH BLAH BLAH BLAH BLAH BLAH BLAH BLAH BLAH
MOM...
SCOTT and BORGMAN
BLAH BLAH BLAH BLAH BLAH BLAH BLAH BLAH BLAH BLAH BLAH BLAH
MOM!
BLAH BLAH BLAH BLAH BLAH BLAH BLAH BLAH BLAH BLAH BLAH BLAH
MOM!
TAP TAP
BLAH BLAH BLAH BLAH
MOM!
BLAH BLAH BLAH
BLAH
WHEN YOUR MOTHER GETS GOING, IT CAN BE HARD TO GET A WORD IN EDGEWISE.
TELL ME ABOUT IT.

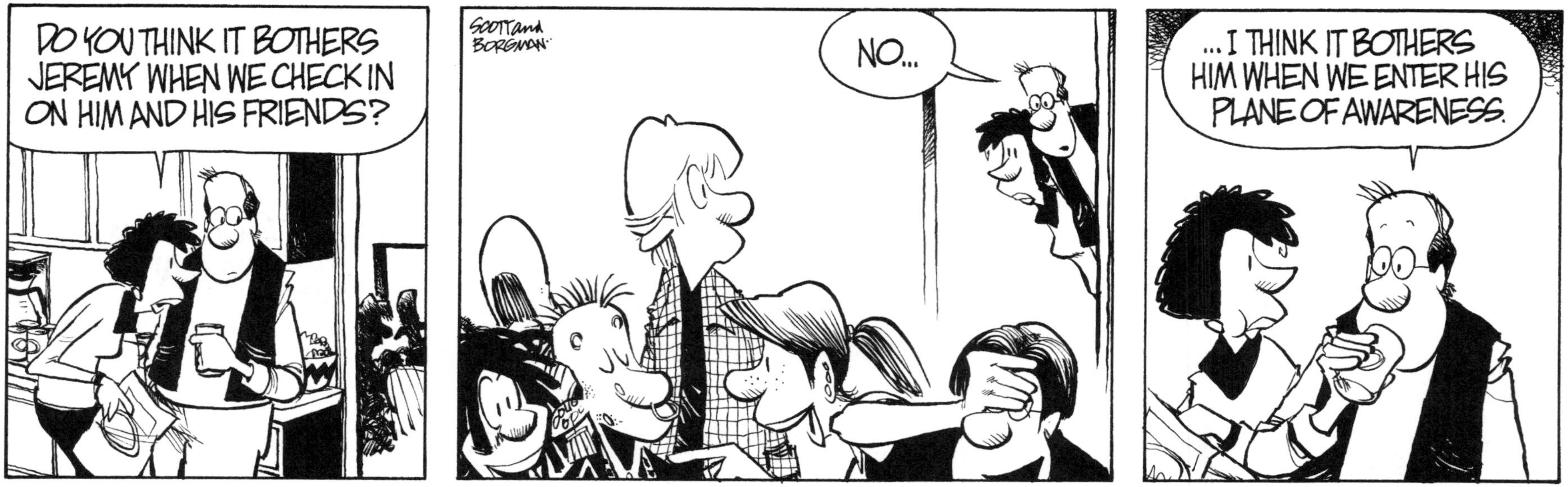
DO YOU THINK IT BOTHERS JEREMY WHEN WE CHECK IN ON HIM AND HIS FRIENDS?
NO...
...I THINK IT BOTHERS HIM WHEN WE ENTER HIS PLANE OF AWARENESS.

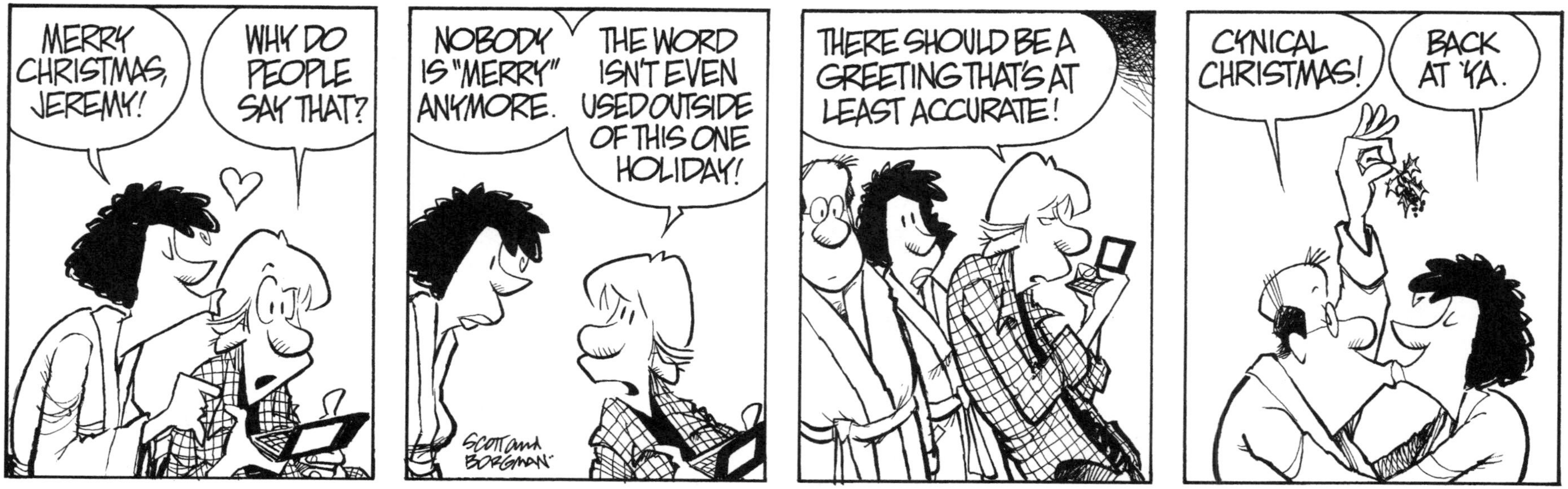
MERRY CHRISTMAS, JEREMY!
WHY DO PEOPLE SAY THAT?
NOBODY IS "MERRY" ANYMORE.
THE WORD ISN'T EVEN USED OUTSIDE OF THIS ONE HOLIDAY!
THERE SHOULD BE A GREETING THAT'S AT LEAST ACCURATE!
CYNICAL CHRISTMAS!
BACK AT 'YA.

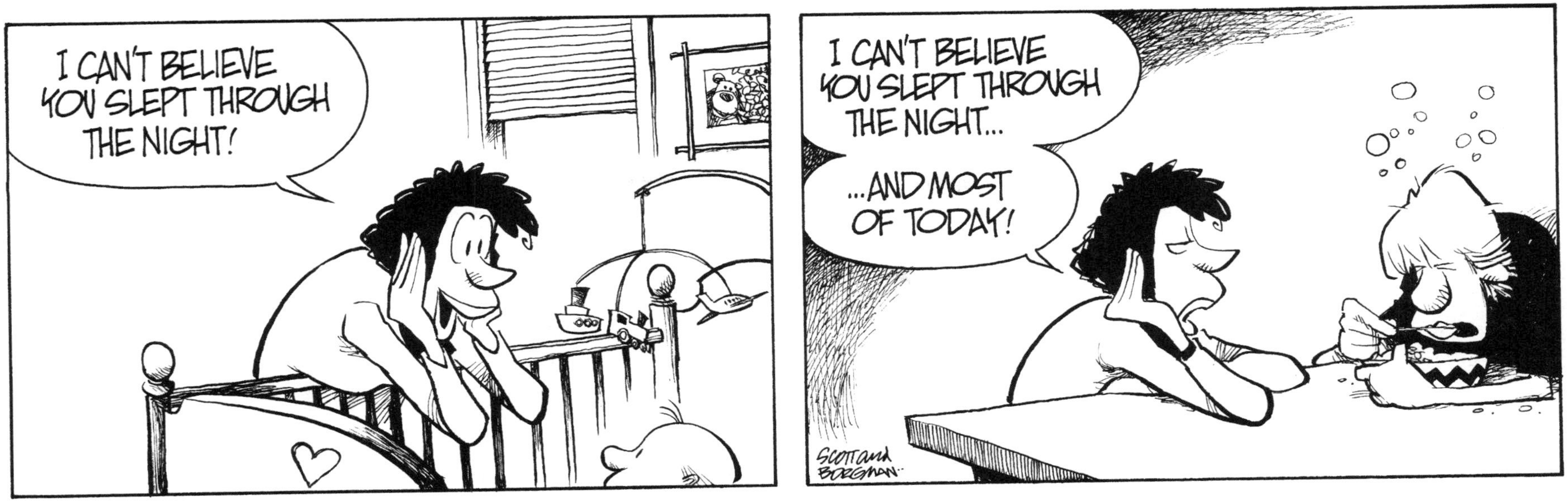
I CAN'T BELIEVE YOU SLEPT THROUGH THE NIGHT!
I CAN'T BELIEVE YOU SLEPT THROUGH THE NIGHT...
...AND MOST OF TODAY!
SCOTT and BORGMAN

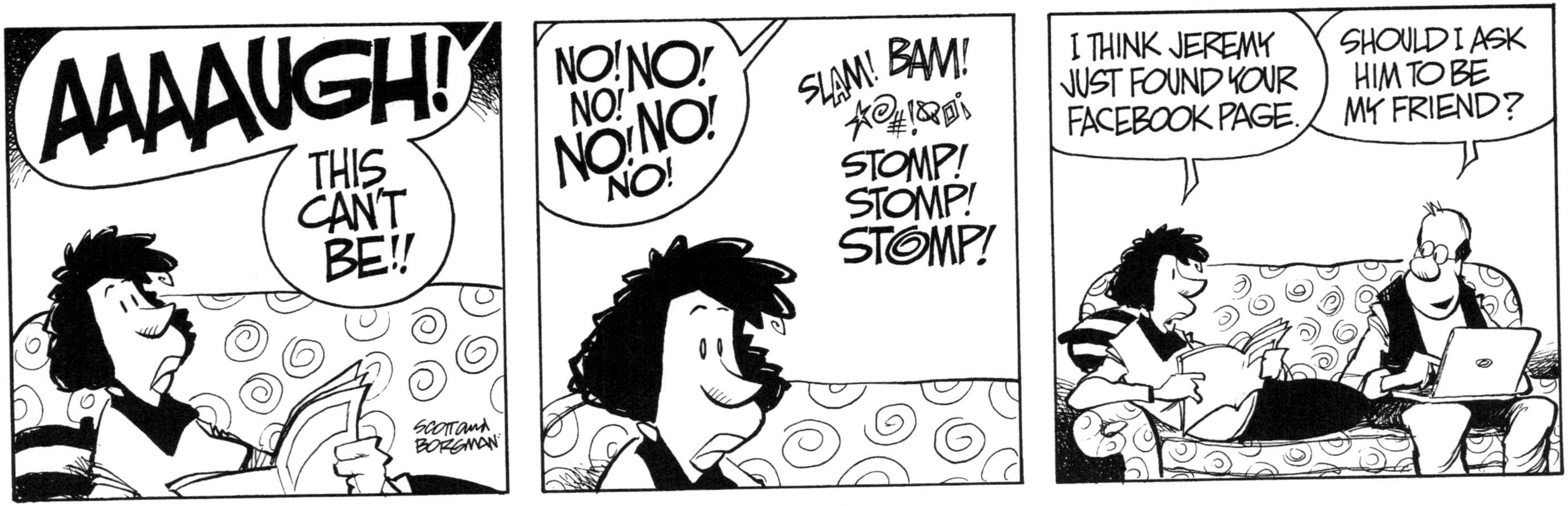
AAAAUGH!
THIS CAN'T BE!!
SCOTT and BORGMAN
NO! NO! NO! NO! NO! NO!
SLAM! BAM!
STOMP! STOMP! STOMP!
I THINK JEREMY JUST FOUND YOUR FACEBOOK PAGE.
SHOULD I ASK HIM TO BE MY FRIEND?

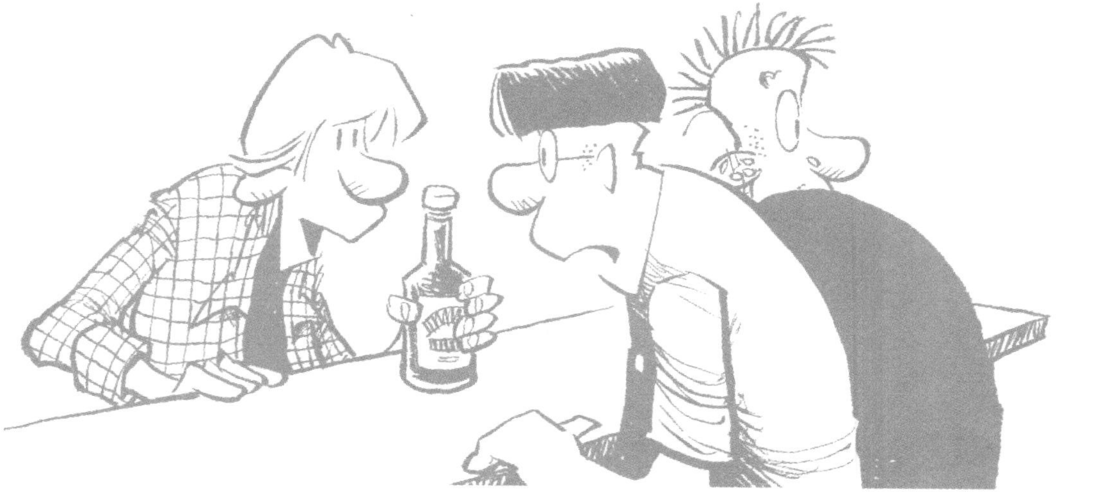

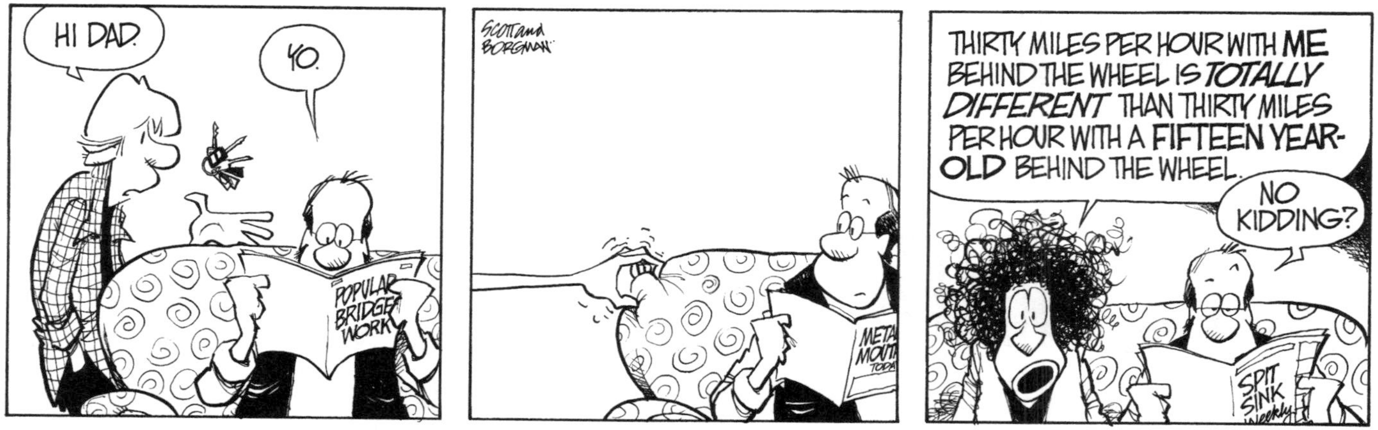
HI DAD.
YO.
SCOTT and BORGMAN
POPULAR BRIDGEWORK
METAL MOUTH TODAY
THIRTY MILES PER HOUR WITH **ME** BEHIND THE WHEEL IS ***TOTALLY DIFFERENT*** THAN THIRTY MILES PER HOUR WITH A **FIFTEEN YEAR-OLD** BEHIND THE WHEEL.
NO KIDDING?
SPIT SINK Weekly

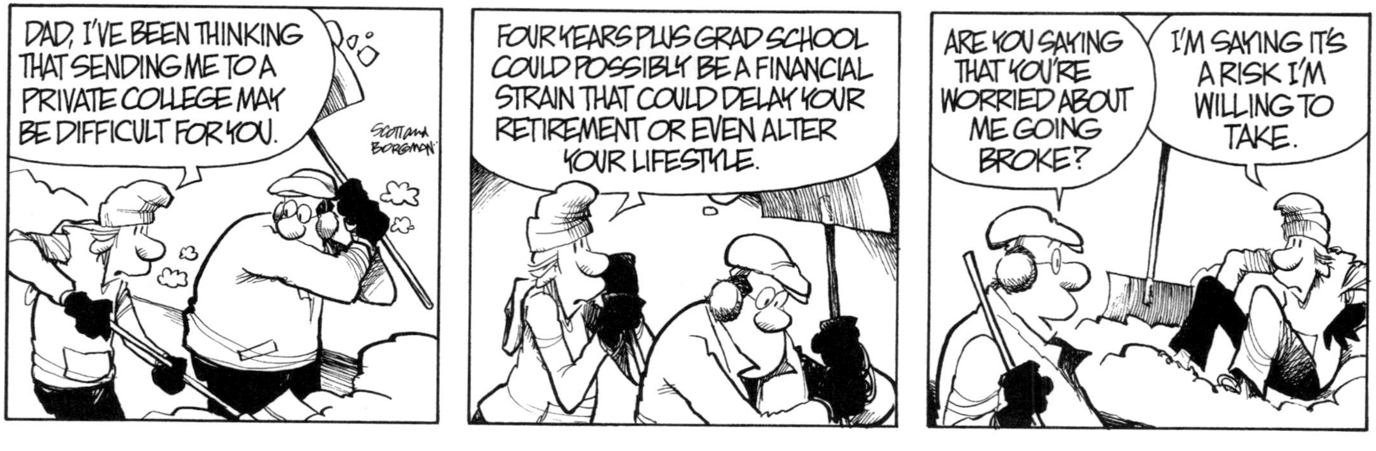
DAD, I'VE BEEN THINKING THAT SENDING ME TO A PRIVATE COLLEGE MAY BE DIFFICULT FOR YOU.
SCOTT and BORGMAN
FOUR YEARS PLUS GRAD SCHOOL COULD POSSIBLY BE A FINANCIAL STRAIN THAT COULD DELAY YOUR RETIREMENT OR EVEN ALTER YOUR LIFESTYLE.
ARE YOU SAYING THAT YOU'RE WORRIED ABOUT ME GOING BROKE?
I'M SAYING IT'S A RISK I'M WILLING TO TAKE.

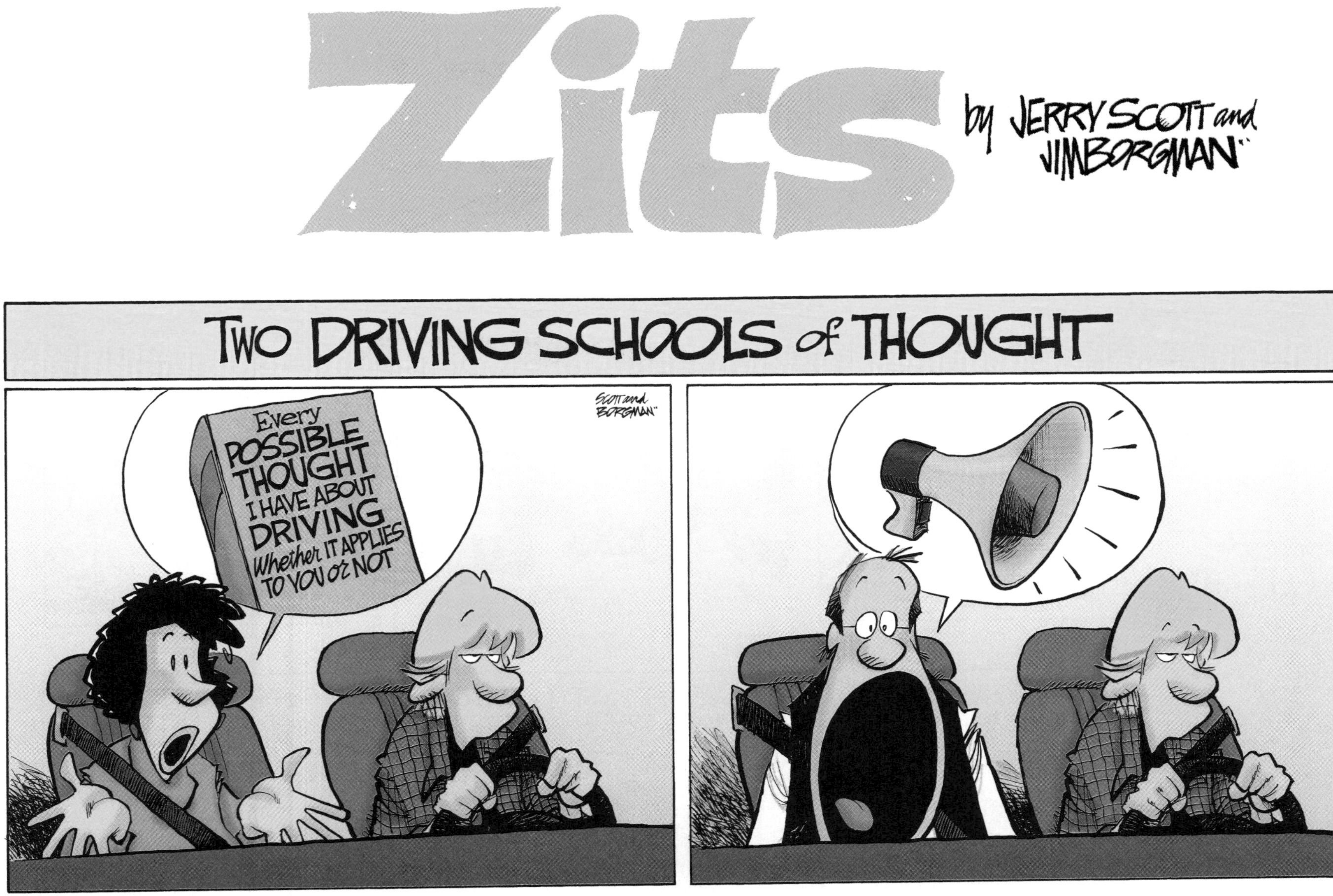
Zits
by JERRY SCOTT and JIM BORGMAN
TWO DRIVING SCHOOLS of THOUGHT
SCOTT and BORGMAN
Every POSSIBLE THOUGHT I HAVE ABOUT DRIVING Whether IT APPLIES TO YOU or NOT

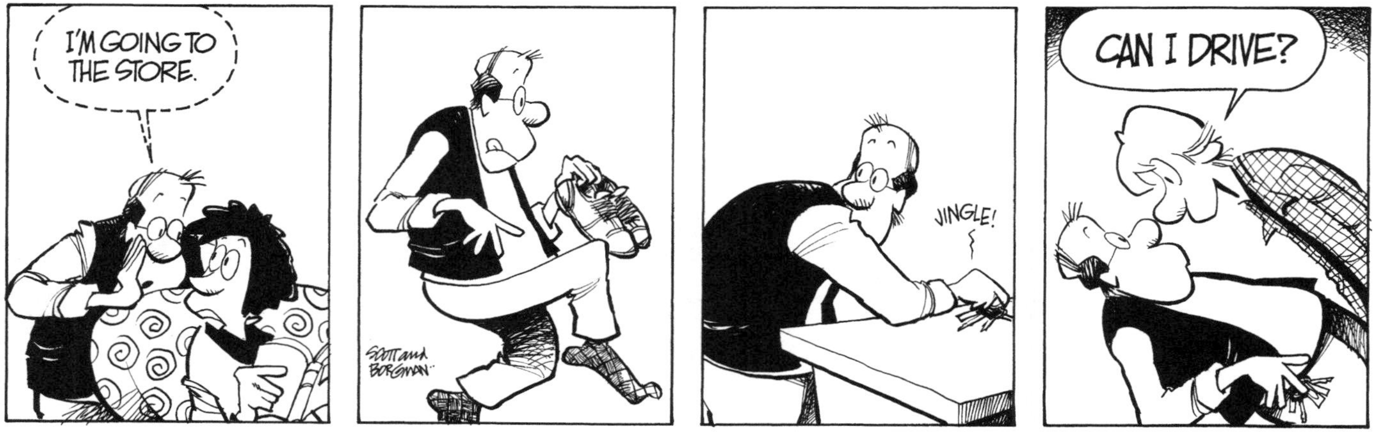
I'M GOING TO THE STORE.
SCOTT and BORGMAN
JINGLE!
CAN I DRIVE?

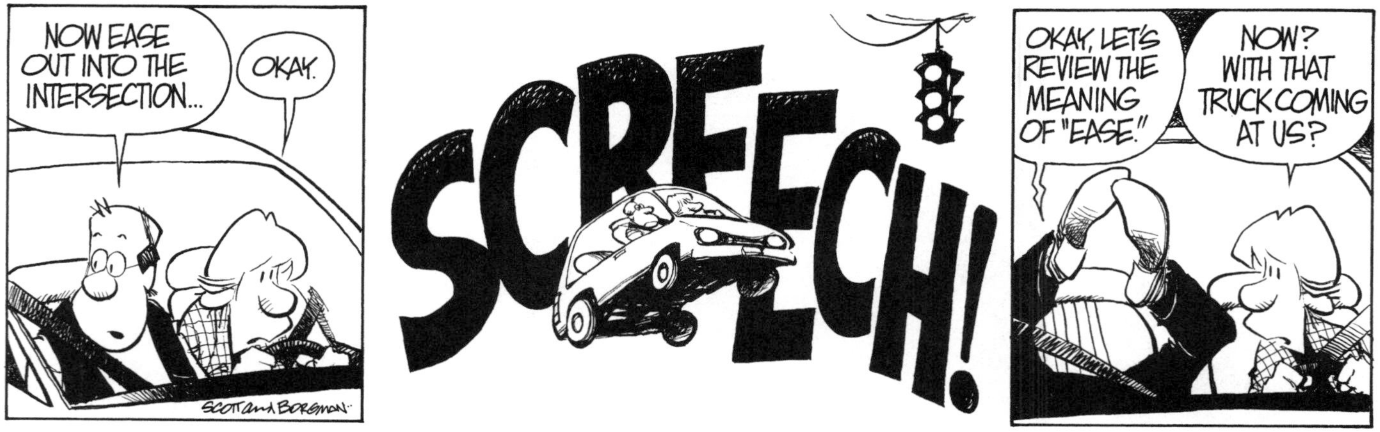
NOW EASE OUT INTO THE INTERSECTION...
OKAY.
SCOTT and BORGMAN
SCREECH!
OKAY, LET'S REVIEW THE MEANING OF "EASE."
NOW? WITH THAT TRUCK COMING AT US?

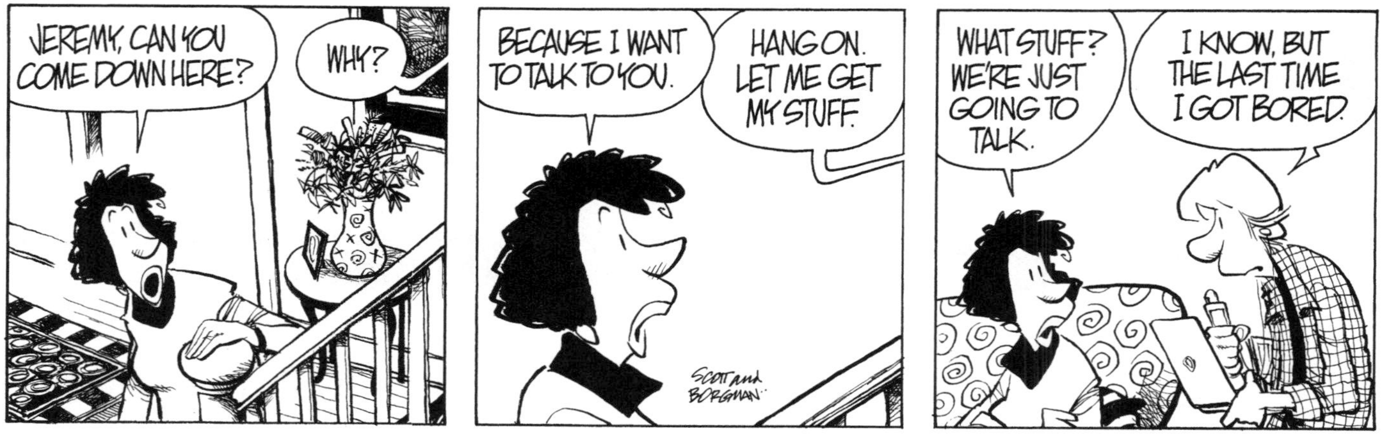
JEREMY, CAN YOU COME DOWN HERE?
WHY?
BECAUSE I WANT TO TALK TO YOU.
HANG ON. LET ME GET MY STUFF.
SCOTT and BORGMAN
WHAT STUFF? WE'RE JUST GOING TO TALK.
I KNOW, BUT THE LAST TIME I GOT BORED.

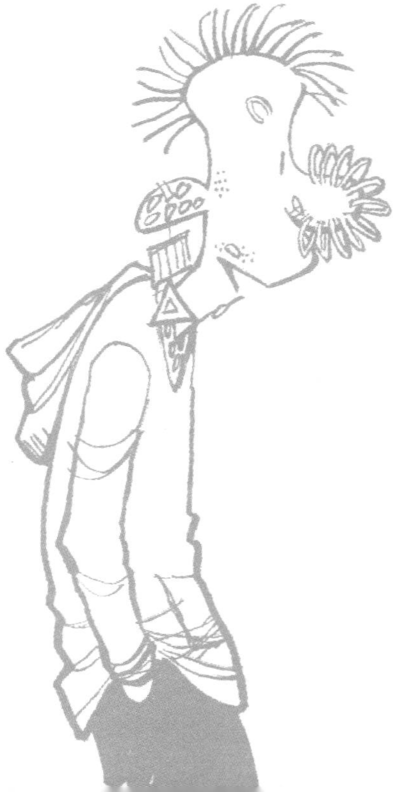

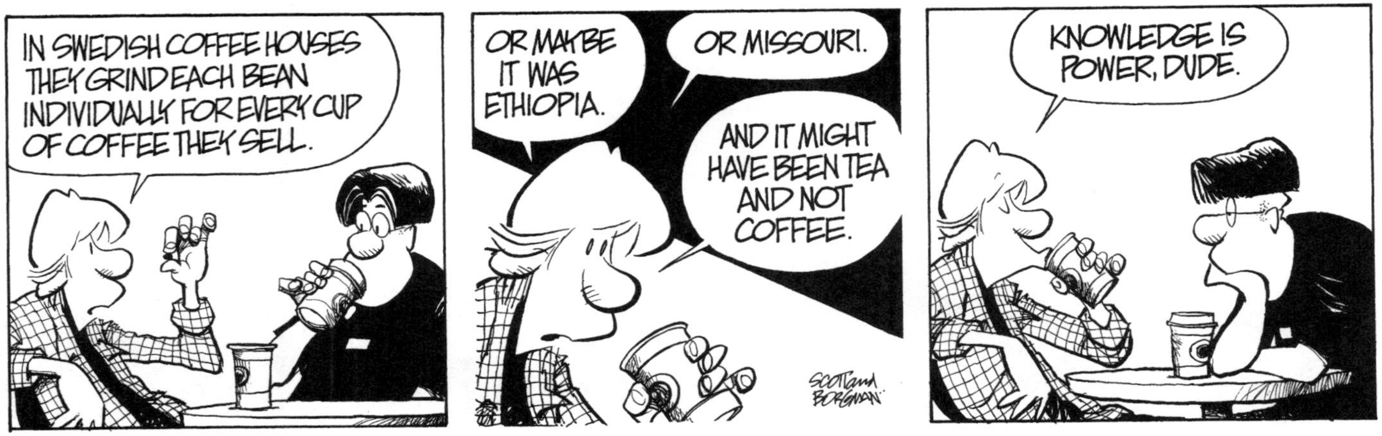
IN SWEDISH COFFEE HOUSES THEY GRIND EACH BEAN INDIVIDUALLY FOR EVERY CUP OF COFFEE THEY SELL.
OR MAYBE IT WAS ETHIOPIA.
OR MISSOURI.
AND IT MIGHT HAVE BEEN TEA AND NOT COFFEE.
KNOWLEDGE IS POWER, DUDE.

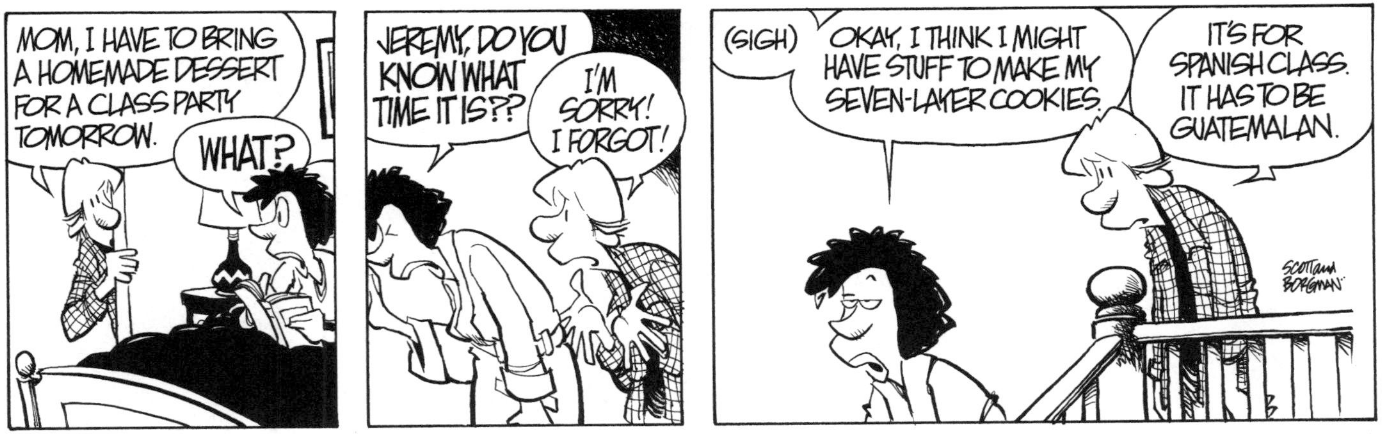
MOM, I HAVE TO BRING A HOMEMADE DESSERT FOR A CLASS PARTY TOMORROW.
WHAT?
JEREMY, DO YOU KNOW WHAT TIME IT IS??
I'M SORRY! I FORGOT!
(SIGH)
OKAY, I THINK I MIGHT HAVE STUFF TO MAKE MY SEVEN-LAYER COOKIES.
IT'S FOR SPANISH CLASS. IT HAS TO BE GUATEMALAN.

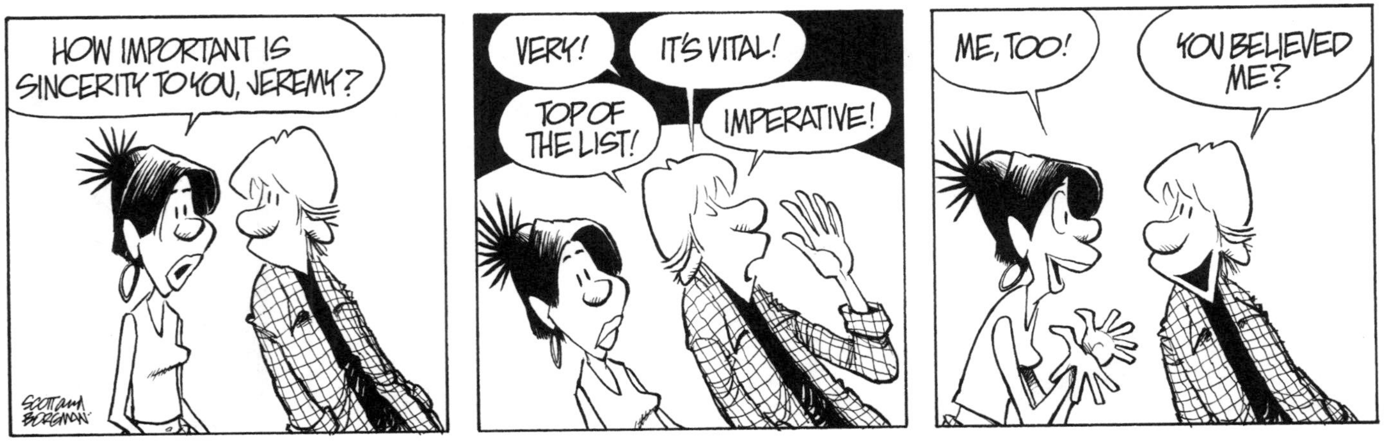
HOW IMPORTANT IS SINCERITY TO YOU, JEREMY?
VERY!
IT'S VITAL!
TOP OF THE LIST!
IMPERATIVE!
ME, TOO!
YOU BELIEVED ME?

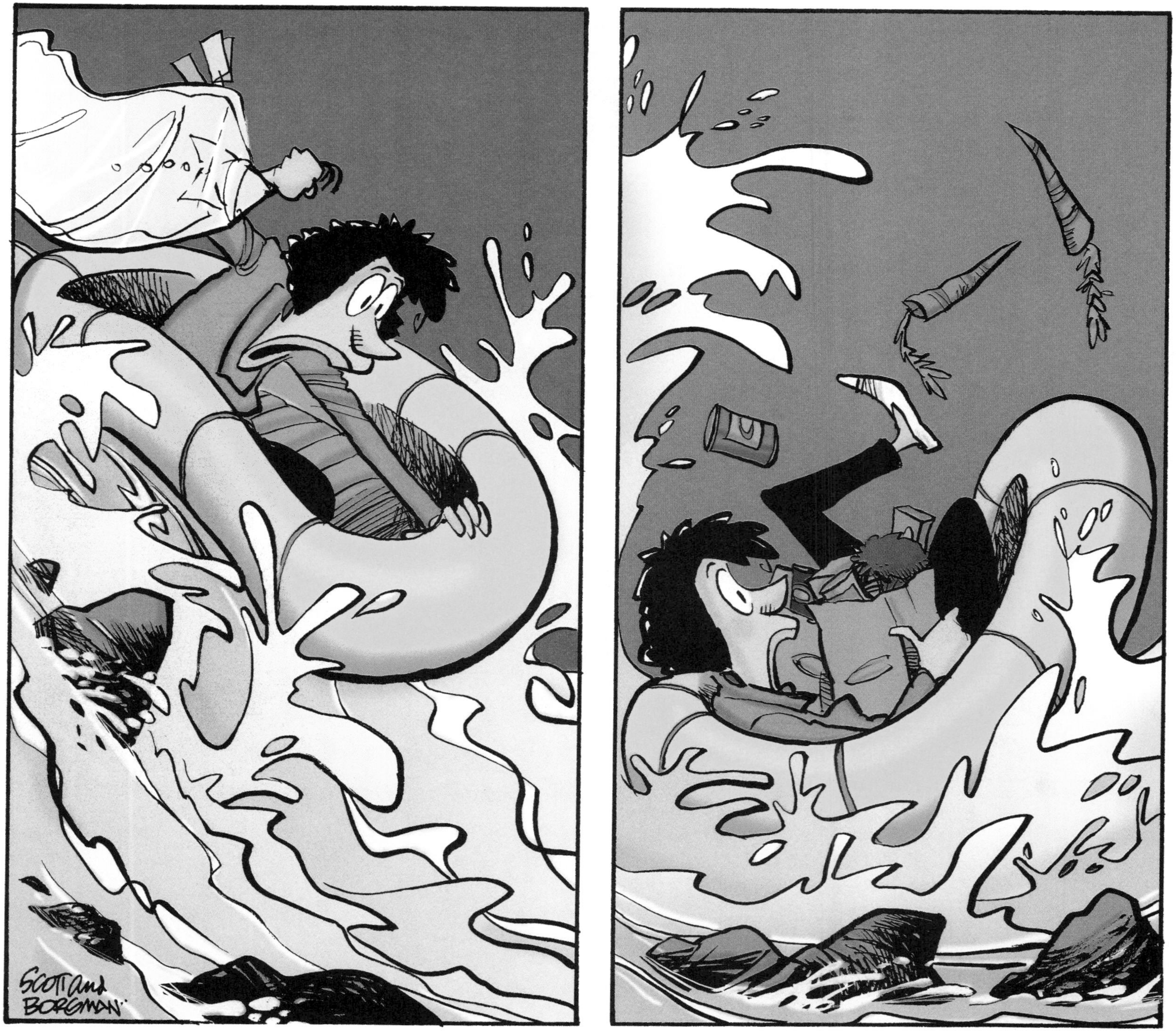
SCOTT and BORGMAN

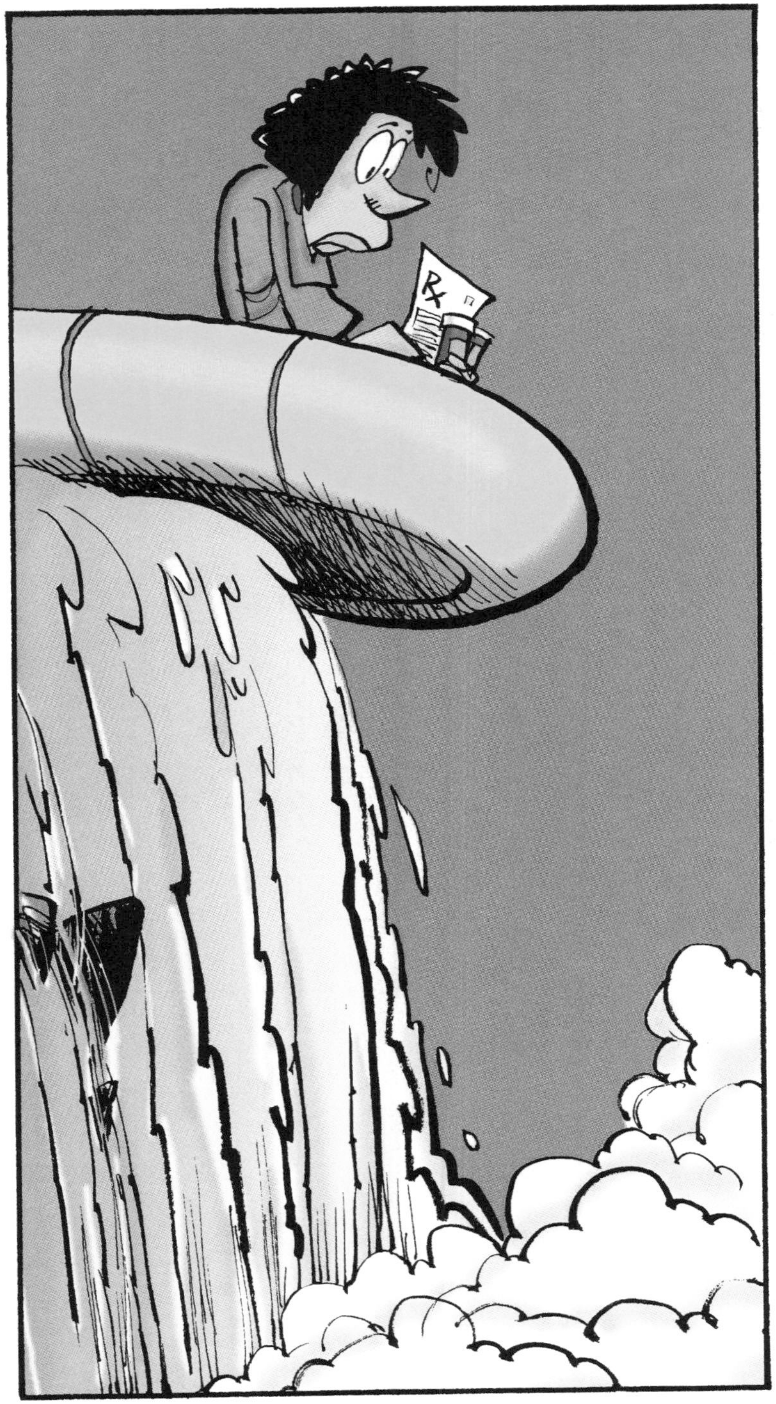

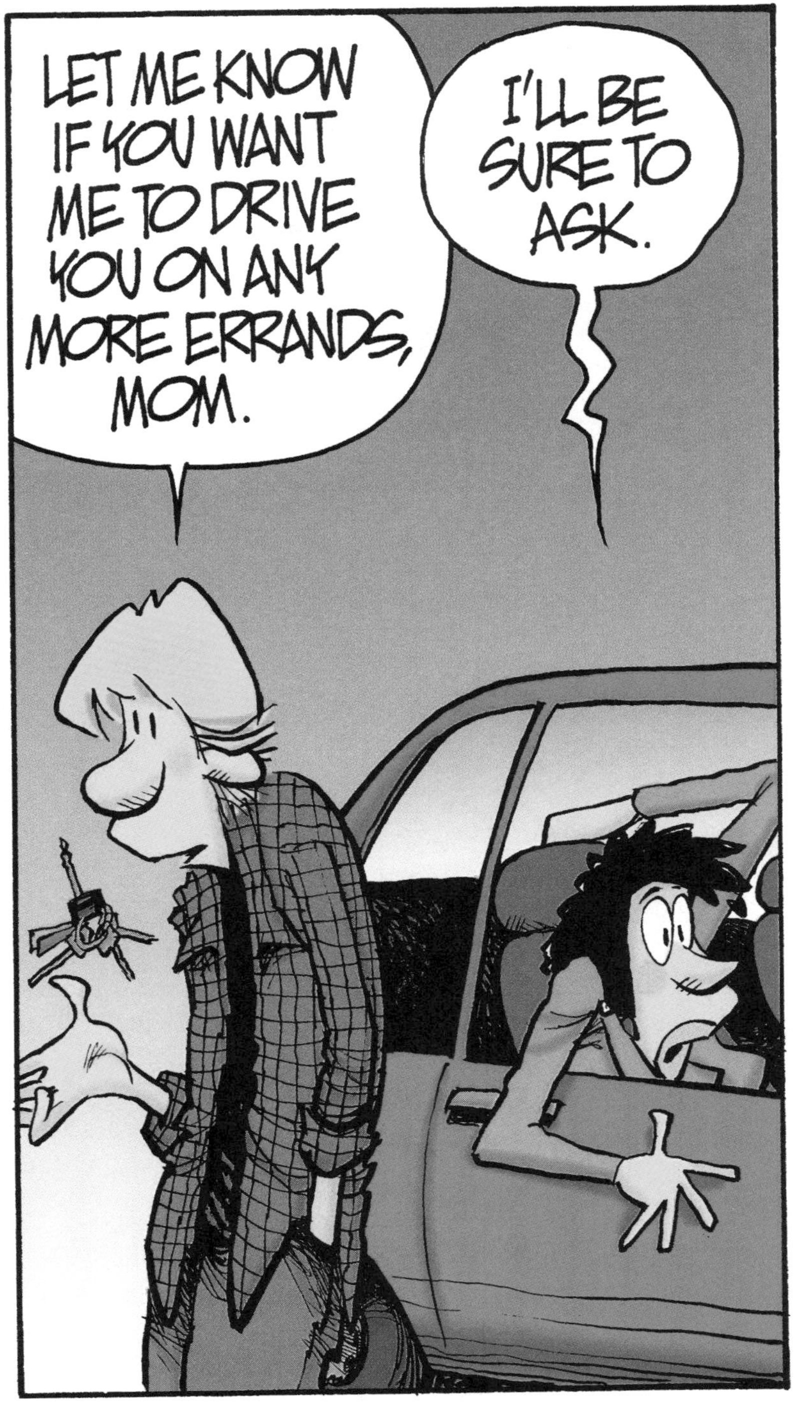
LET ME KNOW IF YOU WANT ME TO DRIVE YOU ON ANY MORE ERRANDS, MOM.
I'LL BE SURE TO ASK.

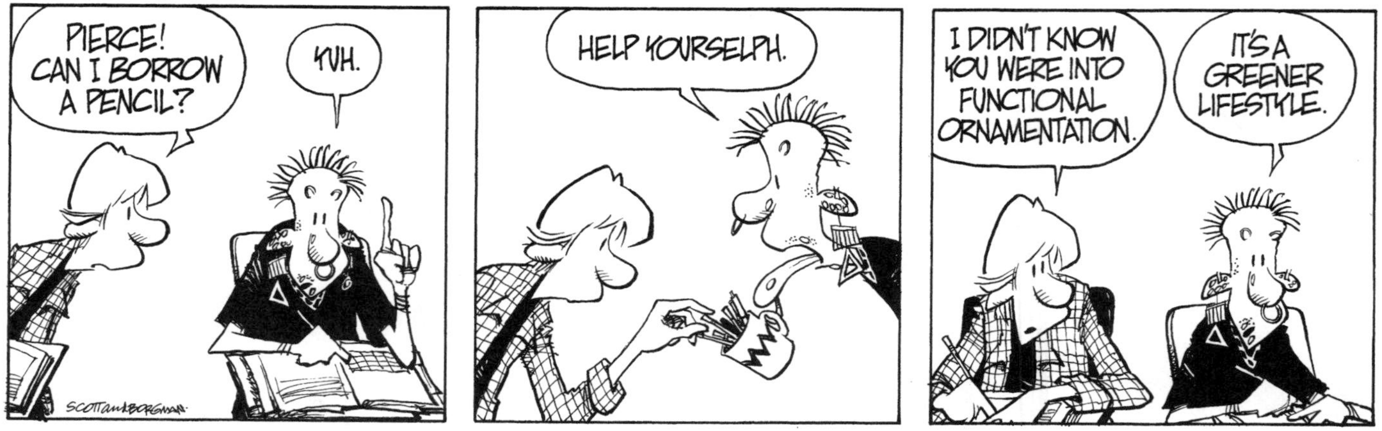
PIERCE! CAN I BORROW A PENCIL?
YUH.
SCOTT and BORGMAN
HELP YOURSELPH.
I DIDN'T KNOW YOU WERE INTO FUNCTIONAL ORNAMENTATION.
IT'S A GREENER LIFESTYLE.

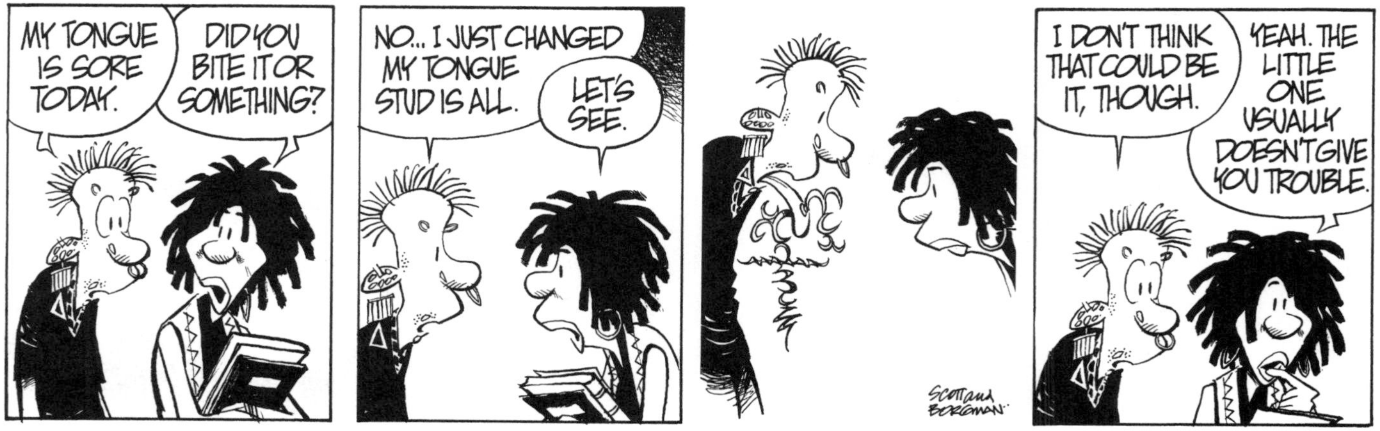
MY TONGUE IS SORE TODAY.
DID YOU BITE IT OR SOMETHING?
NO... I JUST CHANGED MY TONGUE STUD IS ALL.
LET'S SEE.
SCOTT and BORGMAN
I DON'T THINK THAT COULD BE IT, THOUGH.
YEAH. THE LITTLE ONE USUALLY DOESN'T GIVE YOU TROUBLE.

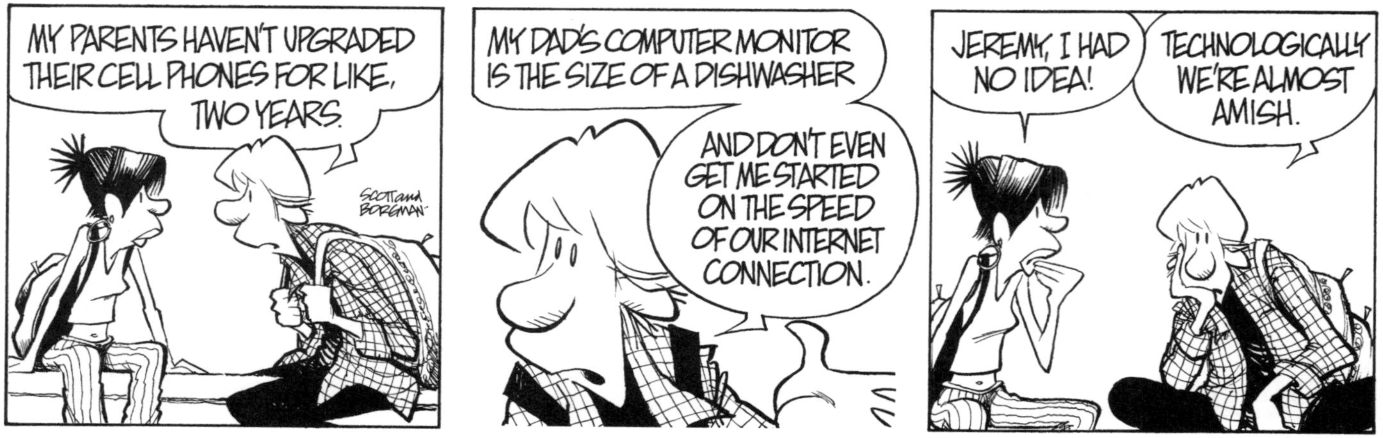
MY PARENTS HAVEN'T UPGRADED THEIR CELL PHONES FOR LIKE, TWO YEARS.
SCOTT and BORGMAN
MY DAD'S COMPUTER MONITOR IS THE SIZE OF A DISHWASHER
AND DON'T EVEN GET ME STARTED ON THE SPEED OF OUR INTERNET CONNECTION.
JEREMY, I HAD NO IDEA!
TECHNOLOGICALLY WE'RE ALMOST AMISH.

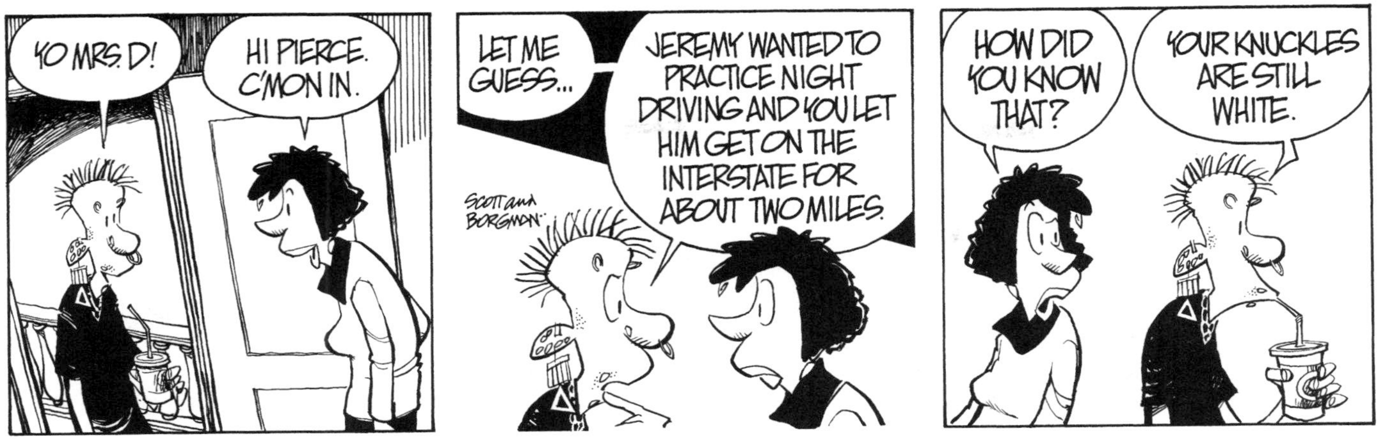
YO MRS. D!
HI PIERCE. C'MON IN.
LET ME GUESS...
JEREMY WANTED TO PRACTICE NIGHT DRIVING AND YOU LET HIM GET ON THE INTERSTATE FOR ABOUT TWO MILES.
SCOTT and BORGMAN
HOW DID YOU KNOW THAT?
YOUR KNUCKLES ARE STILL WHITE.

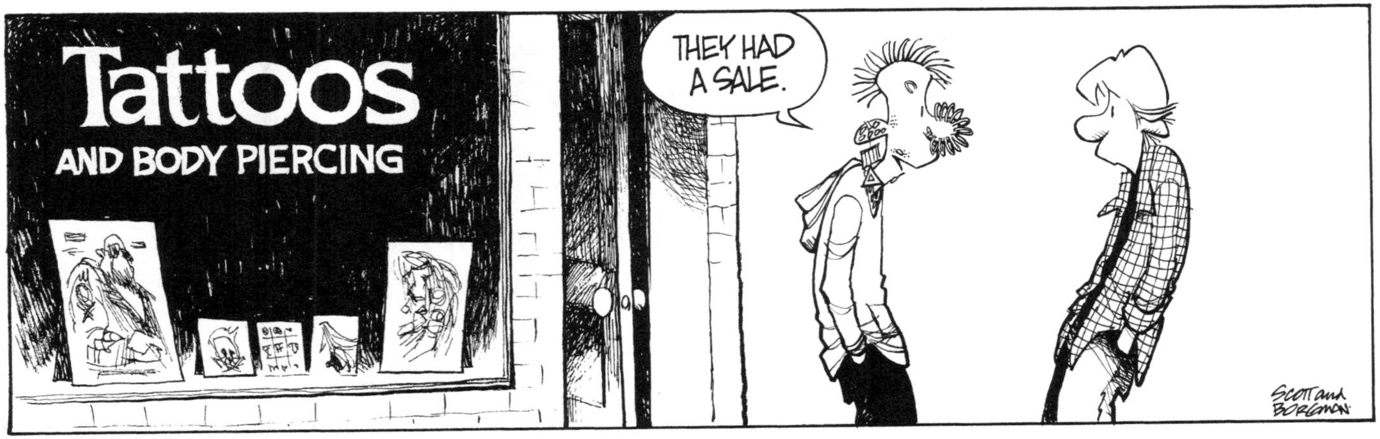
Tattoos
AND BODY PIERCING
THEY HAD A SALE.
SCOTT and BORGMAN

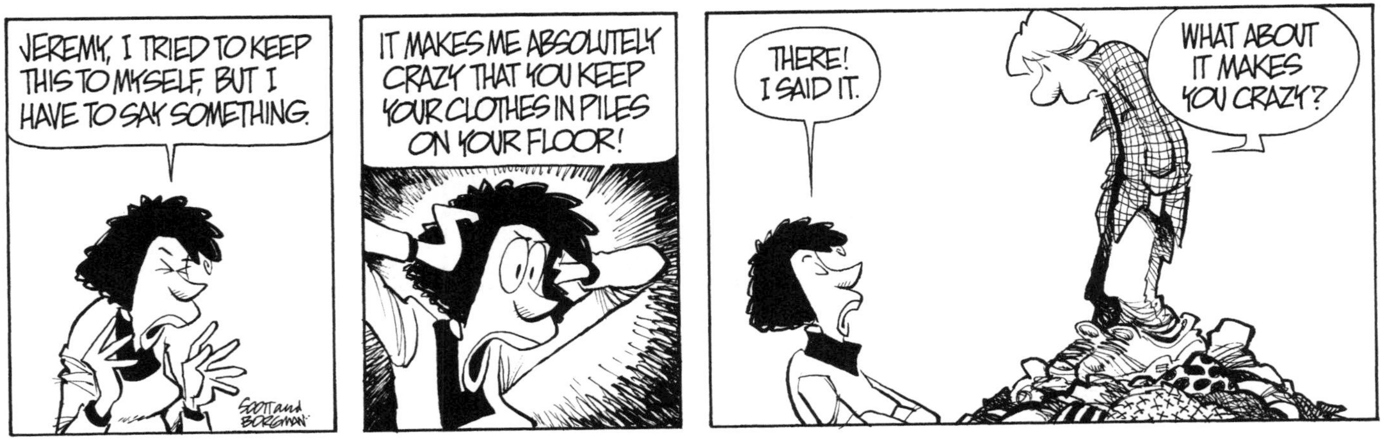
JEREMY, I TRIED TO KEEP THIS TO MYSELF, BUT I HAVE TO SAY SOMETHING.
SCOTT and BORGMAN
IT MAKES ME ABSOLUTELY CRAZY THAT YOU KEEP YOUR CLOTHES IN PILES ON YOUR FLOOR!
THERE! I SAID IT.
WHAT ABOUT IT MAKES YOU CRAZY?

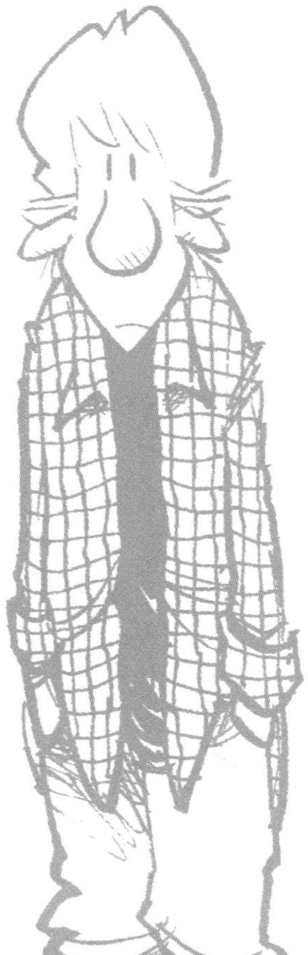

Zits

by JERRY SCOTT and JIM BORGMAN

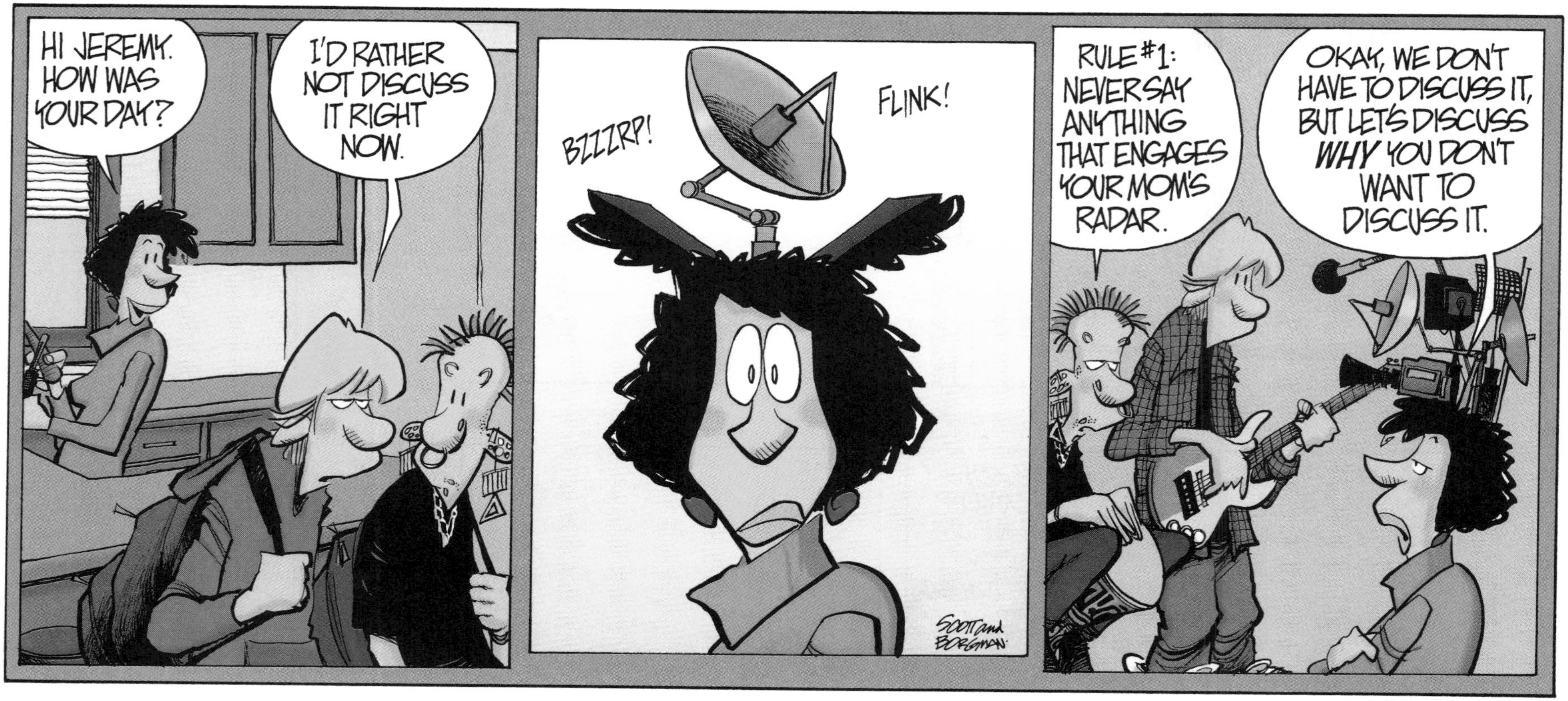
HI JEREMY. HOW WAS YOUR DAY?
I'D RATHER NOT DISCUSS IT RIGHT NOW.
BZZZRP!
FLINK!
SCOTT and BORGMAN
RULE #1: NEVER SAY ANYTHING THAT ENGAGES YOUR MOM'S RADAR.
OKAY, WE DON'T HAVE TO DISCUSS IT, BUT LET'S DISCUSS WHY YOU DON'T WANT TO DISCUSS IT.

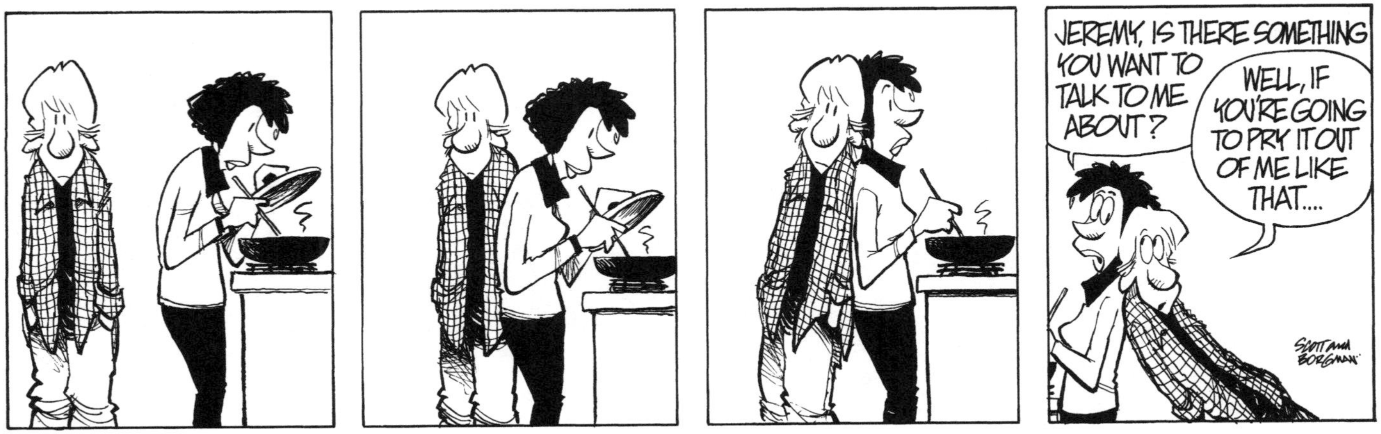
JEREMY, IS THERE SOMETHING YOU WANT TO TALK TO ME ABOUT?
WELL, IF YOU'RE GOING TO PRY IT OUT OF ME LIKE THAT....

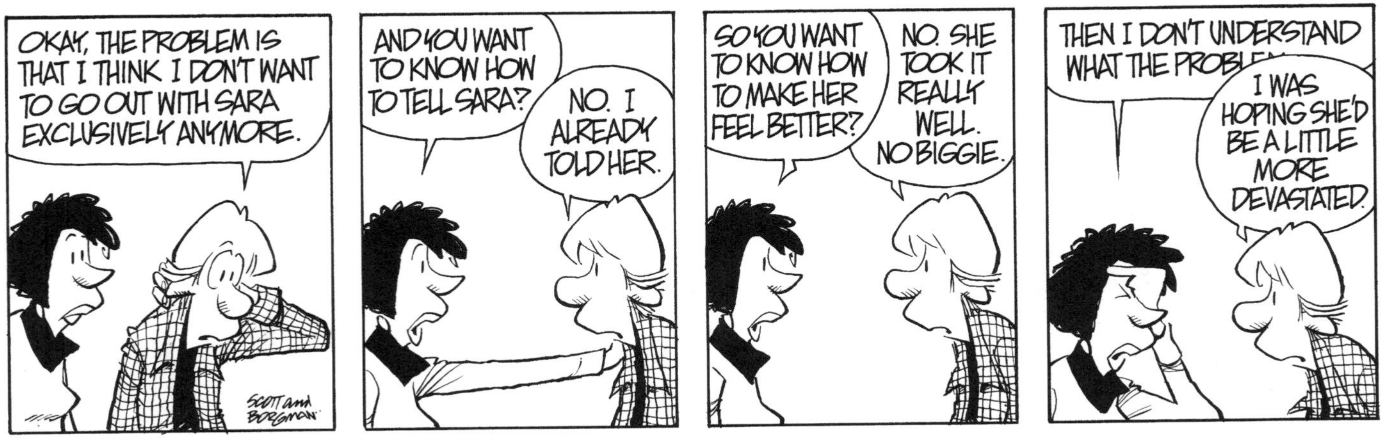
OKAY, THE PROBLEM IS THAT I THINK I DON'T WANT TO GO OUT WITH SARA EXCLUSIVELY ANYMORE.
AND YOU WANT TO KNOW HOW TO TELL SARA?
NO. I ALREADY TOLD HER.
SO YOU WANT TO KNOW HOW TO MAKE HER FEEL BETTER?
NO. SHE TOOK IT REALLY WELL. NO BIGGIE.
THEN I DON'T UNDERSTAND WHAT THE PROBL
I WAS HOPING SHE'D BE A LITTLE MORE DEVASTATED.

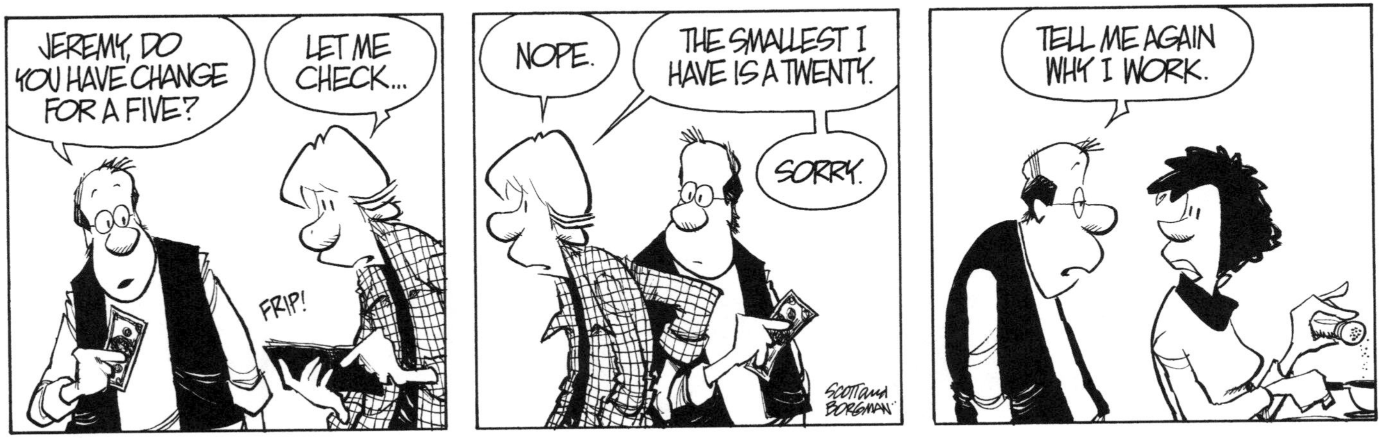
JEREMY, DO YOU HAVE CHANGE FOR A FIVE?
LET ME CHECK...
FRIP!
NOPE.
THE SMALLEST I HAVE IS A TWENTY.
SORRY.
TELL ME AGAIN WHY I WORK.

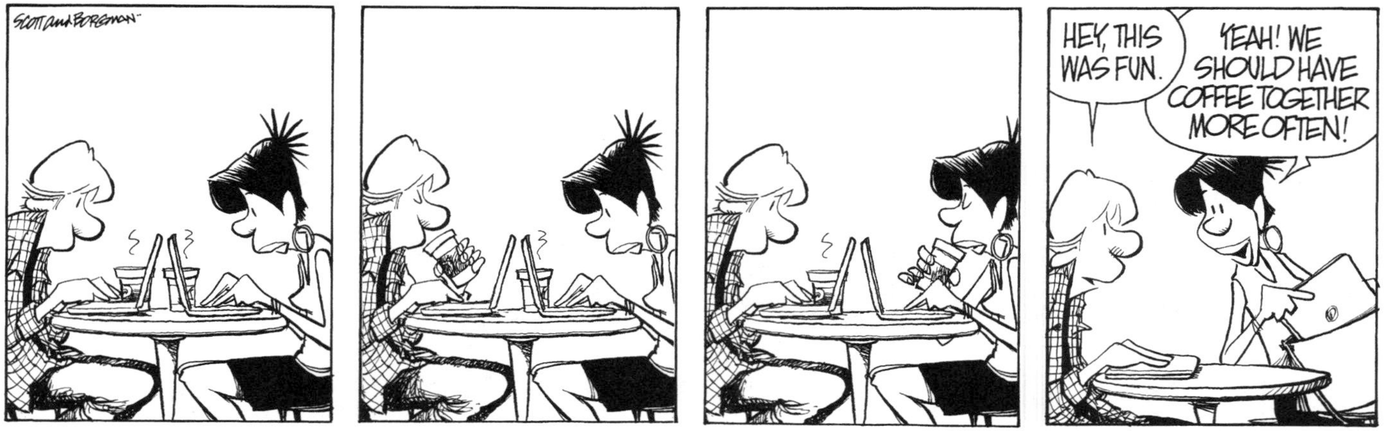
SCOTT and BORGMAN
HEY, THIS WAS FUN.
YEAH! WE SHOULD HAVE COFFEE TOGETHER MORE OFTEN!

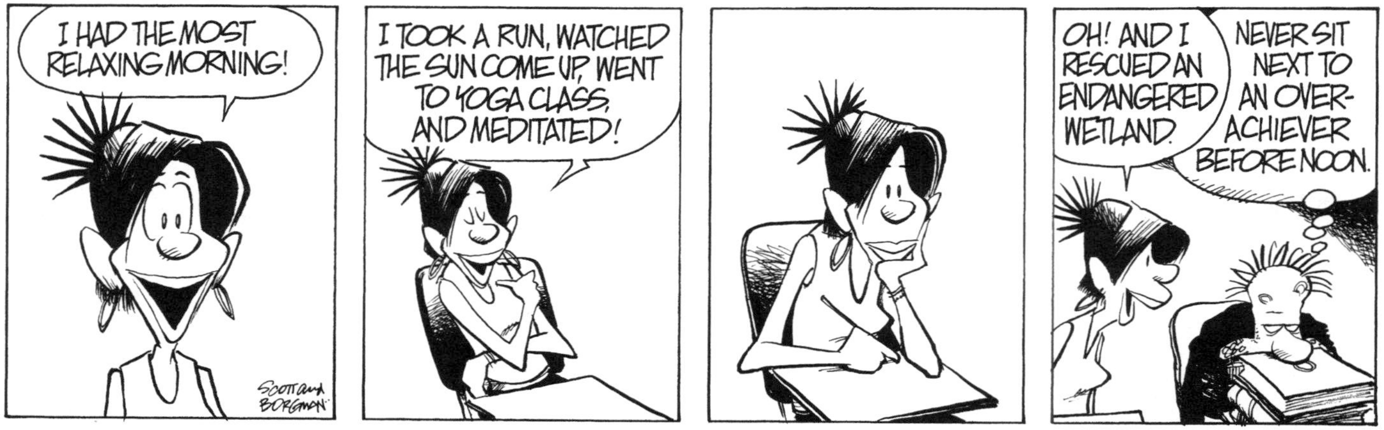
I HAD THE MOST RELAXING MORNING!
SCOTT and BORGMAN
I TOOK A RUN, WATCHED THE SUN COME UP, WENT TO YOGA CLASS, AND MEDITATED!
OH! AND I RESCUED AN ENDANGERED WETLAND.
NEVER SIT NEXT TO AN OVER-ACHIEVER BEFORE NOON.

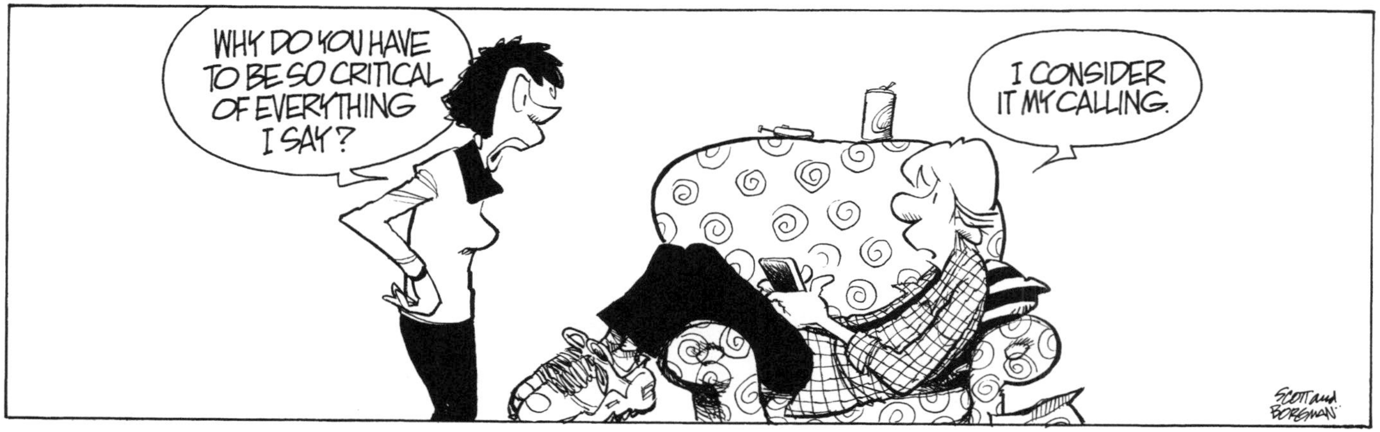
WHY DO YOU HAVE TO BE SO CRITICAL OF EVERYTHING I SAY?
I CONSIDER IT MY CALLING.
SCOTT and BORGMAN

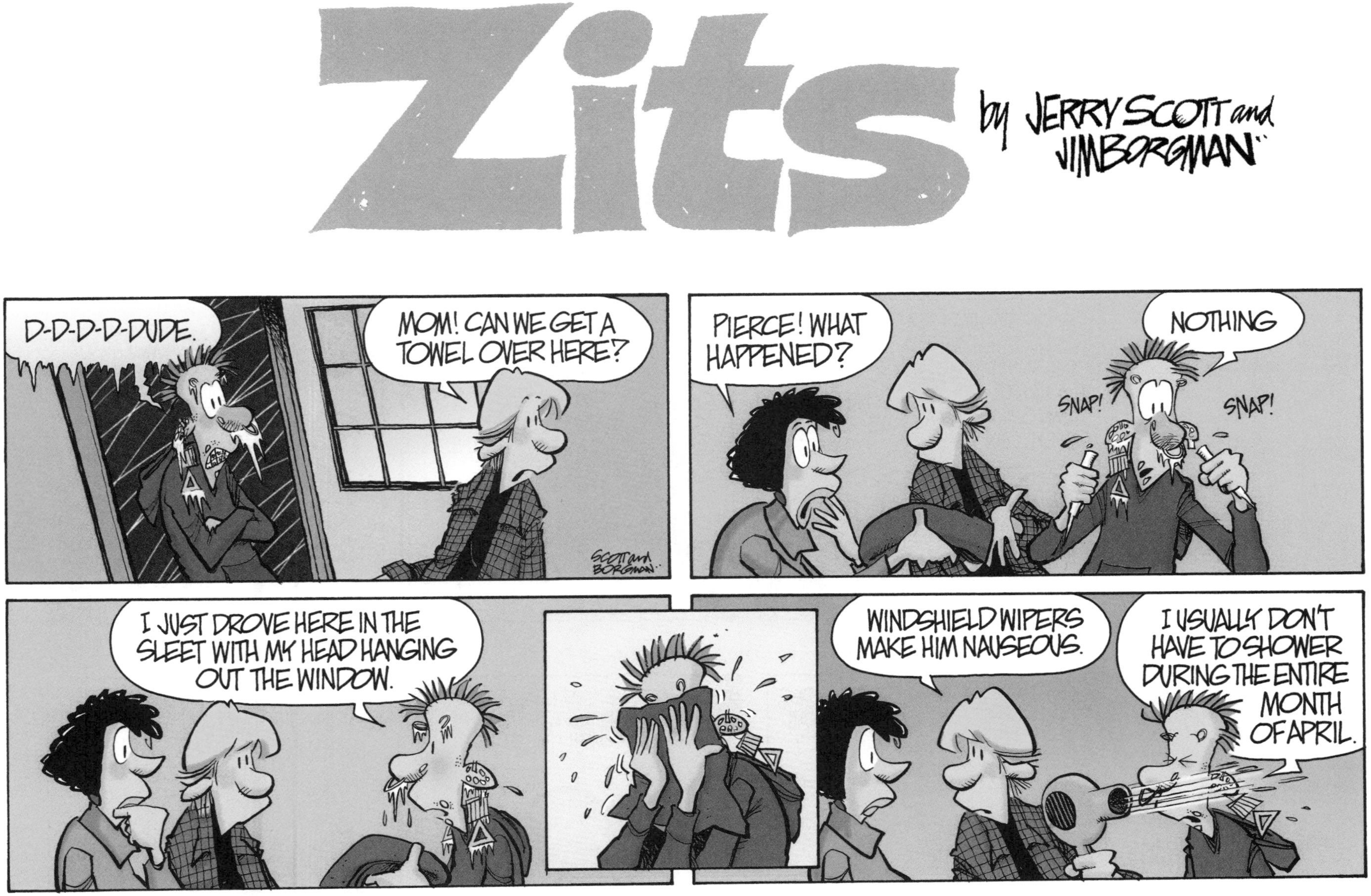
Zits
by JERRY SCOTT and JIM BORGMAN
D-D-D-D-DUDE.
MOM! CAN WE GET A TOWEL OVER HERE?
SCOTT and BORGMAN
PIERCE! WHAT HAPPENED?
NOTHING
SNAP!
SNAP!
I JUST DROVE HERE IN THE SLEET WITH MY HEAD HANGING OUT THE WINDOW.
WINDSHIELD WIPERS MAKE HIM NAUSEOUS.
I USUALLY DON'T HAVE TO SHOWER DURING THE ENTIRE MONTH OF APRIL.

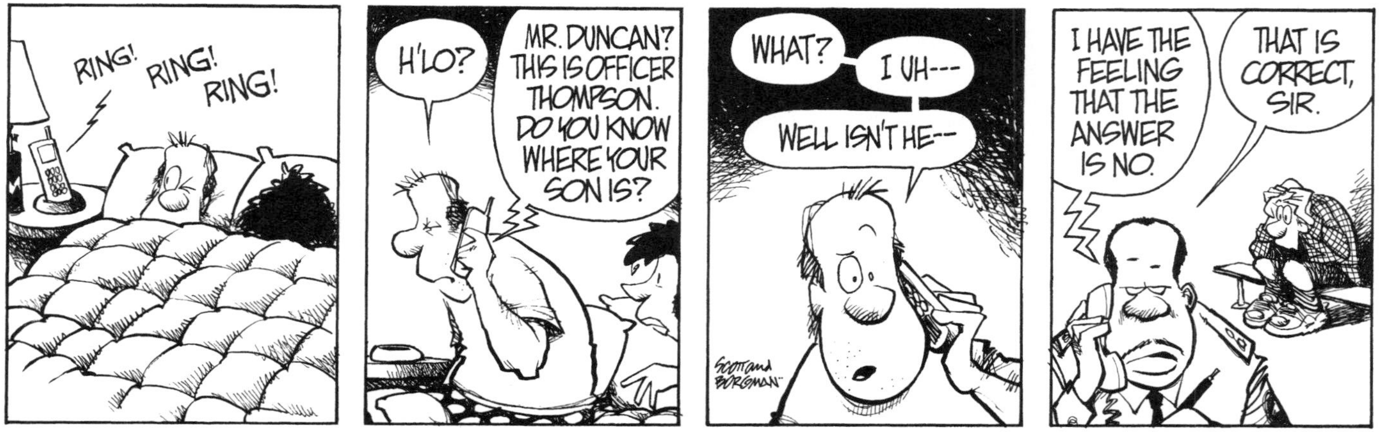
RING!
RING!
RING!
H'LO?
MR. DUNCAN? THIS IS OFFICER THOMPSON. DO YOU KNOW WHERE YOUR SON IS?
WHAT?
I UH---
WELL ISN'T HE--
SCOTT and BORGMAN
I HAVE THE FEELING THAT THE ANSWER IS NO.
THAT IS CORRECT, SIR.

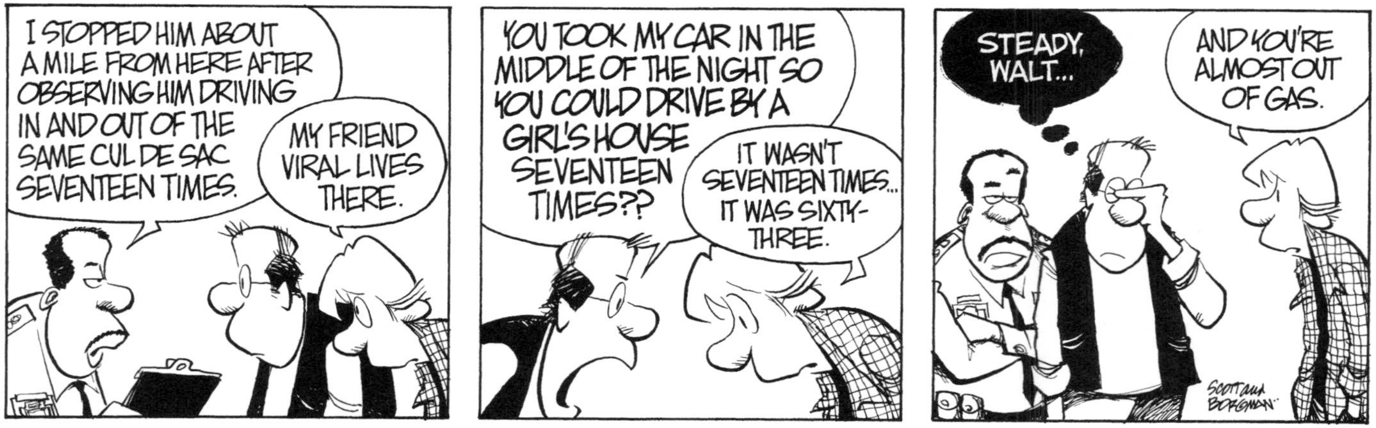
I STOPPED HIM ABOUT A MILE FROM HERE AFTER OBSERVING HIM DRIVING IN AND OUT OF THE SAME CUL DE SAC SEVENTEEN TIMES.
MY FRIEND VIRAL LIVES THERE.
YOU TOOK MY CAR IN THE MIDDLE OF THE NIGHT SO YOU COULD DRIVE BY A GIRL'S HOUSE SEVENTEEN TIMES??
IT WASN'T SEVENTEEN TIMES... IT WAS SIXTY-THREE.
STEADY, WALT...
AND YOU'RE ALMOST OUT OF GAS.
SCOTT and BORGMAN

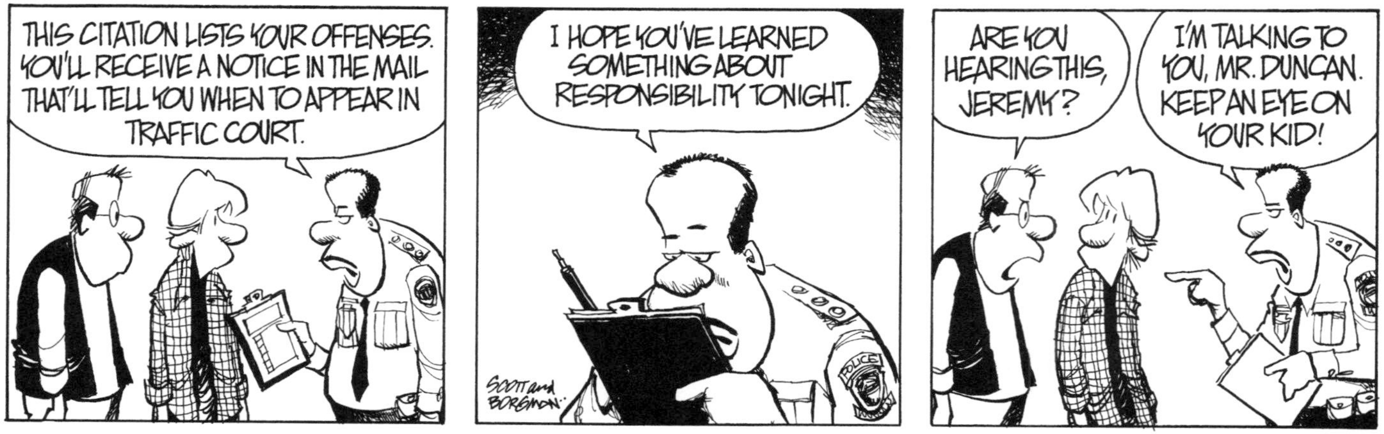
THIS CITATION LISTS YOUR OFFENSES. YOU'LL RECEIVE A NOTICE IN THE MAIL THAT'LL TELL YOU WHEN TO APPEAR IN TRAFFIC COURT.
I HOPE YOU'VE LEARNED SOMETHING ABOUT RESPONSIBILITY TONIGHT.
SCOTT and BORGMAN
POLICE
ARE YOU HEARING THIS, JEREMY?
I'M TALKING TO YOU, MR. DUNCAN. KEEP AN EYE ON YOUR KID!

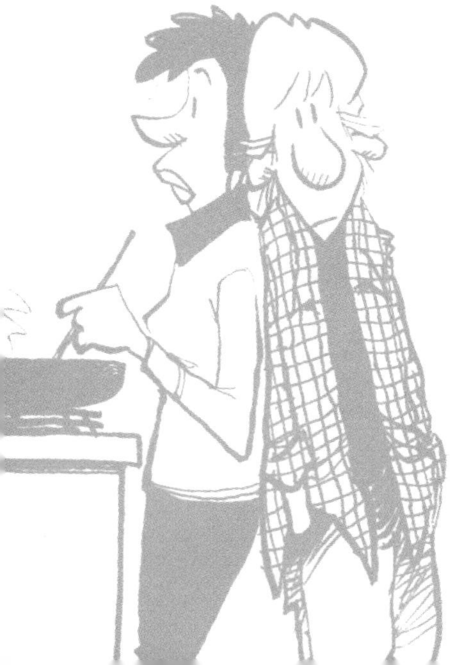

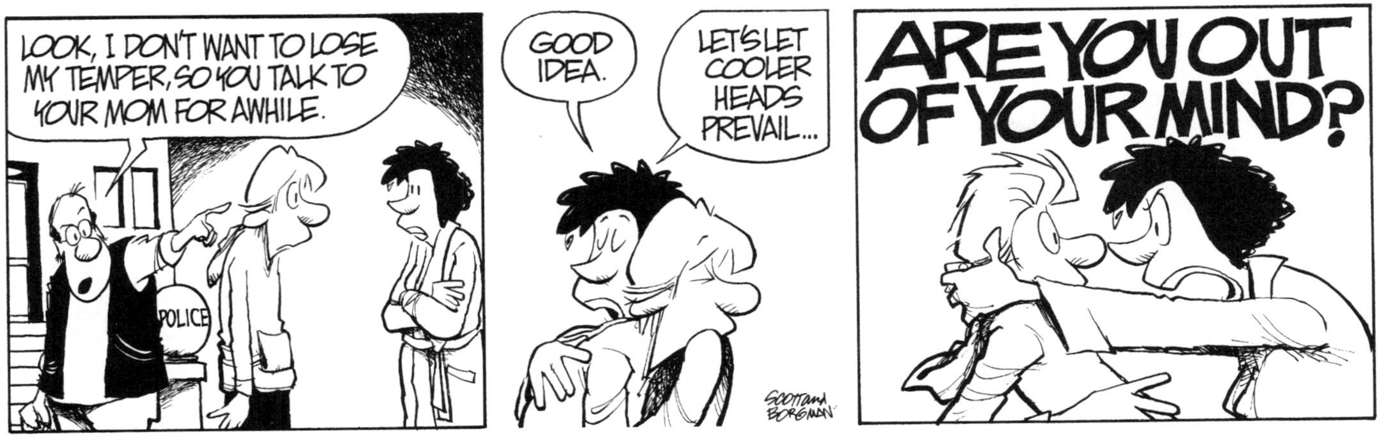
LOOK, I DON'T WANT TO LOSE MY TEMPER, SO YOU TALK TO YOUR MOM FOR AWHILE.
POLICE
GOOD IDEA.
LET'S LET COOLER HEADS PREVAIL...
ARE YOU OUT OF YOUR MIND?

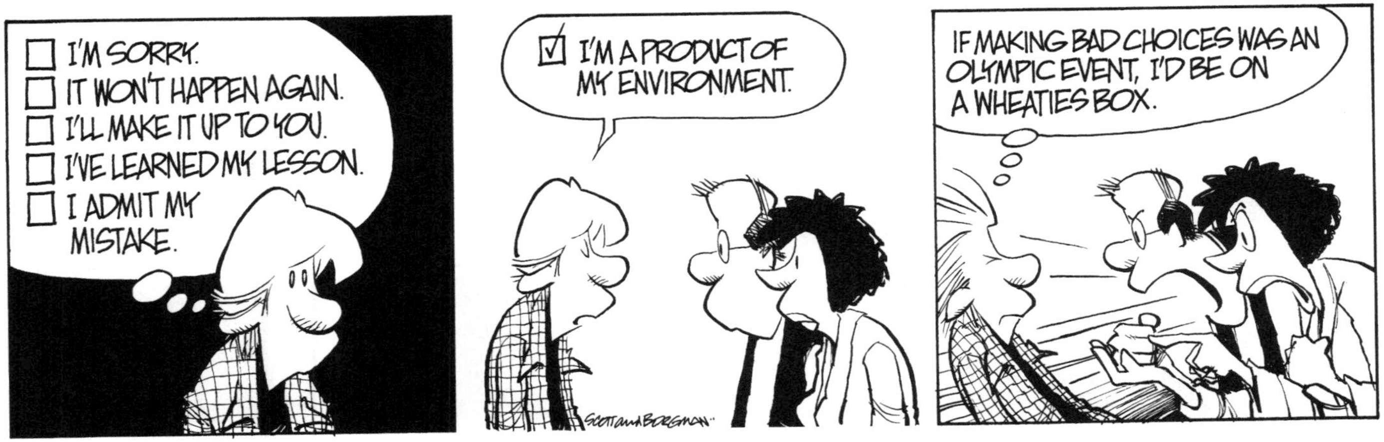
☐ I'M SORRY.
☐ IT WON'T HAPPEN AGAIN.
☐ I'LL MAKE IT UP TO YOU.
☐ I'VE LEARNED MY LESSON.
☐ I ADMIT MY MISTAKE.
☑ I'M A PRODUCT OF MY ENVIRONMENT.
IF MAKING BAD CHOICES WAS AN OLYMPIC EVENT, I'D BE ON A WHEATIES BOX.

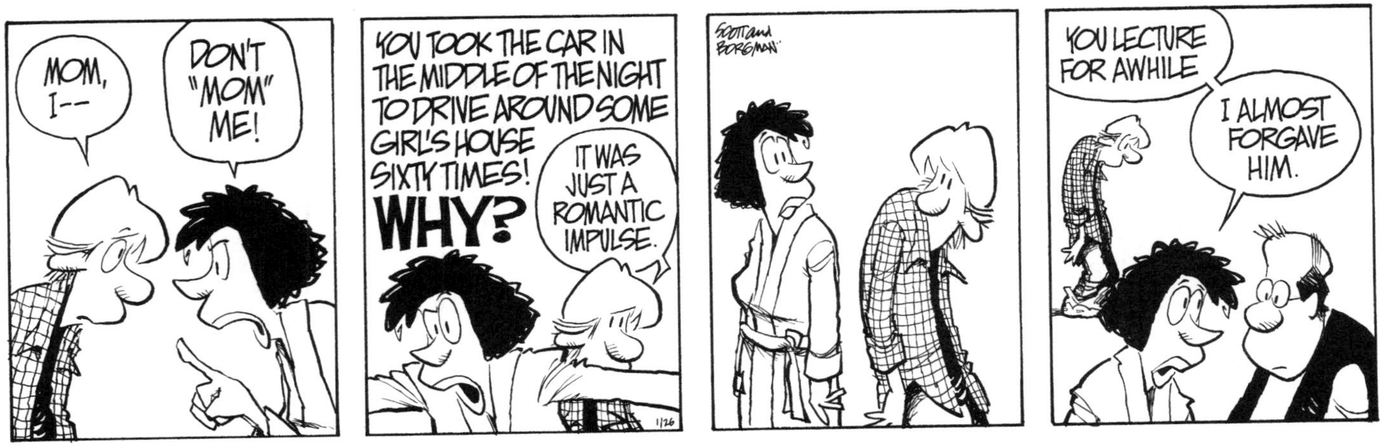
MOM, I--
DON'T "MOM" ME!
YOU TOOK THE CAR IN THE MIDDLE OF THE NIGHT TO DRIVE AROUND SOME GIRL'S HOUSE SIXTY TIMES! WHY?
IT WAS JUST A ROMANTIC IMPULSE.
YOU LECTURE FOR AWHILE
I ALMOST FORGAVE HIM.

Zits

by JERRY SCOTT and JIM BORGMAN

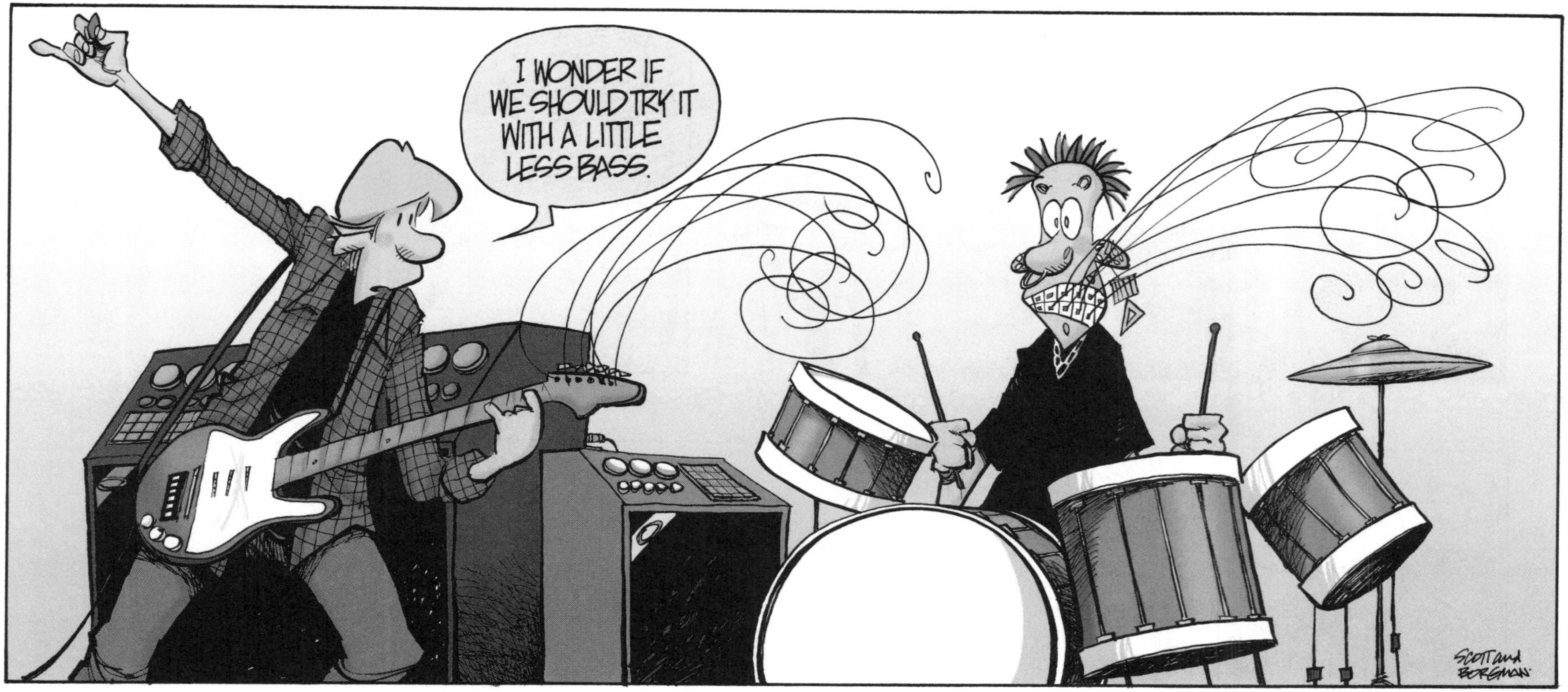
I WONDER IF WE SHOULD TRY IT WITH A LITTLE LESS BASS.
SCOTT and BORGMAN

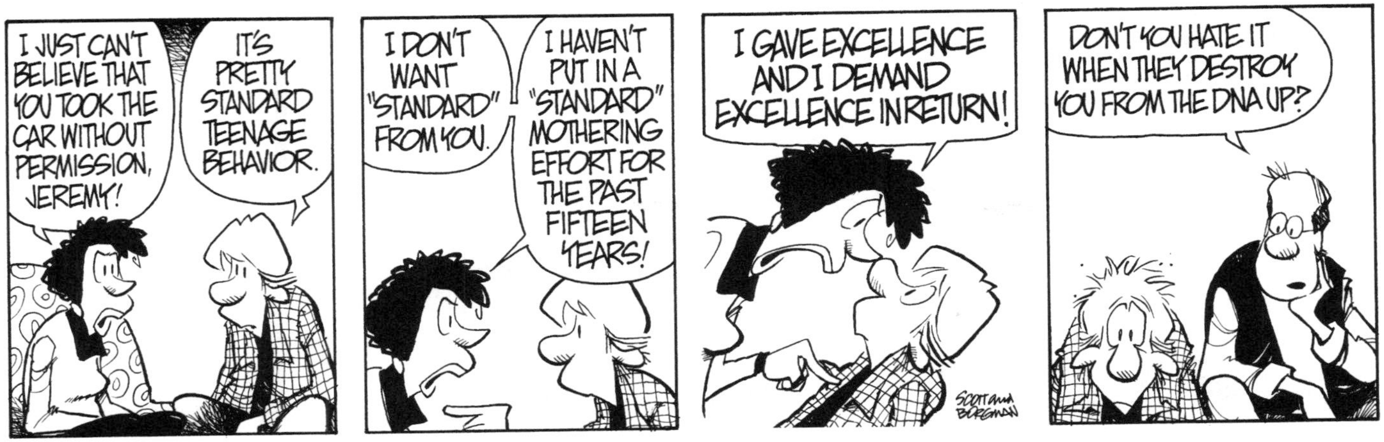
I JUST CAN'T BELIEVE THAT YOU TOOK THE CAR WITHOUT PERMISSION, JEREMY!
IT'S PRETTY STANDARD TEENAGE BEHAVIOR.
I DON'T WANT "STANDARD" FROM YOU.
I HAVEN'T PUT IN A "STANDARD" MOTHERING EFFORT FOR THE PAST FIFTEEN YEARS!
I GAVE EXCELLENCE AND I DEMAND EXCELLENCE IN RETURN!
DON'T YOU HATE IT WHEN THEY DESTROY YOU FROM THE DNA UP?

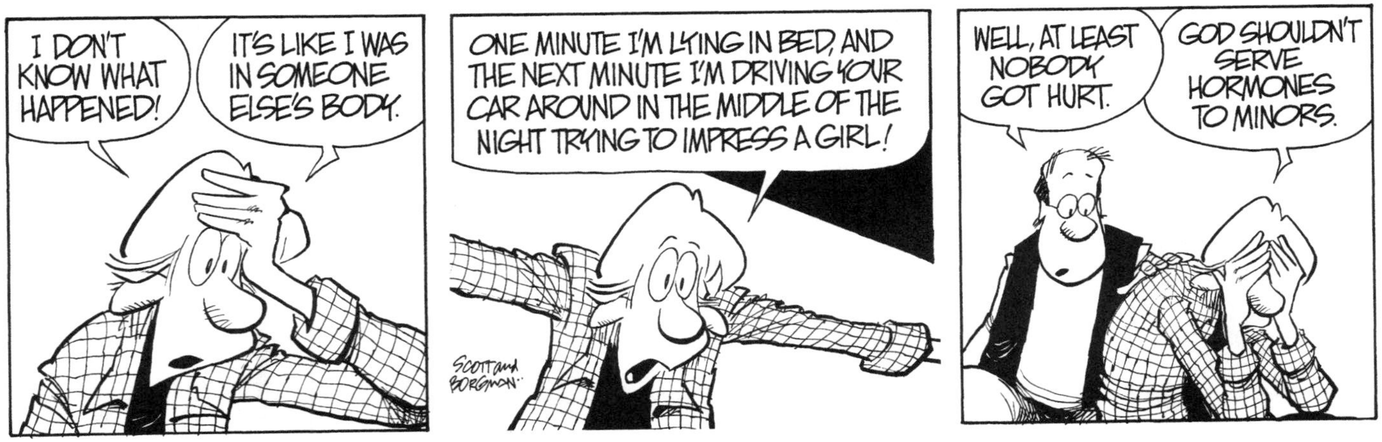
I DON'T KNOW WHAT HAPPENED!
IT'S LIKE I WAS IN SOMEONE ELSE'S BODY.
ONE MINUTE I'M LYING IN BED, AND THE NEXT MINUTE I'M DRIVING YOUR CAR AROUND IN THE MIDDLE OF THE NIGHT TRYING TO IMPRESS A GIRL!
WELL, AT LEAST NOBODY GOT HURT.
GOD SHOULDN'T SERVE HORMONES TO MINORS.

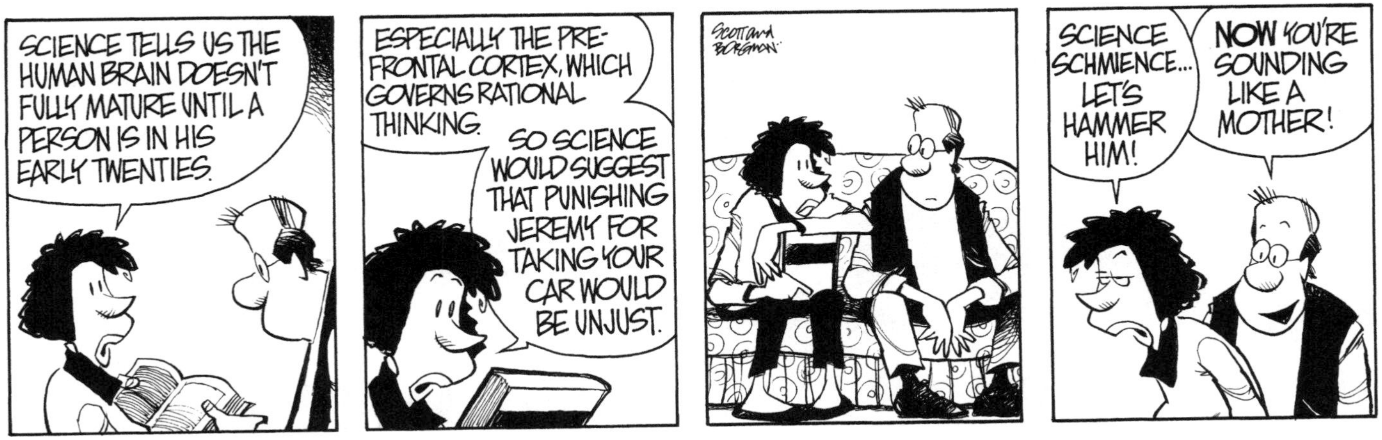
SCIENCE TELLS US THE HUMAN BRAIN DOESN'T FULLY MATURE UNTIL A PERSON IS IN HIS EARLY TWENTIES.
ESPECIALLY THE PRE-FRONTAL CORTEX, WHICH GOVERNS RATIONAL THINKING.
SO SCIENCE WOULD SUGGEST THAT PUNISHING JEREMY FOR TAKING YOUR CAR WOULD BE UNJUST.
SCIENCE SCHMIENCE... LET'S HAMMER HIM!
NOW YOU'RE SOUNDING LIKE A MOTHER!

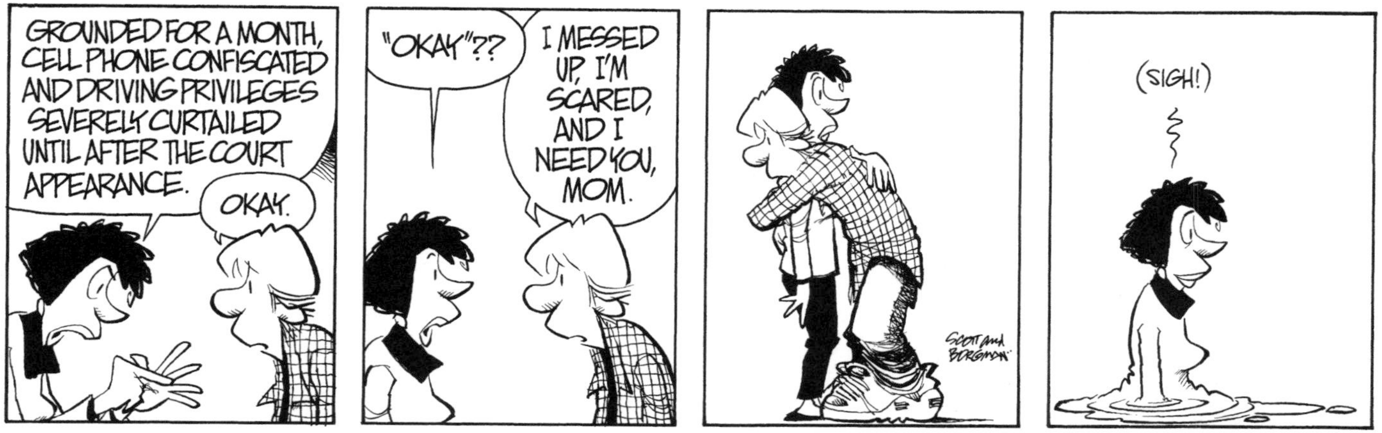
GROUNDED FOR A MONTH, CELL PHONE CONFISCATED AND DRIVING PRIVILEGES SEVERELY CURTAILED UNTIL AFTER THE COURT APPEARANCE.
OKAY.
"OKAY"??
I MESSED UP, I'M SCARED, AND I NEED YOU, MOM.
(SIGH!)

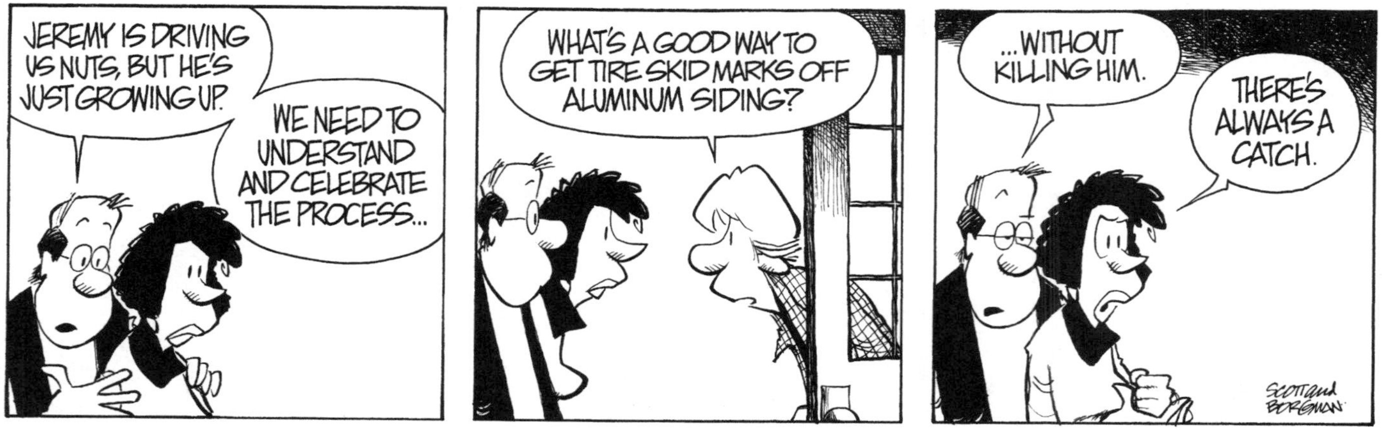
JEREMY IS DRIVING US NUTS, BUT HE'S JUST GROWING UP.
WE NEED TO UNDERSTAND AND CELEBRATE THE PROCESS...
WHAT'S A GOOD WAY TO GET TIRE SKID MARKS OFF ALUMINUM SIDING?
...WITHOUT KILLING HIM.
THERE'S ALWAYS A CATCH.

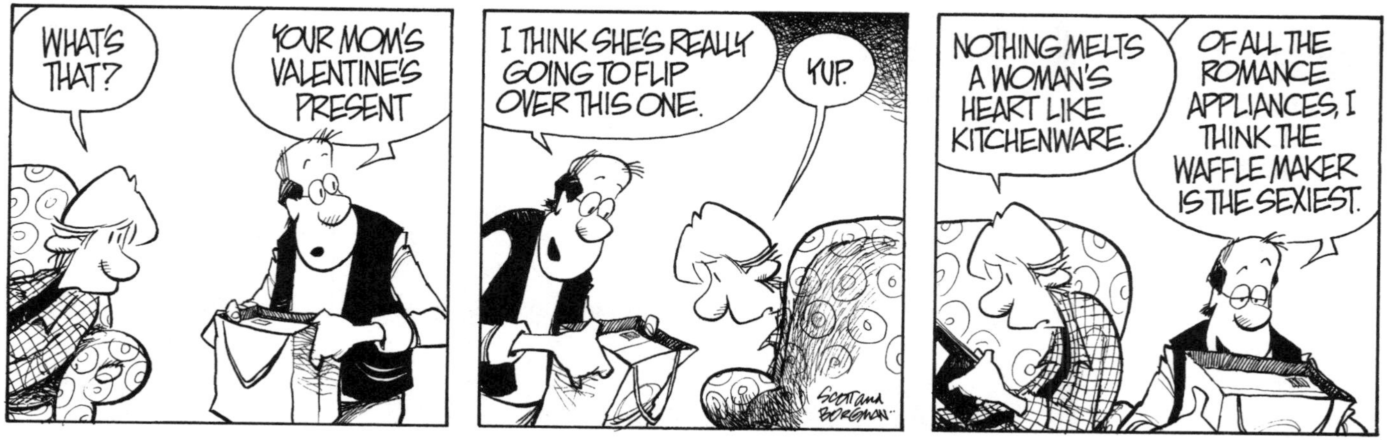
WHAT'S THAT?
YOUR MOM'S VALENTINE'S PRESENT
I THINK SHE'S REALLY GOING TO FLIP OVER THIS ONE.
YUP.
NOTHING MELTS A WOMAN'S HEART LIKE KITCHENWARE.
OF ALL THE ROMANCE APPLIANCES, I THINK THE WAFFLE MAKER IS THE SEXIEST.

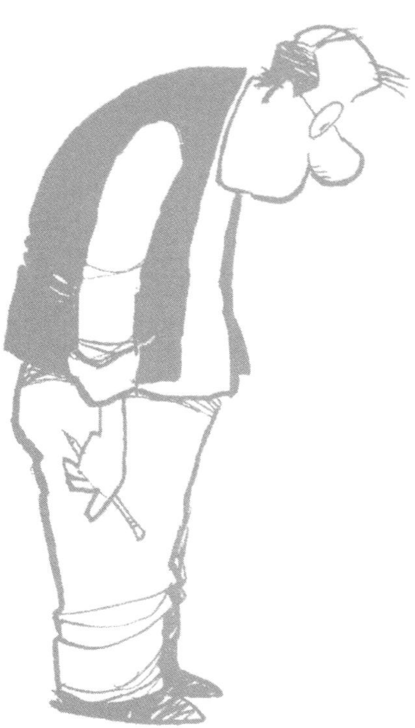

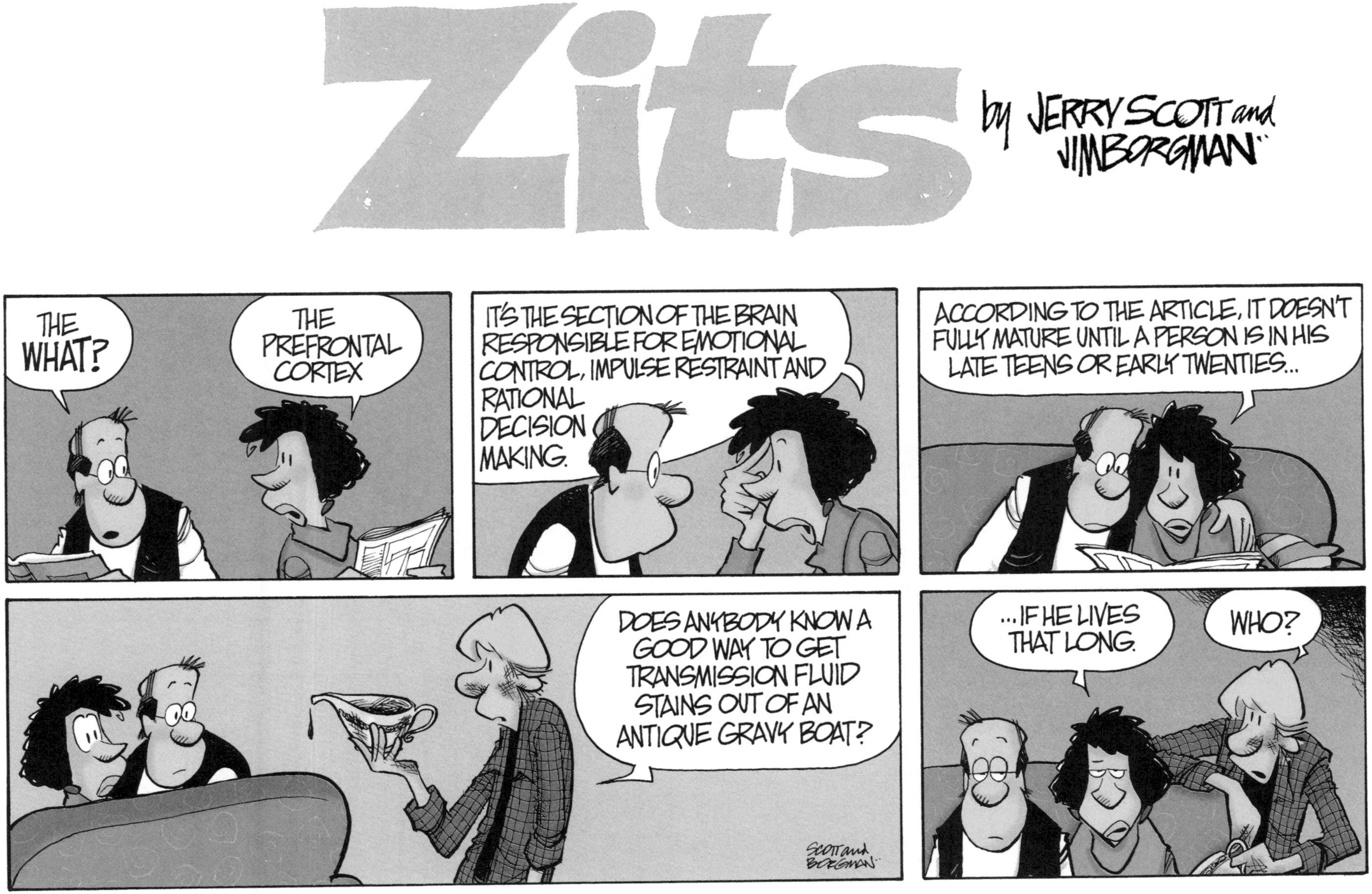
Zits
by JERRY SCOTT and JIMBORGMAN
THE WHAT?
THE PREFRONTAL CORTEX
IT'S THE SECTION OF THE BRAIN RESPONSIBLE FOR EMOTIONAL CONTROL, IMPULSE RESTRAINT AND RATIONAL DECISION MAKING.
ACCORDING TO THE ARTICLE, IT DOESN'T FULLY MATURE UNTIL A PERSON IS IN HIS LATE TEENS OR EARLY TWENTIES...
DOES ANYBODY KNOW A GOOD WAY TO GET TRANSMISSION FLUID STAINS OUT OF AN ANTIQUE GRAVY BOAT?
SCOTT and BORGMAN
...IF HE LIVES THAT LONG.
WHO?

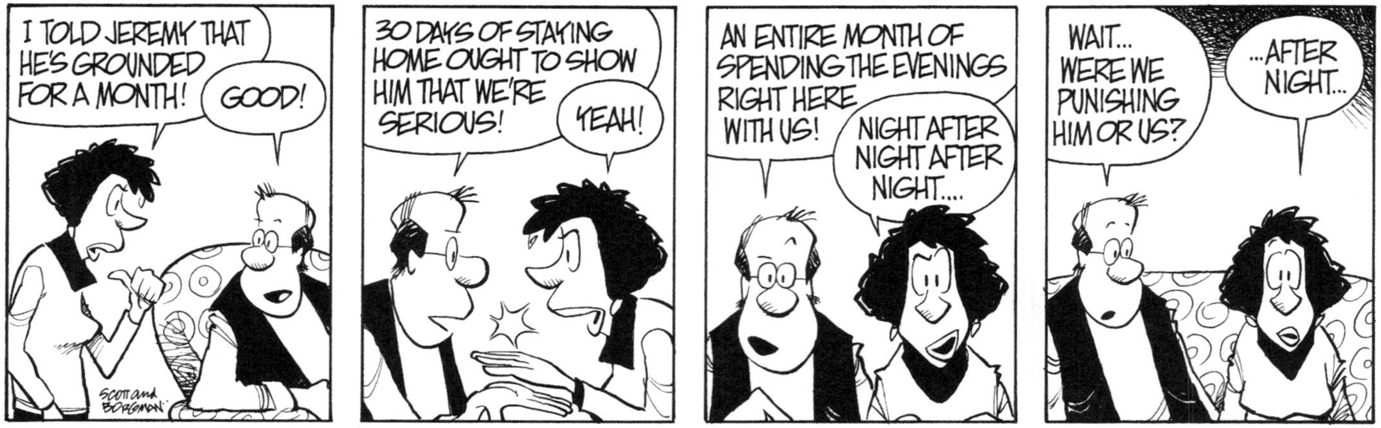
I TOLD JEREMY THAT HE'S GROUNDED FOR A MONTH!
GOOD!
30 DAYS OF STAYING HOME OUGHT TO SHOW HIM THAT WE'RE SERIOUS!
YEAH!
AN ENTIRE MONTH OF SPENDING THE EVENINGS RIGHT HERE WITH US!
NIGHT AFTER NIGHT AFTER NIGHT....
WAIT... WERE WE PUNISHING HIM OR US?
...AFTER NIGHT...

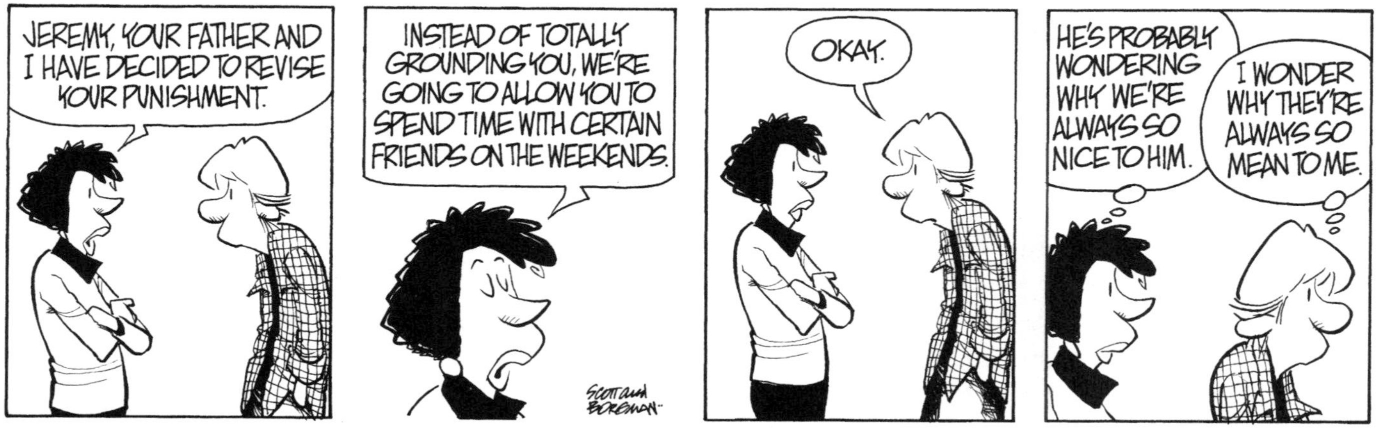
JEREMY, YOUR FATHER AND I HAVE DECIDED TO REVISE YOUR PUNISHMENT.
INSTEAD OF TOTALLY GROUNDING YOU, WE'RE GOING TO ALLOW YOU TO SPEND TIME WITH CERTAIN FRIENDS ON THE WEEKENDS.
OKAY.
HE'S PROBABLY WONDERING WHY WE'RE ALWAYS SO NICE TO HIM.
I WONDER WHY THEY'RE ALWAYS SO MEAN TO ME.

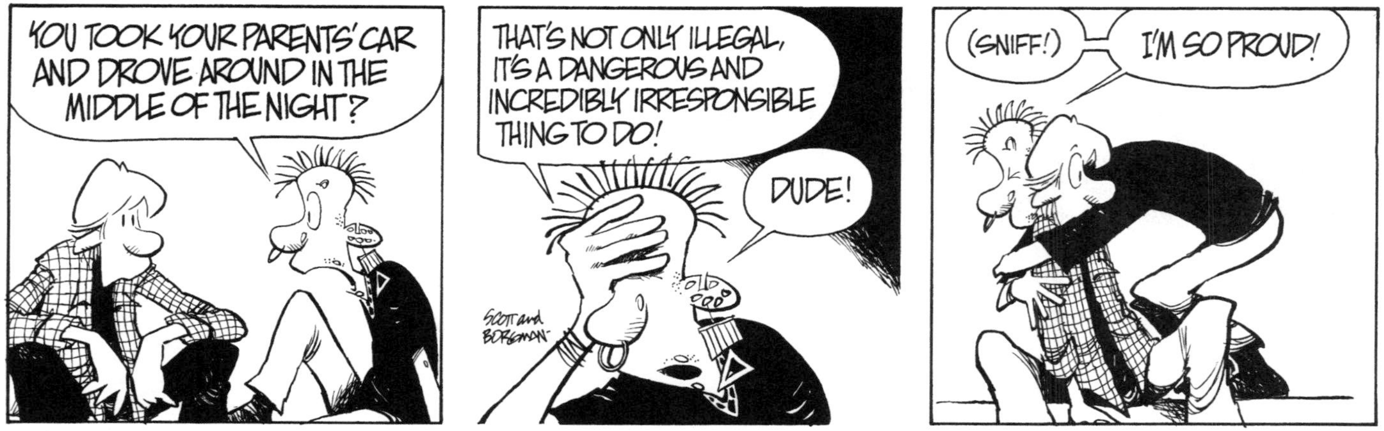
YOU TOOK YOUR PARENTS' CAR AND DROVE AROUND IN THE MIDDLE OF THE NIGHT?
THAT'S NOT ONLY ILLEGAL, IT'S A DANGEROUS AND INCREDIBLY IRRESPONSIBLE THING TO DO!
DUDE!
(SNIFF!)
I'M SO PROUD!

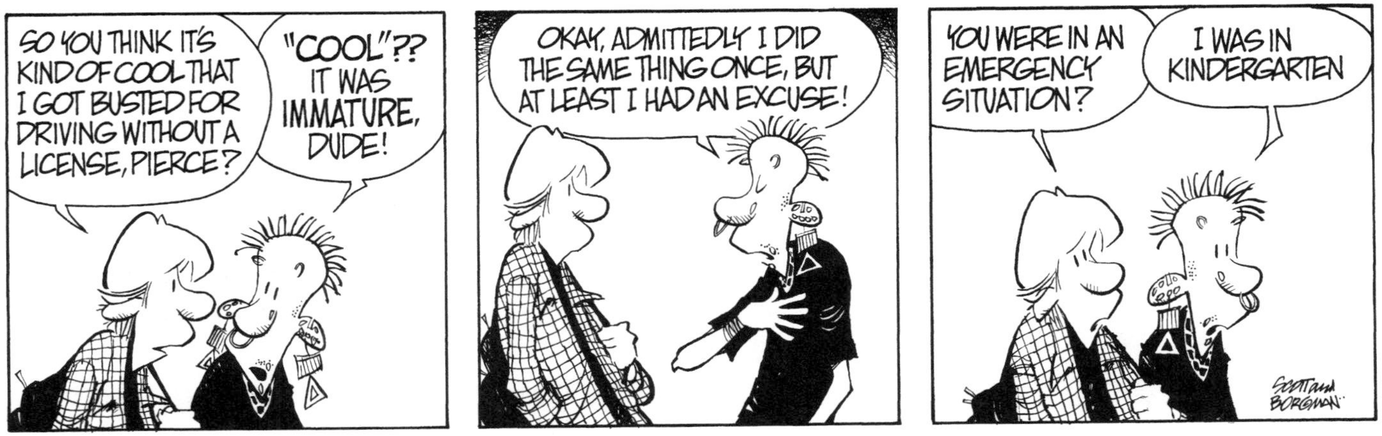
SO YOU THINK IT'S KIND OF COOL THAT I GOT BUSTED FOR DRIVING WITHOUT A LICENSE, PIERCE?
"COOL"?? IT WAS IMMATURE, DUDE!
OKAY, ADMITTEDLY I DID THE SAME THING ONCE, BUT AT LEAST I HAD AN EXCUSE!
YOU WERE IN AN EMERGENCY SITUATION?
I WAS IN KINDERGARTEN
SCOTT AND BORGMAN

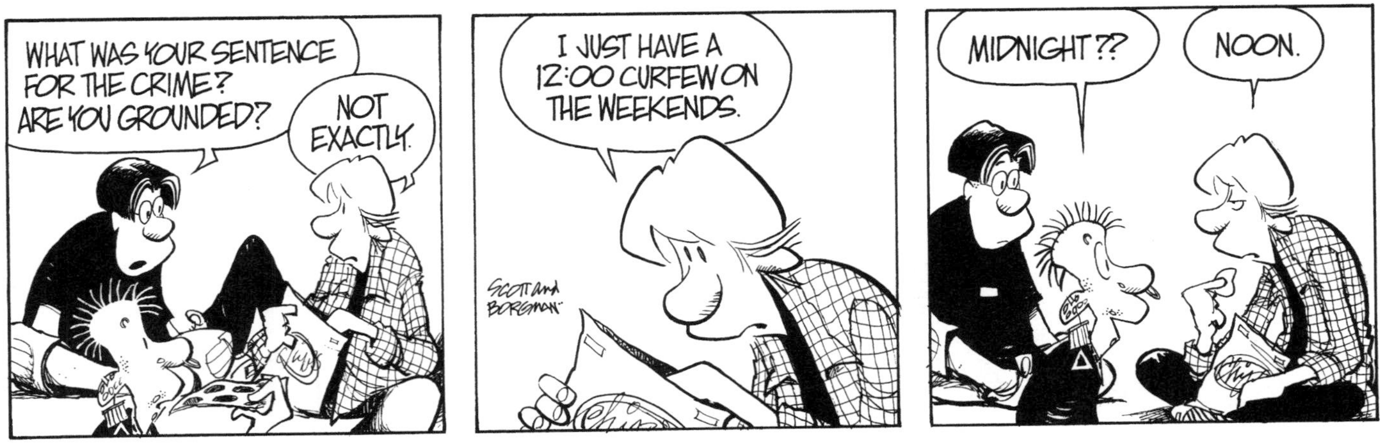
WHAT WAS YOUR SENTENCE FOR THE CRIME? ARE YOU GROUNDED?
NOT EXACTLY.
SCOTT AND BORGMAN
I JUST HAVE A 12:00 CURFEW ON THE WEEKENDS.
MIDNIGHT??
NOON.

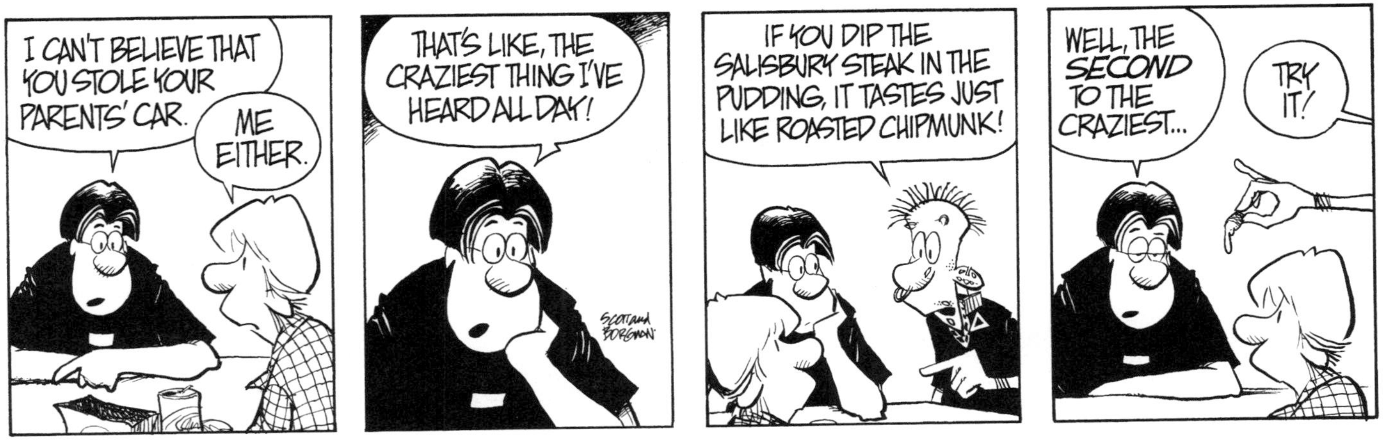
I CAN'T BELIEVE THAT YOU STOLE YOUR PARENTS' CAR.
ME EITHER.
THAT'S LIKE, THE CRAZIEST THING I'VE HEARD ALL DAY!
SCOTT AND BORGMAN
IF YOU DIP THE SALISBURY STEAK IN THE PUDDING, IT TASTES JUST LIKE ROASTED CHIPMUNK!
WELL, THE SECOND TO THE CRAZIEST...
TRY IT!

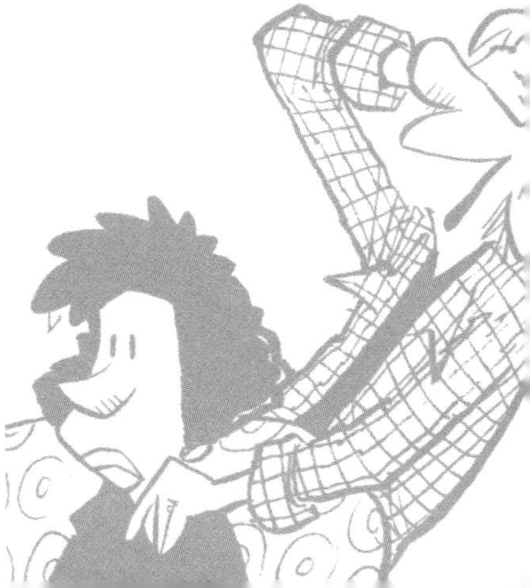

Zits

by JERRY SCOTT and JIM BORGMAN

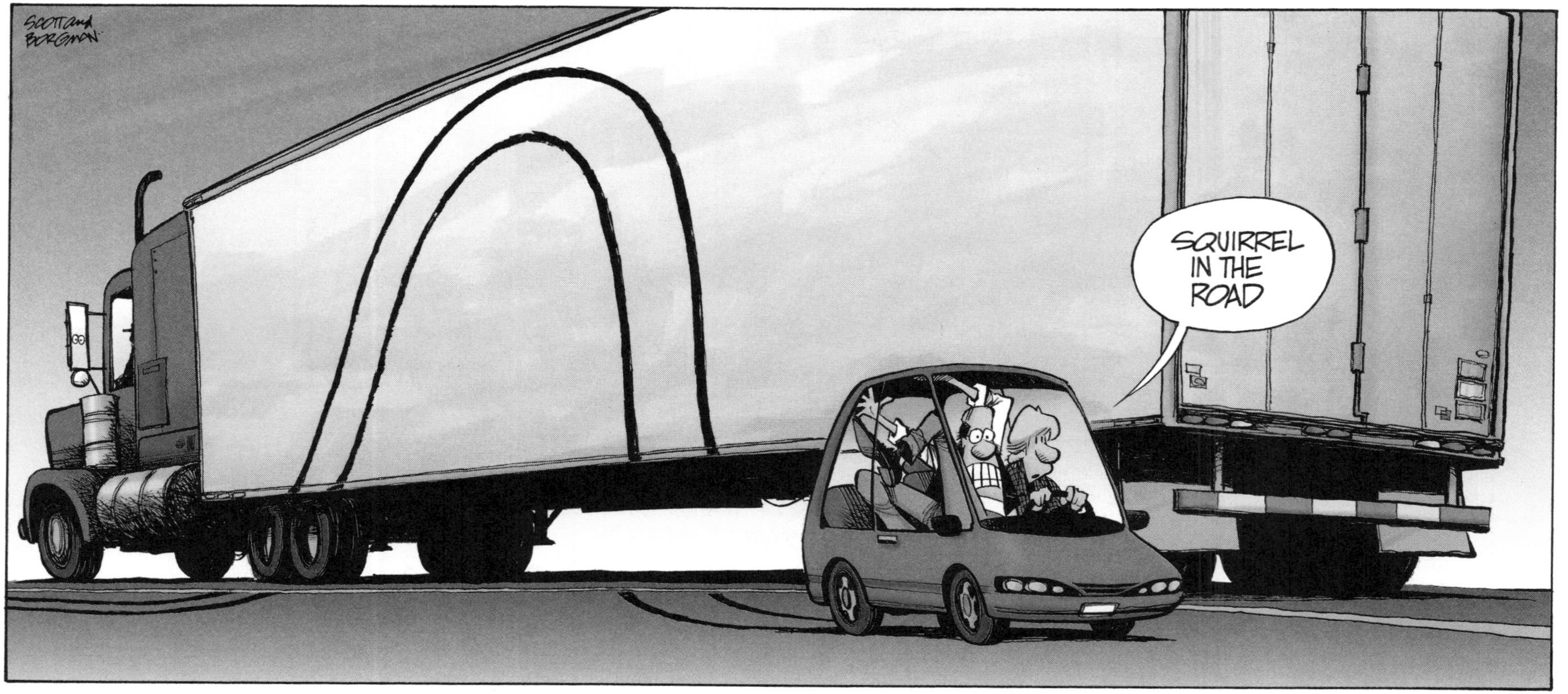
SCOTT and BORGMAN
SQUIRREL IN THE ROAD

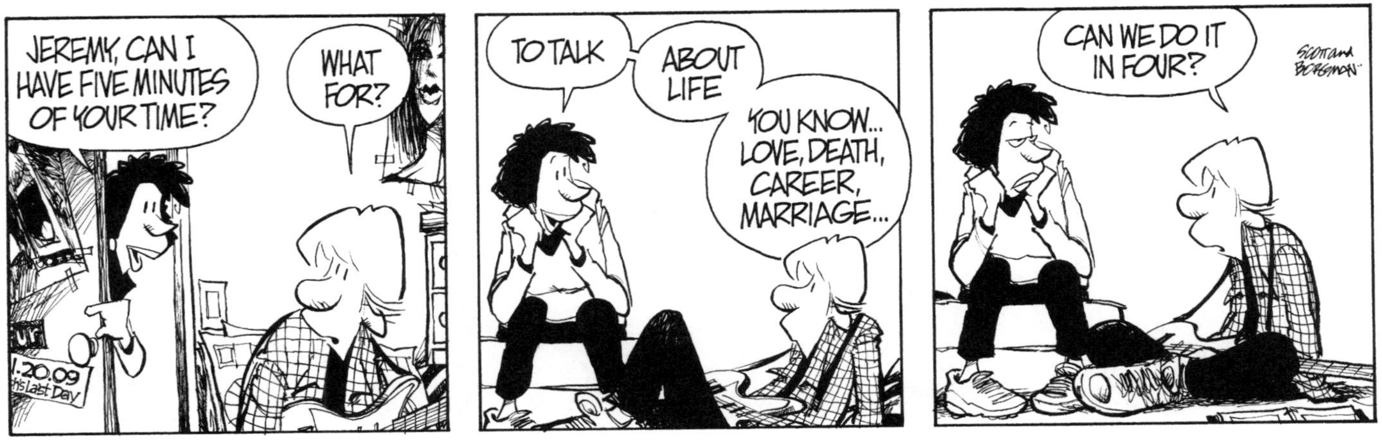
JEREMY, CAN I HAVE FIVE MINUTES OF YOUR TIME?
WHAT FOR?
TO TALK
ABOUT LIFE
YOU KNOW... LOVE, DEATH, CAREER, MARRIAGE...
CAN WE DO IT IN FOUR?
SCOTT and BORGMAN

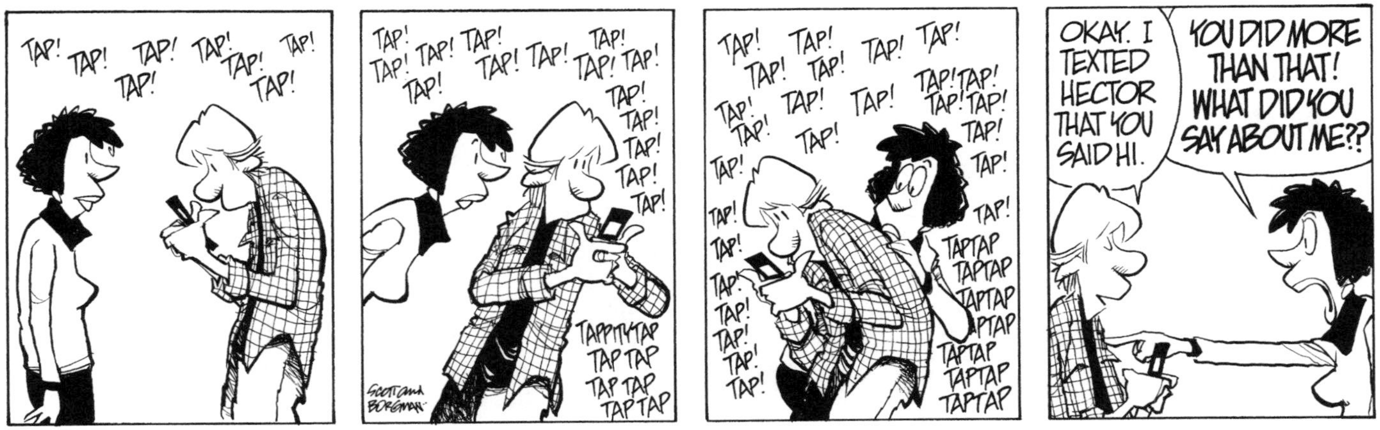
TAP! TAP! TAP! TAP! TAP! TAP! TAP! TAP!
TAP! TAP! TAP! TAP! TAP! TAP! TAP! TAP! TAP! TAP! TAP! TAP! TAP! TAP! TAP!
TAPPITYTAP TAP TAP TAP TAP TAP TAP
SCOTT and BORGMAN
TAP! TAP! TAP! TAP! TAP! TAP! TAP! TAP! TAP! TAP! TAP! TAP! TAP! TAP! TAP! TAP! TAP! TAP! TAP! TAP! TAP! TAP! TAP! TAP! TAP! TAP!
TAPTAP TAPTAP TAPTAP TAPTAP TAPTAP TAPTAP TAPTAP
OKAY. I TEXTED HECTOR THAT YOU SAID HI.
YOU DID MORE THAN THAT! WHAT DID YOU SAY ABOUT ME??

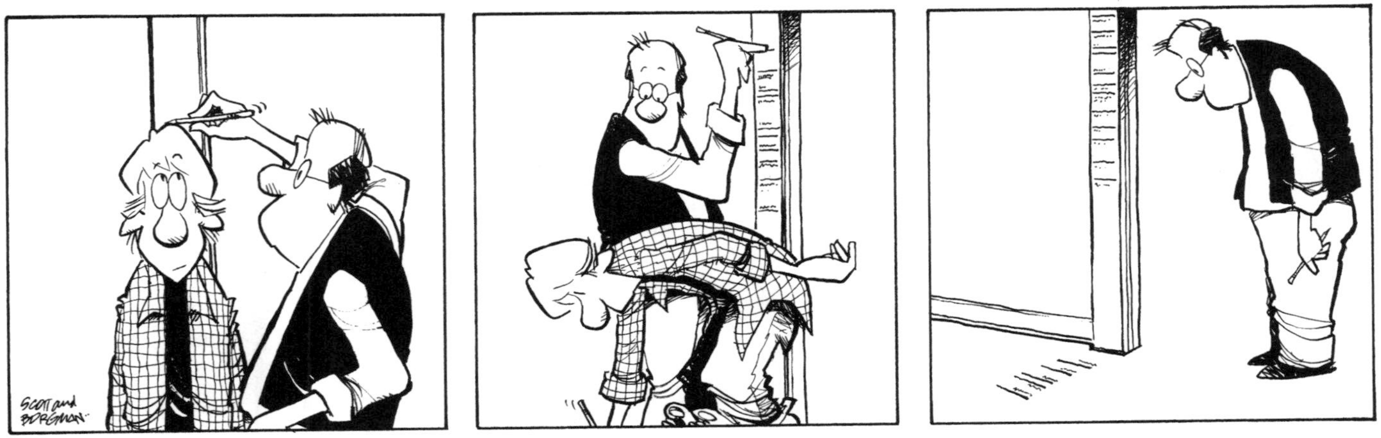
SCOTT and BORGMAN

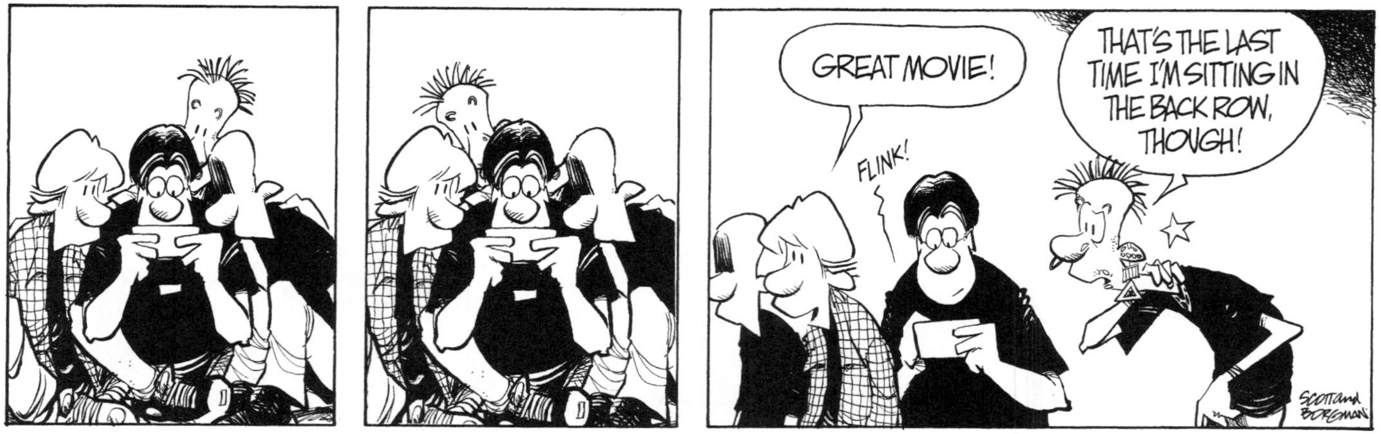
GREAT MOVIE!
FLINK!
THAT'S THE LAST TIME I'M SITTING IN THE BACK ROW, THOUGH!

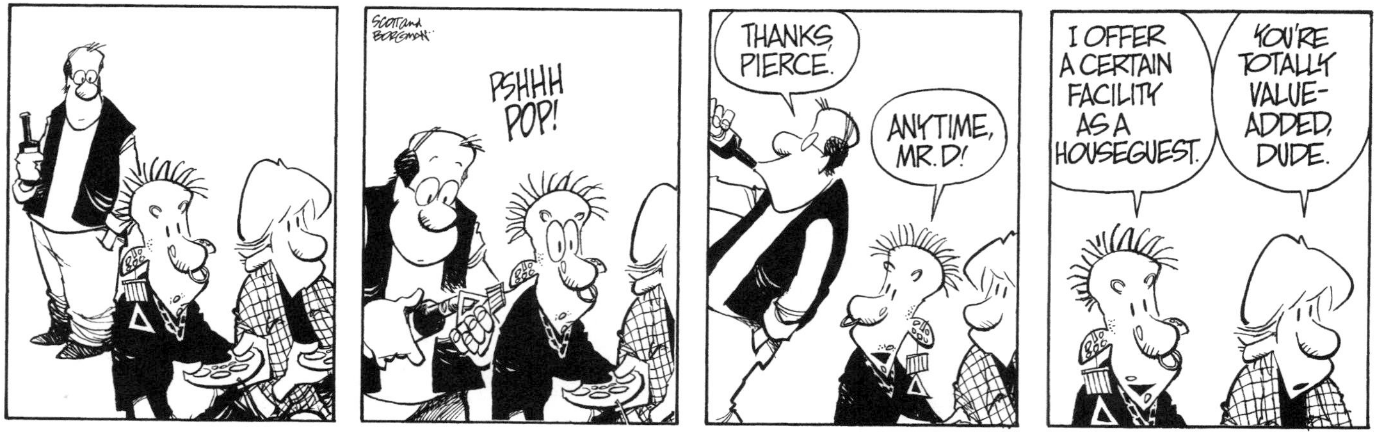
PSHHH POP!
THANKS, PIERCE.
ANYTIME, MR. D!
I OFFER A CERTAIN FACILITY AS A HOUSEGUEST.
YOU'RE TOTALLY VALUE-ADDED, DUDE.

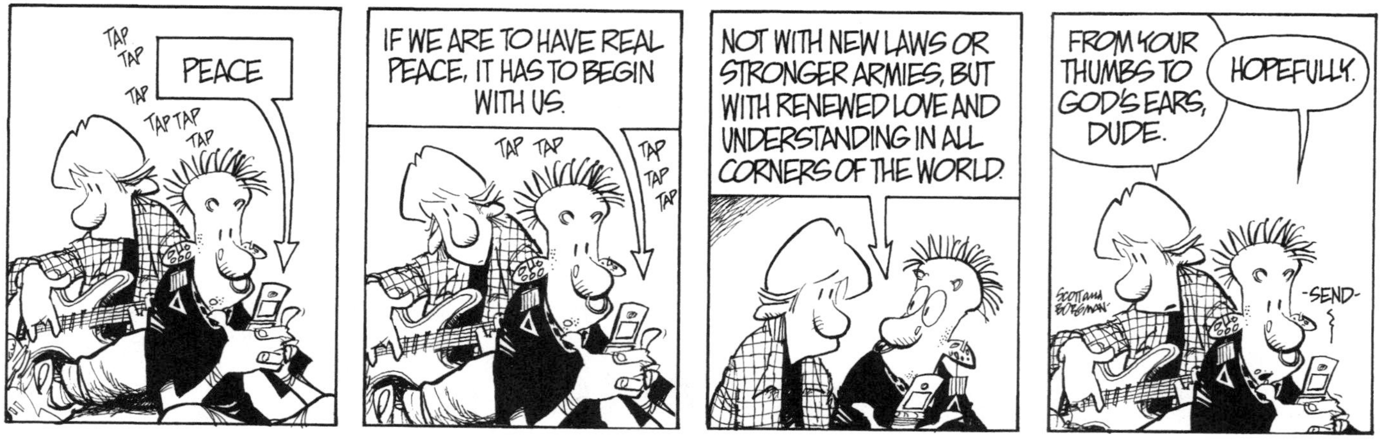
TAP TAP TAP TAP TAP TAP
PEACE
IF WE ARE TO HAVE REAL PEACE, IT HAS TO BEGIN WITH US.
TAP TAP
TAP TAP TAP
NOT WITH NEW LAWS OR STRONGER ARMIES, BUT WITH RENEWED LOVE AND UNDERSTANDING IN ALL CORNERS OF THE WORLD.
FROM YOUR THUMBS TO GOD'S EARS, DUDE.
HOPEFULLY.
-SEND-

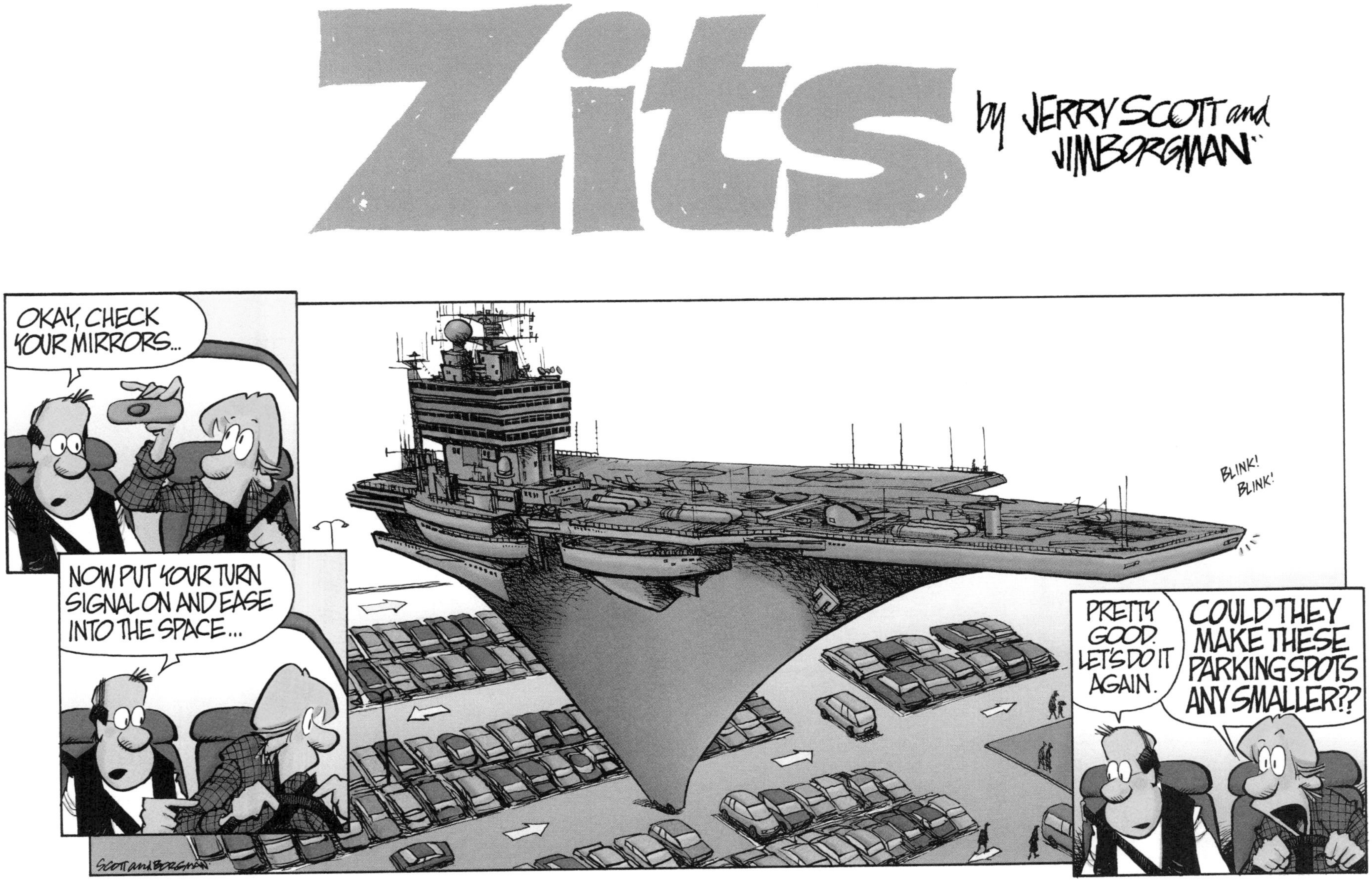
Zits
by JERRY SCOTT and JIM BORGMAN
OKAY, CHECK YOUR MIRRORS...
NOW PUT YOUR TURN SIGNAL ON AND EASE INTO THE SPACE...
BLINK! BLINK!
PRETTY GOOD. LET'S DO IT AGAIN.
COULD THEY MAKE THESE PARKING SPOTS ANY SMALLER??
SCOTT and BORGMAN

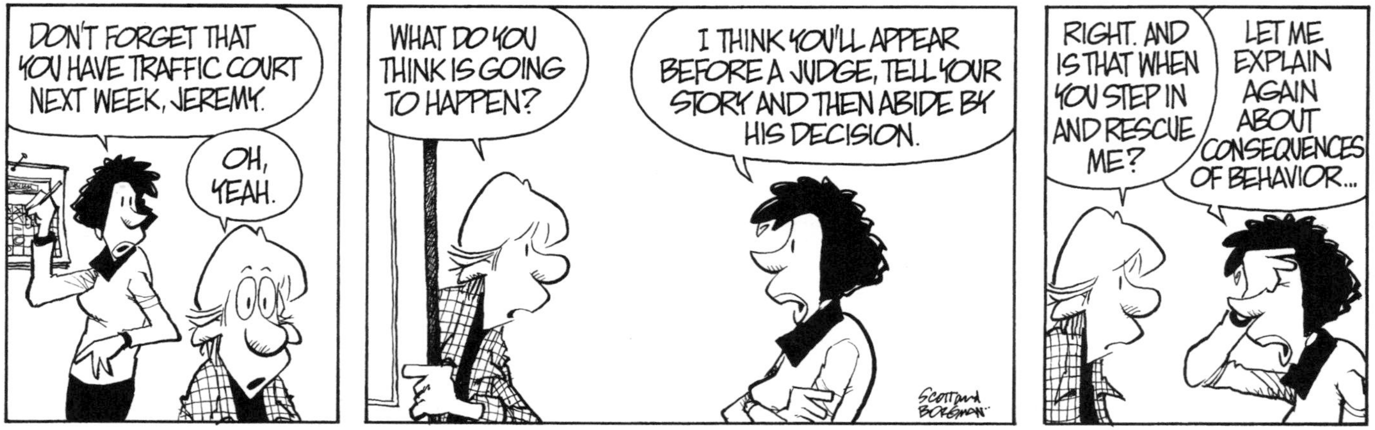
DON'T FORGET THAT YOU HAVE TRAFFIC COURT NEXT WEEK, JEREMY.
OH, YEAH.
WHAT DO YOU THINK IS GOING TO HAPPEN?
I THINK YOU'LL APPEAR BEFORE A JUDGE, TELL YOUR STORY AND THEN ABIDE BY HIS DECISION.
RIGHT. AND IS THAT WHEN YOU STEP IN AND RESCUE ME?
LET ME EXPLAIN AGAIN ABOUT CONSEQUENCES OF BEHAVIOR...

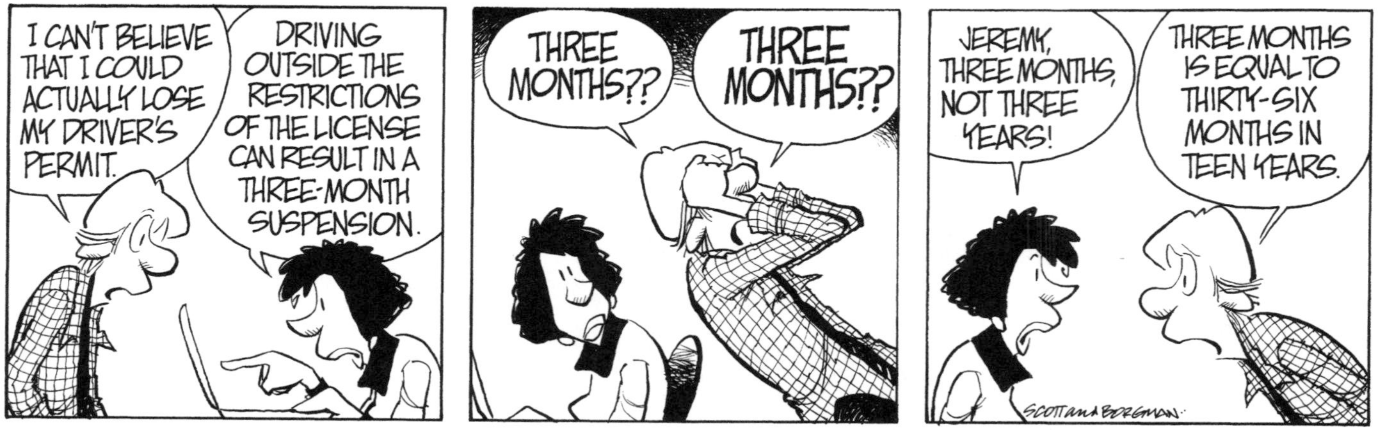
I CAN'T BELIEVE THAT I COULD ACTUALLY LOSE MY DRIVER'S PERMIT.
DRIVING OUTSIDE THE RESTRICTIONS OF THE LICENSE CAN RESULT IN A THREE-MONTH SUSPENSION.
THREE MONTHS??
THREE MONTHS??
JEREMY, THREE MONTHS, NOT THREE YEARS!
THREE MONTHS IS EQUAL TO THIRTY-SIX MONTHS IN TEEN YEARS.

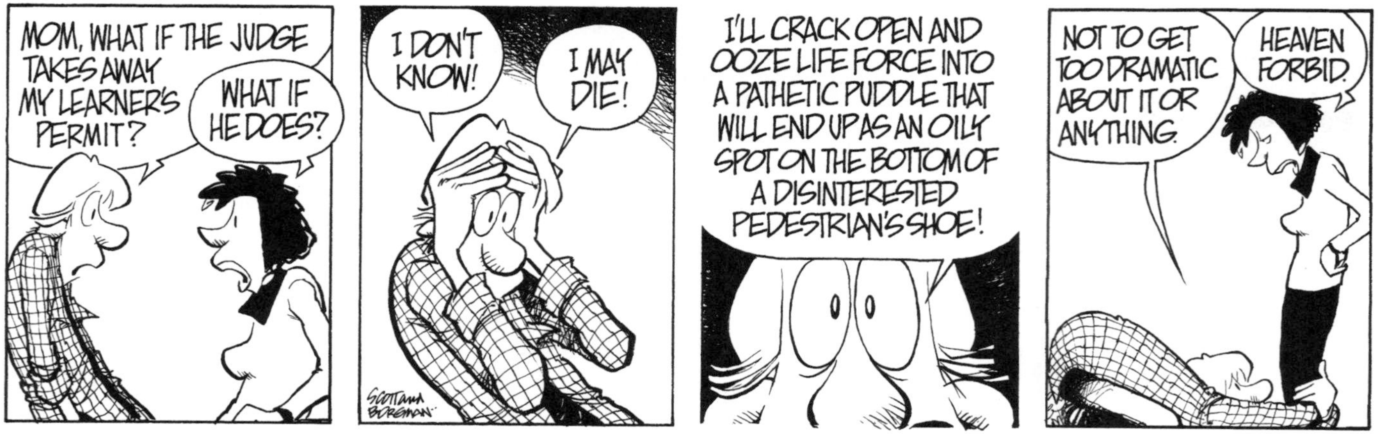
MOM, WHAT IF THE JUDGE TAKES AWAY MY LEARNER'S PERMIT?
WHAT IF HE DOES?
I DON'T KNOW!
I MAY DIE!
I'LL CRACK OPEN AND OOZE LIFE FORCE INTO A PATHETIC PUDDLE THAT WILL END UP AS AN OILY SPOT ON THE BOTTOM OF A DISINTERESTED PEDESTRIAN'S SHOE!
NOT TO GET TOO DRAMATIC ABOUT IT OR ANYTHING.
HEAVEN FORBID.

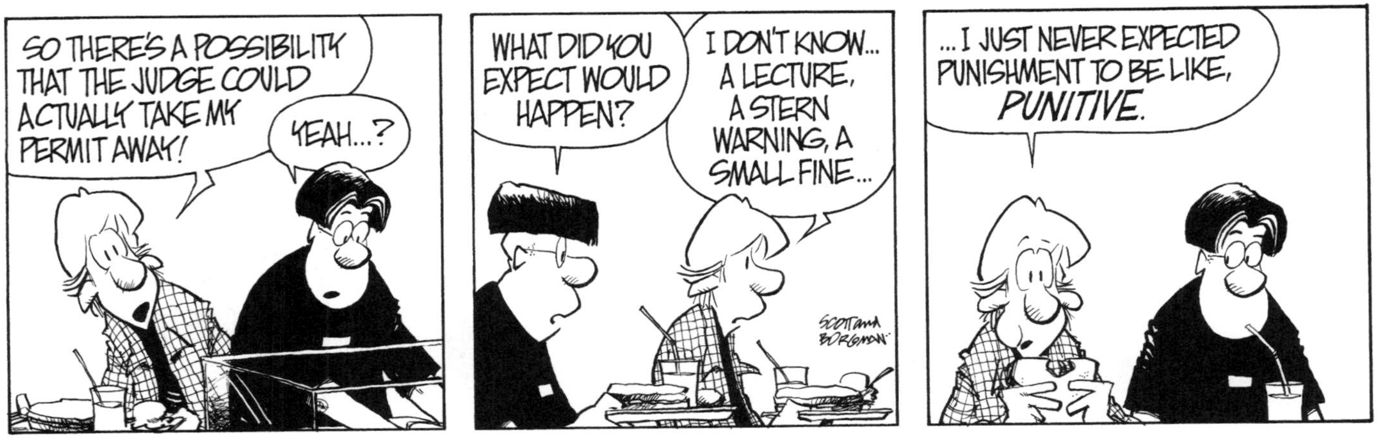
SO THERE'S A POSSIBILITY THAT THE JUDGE COULD ACTUALLY TAKE MY PERMIT AWAY!
YEAH...?
WHAT DID YOU EXPECT WOULD HAPPEN?
I DON'T KNOW... A LECTURE, A STERN WARNING, A SMALL FINE...
SCOTT and BORGMAN
...I JUST NEVER EXPECTED PUNISHMENT TO BE LIKE, *PUNITIVE*.

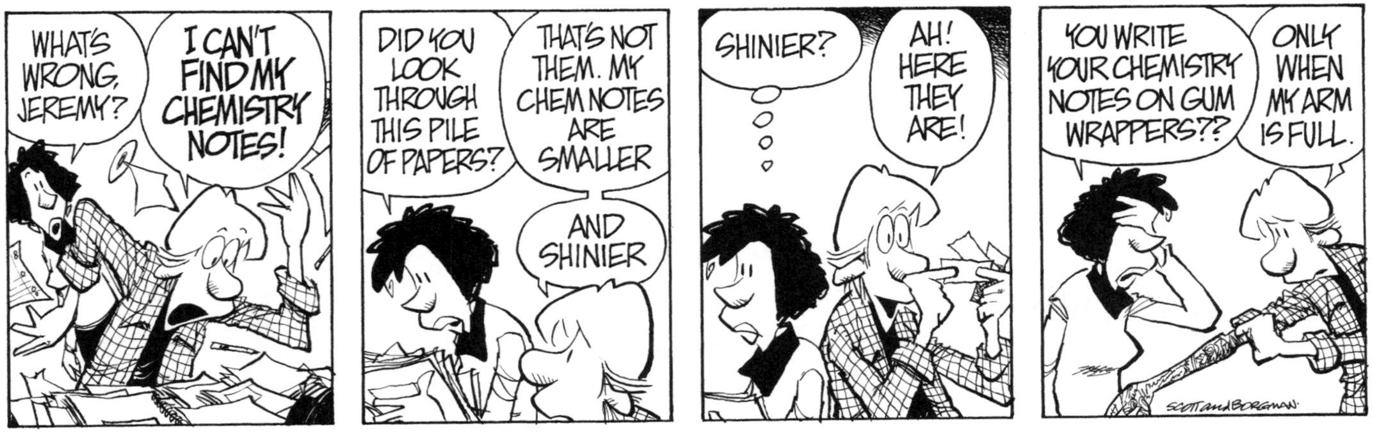
WHAT'S WRONG, JEREMY?
I CAN'T FIND MY CHEMISTRY NOTES!
DID YOU LOOK THROUGH THIS PILE OF PAPERS?
THAT'S NOT THEM. MY CHEM NOTES ARE SMALLER
AND SHINIER
SHINIER?
AH! HERE THEY ARE!
YOU WRITE YOUR CHEMISTRY NOTES ON GUM WRAPPERS??
ONLY WHEN MY ARM IS FULL.
SCOTT and BORGMAN

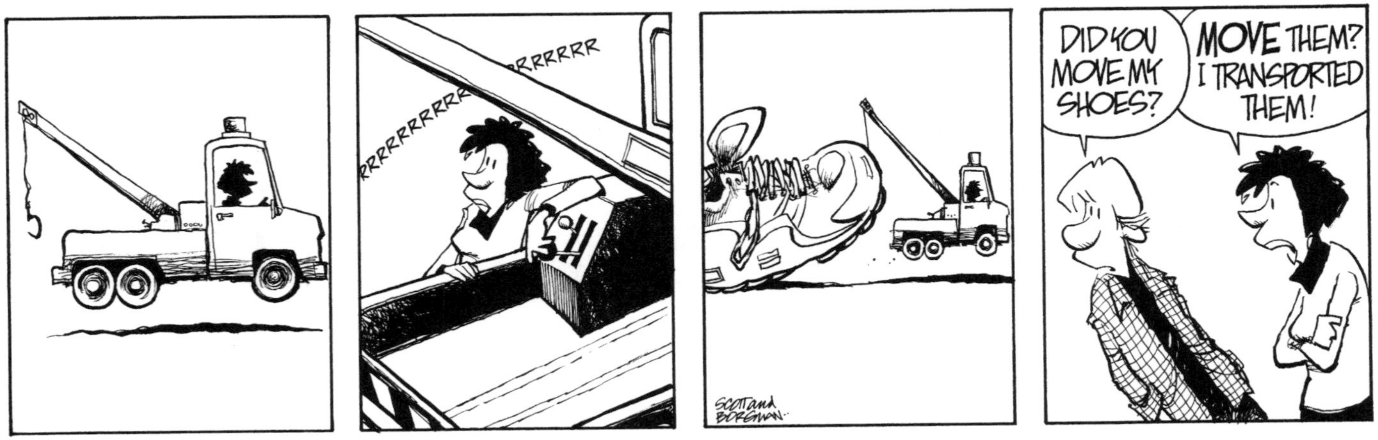
RRRRRRRRR RRRRRR
SCOTT and BORGMAN
DID YOU MOVE MY SHOES?
MOVE THEM? I TRANSPORTED THEM!

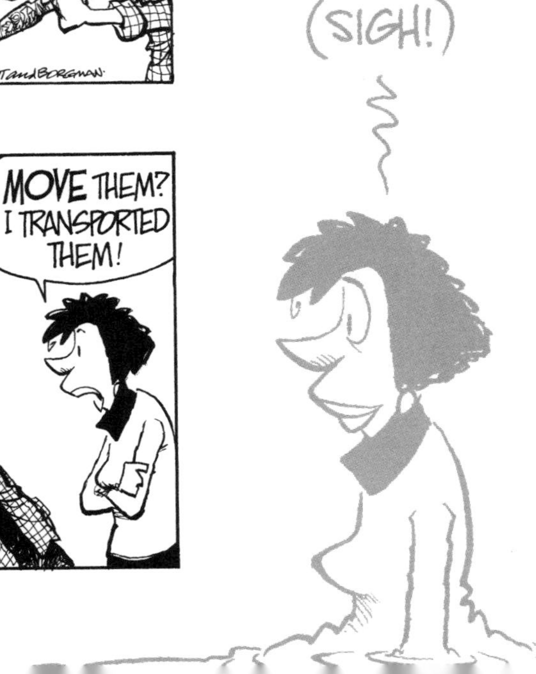
(SIGH!)

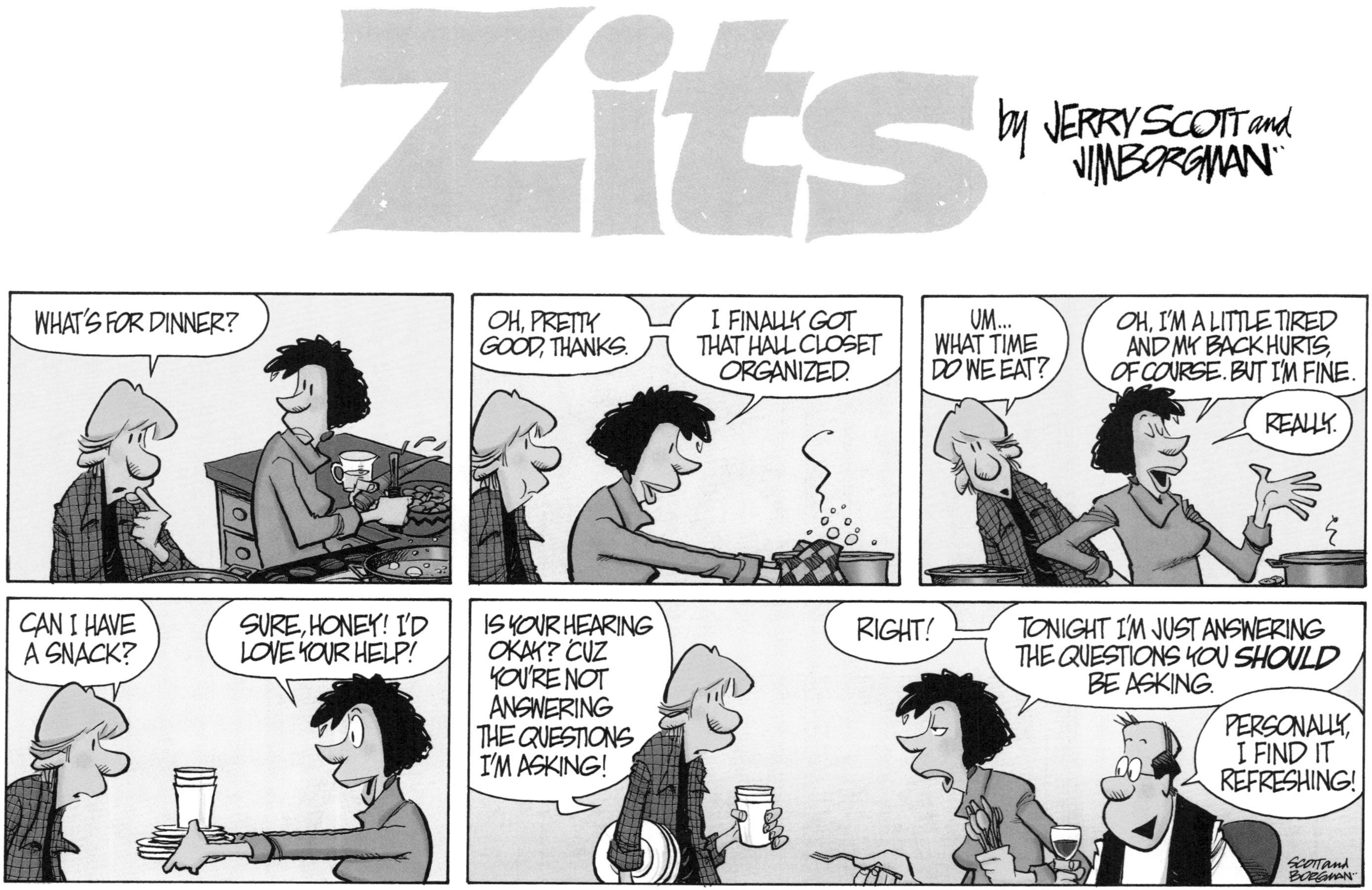
Zits
by JERRY SCOTT and JIM BORGMAN
WHAT'S FOR DINNER?
OH, PRETTY GOOD, THANKS.
I FINALLY GOT THAT HALL CLOSET ORGANIZED.
UM... WHAT TIME DO WE EAT?
OH, I'M A LITTLE TIRED AND MY BACK HURTS, OF COURSE. BUT I'M FINE.
REALLY.
CAN I HAVE A SNACK?
SURE, HONEY! I'D LOVE YOUR HELP!
IS YOUR HEARING OKAY? 'CUZ YOU'RE NOT ANSWERING THE QUESTIONS I'M ASKING!
RIGHT!
TONIGHT I'M JUST ANSWERING THE QUESTIONS YOU SHOULD BE ASKING.
PERSONALLY, I FIND IT REFRESHING!
SCOTT and BORGMAN

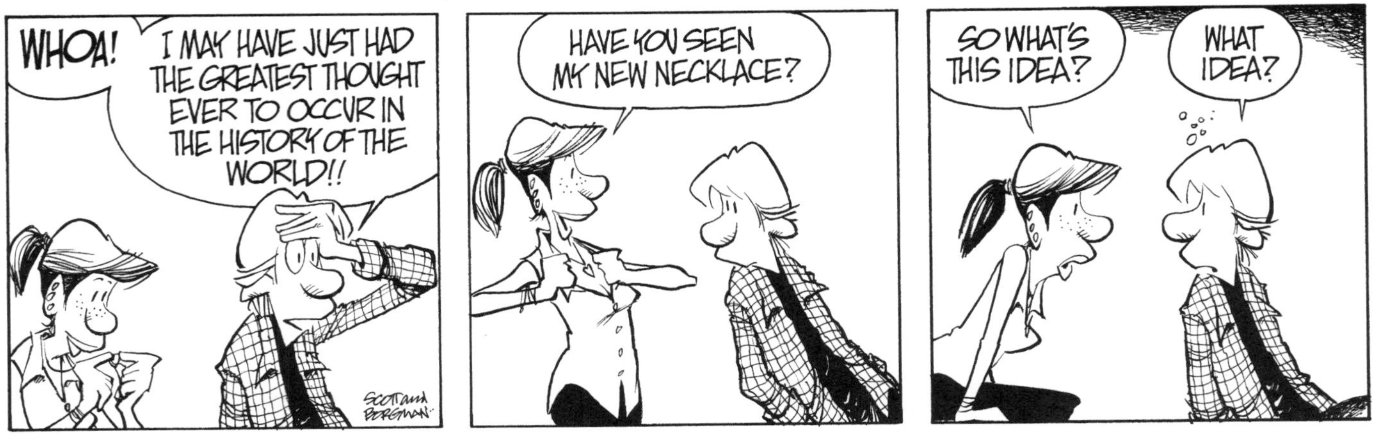
WHOA!
I MAY HAVE JUST HAD THE GREATEST THOUGHT EVER TO OCCUR IN THE HISTORY OF THE WORLD!!
HAVE YOU SEEN MY NEW NECKLACE?
SO WHAT'S THIS IDEA?
WHAT IDEA?

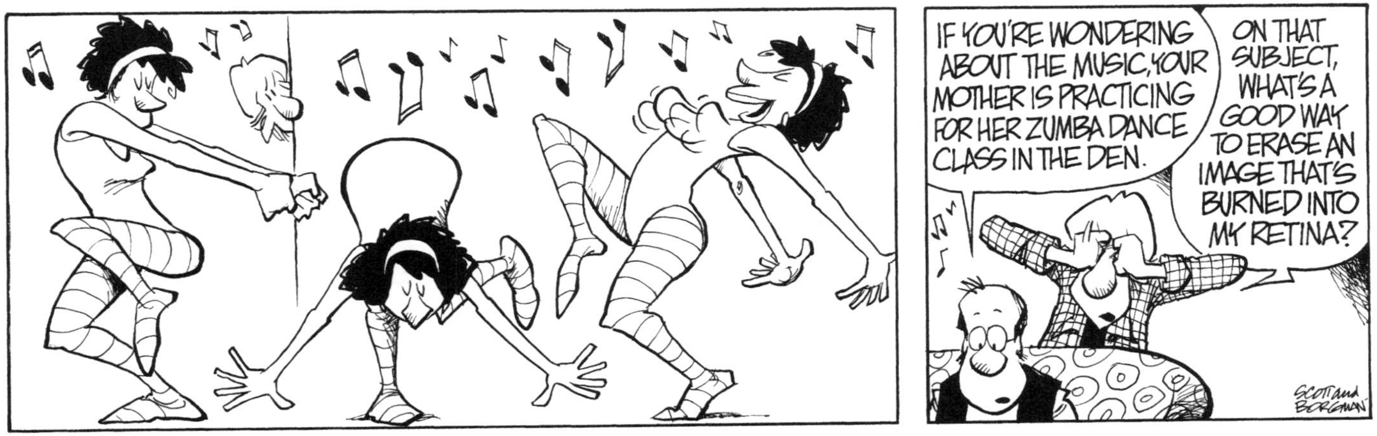
IF YOU'RE WONDERING ABOUT THE MUSIC, YOUR MOTHER IS PRACTICING FOR HER ZUMBA DANCE CLASS IN THE DEN.
ON THAT SUBJECT, WHAT'S A GOOD WAY TO ERASE AN IMAGE THAT'S BURNED INTO MY RETINA?

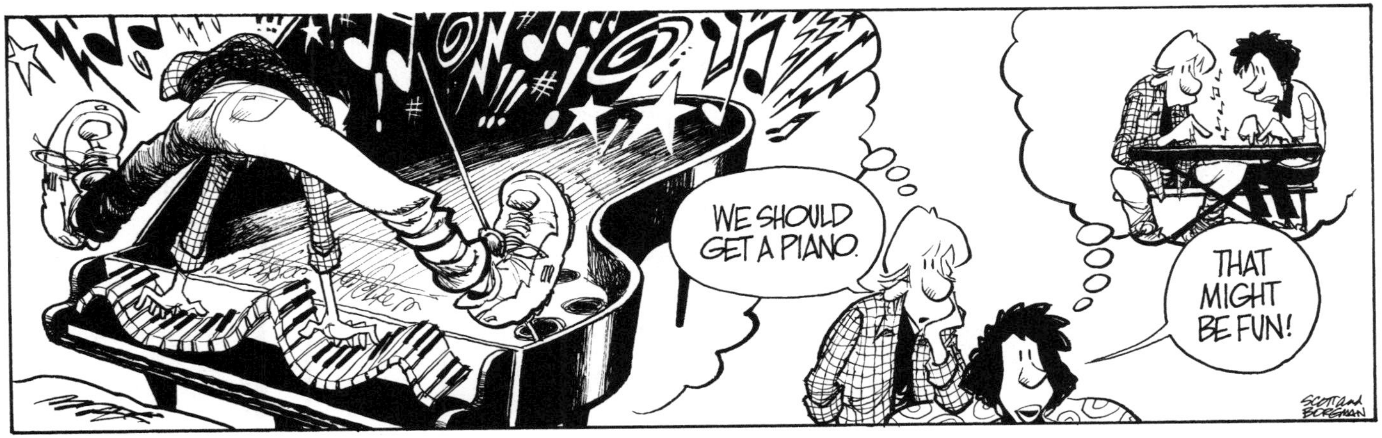
WE SHOULD GET A PIANO.
THAT MIGHT BE FUN!

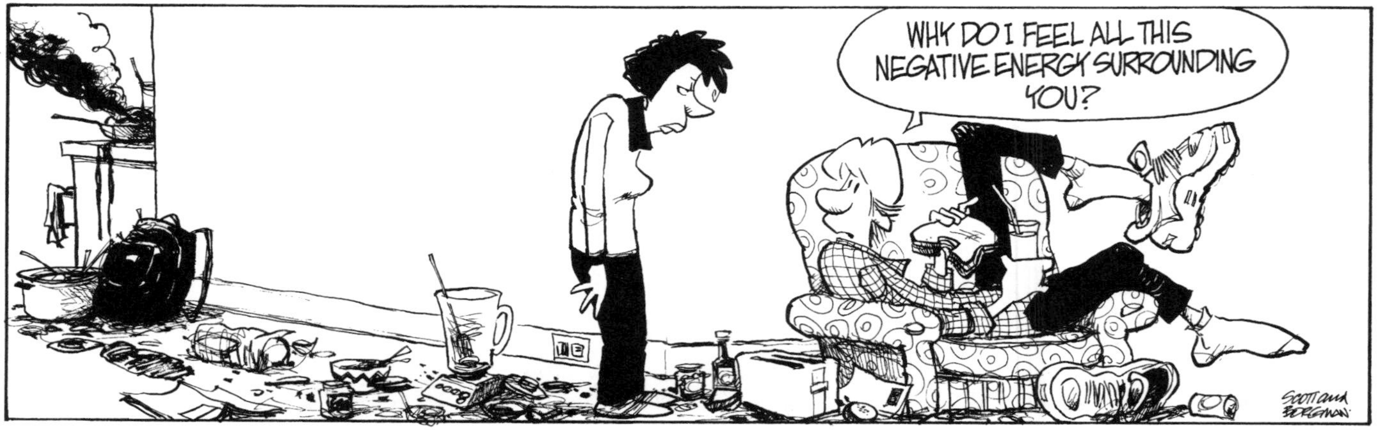
WHY DO I FEEL ALL THIS NEGATIVE ENERGY SURROUNDING YOU?
SCOTT and BORGMAN

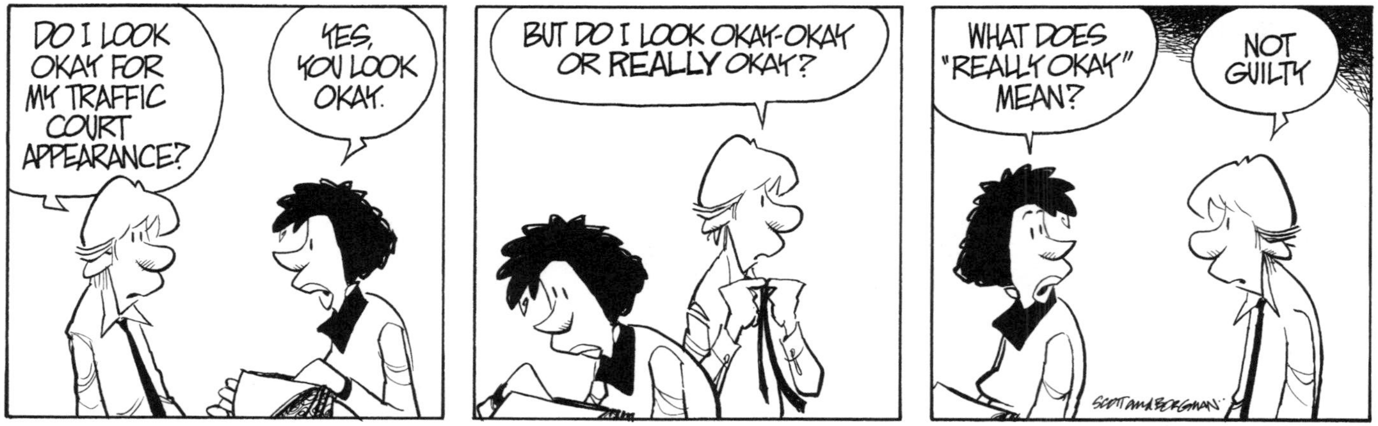
DO I LOOK OKAY FOR MY TRAFFIC COURT APPEARANCE?
YES, YOU LOOK OKAY.
BUT DO I LOOK OKAY-OKAY OR REALLY OKAY?
WHAT DOES "REALLY OKAY" MEAN?
NOT GUILTY
SCOTT and BORGMAN

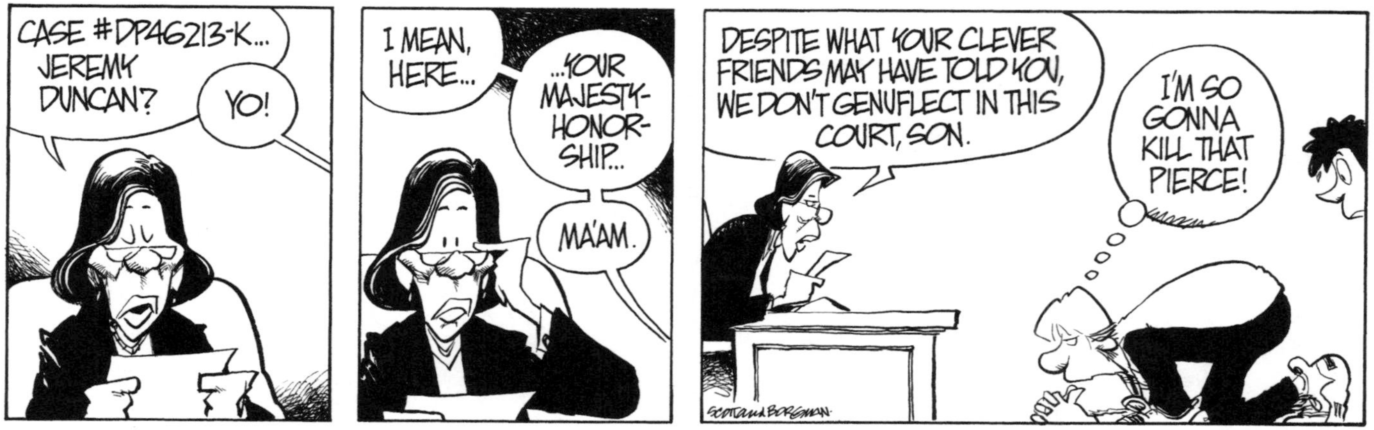
CASE #DP46213-K... JEREMY DUNCAN?
YO!
I MEAN, HERE...
...YOUR MAJESTY-HONOR-SHIP...
MA'AM.
DESPITE WHAT YOUR CLEVER FRIENDS MAY HAVE TOLD YOU, WE DON'T GENUFLECT IN THIS COURT, SON.
I'M SO GONNA KILL THAT PIERCE!
SCOTT and BORGMAN

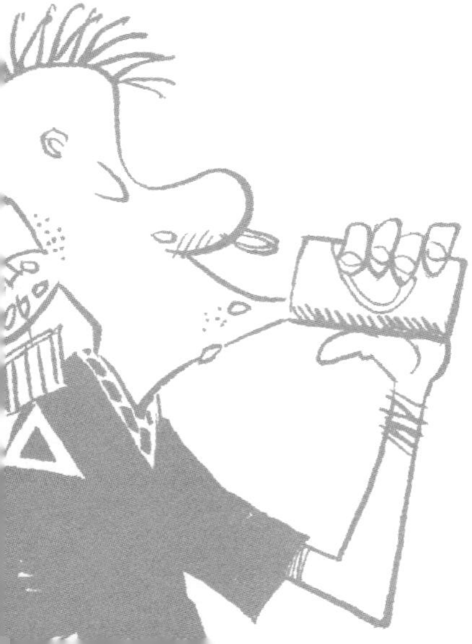

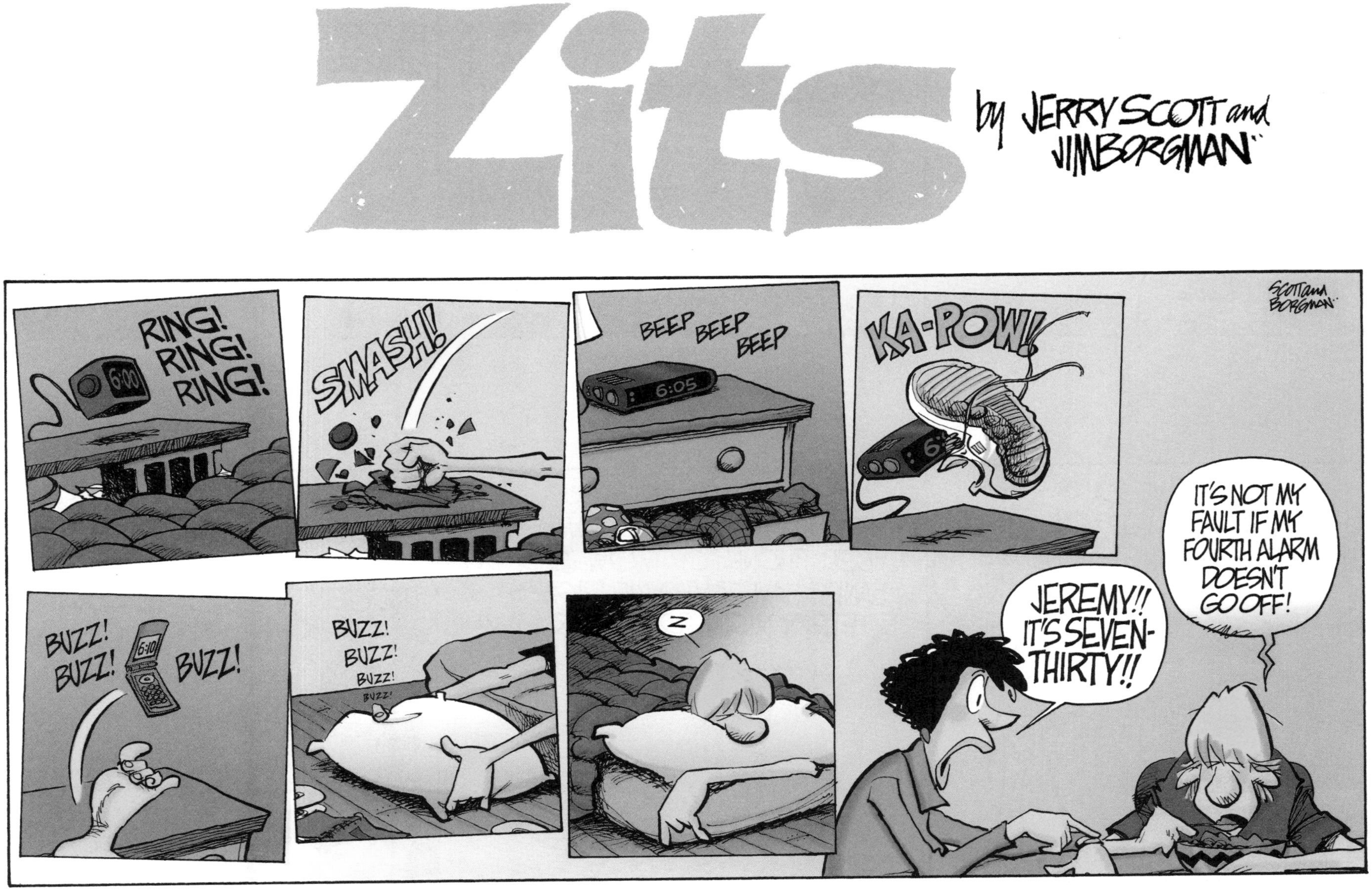
Zits
by JERRY SCOTT and JIM BORGMAN
SCOTT and BORGMAN
RING! RING! RING!
6:00
SMASH!
BEEP BEEP BEEP
6:05
KA-POW!!
BUZZ! BUZZ! BUZZ!
6:10
BUZZ! BUZZ! BUZZ! BUZZ!
Z
JEREMY!! IT'S SEVEN-THIRTY!!
IT'S NOT MY FAULT IF MY FOURTH ALARM DOESN'T GO OFF!

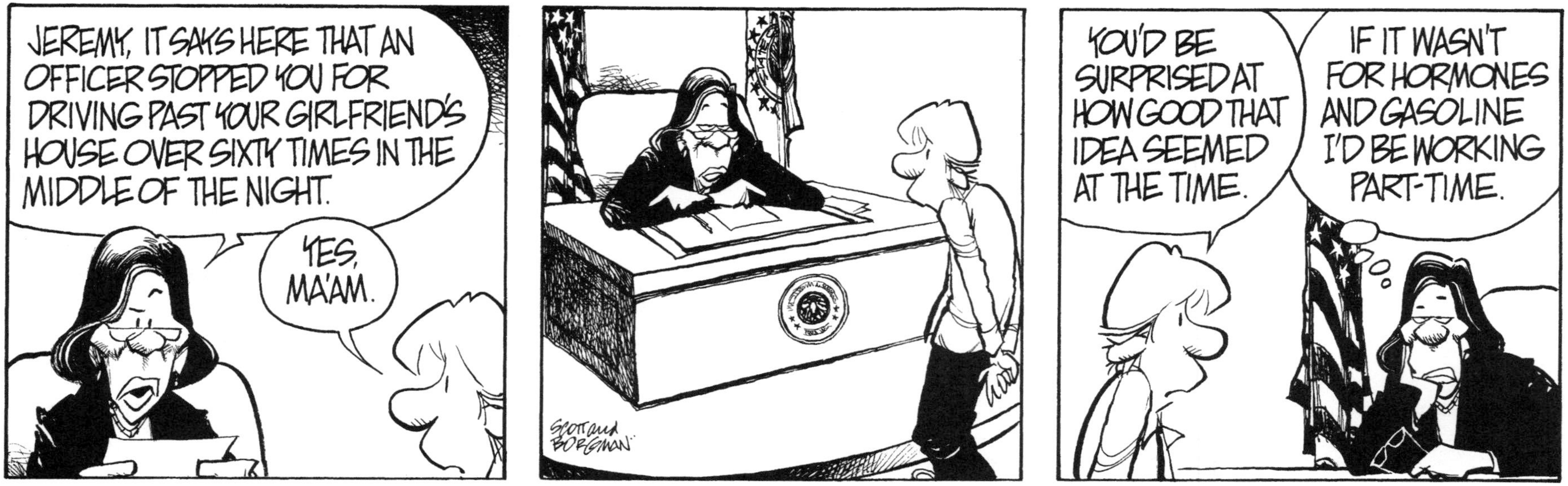
JEREMY, IT SAYS HERE THAT AN OFFICER STOPPED YOU FOR DRIVING PAST YOUR GIRLFRIEND'S HOUSE OVER SIXTY TIMES IN THE MIDDLE OF THE NIGHT.
YES, MA'AM.
SCOTT and BORGMAN
YOU'D BE SURPRISED AT HOW GOOD THAT IDEA SEEMED AT THE TIME.
IF IT WASN'T FOR HORMONES AND GASOLINE I'D BE WORKING PART-TIME.

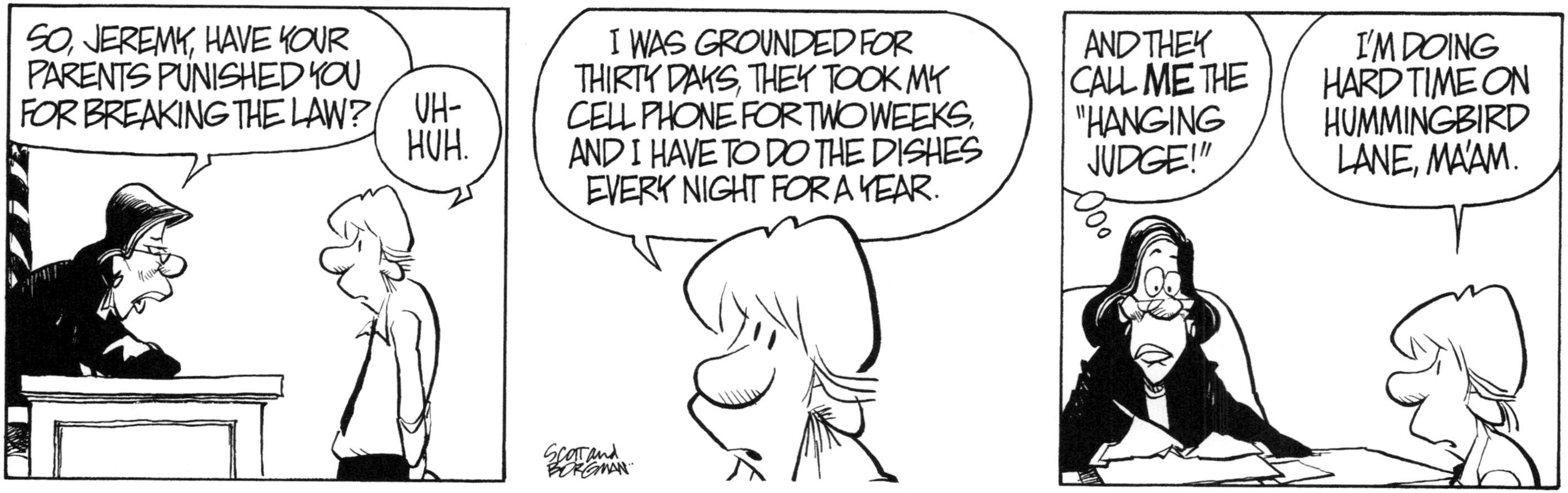
SO, JEREMY, HAVE YOUR PARENTS PUNISHED YOU FOR BREAKING THE LAW?
UH-HUH.
I WAS GROUNDED FOR THIRTY DAYS, THEY TOOK MY CELL PHONE FOR TWO WEEKS, AND I HAVE TO DO THE DISHES EVERY NIGHT FOR A YEAR.
SCOTT and BORGMAN
AND THEY CALL **ME** THE "HANGING JUDGE!"
I'M DOING HARD TIME ON HUMMINGBIRD LANE, MA'AM.

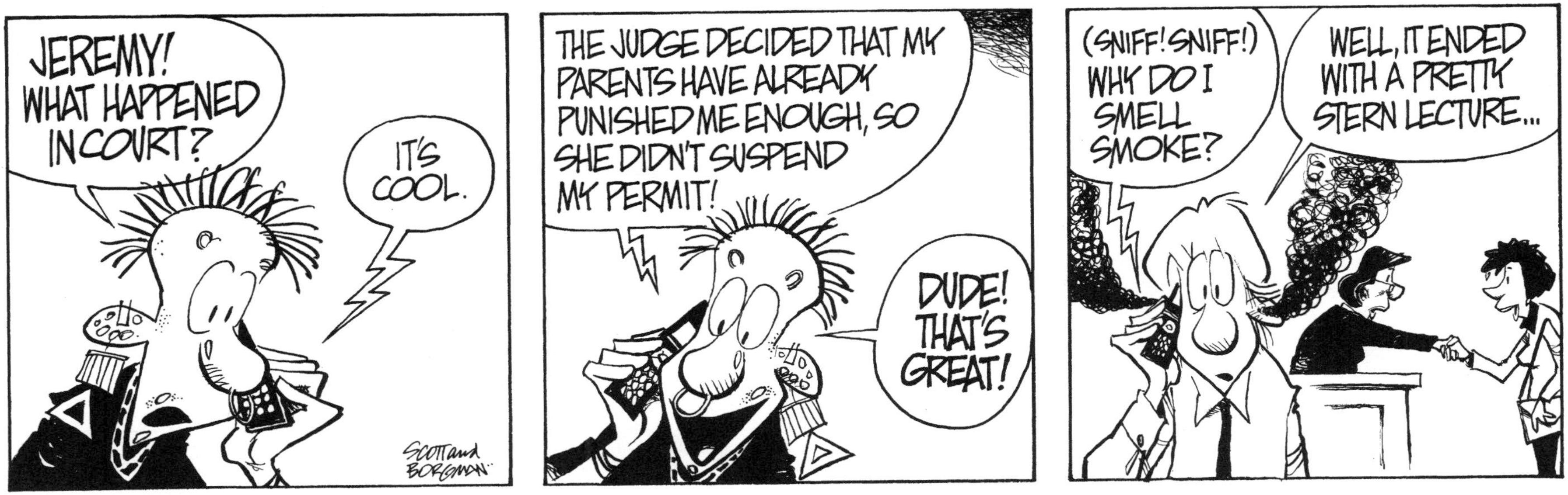
JEREMY! WHAT HAPPENED IN COURT?
IT'S COOL.
SCOTT and BORGMAN
THE JUDGE DECIDED THAT MY PARENTS HAVE ALREADY PUNISHED ME ENOUGH, SO SHE DIDN'T SUSPEND MY PERMIT!
DUDE! THAT'S GREAT!
(SNIFF! SNIFF!) WHY DO I SMELL SMOKE?
WELL, IT ENDED WITH A PRETTY STERN LECTURE...

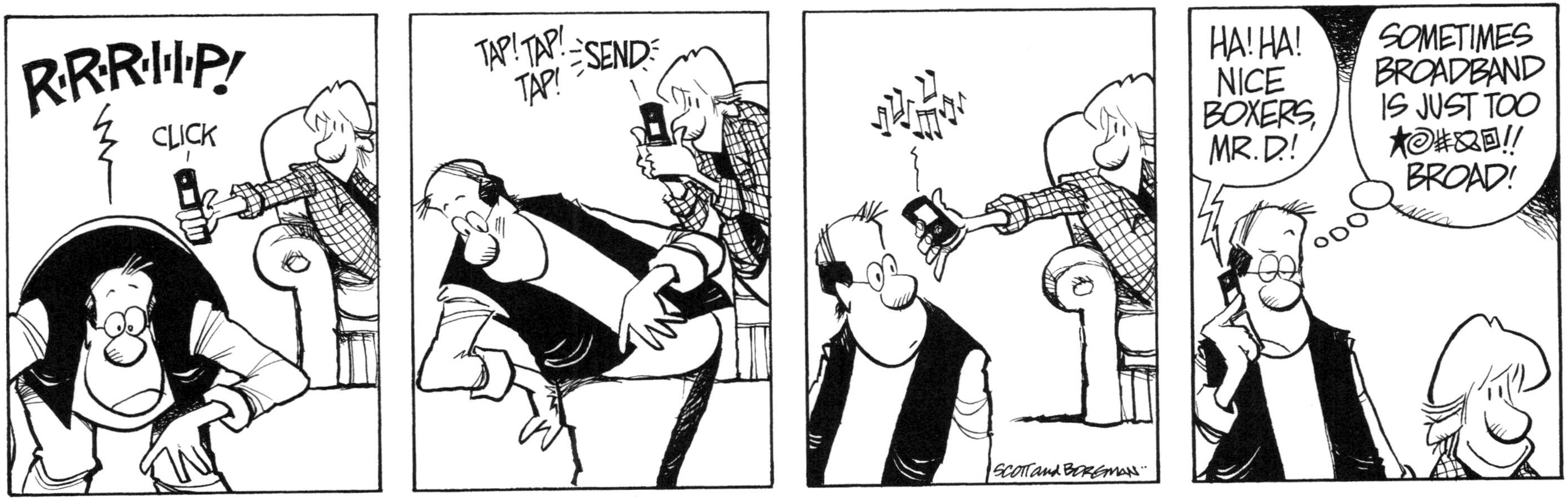
R-R-R-I-I-P!
CLICK
TAP! TAP! TAP!
SEND
SCOTT and BORGMAN
HA! HA! NICE BOXERS, MR. D!
SOMETIMES BROADBAND IS JUST TOO ★@#&□!! BROAD!

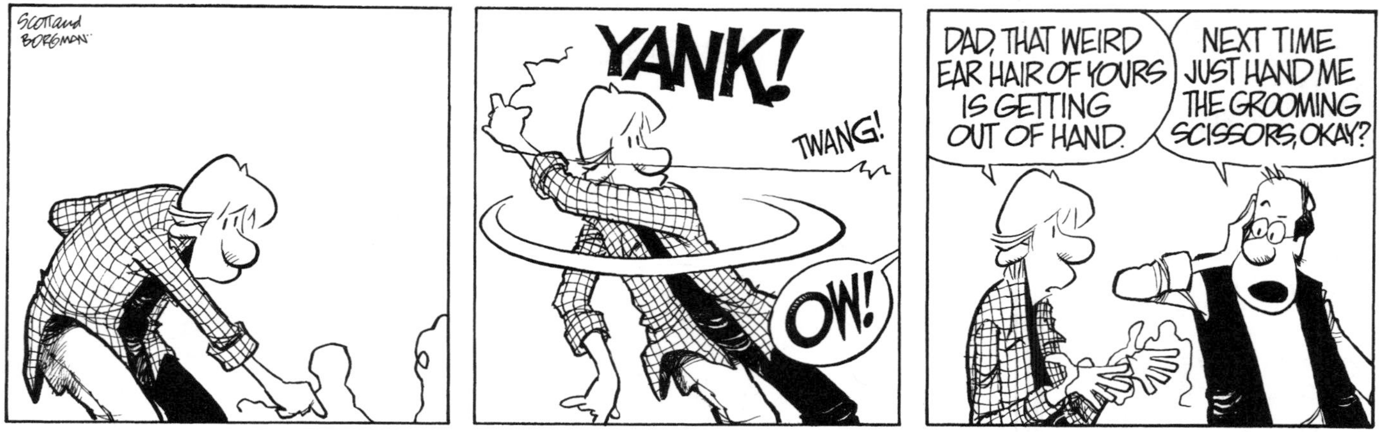
SCOTT and BORGMAN
YANK!
TWANG!
OW!
DAD, THAT WEIRD EAR HAIR OF YOURS IS GETTING OUT OF HAND.
NEXT TIME JUST HAND ME THE GROOMING SCISSORS, OKAY?

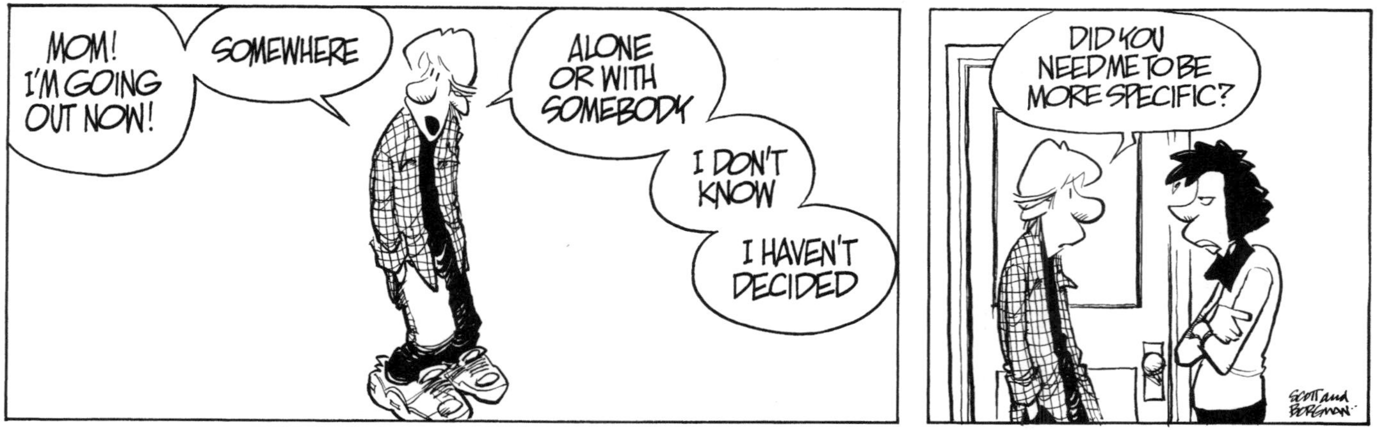
MOM! I'M GOING OUT NOW!
SOMEWHERE
ALONE OR WITH SOMEBODY
I DON'T KNOW
I HAVEN'T DECIDED
DID YOU NEED ME TO BE MORE SPECIFIC?
SCOTT and BORGMAN

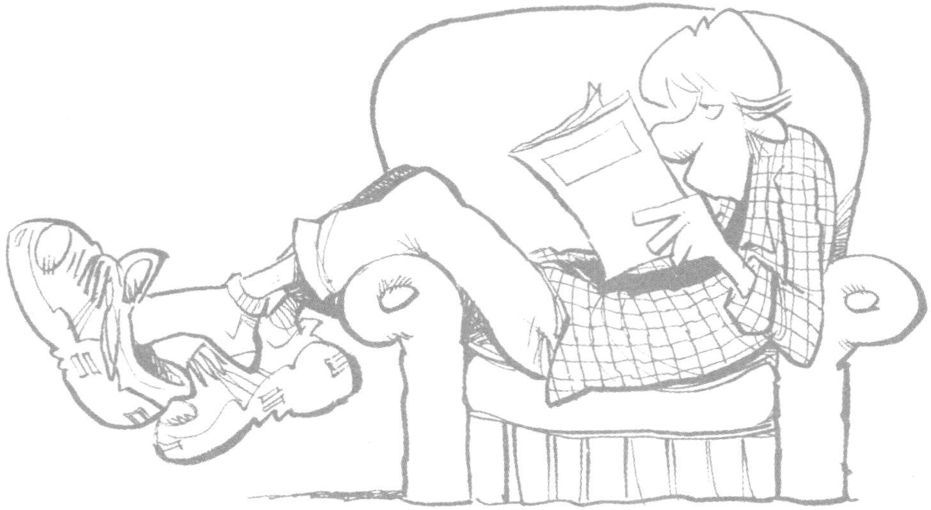

Zits

by JERRY SCOTT and JIM BORGMAN

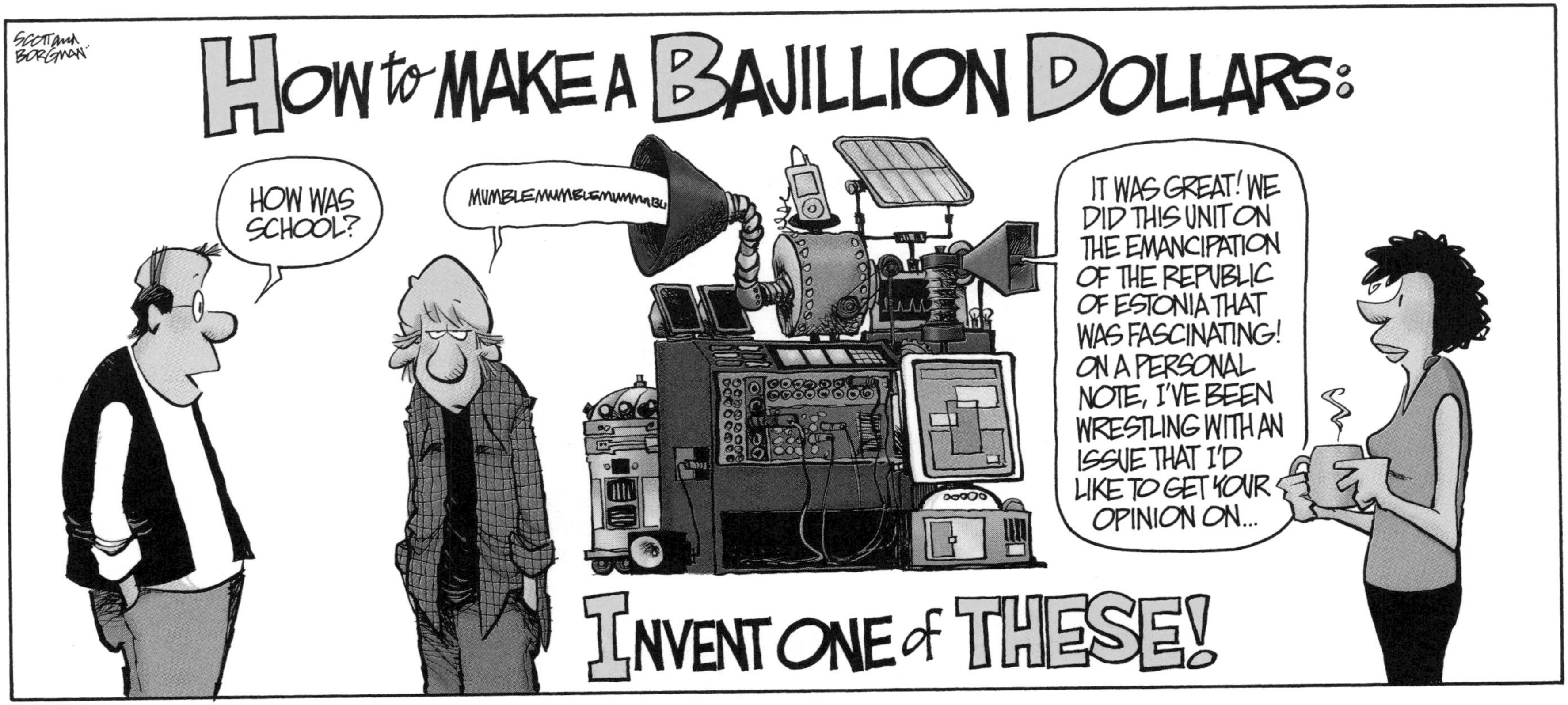
SCOTT and BORGMAN
HOW to MAKE A BAJILLION DOLLARS:
HOW WAS SCHOOL?
MUMBLEMUMBLEMUMMMBLU
IT WAS GREAT! WE DID THIS UNIT ON THE EMANCIPATION OF THE REPUBLIC OF ESTONIA THAT WAS FASCINATING! ON A PERSONAL NOTE, I'VE BEEN WRESTLING WITH AN ISSUE THAT I'D LIKE TO GET YOUR OPINION ON...
INVENT ONE of THESE!

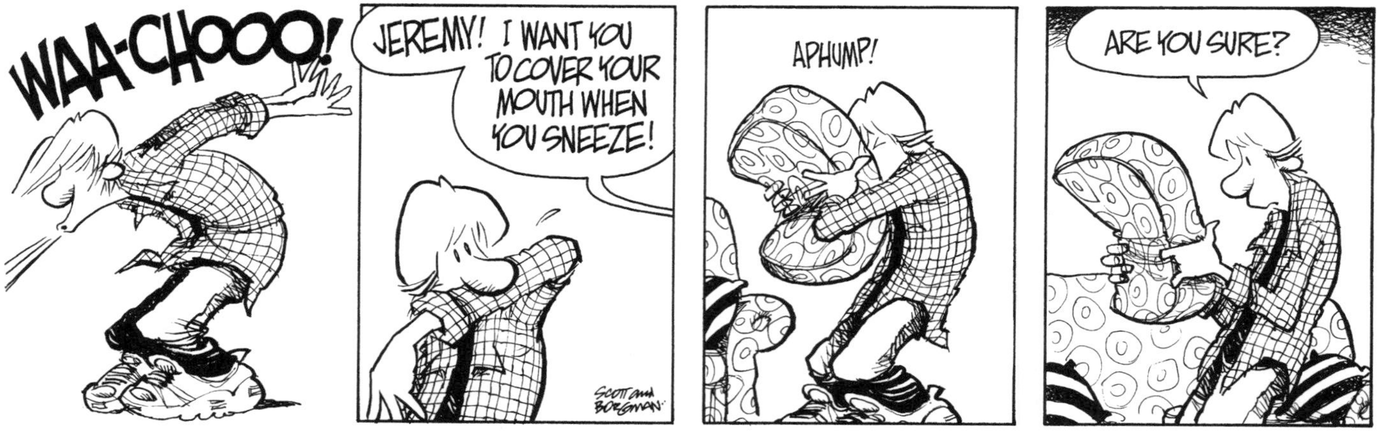
WAA-CHOOO!
JEREMY! I WANT YOU TO COVER YOUR MOUTH WHEN YOU SNEEZE!
SCOTT and BORGMAN
APHUMP!
ARE YOU SURE?

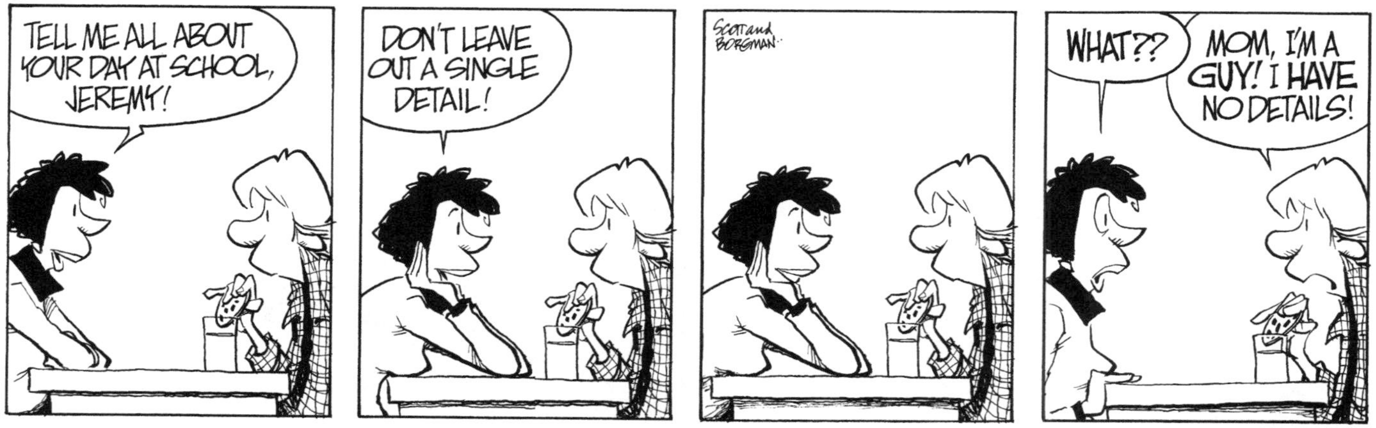
TELL ME ALL ABOUT YOUR DAY AT SCHOOL, JEREMY!
DON'T LEAVE OUT A SINGLE DETAIL!
SCOTT and BORGMAN
WHAT??
MOM, I'M A GUY! I HAVE NO DETAILS!

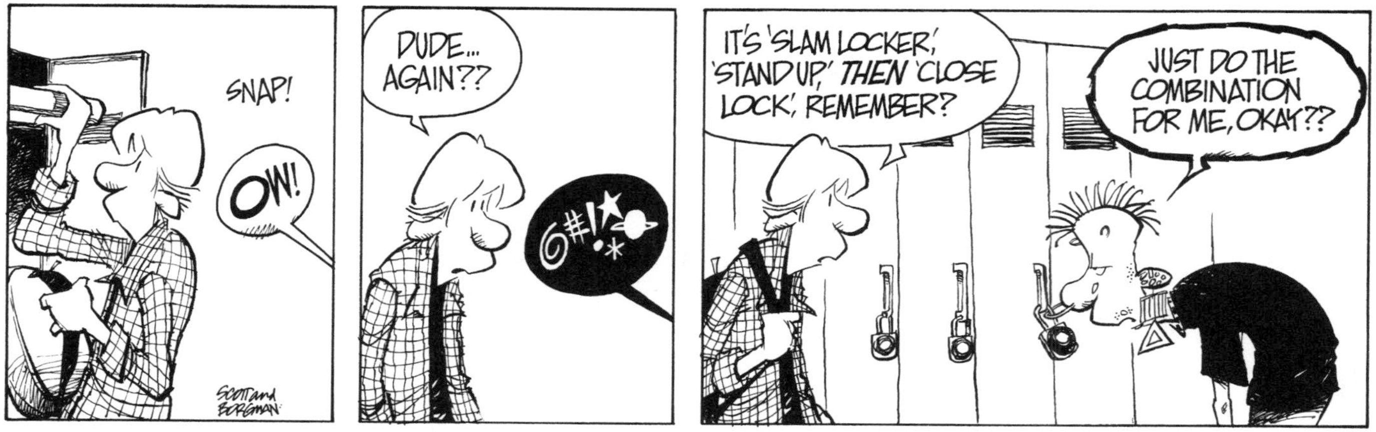
SNAP!
OW!
SCOTT and BORGMAN
DUDE... AGAIN??
IT'S 'SLAM LOCKER,' 'STAND UP,' THEN 'CLOSE LOCK,' REMEMBER?
JUST DO THE COMBINATION FOR ME, OKAY??

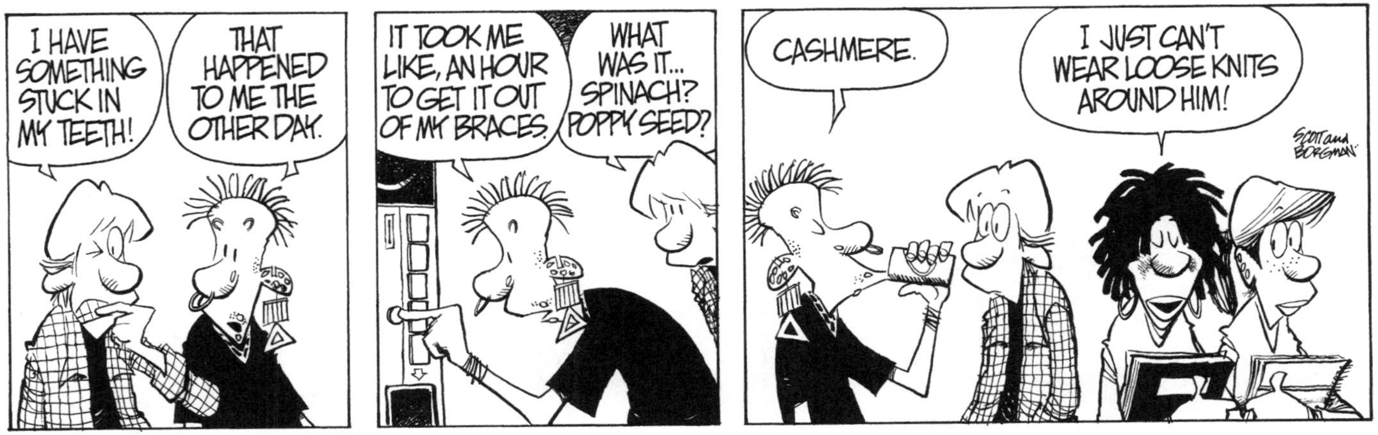
I HAVE SOMETHING STUCK IN MY TEETH!
THAT HAPPENED TO ME THE OTHER DAY.
IT TOOK ME LIKE, AN HOUR TO GET IT OUT OF MY BRACES.
WHAT WAS IT... SPINACH? POPPY SEED?
CASHMERE.
I JUST CAN'T WEAR LOOSE KNITS AROUND HIM!
SCOTT and BORGMAN

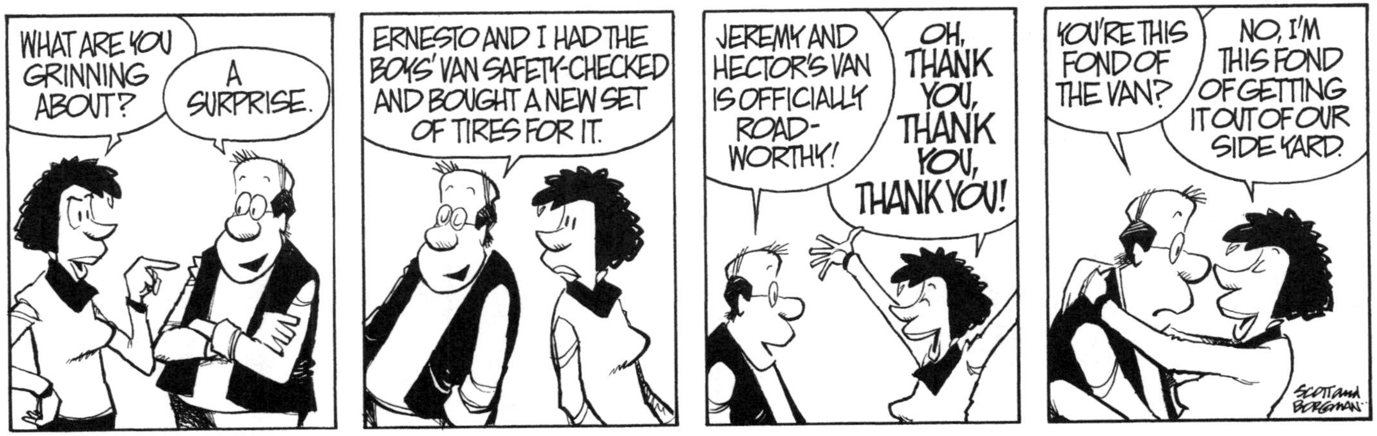
WHAT ARE YOU GRINNING ABOUT?
A SURPRISE.
ERNESTO AND I HAD THE BOYS' VAN SAFETY-CHECKED AND BOUGHT A NEW SET OF TIRES FOR IT.
JEREMY AND HECTOR'S VAN IS OFFICIALLY ROAD-WORTHY!
OH, THANK YOU, THANK YOU, THANK YOU!
YOU'RE THIS FOND OF THE VAN?
NO, I'M THIS FOND OF GETTING IT OUT OF OUR SIDE YARD.
SCOTT and BORGMAN

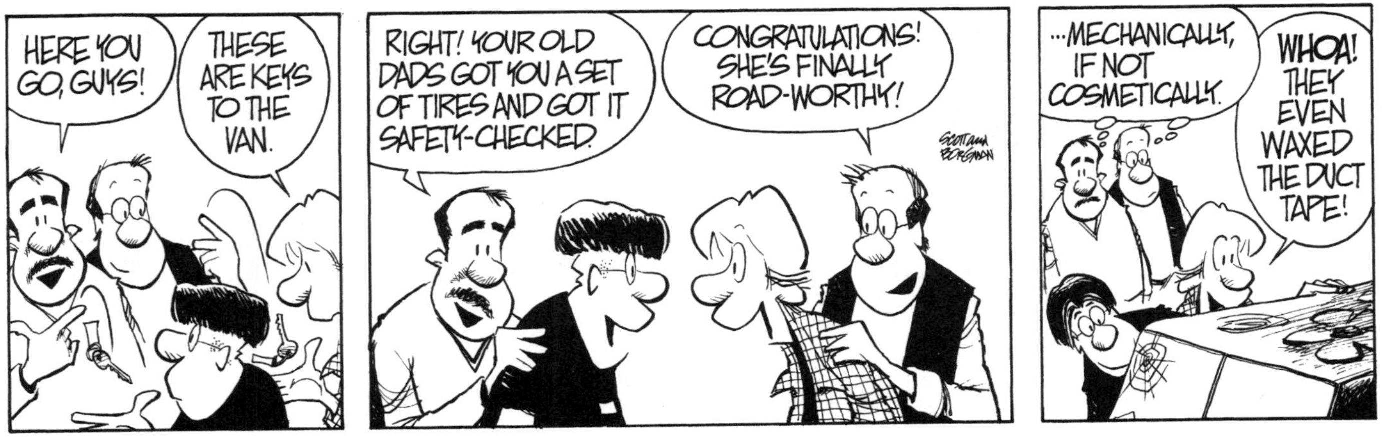
HERE YOU GO, GUYS!
THESE ARE KEYS TO THE VAN.
RIGHT! YOUR OLD DADS GOT YOU A SET OF TIRES AND GOT IT SAFETY-CHECKED.
CONGRATULATIONS! SHE'S FINALLY ROAD-WORTHY!
SCOTT and BORGMAN
...MECHANICALLY, IF NOT COSMETICALLY.
WHOA! THEY EVEN WAXED THE DUCT TAPE!

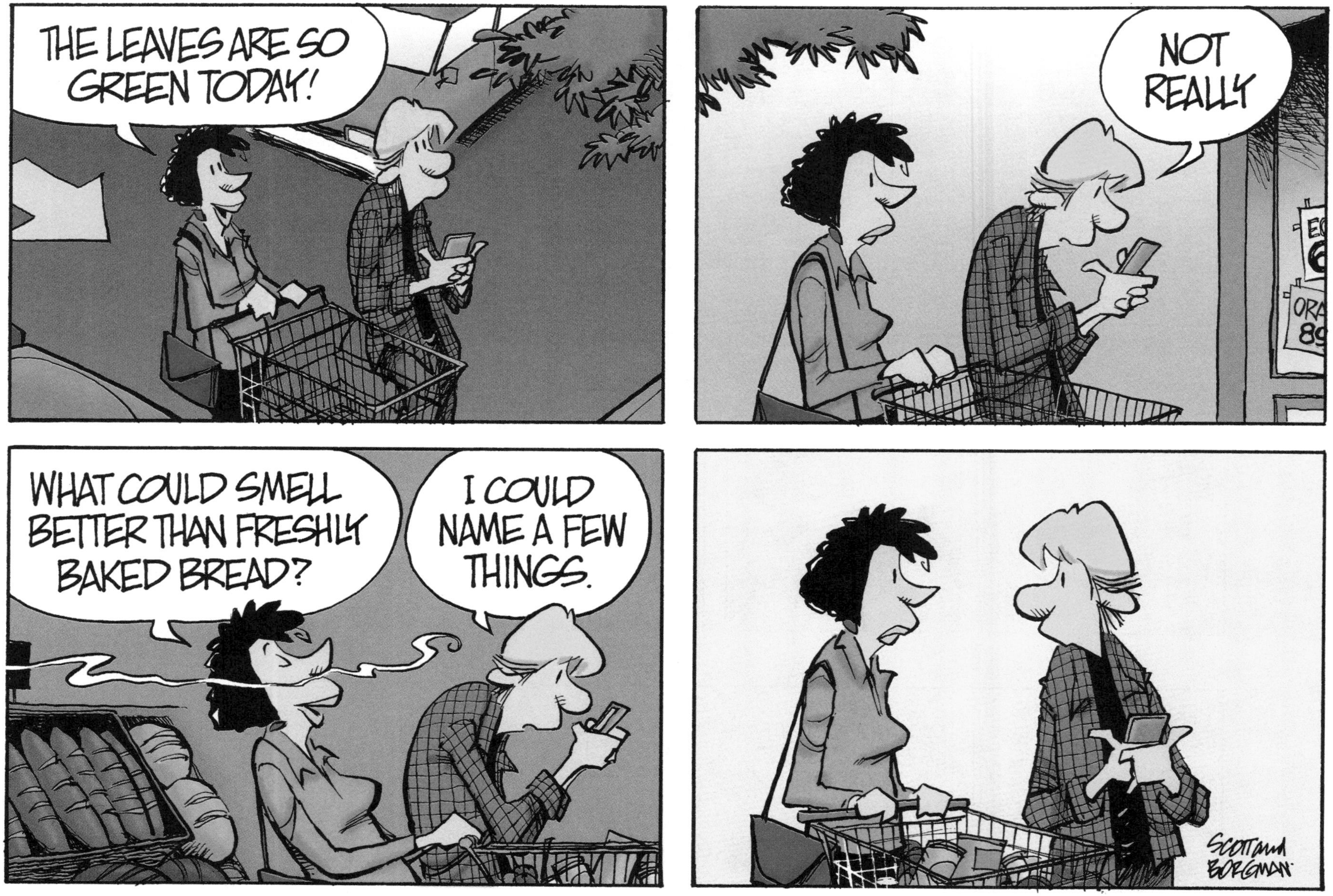
THE LEAVES ARE SO GREEN TODAY!
NOT REALLY
WHAT COULD SMELL BETTER THAN FRESHLY BAKED BREAD?
I COULD NAME A FEW THINGS.
SCOTT and BORGMAN

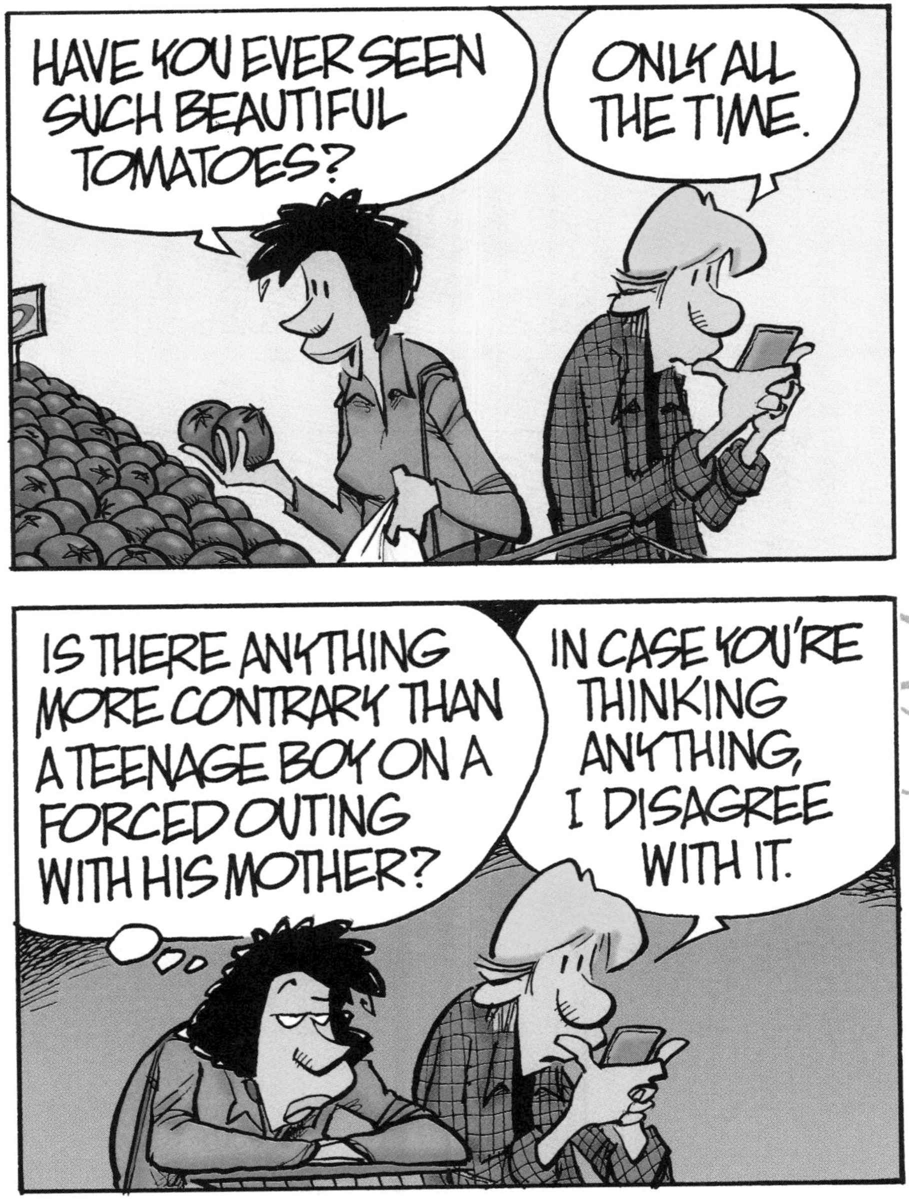
HAVE YOU EVER SEEN SUCH BEAUTIFUL TOMATOES?
ONLY ALL THE TIME.
IS THERE ANYTHING MORE CONTRARY THAN A TEENAGE BOY ON A FORCED OUTING WITH HIS MOTHER?
IN CASE YOU'RE THINKING ANYTHING, I DISAGREE WITH IT.

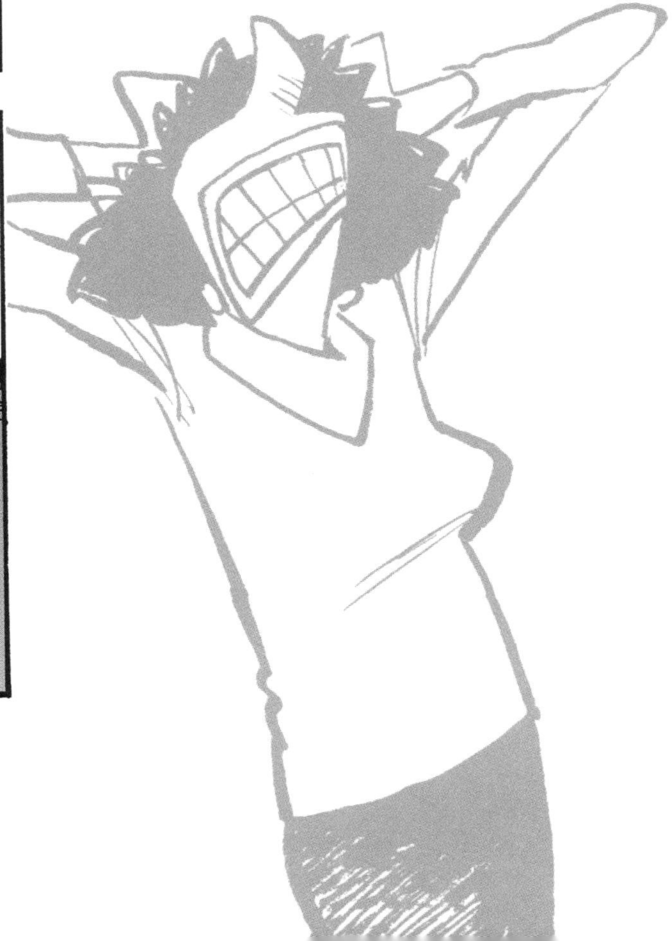

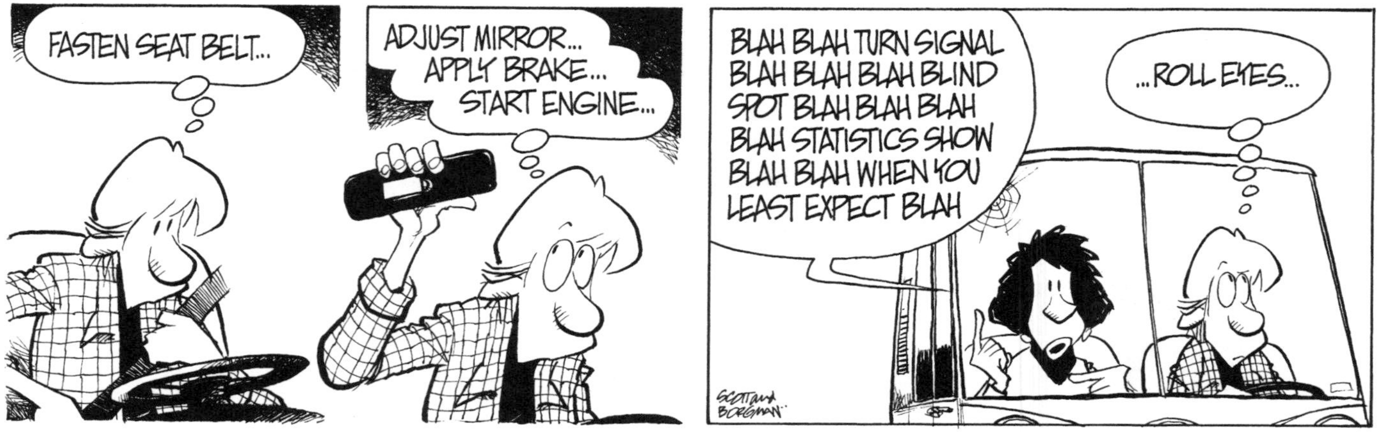
FASTEN SEAT BELT...
ADJUST MIRROR... APPLY BRAKE... START ENGINE...
BLAH BLAH TURN SIGNAL BLAH BLAH BLAH BLIND SPOT BLAH BLAH BLAH BLAH STATISTICS SHOW BLAH BLAH WHEN YOU LEAST EXPECT BLAH
...ROLL EYES...
SCOTT and BORGMAN

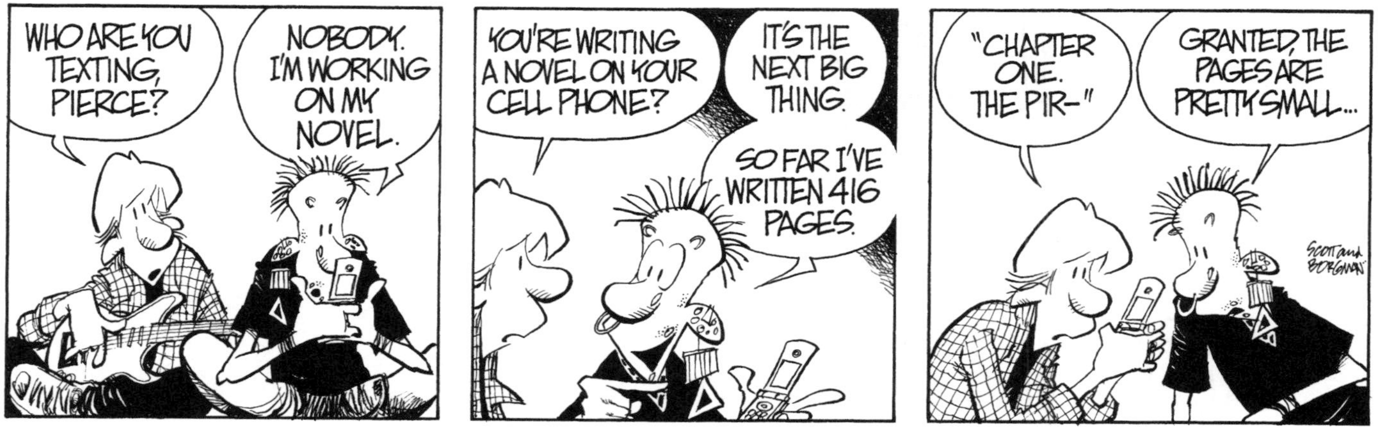
WHO ARE YOU TEXTING, PIERCE?
NOBODY. I'M WORKING ON MY NOVEL.
YOU'RE WRITING A NOVEL ON YOUR CELL PHONE?
IT'S THE NEXT BIG THING.
SO FAR I'VE WRITTEN 416 PAGES.
"CHAPTER ONE. THE PIR-"
GRANTED, THE PAGES ARE PRETTY SMALL...
SCOTT and BORGMAN

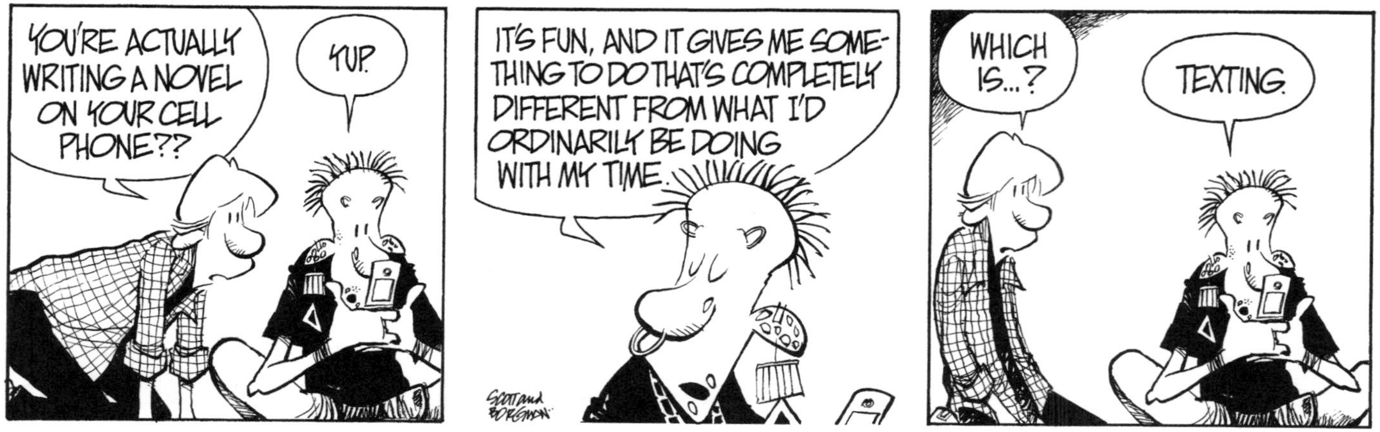
YOU'RE ACTUALLY WRITING A NOVEL ON YOUR CELL PHONE??
YUP.
IT'S FUN, AND IT GIVES ME SOMETHING TO DO THAT'S COMPLETELY DIFFERENT FROM WHAT I'D ORDINARILY BE DOING WITH MY TIME.
WHICH IS...?
TEXTING.
SCOTT and BORGMAN

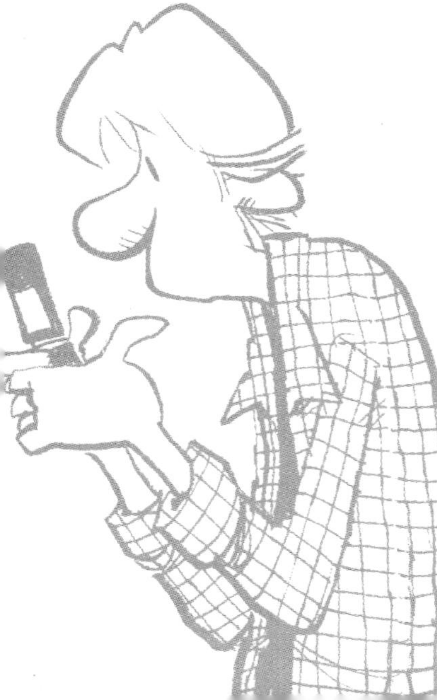

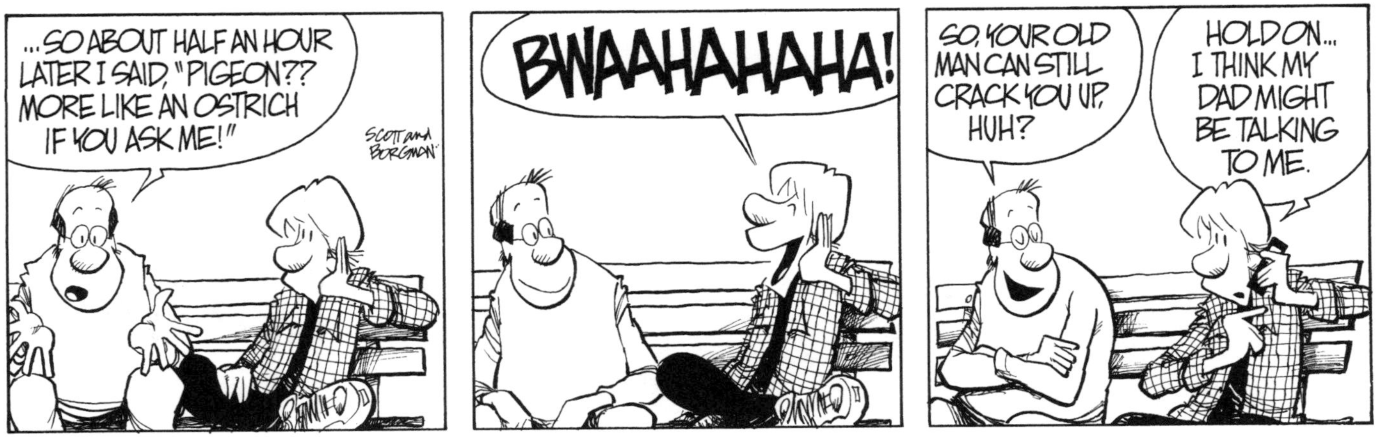
...SO ABOUT HALF AN HOUR LATER I SAID, "PIGEON?? MORE LIKE AN OSTRICH IF YOU ASK ME!"
BWAAHAHAHA!
SO, YOUR OLD MAN CAN STILL CRACK YOU UP, HUH?
HOLD ON... I THINK MY DAD MIGHT BE TALKING TO ME.

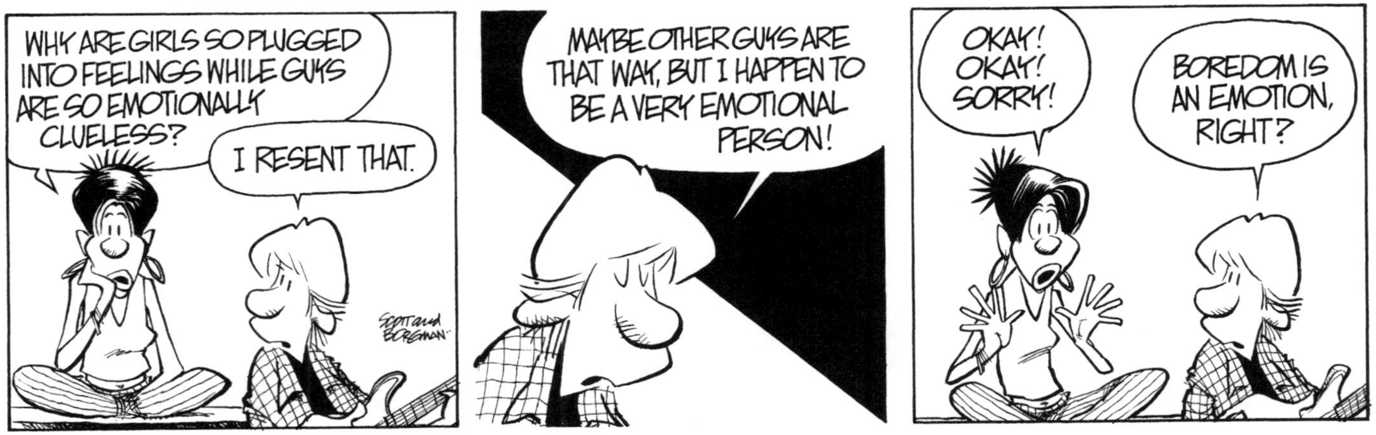
WHY ARE GIRLS SO PLUGGED INTO FEELINGS WHILE GUYS ARE SO EMOTIONALLY CLUELESS?
I RESENT THAT.
MAYBE OTHER GUYS ARE THAT WAY, BUT I HAPPEN TO BE A VERY EMOTIONAL PERSON!
OKAY! OKAY! SORRY!
BOREDOM IS AN EMOTION, RIGHT?

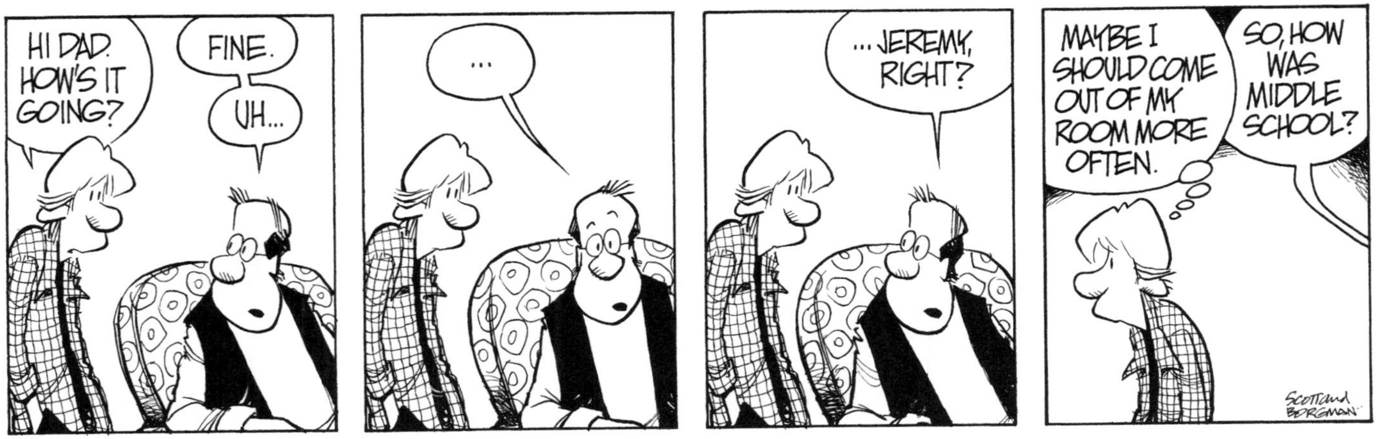
HI DAD. HOW'S IT GOING?
FINE.
UH...
...
...JEREMY, RIGHT?
MAYBE I SHOULD COME OUT OF MY ROOM MORE OFTEN.
SO, HOW WAS MIDDLE SCHOOL?

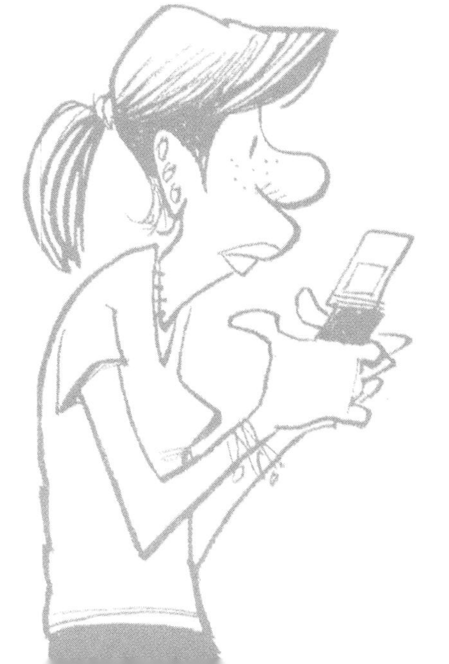

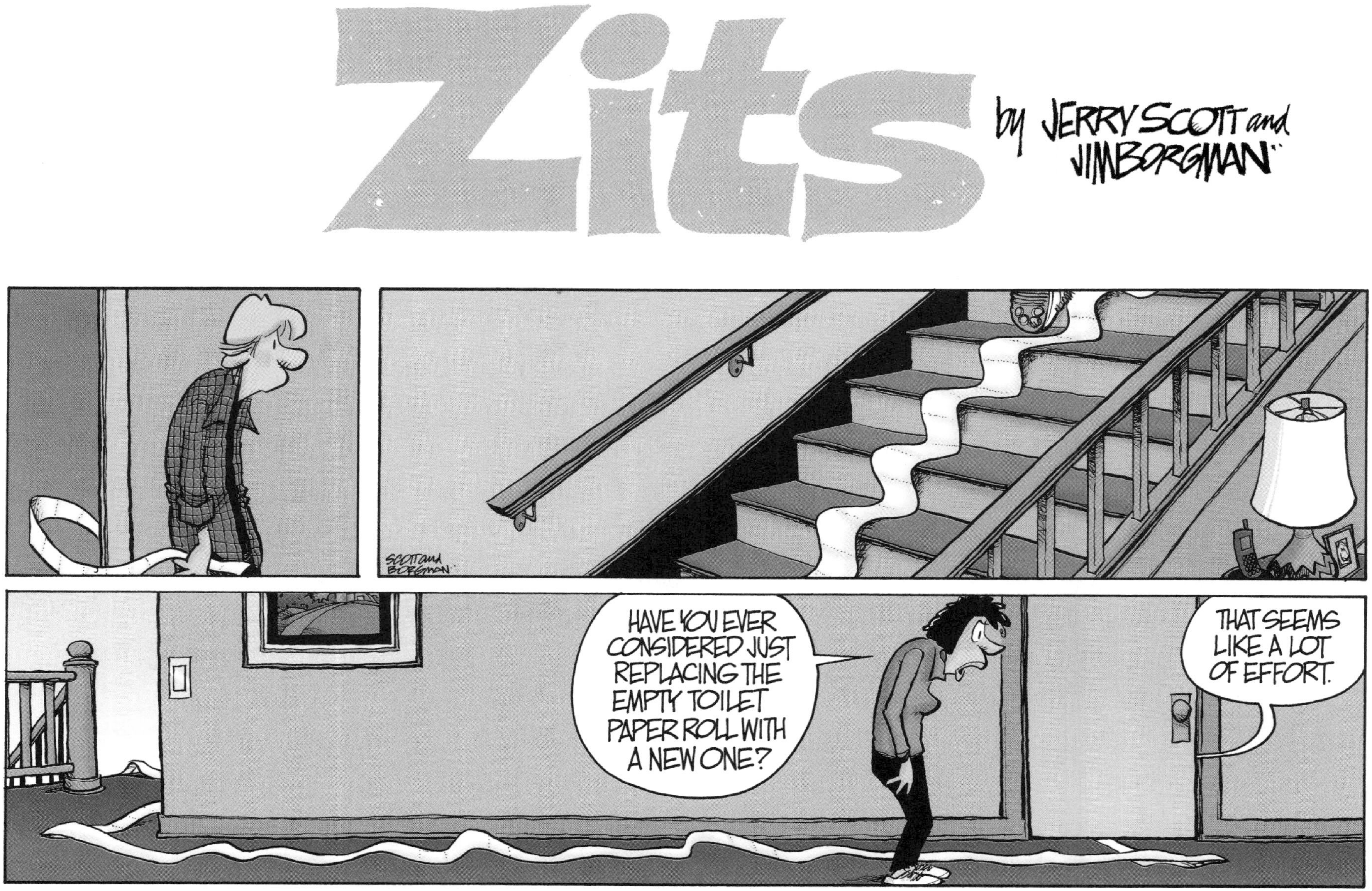
Zits
by JERRY SCOTT and JIM BORGMAN
SCOTT and BORGMAN
HAVE YOU EVER CONSIDERED JUST REPLACING THE EMPTY TOILET PAPER ROLL WITH A NEW ONE?
THAT SEEMS LIKE A LOT OF EFFORT.

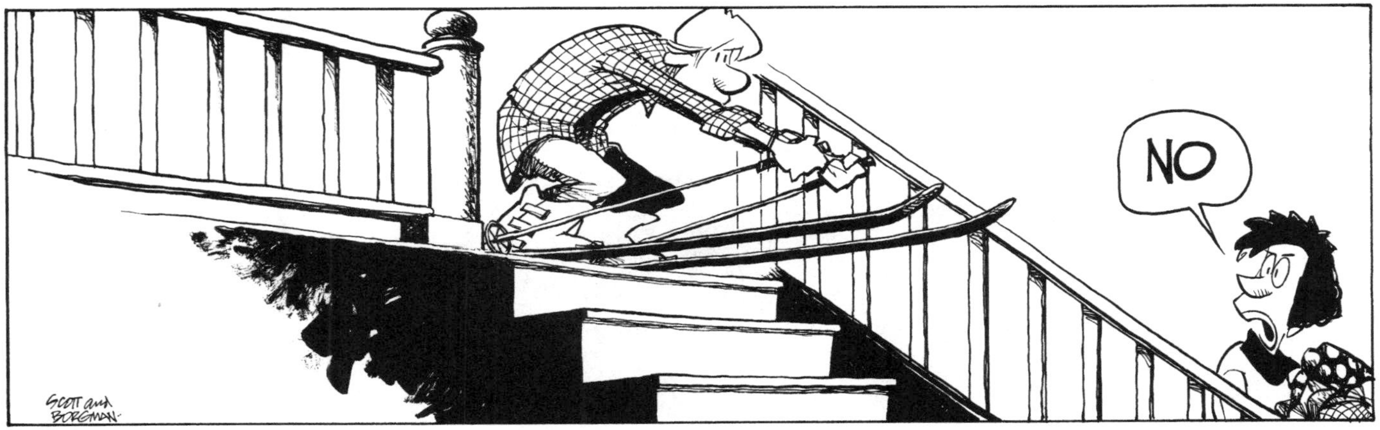
NO
SCOTT and BORGMAN

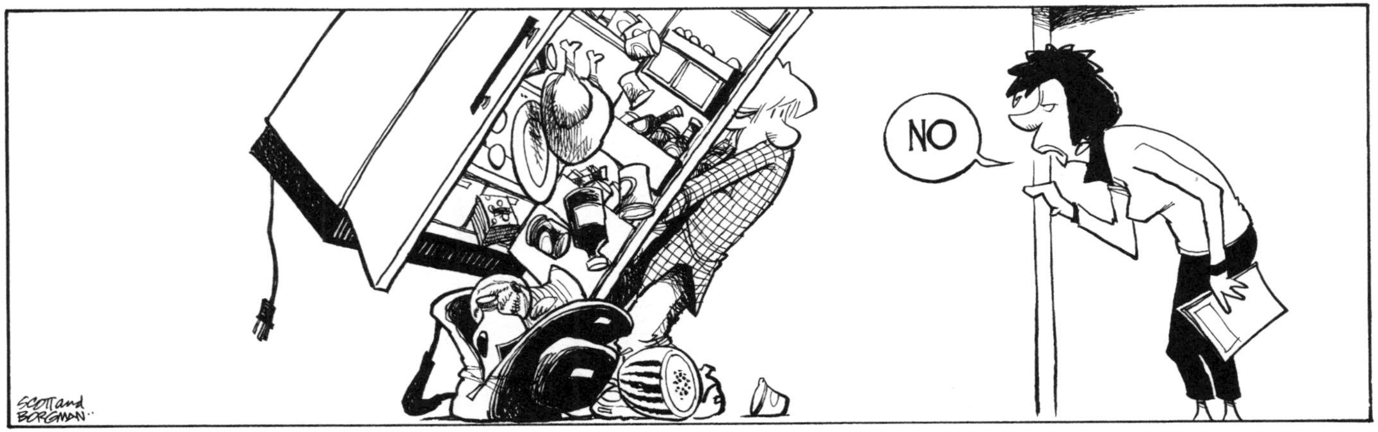
NO
SCOTT and BORGMAN

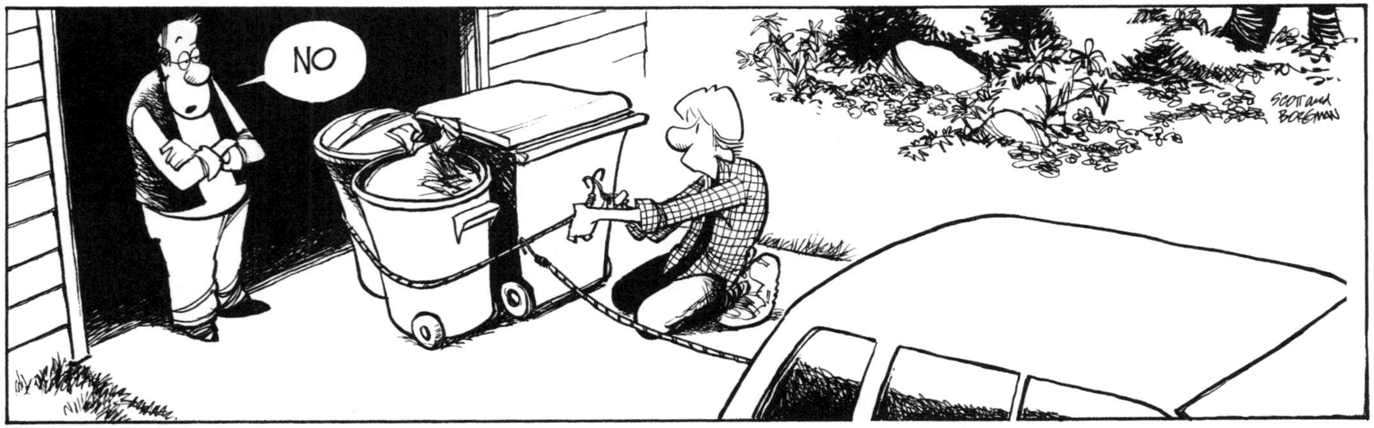
NO
SCOTT and BORGMAN

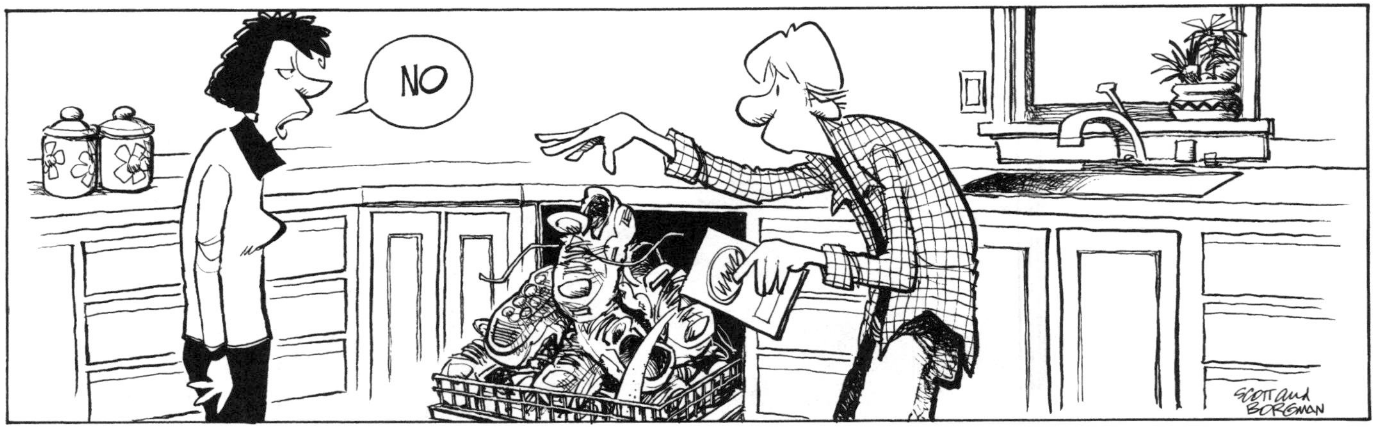
NO
SCOTT and BORGMAN

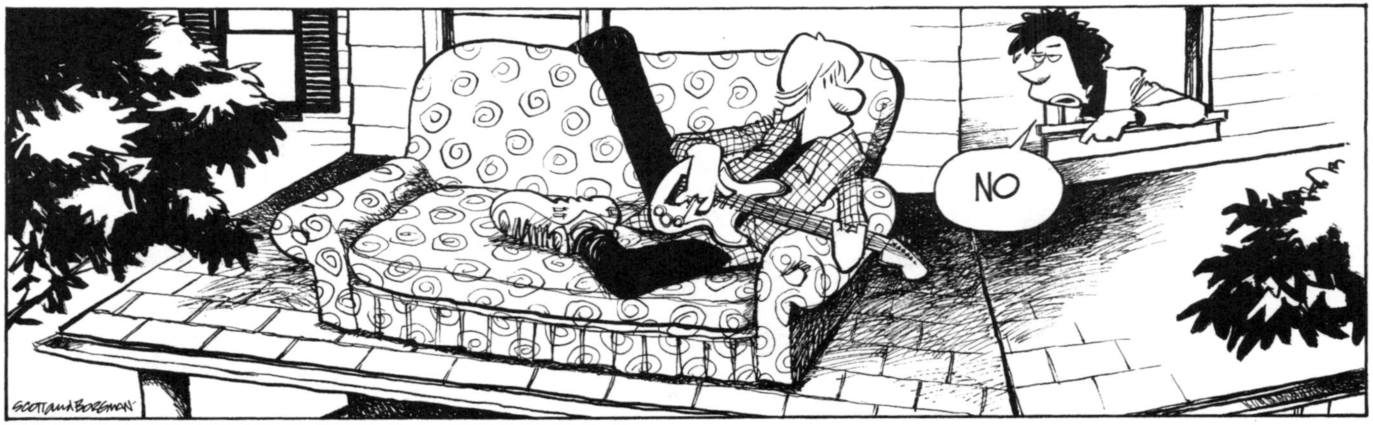
NO
SCOTT and BORGMAN

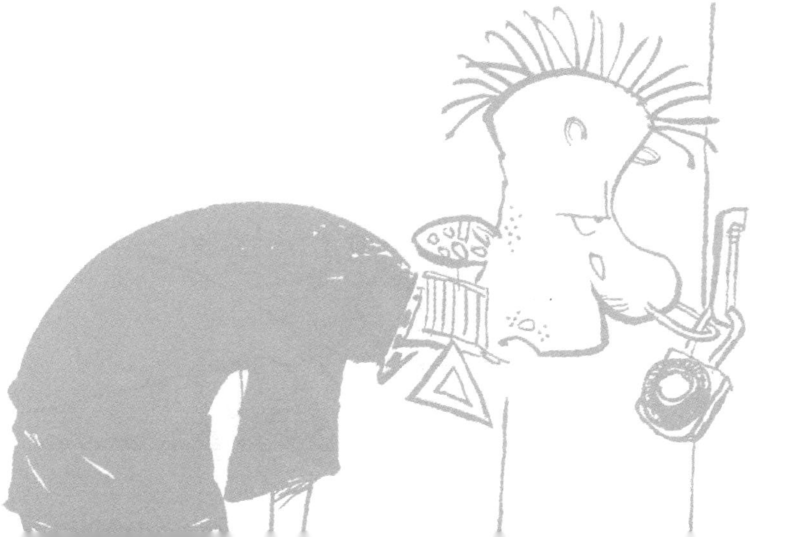

SCOTT and BORGMAN
NO

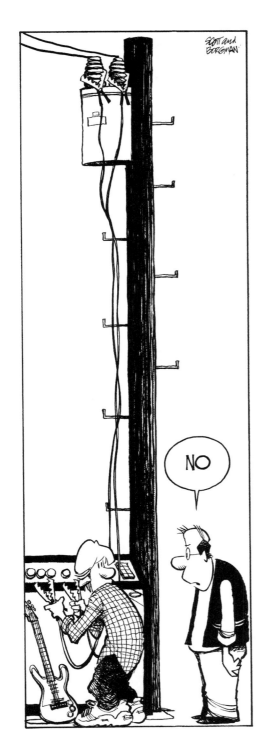

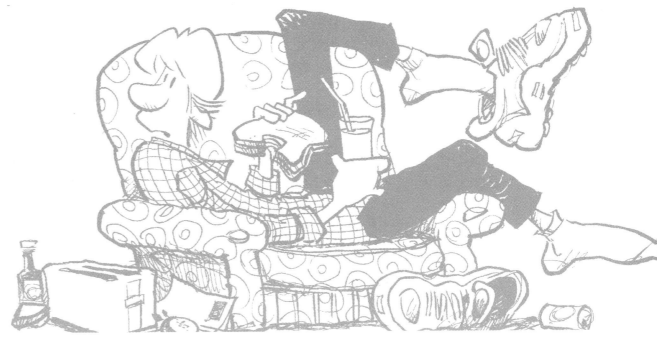

TWANG!

DANG!

WHAT'S WRONG?

I BROKE ANOTHER G STRING.

SCOTT and BORGMAN

PLEASE LET US BE TALKING ABOUT GUITARS! PLEASE LET US BE TALKING ABOUT GUITARS!

WANNA SEE?

TAP! TAP! TAP! TAP! TAP! TAP! TAP! TAP! TAP! TAP! TAP! TAP! TAP! TAP!

SCOTT and BORGMAN

SARA: HI

JEREMY: HI

GLAD TO SEE YOU GUYS ARE STILL TALKING.

NEVER CLOSER.

JEREMY, WHY CAN'T YOU PUT THESE IN THE DISHWASHER INSTEAD OF THE SINK?

PHYSIOLOGY.

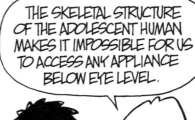

THE SKELETAL STRUCTURE OF THE ADOLESCENT HUMAN MAKES IT IMPOSSIBLE FOR US TO ACCESS ANY APPLIANCE BELOW EYE LEVEL.

SHE ASKS BUT SHE DOESN'T LISTEN.

MAYBE SHE WASN'T ASKING.

SCOTT and BORGMAN

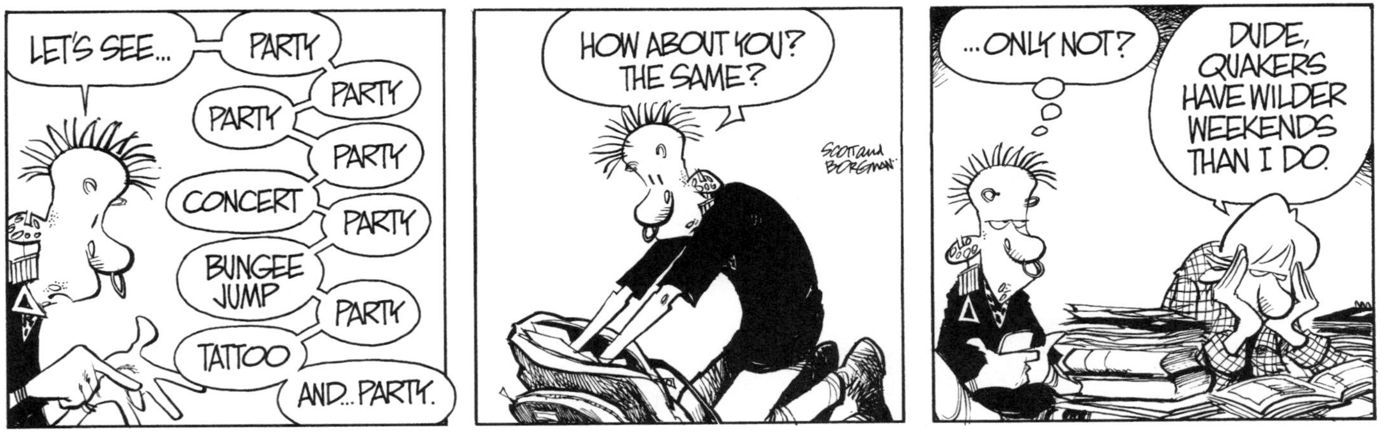
LET'S SEE...
PARTY
PARTY
PARTY
PARTY
CONCERT
PARTY
BUNGEE JUMP
PARTY
TATTOO
AND... PARTY.
HOW ABOUT YOU? THE SAME?
...ONLY NOT?
DUDE, QUAKERS HAVE WILDER WEEKENDS THAN I DO.

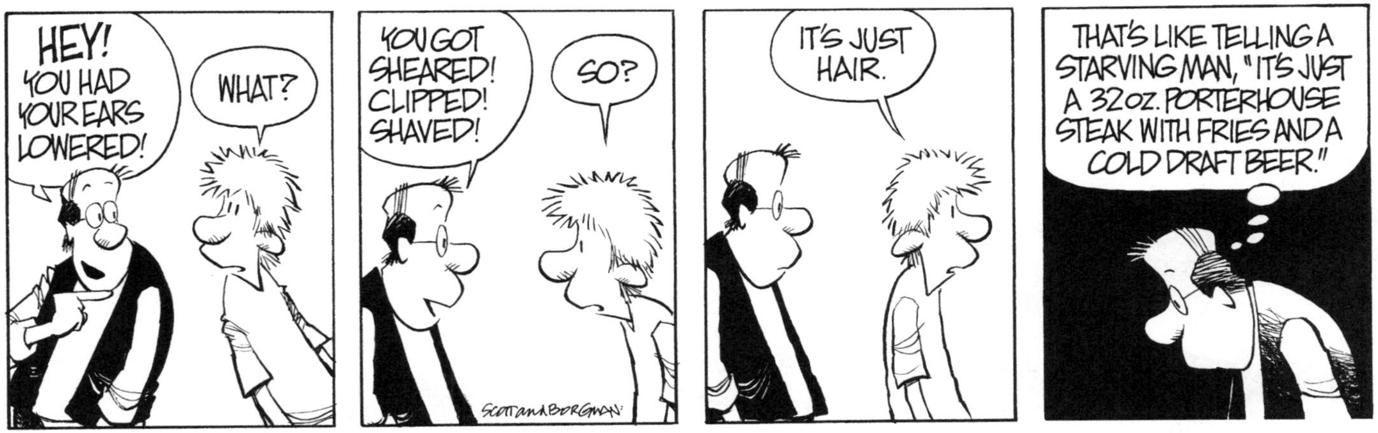
HEY! YOU HAD YOUR EARS LOWERED!
WHAT?
YOU GOT SHEARED! CLIPPED! SHAVED!
SO?
IT'S JUST HAIR.
THAT'S LIKE TELLING A STARVING MAN, "IT'S JUST A 32 oz. PORTERHOUSE STEAK WITH FRIES AND A COLD DRAFT BEER."

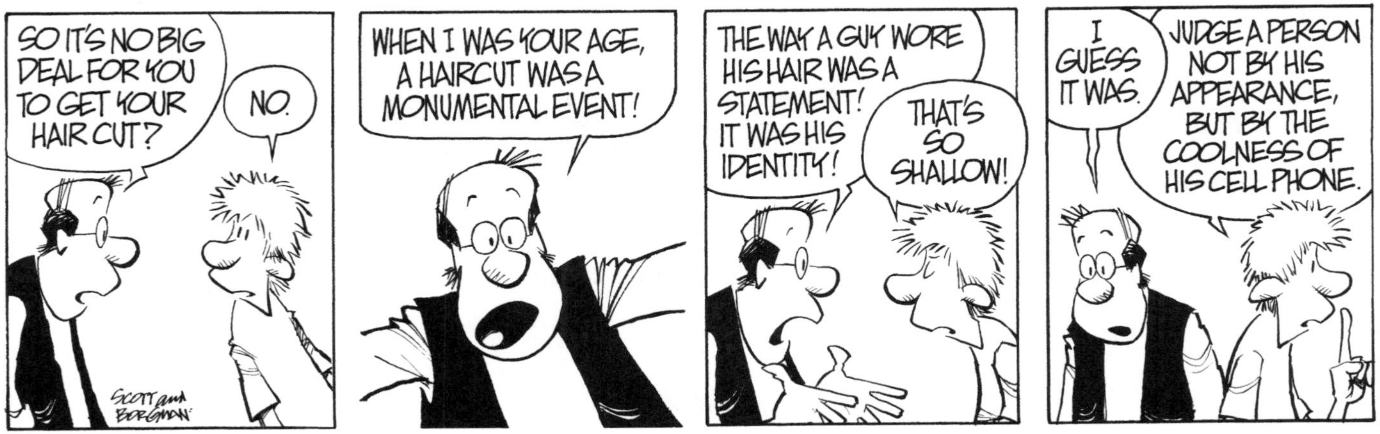
SO IT'S NO BIG DEAL FOR YOU TO GET YOUR HAIR CUT?
NO.
WHEN I WAS YOUR AGE, A HAIRCUT WAS A MONUMENTAL EVENT!
THE WAY A GUY WORE HIS HAIR WAS A STATEMENT! IT WAS HIS IDENTITY!
THAT'S SO SHALLOW!
I GUESS IT WAS.
JUDGE A PERSON NOT BY HIS APPEARANCE, BUT BY THE COOLNESS OF HIS CELL PHONE.

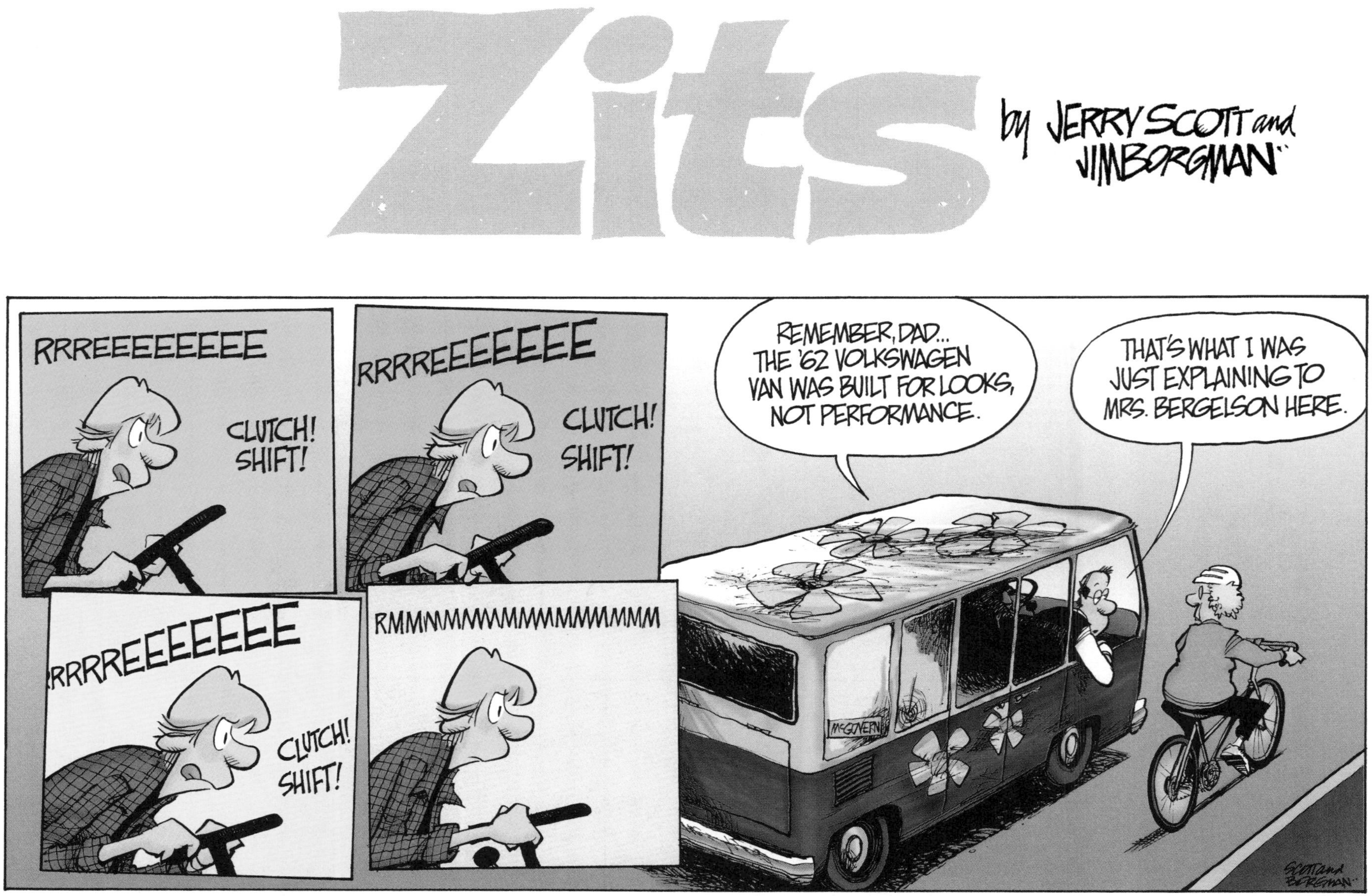
Zits
by JERRY SCOTT and JIM BORGMAN
RRREEEEEEEEE
CLUTCH! SHIFT!
RRRREEEEEEEE
CLUTCH! SHIFT!
RRRREEEEEEEE
CLUTCH! SHIFT!
RMMMMMMMMMMMMMMMM
REMEMBER, DAD... THE '62 VOLKSWAGEN VAN WAS BUILT FOR LOOKS, NOT PERFORMANCE.
THAT'S WHAT I WAS JUST EXPLAINING TO MRS. BERGELSON HERE.
McGOVERN
SCOTT and BORGMAN

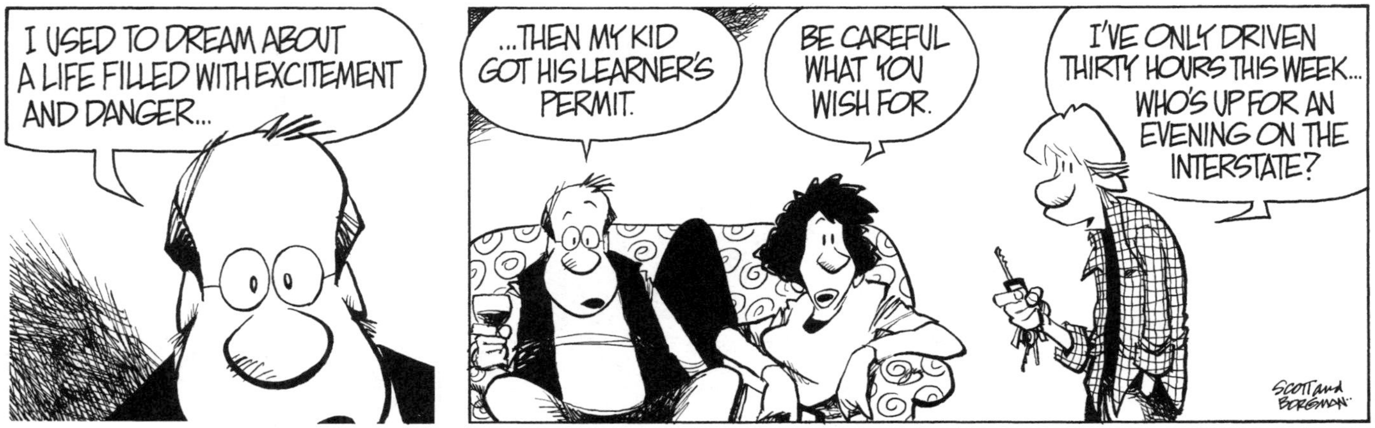
I USED TO DREAM ABOUT A LIFE FILLED WITH EXCITEMENT AND DANGER...
...THEN MY KID GOT HIS LEARNER'S PERMIT.
BE CAREFUL WHAT YOU WISH FOR.
I'VE ONLY DRIVEN THIRTY HOURS THIS WEEK... WHO'S UP FOR AN EVENING ON THE INTERSTATE?
SCOTT and BORGMAN

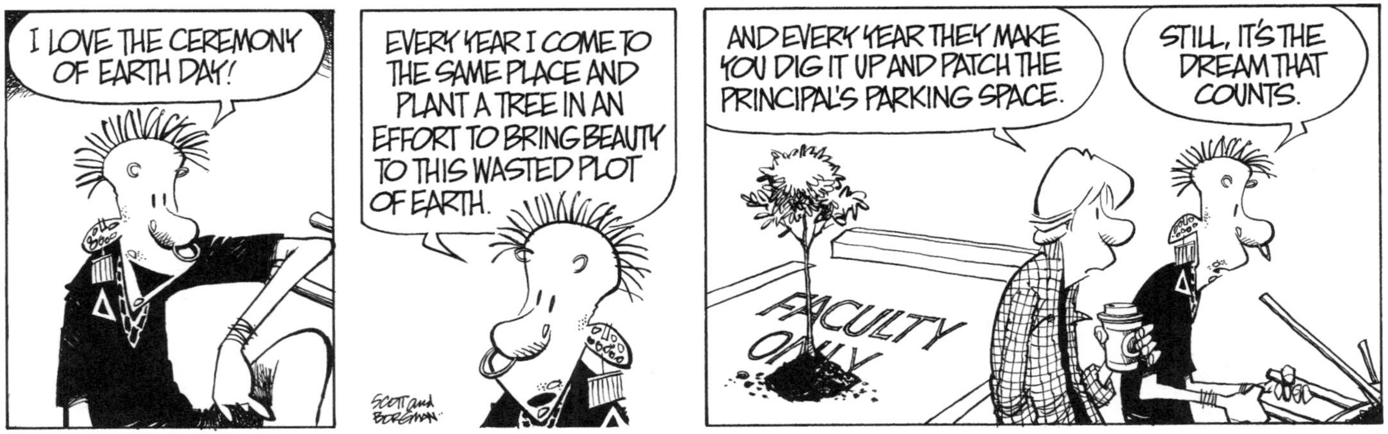
I LOVE THE CEREMONY OF EARTH DAY!
EVERY YEAR I COME TO THE SAME PLACE AND PLANT A TREE IN AN EFFORT TO BRING BEAUTY TO THIS WASTED PLOT OF EARTH.
SCOTT and BORGMAN
AND EVERY YEAR THEY MAKE YOU DIG IT UP AND PATCH THE PRINCIPAL'S PARKING SPACE.
STILL, IT'S THE DREAM THAT COUNTS.
FACULTY ONLY

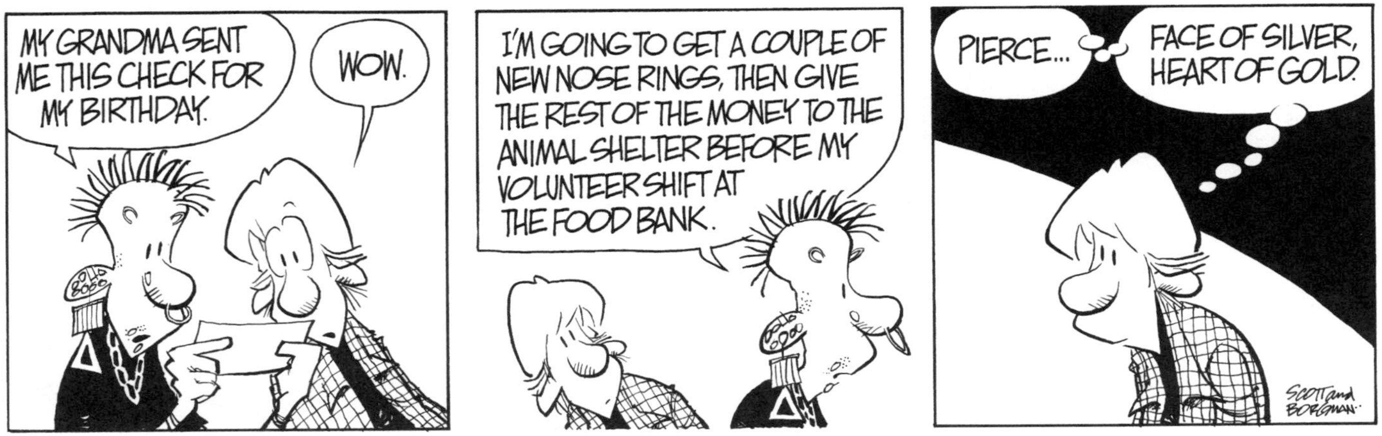
MY GRANDMA SENT ME THIS CHECK FOR MY BIRTHDAY.
WOW.
I'M GOING TO GET A COUPLE OF NEW NOSE RINGS, THEN GIVE THE REST OF THE MONEY TO THE ANIMAL SHELTER BEFORE MY VOLUNTEER SHIFT AT THE FOOD BANK.
PIERCE...
FACE OF SILVER, HEART OF GOLD.
SCOTT and BORGMAN

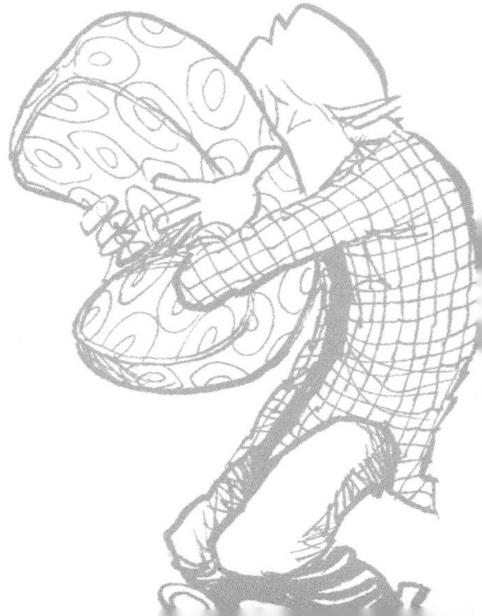

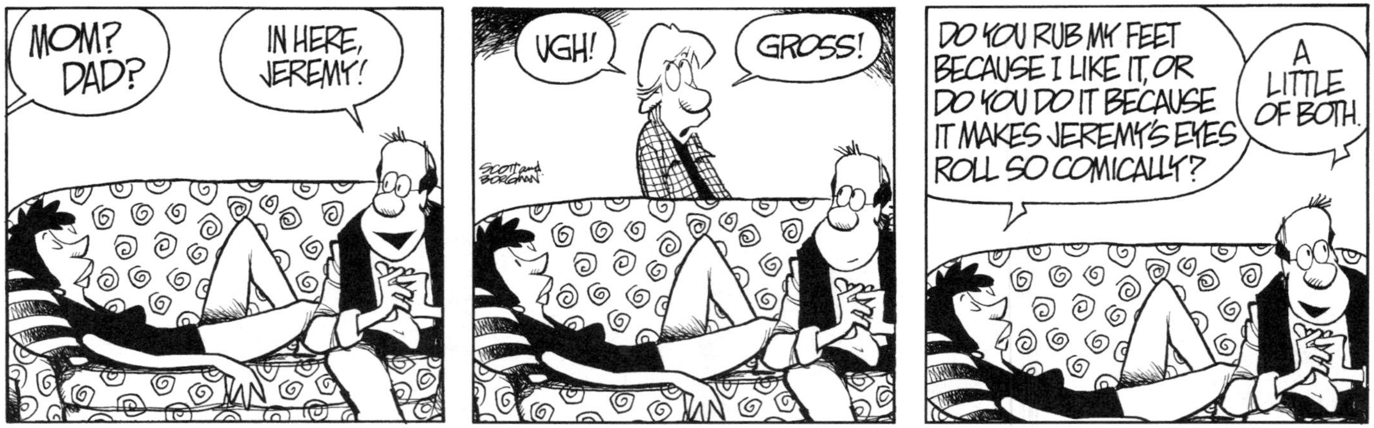
MOM? DAD?
IN HERE, JEREMY!
SCOTT and BORGMAN
UGH!
GROSS!
DO YOU RUB MY FEET BECAUSE I LIKE IT, OR DO YOU DO IT BECAUSE IT MAKES JEREMY'S EYES ROLL SO COMICALLY?
A LITTLE OF BOTH.

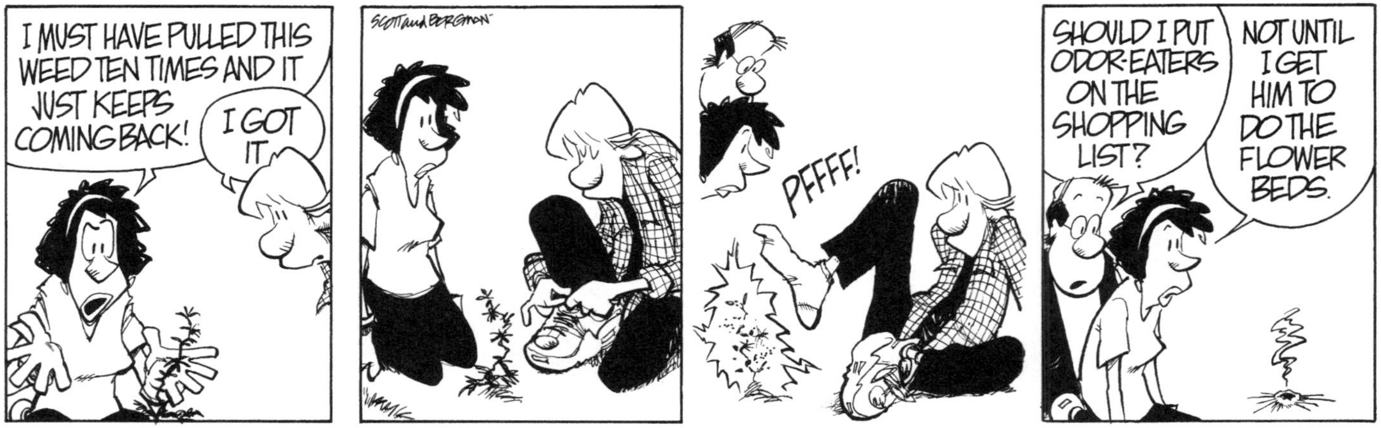
I MUST HAVE PULLED THIS WEED TEN TIMES AND IT JUST KEEPS COMING BACK!
I GOT IT.
SCOTT and BORGMAN
PFFFF!
SHOULD I PUT ODOR-EATERS ON THE SHOPPING LIST?
NOT UNTIL I GET HIM TO DO THE FLOWER BEDS.

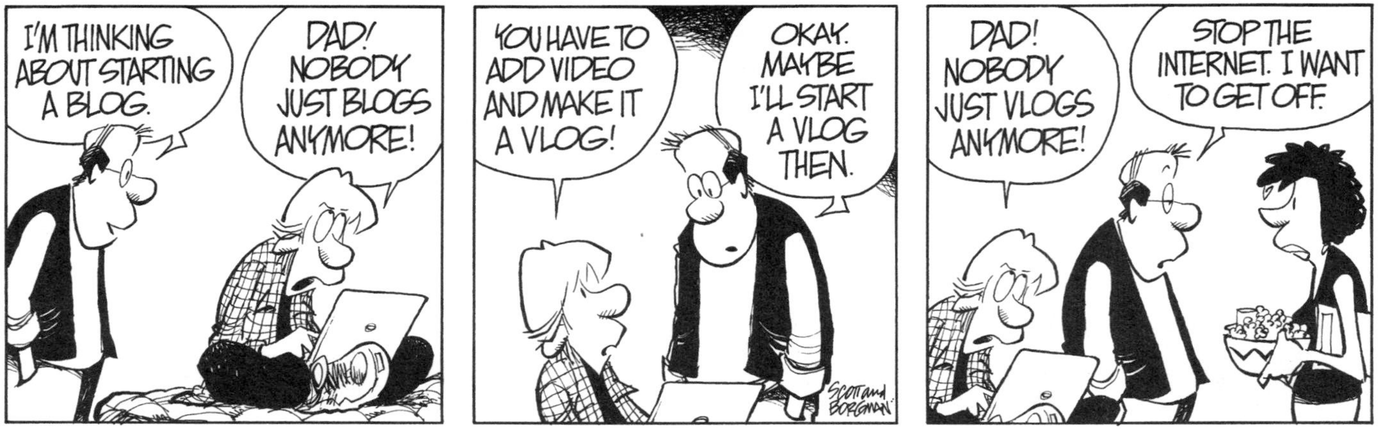
I'M THINKING ABOUT STARTING A BLOG.
DAD! NOBODY JUST BLOGS ANYMORE!
YOU HAVE TO ADD VIDEO AND MAKE IT A VLOG!
OKAY. MAYBE I'LL START A VLOG THEN.
SCOTT and BORGMAN
DAD! NOBODY JUST VLOGS ANYMORE!
STOP THE INTERNET. I WANT TO GET OFF.

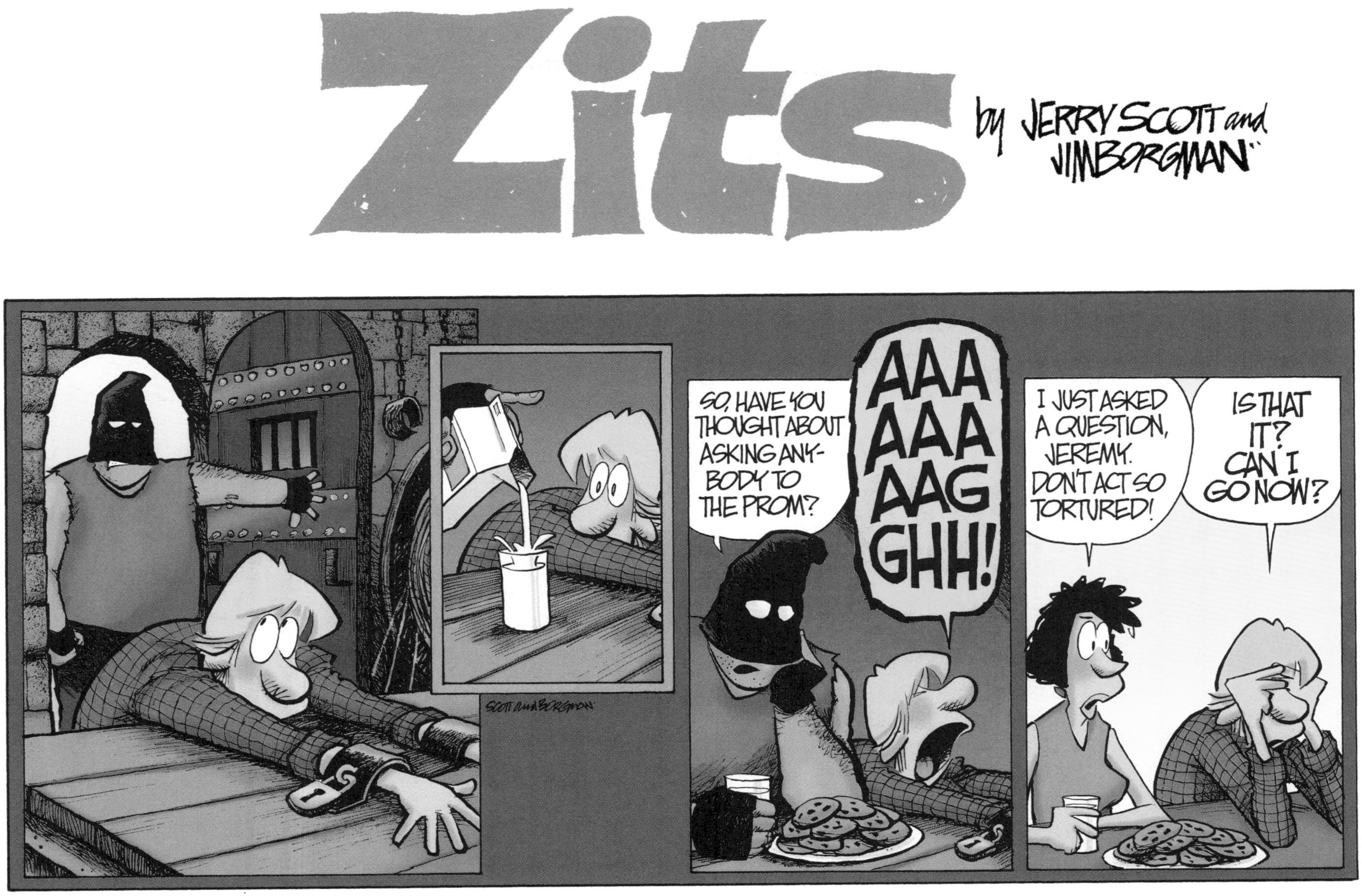
Zits
by JERRY SCOTT and JIM BORGMAN
SO, HAVE YOU THOUGHT ABOUT ASKING ANY-BODY TO THE PROM?
AAAAAAAAGGHH!
I JUST ASKED A QUESTION, JEREMY. DON'T ACT SO TORTURED!
IS THAT IT? CAN I GO NOW?

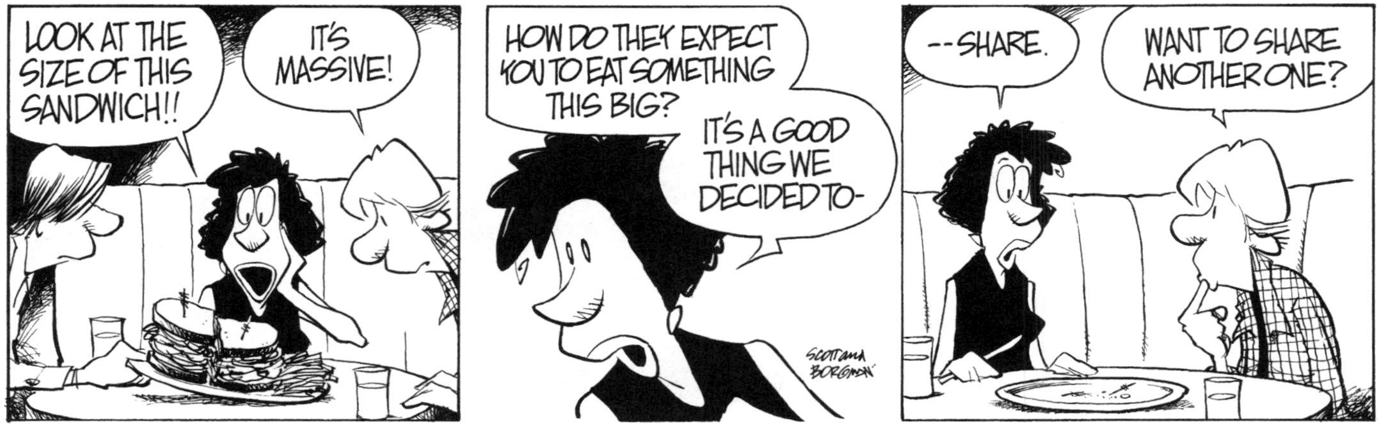
LOOK AT THE SIZE OF THIS SANDWICH!!
IT'S MASSIVE!
HOW DO THEY EXPECT YOU TO EAT SOMETHING THIS BIG?
IT'S A GOOD THING WE DECIDED TO-
--SHARE.
WANT TO SHARE ANOTHER ONE?
SCOTT AND BORGMAN

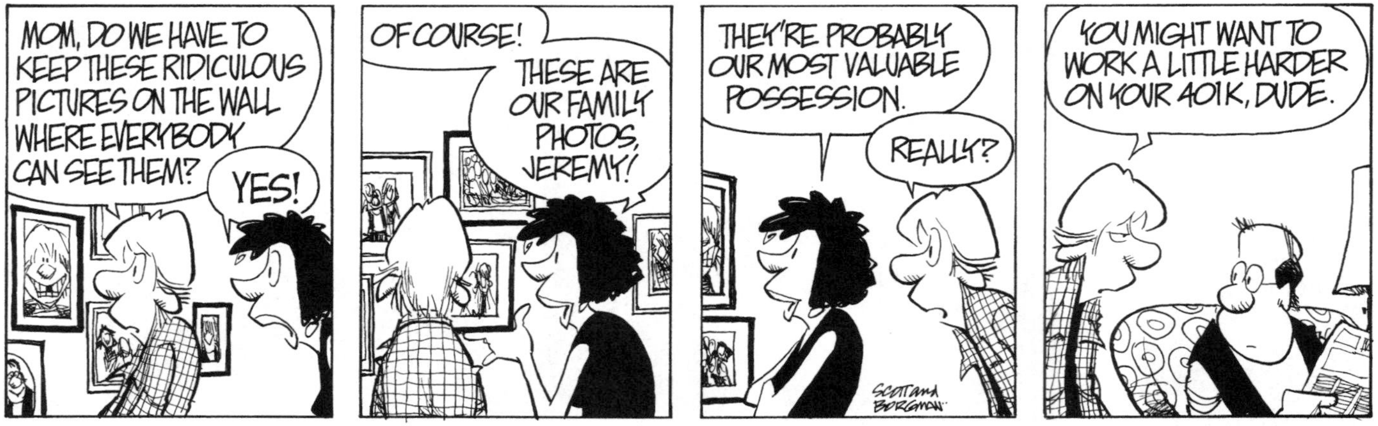
MOM, DO WE HAVE TO KEEP THESE RIDICULOUS PICTURES ON THE WALL WHERE EVERYBODY CAN SEE THEM?
YES!
OF COURSE!
THESE ARE OUR FAMILY PHOTOS, JEREMY!
THEY'RE PROBABLY OUR MOST VALUABLE POSSESSION.
REALLY?
SCOTT AND BORGMAN
YOU MIGHT WANT TO WORK A LITTLE HARDER ON YOUR 401K, DUDE.

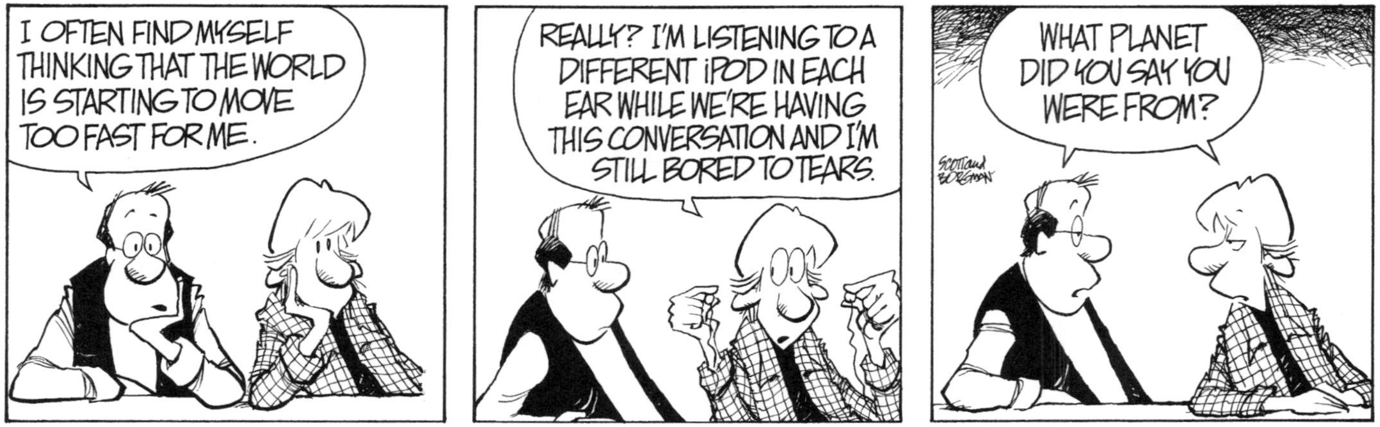
I OFTEN FIND MYSELF THINKING THAT THE WORLD IS STARTING TO MOVE TOO FAST FOR ME.
REALLY? I'M LISTENING TO A DIFFERENT iPOD IN EACH EAR WHILE WE'RE HAVING THIS CONVERSATION AND I'M STILL BORED TO TEARS.
WHAT PLANET DID YOU SAY YOU WERE FROM?
SCOTT AND BORGMAN

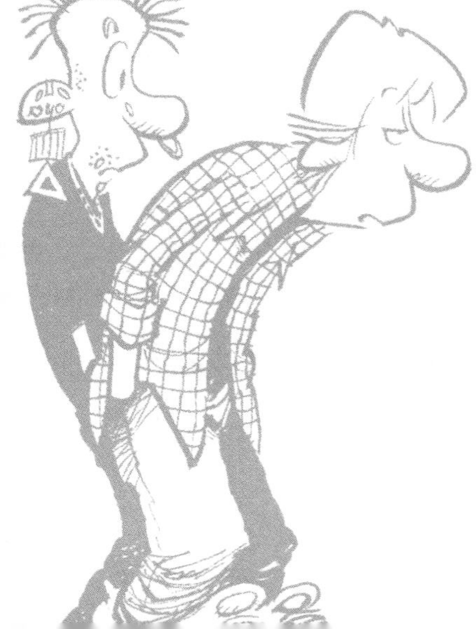

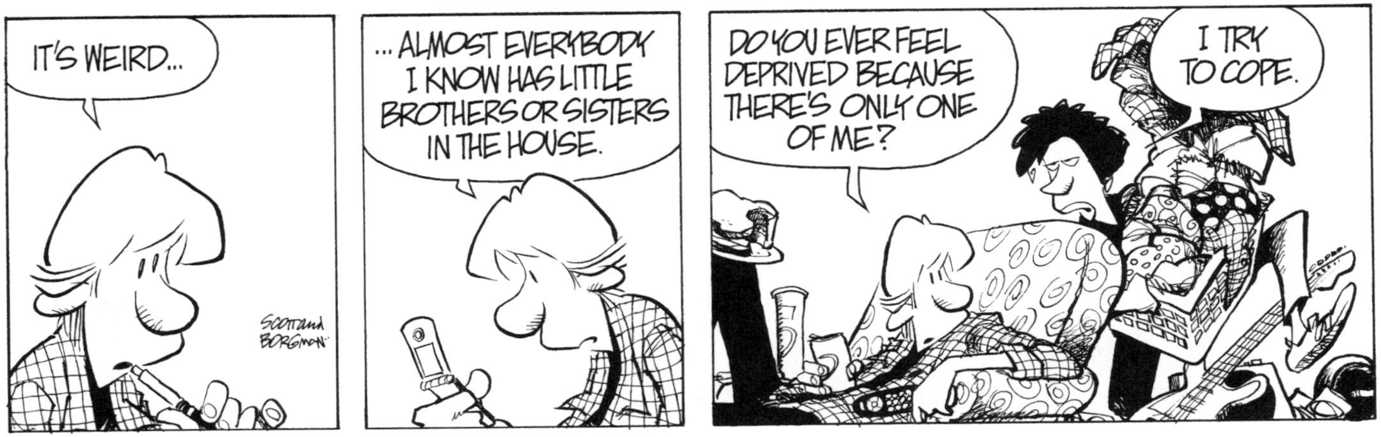
IT'S WEIRD...
... ALMOST EVERYBODY I KNOW HAS LITTLE BROTHERS OR SISTERS IN THE HOUSE.
DO YOU EVER FEEL DEPRIVED BECAUSE THERE'S ONLY ONE OF ME?
I TRY TO COPE.

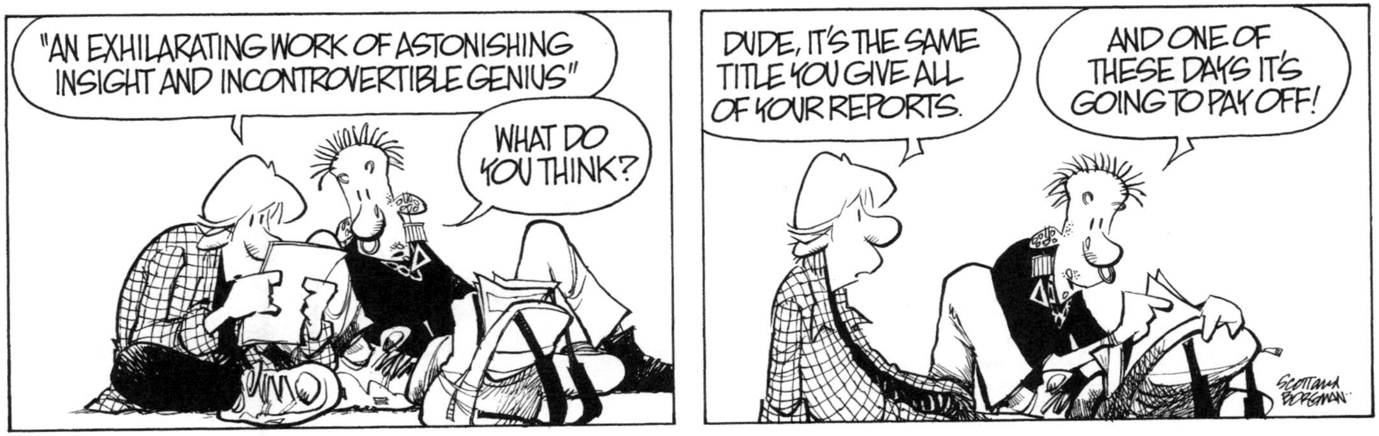
"AN EXHILARATING WORK OF ASTONISHING INSIGHT AND INCONTROVERTIBLE GENIUS"
WHAT DO YOU THINK?
DUDE, IT'S THE SAME TITLE YOU GIVE ALL OF YOUR REPORTS.
AND ONE OF THESE DAYS IT'S GOING TO PAY OFF!

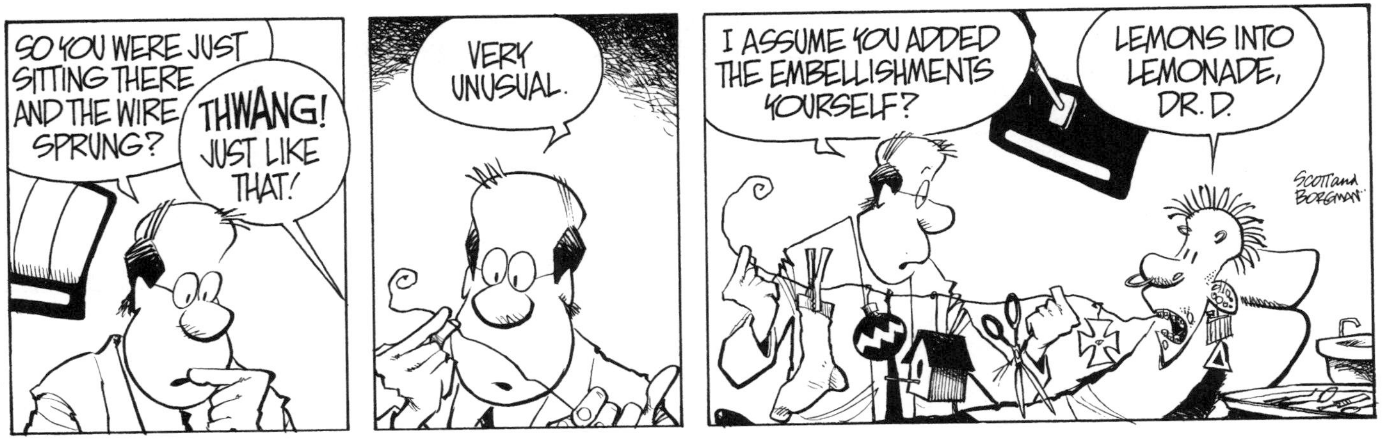
SO YOU WERE JUST SITTING THERE AND THE WIRE SPRUNG?
THWANG! JUST LIKE THAT!
VERY UNUSUAL.
I ASSUME YOU ADDED THE EMBELLISHMENTS YOURSELF?
LEMONS INTO LEMONADE, DR. D.

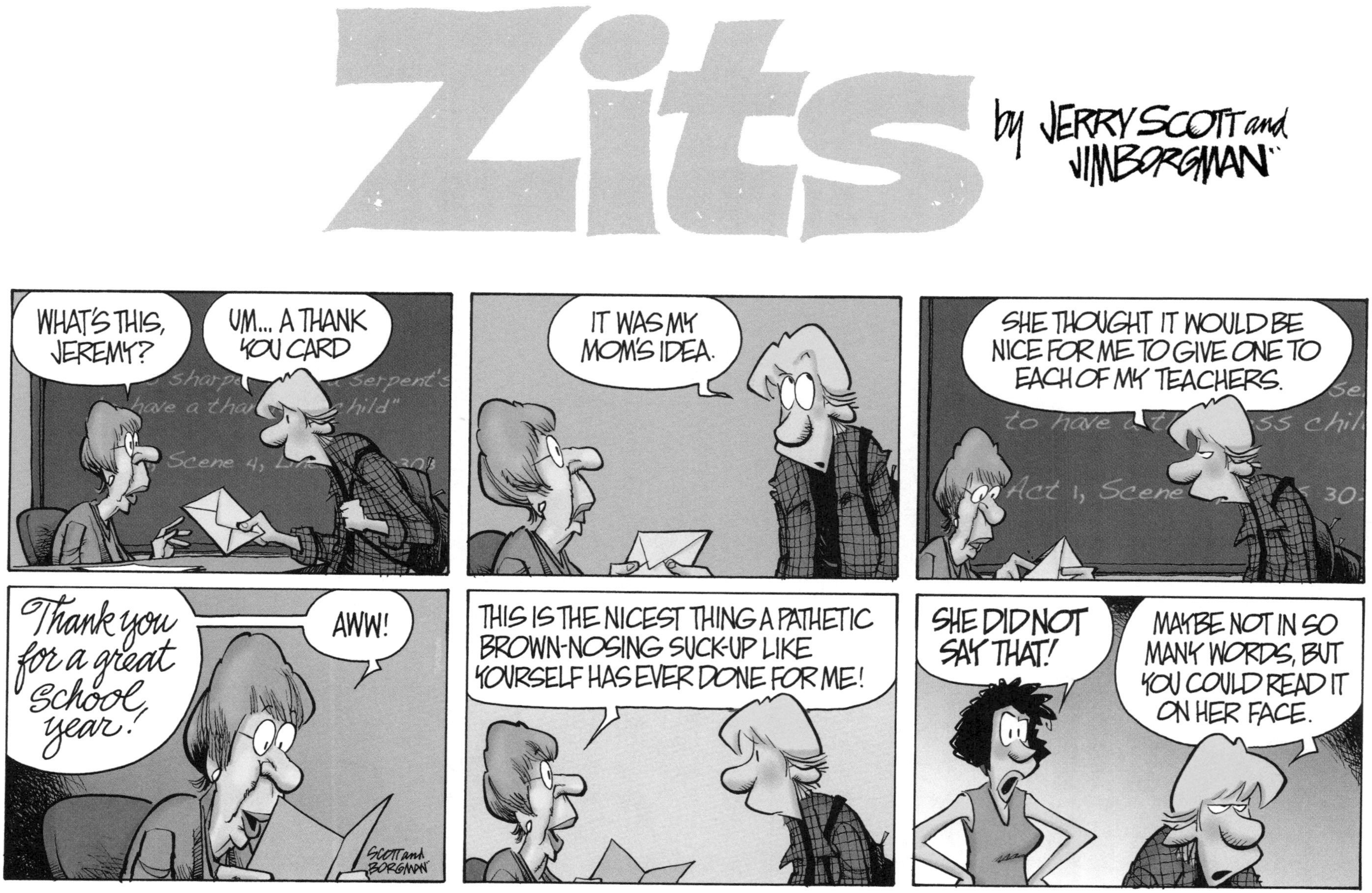
Zits
by JERRY SCOTT and JIM BORGMAN
WHAT'S THIS, JEREMY?
UM... A THANK YOU CARD
IT WAS MY MOM'S IDEA.
SHE THOUGHT IT WOULD BE NICE FOR ME TO GIVE ONE TO EACH OF MY TEACHERS.
Thank you for a great school year!
AWW!
THIS IS THE NICEST THING A PATHETIC BROWN-NOSING SUCK-UP LIKE YOURSELF HAS EVER DONE FOR ME!
SHE DID NOT SAY THAT!
MAYBE NOT IN SO MANY WORDS, BUT YOU COULD READ IT ON HER FACE.
SCOTT and BORGMAN

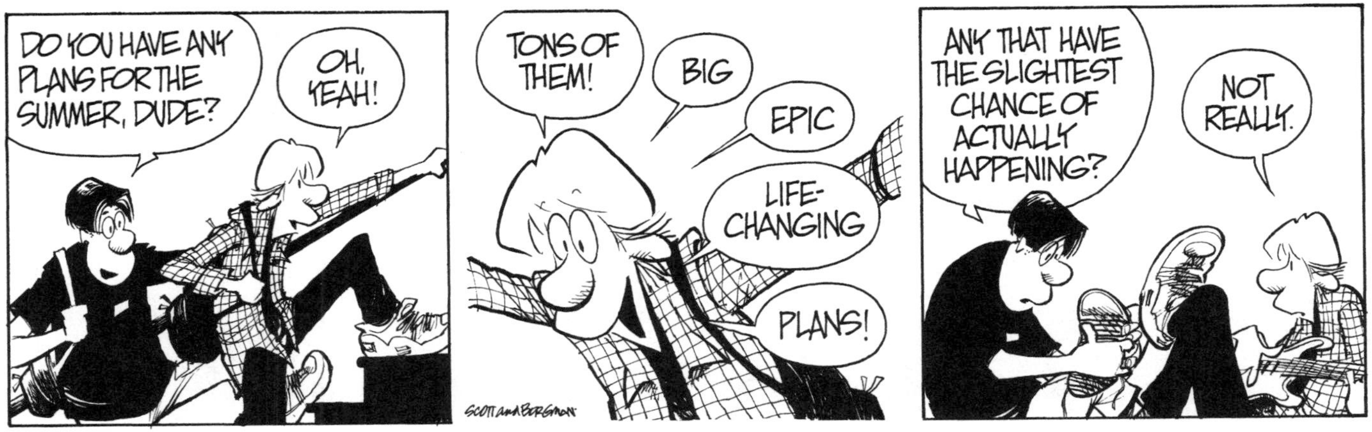
DO YOU HAVE ANY PLANS FOR THE SUMMER, DUDE?
OH, YEAH!
TONS OF THEM!
BIG
EPIC
LIFE-CHANGING
PLANS!
ANY THAT HAVE THE SLIGHTEST CHANCE OF ACTUALLY HAPPENING?
NOT REALLY.

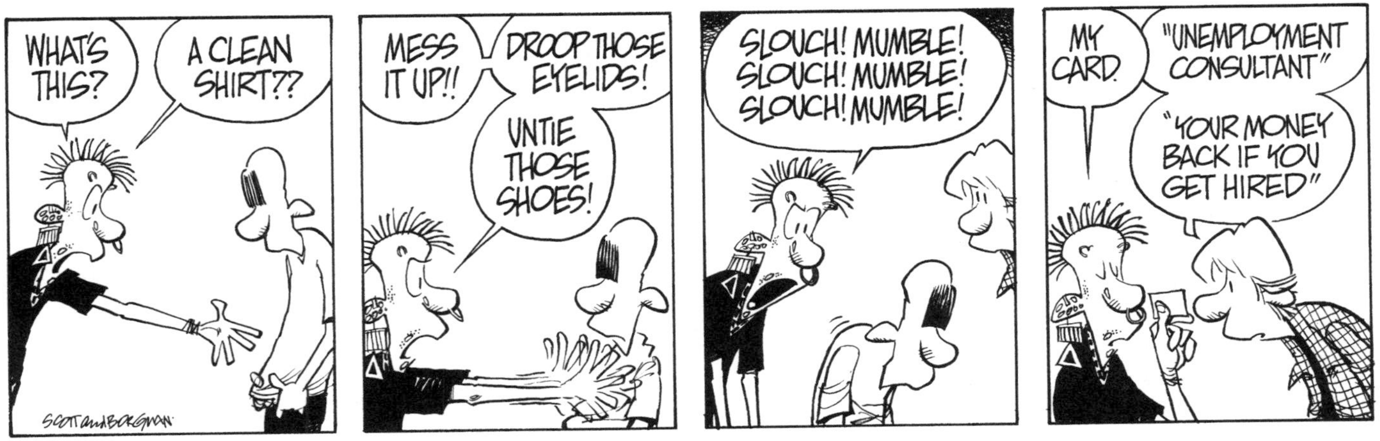
WHAT'S THIS?
A CLEAN SHIRT??
MESS IT UP!!
DROOP THOSE EYELIDS!
UNTIE THOSE SHOES!
SLOUCH! MUMBLE! SLOUCH! MUMBLE! SLOUCH! MUMBLE!
MY CARD.
"UNEMPLOYMENT CONSULTANT"
"YOUR MONEY BACK IF YOU GET HIRED"

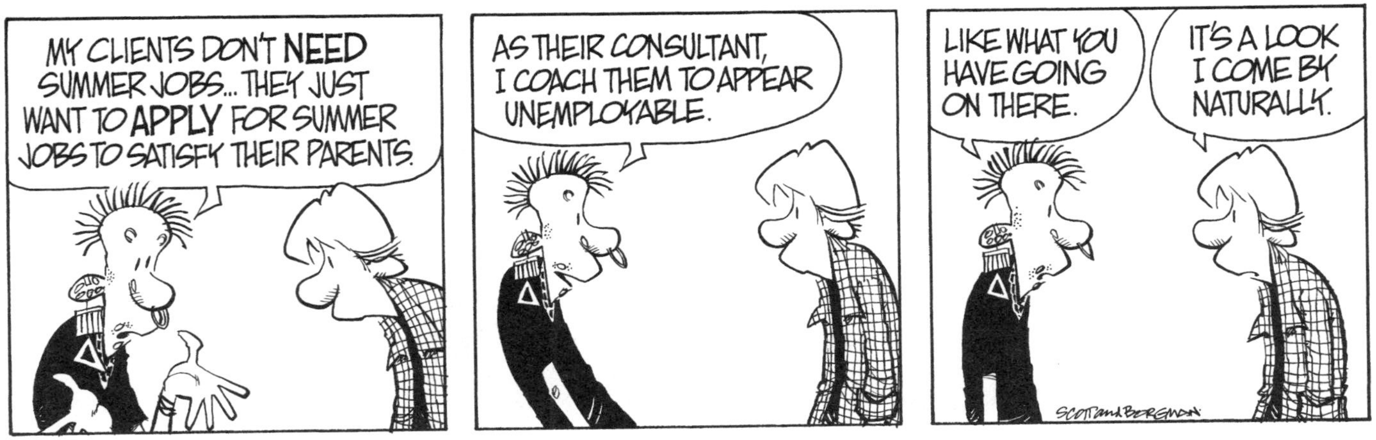
MY CLIENTS DON'T NEED SUMMER JOBS... THEY JUST WANT TO APPLY FOR SUMMER JOBS TO SATISFY THEIR PARENTS.
AS THEIR CONSULTANT, I COACH THEM TO APPEAR UNEMPLOYABLE.
LIKE WHAT YOU HAVE GOING ON THERE.
IT'S A LOOK I COME BY NATURALLY.

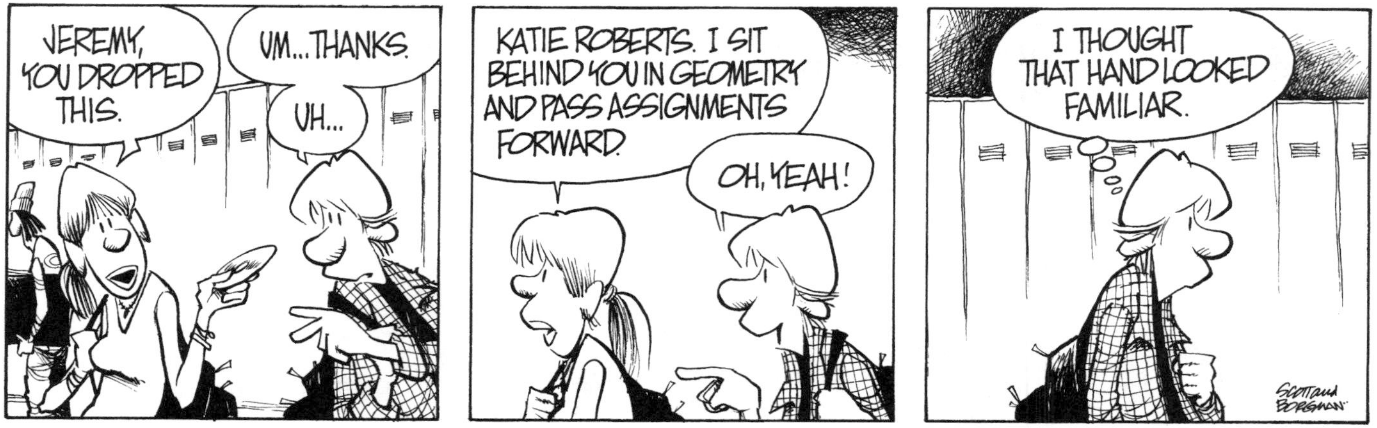
JEREMY, YOU DROPPED THIS.
UM... THANKS.
UH...
KATIE ROBERTS. I SIT BEHIND YOU IN GEOMETRY AND PASS ASSIGNMENTS FORWARD.
OH, YEAH!
I THOUGHT THAT HAND LOOKED FAMILIAR.

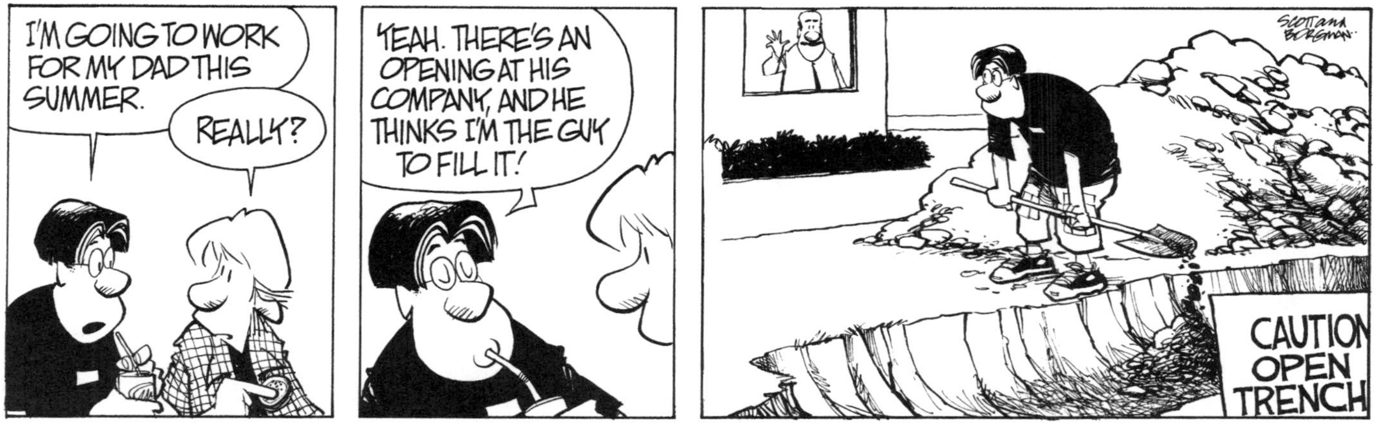
I'M GOING TO WORK FOR MY DAD THIS SUMMER.
REALLY?
YEAH. THERE'S AN OPENING AT HIS COMPANY, AND HE THINKS I'M THE GUY TO FILL IT!
CAUTION OPEN TRENCH

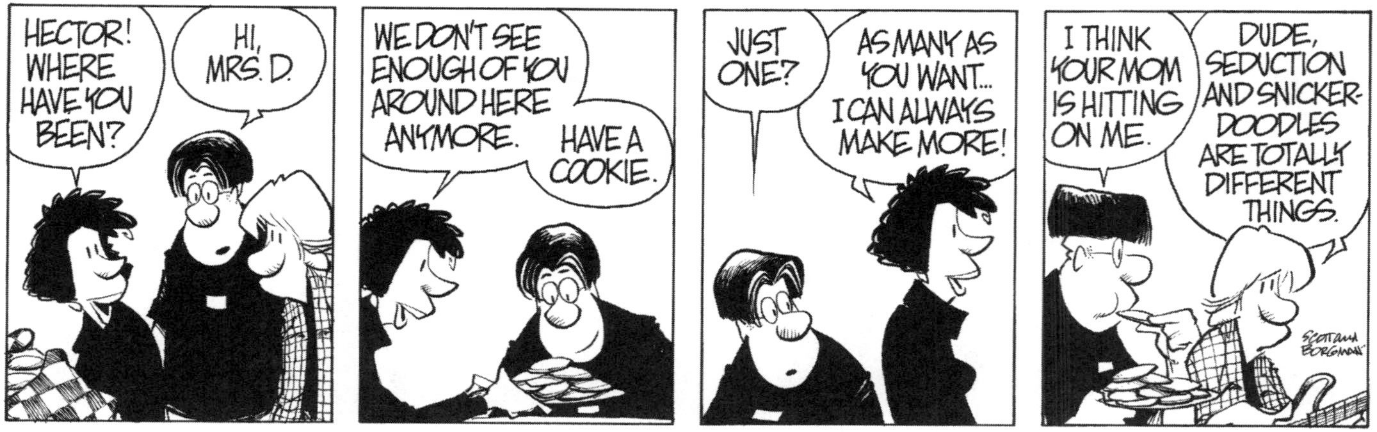
HECTOR! WHERE HAVE YOU BEEN?
HI, MRS. D.
WE DON'T SEE ENOUGH OF YOU AROUND HERE ANYMORE.
HAVE A COOKIE.
JUST ONE?
AS MANY AS YOU WANT... I CAN ALWAYS MAKE MORE!
I THINK YOUR MOM IS HITTING ON ME.
DUDE, SEDUCTION AND SNICKER-DOODLES ARE TOTALLY DIFFERENT THINGS.

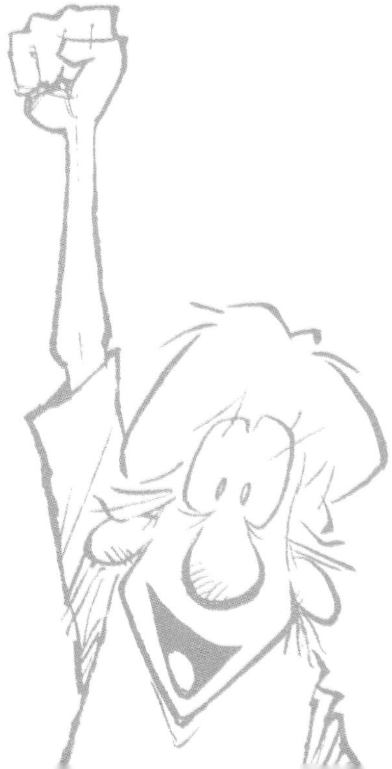

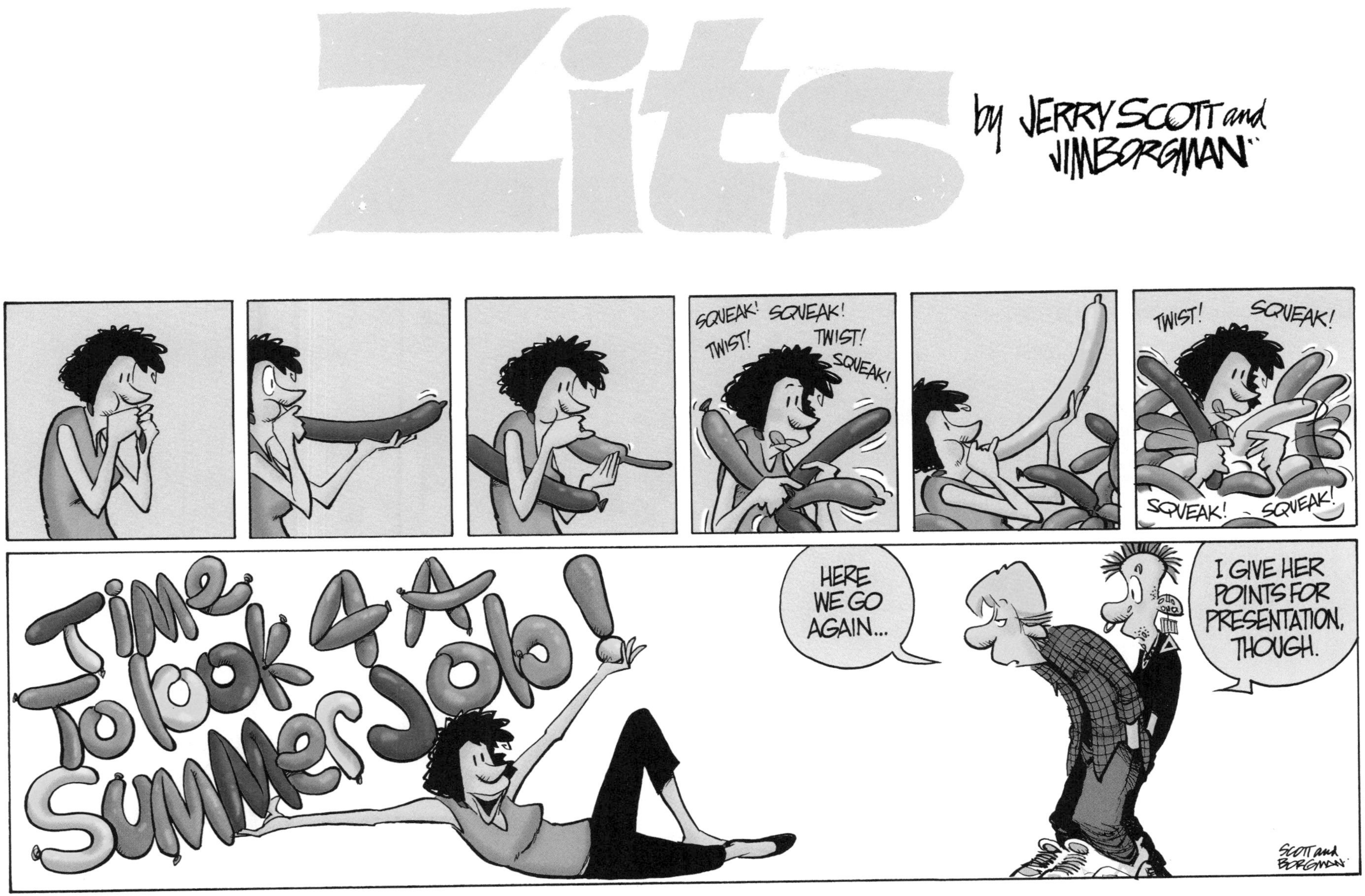
Zits
by JERRY SCOTT and JIM BORGMAN
SQUEAK! SQUEAK!
TWIST! TWIST!
SQUEAK!
TWIST! SQUEAK!
SQUEAK! SQUEAK!
Time To look 4 A Summer Job!
HERE WE GO AGAIN...
I GIVE HER POINTS FOR PRESENTATION, THOUGH.
SCOTT and BORGMAN

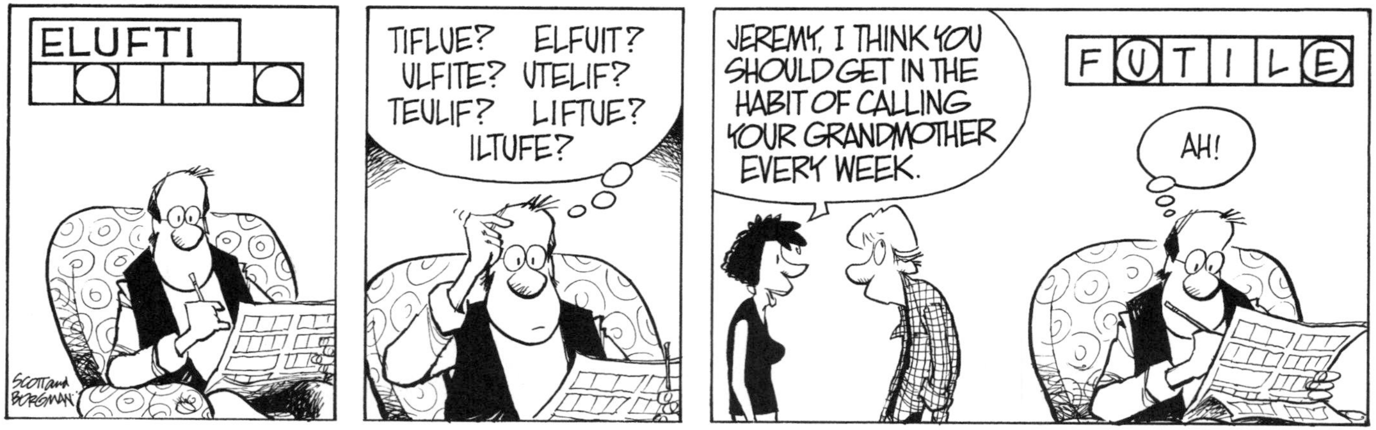
ELUFTI
TIFLUE? ELFUIT?
ULFITE? UTELIF?
TEULIF? LIFTUE?
ILTUFE?
JEREMY, I THINK YOU SHOULD GET IN THE HABIT OF CALLING YOUR GRANDMOTHER EVERY WEEK.
FUTILE
AH!

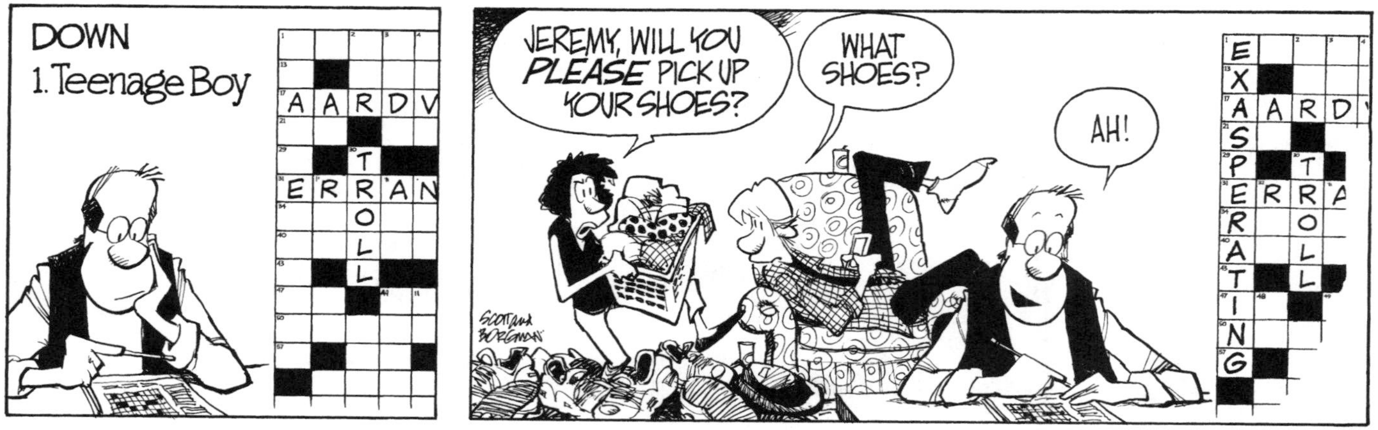
DOWN
1. Teenage Boy
AARDV
ERRAN
TROLL
JEREMY, WILL YOU *PLEASE* PICK UP YOUR SHOES?
WHAT SHOES?
AH!
EXASPERATING

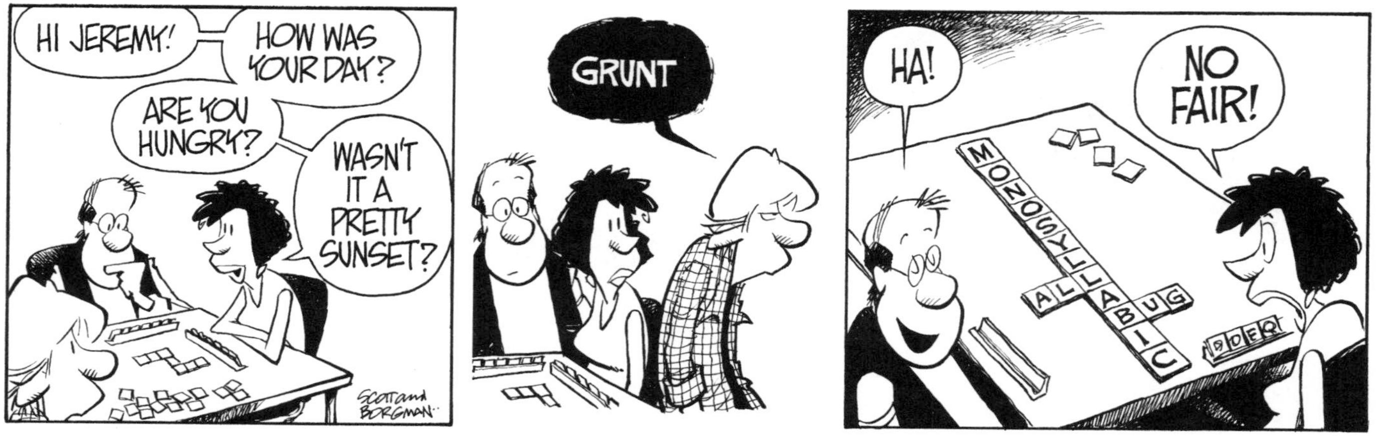
HI JEREMY!
HOW WAS YOUR DAY?
ARE YOU HUNGRY?
WASN'T IT A PRETTY SUNSET?
GRUNT
HA!
NO FAIR!
MONOSYLLABIC
ALL
BUG

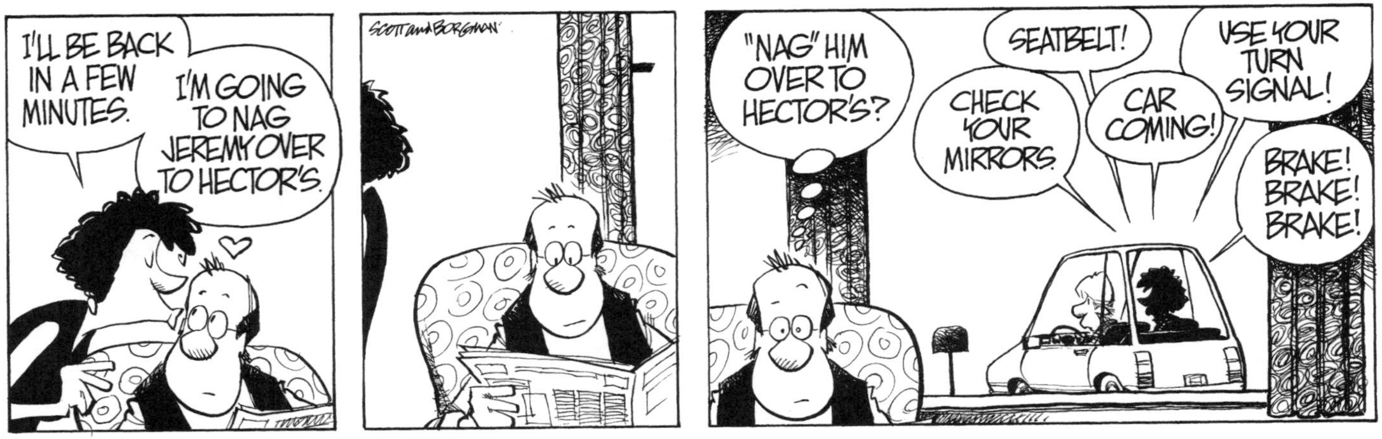
I'LL BE BACK IN A FEW MINUTES.
I'M GOING TO NAG JEREMY OVER TO HECTOR'S.
"NAG" HIM OVER TO HECTOR'S?
CHECK YOUR MIRRORS.
SEATBELT!
CAR COMING!
USE YOUR TURN SIGNAL!
BRAKE! BRAKE! BRAKE!

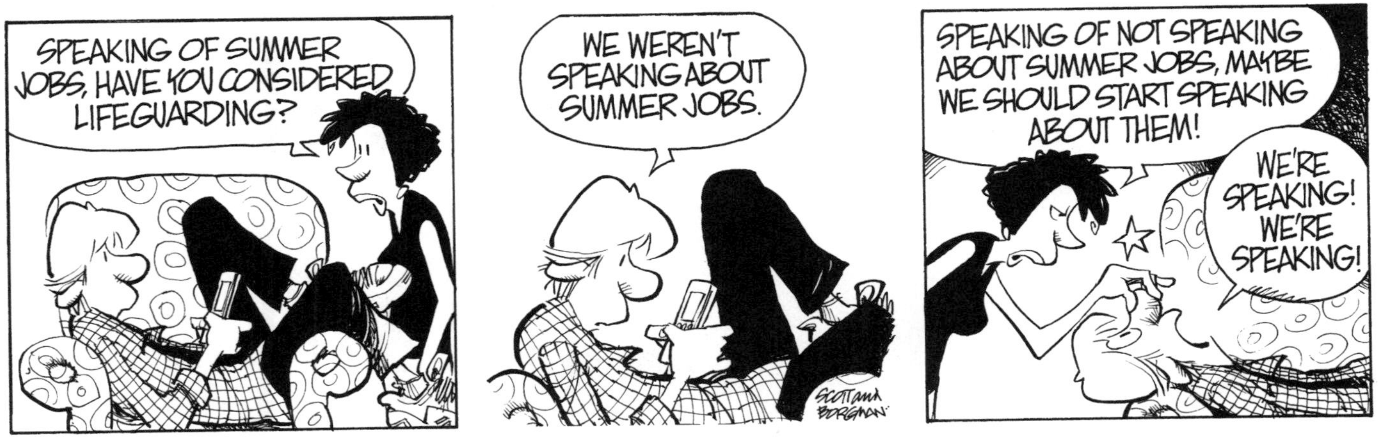
SPEAKING OF SUMMER JOBS, HAVE YOU CONSIDERED LIFEGUARDING?
WE WEREN'T SPEAKING ABOUT SUMMER JOBS.
SPEAKING OF NOT SPEAKING ABOUT SUMMER JOBS, MAYBE WE SHOULD START SPEAKING ABOUT THEM!
WE'RE SPEAKING! WE'RE SPEAKING!

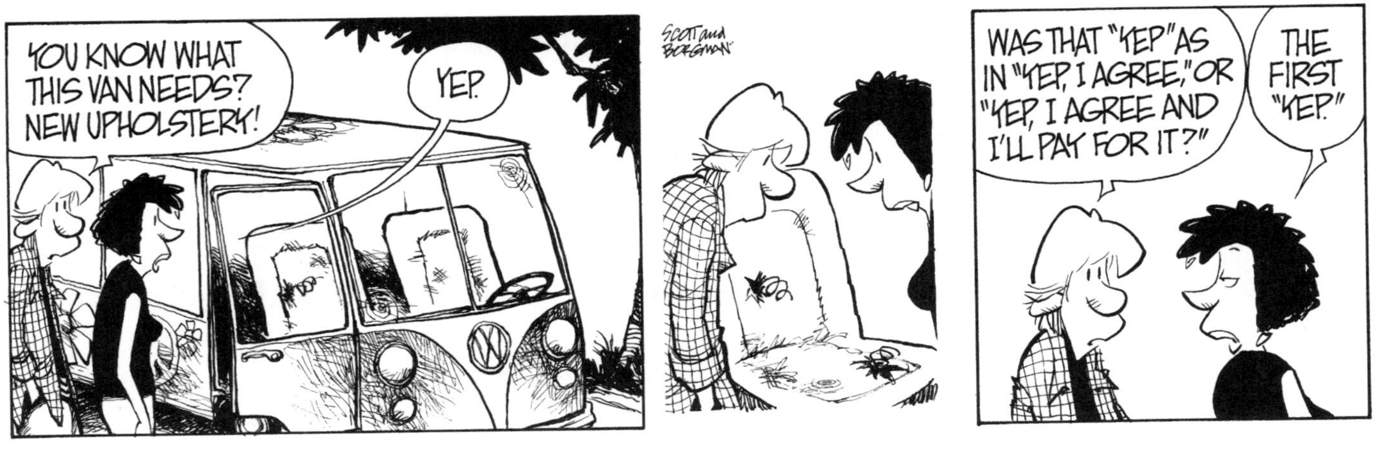
YOU KNOW WHAT THIS VAN NEEDS? NEW UPHOLSTERY!
YEP.
WAS THAT "YEP" AS IN "YEP, I AGREE," OR "YEP, I AGREE AND I'LL PAY FOR IT?"
THE FIRST "YEP."

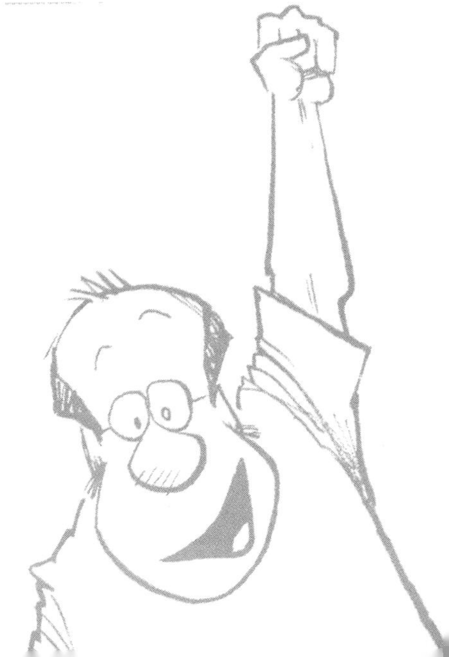

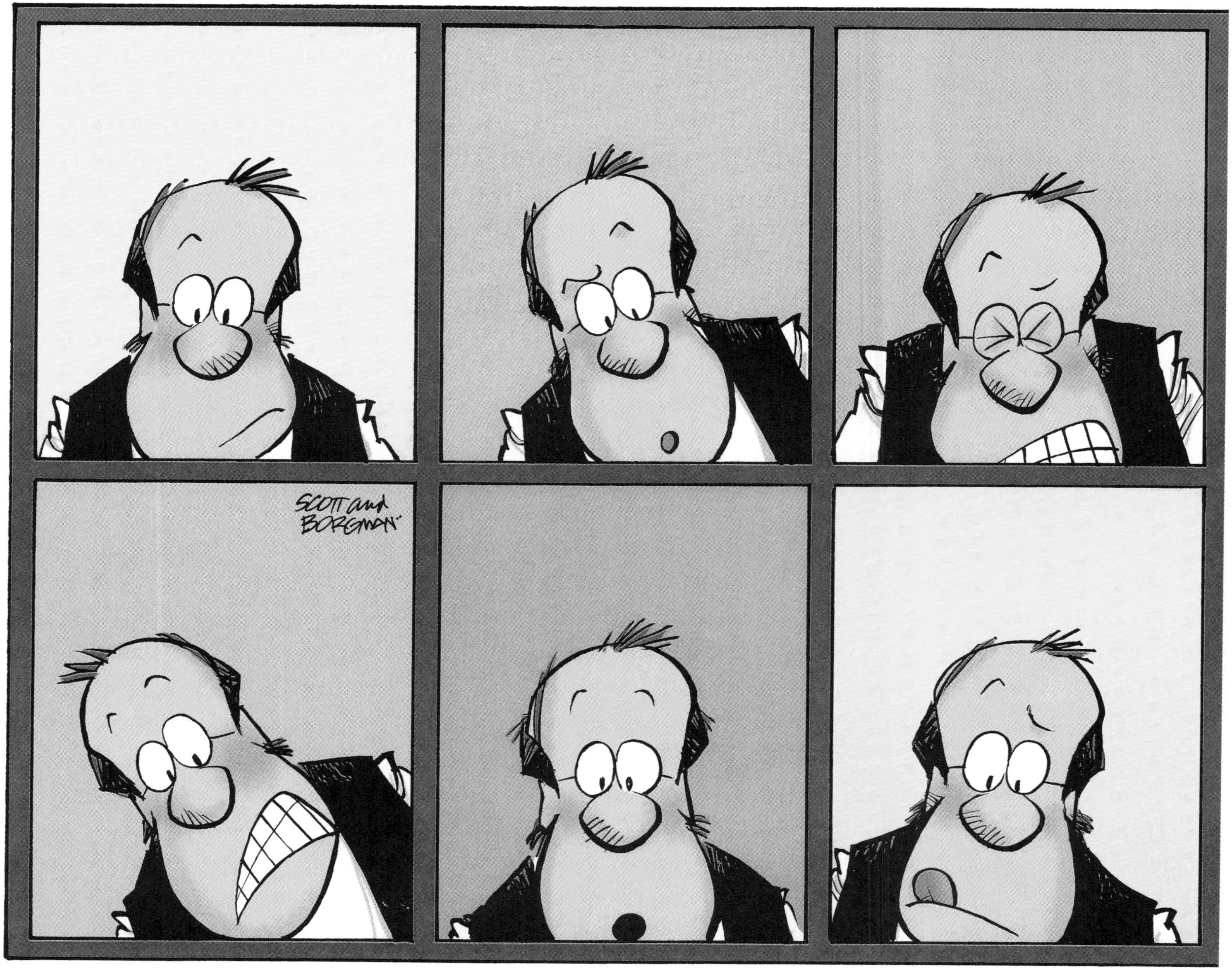
SCOTT and
BORGMAN

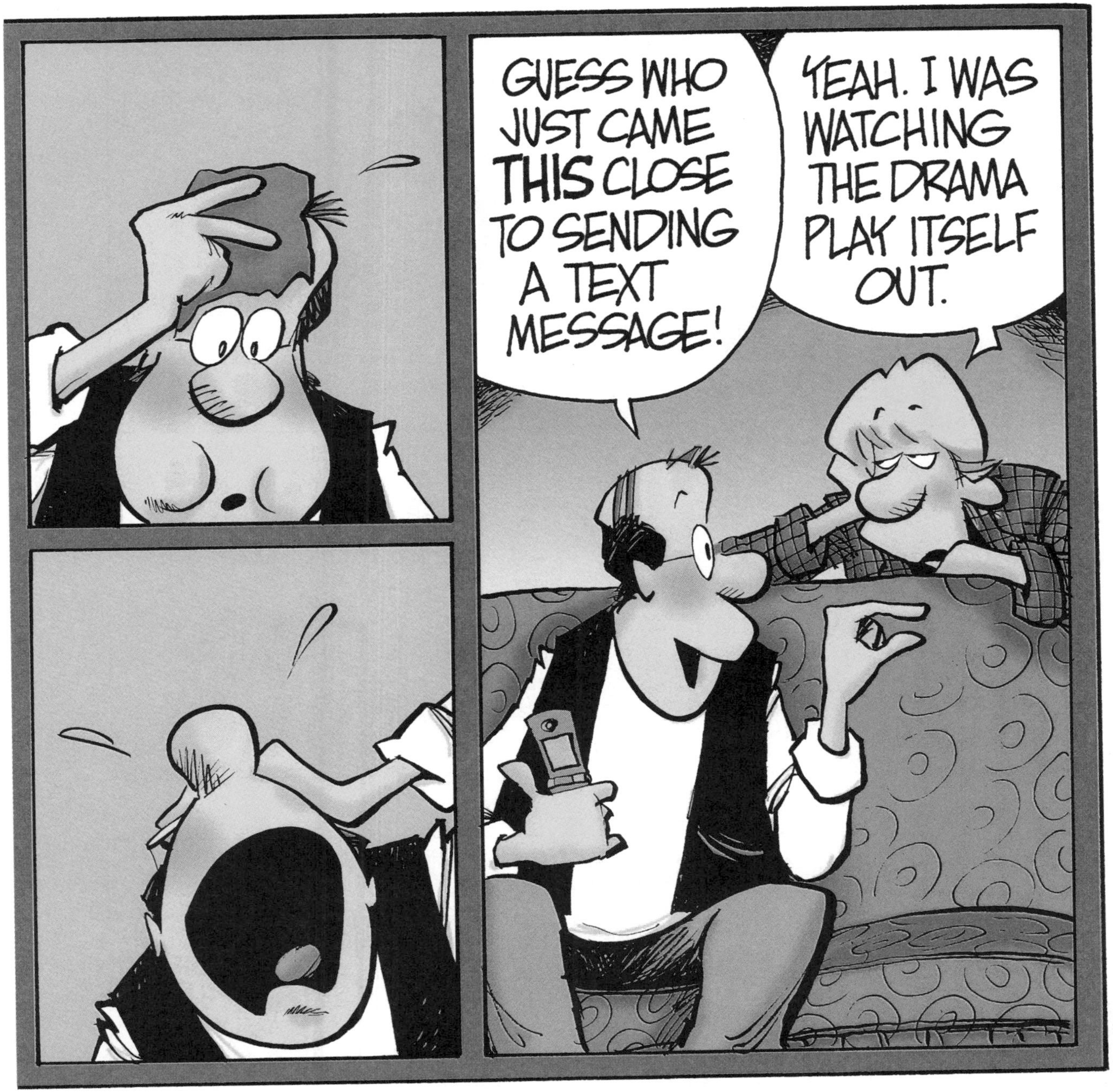
GUESS WHO JUST CAME THIS CLOSE TO SENDING A TEXT MESSAGE!
YEAH. I WAS WATCHING THE DRAMA PLAY ITSELF OUT.

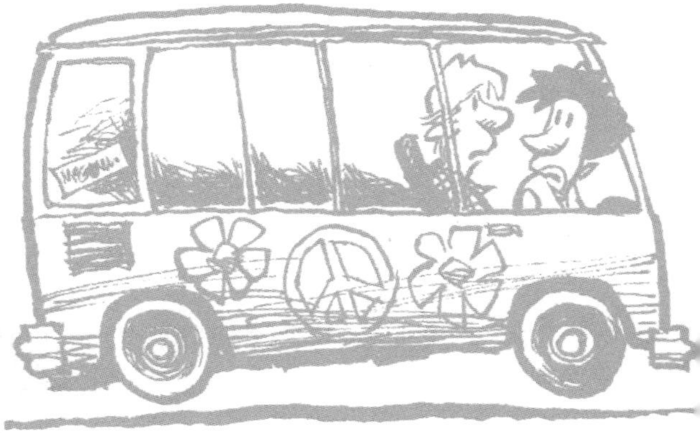

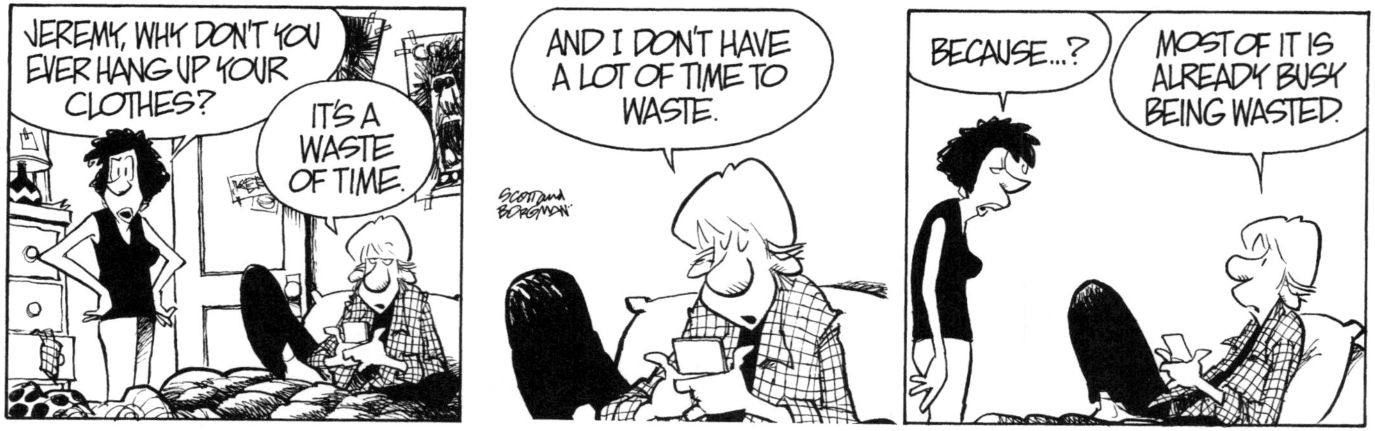
JEREMY, WHY DON'T YOU EVER HANG UP YOUR CLOTHES?
IT'S A WASTE OF TIME.
AND I DON'T HAVE A LOT OF TIME TO WASTE.
BECAUSE...?
MOST OF IT IS ALREADY BUSY BEING WASTED.

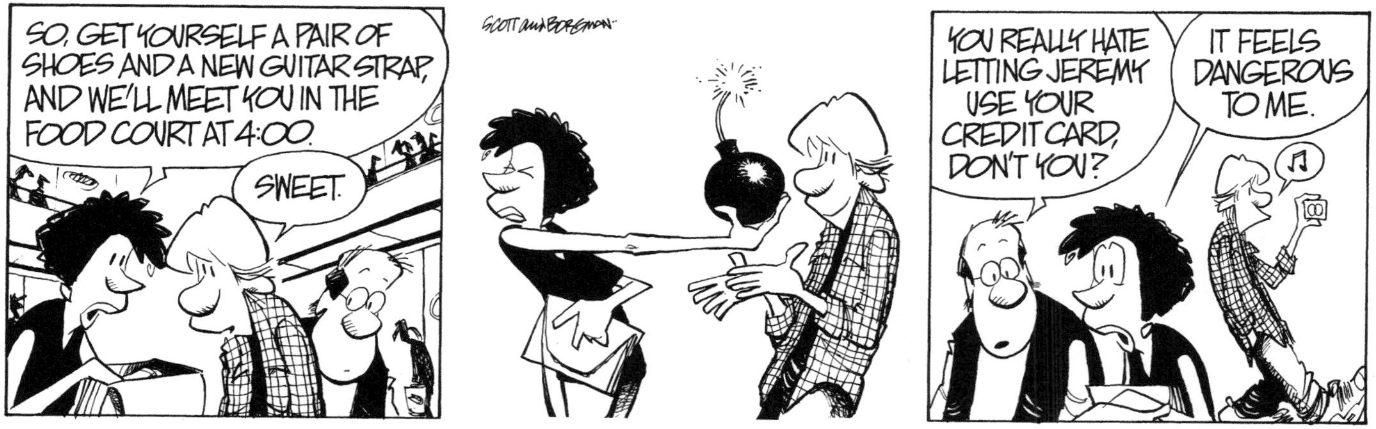
SO, GET YOURSELF A PAIR OF SHOES AND A NEW GUITAR STRAP, AND WE'LL MEET YOU IN THE FOOD COURT AT 4:00.
SWEET.
YOU REALLY HATE LETTING JEREMY USE YOUR CREDIT CARD, DON'T YOU?
IT FEELS DANGEROUS TO ME.

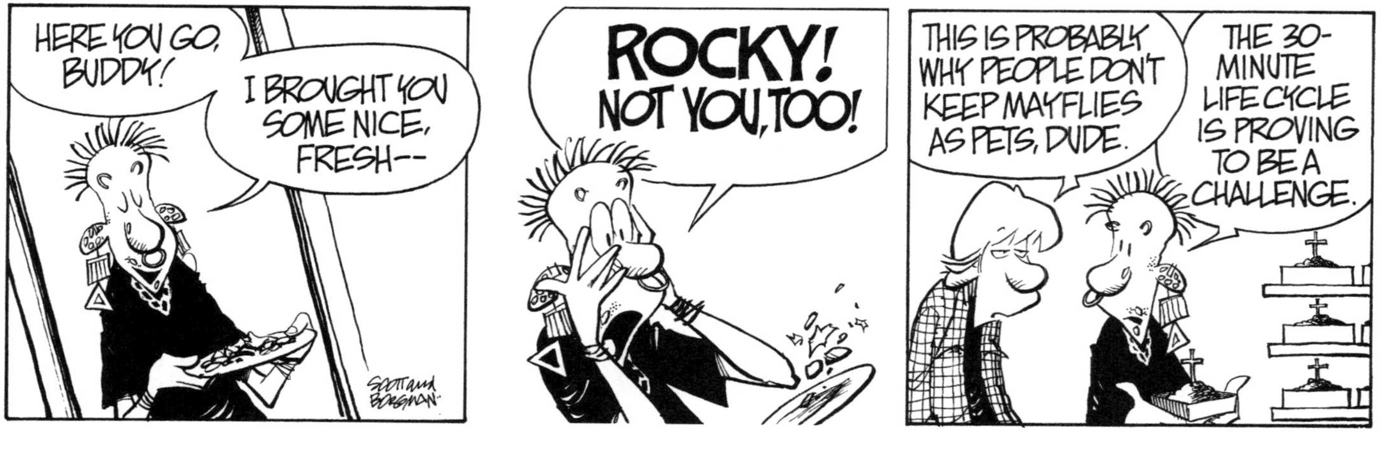
HERE YOU GO, BUDDY!
I BROUGHT YOU SOME NICE, FRESH--
ROCKY! NOT YOU, TOO!
THIS IS PROBABLY WHY PEOPLE DON'T KEEP MAYFLIES AS PETS, DUDE.
THE 30-MINUTE LIFE CYCLE IS PROVING TO BE A CHALLENGE.

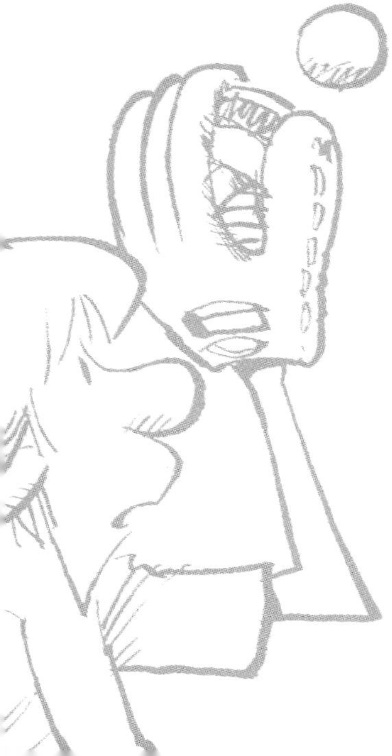

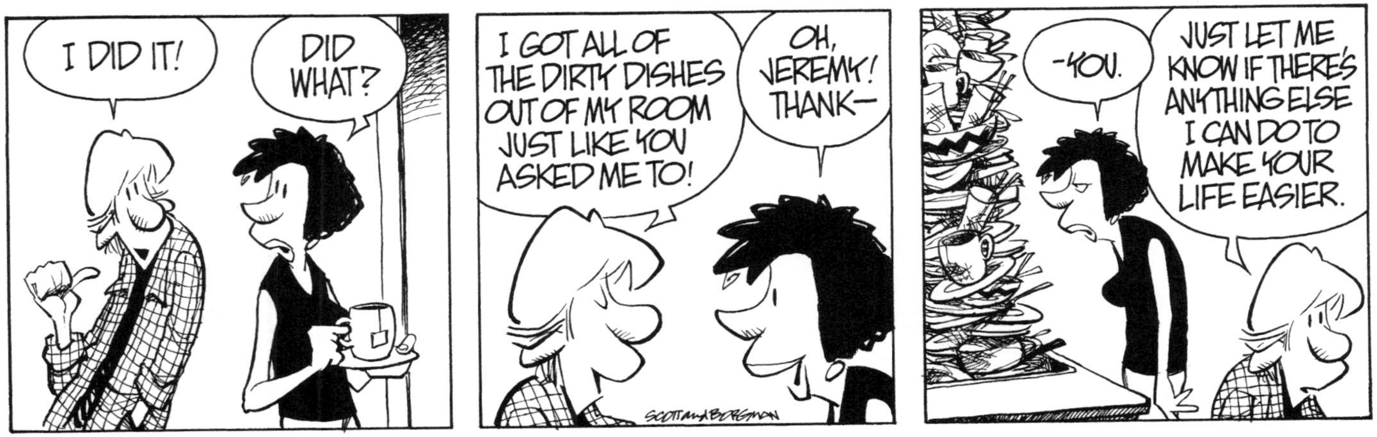
I DID IT!
DID WHAT?
I GOT ALL OF THE DIRTY DISHES OUT OF MY ROOM JUST LIKE YOU ASKED ME TO!
OH, JEREMY! THANK—
-YOU.
JUST LET ME KNOW IF THERE'S ANYTHING ELSE I CAN DO TO MAKE YOUR LIFE EASIER.

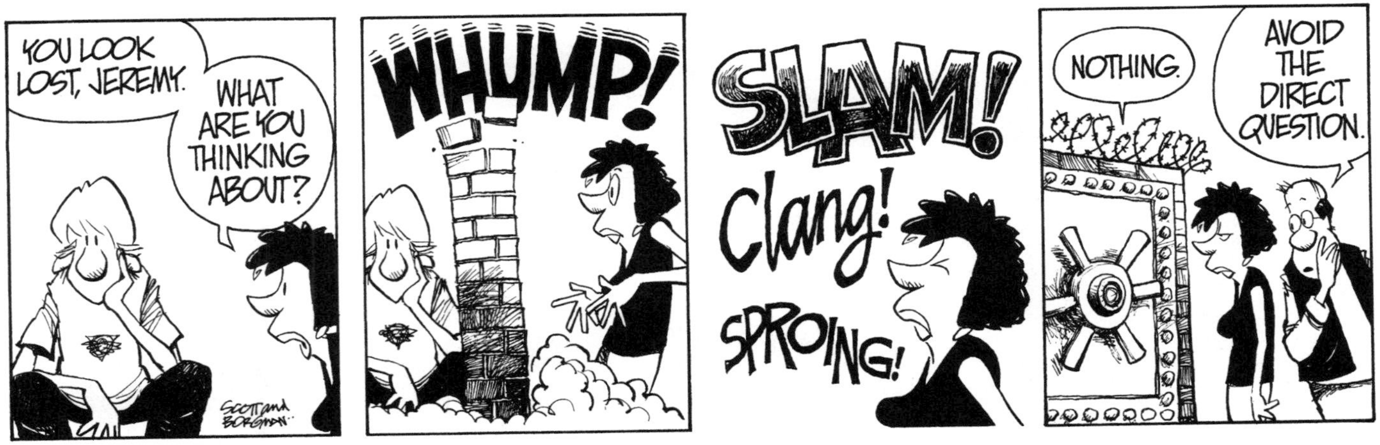
YOU LOOK LOST, JEREMY.
WHAT ARE YOU THINKING ABOUT?
WHUMP!
SLAM!
Clang!
SPROING!
NOTHING.
AVOID THE DIRECT QUESTION.

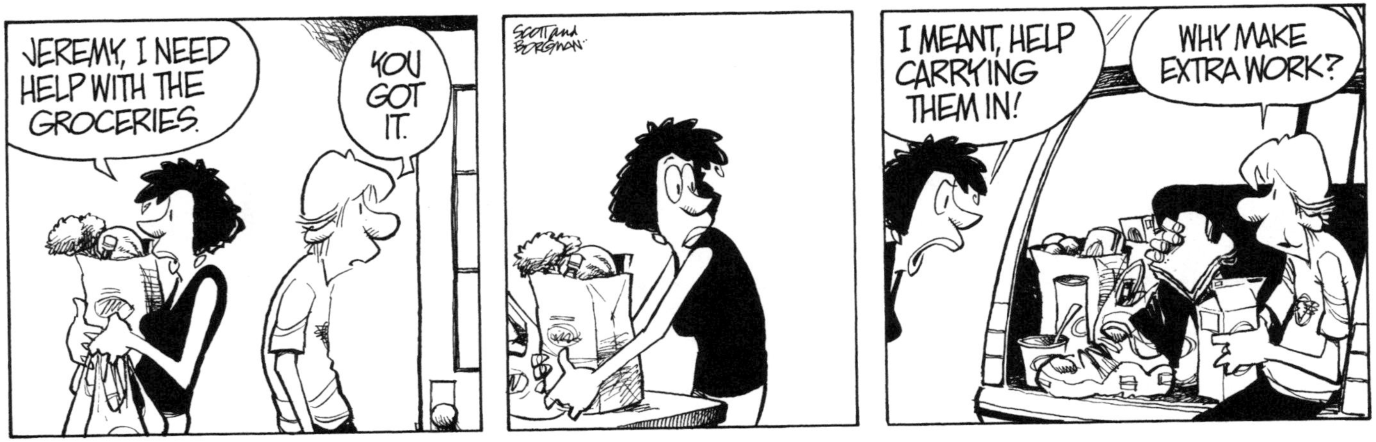
JEREMY, I NEED HELP WITH THE GROCERIES.
YOU GOT IT.
I MEANT, HELP CARRYING THEM IN!
WHY MAKE EXTRA WORK?

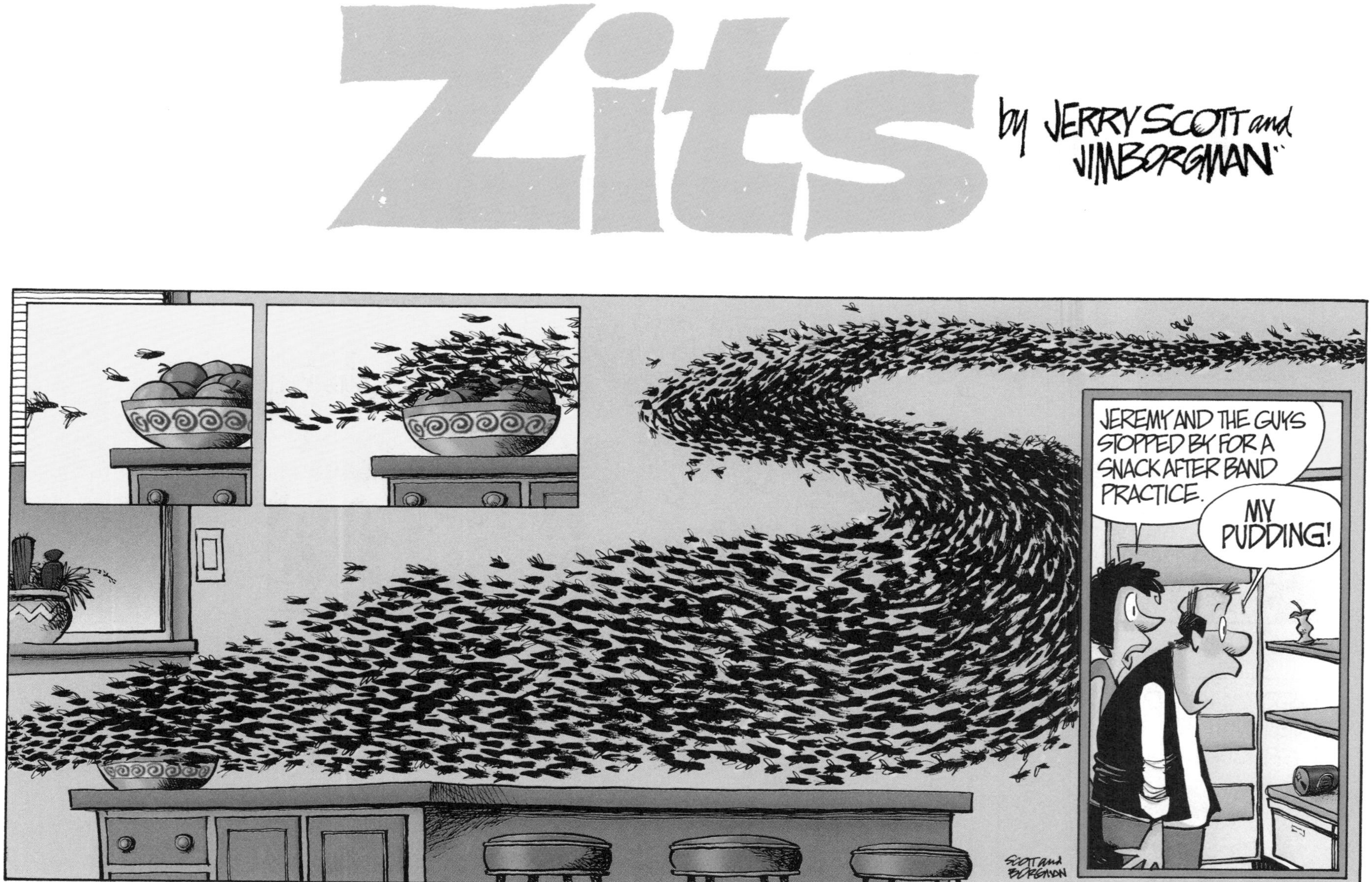
Zits
by JERRY SCOTT and JIM BORGMAN
JEREMY AND THE GUYS STOPPED BY FOR A SNACK AFTER BAND PRACTICE.
MY PUDDING!
SCOTT and BORGMAN

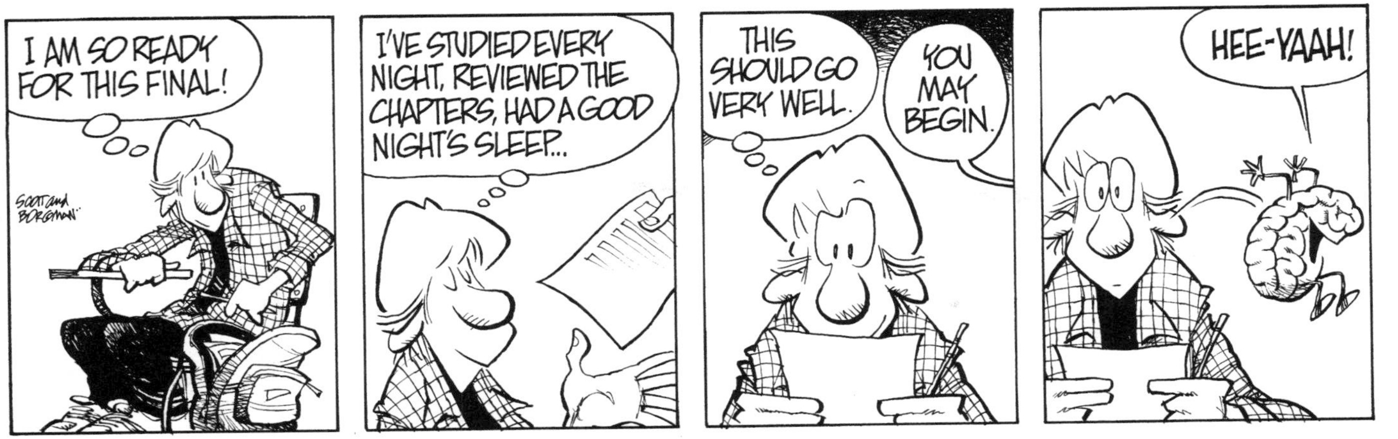
I AM SO READY FOR THIS FINAL!
I'VE STUDIED EVERY NIGHT, REVIEWED THE CHAPTERS, HAD A GOOD NIGHT'S SLEEP...
THIS SHOULD GO VERY WELL.
YOU MAY BEGIN.
HEE-YAAH!

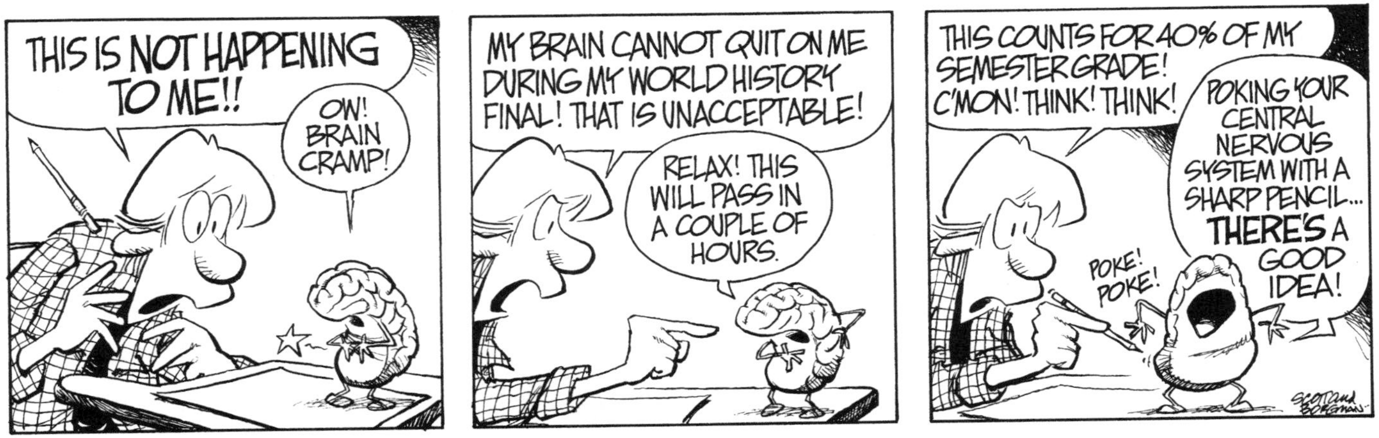
THIS IS NOT HAPPENING TO ME!!
OW! BRAIN CRAMP!
MY BRAIN CANNOT QUIT ON ME DURING MY WORLD HISTORY FINAL! THAT IS UNACCEPTABLE!
RELAX! THIS WILL PASS IN A COUPLE OF HOURS.
THIS COUNTS FOR 40% OF MY SEMESTER GRADE! C'MON! THINK! THINK!
POKE! POKE!
POKING YOUR CENTRAL NERVOUS SYSTEM WITH A SHARP PENCIL... THERE'S A GOOD IDEA!

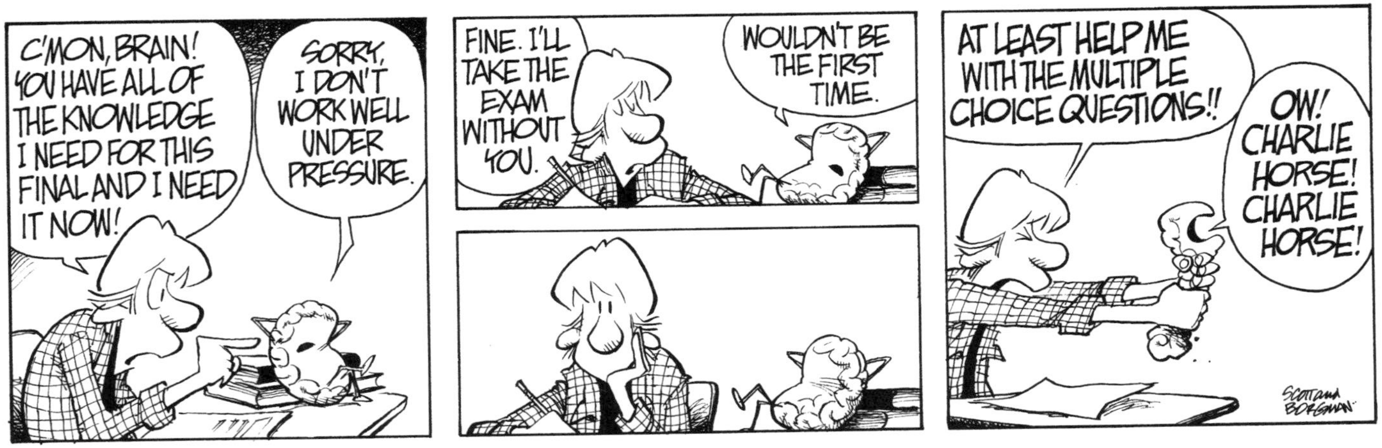
C'MON, BRAIN! YOU HAVE ALL OF THE KNOWLEDGE I NEED FOR THIS FINAL AND I NEED IT NOW!
SORRY, I DON'T WORK WELL UNDER PRESSURE.
FINE. I'LL TAKE THE EXAM WITHOUT YOU.
WOULDN'T BE THE FIRST TIME.
AT LEAST HELP ME WITH THE MULTIPLE CHOICE QUESTIONS!!
OW! CHARLIE HORSE! CHARLIE HORSE!

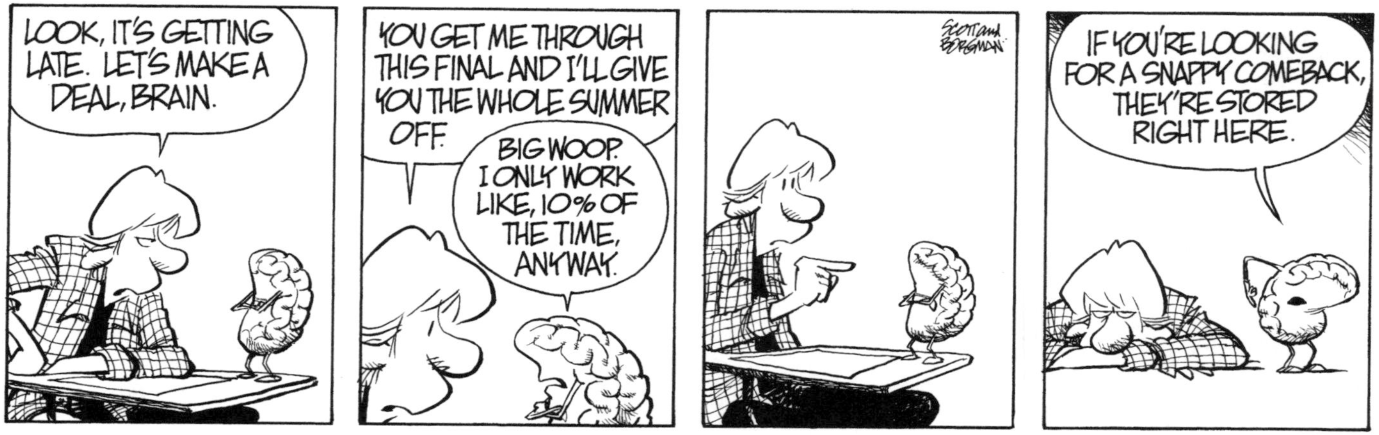
LOOK, IT'S GETTING LATE. LET'S MAKE A DEAL, BRAIN.
YOU GET ME THROUGH THIS FINAL AND I'LL GIVE YOU THE WHOLE SUMMER OFF.
BIG WOOP. I ONLY WORK LIKE, 10% OF THE TIME, ANYWAY.
IF YOU'RE LOOKING FOR A SNAPPY COMEBACK, THEY'RE STORED RIGHT HERE.

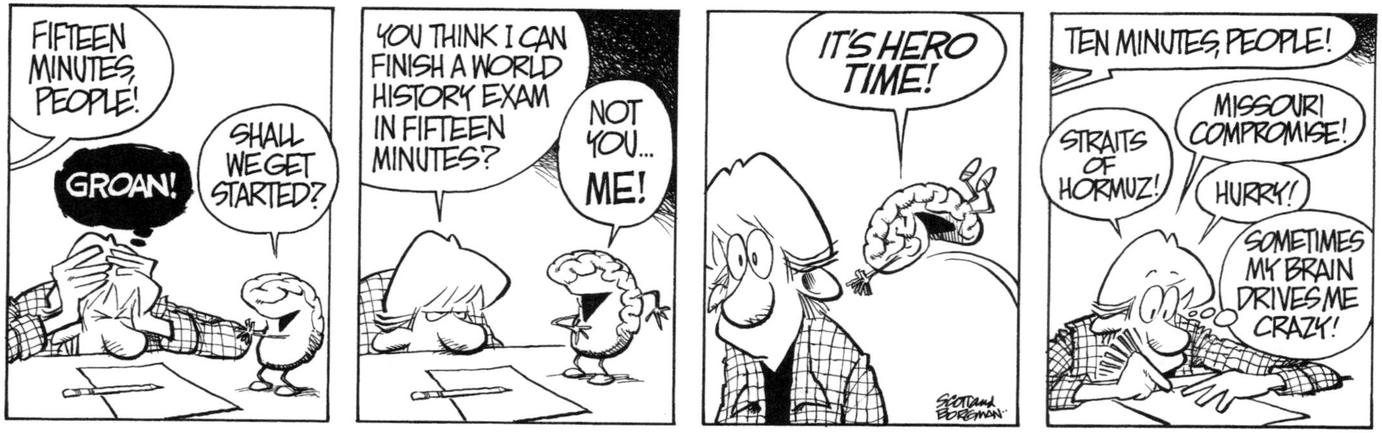
FIFTEEN MINUTES, PEOPLE!
GROAN!
SHALL WE GET STARTED?
YOU THINK I CAN FINISH A WORLD HISTORY EXAM IN FIFTEEN MINUTES?
NOT YOU... ME!
IT'S HERO TIME!
TEN MINUTES, PEOPLE!
STRAITS OF HORMUZ!
MISSOURI COMPROMISE!
HURRY!
SOMETIMES MY BRAIN DRIVES ME CRAZY!

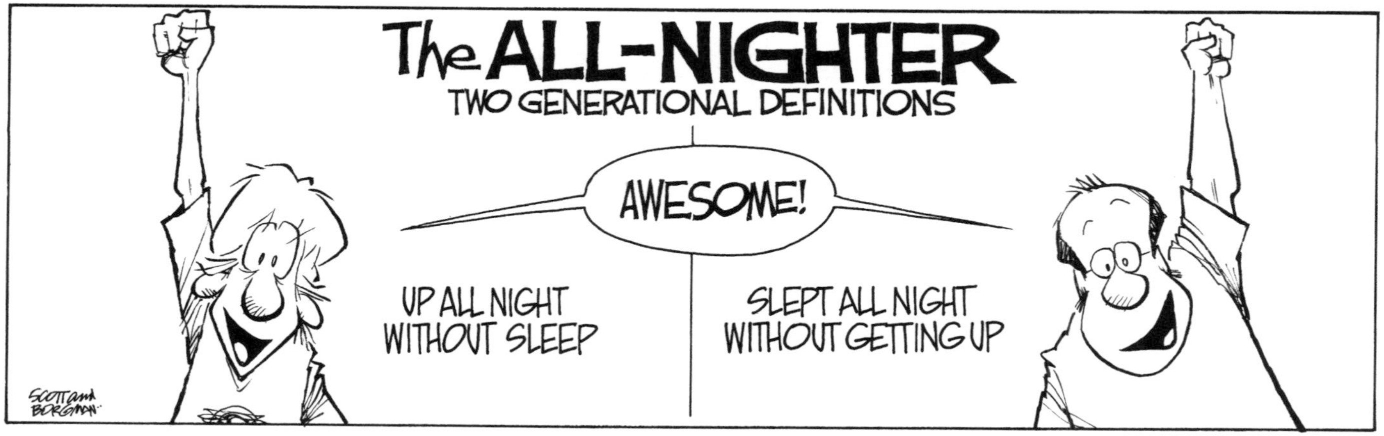
The ALL-NIGHTER
TWO GENERATIONAL DEFINITIONS
AWESOME!
UP ALL NIGHT WITHOUT SLEEP
SLEPT ALL NIGHT WITHOUT GETTING UP

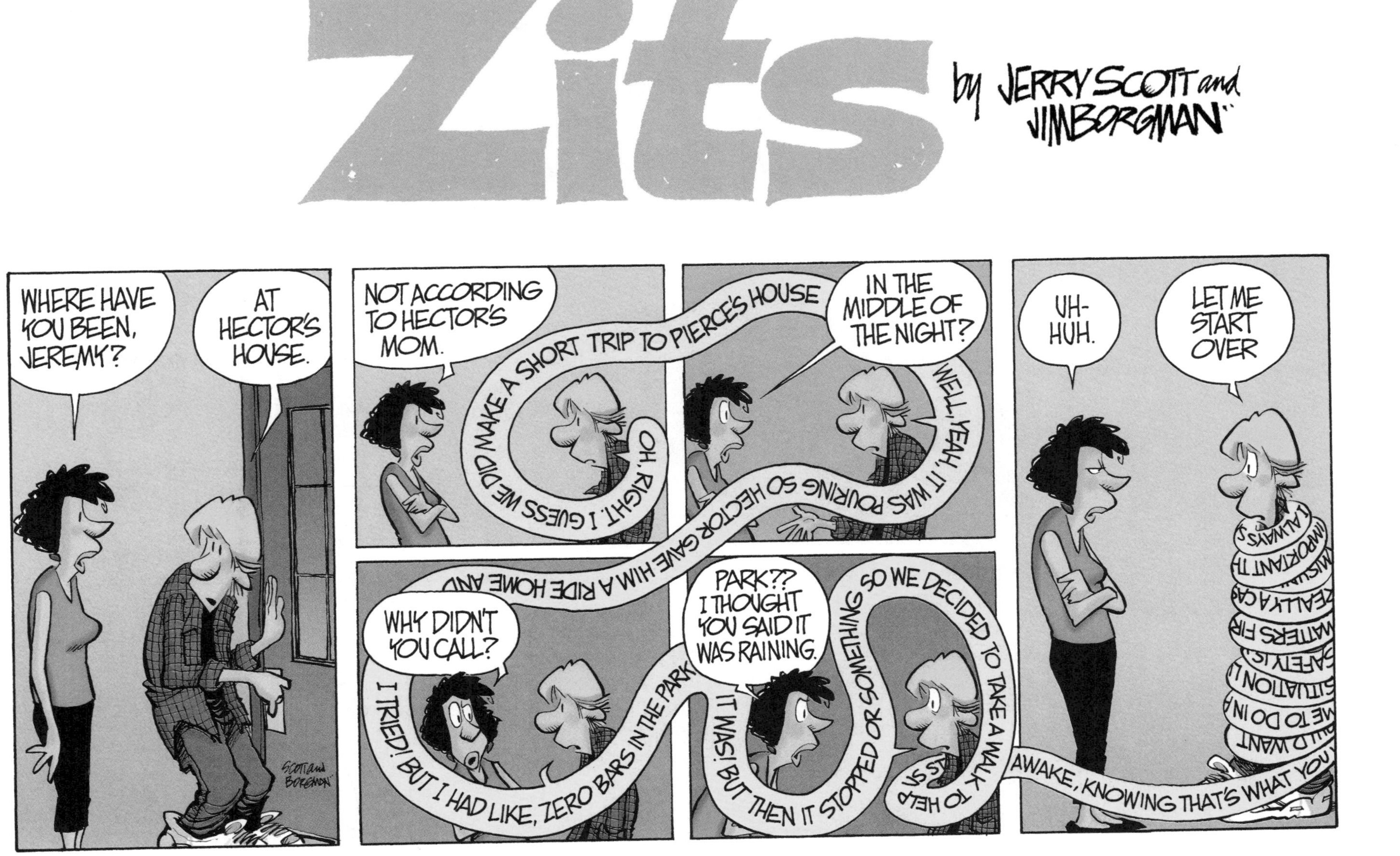
Zits
by JERRY SCOTT and JIM BORGMAN
WHERE HAVE YOU BEEN, JEREMY?
AT HECTOR'S HOUSE.
SCOTT and BORGMAN
NOT ACCORDING TO HECTOR'S MOM.
OH, RIGHT. I GUESS WE DID MAKE A SHORT TRIP TO PIERCE'S HOUSE
IN THE MIDDLE OF THE NIGHT?
WELL, YEAH. IT WAS POURING SO HECTOR GAVE HIM A RIDE HOME AND
WHY DIDN'T YOU CALL?
I TRIED! BUT I HAD LIKE, ZERO BARS IN THE PARK
PARK?? I THOUGHT YOU SAID IT WAS RAINING.
IT WAS! BUT THEN IT STOPPED OR SOMETHING SO WE DECIDED TO TAKE A WALK TO HELP US ST
AWAKE, KNOWING THAT'S WHAT YOU
UH-HUH.
LET ME START OVER
I ALWAYS
IMPORTANT TH
REALLY A CA
MATTERS FIR
SAFETY IS
SITUATION
ME TO DO IN A
D WANT

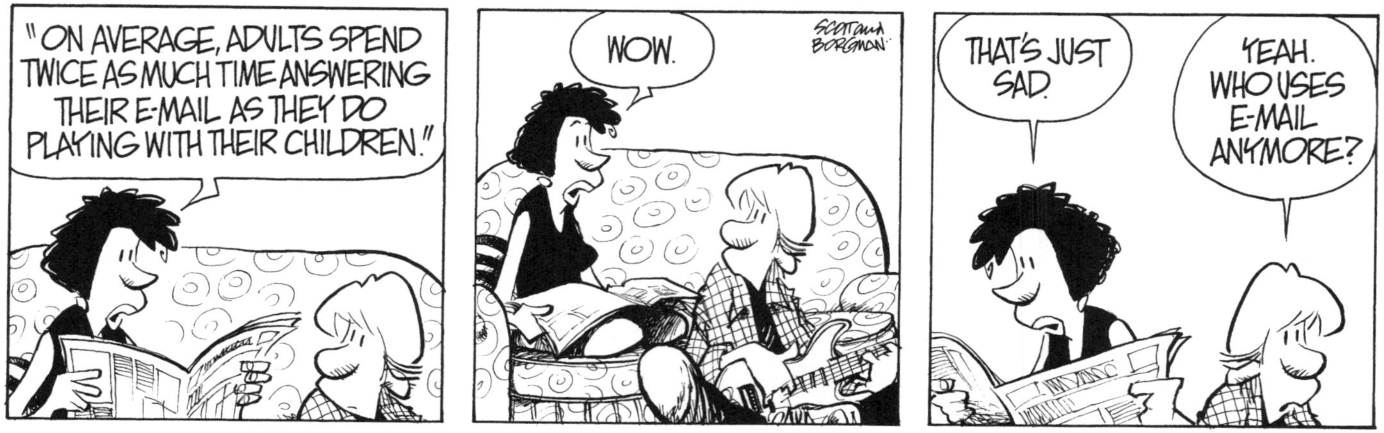
"ON AVERAGE, ADULTS SPEND TWICE AS MUCH TIME ANSWERING THEIR E-MAIL AS THEY DO PLAYING WITH THEIR CHILDREN."
WOW.
SCOTT and BORGMAN
THAT'S JUST SAD.
YEAH. WHO USES E-MAIL ANYMORE?

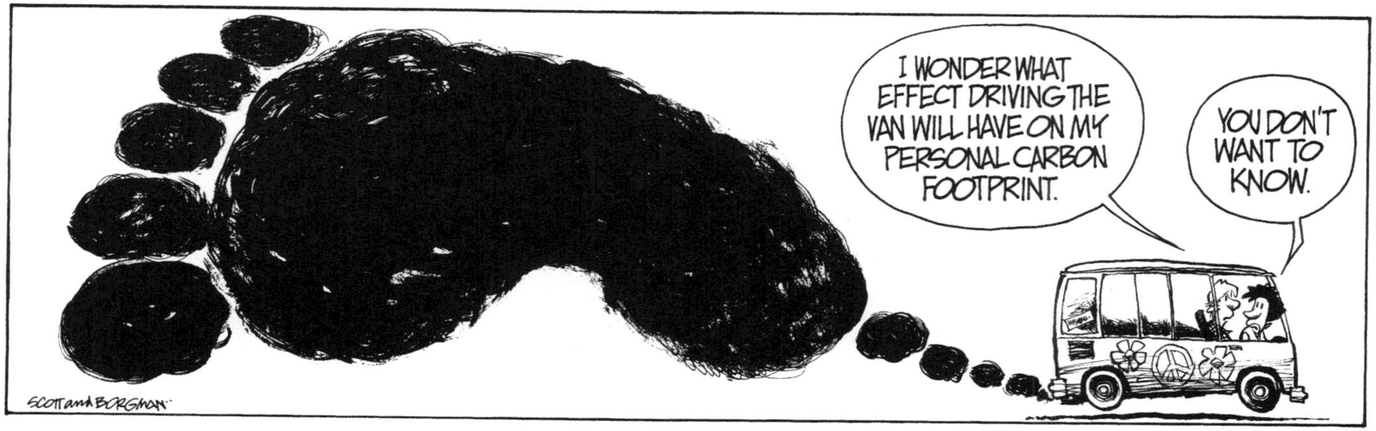
I WONDER WHAT EFFECT DRIVING THE VAN WILL HAVE ON MY PERSONAL CARBON FOOTPRINT.
YOU DON'T WANT TO KNOW.
SCOTT and BORGMAN

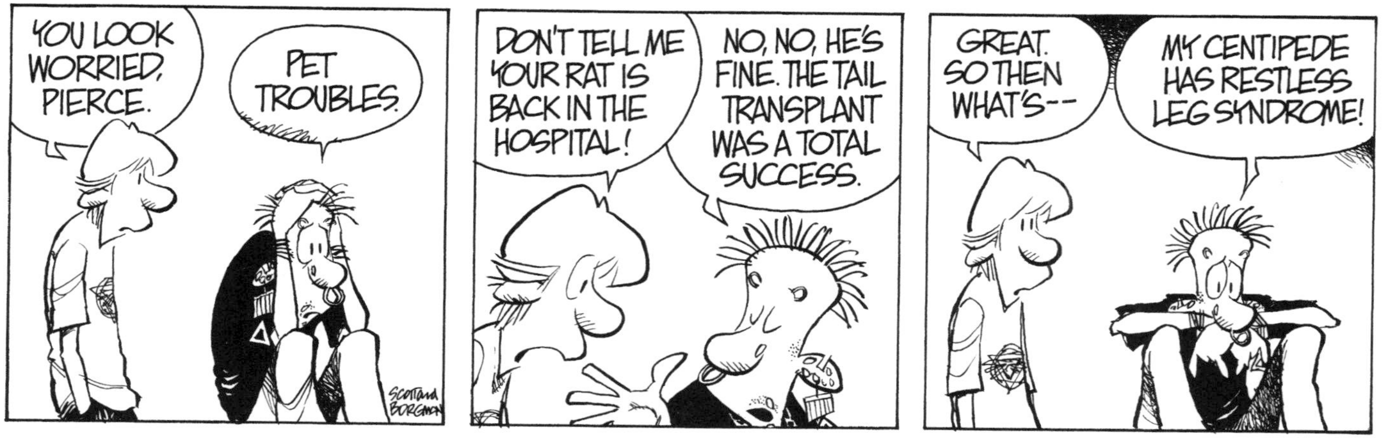
YOU LOOK WORRIED, PIERCE.
PET TROUBLES.
SCOTT and BORGMAN
DON'T TELL ME YOUR RAT IS BACK IN THE HOSPITAL!
NO, NO, HE'S FINE. THE TAIL TRANSPLANT WAS A TOTAL SUCCESS.
GREAT. SO THEN WHAT'S--
MY CENTIPEDE HAS RESTLESS LEG SYNDROME!

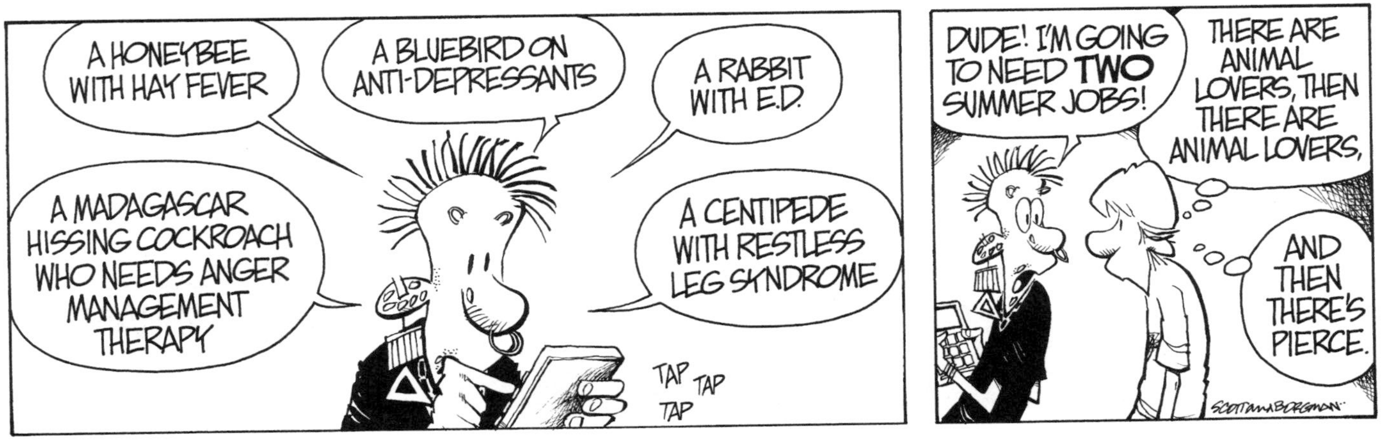
A HONEYBEE WITH HAY FEVER
A BLUEBIRD ON ANTI-DEPRESSANTS
A RABBIT WITH E.D.
A MADAGASCAR HISSING COCKROACH WHO NEEDS ANGER MANAGEMENT THERAPY
A CENTIPEDE WITH RESTLESS LEG SYNDROME
TAP TAP TAP
DUDE! I'M GOING TO NEED **TWO** SUMMER JOBS!
THERE ARE ANIMAL LOVERS, THEN THERE ARE ANIMAL LOVERS,
AND THEN THERE'S PIERCE.
SCOTT AND BORGMAN

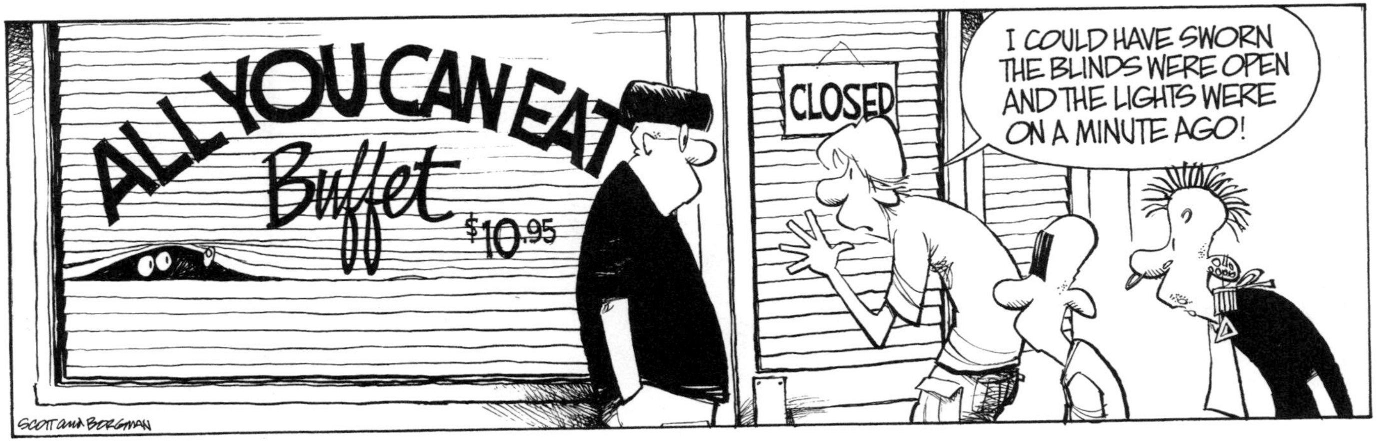
ALL YOU CAN EAT
Buffet
$10.95
CLOSED
I COULD HAVE SWORN THE BLINDS WERE OPEN AND THE LIGHTS WERE ON A MINUTE AGO!
SCOTT AND BORGMAN

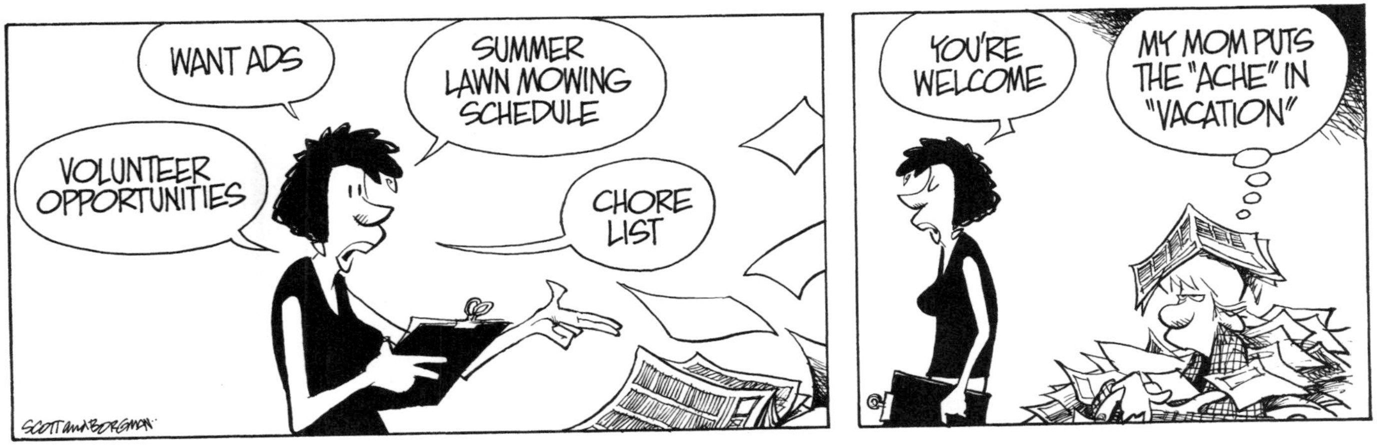
WANT ADS
SUMMER LAWN MOWING SCHEDULE
VOLUNTEER OPPORTUNITIES
CHORE LIST
YOU'RE WELCOME
MY MOM PUTS THE "ACHE" IN "VACATION"
SCOTT AND BORGMAN

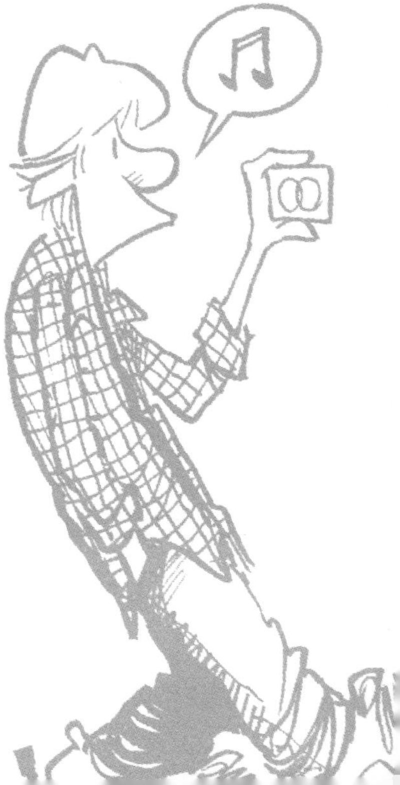

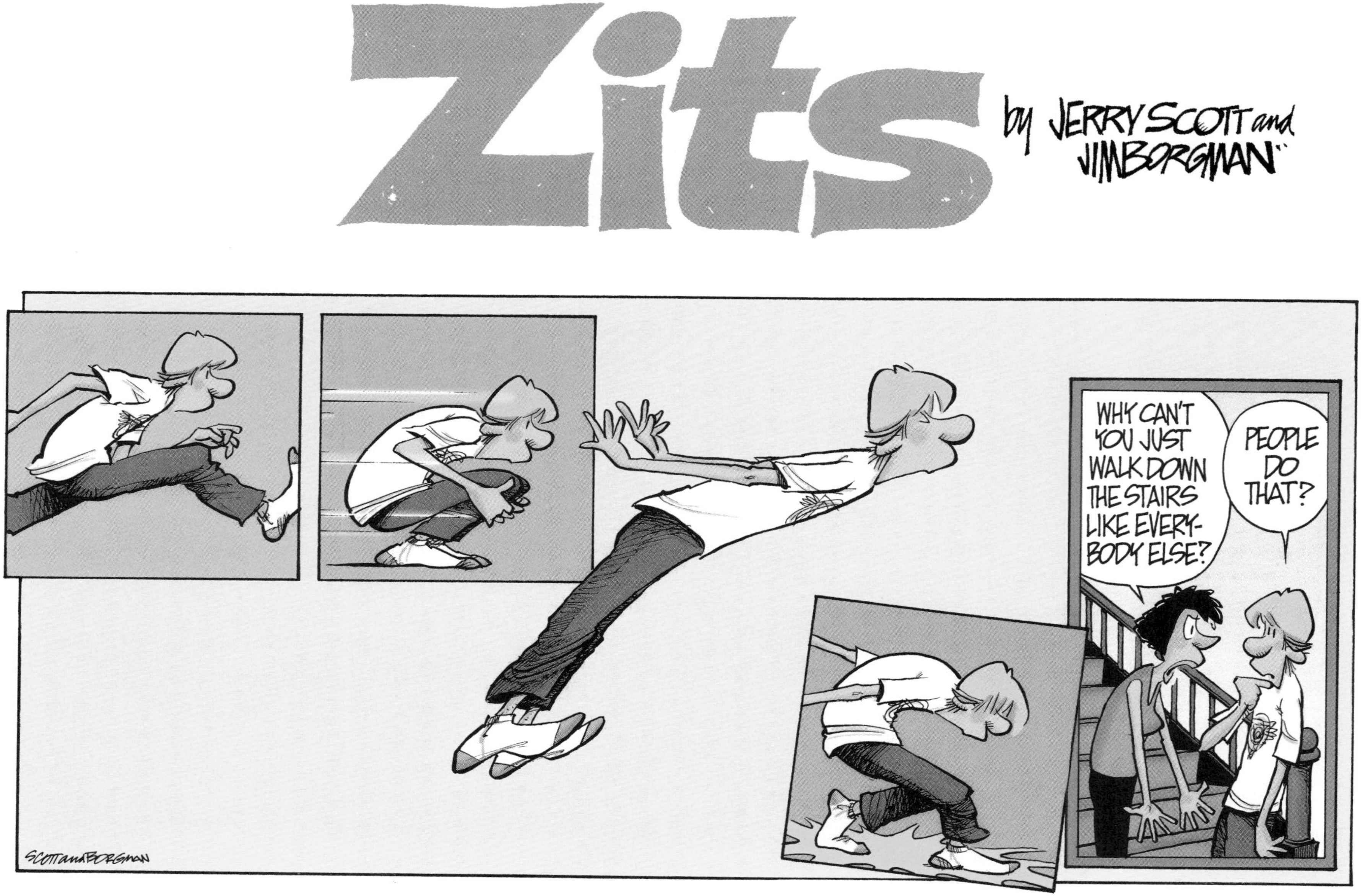
Zits
by JERRY SCOTT and JIM BORGMAN
WHY CAN'T YOU JUST WALK DOWN THE STAIRS LIKE EVERYBODY ELSE?
PEOPLE DO THAT?
SCOTT and BORGMAN

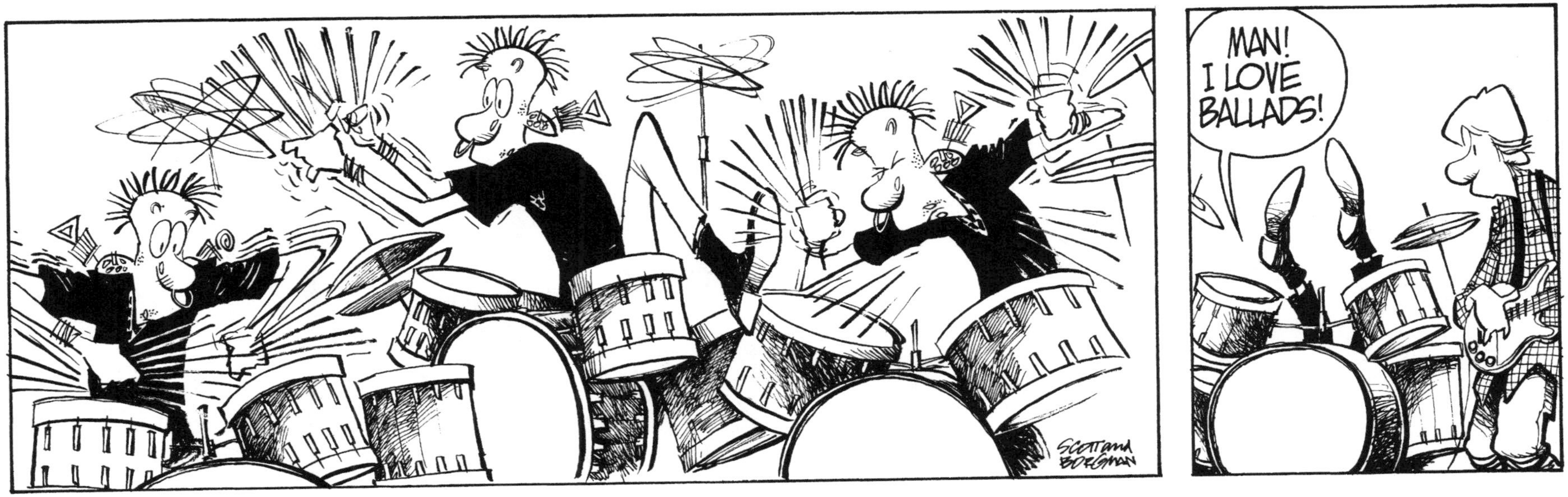
MAN! I LOVE BALLADS!

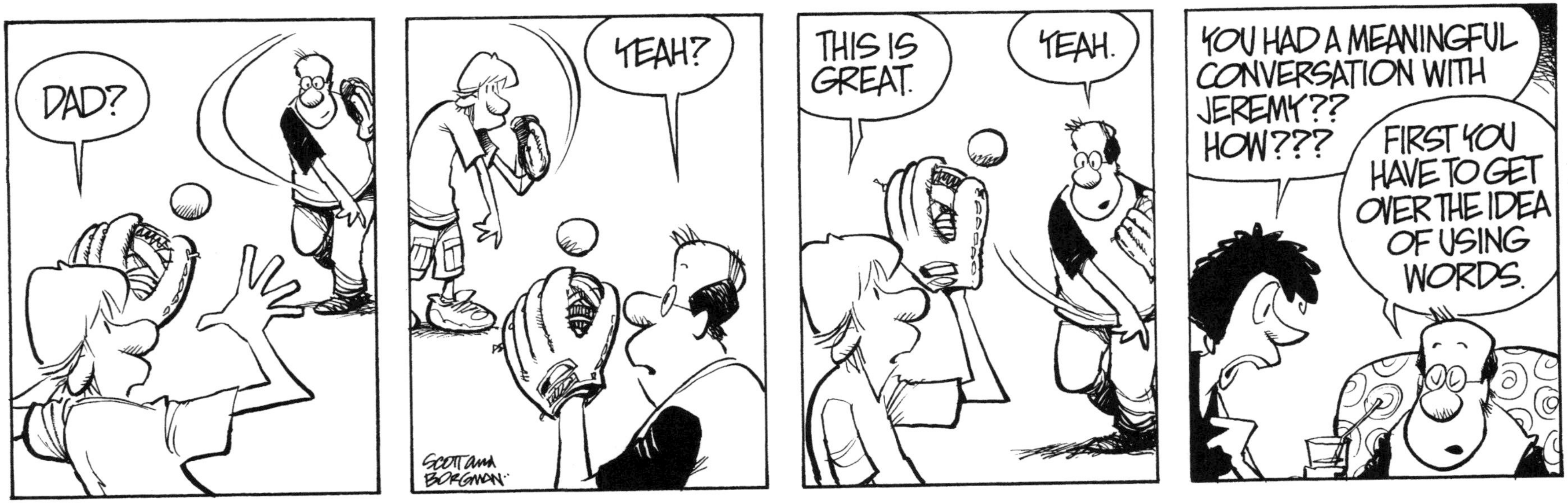
DAD?
YEAH?
THIS IS GREAT.
YEAH.
YOU HAD A MEANINGFUL CONVERSATION WITH JEREMY?? HOW???
FIRST YOU HAVE TO GET OVER THE IDEA OF USING WORDS.

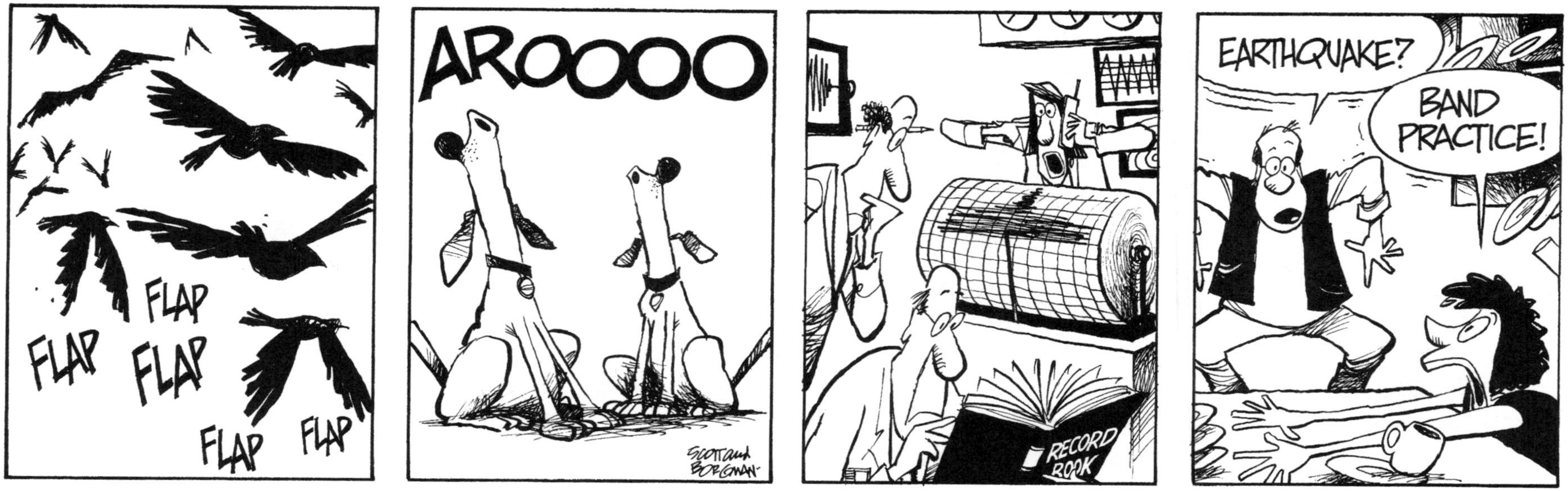
FLAP
FLAP
FLAP
FLAP
FLAP
AROOOO
RECORD BOOK
EARTHQUAKE?
BAND PRACTICE!

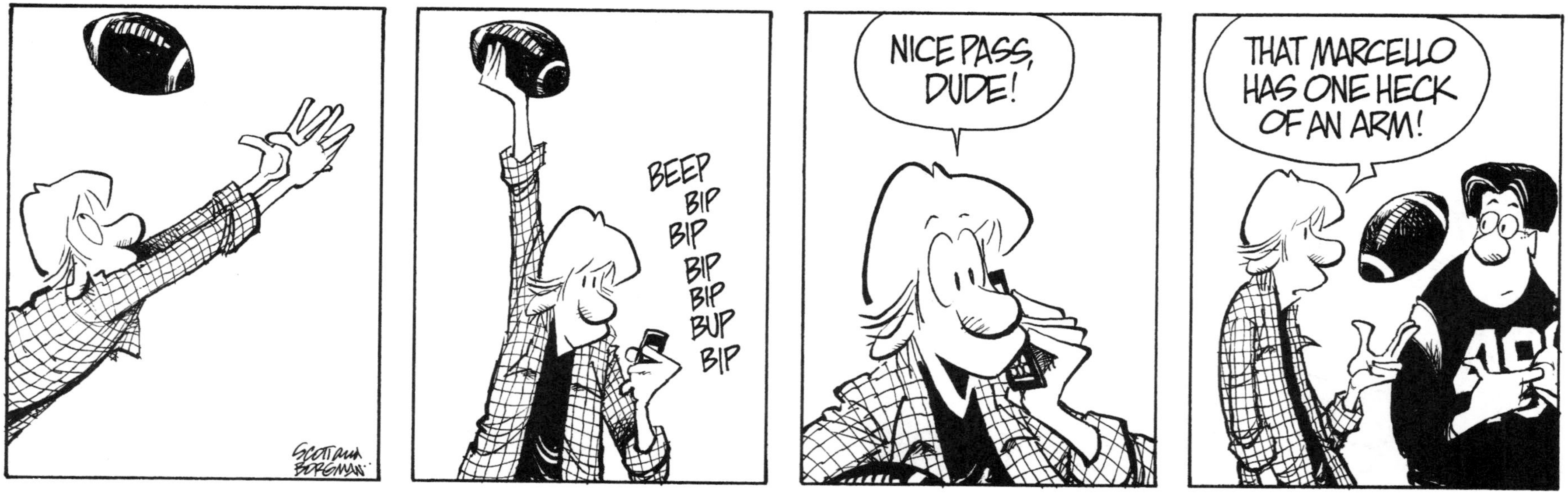
BEEP
BIP
BIP
BIP
BIP
BIP
BUP
BIP
NICE PASS, DUDE!
THAT MARCELLO HAS ONE HECK OF AN ARM!

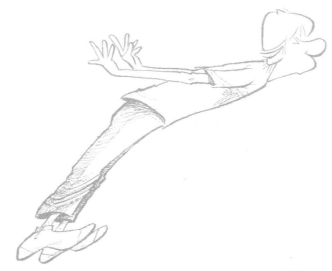

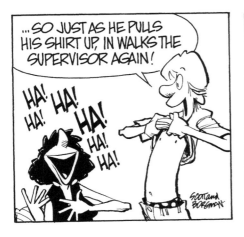

...SO JUST AS HE PULLS HIS SHIRT UP, IN WALKS THE SUPERVISOR AGAIN!
HA! HA! HA! HA! HA! HA!
SCOTT and BORGMAN
I'M HAVING SUCH A GOOD TIME, JEREMY!
ME, TOO.
WHY ARE YOU BEING SO FUNNY AND ENGAGING TODAY?
NOBODY'S LOOKING.

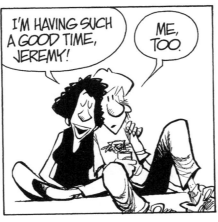

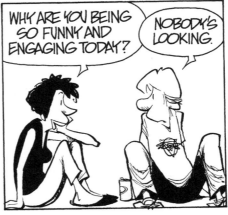

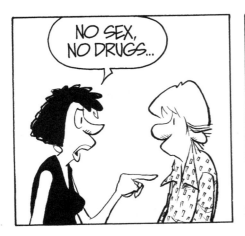

NO SEX, NO DRUGS...
...AND ONLY ROCK AND ROLL FROM THE SIXTIES AND SEVENTIES!
HAS ANYONE SUFFERED MORE THAN ME?
YOU MEAN IN RECORDED HISTORY, OR JUST FOR THIS DANCE?
SCOTT and BORGMAN

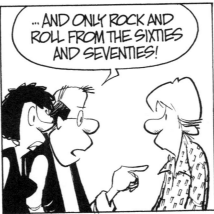

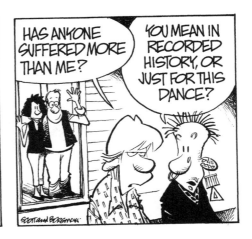

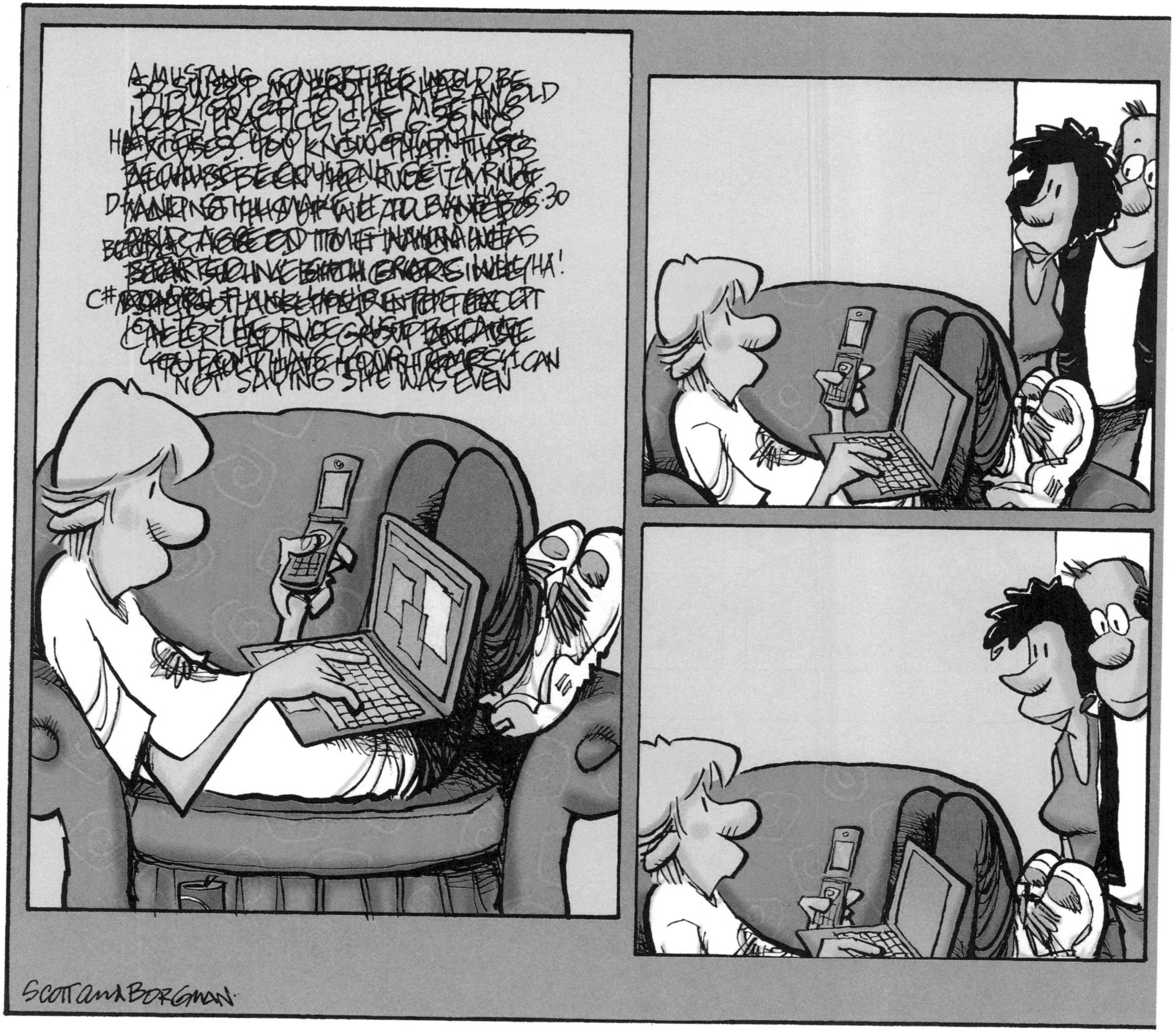
A MUSTANG CONVERTIBLE WOULD BE
NOT SAYING SHE WAS EVEN
SCOTT and BORGMAN

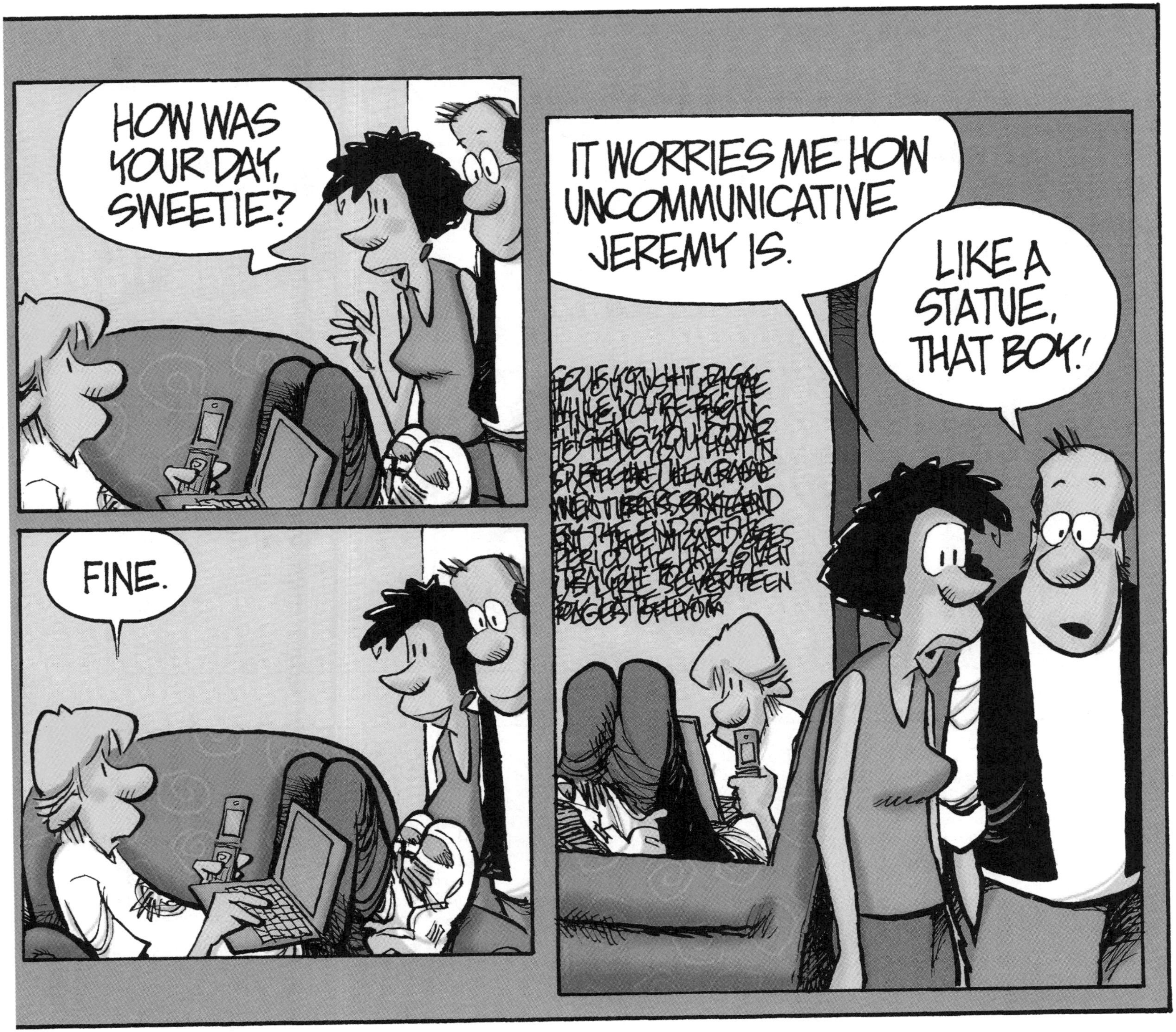
HOW WAS YOUR DAY, SWEETIE?
FINE.
IT WORRIES ME HOW UNCOMMUNICATIVE JEREMY IS.
LIKE A STATUE, THAT BOY!

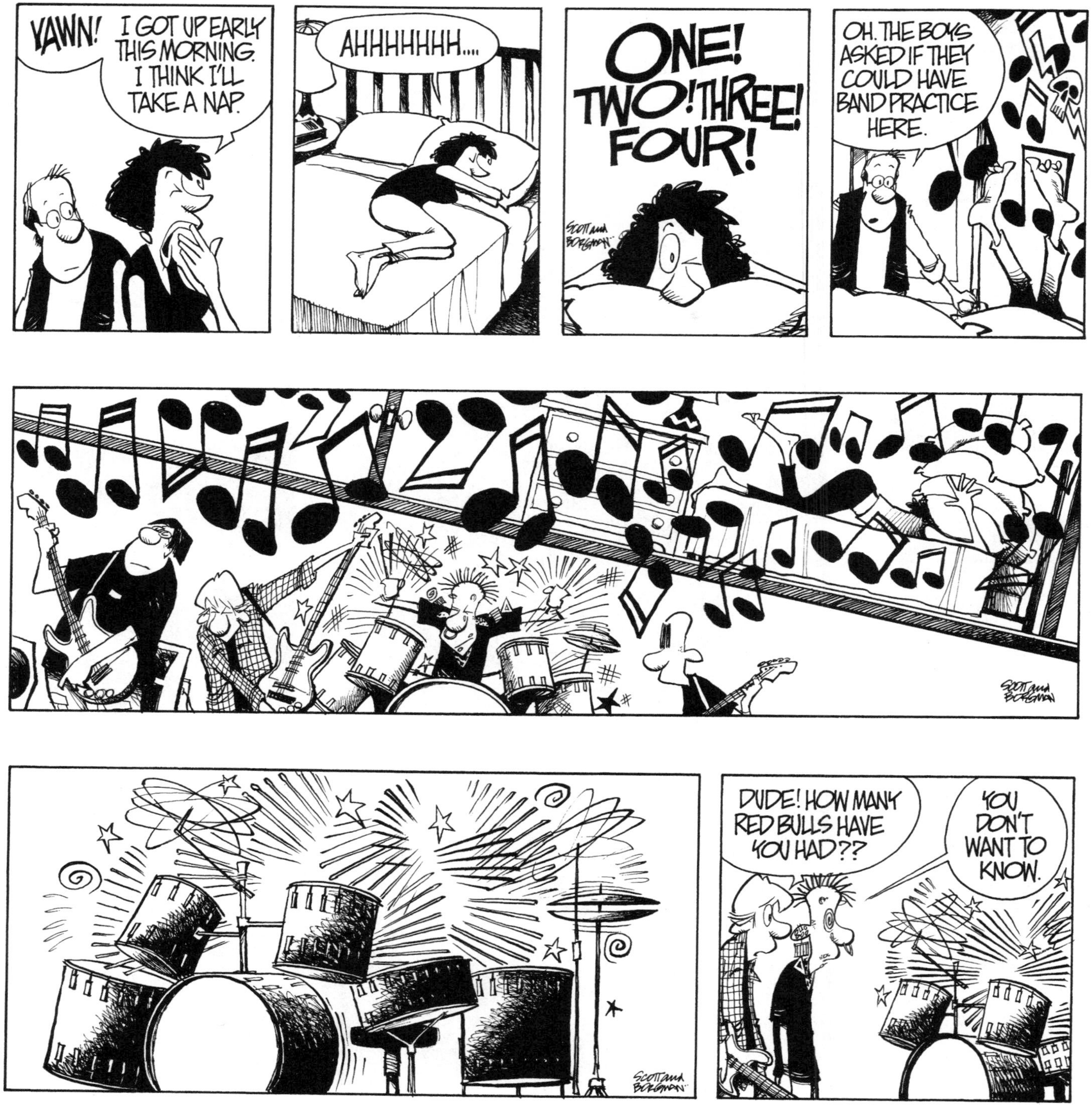
YAWN!
I GOT UP EARLY THIS MORNING. I THINK I'LL TAKE A NAP.
AHHHHHHH....
ONE! TWO! THREE! FOUR!
OH. THE BOYS ASKED IF THEY COULD HAVE BAND PRACTICE HERE.
DUDE! HOW MANY RED BULLS HAVE YOU HAD??
YOU DON'T WANT TO KNOW.

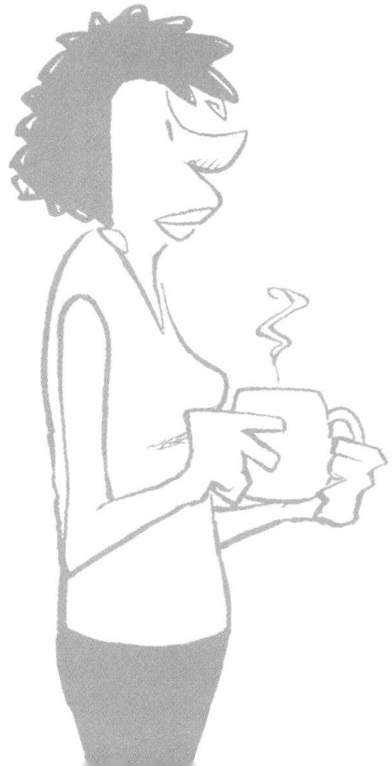

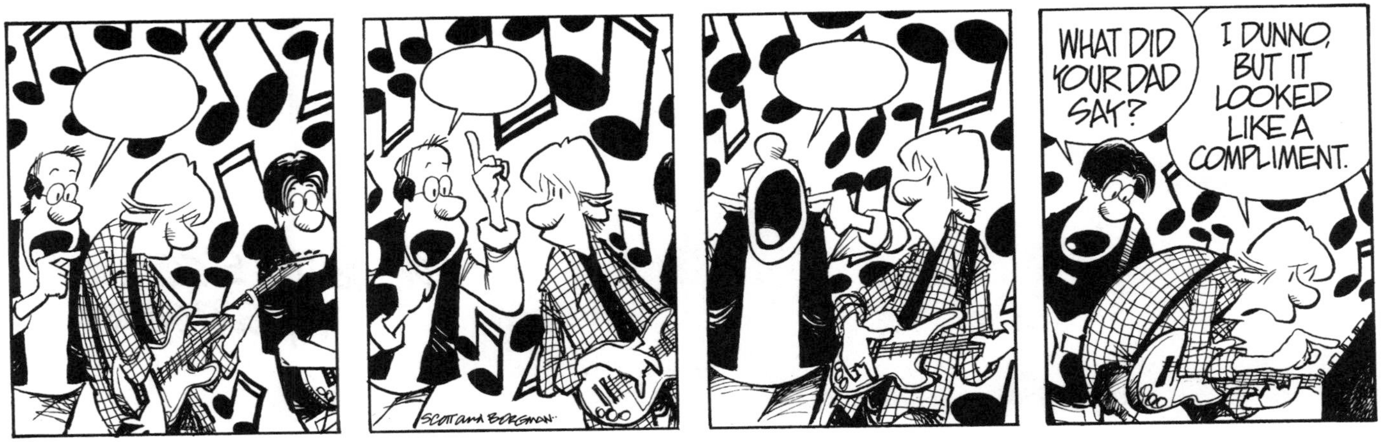
WHAT DID YOUR DAD SAY?
I DUNNO, BUT IT LOOKED LIKE A COMPLIMENT.

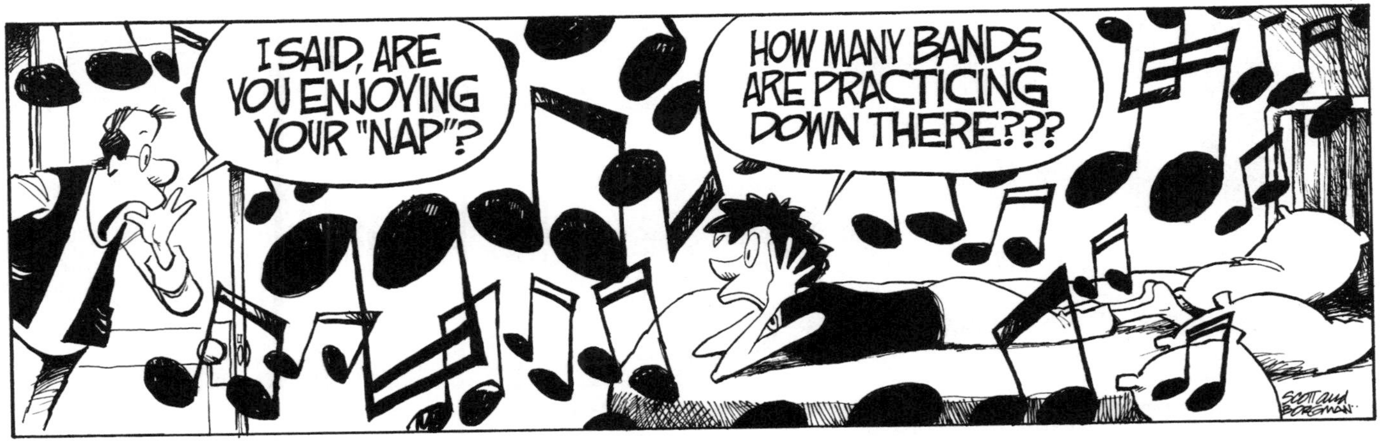
I SAID, ARE YOU ENJOYING YOUR "NAP"?
HOW MANY BANDS ARE PRACTICING DOWN THERE???

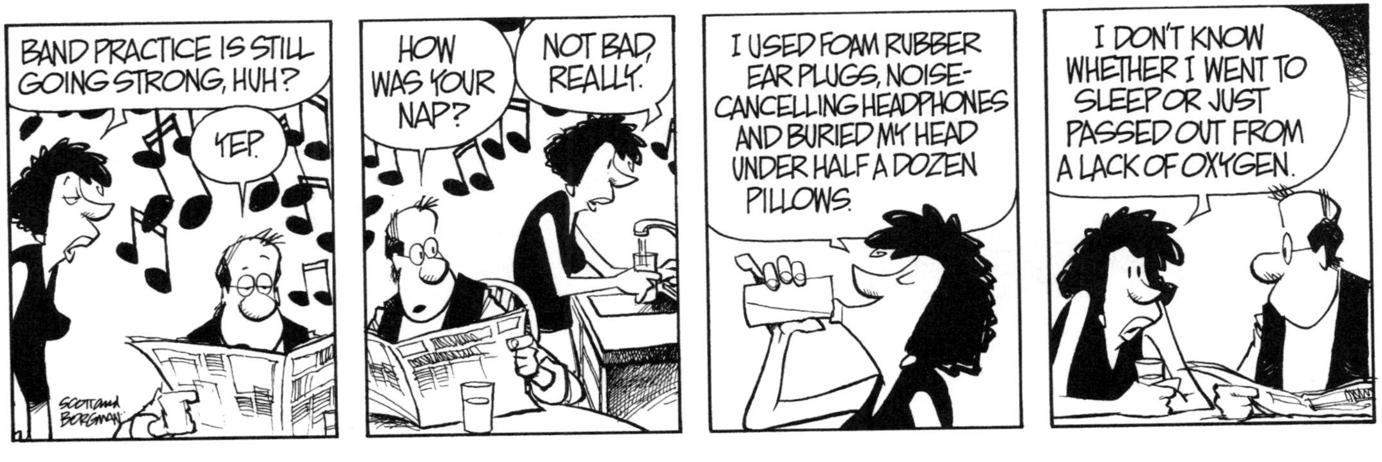
BAND PRACTICE IS STILL GOING STRONG, HUH?
YEP.
HOW WAS YOUR NAP?
NOT BAD, REALLY.
I USED FOAM RUBBER EAR PLUGS, NOISE-CANCELLING HEADPHONES AND BURIED MY HEAD UNDER HALF A DOZEN PILLOWS.
I DON'T KNOW WHETHER I WENT TO SLEEP OR JUST PASSED OUT FROM A LACK OF OXYGEN.

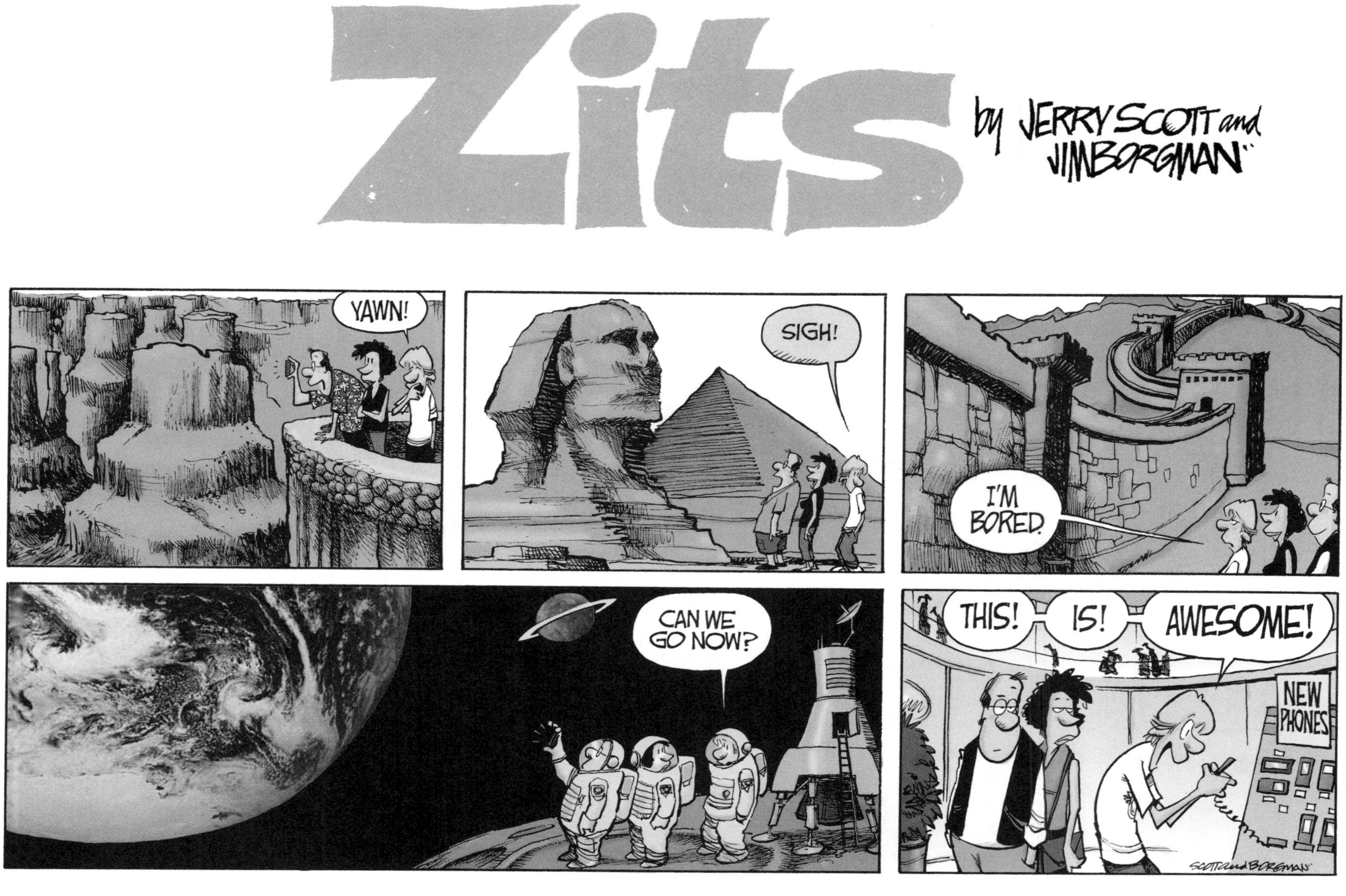
Zits
by JERRY SCOTT and JIM BORGMAN
YAWN!
SIGH!
I'M BORED.
CAN WE GO NOW?
THIS!
IS!
AWESOME!
NEW PHONES
SCOTT and BORGMAN

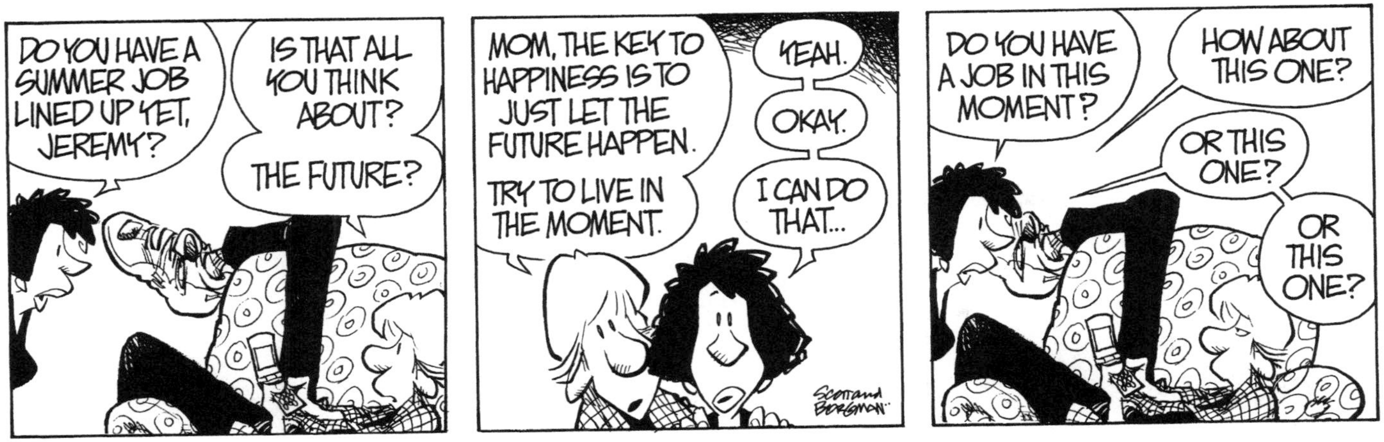
DO YOU HAVE A SUMMER JOB LINED UP YET, JEREMY?
IS THAT ALL YOU THINK ABOUT?
THE FUTURE?
MOM, THE KEY TO HAPPINESS IS TO JUST LET THE FUTURE HAPPEN.
TRY TO LIVE IN THE MOMENT.
YEAH.
OKAY.
I CAN DO THAT...
SCOTT AND BORGMAN
DO YOU HAVE A JOB IN THIS MOMENT?
HOW ABOUT THIS ONE?
OR THIS ONE?
OR THIS ONE?

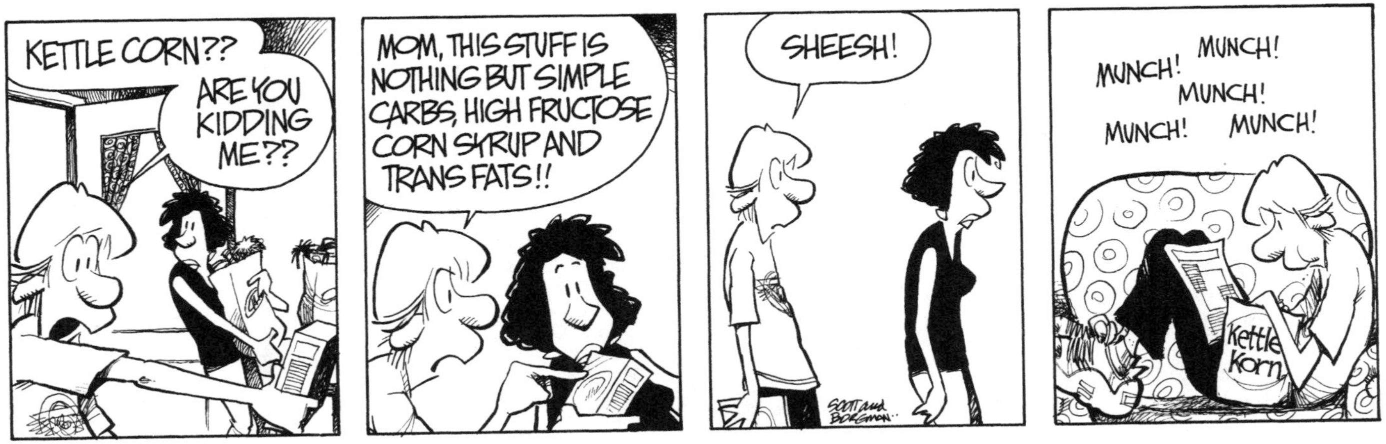
KETTLE CORN??
ARE YOU KIDDING ME??
MOM, THIS STUFF IS NOTHING BUT SIMPLE CARBS, HIGH FRUCTOSE CORN SYRUP AND TRANS FATS!!
SHEESH!
SCOTT AND BORGMAN
MUNCH! MUNCH!
MUNCH!
MUNCH! MUNCH!
Kettle Korn

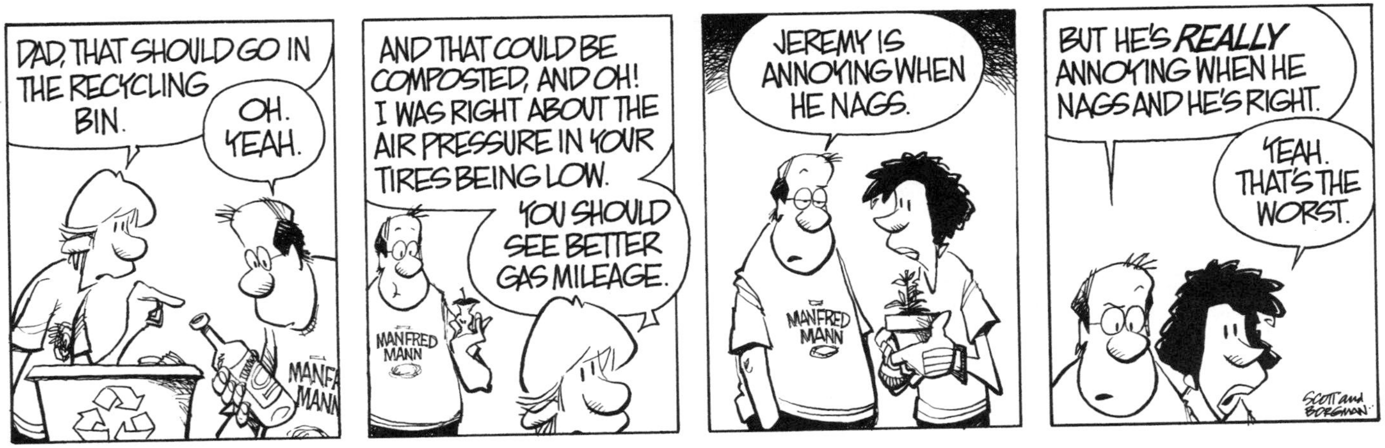
DAD, THAT SHOULD GO IN THE RECYCLING BIN.
OH. YEAH.
MANFRED MANN
AND THAT COULD BE COMPOSTED, AND OH! I WAS RIGHT ABOUT THE AIR PRESSURE IN YOUR TIRES BEING LOW.
YOU SHOULD SEE BETTER GAS MILEAGE.
MANFRED MANN
JEREMY IS ANNOYING WHEN HE NAGS.
MANFRED MANN
BUT HE'S ***REALLY*** ANNOYING WHEN HE NAGS AND HE'S RIGHT.
YEAH. THAT'S THE WORST.
SCOTT AND BORGMAN

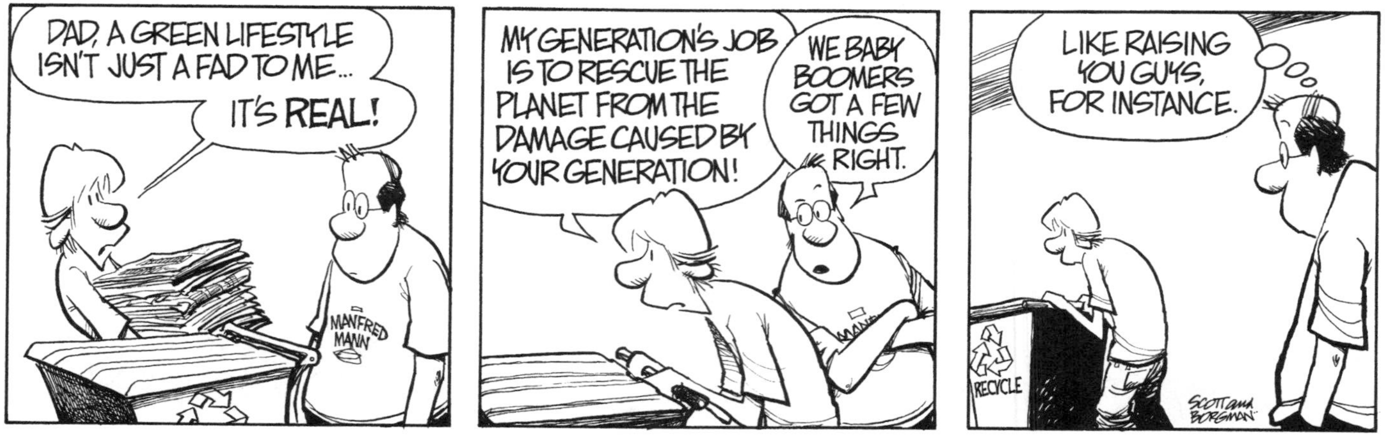
DAD, A GREEN LIFESTYLE ISN'T JUST A FAD TO ME...
IT'S REAL!
MANFRED MANN
MY GENERATION'S JOB IS TO RESCUE THE PLANET FROM THE DAMAGE CAUSED BY YOUR GENERATION!
WE BABY BOOMERS GOT A FEW THINGS RIGHT.
LIKE RAISING YOU GUYS, FOR INSTANCE.
RECYCLE
SCOTT and BORGMAN

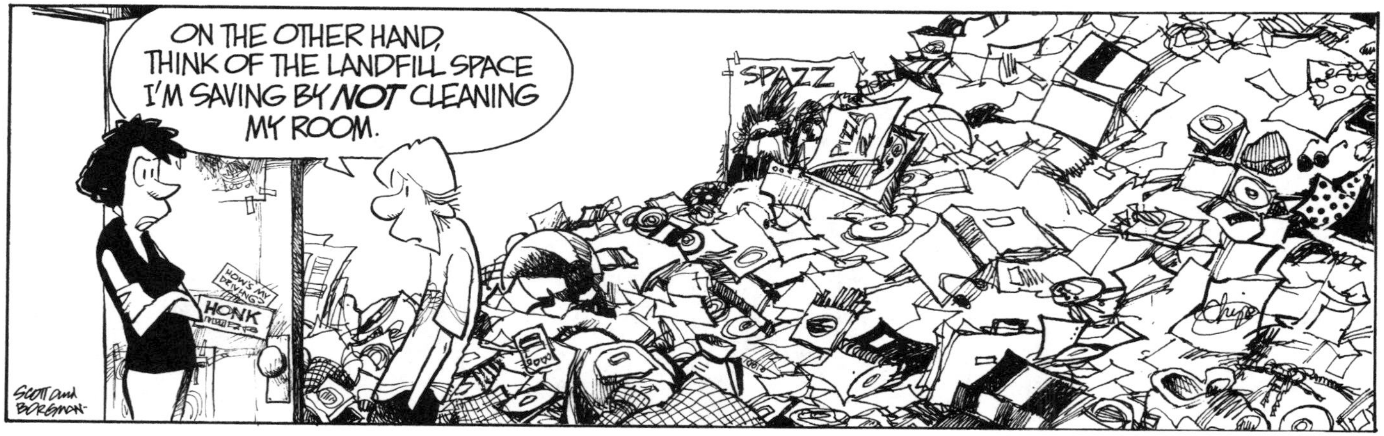
ON THE OTHER HAND, THINK OF THE LANDFILL SPACE I'M SAVING BY NOT CLEANING MY ROOM.
SPAZZ
PIZZA
HOW'S MY DRIVING?
HONK
SCOTT and BORGMAN

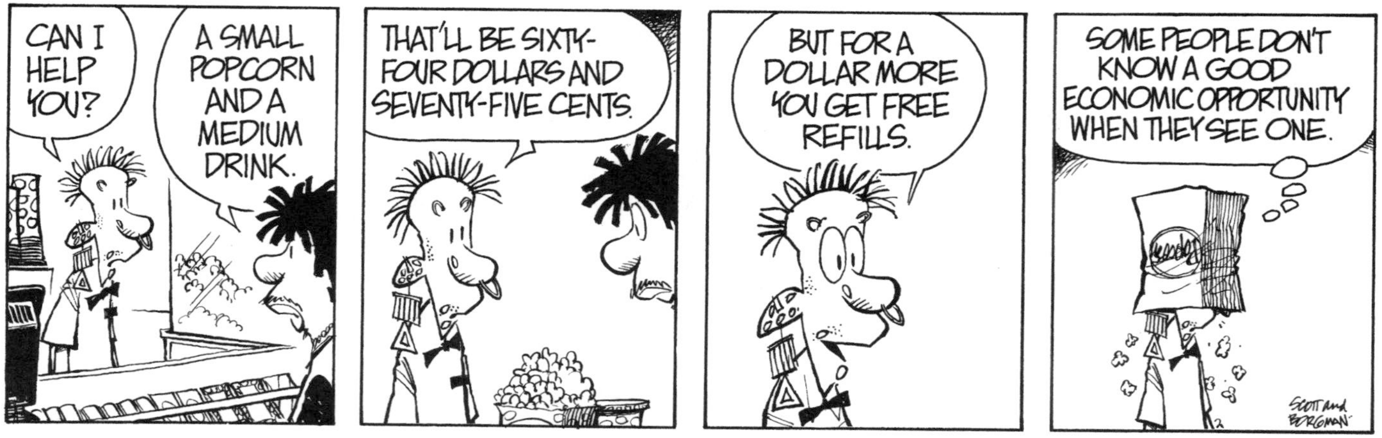
CAN I HELP YOU?
A SMALL POPCORN AND A MEDIUM DRINK.
THAT'LL BE SIXTY-FOUR DOLLARS AND SEVENTY-FIVE CENTS.
BUT FOR A DOLLAR MORE YOU GET FREE REFILLS.
SOME PEOPLE DON'T KNOW A GOOD ECONOMIC OPPORTUNITY WHEN THEY SEE ONE.
SCOTT and BORGMAN

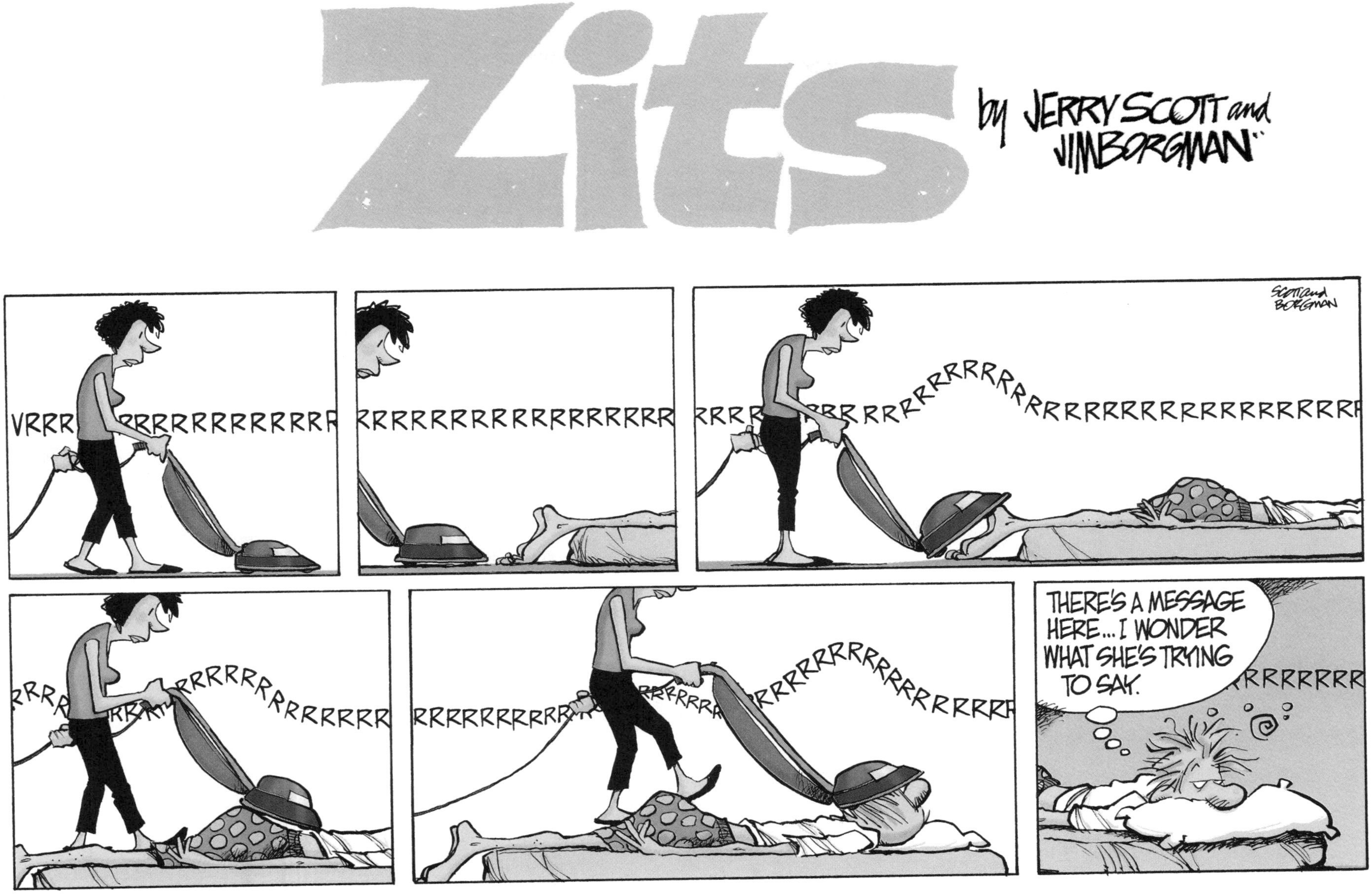
Zits
by JERRY SCOTT and JIM BORGMAN
SCOTT and BORGMAN
VRRRRRRRRRRRRRRRRR
RRRRRRRRRRRRRRRRRR
RRRRRRRRRRRRRRRRRRRRRRRRRRRRRRRRRRRR
RRRRRRRRRRRRRRRRRR
RRRRRRRRRRRRRRRRRRRRRRRRRRRRRRRRR
THERE'S A MESSAGE HERE... I WONDER WHAT SHE'S TRYING TO SAY.
RRRRRRRR

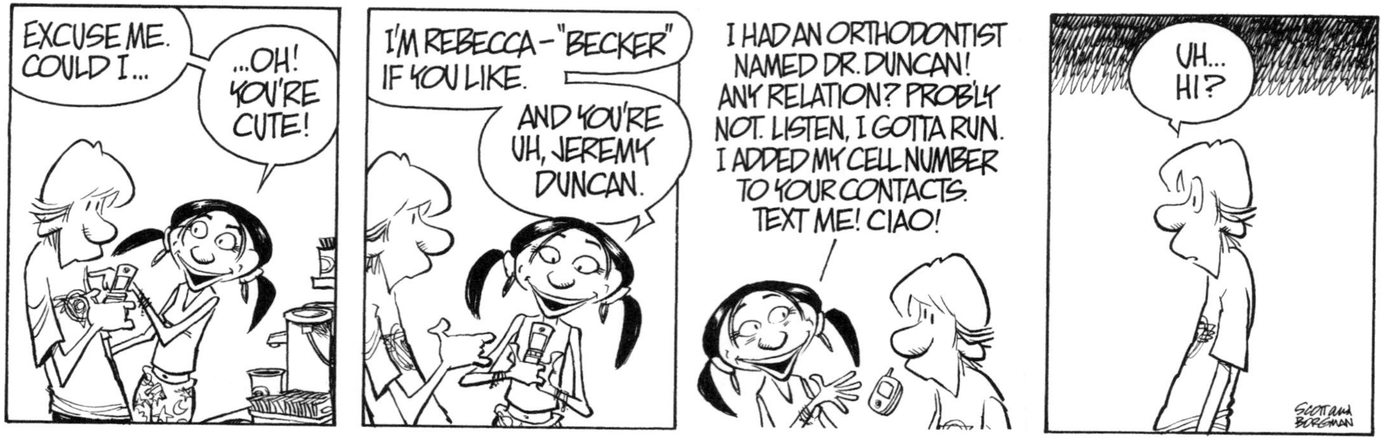
EXCUSE ME. COULD I...
...OH! YOU'RE CUTE!
I'M REBECCA - "BECKER" IF YOU LIKE.
AND YOU'RE UH, JEREMY DUNCAN.
I HAD AN ORTHODONTIST NAMED DR. DUNCAN! ANY RELATION? PROB'LY NOT. LISTEN, I GOTTA RUN. I ADDED MY CELL NUMBER TO YOUR CONTACTS. TEXT ME! CIAO!
UH... HI?
SCOTT and BORGMAN

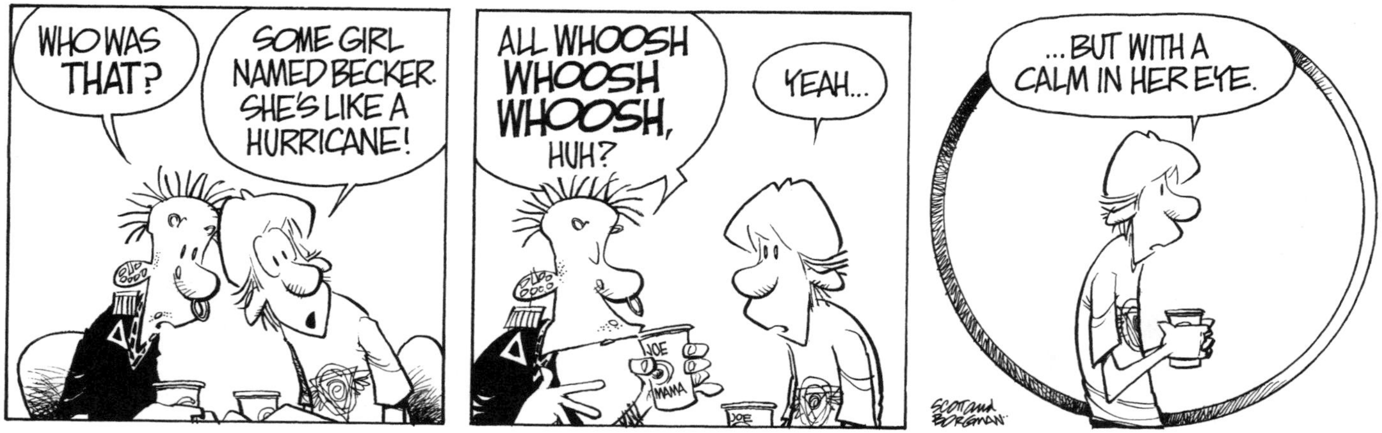
WHO WAS THAT?
SOME GIRL NAMED BECKER. SHE'S LIKE A HURRICANE!
ALL WHOOSH WHOOSH WHOOSH, HUH?
YEAH...
JOE MAMA
...BUT WITH A CALM IN HER EYE.
SCOTT and BORGMAN

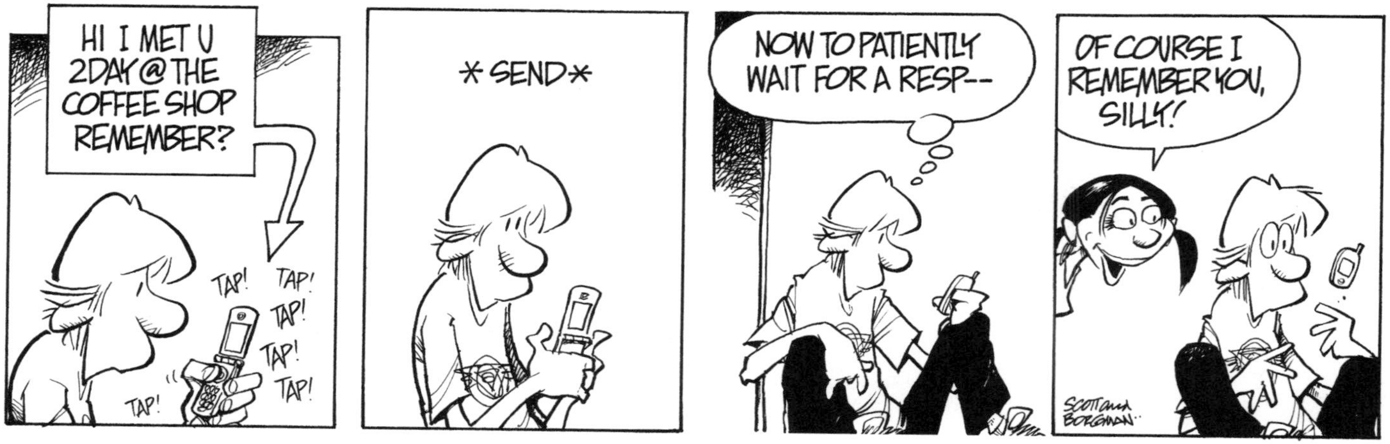
HI I MET U 2DAY @ THE COFFEE SHOP REMEMBER?
TAP! TAP! TAP! TAP! TAP! TAP!
SEND
NOW TO PATIENTLY WAIT FOR A RESP--
OF COURSE I REMEMBER YOU, SILLY!
SCOTT and BORGMAN

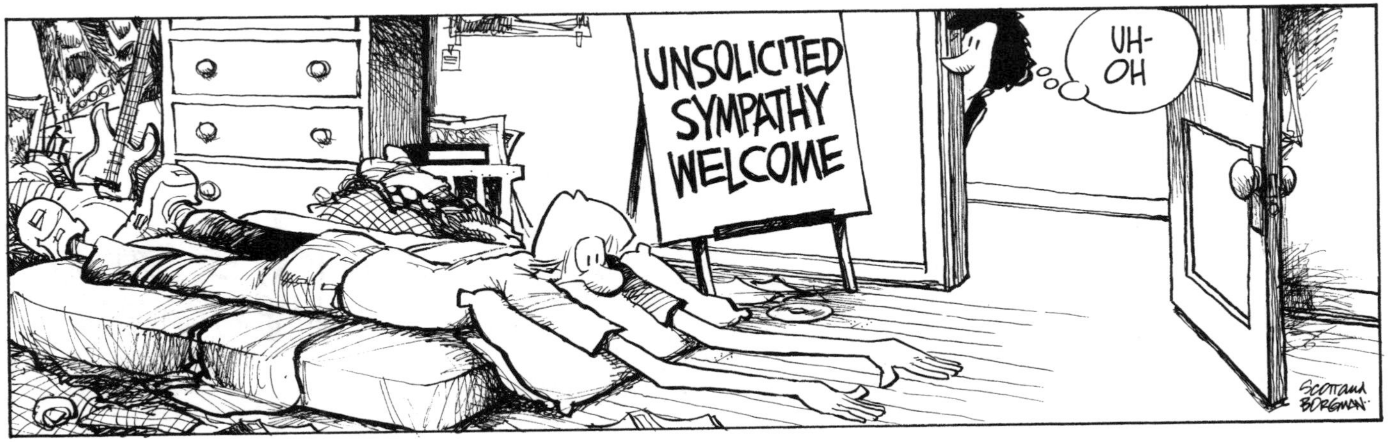
UNSOLICITED SYMPATHY WELCOME
UH-OH
SCOTT and BORGMAN

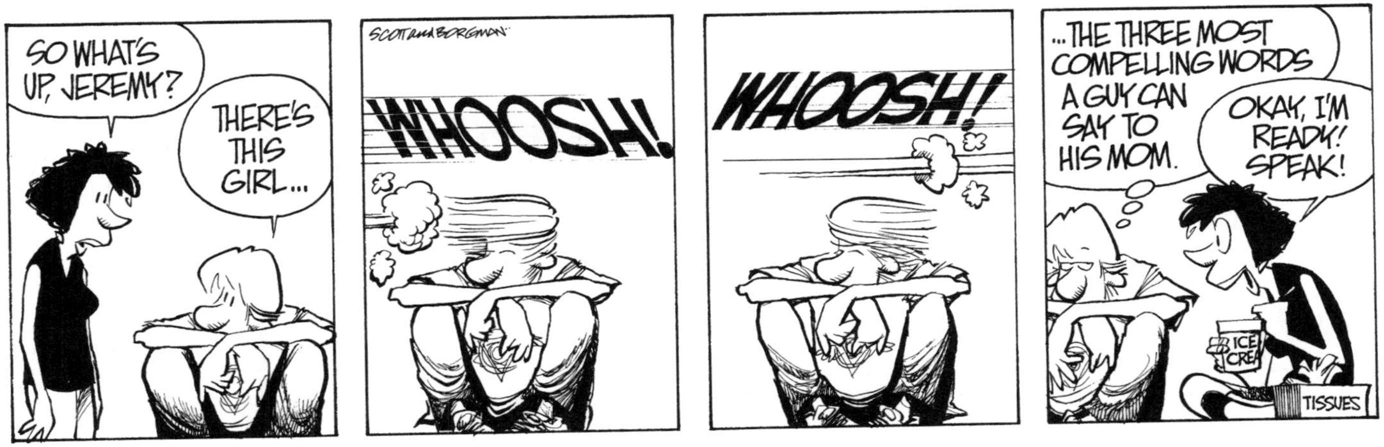
SO WHAT'S UP, JEREMY?
THERE'S THIS GIRL...
SCOTT and BORGMAN
WHOOSH!
WHOOSH!
...THE THREE MOST COMPELLING WORDS A GUY CAN SAY TO HIS MOM.
OKAY, I'M READY! SPEAK!
ICE CREA
TISSUES

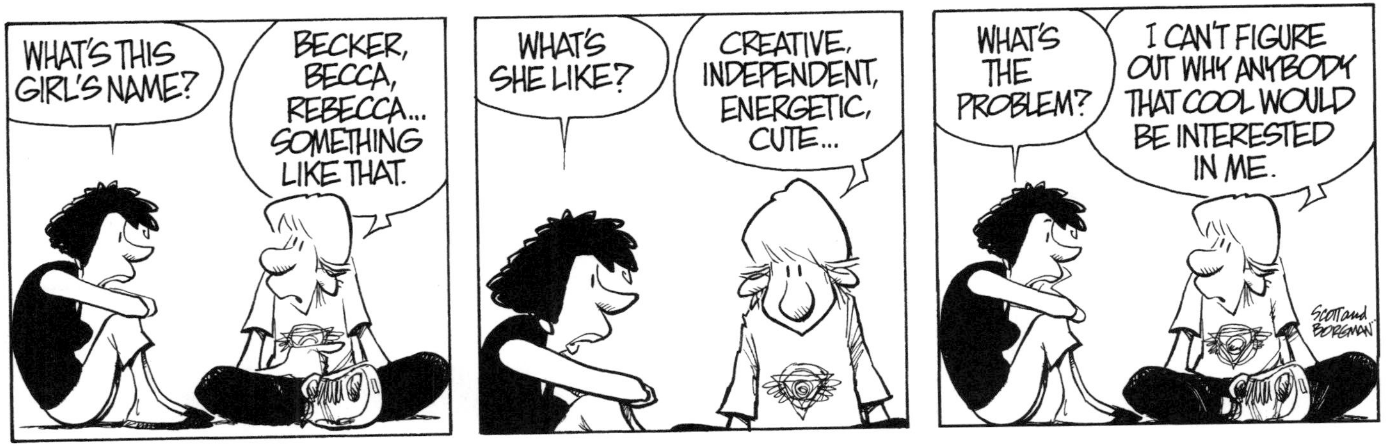
WHAT'S THIS GIRL'S NAME?
BECKER, BECCA, REBECCA... SOMETHING LIKE THAT.
WHAT'S SHE LIKE?
CREATIVE, INDEPENDENT, ENERGETIC, CUTE...
WHAT'S THE PROBLEM?
I CAN'T FIGURE OUT WHY ANYBODY THAT COOL WOULD BE INTERESTED IN ME.
SCOTT and BORGMAN

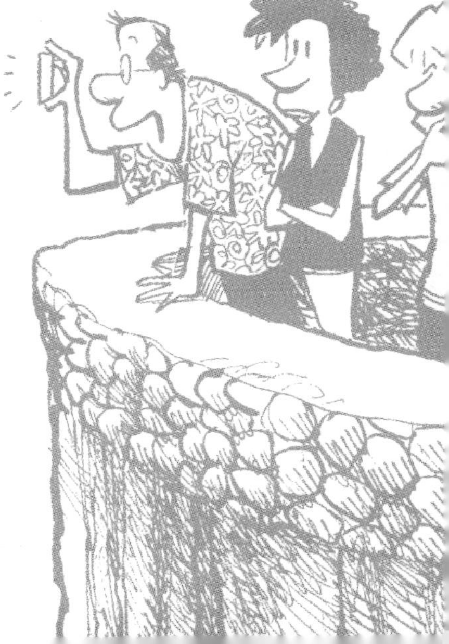

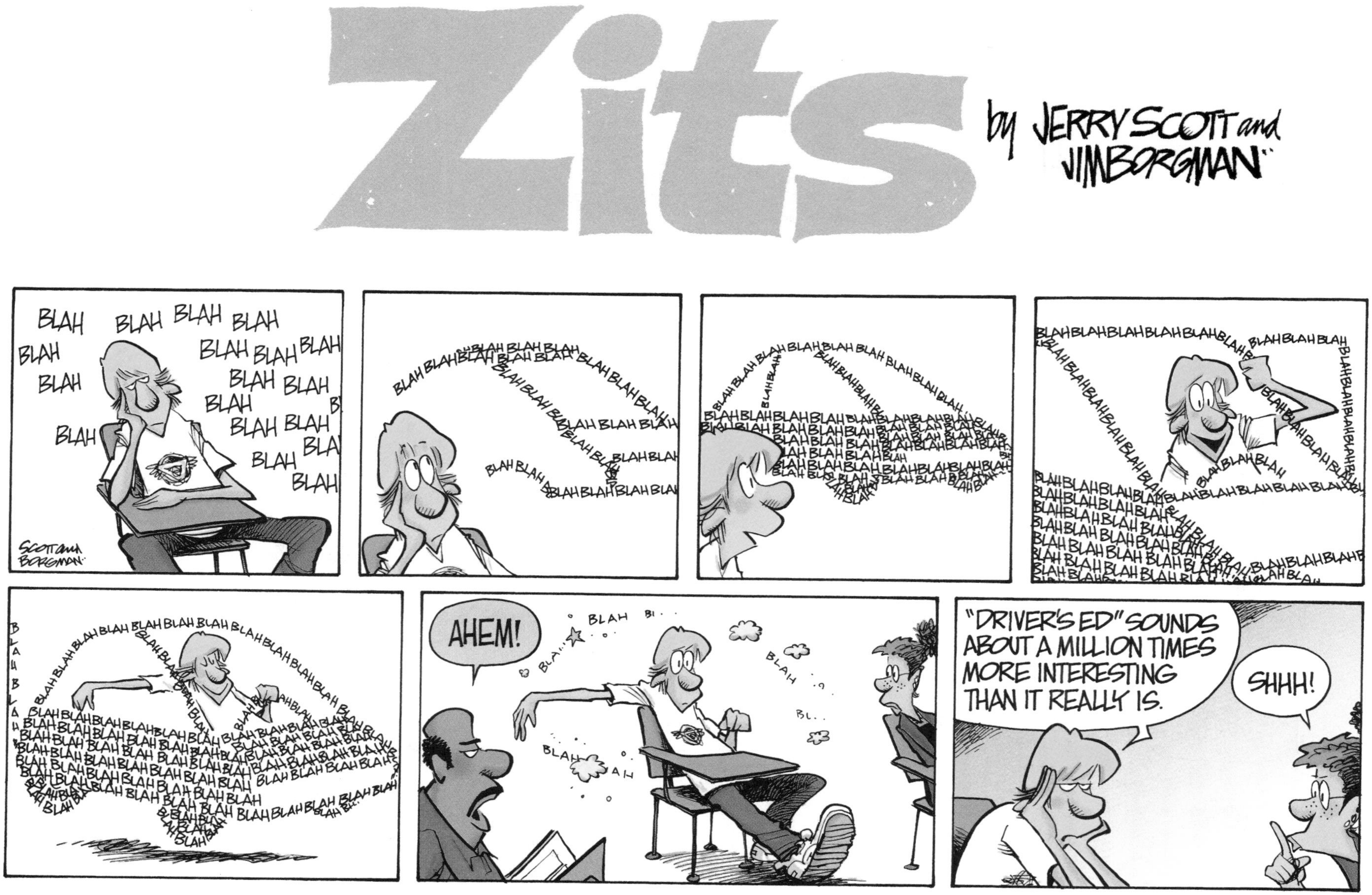
Zits
by JERRY SCOTT and JIM BORGMAN
BLAH BLAH BLAH BLAH
BLAH BLAH BLAH BLAH BLAH BLAH BLAH BLAH BLAH BLAH BLAH BLAH BLAH
SCOTT and BORGMAN
AHEM!
BLAH
"DRIVER'S ED" SOUNDS ABOUT A MILLION TIMES MORE INTERESTING THAN IT REALLY IS.
SHHH!

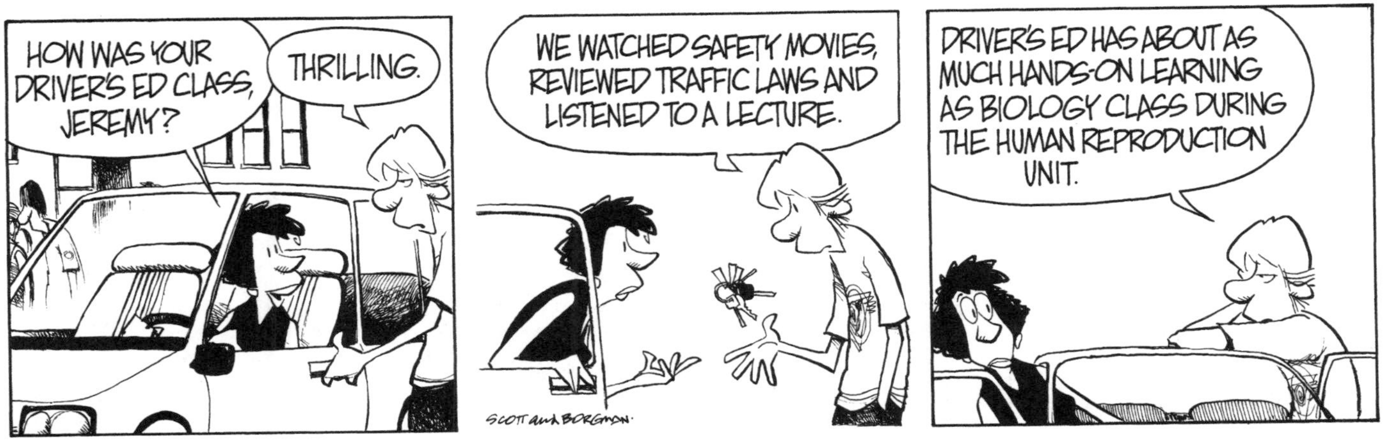
HOW WAS YOUR DRIVER'S ED CLASS, JEREMY?
THRILLING.
WE WATCHED SAFETY MOVIES, REVIEWED TRAFFIC LAWS AND LISTENED TO A LECTURE.
SCOTT and BORGMAN
DRIVER'S ED HAS ABOUT AS MUCH HANDS-ON LEARNING AS BIOLOGY CLASS DURING THE HUMAN REPRODUCTION UNIT.

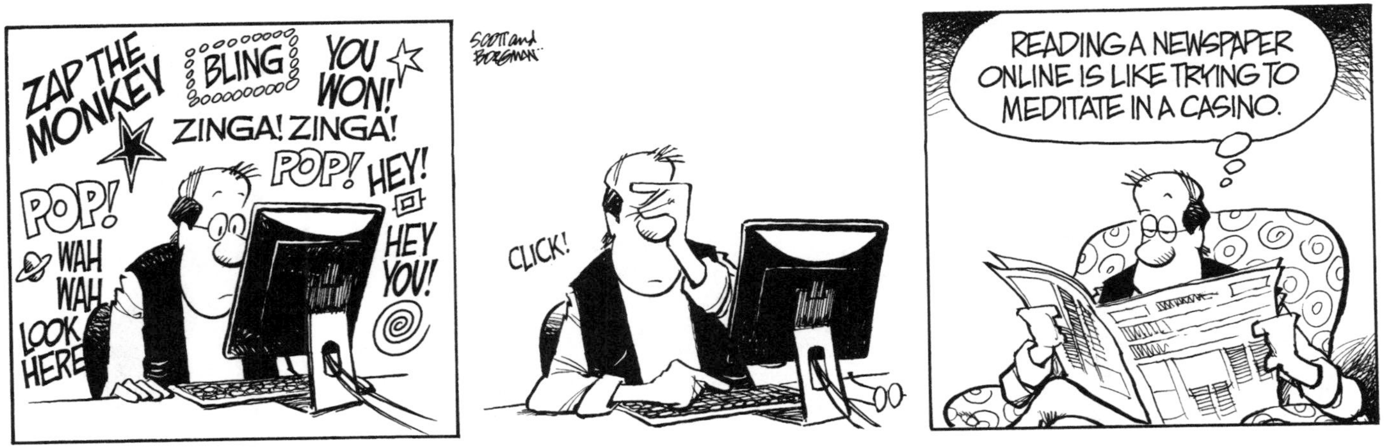
ZAP THE MONKEY
BLING
YOU WON!
ZINGA! ZINGA!
POP!
POP!
HEY!
WAH WAH
HEY YOU!
LOOK HERE
SCOTT and BORGMAN
CLICK!
READING A NEWSPAPER ONLINE IS LIKE TRYING TO MEDITATE IN A CASINO.

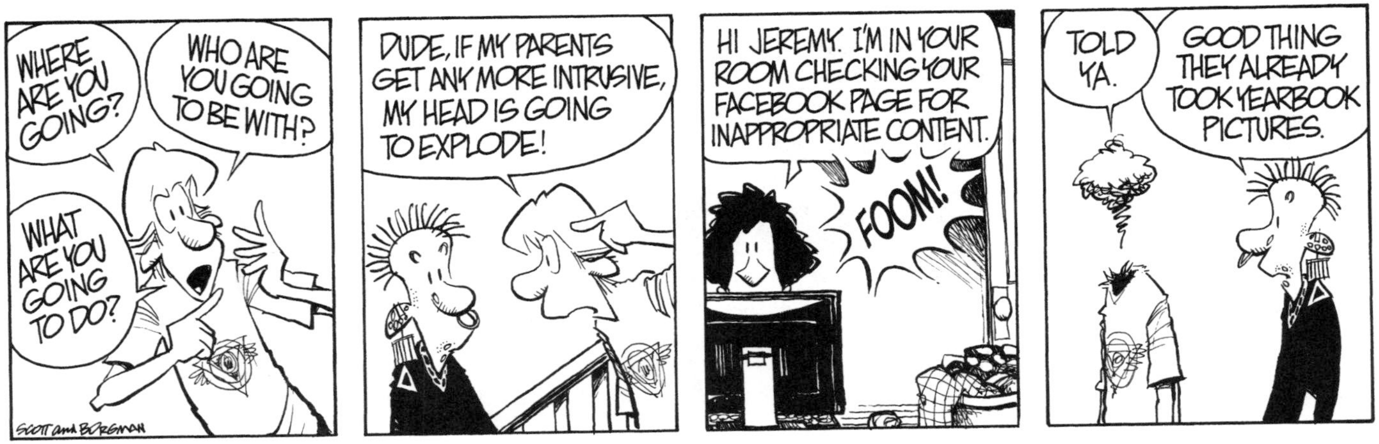
WHERE ARE YOU GOING?
WHO ARE YOU GOING TO BE WITH?
WHAT ARE YOU GOING TO DO?
SCOTT and BORGMAN
DUDE, IF MY PARENTS GET ANY MORE INTRUSIVE, MY HEAD IS GOING TO EXPLODE!
HI JEREMY. I'M IN YOUR ROOM CHECKING YOUR FACEBOOK PAGE FOR INAPPROPRIATE CONTENT.
FOOM!
TOLD YA.
GOOD THING THEY ALREADY TOOK YEARBOOK PICTURES.

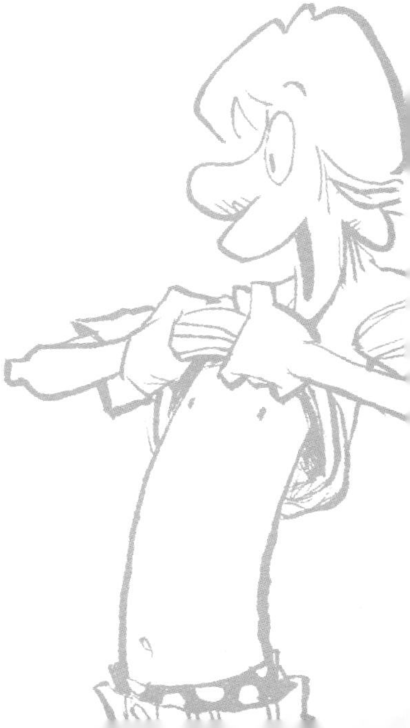

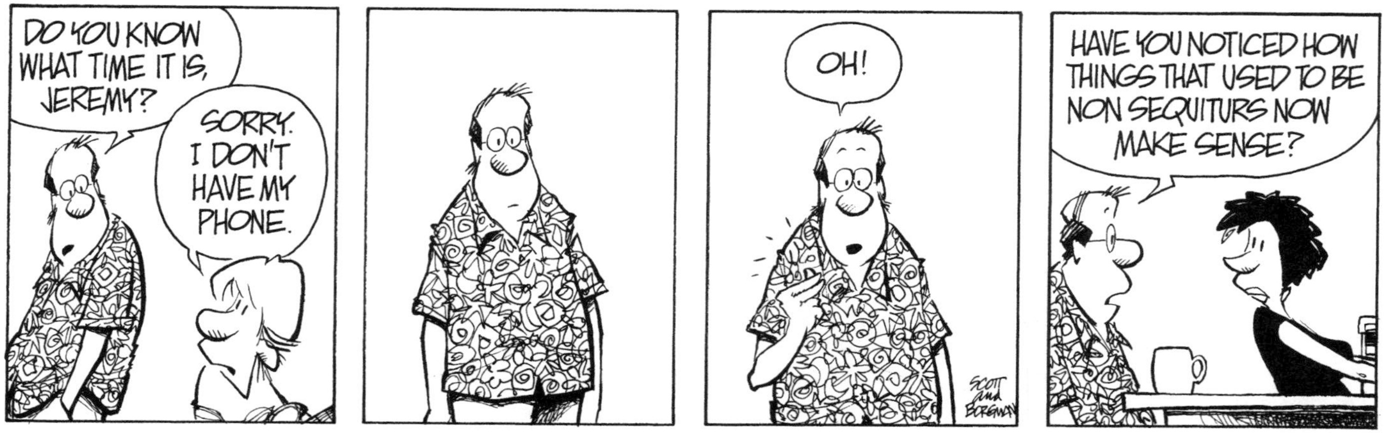
DO YOU KNOW WHAT TIME IT IS, JEREMY?
SORRY. I DON'T HAVE MY PHONE.
OH!
HAVE YOU NOTICED HOW THINGS THAT USED TO BE NON SEQUITURS NOW MAKE SENSE?

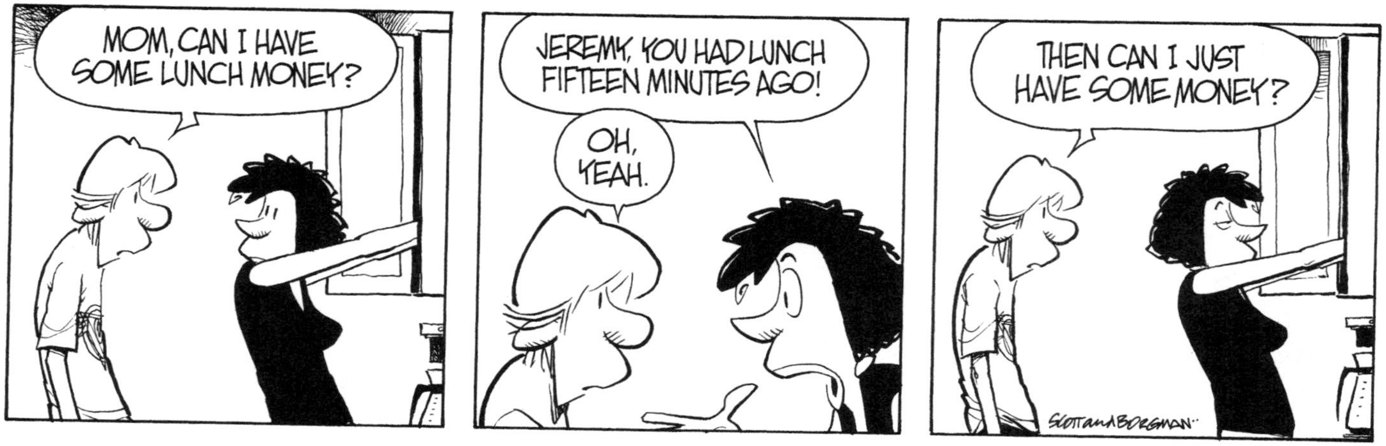
MOM, CAN I HAVE SOME LUNCH MONEY?
JEREMY, YOU HAD LUNCH FIFTEEN MINUTES AGO!
OH, YEAH.
THEN CAN I JUST HAVE SOME MONEY?

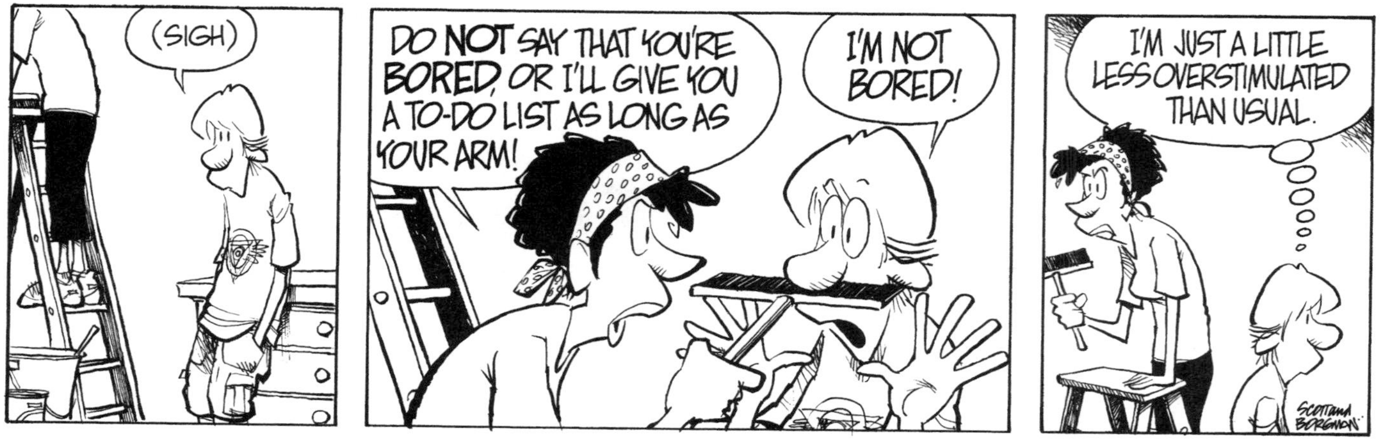
(SIGH)
DO NOT SAY THAT YOU'RE BORED, OR I'LL GIVE YOU A TO-DO LIST AS LONG AS YOUR ARM!
I'M NOT BORED!
I'M JUST A LITTLE LESS OVERSTIMULATED THAN USUAL.

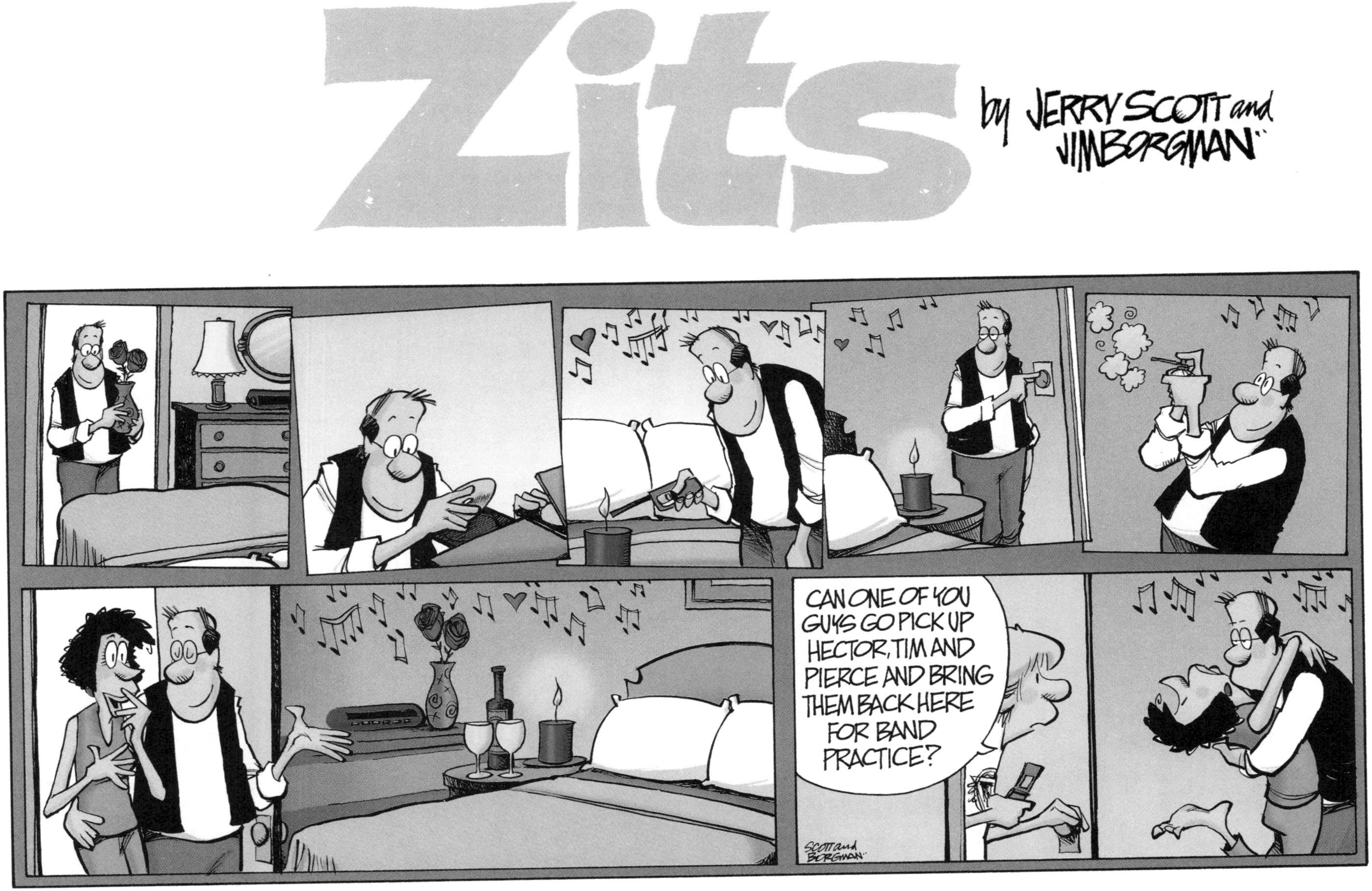
Zits
by JERRY SCOTT and JIM BORGMAN
CAN ONE OF YOU GUYS GO PICK UP HECTOR, TIM AND PIERCE AND BRING THEM BACK HERE FOR BAND PRACTICE?
SCOTT and BORGMAN

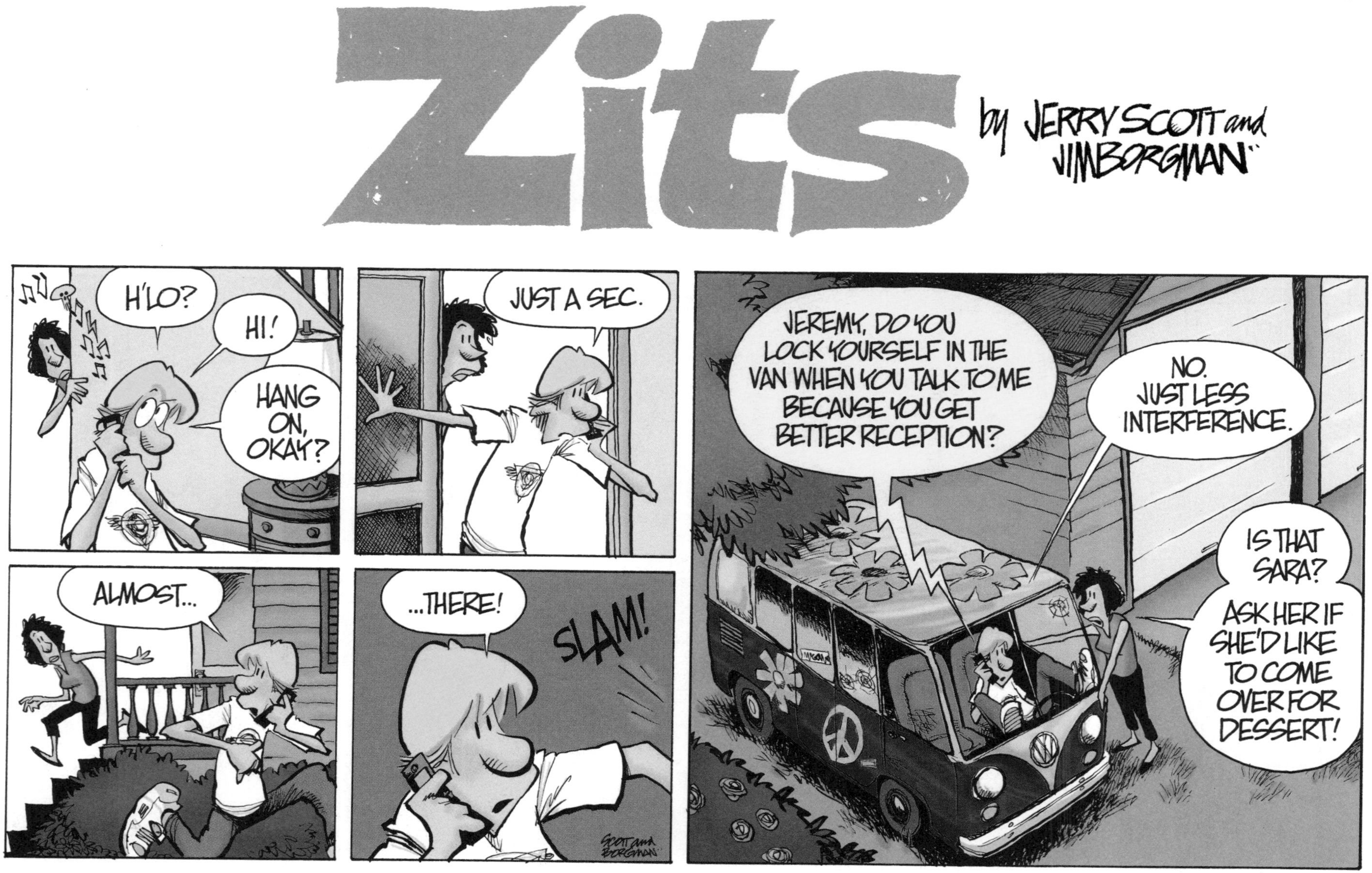
Zits
by JERRY SCOTT and JIM BORGMAN
H'LO?
HI!
HANG ON, OKAY?
JUST A SEC.
ALMOST...
...THERE!
SLAM!
JEREMY, DO YOU LOCK YOURSELF IN THE VAN WHEN YOU TALK TO ME BECAUSE YOU GET BETTER RECEPTION?
NO. JUST LESS INTERFERENCE.
IS THAT SARA?
ASK HER IF SHE'D LIKE TO COME OVER FOR DESSERT!